Deep Learning in Science

This is the first rigorous, self-contained treatment of the theory of deep learning. Starting with the foundations of the theory and building it up, this is essential reading for any scientists, instructors, and students interested in artificial intelligence and deep learning. It provides guidance on how to think about scientific questions, and leads readers through the history of the field and its fundamental connections to neuroscience. The author discusses many applications to beautiful problems in the natural sciences, in physics, chemistry, and biomedicine. Examples include the search for exotic particles and dark matter in experimental physics, the prediction of molecular properties and reaction outcomes in chemistry, and the prediction of protein structures and the diagnostic analysis of biomedical images in the natural sciences. The text is accompanied by a full set of exercises at different difficulty levels and encourages out-of-the-box thinking.

Pierre Baldi is Distinguished Professor of Computer Science at University of California, Irvine. His main research interest is understanding intelligence in brains and machines. He has made seminal contributions to the theory of deep learning and its applications to the natural sciences, and has written four other books.

Deep Learning in Science

PIERRE BALDI

University of California, Irvine

CAMBRIDGE
UNIVERSITY PRESS

University Printing House, Cambridge CB2 8BS, United Kingdom

One Liberty Plaza, 20th Floor, New York, NY 10006, USA

477 Williamstown Road, Port Melbourne, VIC 3207, Australia

314–321, 3rd Floor, Plot 3, Splendor Forum, Jasola District Centre, New Delhi – 110025, India

79 Anson Road, #06–04/06, Singapore 079906

Cambridge University Press is part of the University of Cambridge.

It furthers the University's mission by disseminating knowledge in the pursuit of
education, learning, and research at the highest international levels of excellence.

www.cambridge.org
Information on this title: www.cambridge.org/9781108845359
DOI: 10.1017/9781108955652

First published 2021

Printed in Singapore by Markono Print Media Pte Ltd

A catalogue record for this publication is available from the British Library.

ISBN 978-1-108-84535-9 Hardback

To Cristina, Julia Melody, and Marco Jazz

Contents

Preface

By and large, this book grew out of research conducted in my group as well as classes and lectures given at the University of California, Irvine (UCI) and elsewhere over the years. It can be used as a textbook for an undergraduate or graduate course in machine learning, or as an introduction to the topic for scientists from other fields. Basic prerequisites for understanding the material include college-level algebra, calculus, and probability. Familiarity with information theory, statistics, coding theory, and computational complexity at an elementary level are also helpful. I have striven to focus primarily on fundamental principles and provide a treatment that is both self-contained and rigorous, sometimes referring to the literature for well-known technical results, or to the exercises, which are an integral part of the book.

In writing this book, one of my goals has been to provide a rigorous treatment from first principles, as much as possible, in a still rapidly evolving field. This is one of the meanings of "in science" in the title. In this regard, the flow of the book is dictated primarily by complexity issues, going from shallow networks in their different forms, to deep feedforward networks, to recurrent and recursive networks. Two-layer networks, of which autoencoders are the prototypical example, provide the hinge between shallow and deep learning. For each kind of network, it is useful to consider special "hardware" cases, such as networks of linear units. Contrary to widespread belief, the linear case is often interesting and far from trivial. But this is not the only case where using a particular hardware model is helpful. Another example is the use of unrestricted Boolean units, another model that may seem trivial at first sight, but which leads to useful insights for both autoencoders and deep architectures. Yet another important example is provided by networks of linear or polynomial threshold gates.

A second characteristic of this book is its connection to biology. Neural networks, deep learning, and the entire field of AI are deeply rooted in biology, in trying to understand how the brain works and the space of possible strategies to replicate and surpass its capabilities. This is evident in Turing's foundational work on Turing machines, guided by the fundamental intuition of a brain capable of having only a finite number of states [736] and in the vocabulary of computer science, which is full of words clearly rooted in biology such as AI, machine learning, memory, computer vision, computer virus, genetic algorithms, and so forth. It is regrettable to see young students and practitioners of machine learning misled to believe that artificial neural networks have little to do with biology, or that machine learning is the set of techniques used to maximize engineering or business goals, such as advertising revenues for search engines. In addition, not only computers and neural networks are inspired by biology, but they are of course also being successfully used to analyze biological data, for instance high-throughput omic data, and through one of these surprising self-recursions only mankind seems to have produced, the results of these bioinformatics and systems biology analyses are progressively informing our understanding of the brain, helping to reveal for instance key gene expression and protein mechanisms involved in synaptic formation and biological memory.

A third characteristic of this book is precisely in the applications. The second meaning of "in science" in the title is "for science". I have focused on applications of deep learning to the natural sciences – primarily physics, chemistry, and biology for the past three decades or so. These applications are expanding rapidly today, but were almost nonexistent in the 1980s. Plenty of textbooks and other material can be found dealing with applications of neural networks to problems in engineering and other related areas.

A fourth characteristic is the emphasis placed on storage, specifically on the neural-style of information storage, in fundamental contrast to the Turing-style of information storage, ironically introduced by Turing precisely while thinking about the brain. This theme goes together with the importance of recognizing the virtualization process hidden behind most of today's neural network applications. In most applications of neural networks today, there are no neurons and no synapses, only their digital mirage. This comes at a price that can only be understood by thinking about "learning in the machine", as opposed to machine learning. In a physical neural system, learning rules must be local both in space and time. Among other things, this locality principle helps clarify the relationship between Hebbian learning and backpropagation and explains why Hebbian learning applied to feedforward convolutional architectures has never worked. It also naturally leads to random backpropagation and recirculation algorithms, important topics that are poorly known because they are not particularly useful for current applications. For readers primarily interested in applications, or for courses with tight time limitations, I recommend using the abbreviated sequence of chapters: 2, 3, 6, and 10, covering most of the practical aspects.

Finally, the field of neural networks has been polluted by fads and a significant amount of cronyism and collusion over the past few decades, that a fragmented, multigenerational, and often unaware community could do little to stop. Cronyism and collusion are nothing new in human affairs, but they have distorted and slowed down the development of the field through the subtle control and manipulation of conferences, publications, academic and corporate research departments, and other avenues of power and dissemination. Readers should read more widely, check what has been published – where and when – and decide for themselves which results are supported by mathematical proofs or sound simulations, and which are not. In the end, towering over human affairs, all that matters are the beauty of deep learning and the underlying mysteries it is intimately connected to: from whether silicon can be conscious to the fundamental nature of the universe.

About the Exercises

The exercises vary in difficulty substantially. Should you become frustrated at trying to solve one of them, remind yourself that it is only when you are struggling with a problem that your brain is really learning something.

In order to solve some of the problems in the book, or more broadly to think about scientific and other questions, I recommend that my students systematically try at least four different approaches. The first of course is to simplify. When a question seems too difficult at first, look for special or simpler cases. When trying to understand a theorem, look at the case of "small n", or fix the values of certain parameters, or switch to the linear case, or try to interpolate. The second is the opposite way of thinking: generalize, abstract, or extrapolate. Are there other situations that bear some similarity to the current problem? How can a result be applied to more general cases? Can the conditions under which a theorem is true be relaxed? The third way of thinking is "to take the limit", to look at what happens at the boundaries of a certain domain, under extreme conditions, to let n go to zero, or to infinity. And finally, the fourth way is always to invert, look at things somehow from an opposite perspective. Thus, for example, when thinking about an autoencoder, one may want first to simplify it by studying how to solve the top layer given the lower layer, which is usually an easier problem; and then to invert this approach by studying how the lower layer can be solved given the top layer, which is usually a harder problem.

Of course these four principles are not a panacea to every situation and, for instance, identifying the right form of "inversion" in a given situation may not be obvious. However, the discipline of trying to apply these four principles in a systematic manner can be helpful and, incidentally, remains a major challenge for Artificial Intelligence (AI).

Acknowledgments

The number of people I am indebted to keeps growing every year, and I can only mention a few of them.

- As a graduate student at Caltech (1983-1986) and visiting lecturer at UCSD (1986-1988), I was fortunate to be able to participate and contribute to the early beginnings of neural networks in the 1980s. Being at those two universities, which were the hotbeds of neural networks research at the time, resulted to a large extent from a series of chance encounters with several individuals, of whom I can only mention two: Brian Ekin and Gill Williamson. Brian, who I met by chance in Paris, told me to apply to Caltech, a name I had never heard before. And while bartendering for an alumni reunion in the basement of the Caltech Athenaeum, I met Gill Williamson who was a Professor at UCSD and, while still sober, offered me my first academic job.

- From those early times, I wish also to acknowledge two kind mentors – Edward Posner and Walter Heiligenberg – both of whom died prematurely in tragic transportation accidents; as well as some of my early collaborators and friends including: Amir Atiya, Eric Baum, Joachim Buhmann, Yves Chauvin, Paolo Frasconi, Kurt Hornik, Ron Meir, Fernando Pineda, Yosi Rinott, and Santosh Venkatesh.

- From more recent times, I wish to acknowledge past and present faculty colleagues at UCI in AI and machine learning, including: Rina Dechter, Charless Fowlkes, Roy Fox, Richard Granger, Alexander Ihler, Dennis Kibler, Richard Lathrop, Stephan

Mandt, Eric Mjoslness, Ioannis Panageas, Michael Pazzani, Deva Ramanan, Sameer Singh, Padhraic Smyth, Erik Sudderth, Max Welling, and Xiaohui Xie.

- Successful applications of deep learning to the sciences vitally require interdisciplinary collaborations. I am deeply grateful to all my collaborators from the natural sciences. Among the current active ones at UCI, I only have space to mention: Roman Vershynin (Mathematics) and Babak Shahbaba (Statistics), Daniel Whiteson and Jianming Bian, together with Simona Murgia, Franklin Dollar, and Steven Barwick (Physics), Michael Pritchard (Earth Sciences), David Van Vranken and Ann Marie Carlton (Chemistry), and Paolo Sassone-Corsi, Marcelo Wood, and Amal Alachkar (Biology). As I was about to send the final draft to Cambridge University Press, Paolo unexpectedly died and I wish to honor his memory here. He was an outstanding scientist, friend, and collaborator.

- Together with my external collaborators, I am also deeply grateful to current and past students and postdoctoral fellows in my research group, who have contributed in so many ways to this book over the years, including: Forest Agostinelli, Alessio Andronico, Chloe Azencott, Kevin Bache, Pierre-François Baisnée, Ryan Benz, Vincenzo Bonnici, Martin Brandon, Andrew Brethorst, Jocelyne Bruand, Francesco Ceccarelli, Nicholas Ceglia, Ivan Chang, Jonathan Chen, Siwei Chen, Jianlin Cheng, Davide Chicco, Julian Collado, Kenneth Daily, Ekaterina Deyneka, Pietro Di Lena, Yimeng Dou, David Fooshee, Clovis Galliez, Steven Hampson, Lars Hertel, Qian-Nan Hu, Raja Jurdak, Matt Kayala, John B. Lanier, Christine Lee, Lingge Li, Erik Linstead, Junze Liu, Yadong Lu, Alessandro Lusci, Christophe Magnan, Antonio Maratea, Stephen McAleer, Ken Nagata, Francesco Napolitano, Ramzi Nasr, Jordan Ott, Vishal Patel, Gianluca Pollastri, Liva Ralaivola, Arlo Randall, Paul Rigor, Alex Sadovsky, Peter Sadowski, Muntaha Samad, Hiroto Saigo, Siyu Shao, Alexander Shmakov, Suman Sundaresh, S. Joshua Swamidass, Mike Sweredoski, Amin Tavakoli, Gregor Urban, Alessandro Vullo, Eric Wang, Lin Wu, Yu Liu, and Michael Zeller.

- I am equally grateful to Janet Ko, who has assisted me and other faculty, for so many years with her loyalty and outstanding administrative skills, always shielding scientific research from bureaucracy.

- As far as the book itself is directly concerned, two chapters and the appendix reuse material from three previously published articles [72, 634, 262] and I thank the publishers – Springer and Annual Reviews – for their permissions. I wish also to thank Annie Vogel-Cierna for providing me two of the microscopy images in the last chapter.

- This book was finished during the COVID-19 pandemic. It has been a real pleasure to work with the staff of Cambridge University Press, and in particular with David Tranah. I thank them for their outstanding support and professionalism, and their deep understanding of academic publishing.

- Last but not least, I am deeply grateful to my close friends and to my family.

1   Introduction

La gymnastique cerebrale n'est pas susceptible d'ameliorer l'organisation du cerveau en augmentant le nombre de cellules, car, on le sait, les elements nerveux ont perdu depuis l'epoque embryonnaire la propriety de proliferer; mais on peut admettre comme une chose tres vraisemblable que l'exercice mental suscite dans les regions cerebrales plus sollicitees un plus grand developpment de l'appareil protoplasmique et du systeme des collaterales nerveuses. De la sorte, des associations deja creees entre certains groupes de cellules se renforceraient notablement au moyen de la multiplication des ramilles terminales des appendices protoplasmiques et des collaterals nerveuses; mais, en outre, des connexions intercellulaires tout a fait nouvelles pourraient s'etablir grace a la neoformation de collaterales et d'expansions protoplasmiques. [Santiago Ramón y Cajal [165]]

The long-term research goal behind this book is to understand intelligence in brains and machines. Intelligence, like consciousness, is one of those words that:

(1) was coined a long time ago, when our scientific knowledge of the world was still fairly primitive;
(2) is not well defined, but has been and remains very useful both in everyday communication and scientific research; and
(3) for which seeking a precise definition today is premature, and thus not particularly productive.

Thus, rather than trying to define intelligence, we may try to gain a broader perspective on intelligent systems, by asking which systems are "intelligent", and how they came about on planet Earth. For this purpose, imagine an alien from an advanced civilization on a distant galaxy charged with reporting to her alien colleagues on the state of intelligent systems on planet Earth. How would she summarize her main findings?

1.1   Carbon-Based and Silicon-Based Computing

At a fundamental level, intelligent systems must be able to both compute and store information, and thus it is likely that the alien would organize her summary along these two axes. Along the computing axis, the first main finding she would have to report is that currently there are two computing technologies that are dominant on Earth: carbon-based computing implemented in all living systems, and silicon-based computing implemented in a growing number of devices ranging from sensors, to cellphones, to laptops, to computer clusters and clouds. Carbon-based computing has a 3.8 billion-year-long history, driven by evolution. In contrast, silicon-based computing is less than 100 years old, with a history driven by human (hence carbon-based) design rather than evolution. Other computing technologies, from DNA computing to quantum computing, currently play minor roles, although quantum computing can be expected to significantly expand in the coming two decades.

Along the storage axis, the main finding the alien would have to report is that there are at least two different styles of storage: the digital/Turing-tape style, and the neural style which is at the center of this book (Figure 1.1). In the digital style, information is stored neatly at different discrete locations, or memory addresses, of a physical substrate. In the neural style of computing, information is stored in a messy way, through some kind of holographic process, which distributes information across a large number of synapses. Think of how you may store your telephone number in a computer as opposed to your brain. In Turing machines, storage and processing are physically separate and information must be transferred from the storage unit to the computing unit for processing. In neural machines, storage and processing are intimately intertwined. In the digital style, storage tends to be transparent and lossless. In the neural style, storage tends to be opaque and lossy.

Remarkably, carbon-based computing discovered both ways of storing information. It first discovered the digital style of storage, using chemical processes, by storing information using DNA and RNA molecules which, to a first degree of approximation, can be viewed as finite tapes containing symbols from a four-letter alphabet at each position. Indeed, biological systems store genetic information, primarily about genes and their control, at precise addresses along their DNA/RNA genome. And every cell can be viewed as a formidable computer which, among other things, continuously measures and adjusts the concentration of thousands of different molecules. It took roughly 3.3 billion years of evolution of carbon-based digital computing for it to begin to discover the neural style of information processing, by developing the first primitive nervous circuits and brains, using tiny electrical signals to communicate information between neurons. Thus, about 500 million years ago it also began to discover the neural style of information storage, distributing information across synapses. In time, this evolutionary process led to the human brain in the last million year or so, and to language in the last few hundred thousand years.

It is only over the very last 100 years, using precisely these tiny electrical signals and synapses, that the human brain invented silicon-based computing which, perhaps not too surprisingly, also uses tiny electrical signals to process information. In some sense, the evolution of storage in silicon-based computing is an accelerated recapitulation of the evolution of storage in carbon-based computing. Silicon-based computing rapidly adopted the digital Turing style of storage and computing we are so familiar with. As an aside, it is, ironically, striking that the notion of tape storage was introduced by Turing precisely while thinking about modeling the brain which uses a different style of storage. Finally, in the last seven decades or so, human brains started trying to simulate on digital computers, or implement in neuromorphic chips, the neural style of computing using silicon-based hardware, beginning the process of building intelligent machines (Figure 1.1). While true neuromorphic computing in silicon substrate is an active area of research, it must be stressed that the overwhelming majority of neural network implementations today are produced by a process of virtualization, simulating the neural style of computing and storage on digital, silicon-based, machines. Thus, for most of these neural networks, there are no neurons or synapses, but only fantasies of these objects stored in well-organized digital memory arrays. Silicon computing is fast enough that we often forget that we are running a neural fantasy. As we shall see later in this book, thinking about this virtualization and about computing in native neural systems, rather than their digital simulations, will be key to better understand neural information processing.

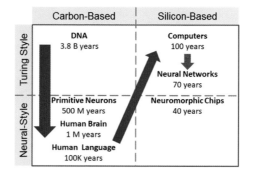

Figure 1.1 Evolution of computing and intelligence on planet Earth with approximate time scales. Computing on Earth can be organized along two axis: processing (carbon-based vs. silicon-based) and storage style (Turing vs. neural). Evolution began with carbon-based processing and Turing-style storage approximately 3.8B years ago. Primitive neurons and brains began emerging 500M years ago. Primate brains are a few million years old and human language is a few hundred thousand years old. Over the last 100 years or so, human brains developed silicon-based computing and computers rooted in the idea of Turing machines. AI and ANNs (artificial neural networks) have been developed over the last 70 years or so (red arrow). Most neural networks used today are virtual, in the sense that they are implemented in digital machines using the Turing style of storage. Neuromorphic chips, with mostly Turing-style but occasionally also neural-style of storage, have been in development for the past 40 years. Likewise, over the past 40 years, digital computers and artificial neural networks have been applied to biology, from molecular biology and evolution to neuroscience, to better understand carbon-based computing (arrow not shown).

Today, the carbon-based and silicon-based computing technologies are vastly different and carbon-based computing is still in many ways far more sophisticated. The differences are at all levels: physical sizes, time scales, energy requirements, and overall architectures. For instance, the human brain occupies slightly less than two liters of space and uses on the order of 20–40 W of power, roughly the equivalent of a light bulb, to effortlessly pass the Turing test of human conversation. In comparison, some of our supercomputers with their basketball-court size use three to four orders of magnitude more energy – something on the order of 100,000 W – to match, or slightly outperform, humans on a single task like the game of Jeopardy or GO, while miserably failing at passing the Turing test. This huge difference in energy consumption has a lot to do with the separation of storage and computing in silicon computers, versus their intimate and inextricable intertwining in the brain.

In spite of these differences, in the quest for intelligence these two computing technologies have converged on two key ideas, not unlike the well-known analogy in the quest of flight, where birds and airplanes have converged on the idea of using wings. In addition to using tiny electrical signals, both carbon-based and silicon-based intelligent systems have converged on the use of learning, including evolutionary learning and lifetime learning, in order to build systems that can deliver intelligent behavior and adapt to variations and changes in their environments. Thus it should not be too surprising that machine learning is today one of the key and most successful areas of artificial intelligence, and has been so for at least four decades.

As we have seen, on the silicon-side humans are learning how to emulate the neural-style of storing information. As an aside, and as an exercise in inversion, one may wonder whether evolution discovered how to emulate the Turing style of storage, for a second time, in brains. There is some evidence of that in our symbolic processing in general, in the discovery of individuals with superior autobiographical memory, or hyperthymesia [441, 644], who tend to index their life by dates, and in "enfants savants" and other individuals with superior arithmetic and other related capabilities, often connected to autism spectrum disorders (e.g. [383, 268, 370]). Unfortunately, we still know too little about information storage in the brain to really address this question, which touches on some of the main challenges for AI today.

1.2   Early Beginnings Until the Late 1940s

We now turn to a brief history of neural networks and deep learning. The goal here is not to be comprehensive, but simply to connect some of the most salient historical points in order to gain a useful perspective on the field. Additional pointers can be found, for instance, in [653]. Although one can trace the beginnings of artificial intelligence back to the Greek philosophers and even more ancient times, a more precise beginning that is relevant for this book can be identified by considering shallow learning as the precursor of deep learning. And shallow learning began with the discovery of linear regression in the late 1700s.

1.2.1   Linear Regression

The discovery of linear regression in the late 1700s resulted from the work of Carl Friedrich Gauss (1777–1855) and Adrien-Marie Legendre (1752–1833). Many if not most of the features of machine learning and deep learning are already present in the basic linear regression framework (Figure 1.2), such as having:

(1) an initial set of data points;

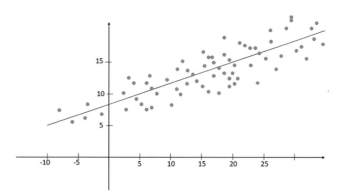

Figure 1.2 Linear regression in two dimensions.

(2) a class of possible models;

(3) a problem of model fitting;

(4) a problem of prediction using fitted models;

(5) a problem of model comparison; and so forth.

All these features are present in the deep learning framework of today, and by and large a cynic could say that most of deep learning today is akin to linear regression on steroids. However there are two fundamental points where linear regression is misleading. First, there is a closed mathematical formula for the coefficients of the "best" model, which will be reviewed in a coming chapter. In deep learning the models are more complex and there is no analytical formula; the parameters of the model must be learnt progressively through a process of optimization. Second, and especially in two or three dimensions, the linear model is easily interpretable and our visual system can see the data points and the model. In deep learning one is typically fitting non-linear surfaces in high-dimensional spaces, a process that cannot be visualized directly, and the parameters of the models tend to be more opaque. However, even in the simple case of a linear model, or a linear neuron, opacity is already present due to the neural style of storage: information about the data is stored, through a shattering process, in the coefficients of the linear model. This storage process is irreversible: one cannot retrieve the original points from the coefficients. Only some of their basic statistical properties, such as means and covariances (the sufficient statistics), are retained.

Of course, in addition to using non-linear models, deep learning today is often applied in situations characterized by very large numbers of data points in high-dimensional spaces (e.g. 1 billion humans in genome/DNA space or in photo/pixel space), where traditional linear regression has rarely ventured, for obvious historical and technical reasons.

1.2.2   Neuroscience Origins

Next, having traced the beginning of shallow (linear) learning, we can now turn to the true beginnings of deep learning. Machine learning and artificial intelligence as we know them today began to be developed in the late 1940s and early 1950s. They were fundamentally inspired by questions and knowledge available at the time about the brain. Thus it is useful to briefly summarize the state of neuroscience around 1950. Although we know much more today, many of the basic principles were already in place by 1950.

Briefly, by 1950 scientists had already gathered a good deal of essential information about the brain, its structure, and its function. Charles Darwin (1809–1882)'s *On the Origin of Species* had been published almost a century earlier in 1859. Thus they were well aware of the fact that the human brain has been shaped by evolutionary forces and that "nothing in biology makes sense except in the light of evolution"[1]. And in as much evolution operates by tinkering, rather than design, they could expect the brain to have a messy structure. Information about the coarse anatomy of the brain and some of its different components was also known. For instance, since the work of Pierre Paul Broca (1824–1880), Carl Wernicke (1848–1905), and others in the 19th century, the existence of very specialized areas for speech production and comprehension, as well as other functions was known, although not with the level of detail we have today. The detailed anatomical work of Santiago Ramón y Cajal (1852–1934), using staining methods that had been pioneered by Camillo Golgi (1843–1926), had revealed the delicate architecture of the brain, the various cortical layers, and the remarkable arborization and shape of different kinds of neurons, from pyramidal cells in the cortex to Purkinje cells in the cerebellum. The word "synapse", describing the contacts neurons make with each other, had been introduced by Charles Sherrington (1857–1952). Anesthetic and other drugs that can chemically alter brain states and consciousness were also well known. Finally the studies of Alan Hodgkin (1914–1998) and Andrew Huxley (1917–2012) of how neurons transmit electric signals along their axons started before, and interrupted by, the Second World War, had resumed and resulted in the publication of the famous Hodgkin–Huxley model in 1952.

At the same time, on the theoretical side, mathematicians from George Boole (1815–1864), to Georg Cantor (1845–1918), to Kurt Gödel (1906–1978), and especially Alan Turing (1912–1954) had laid the foundations of logic, computability, and computer science. The mathematician John von Neumann (1903–1957) had designed the basic computer architecture still in use today, participated in the development of one of the first computers, studied cellular and self-reproducing automata, and written a little book *The Computer and the Brain* (originally unfinished and published first in 1958 after his death) [770]. Claude Shannon (1916–2001) had laid the foundations of information theory in *A Mathematical Theory of Communication* published in 1948. Perhaps most notably for this book, Warren McCulloch (1898–1969) and Walter Pitts (1923–1969) had published *A Logical Calculus of the Ideas Immanent in Nervous Activity* in 1943 and,

---

[1] This is the title of an essay published a little later, in 1973, by evolutionary biologist Theodosius Dobzhansky (1900–1975).

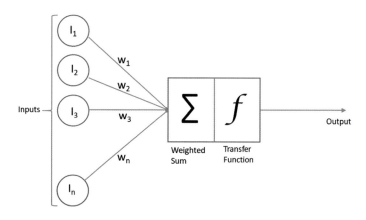

Figure 1.3 Simple neuronal model with n inputs and n synaptic weights. The neuron operates by computing the weighted sum of its inputs, also called the activation, and then passing it through a transfer function, also called activation function, to produce its output. Crucially, this computing units comes with its own storage unit. Information is stored in the synaptic weights.

together with their subsequent work, started to introduce a simple neural model, which is essentially what is still used today in most deep learning applications (Figure 1.3).

It is against this rich intellectual backdrop, that scientists could begin to think in more precise ways about learning and memory and try to seek detailed mechanistic explanations for Ivan Pavlov (1849–1936)'s experiments on conditioning reflexes or, more broadly, the question of neural storage: how and where one stores information in the brain, such as one's name or telephone number.

A back of the envelope calculation shows that long-term memories cannot be encoded in permanent electrical signals reverberating throughout the brain. As a result, long-term memory bits must ultimately be encoded in the structure and biochemical composition of the brain, not its electrical activity, and synapses are the ideal place where this encoding ought to take place, in order to be able to rapidly influence neural activity during recall and other tasks. The hypothesis that memories may be encoded in synapses can be traced back at least to an article by Cajal [165], where it is hinted in broad strokes, the term synapse not having been created yet. This is the quote given at the beginning of this chapter, which can roughly be translated by: "Mental exercise is not likely to improve the organization of the brain by increasing the number of cells because, as we know, nerve cells have lost the ability to replicate since the embryonic stage; but one can accept as being very likely that mental exercise triggers the growth of the protoplasmic apparatus and branching network of arborizations in the areas that are most activated. In this way, associations already created between certain groups of cells become reinforced in particular through the expansion of terminal arborizations and connections; in addition, entirely new connections between cells could be created through the formation of new branches and new protoplasmic expansions.".

Thus the simple idea was born that learning and memory must be implemented some-how at the level of synapses (their position, shape, composition, creation/elimination,

Table 1.1 Length scales: in the human brain, and the brain rescaled by a factor of 10^6.

Object	Scale in Meters	Rescaled by 10^6	Rescaled Object
Diameter of Atom	10^{-10}	10^{-4}	Hair
Diameter of DNA	10^{-9}	10^{-3}	
Diameter of Synapse	10^{-7}	10^{-1}	Fist
Diameter of Axon	10^{-6}	10^0	
Diameter of Neuron	10^{-5}	10^1	Room
Length of Axon	10^{-3}–10^0	10^3–10^6	Park-Nation
Length of Brain	10^{-1}	10^5	State
Length of Body	10^0	10^6	Nation

strengthening/weakening) – and roughly remains the guiding model even today. Needless to say, we have gained a much better appreciation of the biochemical processes involved in synaptic modifications, including complex patterns of gene expression and epigenetic modifications, and the complex production, transport, sequestration, and degradation of protein, RNA, and other molecular species (e.g. [317, 488, 767, 568, 713]).

Furthermore, one may conjecture that the essence of the learning algorithms for modifying synapses must be relatively simple since they are shared by vertebrates and invertebrates (e.g. Aplysia) and thus were discovered very early by evolution. This is not to say, of course, that the actual implementation of the algorithms in biological wetware may not be extremely complicated, requiring again changes in gene expression, epigenetic modifications, and many other cellular processes. But the basic underlying algorithms ought to be relatively simple, and thus began the quests for such algorithms.

1.2.3   The Deep Learning Problem

While elegant in its simplicity and power, the idea that changes in synapses over time and in different parts of the brain, intimately coupled with electrical activity, is ultimately responsible for learning and memory formation faces a formidable challenge which is not immediately apparent given the very small length-scale of synapses. To clearly see this challenge, it is useful to rescale synapses by a factor of one million (Table 1.1) to obtain a better visualization of the problem. With this rescaling, a synapse becomes the size of a human fist (10 centimeters), the body of a neuron the size of a house (~30 meters), the brain a sphere with radius ~100 kilometers, and the longest axons can run about 10^6 meters, or 1,000 kilometers. Imagine now the task of an individual who is trying to learn how to play tennis, or how to play the violin. How can a fist-sized motor synapse in Los Angeles adjust itself, deciding for instance whether to strengthen or weaken itself, to better control a tennis racket or a bow that is located in San Francisco? The synapse in Los Angeles knows nothing about tennis, or music, or the laws of mechanics, and it is essentially a blind machine: it can only sense its immediate biochemical environment on the scale of its diameter. *This is the epicenter of the deep learning problem.*

More broadly, how can very large numbers of essentially blind synapses, deeply buried inside a jungle of interconnected neurons, adjust themselves in a coordinated manner to produce memories and human intelligent behavior?

1.2.4   Hebbian Learning

Donald Hebb (1904–1985) is credited with being one of the first to sense this deep mystery, still largely unsolved today, and to attempt to provide one of the first ideas for a possible solution in his book *The Organization of Behavior*, which appeared in 1949. Hebb, who was primarily a psychologist, did not use any mathematical formalism and stated his ideas in rather vague terms. Buried in his book, one can find the statement: "*Let us assume that the persistence or repetition of a reverberatory activity (or 'trace') tends to induce lasting cellular changes that add to its stability. When an axon of cell A is near enough to excite cell B and repeatedly or persistently takes part in firing it, some growth process or metabolic change takes place in one or both cells such that A's efficiency, as one of the cells firing B, is increased*". This is often paraphrased in compact form by: "Neurons that fire together, wire together".

While not mathematically precise, Hebb's conceptualization is the first to propose a general purpose, seemingly unsupervised, algorithm for the adjustment of synapses on a large-scale. As previously mentioned, the detailed molecular implementation of learning and memory algorithms in the brain is very complex, regardless of the potential simplicity of the underlying algorithms (as additional references to a vast literature, see for instance [324, 323, 789, 758]). However Hebb's basic insight has remained an important source of inspiration for machine learning, deep learning, and neuroscience. However, it is not clear at all how the large-scale application of Hebbian learning could lead to coherent memories and intelligent behavior. This problem will be examined in a later chapter of this book.

There are several ways of providing a precise mathematical implementation of Hebb's vague idea of self-organized learning. Without going into details yet, the most simple embodiment is given by learning rules of the form:

$$\Delta w_{ij} \propto O_i O_j \quad \text{or} \quad \Delta w_{ij} \propto (O_i - \mu_i)(O_j - \mu_j) \tag{1.1}$$

where w_{ij} denotes the strength of the synaptic connection from neuron j to neuron i, $\propto$ denotes proportionality, O_i represents the output of the postsynaptic neuron with corresponding average μ_i, O_j represents the output of the presynaptic neuron with corresponding average μ_j. The term Δw_{ij} represents the incremental change resulting from the activity of the pre- and post-synatpic neurons. Obviously a more complete formulation would have to include other important details, which will be discussed later, such as the time scales over which these quantities are computed and the interpretation of the outputs (e.g. in terms of firing rates). For the time being, it is worth noting two things in this formulation. First, the learning rule is a quadratic polynomial in the outputs of the two neighboring neurons. Second, as described, this formulation of Hebb's rule is symmetric in that it does not depend on whether the connection runs from the axon of neuron i to the dendrites of neuron j, or vice versa.

1.3   From 1950 to 1980

1.3.1   Shallow Non-Linear Learning

A few years later, Frank Rosenblatt (1928–1971) proposed the first learning algorithm for a neuron represented by a linear threshold function (or perceptron) [618], the perceptron learning algorithm. If a single layer of n perceptrons is given, it is easy to see that each perceptron learns independently from the other perceptrons. In Chapter 7, we will prove that, for such a layer, the perceptron learning algorithm can be rewritten in the form:

$$\Delta w_{ij} \propto (T_i - O_i)I_j \tag{1.2}$$

where Δw_{ij} is the change in the synaptic weight w_{ij} connecting input j to output i, T_i is the binary target for output i, $O_i = f(S_i) = \sum_j f(w_{ij}I_j)$ where f is a threshold function, I_j is the jth component of the input, and all these quantities are computed on-line, i.e. for each training example. The perceptron algorithm can be viewed as a supervised Hebbian algorithm in that it requires a target T_i for each output unit i and each training example, but is written as a product of a postsynaptic term $T_i - O_i$ and a presynaptic term I_j. Again note that this learning rule is a quadratic function of the input, output, and target variables. As we shall see, when the data is linearly separable with respect to each output, the perceptron learning algorithm is capable of finding n suitable hyperplanes that correcly separate the data.

A slightly more general version of the perceptron algorithm, the Delta rule, was introduced by Bernard Widrow and Marcian Hoff [786] in the form:

$$\Delta w_{ij} \propto (T_i - O_i)g'(S_i)I_j \tag{1.3}$$

where the new term $g'(S_i)$ represents the derivative of the transfer function g, and $O_i = g(S_i)$. This again can be viewed as a supervised Hebbian rule for shallow (one-layer) differentiable networks, and it is easy to see that the Widrow–Hoff rule performs gradient descent with respect to the least square error function $\mathcal{E} = \frac{1}{2}\sum_i (T_i - O_i)^2$.

1.3.2   First Forays into Deep Architectures and their Challenges

In the following two decades, some progress was made through a number of individual efforts, but with little global coordination. On the neuroscience side, David Hubel (1926–2013) and Torsten Wiesel began probing the mysteries of the visual system. As the man who introduced the term synapse had put it: "*A shower of little electrical leaks conjures up for me, when I look, the landscape; the castle on the height, or when I look at him, my friend's face and how distant he is from me they tell me. Taking their word for it, I go forward and my other senses confirm that he is there.*" (Charles Sherrington in *Man on his Nature*, 1940). Huber and Wiesel published the results of some of their famous experiments [365] showing that, under anesthesia and very specific stimulus conditions, there are neurons in the early stages of the cat visual cortex that behave like feature detectors by responding, for instance, to bars of a particular orientation at a particular location in the visual field. Furthermore, these feature detector neurons are organized into fairly regular arrays covering both the entire visual field and the space of features (e.g. bars at all possible orientations).

On the computational side, Alexey Ivakhnenko (1913–2007) in Russia seems to have been among the first to formally consider multi-layer architectures of simple processing units, and deep learning algorithms for training them [371, 372], such as gradient descent, although the influence of his work at the time seems to have been limited. The idea of gradient descent goes back at least to the work of Augustin-Louis Cauchy (1789–1857) in 1847 and Jacques Hadamard (1865–1963) in 1908. As we shall see, deriving gradient descent in systems with multiple layers requires the chain rule of calculus, which itself goes back to Gottfried Leibniz (1646–1716) and Isaac Newton (1643–1727). It is also in Russia, around the same period that Vladimir Vapnik and Alexey Chervonenkis (1938–2014) began to develop their statistical theory of learning ([752, 750, 751] and references therein).

More influential at the time were Marvin Minsky (1927–2016) and Seymour Papert with their 1969 book [503] proving a number of interesting results about perceptrons. In this book, they also raised concerns regarding the possibility of finding good learning algorithms for deep (multi-layer) perceptrons: *"The perceptron has shown itself worthy of study despite (and even because of!) its severe limitations. It has many features to attract attention: its linearity; its intriguing learning theorem; its clear paradigmatic simplicity as a kind of parallel computation. There is no reason to suppose that any of these virtues carry over to the many-layered version."* While such statements may have not encouraged research in neural networks, claims that this brought neural network research to a halt have been exaggerated, as can be seen from the literature. Even in the original perceptron book, right after the sentence above, the authors wrote the following hedging sentence: *"Nevertheless, we consider it to be an important research problem to elucidate (or reject) our intuitive judgment that the extension to multilayer systems is sterile. Perhaps some powerful convergence theorem will be discovered, or some profound reason for the failure to produce an interesting 'learning theorem' for the multilayered machine will be found"*.

Finally, in Japan, throughout the 1960s and 1970s Kehiko Fukushima began to think about computer vision architectures inspired by neurobiology and in particular the work of Hubel and Wiesel [286, 287, 289]. This line of work culminated in the neocognitron model [288], essentially a multi-layer convolutional neural network, whereby local operations, such as detection of particular features over a small patch, are repeated at each location of the input image, effectively convolving the image with the corresponding feature detector, and providing a foundation for enabling translation invariant recognition. Unfortunately the computer power to train convolutional neural networks was not readily available at the time. However, and even more fundamentally, Fukushima proposed to solve vision problems using the wrong learning algorithm: he proposed to learn the parameters of the neocognitron in a self-organized way using Hebbian learning. This approach never materialized in practice and the reasons behind this will play an important role later in the book. In particular, we will show that Hebbian learning applied to a feedforward convolutional neural network cannot solve vision tasks [102].

Needless to say, there were many other developments in the period 1950–1980 that were directly relevant but cannot be surveyed, for instance, the development of complexity theory and the concept of NP-completeness [293], or additional work on neural networks by other scientists, such as Shun Ichi Amari [22, 23] or Stephen Grossberg [313, 314, 255, 315]).

1.4   From 1980 to Today

The machine learning expansion of the past few decades started in the 1980s, under the influence of several clusters of researchers, which originally worked fairly independently of each other and whose influences progressively merged. Three of these clusters were based in Southern California, the exception being Leslie Valiant at Harvard who was laying some of the foundations of computational learning theory by developing the probably approximately correct (PAC) framework [743]. Around the same time, Judea Pearl at UCLA was developing the theory and algorithms for Bayesian networks [567]. At Caltech, John Hopfield developed a discrete model of associative memory [355], followed by an analog version for optimization and other purposes [357, 720], that were particularly influential at the time. For one, these models established important connections to statistical mechanics, in particular the theory of spin glasses, and brought many physicists to the field from around the world. Other faculty members at the time at Caltech that were drawn into neural networks included Edward Posner, Robert McEliece, Demetri Psaltis, Yaser Abu-Mostafa, and Carver Mead who used analog VLSI to build some of the first analog neuromorphic circuits [496, 470, 495] with Misha Mahowald (1963–1996). Hopfield's connections also brought an influx of scientists and research from the Bell Laboratories. The fourth cluster, and perhaps the one which over time contributed the most to practical applications of neural networks, was the Parallel Distributed Processing (PDP) group at UCSD (and also CMU) led by David Rumelhart and James McClelland [490]. The PDP group made several contributions that are studied in detail in this book including the concepts of supervised and unsupervised learning, autoencoders and Boltzmann machines [9], and of course it co-developed and popularized the backpropagation learning algorithm, basically stochastic gradient descent for neural networks using the chain rule of calculus [627].

The basic backpropagation learning rule can be written as:

$$\Delta w_{ij} \propto B_i O_j \qquad (1.4)$$

where O_j is the output of the presynaptic neuron and B_i is a postsynaptic backpropagated error obtained by applying the chain rule. While in this form the rule still seems to have a supervised Hebbian flavor with a quadratic form, it is important to note that the backpropagated error B_i is not the activity of the postsynaptic neuron. This again will have important consequences in later analyses.

Backpropagation is the single most important and most practical algorithm in this book, and the PDP group played a role in demonstrating its capabilities and promoting its early adoption in the mid-1980s. Terry Sejnowski, for instance, used it to pioneer several applications in speech synthesis (NETtalk)[665] and protein secondary structure prediction [588]. Finally, using backpropagation, it became possible to train the convolutional neural networks that Fukishima had originally proposed, in applications such as handwritten character recognition [219] or biometric fingerprint recognition [76].

The mid-1980s also correspond to the time when the first sustained machine learning conferences started, originally run by a combination of scientists from Caltech, Bell Labs, and the PDP group; beginning with a meeting in Santa Barbara, CA in 1985, followed by the first annual, by-invitation only Snowbird, UT conference in 1986 which also led to the first NIPS – now renamed NeurIPS – conference in Denver, CO and the establishment of the NIPS Foundation by Edward Posner in 1987.

By the end of the 1980s, the word "HMMs" (hidden Markov models), coming from the scientists using them in speech recognition, could be heard with increasing frequency at these conferences. In a few short years, this led to several developments including:

(1) the development of HMMs for bioinformatics applications which ushered machine learning methods into biology at the time of the human genome sequencing project [423, 79];
(2) the first attempts at combining graphical models with neural networks leading to, for instance, hybrid HMM/Neural Network (NN) and recursive neural networks [78, 99, 280];
(3) the recognition that HMMs and their learning algorithms (e.g. the EM algorithm) were special cases of a more general theory of graphical models [689] and probabilistic inference, the foundations of which had already been laid by Judea Pearl and several others.

Thus the 1990s saw a rapid expansion of research in all areas of probabilistic graphical models [696, 282, 386, 417, 234], which for almost a decade became the dominant topic at NIPS, and more broadly in machine learning. Somewhat like "HMMs", SVMs (support vector machines) [211, 217] – a sophisticated form of shallow learning – started at some point to gain popularity and led to a rapid expansion of research in the more general area of kernel methods [656, 657], which also became a dominant topic in machine learning for another decade or so.

Although graphical models and kernel methods were the dominant topics in the 1990s and 2000s, the idea of a second "neural network winter" has been overblown, just like the first one, and for similar reasons. A simple inspection of the literature shows that research on neural networks by several groups around the world continued unabated, leading to several new results. Among many others, these include: the development of LSTMs (long–short term memory units) [348]; the development of recursive deep learning methods [280]; and the application of recursive neural networks to a host of problems ranging from protein secondary structure prediction [75, 579], to protein contact map prediction [88, 237], and to the game of GO [791, 792], to name just a few.

Starting around 2011, convolutional neural networks implemented on Graphical Processing Units (GPUs) were used to win international computer vision competitions, such as the IJCNN 2011 traffic site recognition contest [199], achieving super-human performance levels. A successful application of GPUs and convolutional neural networks to

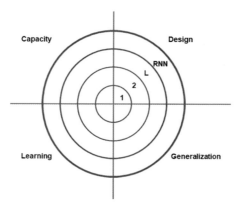

Figure 1.4 Roadmap. Concentric circles correspond to neural networks of increasing complexity, starting from single neurons, going to feedforward neural networks with increasing number L of layers, and then to recurrent and recursive neural networks. The sectors provide examples of important topics that need to be investigated for each level of complexity.

the ImageNet benchmark data set [422], involving million of images across thousands of categories, contributed significantly to a broader recognition of neural networks and their rebranding as "deep learning".

The current period of expansion of neural networks and deep learning into most areas of science and technology is driven by three major technological factors:

(1) the availability of unprecedented computing power, primarily in the form of GPUs;
(2) the availability of large training sets, thanks to progress in sensors, databases, the Internet, open-source projects, and so forth – although it is important to note that deep learning methods can also be adapted and deployed in scenarios where data is less abundant; and
(3) the development of well-maintained, industrial-strength, software libraries for neural networks such as TensorFlow, PyTorch, and Keras.

1.5   Roadmap

A mental roadmap for the rest of this book is depicted in Figure 1.4. We will start from the center of the bullseye and progressively expand towards the periphery. The concentric circles correspond to networks of increasing power and complexity, starting from feedforward networks with one layer, two layers, an arbitrary number L layers, and then recurrent and recursive networks. In the angular dimension, the sectors correspond to fundamental topics that need to be studied for each level of complexity. Examples of sectors we will study include the design and capacity of these networks, the corresponding learning algorithms and generalization capabilities. There is not yet a complete theory for each one of the resulting "boxes", however, as we shall see, there is substantial theory for many of them. The flip side of deep learning being like linear regression on steroids is that, like linear regression, it can be applied to essentially any domain provided one is willing to collaborate with domain experts. There are plenty of applications of deep learning to engineering and other problems that are covered in many articles and in other books. Here we will focus on applications of deep learning to problems in the natural sciences.

1.6   Exercises

EXERCISE 1.1   Identify as many other forms of computing as possible and evaluate their current status.

EXERCISE 1.2   Identify and discuss different forms of virtualization that may be contained in Figure 1.1.

EXERCISE 1.3   Why may it not be too surprising to find that both brains and computers use electrical signals to process information?

EXERCISE 1.4   Provide a back-of-the-envelope calculation for estimating the energetic cost of storing information, over the long-term, using patterns of electrical activity in brains or computers.

EXERCISE 1.5   Provide a back-of-the-envelope calculation for estimating how much power the brain requires for its operation, and compare it to the power required by the entire organism.

EXERCISE 1.6   Provide a back-of-the-envelope calculation for estimating how much power is required to power a desktop, versus a supercomputer, versus a server farm.

EXERCISE 1.7   The olfactory cortex appears to be close to the nose, and the auditory cortex appears to be close to the ears. Provide plausible explanations for why our primary visual cortex is located in the back of our heads, far away from the eyes.

2 Basic Concepts

In this chapter, we introduce the basic neural network models used throughout the book, which date back to ideas developed in the 1940s and 1950s, as described in the previous chapter. The basic idea is to view neural networks as parallel distributed processing systems consisting of interconnected networks of simple processing units, or "neurons". The connections have parameters, or "synaptic weights", and learning and memory processes are implemented through algorithms for adjusting these synaptic weights to influence the activity of the units in a suitable way.

The relation of these models to biological neural networks is briefly discussed at the end of the book. However, regardless of how strong the connection is, these models are the simplest and best approach we have found so far to explore the style of computing adopted by biological neural systems. This style is radically different from the style of standard computers with: holographic-based instead of tape-based information storage, and intimate colocation and intertwining of memory and computation, instead of their clear separation in digital systems.

2.1 Synapses

Biological synapses are difficult to study – among other things their size is in a range difficult to analyze with traditional instruments, roughly half way between the size of molecules and cells. However new technologies are continuously being developed and are revealing how complex and dynamical biological synapses are, how they exist in different types, how they are dependent on many cellular phenomena (e.g. gene expression, molecular transport), and how they can be characterized by several attributes (e.g. shape, surface, volume, composition). It also seems to be common for a biological neuron to have more than one synaptic contact onto a neuron to which it is connected, and synapses are organized along dendritic trees with complex geometries. It is not clear how much of this complexity is essential to neural computation, and how much is the result of having to deal with all the constraints posed by carbon-based computing.

In this book, most of the time, we take the simplified view that a neuron i can only receive one synaptic connection from neuron j, and this connection is characterized by a single real-valued parameter w_{ij}, representing the synaptic strength or efficacy. If neuron j has multiple synapses onto neuron i, we consider that they have been lumped together into the value w_{ij} which globally captures how strongly neuron j influences neuron i. However, by simplifying a synapse to a single number w_{ij}, we are able to focus on the most fundamental problem of learning and memory: how is information about the world stored in w_{ij}?

Before we treat the learning problem, a fundamental question is how many bits of information can be stored in a synapse. Within the models considered in this book, we will see that this fundamental question has a precise answer. Although most of the time we will work with real-valued (or rational-valued) synapses as an approximation, obviously in a physical neural system there may be limits on the dynamic range and precision of w_{ij}. And thus it can be instructive to consider also cases where w_{ij} has a finite range or a limited precision of a few bits, possibly down to a single bit [111]. In some cases, one may want to include a constraint on the sign of w_{ij}, for instance not allowing excitatory synapses to become inhibitory or vice versa. These cases will occasionally be treated and, while real-valued synapses are convenient to use in theoretical calculations and computer simulations, one should never take them to imply that an infinite amount of information can be stored at each synapse.

In order to build more intelligent systems using neural networks, it is likely that the current synaptic model will have to be expanded and new mechanisms included. For example, think about situations where one is reading the end of a long paragraph and must remember its beginning, or walking in a new environment and must remember one's path. It is unlikely that this kind of short-term information, corresponding to periods of seconds to minutes, is stored in neural activity alone. A more likely scenario is that this information is stored, at least in part, in fast synaptic weights, thus requiring the introduction of synapses with different time scales as well as erasing mechanisms. Another example of new mechanism could be the introduction of computational circuits within groups of synapses (e.g. [582]), or synapses that can modulate other synapses, giving rise to neural networks that can modulate the function of other neural networks.

2.2 Units or Neurons

In this book, we consider neural networks, consisting of simple computing elements called "units", or "gates", or "neurons". A unit with n inputs $I_1, \ldots, I_n$ and n corresponding synapses, computes an output $O = f(I_1, \ldots, I_n, w_1, \ldots, w_n)$. Most of the time, we will consider that the operation of the unit can be decomposed into two steps: the computation of a simple activation $S = g(I_1, \ldots, I_n, w_1, \ldots, w_n)$, followed by the application of a transfer (or activation) function f to produce the output $O = f(S)$.

2.3 Activations

In most cases, we will use the linear activation:

$$S = \sum_{i=1}^{n} w_i I_i \quad \text{or} \quad S = \sum_{i=0}^{n} w_i I_i. \tag{2.1}$$

In this notation, the parameter w_i represents the synaptic strength of the connection of the ith input to the unit. Furthermore, we assume that I_0 is always set to 1 and w_0 is called the bias of the unit. In other words, the activation is simply the weighted average of all the inputs weighted by the synaptic weights, or the dot product between the input vector and the vector of synaptic weights. There is evidence that neuronal dendrites may be well suited to computing dot products [575]. Although several different non-linear transfer functions will be considered in the next section, equating the dot product to zero defines a fundamental hyperplane that partitions the neuron's input space into two halves and provides the direction of affine hyperplanes where the dot product remains constant.

In the search for greater biological realism, or more powerful computing units, it is also natural to introduce polynomial activations where S is a polynomial P of degree d in the input variables. For instance, if P is a homogeneous polynomial of degree two, then:

$$S = \sum_{i,j} v_{ij} I_i I_j. \tag{2.2}$$

Note that here v_{ij} is an interaction weight between I_i and I_j. More generally, polynomial activations of degree d require synaptic weights associated with the product of up to d inputs. As we shall see in Chapter 6, quadratic activation functions are one way of implementing gating or attention mechanisms.

2.4   Transfer Functions

Different kinds of computing units are obtained by using different kinds of transfer functions f to compute the output $O = f(S)$. We briefly review the most common ones.

2.4.1   Identity and Linear Transfer Functions

In this case, $f(S) = S$ or $f(S) = aS + b$ for some real numbers a and b. When the bias is included in the activation S through w_0, these two transfer functions are interchangeable by adjusting the weights w_i accordingly. Thus, in many cases, only $f(S) = S$ needs to be considered or implemented. If the activation S is linear ($d = 1$), this yields a linear unit. As a special case, a pooling unit that computes the average of its inputs is of course a linear unit. Networks of linear units are often dismissed as being uninteresting. As we shall see, this is far from being the case. However it is essential to introduce and study non-linear transfer functions.

2.4.2   Polynomial Transfer Functions

In this case, the activation function can be a polynomial Q of degree d. In fact, most other non-linear transfer functions described below can be well approximated, at least over a finite range, by a polynomial transfer function for a suitable degree d, depending on the precision required. Note that in general, polynomial activations and polynomial transfer functions are not equivalent, even when their degree is the same.

2.4.3 Max (Pool) Transfer Functions

Sometimes, for instance in convolutional architectures for vision problems to be described below, it can be useful to use max pooling units of the form:

$$O = \max(I_1, \ldots, I_n). \tag{2.3}$$

Note that although listed here as a different kind of transfer function, within the general framework described above this corresponds rather to a different kind of non-linear activation function, although the distinction is not consequential.

2.4.4 Threshold Transfer Functions

A threshold (or step) function has the form:

$$f(S) = \begin{cases} 1 & \text{if } S > 0 \\ 0 & \text{otherwise,} \end{cases} \tag{2.4}$$

using a $\{0, 1\}$ formalism (also called Heaviside function), or:

$$f(S) = \begin{cases} +1 & \text{if } S > 0 \\ -1 & \text{otherwise,} \end{cases} \tag{2.5}$$

using a $\{-1, +1\}$ formalism. The latter can also be written as $f(S) = \text{sgn}(S)$. [Note that usually $\text{sgn}(0) = 0$ but the decision of what to do when S is exactly equal to 0 is usually not consequential.] Usually the two formalisms are equivalent using the affine transformations $t(x) = 2x - 1$ to go from $\{0, 1\}$ to $\{-1, +1\}$, or $t(x) = (x + 1)/2$ to go from $\{-1, +1\}$ to $\{0, 1\}$. However, it is always good to check the equivalence and look at its effects on the synaptic weights. Unless otherwise stated, we will use the $\{-1, +1\}$ formalism. If S is linear, then this case leads to the notion of a linear threshold function. If in addition the inputs are binary, this leads to the notion of a Boolean threshold gate, a particular kind of Boolean function. Likewise, if S is a polynomial of degree d, then this leads to the notion of a polynomial or algebraic threshold function of degree d. If in addition the inputs are binary, this leads to the notion of Boolean polynomial threshold gate of degree d.

To be more specific, we consider the n-dimensional hypercube $H^n = \{-1, 1\}^n$. A homogeneous Boolean linear threshold gate f of n variables is a Boolean function over H^n of the form:

$$f(I_1, \ldots, I_n) = \text{sgn}\left(\sum_{i=1}^{n} w_i I_i\right). \tag{2.6}$$

A non-homogenous Boolean linear threshold gate has an additional bias w_0 and is given by:

$$f(I_1, \ldots, I_n) = \text{sgn}\left(w_0 + \sum_{i=1}^{n} w_i I_i\right) = \text{sgn}\left(\sum_{i=0}^{n} w_i I_i\right), \tag{2.7}$$

assuming that $I_0 = 1$.

Likewise, a homogeneous Boolean polynomial threshold gate of degree d is a Boolean function over H given by:

$$f(I_1, \ldots, I_n) = \text{sgn}\left(\sum_{J \in \mathcal{J}_d} w_J I^J\right),\tag{2.8}$$

where $\mathcal{J}_d$ denotes all the subsets of size d of $\{1, 2, \ldots, n\}$. If $J = \{j_1, j_2, \ldots, j_d\}$ is such a subset, then $I^J = I_{j_1} I_{j_2} \cdots I_{j_d}$, and $w = (w_J)$ is the vector of weights representing interactions of degree d. Note that if the variables are valued in $\{-1, 1\}$, then for any index i, $I_i^2 = +1$ and therefore integer exponents greater than 1 can be ignored. Alternatively, one can also define homogeneous polynomial threshold functions where the polynomial is homogenous over $\mathbb{R}^n$ rather than H^n. A non-homogenous Boolean polynomial threshold gate of degree d is given by the same expression:

$$f(I_1, \ldots, I_n) = \text{sgn}\left(\sum_{J \in \mathcal{J}_{\leq d}} w_J x^J\right).\tag{2.9}$$

This time $\mathcal{J}_{\leq d}$ represents all possible subsets of $\{1, 2, \ldots, n\}$ of size d or less, including possibly the empty set associated with a bias term. Note that for most practical purposes, including developing more complex models of synaptic integration, one is interested in fixed, relatively small values of d.

As we shall see, it is useful to consider networks of Boolean threshold gates and compare their properties to networks consisting of other Boolean gates, such as unrestricted Boolean gates, or standard Boolean gates (AND, OR, NOT). In particular, it is important to keep in mind the fundamental difference between a linear threshold gate and a standard gate. A standard gate does not have a memory, or at best one could say that it has a frozen memory associated with the list of patterns it maps to one. In contrast, the units we consider in this book have an adaptive memory embodied in the synaptic weights. Instead of being frozen, their input-output function varies as a function of the information stored in the weights. The adaptive storage is the fundamental difference, and not whether a certain class of transfer functions is better than another one.

2.4.5   Rectified and Piecewise Linear Transfer Functions

The rectified linear transfer function, often called ReLU (Rectified Linear Unit), is a piecewise linear transfer function corresponding to:

$$O = f(S) = \max(0, S).\tag{2.10}$$

Thus the function is equal to 0 if $S \leq 0$, and equal to the identity function $f(x) = x$ if $S \geq 0$. The ReLU transfer function is differentiable everywhere except for $S = 0$ and one of its key advantages, which will become important during gradient descent learning, is that its derivative is very simple: it is either 0 or 1. Leaky ReLU transfer functions have a small non-zero slope for $S \leq 0$. More generally, it is possible to consider more general piecewise linear (PL) transfer functions with multiple hinges and different slopes between the hinges (e.g. [13]). Useful sub-classes are the even PLs satisfying $f(-x) = f(x)$, and the odd PLs satisfying $f(-x) = -f(x)$. As we shall see, it is also possible to learn the parameters of the transfer functions, in this case the location of the hinges or the slope of the linear segments, resulting in adaptive PLs (APLs). If needed, there are also continuously differentiable approximation to PLs using polynomial transfer functions of suitable degree or, other approximations. For instance, the ReLU can be approximated by the integral of the logistic function described below.

2.4.6 Sigmoidal Transfer Functions

Sigmoidal transfer functions can be viewed as continuous differentiable versions of threshold transfer functions. Over the $(0, 1)$ range, it is common to use the logistic function:

$$f(S) = \frac{1}{1 + e^{-S}}.$$ (2.11)

As we shall see, in many cases $f(S)$ can be interpreted as a probability. The derivative of the logistic function satisfies: $f'(S) = f(S)(1 - f(S))$. If necessary, the location and slope of the fast growing region can be changed by using the slightly more general form:

$$f(S) = \frac{1}{1 + Ce^{-\lambda S}},$$ (2.12)

where C and λ are additional parameters. In this case, $f'(S) = \lambda f(S)(1 - f(S))$. Over the $(-1, +1)$ range, it is common to use the tanh transfer function:

$$f(S) = \tanh S = \frac{e^S - e^{-S}}{e^S + e^{-S}},$$ (2.13)

which satisfies $f'(S) = 1 - \tanh^2 S = 1 - (f(S))^2$. Other sigmoidal functions that are more rarely used include: $f(S) = \arctan S$ and $f(S) = S/\sqrt{1 + S^2}$ and their parameterized variations.

2.4.7 Softmax Transfer Functions

Starting from the vector $(I_1, \ldots, I_n)$ it is sometimes desirable to produce an n-dimensional output probability vector $(O_1, \ldots, O_n)$, satisfying for every i $O_i \geq 0$, and $\sum_i O_i = 1$. This is typically the case in classification problems where multiple classes are present and O_i can be interpreted as the probability of membership in class i. The softmax, or normalized exponential, transfer function (with a slight abuse of language) can be written as:

$$O_i = \frac{e^{I_i}}{\sum_j e^{I_j}},$$ (2.14)

or

$$O_i = \frac{e^{\lambda I_i}}{\sum_j e^{\lambda I_j}},$$ (2.15)

with an additional parameter $\lambda > 0$, which plays the role of an inverse temperature in relation to the Boltzmann distribution in statistical mechanics (see below). At high temperature, $\lambda \to 0$ and the distribution approaches the uniform distribution. At low temperature, $\lambda \to \infty$ and the distribution becomes increasingly concentrated where the maximum of I_j occurs. When $n = 2$, each output can be written as a logistic function of the corresponding difference of the inputs: $O_1 = 1/(1 + e^{-(I_1 - I_2)})$. For every i, the partial derivatives of the softmax transfer function satisfy: $\partial O_i / \partial I_i = O_i(1 - O_i)$ and for $j \neq i$ $\partial O_i / \partial I_j = -O_i O_j$. When there is a temperature parameter, these formula must be multiplied by the factor λ. Note also that there are many other ways of producing probability vectors, for instance: $O_i = I_i^2 / \sum_j I_j^2$.

2.5   Discrete versus Continuous Time

In most engineering applications of neural networks today, neural networks are simulated on digital machines where time is simply ignored. More precisely, time considerations are handled artificially by external computer programs that decide when to update the activity of each neuron, when to update each synaptic weight, and so forth using a discretized version of time. Quantities, such as how long it takes for a signal to propagate from one neuron to the next, or for a synapse or neuron to update itself, are completely ignored.

However, in a physical neural system, time is continuous and its role is essential. Various continuous-time models of neurons exist, and can themselves be simulated on digital machines. However these models are seldom used in current applications and will not be treated extensively in this book. Usually the continuous-time aspect of these systems is modeled using differential equations that may lead to neuronal activities that are either smoothly continuous or produce spikes at precise times. For example, [69], we can consider a network of n interacting neurons, where each neuron i is described by a smooth activation function $S_i(t)$, which can be thought of as a "voltage" and a smooth output function $O_i(t)$, governed by the equations:

$$\frac{dS_i}{dt} = -\frac{S_i}{\tau_i} + \sum_j w_{ij} O_j + I_i \quad \text{and} \quad O_i = f_i(S_i), \tag{2.16}$$

where τ_i is the time constant of neuron i, I_i is an external input to neuron i, and f_i is the transfer function of neuron i, for instance a logistic or tanh function. The logistic output could be further interpreted as a short-term average firing rate, or as the probability of producing a spike if a continuous-time spiking model is required.

A different version of this model can be written as:

$$\frac{dS_i}{dt} = -\frac{S_i}{\tau_i} + \alpha_i f_i \left(\sum_j w_{ij} S_j \right) + I_i \quad \text{and} \quad O_i = f_i(S_i). \tag{2.17}$$

It is easy to show that provided all the time constants are identical ($\tau_i = \tau$) and the matrix (w_{ij}) is invertible, the systems described by Equations 2.16 and 2.17 are equivalent. The discretization of Equation 2.17 with $\tau_i = \alpha_i = \Delta t = 1$ yields back the standard discrete models described above.

These single-compartment models were already well-known in the 1970s and 1980s [22, 664, 355, 204] and they were applied to, for instance, combinatorial optimization problems [356, 357] and speech recognition [720]. More detailed models of biological neurons, using multiple compartments, were also developed in the early 1980s and continue to be developed today [415, 141, 342, 142, 170]. The issues of whether spikes play a fundamental computational role, or other auxiliary roles, such as energy conservation, is still not clear. Spiking models are also used in neuromorphic chips. While detailed compartmental models of spiking neurons may be too slow to simulate for applicaitons, there are several simplified spiking models that enable the simulations of large spiking networks on digital machines, from the early model of FitzHugh–Nagumo [275, 527] to its modern descendants [373].

2.6   Networks and Architectures

Now that the basic models for units and synapses are in place, we want to think about the circuits that can be built with them. The words circuit, network, and architecture are used more or less interchangeably in the field, although they sometimes have slightly different connotations. The word architecture, for instance, is often associated with a notion of "design"; often it is also used to refer to the topology (i.e. the underlying directed graph) of a network, irrespective of the particular values of the synaptic weights.

To learn complex tasks, it is natural to consider large neural networks with both visible and hidden units. The visible units are the units at the periphery of the architecture, where "external" inputs can be applied, or outputs can be produced. All the other units are called non-visible units, or hidden units.

2.6.1   The Proper Definition of Deep

In loose terms, the depth of a circuit or network refers to the number of processing stages that are required to transform an input into an output. In circuit theory [201], the word deep typically refers to circuits where the depth scales like n^α ($\alpha > 0$), where n denotes the size of the input vectors. This is not the definition used in this book.

In neural networks, the word "deep" is meant to establish a contrast with "shallow" methods, epitomized by simple kernel methods [657]. Some have used loose definitions of depth (e.g. at least half a dozen layers), or arbitrary cutoffs (e.g. at least three layers). Instead, it is preferable to use a simple but precise definition.

As we shall see, the learning problem is relatively easy when there are no hidden units. However, as soon as there are hidden units, the question of how to train their incoming weights becomes tricky. This is sometimes referred to as the credit assignment problem in the literature. For these reasons, in this book, we define as shallow any architecture that contains only visible units, and as deep any architecture that contains at least one hidden unit.

Hence in the next chapter we will first study shallow architectures, with no hidden units. In the meantime, it is worth defining a few broad classes of architectures and establish the corresponding notation.

2.6.2   Feedforward Architectures

A feedforward architecture with n neurons is an architecture that does not contain any directed cycles. Alternatively, it is an architecture where the neurons can be numbered in such a way that a connection from neuron i to neuron j can exist if and only if $i < j$. The source and sink neurons are visible and correspond to inputs and outputs respectively. All other neurons are hidden. In a feedforward architecture, the numbering of the neurons can also provide a natural ordering for updating them. The first part of the book focuses on feedforward architectures.

2.6.3   Recurrent Architectures

A recurrent architecture is any architecture that contains at least one directed cycle. To define how the architecture operates, one must also specify in which order the neurons are updated (e.g. synchronously, stochastically, according to a fixed order). By discretizing time and using synchronous updates, a recurrent architecture with n neurons can always be "unfolded in time" into a feedforward layered architecture (see Chapter 9), where each layer has n neurons, and the depth of the unfolded architecture is equal to the number of time steps.

2.6.4   Layered Architectures

A layered architecture is an architecture where the units have been grouped into layers. Both feedforward and recurrent architectures can be layered, or not. In a layered feedforward architecture, connections typically run from one layer to the next. Neighboring layers are said to be fully connected if every neuron in one layer is connected to every neuron in the next layer. Otherwise the two layers are partially connected. Depending on the degree of connectivity of the layers and their arrangement, the layers can also be described as sparsely connected, or locally connected. In locally connected architectures, a neuron in one layer may receive connections only from a (small) neighborhood in the previous layer. A layered architecture may skip connections, connecting two non-consecutive layers. Intra-layer connections are also possible, and often observed in biology (e.g."inhibitory interneurons") but these are rarely used in current practical applications.

In general, a feedforward architecture with L layers of neurons (including both input and output neurons) will be denoted by:

$$A(n_1, n_2, \ldots, n_L), \tag{2.18}$$

where n_1 is the number of inputs, n_L is the number of outputs, and n_h is the number of units in hidden layer h. For instance, if we write $A(n_0, \ldots, n_L)$ the architecture has $L + 1$ layers and the input layer has size n_0. Likewise, $A(n, m, p)$ is an architecture with n input units, m hidden units, and p output units. Two layers l_1 and l_2 ($l_1 < l_2$) are said to be fully connected if every unit in layer l_1 is connected to every unit in layer l_2. A weight running from unit j in layer k to unit i in layer $h \geq k$ will be denoted by w_{ij}^{hk}.

This notation allows both skip connections and intra-layer connections. In this case, the output of unit i in layer h can be written as:

$$O_i^h = f_i^h(S_i^h) = f_i^h\left(\sum_{k \le h}\sum_{j=1}^{n_k} w_{ij}^{hk} O_j^k\right), \tag{2.19}$$

where f_i^h is the transfer function of the unit. However, in general, there is not much benefit to be derived by allowing skip connections and, if necessary, it is usually easy to adapt a result obtained in the non-skip case to the skip case. Most often, we will also disallow intra-layer connections and assume that all the transfer functions in one layer are identical. Under these assumptions, we can simplify the notation slightly by denoting a weight running from unit j in layer $h - 1$ to unit i in layer h by w_{ij}^h, keeping only the target layer as an upper index. Thus, in this most typical case:

$$O_i^h = f(S_i^h) = f\left(\sum_{j=1}^{n_{h-1}} w_{ij}^h O_j^{h-1}\right). \tag{2.20}$$

If each layer is fully connected to the next, then the total number of weights is given by:

$$W = \sum_{h=1}^{L-1}(n_h + 1)n_{h+1} \approx \sum_{h=1}^{L-1} n_h n_{h+1}, \tag{2.21}$$

where the approximation on the right ignores the biases of the units.

2.6.5 Weight Sharing, Convolutional, and Siamese Architectures

It is sometimes useful to constrain two different connections in a neural network to have the same synaptic strength. This may be difficult to realize, or even implausible, in a physical neural system. However it is easy to implement in digital simulations. This so-called weight-sharing technique is often used and one of its benefits is to reduce the number of free parameters that need to be learnt. This technique is most commonly used in the context of convolutional architectures, for computer vision and other applications. Convolutional neural networks, originally inspired by the work of Hubel and Wiesel, contain entire layers of locally connected units that share the exact same pattern of connection weights. Thus these units apply the same transformation (e.g. vertical edge detection) at all possible locations of the input field, as in a convolution operation. Furthermore, within the same level of the architecture, multiple such layers can co-exist to detect different features (e.g. edge detection at all possible orientations). In these architectures, the total number of parameters is greatly reduced by the weight sharing approach and, even more so, by having local connectivity patterns between layers, as opposed to full connectivity.

The weight-sharing technique is also used in other standard architectures. For instance, it is used in Siamese architectures where the outputs of two identical networks, sharing all their connections, are fed into a final "comparator" network. Siamese architectures are used when two similar input objects need to be processed in a similar way and then compared to assess their similarity, or to order them. This is the case, for instance, when comparing two fingerprint images [76], or when ranking possible source–sink pairs in predicting elementary chemical reactions [396, 397].

Several other kinds of architectures exist, such as autoencoder, ensemble, and adversarial architectures – these will be introduced later in the book. Armed with these basic architectural notions, it is natural to ask at least three fundamental questions:

(1) capacity: what can be done with a given architecture?
(2) design: how can one design architecture be suitable for a given problem?
(3) learning: how can one find suitable weight values for a given architecture?

These questions will occupy much of the rest of this book and will have to be examined multiple times for different kinds of architectures and situations. Here we introduce some of the basic concepts that will be used to deal with the questions of capacity, design, and learning.

2.7   Functional and Cardinal Capacity of Architectures

A basic framework for the study of learning complexity is to consider that there is a function h that one wishes to learn and a class of functions or hypotheses A that is available to the learner. The function h may be known explicitly or through examples and often h is not in A. The class A, for instance, could be all the functions that can be implemented by a given neural network architecture as the synaptic weights are varied. Starting from some initial function in A, often selected at random, learning is often cast as the process of finding functions in A that are as close as possible to h in some sense (Figure 2.1). Obviously how well h can be learnt critically depends on the class A and thus it is natural to seek to define a notion of "capacity" for any class A.

Ideally, one would like to be able to describe the *functional capacity* of a neural network architecture, i.e. completely characterize the class of functions that it can compute as its synaptic weights are varied. In Chapter 4, we will show that networks with a single hidden layer of arbitrary size have universal approximation properties, in the sense that they can approximate any reasonably smooth function. We will also resolve the functional capacity of feedforward linear and unrestricted Boolean architectures. However, in most of the other cases, the problem of resolving the functional capacity remains open.

In part as a proxy, we will use a simpler notion of capacity, the *cardinal capacity*, or just capacity when the context is clear. The cardinal capacity $C(A)$ of a class A of functions (Figure 2.1) is simply the logarithms base two of the size or volume of A, in other words:

$$C(A) = \log_2 |A|. \tag{2.22}$$

Given an architecture $A(n_1, \ldots, n_L)$ we will denote its capacity by $C(n_1, \ldots, n_L)$. To measure capacity in a continuous setting, one must define $|A|$ in some measure-theoretic sense. In the coming chapters, we will simplify the problem by using threshold gate

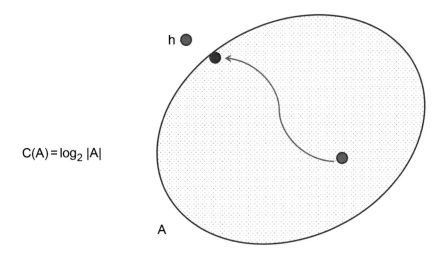

Figure 2.1 Learning framework where h is the function to be learnt and A is the available class of hypotheses or approximating functions.

neurons, so that the class A is finite (provided the inputs are restricted to be binary, or in any other finite set) and therefore we can simply let $|A|$ be the number of functions contained in A. We will show that in this discrete setting the cardinal capacity of many architectures can be estimated.

There are other notions of capacity, besides functional and cardinal capacity, that will be examined in later chapters. The kind of capacity that is being discussed should either be specified or clear from the context. But, in general, the default usage will refer to the cardinal capacity. The fundamental reason why the cardinal capacity is important is that it can be viewed as the number of bits required to specify, or communicate, an element of A. More precisely, it is the minimum average number of bits required to specify an element of A in the worst case of a uniform distribution over A. Another way to look at learning is to view it as a communication process by which information about the "world" is communicated to, and stored in, the synapses of a network. Thus the cardinal capacity provides an estimate of the number of bits that must be communicated to the architecture, and stored in the synaptic weights, so that it can implement the right function.

To address questions of design, as well as other questions, a sound statistical framework is useful. Perhaps the most elegant statistical framework is the Bayesian framework. In particular, in Chapter 3 we will show how the Bayesian framework allows one to solve the design question for shallow networks, as well as for the top layer of any architecture, under a broad set of conditions. Thus next we provide a very brief introduction to the Bayesian statistical framework.

2.8   The Bayesian Statistical Framework

One of the most elegant and coherent frameworks to cope with data is the Bayesian statistical framework. To begin, it is useful to review the axiomatic foundations of the Bayesian statistical framework ([215, 648, 376, 124]). Broadly speaking there are at least two related kinds of axiomatic frameworks. The first kind is based on "monetary" notions, such as utility and betting. As we do not think, perhaps naively, that monetary considerations are essential to science and statistics, we choose the second framework, based on the notion of "degrees of belief".

The starting point for this framework is to consider an observer who has some background knowledge $\mathcal{B}$ and observes some data D. The observer is capable of generating hypotheses or models, from a certain class of hypotheses or models. The process by which these models are generated, or by which the class of models is changed, are outside the immediate scope of the framework.

Bayesian analysis is concerned with the assessment of the quality of the hypotheses given the data and the background model. Given any hypothesis H, the fundamental object of Bayesian statistics is the "observer's degree of belief" $\pi(H|D, \mathcal{B})$ in H, given D and $\mathcal{B}$. If the background knowledge $\mathcal{B}$ changes, the degree of belief may change, which is one of the main reasons why this approach is sometimes called "subjective" (incidentally, a major marketing error of the Bayesian camp and a main argument for the detractors of this approach). Although "subjective", the approach aims to be rational in the sense that the fundamental object $\pi(H|D, \mathcal{B})$ should satisfy a set of reasonable axioms. Usually three axioms are imposed on $\pi(H|D, \mathcal{B})$.

First π should be transitive, in the sense that given three hypotheses H_1, H_2, and H_3, if $\pi(H_1|D, \mathcal{B}) \leq \pi(H_2|D, \mathcal{B})$ and $\pi(H_2|D, \mathcal{B}) \leq \pi(H_3|D, \mathcal{B})$, then:

$$\pi(H_1|D, \mathcal{B}) \leq \pi(H_3|D, \mathcal{B}). \tag{2.23}$$

Here $X \leq Y$ is meant to represent that hypothesis Y is preferable to hypothesis X. The transitivity hypothesis essentially allows mapping degrees of beliefs to real numbers and replacing $\leq$ with $\leq$.

The second axiom states that there exists a function $f(x)$ establishing a systematic relationship between the degree of belief in an hypothesis H and the degree of belief in its negation $\neg H$. Intuitively, the greater the belief in H, the smaller the belief in $\neg H$ should be. In other words:

$$\pi(H|D, \mathcal{B}) = f(\pi(\neg H|D, \mathcal{B})). \tag{2.24}$$

Finally, the third axiom states that given two hypotheses H_1 and H_2, there exists a function $F(x, y)$ establishing a systematic relationship such that:

$$\pi(H_1, H_2|D, \mathcal{B}) = F[\pi(H_1|D, \mathcal{B}), \pi(H_2|H_1, D, \mathcal{B})]. \tag{2.25}$$

The fundamental theorem that results from these axioms is that degrees of beliefs can be represented by real numbers and that if these numbers are re-scaled to the $[0, 1]$ interval, then $\pi(H|D, \mathcal{B})$ must obey all the rules of probability. In particular, $f(x) = 1 - x$ and

$F(x, y) = xy$. As a result, in what follows we will use the notation $P(H|D, \mathcal{B})$ and call it the probability of H given D and $\mathcal{B}$.

In particular, when re-scaled to $[0, 1]$, degrees of belief must satisfy Bayes' theorem:

$$P(H|D, \mathcal{B}) = \frac{P(D|H, \mathcal{B})P(H|\mathcal{B})}{P(D|\mathcal{B})}, \tag{2.26}$$

where $P(H|\mathcal{B})$ is called the prior of the hypothesis, $P(D|H, \mathcal{B})$ the likelihood of the data, and $P(D|\mathcal{B})$ the evidence. Bayes' theorem is the fundamental tool of inversion in probability and allows one to express the posterior as a function of the likelihood.

Thus, in essence, in this framework probabilities are viewed very broadly as degrees of beliefs assigned to statements (or hypotheses or models) about the world, rather than the special case of frequencies associated with repeatable events. Note that a model M can be reduced to a binary hypothesis H by asking whether M fits the data within some level of error ϵ. In general, the goal in the Bayesian framework is to estimate the posterior distribution, as well as the expectation of relevant quantities with respect to the posterior. The framework can also be applied iteratively in time, with the posterior at a given iteration becoming the prior at the following iteration, when new data is received, thus providing a natural way to update one's beliefs.

In practical situations, the elegance and flexibility of the Bayesian framework is often faced with two well-known challenges:
(1) the choice of the prior degree of belief $P(H|\mathcal{B})$; and
(2) the actual computation of the posterior $P(H|D, \mathcal{B})$, and any related expectations, which may not always be solvable analytically and may require Monte Carlo approaches ([296, 300]).

In the cases relevant to this book, one is interested in a class of models $M(w)$ parameterized by a vector of parameters w. Working with the full posterior distribution $P(w|D, \mathcal{B})$ can be challenging and thus in practice one must often resort to point-estimation approaches, such as finding the parameters with the highest posterior probability – or maximum *a posteriori* (MAP) estimation corresponding to (dropping $\mathcal{B}$ for simplicity):

$$\max_w P(w|D) \Leftrightarrow \max_w \log P(w|D) \Leftrightarrow \min_w -\log P(w|D). \tag{2.27}$$

Using Bayes' theorem, this yields:

$$\max_w P(w|D) \Leftrightarrow \min_w -\log P(D|w) - \log P(w) + P(D). \tag{2.28}$$

The evidence $P(D)$ does not depend on w and thus can be omitted from this first level of analysis, so that:

$$\max_w P(w|D) \Leftrightarrow \min_w -\log P(D|w) - \log P(w). \tag{2.29}$$

When the prior term can be ignored, as in the case of a uniform prior over a compact set, this problem reduces to maximum likelihood (ML) estimation:

$$\max_w P(D|w) \Leftrightarrow \min_w -\log P(D|w). \tag{2.30}$$

2.8.1   Variational Approaches

This section requires some notions from information theory that are given in Section 2.9. One may want to skip this and return to it after reading that section on information theory. The Bayesian framework can be applied at multiple levels not only in time, but also across levels of modeling. For example, suppose that one is interested in modeling (and approximating) a probability distribution $R(x)$ over some space X, which itself could be for instance the posterior obtained from a previous level of modeling. Thus we view R as the "data", and we model this data using a family of distributions $Q = (Q_\theta(x))$ parameterized by some parameter vector θ. In general, Q_θ consists of a family of relatively simple distributions, such as factorial distributions and distributions from the exponential family [153]. In terms of point estimation, we thus wish to estimate:

$$\min_\theta \left(- \log P(R|Q_\theta) - \log P(Q_\theta) \right) . \tag{2.31}$$

For the prior $P(Q_\theta)$ it is reasonable to choose an entropic prior (see Section 2.9) where $P(Q_\theta)$ is proportional to $e^{-H(Q_\theta)}$ and $H(Q_\theta)$ is the entropy of Q (as an exercise, check that it does not matter whether one uses natural logarithms or logarithms base 2). Thus:

$$- \log P(Q_\theta) = H(Q_\theta) + C = - \sum_x Q_\theta(x) \log(Q_\theta(x)) + C, \tag{2.32}$$

where C is a constant that is not relevant for the optimization. For the log-likelihood term:

$$- \log P(R|Q_\theta) = - \sum_x Q_\theta(x) \log R(x), \tag{2.33}$$

up to constant terms. This is essentially derived from a multinomial likelihood of the form: $\prod_x R(x)^{Q_\theta(x)}$.

This general approach is commonly called the variational approach. It is often described directly, in a less principled way, as trying to find a distribution Q_θ to approximate R by minimizing the relative entropy KL (Q_θ, R):

$$\min_Q \text{KL} (Q_\theta, R) = \min_\theta \sum_x Q_\theta \log Q_\theta - \sum_x Q \log R. \tag{2.34}$$

Notice, more broadly, that the same Bayesian ideas can be applied more generally to the approximation of functions in analysis [238, 123]. For instance, from a data modeling perspective, approximation formula like Taylor expansions can be derived from the Bayesian framework.

We now turn to the basic concepts of information theory which play a fundamental role in deep learning and neural networks, not surprisingly, since one of the fundamental aspects of deep learning is the storage of information in synapses. These basic concepts are probabilistic in nature.

2.9   Information Theory

What we call Information Theory was originally developed by Shannon in 1948. Shannon's fundamental insight was to avoid getting bogged down in semantic issues – what does a message means to me – and rather think of information in terms of communication – the problem of "reproducing at one point either exactly or approximately a message selected at another point" [669]. The three most fundamental concepts in information theory are those of entropy, relative entropy, and mutual information. We review them succinctly, more complete treatments can be found, for example, in [129, 213, 491]. Throughout this section, we will consider random variables X and Y with distributions $P(x)$ and $Q(y)$. When needed, we will also consider the joint distribution $R(x, y)$.

Given any random variable X with distribution $P(x)$, the entropy $H(X)$ is defined by:

$$H(X) = -\sum_x P(x) \log_2 P(x).$$
(2.35)

Using logarithms in base 2 ensures that the entropy is measured in bits. The entropy is the average number of bits of information gained by observing an outcome of X. It is also the minimum average number of bits needed to transmit the outcome in the absence of noise. Obviously $H(X) \geq 0$ and the entropy is maximal for a uniform distribution, and minimal for a distribution concentrated at a single point. Given a second random variable Y with distribution $Q(y)$, the conditional entropy $H(X|Y)$ is defined by the expectation:

$$E_y H(X|Y = y) = -\sum_y Q(y) \sum_x P(X = x|Y = y) \log_2 P(X = x|Y = y).$$
(2.36)

It is easy to check that: $H(X|Y) \leq H(X)$.

Given two distributions $P(x)$ and $Q(x)$ defined over the same space X, the relative entropy or Kullback–Leibler divergence KL (P, Q) between $P(x)$ and $Q(x)$ is defined by:

$$KL\,(P, Q) = \sum_x P(x) \log_2 \frac{P(x)}{Q(x)}.$$
(2.37)

Here and throughout the book, in the continuous case, the summation is to be replaced by an integral. Thus the KL can be interpreted as the expected value with respect to P of the log-likelihood ratio between P and Q. It is also the average additional cost, in terms of bits per symbol, incurred by using the distribution Q instead of the true distribution P. It is not symmetric and thus is not a distance. If necessary, it can easily be made symmetric, although this is rarely needed. Using Jensen's inequality, it is easy to see that KL $(P, Q) \geq 0$, and KL $(P, Q) = 0$ if and only if $P = Q$. Jensen's inequality, which is graphically obvious, states that if f is convex down and X is a random variable then:

$$E(f(X)) \leq f(E(X)),$$
(2.38)

where E denotes the expectation. In addition, KL (P, Q) is convex down with respect to P and Q. The entropy $H(P)$ can be derived from the relative entropy by computing the relative entropy with respect to the uniform distribution $U = (1/n, \ldots, 1/n)$, assuming a finite set of n possible outcomes. Using the definition, one obtains:

$$KL\,(P, U) = \log_2 n - H(P). \tag{2.39}$$

In a Bayesian setting, the relative entropy between the prior and posterior distributions (or vice versa) is called the surprise and it can be used to measure the degree of impact of the data on its observer [369, 82].

To define the mutual information $I(X, Y)$ between X and Y, we use the relative entropy between their joint distribution $R(x, y)$ and the product of the marginal distributions $P(x)$ and $Q(y)$. Both distributions are defined on the same joint space so that:

$$I(X, Y) = KL\,(R, PQ) = \sum_{x,y} R(x, y) \log_2 \frac{R(x, y)}{P(x)Q(y)}. \tag{2.40}$$

A simple calculation shows that:

$$I(X, Y) = D(R, PQ) = H(X) - H(X|Y) = H(Y) - H(Y|X). \tag{2.41}$$

These quantities can be visualized in a Venn diagram where the total information $H(X, Y)$ satisfies:

$$H(X, Y) = H(X|Y) + I(X, Y) + H(Y|X). \tag{2.42}$$

It is easy to check that $I(X, X) = H(X)$. Furthermore, if X and Y are independent, then $I(X, Y) = 0$. The mutual information has a fundamental property, shared with the relative entropy: it is invariant with respect to reparameterization (e.g. rescaling). More precisely, for any invertible functions f and g:

$$I(X, Y) = I(f(X), g(Y)). \tag{2.43}$$

Finally, the data processing inequality states that for any Markov chain $X \rightarrow Y \rightarrow Z$:

$$I(X, Z) \le I(X, Y) \quad \text{and} \quad I(X, Z) \le I(Y, Z); \tag{2.44}$$

in other words, feedforward (or post-) processing cannot increase information.

An interesting application of information theory related to the data processing inequality is the information bottleneck method [524, 733, 677] (see exercises). This method was introduced as an information-theoretic approach for extracting the relevant information an input random variable X provides about an output random variable Y. Given their joint distribution $P(x, y)$, this information is precisely measured by the mutual information $I(X, Y)$. An optimal (compressed) representation Z of X for this task would capture the relevant features of X for predicting Y and discard the irrelevant ones. In statistical terms, the relevant part of X with respect to Y is a *minimal sufficient statistic*. Thus, in the bottleneck framework, we want to simultaneously minimize $I(X, Z)$ to optimize compression, while maximizing $I(Z, Y)$ to optimize prediction. Using Lagrange multipliers, this leads to the optimization problem:

$$\min_{P(z|x)} I(X, Z) - \lambda I(Z, Y), \tag{2.45}$$

where $\lambda \ge 0$ is a Lagrange multiplier controlling the tradeoff between compression and prediction. Another elegant framework related to information theory, which cannot be reviewed here, is information geometry [24], connecting information theory and statistical inference to geometrical invariants and differential geometry.

We have briefly presented some of the key ideas needed to address some of the questions related to capacity and design. Beyond these questions, we remain concerned with the fundamental problem of learning from data, i.e. of extracting and storing information contained in the data about the "world" into the synaptic weights of an architecture. Thus we now briefly consider different kinds of data and learning settings.

2.10 Data and Learning Settings

Over the years different learning paradigms have emerged (e.g. supervised, unsupervised, reinforcement, on-line) and new ones are periodically being introduced. Some of these paradigms get their inspiration from biology, others are unabashedly oriented towards machines. While it is not clear how this taxonomy will evolve and what will be left standing once the fog clears up, here we briefly describe only the most basic paradigms.

One key observation is that, from an engineering perspective, learning from data can be viewed as a different way of writing computer programs, by automatically learning the programs from the data. This is particularly, but not exclusively, useful in situations where we do not know how to write the corresponding program (e.g. how to recognize a cat in an image).

2.10.1 Supervised Learning

Perhaps the clearest setting corresponds to supervised learning. In supervised learning, one assumes that for each input example there is a known desirable target. Thus the data comes in the form of input-target pairs (I, T). Note that both I and T can be multi-dimensional objects, such as pixel values in an input image and the corresponding target categories. Thus, in this case, the data typically consists of a set of such pairs $D = \{(I(t), T(t))\}$ for $t = 1, 2, \ldots, K$ which can be viewed as samples of some function $f(I) = T$ one wishes to learn. We use t as a convenient index here, but not necessarily to indicate a notion of time. Within supervised learning tasks, it is common to distinguish regression tasks where the targets are continuous, or at least numerical, versus classification tasks where the targets are binary, or categorical. The standard approach to supervised learning is to define an error function $\mathcal{E}(w)$ that depends on the weights w of the network and somehow measures the mismatch between the outputs produced by the network and the targets. The goal of learning is to minimize the error $\mathcal{E}(w)$ and we will see in later chapters that the main algorithm for doing so is stochastic gradient descent. In Chapter 3, we will see how to design the error function. A useful observation is that, at least in the cases where the underlying function f is injective, the same data can be used to try to learn the inverse function f^{-1} simply by permuting inputs and targets.

2.10.2 Unsupervised Learning

In unsupervised learning, for each input example there is no target. Thus in general the data will come in the form $D = \{I(t)\}$ for $t = 1, 2, \ldots, K$ and one would like to discover useful patterns in this data. A standard example of unsupervised machine learning task is clustering.

2.10.3   Semi-supervised Learning

The term semi-supervised learning is used to describe situations where both supervised and unsupervised data is available. This is quite common in situations where acquiring labels or targets is difficult or expensive. Thus typically one ends up with a small labeled data set, and a large unlabeled data set and one of the main questions is how to leverage both kinds of data in a useful way.

2.10.4   Self-supervised Learning

Self-supervised learning provides a bridge between supervised and unsupervised learning, by solving unsupervised learning problems using supervised learning methods. In self-supervised learning, the data itself provides the targets for supervised learning. This is the basic idea used behind different kinds of autoencoders, or when one trains a system to predict the next item in a sequence, such as the next image frame in a video sequence in computer vision, or the next word in a text sequence in natural language processing. Likewise, one can train a system to reconstruct an item from a partial version of it, such as completing a sequence from which a word has been deleted, or completing an image from which an object or a patch has been deleted or altered.

2.10.5   Transfer Learning

The term transfer learning is used in general in settings where one is trying to learn multiple tasks, based on the same input data, and where there may be learning synergies between the tasks that may lead to improvements over the obvious strategy of learning each task in isolation. Thus in this setting one typically tries to transfer knowledge from one task to another task, either by learning them simultaneously or sequentially. The implicit underlying assumption is that core elements common to multiple related tasks must exist that are easier to extract and learn when multiple tasks are learnt together, as opposed to each one of them in isolation. Elements of transfer learning are already present in the multi-class classification learning task.

2.10.6   On-line versus Batch Learning

Across the various learning paradigms, learning algorithms can be applied after the presentation of each example (on-line) or after the presentation of the entire training set (batch). Of course all regimes between these two extremes are possible and in practice one often uses so-called mini-batches containing several training examples. The size of these mini-batches plays a role and will be discussed in Chapter 3.

2.10.7   Reinforcement Learning

While common, the settings above may seem somewhat unnatural from a biological standpoint or inapplicable to a large number of situations where there are active "agents" interacting with a "world" that is trying to maximize their utility. In its most basic setting, reinforcement learning assumes that there is an agent which can take a number of actions. Given the current state of the world, the action taken changes the state of the world and a certain reward is obtained. The goal of the agent is to learn how to act in order to maximize some form of long-term reward. Reinforcement learning, and its combinations with neural networks, are studied in the appendix.

2.11   Learning Rules

Within the framework adopted here, learning is the process by which information contained in the training data is communicated and stored in the synaptic weights. Given a synaptic weight w_{ij} connecting neuron j to neuron i, learning algorithms are expressed in terms of formulas, or learning rules, for adjusting w_{ij}. Typically these rules have the iterative form:

$$w_{ij}(k + 1) = w_{ij}(k) + \eta F(R) \quad \text{or} \quad \Delta w_{ij} = \eta F(R). \tag{2.46}$$

Weight changes can occur after the presentation of each example in on-line learning, or after the presentation of batches of a particular size, in batch or mini-batch learning. The parameter η is the learning rate which controls the size of the steps taken at each iteration. The vector R is used here to represent the relevant variables on which learning depends, for instance the activities of the pre- and post-synaptic neurons. The function F provides the functional form of the rule, for instance a polynomial of degree two. As examples, we have already seen three learning rules in the introductory chapter where $F(R)$ is equal to $O_i O_j$ in the simple Hebb rule, $(T - O_i)O_j$ in the perceptron rule, and $B_i O_j$ in the backpropagation rule. Note that all three rules share a common form consisting of a product between a post-synaptic term associated with neuron i and a pre-synaptic term associated with neuron j, in fact equal to the activity of neuron j in all three cases. It will be useful to write such equations in matrix form when considering neurons in two consecutive layers. In this case, using column vectors, the matrix learning rule is given by the outer product between the post-synaptic vector term and the transpose of the pre-synaptic vector term. For instance, in the example above for backpropagation, one can simply write:

$$\Delta w_{ij} = \eta B_i O_j \quad \text{(scalar form)}; \qquad \Delta w = \eta B O^{\text{T}} \quad \text{(matrix form)}, \tag{2.47}$$

where the column vector $B = (B_i)$ runs over the post-synaptic layer, and the column vector $O = (O_j)$ runs over the pre-synaptic layer, and O^{T} denotes transposition. Within this framework, as one varies the choice of R and F, there is potentially a very large space of learning rules to be explored. In later chapters, we will see how this space can be organized and greatly restricted, in particular using the concept of locality for learning rules.

To study the dynamic behavior of learning rules, one can sometimes resort to geometric or convexity considerations. Alternatively, one can try to derive an ordinary or stochastic differential equation. In batch learning, the learning dynamic is deterministic and one can try to solve the difference equation (Equation 2.46) or, assuming a small learning rate ($\eta \approx \Delta t$) the ordinary differential equation:

$$\frac{dw_{ij}}{dt} = E(F(R)), \qquad (2.48)$$

where E denotes expectation taken over one epoch. On-line or mini-batch learning will induce stochastic fluctuations – the smaller the batches the larger the fluctuations – which can be modeled as an additional noise term. We will see examples where this differential equation, or its stochastic version obtained with the addition of a noise term, can be analyzed.

2.12   Computational Complexity Theory

Finally, to complete these preliminaries, we give a very brief introduction to some of the most basic concepts of computational complexity theory. Please refer to standard text books (e.g. [560, 46]) for more complete treatments.

The first important distinction is between what can be computed and what cannot be computed by a Turing machine, or a computer program. For this purpose, basic notions of cardinality are necessary. Two sets, finite or infinite, have the same cardinality if there is a one-to-one correspondence (bijective function) between the two sets. An infinite set S is said to be countable if there exists a one to one function between S and the set $\mathbb{N}$ of all the integers. For instance the sets of all even integers, all signed integers, and all possible fractions are countable. The set of all real numbers $\mathbb{R}$ is not countable. Likewise, it is easy to show that the set of all finite strings over a finite (non-empty) alphabet is countable, while the set of all infinite strings over an alphabet with at least two symbols is not countable. As a result, the set of all functions from $\mathbb{N}$ to $\{0, 1\}$ is not countable, whereas the set of all possible computer programs in Python (or any other computer language) is countable. Therefore, there exists functions from $\mathbb{N}$ to $\{0, 1\}$ that are not computable, i.e. for which it is not possible to write a computer program that computes them. More broadly, there exist decision problems, i.e. problems with a yes/no answer that are not computable. The argument above provides an existential proof of problems that are not computable or decidable. For a constructive proof, a classical example is provided by the halting problem: deciding if a given program will halt or not when applied to a given input. That the halting problem cannot be solved by a computer program can be proven fairly easily by contradiction using a diagonal argument, in essence similar to the argument one uses to prove that the set of all real numbers is not computable (see exercises).

In general, the decision problems considered in this book are computable. The important question is whether they can be computed efficiently. Consider for instance the Traveling Salesman Decision Problem (TSP): given n cities and their pairwise distances, is there a tour traversing all the cities of length less than k? Notice that the problem of finding the shortest tour can easily be reduced to a short (logarithmic) sequence of decision problems by varying k. This decision problem has an easy solution obtained by enumerating all possible tours and their corresponding lengths. However this solution is not efficient, as the number of all possible tours ($n!$) is exponential in n and rapidly exceeds the number of all particles in the known universe as n increases. Thus one is led to define the class P of decision problems that can be solved in polynomial time, i.e. for which there is an algorithm whose running time is bounded by a polynomial function of the input size. The next useful class is called NP (non-deterministic polynomial), this is the class of problems where a proposed solution can be checked in polynomial time. Obviosuly, TSP is in NP: if one is given a particular tour α, by adding the distances along α it is easy to decide in polynomial time if the length of α is less than k or not. Thus TSP is in NP. But is TSP in P? One may conjecture that it is not, but no-one has been able to prove it. Thus one of the most important open problems in mathematics and computer science today is whether $P = NP$ or not? Finally, within the class NP one can define the sub-class NP-complete, consisting of problems that are equivalent to each other, in the sense that any one of them can be transformed into any other one of them through a transformation which has at most a polynomial cost. TSP is in NP-complete as well as hundreds of other such problems [293]. A polynomial solution for any one of these problems would lead to a polynomial solution for all the other ones, simply by using the polynomial transformations that exist between them. Thus to prove that a problem in NP is NP-complete is typically done by polynomial reduction to another NP-complete problem. A problem is NP-hard if it is at least as hard as the hardest problems in NP (i.e. every problem in NP can be polynomially reduced to it). The TSP optimization problem is NP-hard. It is possible to show that training a three-node neural network is NP-complete [132]. In Chapter 5 we will show that optimizing the unrestricted Boolean autoencoder is NP-hard.

2.13   Exercises

EXERCISE 2.1   Define a notion of equivalence between networks of threshold gates using $\{0, 1\}$ values, and network of threshold gates using $\{-1, 1\}$ values with the same architecture. Which weight transformations convert a $\{0, 1\}$ network into an equivalent $\{-1, 1\}$ network, and vice versa? Given any two distinct real numbers a and b, can this be generalized to threshold gates with $\{a, b\}$ values (i.e. the output is a if the activation is below the threshold, and b otherwise). Same questions if the threshold gates are replaced by sigmoidal gates with logistic and tanh transfer functions, respectively.

EXERCISE 2.2   Prove the equivalence between the models described by Equations 2.16 and 2.17 under the proper assumptions.

EXERCISE 2.3   Consider a logistic unit with inputs in the interval $[0, 1]$. Can it be considered equivalent, and if so in which sense, to a tanh unit with inputs in the interval $[-1, 1]$?

EXERCISE 2.4   Which of the following Boolean functions of n arguments can be implemented by a single linear threshold gate with a bias, and why:

(1) OR;

(2) AND;

(3) NOT ($n = 1$);

(4) XOR ($n = 2$) and its n-dimensional generalization PARITY;

(5) SINGLE_u which is the Boolean function equal to $+1$ for the binary vector u, and -1 (or 0) for all other binary vector inputs; and

(6) SELECT_k which is the Boolean function that is equal to the kth component of its input.

Show that for the vast majority of pairs of distinct points x and y on the n-dimensional hypercube, there is no linear threshold functions with value $+1$ on those two points, and value -1 (or 0) on the remaining $2^n - 2$ points.

EXERCISE 2.5   Consider the hypercube of dimension n. 1) Show that any vertex of the hypercube is linearly separable from all the other vertices. 2) Show that any two adjacent vertices of the hypercube are linearly separable from all the other vertices. 3) Show that any three adjacent vertices of the hypercube are linearly separable from all the other vertices. 4) Show that any sub-cube of the hypercube is linearly separable from all the other vertices of the hypercube. A sub-cube of dimension $k \leq n$ has exactly 2^k vertices which share identical coordinates in $n - k$ positions.

EXERCISE 2.6   How many terms are there in a homogenous polynomial of degree d over H^n? How many terms are there in a homogeneous polynomial of degree d over $\mathbb{R}^n$?

EXERCISE 2.7   Consider a Boolean architecture $A(n, 2, 1)$ with n binary inputs, two Boolean functions f and g in the hidden layer, and one output Boolean function $h(f, g)$. Assume that: h is the AND Boolean function, f and g are linear (or polynomial) threshold functions with biases. In addition, we assume that all the positive examples of f have the same activation value. Show that the same overall Boolean function can be implemented by a single linear (or polynomial) threshold function of n variables with bias. [This result will be needed in Chapter 4 to estimate the cardinal capacity of an $A(n, m, 1)$ architecture. Do the units in the hidden layer need to be fully connected to the input layer for this result to be true?

EXERCISE 2.8 (CARDINAL CAPACITY)   Prove that the cardinal capacity of an architecture satisfies the following properties.

Monotonicity: If $n_k \leq m_k$ for all k, then:

$$C(n_1, \ldots, n_L) \leq C(m_1, \ldots, m_L).$$

Sub-additivity: For any $1 < k < L - 1$, we have:

$$C(n_1, \ldots, n_L) \leq C(n_1, \ldots, n_k) + C(n_{k+1}, \ldots, n_L).$$

Contractivity: Capacity may only increase if a layer is duplicated. For example:

$$C(n, m, p) \leq C(n, m, m, m, p).$$

EXERCISE 2.9 (INFORMATION THEORY)   In which sense and why can an event that has probability p be communicated using $-\log_2 p$ bits? Prove that:

(1) $H(X|Y) \leq H(X)$;

(2) $KL(P, Q) \geq 0$ with equality if and only if $P = Q$;

(3) $KL(P, Q)$ is convex in P and Q;

(4) $I(X, Y) = H(X) - H(X|Y)$;

(5) $I(X, X) = H(X)$; and

(6) $I(X, Y)$ is invariant under invertible reparameterizations.

EXERCISE 2.10 (DATA PROCESSING INEQUALITY)   Given a Markov Chain $X \rightarrow Y \rightarrow Z$, prove the data processing inequality, i.e. $I(X, Z) \leq I(X, Y)$. Under which necessary and sufficient conditions can there be equality $I(X, Z) = I(X, Y)$?

EXERCISE 2.11 (INFORMATION BOTTLENECK METHOD)   As described in Section 2.9, consider the minimization problem:

$$\min_{P(z|x)} I(X, Z) - \lambda I(Z, Y). \tag{2.49}$$

Derive a set of consistency equations and an iterative algorithm for solving this problem in general. Further analyze the case where the variables X and Y are jointly multivariate zero-mean Gaussian vectors with covariances Σ_{XX}, Σ_{YY}, and Σ_{XY}.

EXERCISE 2.12   Consider a layered feedforward neural network and let X represent the vector of activities in one of its layers. Assuming that all of the weights of the networks are fixed, how would you define and estimate the mutual information between the input layer and X? Address this problem first in the case of binary variables and then in the case of continuous variables. This is needed for the information plane visualization method described in a later chapter.

EXERCISE 2.13   Recast a Taylor approximation formula such as: "$\cos x \approx 1 - x^2/2$ for x small" in a proper Bayesian framework. In particular describe the data, the family of approximating functions, the prior distribution, and the likelihood function.

EXERCISE 2.14   A law of physics, such as Newton's second law $F = ma$, can be viewed as a hypothesis on how nature works. Given some experimental data D consisting of various measurements of forces, masses, and corresponding accelerations, how would you compute the posterior probability of the hypothesis within a Bayesian framework? How would you compare this hypothesis to an alternative hypothesis, such as $F = ma^{1.001}$?

EXERCISE 2.15   In what sense can the use of an entropic prior be viewed as "reasonable"?

EXERCISE 2.16   Conduct a census, as complete as possible, of all the learning paradigms (e.g. supervised, unsupervised, semi-supervised) found in the literature.

EXERCISE 2.17   Prove that if the set S is infinite, S is countable if and only if there is an injective function from S to $\mathbb{N}$. Prove that the following sets are countable:

(1) the signed numbers ($\mathbb{Z}$);
(2) the rational numbers ($\mathbb{Q}$);
(3) all finite strings over a finite alphabet;
(4) all functions from $\{0, 1\}$ to $\mathbb{N}$;
(5) all finite strings of length m or less, over an infinite but countable alphabet;
(6) all finite strings over an infinite but countable alphabet; and
(7) the union of all possible computer programs and corresponding inputs taken over all existing computer programming languages.

EXERCISE 2.18   Prove the following sets are not countable:
(1) the real numbers ($\mathbb{R}$) (by contradiction, using a diagonal argument);
(2) all infinite strings over a finite alphabet with at least two letters;
(3) all functions from $\mathbb{N}$ to $\{0, 1\}$.

Prove that there exist decision problems that are not computable, i.e. they cannot be solved by a computer program (existential proof). Prove that the halting decision problem – i.e. the problem of deciding whether, given an input, a computer program with halt or not – is not computable by contradiction, using a diagonal argument (constructive proof).

3 Shallow Networks and Shallow Learning

In this chapter we focus on layered feedforward shallow networks, i.e. feedforward networks with no hidden units, and the corresponding shallow learning problem. Thus, we consider $A(n, 1)$ and $A(n, m)$ architectures. We study the questions of design, capacity, and learning in that order. We begin by showing that the Bayesian statistical framework leads to a fairly complete theory of how to design such networks in the supervised learning setting. In particular, it provides a principled and elegant way to derive the transfer functions and the error functions in both the regression and classification cases, in a way that leads to the same simple gradient equations across the cases.

3.1 Supervised Shallow Networks and their Design

We begin with the supervised learning framework with a single unit for regression or classification problems, or k units for classification into k classes. Assume that the data consists of K input-target pairs: $D = \{(I(t), T(t)), \ t = 1, \ldots, K\}$ and w represents the weights. Then, assuming the data pairs are independent of each other and the inputs are independent of the weights, the likelihood has the form:

$$P(D|w) = \prod_{t=1}^{K} P(I(t), T(t)|w) = \prod_{t=1}^{K} P(T(t)|I(t), w) P(I(t)|w), \qquad (3.1)$$

so that:

$$P(D|w) = \prod_{t=1}^{K} P(T(t)|O(t)) P(I(t)), \qquad (3.2)$$

where O is the output of the network. Throughout this section, probabilities for continuous values should be written with the usual notation $P(x < X < x + \Delta x) = P(x)\Delta x$. Here we omit the Δx terms as they play no role in the calculations and the final answers. For simplicity, we also assume that all the inputs have the same probability-$P(I(t)) = c$. Thus, in this case, the maximum likelihood (ML) estimation problem becomes:

$$\min_{w} \mathcal{E} = \min_{w} \sum_{t=1}^{K} \mathcal{E}(t) = \min_{w} \left[-\sum_{t=1}^{K} \log P(T(t)|O(t)) \right], \qquad (3.3)$$

where $\mathcal{E}(t) = -\log P(T(t)|O(t))$ can be viewed as an error function measuring the mismatch between outputs and targets for each training example. The corresponding maximum *a posteriori* (MAP) problem is given by:

$$\min_{w} \mathcal{E}' = \min_{w} \left[-\sum_{t=1}^{K} \log P(T(t)|O(t)) - \log P(w) \right].$$

(3.4)

Next, we must now specify the probabilistic model needed to compute $P(T(t)|O(t))$, as well as $P(w)$. To simplify the notation, we treat a single generic example, dropping the index t. At the end, this procedure will give the error and learning algorithms corresponding to online learning, i.e. example by example. Alternatively, for batch or mini-batch learning, one must remember to sum the corresponding expressions over the corresponding examples.

3.1.1   Regression

In the case of a regression problem, one can use a simple Gaussian model:

$$P(T|O) = \frac{1}{\sqrt{2\pi}\sigma} e^{-(T-O)^2/2\sigma^2}.$$

(3.5)

As a result, the ML equation $\min_w - \log P(T|O)$ is equivalent to the usual least-square problem:

$$\min_{w} \mathcal{E} = \min_{w} \frac{1}{2}(T - O)^2.$$

(3.6)

In the case of regression, the targets are not necessarily bounded, and so it is natural to use a linear unit with $O = S = \sum w_i I_i$. In this case:

$$\partial \mathcal{E}/\partial S = -(T - O).$$

(3.7)

Note that more complex models, where for instance σ is not the same for all the points, can easily be incorporated into this framework and would lead to a weighted least-square problem.

3.1.2   Classification

In the case of binary classification, one can use a simple binomial model, so that:

$$P(T|O) = O^T (1 - O)^{1-T}.$$

(3.8)

As a result, the ML equation $\min_w - \log P(T|O)$ is equal to:

$$\min_{w} \mathcal{E} = \min_{w} - \left[T \log O + (1 - T) \log(1 - O) \right].$$

(3.9)

This is equivalent to minimizing the relative entropy or Kullback–Leibler (KL) divergence between the distributions T and O which is given by:

$$KL(T, O) = T \log T + (1 - T) \log(1 - T) - T \log O - (1 - T) \log(1 - O).$$

(3.10)

In the case of binary classification, since the output O is interpreted as a probability, it is natural to use a logistic unit with $O = f(S) = 1/(1 + e^{-S})$. As a result:

$$\frac{\partial \mathcal{E}}{\partial S} = \frac{\partial \mathcal{E}}{\partial O} \frac{\partial O}{\partial S} = -(T - O).$$

(3.11)

Table 3.1 Summary table for shallow supervised learning for the problems of regression, classification into two classes, and classification into k classes. The corresponding probabilistic models yield the corresponding error functions associated with the negative log-likelihood of the data given the weight parameters. Together with the sensible choice of transfer function f, this leads to simple and identical error derivatives for learning.

Problem	Prob. Model	Error $\mathcal{E}$	Unit	$\partial\mathcal{E}/\partial S$
Reg.	Gaussian	$(T - O)^2/2$ (Quadratic)	Linear	$-(T - O)$
2-Class.	Binomial	$-T \log O - (1 - T) \log(1 - O)$ (KL)	Logistic	$-(T - O)$
k-Class.	Multinomial	$-\sum_{i=1}^{k} T_i \log O_i$ (KL)	Softmax	$-(T - O)$

3.1.3 k-Classification

In the case of classification into k-classes, the straightforward generalization is to use a multinomial model, so that:

$$P(T|O) = \prod_{i=1}^{k} O_i^{T_i}. \tag{3.12}$$

As a result, the ML equation $\min_w - \log P(T|O)$ is given by:

$$\min_w \mathcal{E} = \min_w - \left[\sum_{i=1}^{k} T_i \log O_i \right]. \tag{3.13}$$

This is equivalent to minimizing the relative entropy or Kullback–Leibler (KL) divergence between the distributions T and O which is given by:

$$\text{KL}(T, O) = \sum_{i=1}^{k} T_i \log T_i - \sum_{i=1}^{k} T_i \log O_i. \tag{3.14}$$

In the case of k-class classification, it is natural to use a softmax unit, which generalizes the logistic unit ($k = 2$). With a softmax unit we have $O_i = e^{S_i} / \sum_j e^{S_j}$, where for every i, $S_i = \sum_j w_{ij} I_j$. As a result, for every $i = 1, \ldots, k$ we obtain:

$$\frac{\partial\mathcal{E}}{\partial S_i} = \sum_j \frac{\partial\mathcal{E}}{\partial O_j} \frac{\partial O_j}{\partial S_i} = -(T_i - O_i), \tag{3.15}$$

after some algebra and using the formula for the derivatives from Chapter 2, namely $(\partial O_i/\partial S_i = O_i(1 - O_i)$ and $\partial O_j/\partial S_i = -O_i O_j$ for $j \neq i$).

Thus, in short, the theory dictates which error function and which transfer function to use in both regression and classification cases (Table 3.1). In regression as well as binary classification, the gradient descent learning equation for a single unit can be written as:

$$\Delta w_i = -\eta \frac{\partial\mathcal{E}}{\partial w_i} = -\eta \frac{\partial\mathcal{E}}{\partial S} \frac{\partial S}{\partial w_i} = \eta(T - O)I_i, \tag{3.16}$$

and similarly in k-classification.

3.1.4   Prior Distributions and Regularization

The Bayesian framework allows one to put a prior distribution on the parameters w. Consider a single unit with weight vector $w = (w_i)$ with $0 \le i \le n$ including the bias. A standard approach is to assume uniform or Gaussian prior distributions on the synaptic weights. For instance, in the case of a zero-mean, spherical Gaussian prior distribution (i.e the product of n independent, identical, one-dimensional Gaussian distributions):

$$P(w) = \frac{1}{\sqrt{(2\pi)^n \sigma^{2n}}} e^{-\sum w_i^2 / 2\sigma^2}. \tag{3.17}$$

In the MAP optimization approach, this adds a term of the form $\sum_i w_i^2 / 2\sigma^2$ to the error function and the minimization process. The variance σ^2 determines the relative importance between the terms derived from the likelihood and the prior. Everything else being equal, the larger the value of σ the smaller the influence of the prior. The influence of the prior is to prevent the weights from becoming too large during learning, since large weights incur a large penalty $\sum_i w_i^2$. From an optimization framework, adding terms to the function being optimized to constrain the solutions is called regularization. In this sense, there is an equivalence between using priors and using regularizing terms. The Gaussian prior leads to a quadratic regularizer or an L2 penalty term. From a learning standpoint, in the case of gradient descent, the presence of a Gaussian prior adds a term $-w_i/\sigma^2$ to the gradient descent learning rule for w_i. This is also called "weight decay" in the literature.

Of course other priors or regularizing terms can be applied to the weights. Another regularization that is often used, instead of or in combination with L2 regularization, is the L1 regularization which adds a term of the form: $\lambda \sum_i |w_i|$ to the error function. More generally, one can define Lp regularization for any $p \ge 0$ based on Lp-norms. Other prior distributions or regularization functions can be used in specific cases, for instance in the case where the weights are constrained to have binary values or, more generally, to be limited to a finite set of possible values.

L1 regularization tends to produce sparse solutions where, depending on the strength of the regularizer, a subset of the weights are equal to zero. This can be desirable in some situations, for instance to increase interpretability. Within sparse Bayesian priors alone, L1 is just one of many approaches. The L1 approach was developed early in [645] in relation to geology applications. It was further developed and publicized under the name of LASSO (least absolute shrinkage and selection operator) [729] (see also [730]). Another example of continuous "shrinkage" prior centered at zero is the horseshoe prior [172, 173]. However technically these continuous priors do not have a mass at zero. Thus another alternative direction is to use discrete mixtures [507, 298] where the prior on each weight w_i consists of a mixture of a point mass at $w_i = 0$ with an absolutely continuous distribution.

While priors are useful and can help prevent overfitting, for instance in situations where the amount of training data is limited, the real question is whether a full Bayesian treatment is possible or not. For instance, for prediction purposes, a full Bayesian treatment requires integrating predictions over the posterior distribution. The question then becomes whether this integration process can be carried in exact or approximate form, and how computationally expensive it is. This may not be a problem for single units; but for large networks, in general a full Bayesian approach cannot be carried analytically. In this case, approximations including Markov Chain Monte Carlo methods become necessary. Even so, for large networks, full Bayesian treatments remain challenging and methods based on point-estimates are used instead. The general area at the intersection of Bayesian methods and neural networks continues to be an active research area (e.g. [473, 474, 532, 445]).

3.1.5 Probabilistic Neural Networks

So far we have described feedforward neural networks as being completely deterministic in how they operate: for a given input they always produce the same output in a deterministic way. Whenever desirable, it is easy to create probabilistic neural networks where the input–output relationship is not deterministic, but rather governed by a joint probability distribution determined by the weights of the networks and possibly a few other noise or sampling parameters. Stochasticity can be introduced in different layers of the architecture.

Stochasticity in the input layer is obtained by sampling. If the input is given by the vector $I = (I_1, \ldots, I_n)$, one can interpret each component as being the mean of a normal distribution with standard deviation σ (or any other relevant distribution) and sample accordingly to produce a new input vector $I' = (I_1 + \eta_1, \ldots, I_n + \eta_n)$ which is then fed to the network, in lieu of I. In this case, the noise terms η_i are sampled from a normal distribution $\mathcal{N}(0, \sigma^2)$.

Likewise, stochasticity in the output, or any hidden layer, is obtained by interpreting the neurons activities as parameters of a distribution and then sampling from the corresponding distribution (see also [99]). For instance, in the case of a linear unit, its activity can be interpreted as the mean of a normal distribution, and a sample from that normal distribution can be used as the stochastic output. The standard deviation of the normal distribution is either an external parameter, or an output computed by a different unit. In the case of a logistic unit, its output can be interpreted as a Bernoulli probability p which can be sampled, producing a stochastic output equal to 1 with probability p, and 0 with probability $q = 1 - p$. Introducing such stochasticity in the hidden layer is the key ingredient behind, for instance, variational autoencoders [407].

Other forms of stochasticity can be obtained by adding other forms of noise to the units, or to the connections, as is done for instance during the application of the dropout algorithm [699, 91] during learning. This algorithm is studied in Chapter 6.

3.1.6 Independence of Units During Learning in Shallow Networks

Consider a feedforward shallow network with n_0 inputs and n_1 output units. Even if the units see the same inputs, they operate independently of each other in the sense that the output of any unit does not depend on the output of any other unit. Unless there is a specific mechanism that couples the units during learning, the units learn independently of each other. In particular, if learning is based on minimizing an error function of the form $\mathcal{E} = \sum_{i=1}^{n_1} \mathcal{E}_i$, where $\mathcal{E}_i$ depends on O_i (and possibly a corresponding target T_i in the supervised case) but not on O_j for $j \neq i$, then each unit will learn independently of all the other units. This result, which of course is not true for deep networks, *implies that in shallow networks it is enough to understand the general behavior of one unit in order to understand the behavior of the entire network.* It must be noted that this result is very general and not tied to the existence of an error function. As we shall see in Chapter 7 on local learning, *it is sufficient that the learning rule be local for the units to learn independently of each other in a network with a single adaptive layer.*

Now that we have addressed how to design single-layer architectures we can turn to questions of capacity.

3.2   Capacity of Shallow Networks

3.2.1   Functional Capacity

Because of the independence of the units in a single layer network, it is sufficient to understand the capacity of a single unit. If the activation is linear and the transfer function is the identity (linear unit) then the unit implements a simple linear (or affine) function of the inputs. If the transfer function is the sgn or Heaviside function, or even a sigmoidal function, then we can still visualize the operation of the neuron as being determined by a hyperplane dividing $\mathbb{R}^n$ or H^n into two regions, with the value of the output being $+1$ on one side of the hyperplane – or growing towards $+1$ in the sigmoidal case – and conversely on the opposite side, replacing $+1$ with 0 or -1, depending on the exact transfer function being used. A similar picture is obtained if the activation is ReLU, or even polynomial by replacing the hyperplane by a polynomial surface. Thus, at least in the shallow case, it is possible to get a fairly clear mental picture of the class of functions that can be implemented.

In order to be more quantitative, next we focus primarily on the cardinal capacity of single linear and polynomial Boolean threshold gates. Linear and polynomial threshold functions have been extensively used and studied in complexity theory, machine learning, and network theory; see, for instance, [65, 68, 66, 160, 155, 639, 420, 671, 49, 114, 18, 411, 412, 239, 546, 547, 392] An introduction to polynomial threshold functions can be found in [545, Chapter 5], [40, Chapter 4], and [639]. In the Boolean setting, we know that there are 2^{2^n} Boolean functions of n variables. Some of them can be implemented as linear threshold gates, and some cannot. Thus we wish to estimate the fraction of such Boolean functions that can be realized by linear threshold gates. And similarly, the fraction can be realized by polynomial threshold gates of degree d.

3.2.2   The Capacity of Linear Threshold Gates

As an easy exercise, one can see that a number of well-known Boolean functions of n variables are linearly separable and computable by a single linear threshold gate. For instance (see Figure 3.1), using a $\{-1, +1\}$ encoding of the input variables:

- AND, OR, NOT: The basic Boolean operators are all linearly separable. AND can be implemented using all weights equal to $+1$ and threshold equal to $n - 1$. OR can be implemented using all weights equal to $+1$ and threshold $-(n - 1)$. NOT can be implemented by a linear homogeneous threshold gate with a single weight equal to -1 and threshold 0.
- GEQ_K, LEQ_K (and MAJORITY as a special case): These functions compute whether the total number of $+1$ in the input is larger or smaller than a certain value K. Again they can be implemented using all weights equal to 1 and selecting the appropriate threshold.
- SELECT_k: This is the Boolean function that is equal to the kth component of its input. It can be implemented using $w_k = 1$, $w_i = 0$ for all other weights, and threshold 0.
- SINGLE_u: This is the Boolean function that is equal to $+1$ on a single given vertex $u = (u_1, \ldots, u_n)$ of the hypercube, and -1 on all other vertices. It can be implemented by a linear threshold gate with $w_i = u_i$ and threshold $n - 1$.

However there are also many functions that are not linearly separable. For instance:

- PARITY: This function takes the value $+1$ if the total number of $+1$ component in the input is even, and -1 otherwise.
- XOR: This function takes the value $+1$ only for input vectors that contain exactly one $+1$ component.
- CONNECTED: This function takes the value $+1$ if all the $+1$ component of the input are "together", with or without wrap around. For instance, with $n = 5$, $(+1, +1, +1, -1, -1)$ should be mapped to $+1$, whereas $(+1, -1, +1, -1, +1)$ should me mapped to -1.
- PAIR: Fix two vertices on the hypercube and consider the Boolean function that takes the value $+1$ on those two vertices, and -1 on all the remaining vertices. For the vast majority of such pairs, the corresponding functions is *not* linearly separable.

Thus what we would like to understand is what is the fraction of Boolean functions that can be implemented by linear threshold functions. Equivalently, a Boolean function can be viewed as a coloring of the vertices of the hypercube using two colors: blue and red. We want to estimate the fraction of colorings that are linearly separable.

Recall that in this context, the capacity $C(n, 1)$ is the logarithm base 2 of the number of such colorings. Estimating $C(n, 1)$ is a fundamental problem in the theory of neural networks and it has a relatively long history [40]. Next, we review the main results leaving the proofs as exercises (with additional complements in the references). To state the results, we will use the standard 'little o' and 'big O' notation. As a reminder, given two real-valued functions f and g defined over $\mathbb{R}$ or $\mathbb{N}$, we write $f(x) = O(g(x))$ when $x \to +\infty$ if and only if there exists a constant C and a value x_0 such that: $|f(x)| \leq C|g(x)|$ for all $x \geq x_0$. Similarly, we write $f(x) = o(g(x))$ for $x = a$ if and only if $\lim_{x \to a} f(x)/g(x) = 0$ (here a can be finite or infinite).

The upper bound:

$$C(n, 1) \leq n^2, \qquad \text{for } n > 1, \qquad (3.18)$$

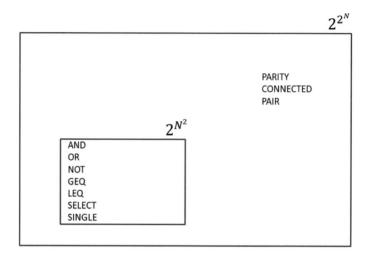

Figure 3.1 Larger box: Set of all Boolean functions of N variables. Smaller box: Subset of all linear threshold Boolean functions of N variables.

has been known since the 1960s (e.g. [214] and references therein). Likewise lower bounds of the form:

$$\alpha n^2 \leq C(n, 1), \qquad \text{for } n > 1 \text{ with } \alpha < 1, \tag{3.19}$$

were also derived in the 1960s. For instance, Muroga proved a lower bound of $n(n-1)/2$ (e.g. [521]), leaving open the question on the correct value of α. The problem of determining the right order was finally settled by Zuev [818, 819] who proved that:

THEOREM 3.1 *The capacity of linear threshold functions satisfies:*

$$C(n, 1) = n^2 \left(1 + o(1)\right), \tag{3.20}$$

as $n \to \infty$.

More precisely, Zuev provided a lower bound of

$$\left(1 - \frac{10}{\log n}\right) \cdot n^2 \leq \log_2 T(n, 1) \leq n^2. \tag{3.21}$$

J. Kahn, J. Komlós, and E. Szemerédi [389, Section 4] further improved this result to:

$$C(n, 1) = n^2 - n \log_2 n \pm O(n). \tag{3.22}$$

Thus in short the capacity of a linear threshold gate is approximately n^2, as opposed to 2^n for the total number of Boolean functions. Zuev's result can be derived from a combination of two results, one in enumerative combinatorics and the other in probability. The combinatorial result is a consequence of Zaslavsky's formula for hyperplane arrangements [807], and the probabilistic result is Odlyzko's theorem on spans of random ± 1 vectors [544]. Odlyzko's theorem, in turn, is based on a result on singularity of random matrices, namely that random matrices with ± 1 entries have full rank with high probability (see also [389, 762]).

Intuitively, Zuev's result is easy to understand from an information-theoretic point of view as it says that a linear threshold gate is fully specified by providing n^2 bits, corresponding to n examples of size n. For instance, these can be the n support vectors, i.e. the n points closest to the separating hyperplane, taken from the largest class (there is one additional bit required to specify the largest class but this is irrelevant for n large).

Finally, it should be clear that $C(n, m) \approx mn^2$. This is simply because the capacity of an $A(n, m)$ architecture of linear threshold gates is equal to the sum of the capacities of each gate, due to their independence.

3.2.3 The Capacity of Polynomial Threshold Gates

The capacity increases if we use separating polynomial hypersurfaces rather than hyperplanes. Any Boolean function of n variables can be expressed as a polynomial of degree at most n. To see this, just write the function f in conjunctive (or disjunctive) normal form, or take the Fourier transform of f. A conjecture of J. Aspnes et al. [49] and C. Wang and A. Williams [772] states that, for most Boolean functions $f(x)$, the lowest degree of $p(x)$ such that $f(x) = \text{sgn}(p(x))$ is either $\lfloor n/2 \rfloor$ or $\lceil n/2 \rceil$. M. Anthony [39] and independently N. Alon (see [639]) proved one half of this conjecture, showing that for most Boolean functions the lower degree of $p(x)$ is at least $\lceil n/2 \rceil$. The other half of the conjecture was settled, in an approximate sense (up to additive logarithmic terms), by R. O'Donnell and R. A. Servedio [546] who gave an upper bound $n/2 + O(\sqrt{n \log n})$ on the degree of $p(x)$.

However here we are more interested in low-degree polynomial threshold functions. While low-degree polynomial threshold functions may be relatively rare within the space of Boolean functions, they are of particular interest both theoretically and practically, due to their functional simplicity and their potential applications in biological modeling and neural network applications. Thus the most important question is: How many low-degree polynomial threshold functions are there? Equivalently, how many different ways are there to partition the Boolean cube by polynomial surfaces of low degree? Equivalently how many bits can effectively be stored in the coefficients of a polynomial threshold function? In short, we want to estimate the cardinal capacity $C_d(n, 1)$ of polynomial threshold gates of n variables of degree d, for fixed degree $d > 1$, as well as slowly increasing values of d. We provide the solution below. The details of the proof can be found in the references (see also exercises).

The history of the solution of this problem parallels in many ways the history of the solution for the case of $d = 1$. An upper bound $C_d(n, 1) \leq n^{d+1}/d!$ was shown in [68], see also [40]. A lower bound $\binom{n}{d+1} \leq C_d(n, 1)$ was derived in [639]. This lower bounds is approximately $n^{d+1}/(d + 1)!$ which leaves a multiplicative gap $O(d)$ between the the upper and lower bounds. The problem was settled in [106] showing the following theorem, which contains Zuev's result as a special case.

THEOREM 3.2   *For any positive integers n and d such that $1 \leq d \leq n^{0.9}$, the capacity* of Boolean polynomial threshold functions of n variables and degree d satisfies[1]

$$\left(1 - \frac{C}{\log n}\right)^d \cdot n\binom{n}{\leq d} \leq C_d(n, 1) \leq n\binom{n}{\leq d}.$$

In this theorem C denotes a positive absolute constant: its value does not depend on n or d. The exponent 0.9 in the constraint on d can be replaced by any constant strictly less than 1 at the cost of changing the absolute constant C. The upper bound in Theorem 3.2 holds for all $1 \leq d \leq n$; it can be derived from counting regions in hyperplane arrangements. The lower bound in Theorem 3.2 uses results on random tensors and Reed–Muller codes [5].

For small degrees d, namely for $d = o(\log n)$, the factor $(1 - C/\log n)^d$ becomes $1 - o(1)$ and Theorem 3.2 yields in this case the asymptotically tight bound on the capacity:

$$C_d(n, 1) = n\binom{n}{\leq d}(1 - o(1)). \tag{3.23}$$

To better understand this bound, note that a general polynomial of degree d has $\binom{n}{\leq d}$ monomial terms. Thus, to communicate a polynomial threshold function, one needs to spend approximately n bits per monomial term. During learning, approximately n bits can be stored per monomial term.

In some situations, it may be desirable to have a simpler estimate of $C_d(n, 1)$ that is free of binomial sums. For this purpose, we can simplify the conclusion of Theorem 3.2 and state it as follows:

THEOREM 3.3   *For any integers n and d such that $n > 1$ and $1 \leq d \leq n^{0.9}$, the number of Boolean polynomial threshold functions $T(n, d)$ satisfies:*

$$\left(1 - \frac{C}{\log n}\right)^d \cdot \frac{n^{d+1}}{d!} < \log_2 T(n, d) < \frac{n^{d+1}}{d!}.$$

The upper bound in Theorem 3.3 actually holds for all $n > 1$, $1 \leq d \leq n$. For small degrees d, namely for $d = o(\log n)$, the factor $(1 - C/\log n)^d$ becomes $1 - o(1)$ and Theorem 3.3 yields in this case the asymptotically tight bound on the capacity:

$$C_d(n, 1) = \frac{n^{d+1}}{d!}(1 - o(1)). \tag{3.24}$$

In summary, polynomial threshold functions of degree d in n variables provide a simple way of stratifying all Boolean functions of these variables (Figure 3.2). In order to specify a polynomial threshold function in n variables and with degree d, one needs approximately $n^{d+1}/d!$ bits. This corresponds to providing the $n^d/d!$ support vectors on the hypercube that are closest to the separating polynomial surface of degree d in the largest class. Equivalently, there are approximately $2^{n^{d+1}/d!}$ different ways of separating the points of the Boolean cube $\{-1, 1\}^n$ into two classes by a polynomial surface of degree d, i.e. the zero set of a polynomial of degree d.

---

[1] Here and in the rest of the book, $\binom{n}{\leq d}$ denotes the binomial sum up to term d, i.e.
$$\binom{n}{\leq d} = \binom{n}{0} + \binom{n}{1} + \cdots + \binom{n}{d}.$$

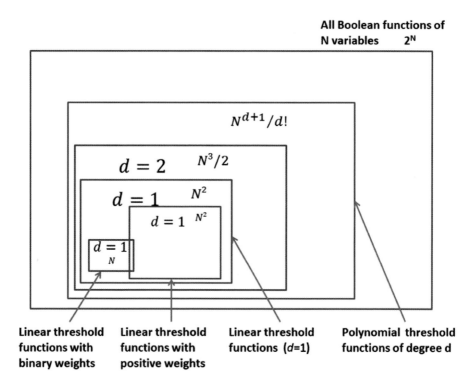

All Boolean functions of N variables 2^N

$N^{d+1}/d!$

$d = 2$ $N^3/2$

$d = 1$ N^2

$d = 1$ N^2

$d = 1$

N

Linear threshold functions with binary weights   **Linear threshold functions with positive weights**   **Linear threshold functions (d=1)**   **Polynomial threshold functions of degree d**

Figure 3.2 Stratified capacity of different classes of Boolean functions of N variables. Linear threshold functions with binary weights have capacity N. Linear threshold functions with positive weights have capacity $N^2 - N$. Linear threshold functions have capacity N^2. Polynomial threshold functions of degree 2 have capacity $N^3/2$. More generally, polynomial threshold functions of degree d have capacity $N^{d+1}/d!$ (fixed or slowly growing d). All these results are up to a multiplicative factor of $(1 + o(1))$. The set of all Boolean functions has capacity exactly equal to 2^N.

3.2.4 The Capacity of Other Units

It is possible to consider other models and compute their capacity (see exercises). For instance, the capacity of linear threshold gates with binary $\{-1, +1\}$ weights $C_B(n, 1)$ is linear rather than quadratic:

$$C_B(n, 1) \approx n. \tag{3.25}$$

By contrast, the capacity of linear threshold gates with positive weights $C_P(n, 1)$ remains quadratic:

$$C_P(n, 1) = n^2 (1 + o(1)). \tag{3.26}$$

Finally, to study the capacity of a ReLU gate, one can imagine concatenating it with a linear threshold gate to produce a binary output. If we consider an $A(n, 1, 1)$ architecture where the hidden unit and the output unit are linear threshold gates, then it is easy to show that the capacity is unchanged, that is:

$$C(n, 1, 1) = C(n, 1). \tag{3.27}$$

If the hidden units is a ReLU, then the capacity increases but still remains quadratic. Thus, with this definition of the capacity $C_{\text{ReLU}}(n, 1)$ of a ReLU unit, one has:

$$C_{\text{ReLU}}(n, 1) = n^2 (1 + o(1)). \tag{3.28}$$

The same approach can be used for other gates with continuous output. As a side note, with this approach, the capacity of a linear unit – obtained by concatenating a linear unit with a threshold unit – is exactly equal to the capacity of a linear threshold gate.

3.3   Shallow Learning

3.3.1   Gradient Descent

One of the most important learning algorithms when there is a well-defined error function $\mathcal{E}$ is gradient descent, which can generally be written as:

$$\Delta w_{ij} = -\eta \frac{\partial \mathcal{E}}{w_{ij}}. \tag{3.29}$$

From the Bayesian statistical framework, we have seen that in the three models for regression, 2-classification, and k-classification the gradient $\partial \mathcal{E}/\partial S$ is the same and equal to $-(T - O)$. Since $\partial S/\partial w_{ij} = I_j$, the gradient descent learning equation for all three cases is given by:

$$\Delta w_j = \eta(T - O)I_j \quad \text{or} \quad \Delta w_{ij} = \eta(T_i - O_i)I_j \quad (k\text{-classification}). \tag{3.30}$$

If we consider an entire output layer of linear units (regression), or logistic units (multiple 2-classifications), then the learning equations for all three cases become identical. As usual, these equations are for a single example and must be summed or averaged over the entire training set (or a minibatch) during any form of batch learning. For instance, in the case of linear regression or logistic regression, the learning equations become:

$$\Delta w_j = \eta \frac{1}{K} \sum_t (T(t) - O(t)) I_j(t), \tag{3.31}$$

where t runs over the batch or minibatch of size K.

Gradient descent learning in shallow networks is relatively easy to analyze due to convexity considerations [615, 145]. We are going to see that the error function in the linear and 2-classification cases are convex in the synaptic weights. We leave the k-classification case as an exercise. Thus, in general, gradient descent learning will converge to a global minimum of the error function in these shallow cases.

To study convexity, it is easy to see from the definition of convexity that a linear combination of convex functions with positive coefficients is also convex. Since the batch error functions are sums of individual-example error functions, it is sufficient to show that the error functions for each training example are themselves convex with respect to the synaptic weights. And in cases where, for each example, the error function is a sum of component-wise error functions (e.g. in vector regression), it is sufficient to deal with each individual component of the error for each example.

3.3.2   The Linear Case

We leave it as an exercise to check that the error function is convex. The linear case, however, corresponds to linear regression and one can analytically derive an expression for the optimal weights. The critical equation is obtained by setting the gradient to zero. Using the matrix notation described in Chapter 2 and the expectation symbol to denote averages over the training set, this yields:

$$E\left((T - O)I^{\mathsf{T}}\right) = 0 \quad \text{or} \quad E(TI^{\mathsf{T}}) - E(WII^{\mathsf{T}}) = 0, \tag{3.32}$$

where W is the matrix of weights. We introduce the two covariance matrices of the data $E(TI^{\mathsf{T}}) = \Sigma_{TI}$ and $E(II^{\mathsf{T}}) = \Sigma_{II}$. Using these matrices, yields the equivalent form: $\Sigma_{TI} = W\Sigma_{II}$. Thus in the general case where Σ_{II} is invertible, the optimal weight matrix is given by:

$$W^* = \Sigma_{TI}\Sigma_{II}^{-1}. \tag{3.33}$$

Note that the same equation applies regardless of whether the output layer contains a single or multiple units. With n input units (possibly including the clamped unit for the bias) and m output units, the matrix W is $m \times n$.

3.3.3   The Logistic Case

To prove convexity in the case of logistic regression with a single logistic unit, we simply show that the Hessian is positive semi-definite. Using the results obtained above it is easy to compute the second-order derivatives, as follows:

$$\frac{\partial^2 \mathcal{E}}{\partial w_i^2} = \frac{\partial}{\partial w_i}\frac{\partial \mathcal{E}}{\partial w_i} = -\frac{\partial}{\partial w_i}(T - O)I_i = I_i\frac{\partial O}{\partial w_i} = I_i^2\frac{\partial O}{\partial S}, \tag{3.34}$$

using $\partial\mathcal{E}/\partial w_i = -(T - O)I_i$ and $\partial O/\partial w_i = \partial O/\partial S \times \partial S/\partial w_i = \partial O/\partial S \times I_i$. Likewise,

$$\frac{\partial^2 \mathcal{E}}{\partial w_i w_j} = \frac{\partial}{\partial w_j}\frac{\partial \mathcal{E}}{\partial w_i} = -\frac{\partial}{\partial w_j}(T - O)I_i = I_i\frac{\partial O}{\partial w_j} = I_iI_j\frac{\partial O}{\partial S}. \tag{3.35}$$

Thus the Hessian H is given by $\frac{\partial O}{\partial S}II^{\mathsf{T}}$. The logistic function is monotone increasing $(\partial O/\partial S > 0)$. Thus for any vector x of dimension n: $x^{\mathsf{T}}Hx = \frac{\partial O}{\partial S}x^{\mathsf{T}}II^{\mathsf{T}}x \geq 0$ and $\mathcal{E}$ is convex.

3.3.4   The Perceptron (Linear Threshold Function) Case

Here we consider a linear threshold function. As mentioned in the Introduction, the perceptron learning rule can be written as a gradient descent rule of the form $\Delta w_i = \eta(T - O)I_i$. However this is not how the rule is usually presented. To see the equivalence between the two forms, let us first notice that as long as the rule is also applied to the bias and all the weights are initialized to zero, then the learning rate is irrelevant. It only influences the scale of the weights and thus of the activation, but not the output of the perceptron. As a result, for simplicity, we can assume that $\eta = 0.5$. Next, note that the term $T - O$ is non-zero only when there is an error, and in this case it is equal to $+2$ or -2. Thus, we can write the more standard, but equivalent, form of the perceptron learning rule:

$$\Delta w = \begin{cases} I, & T = +1 \text{ and } O = -1 \\ -I, & T = -1 \text{ and } O = +1 \\ 0 & \text{otherwise,} \end{cases} \tag{3.36}$$

which holds for any input I. The perceptron learning algorithm initializes the weight vector to zero $w(0) = 0$ and then at each step it selects an element of the training set that is mis-classified and applies the learning rule above. The perceptron learning theorem states that if the data is separable, then the perceptron algorithm will converge to a separating hyperplane in finite time. One may suspect that this may be the case because the rule amounts to applying stochastic gradient descent to a unit with a sigmoidal (logistic or tanh) transfer function, which is similar to a perceptron. In addition, the rule above clearly improves the performance on an example I that is mis-classified. For instance if the target of I is $+1$ and I is mis-classified and selected at step t, then we must have $w(t) \cdot I < 0$ and $w(t + 1) = w(t) + I$. As a result, the performance of the perceptron on example I is improved since $w(t+1) \cdot I = w(t) \cdot I + ||I||^2$, and similarly for mis-classified examples that have a negative target. However none of these arguments is sufficient to give a definitive proof of convergence.

To prove convergence, consider a training set of the form $\{(I(k), T(k)\}$ for $k = 1, \dots, K$. To say that it is linearly separable means that there exists a weight vector w^*, with $||w^*|| = 1$, such that $T(k)w^* \cdot I(k) > 0$ for every k, where "$\cdot$" denotes the dot product. Since the training set is finite, we can let γ correspond to the worst-case margin, i.e. $\gamma = \min_k T(k)w^* \cdot I(k)$. Let also R be the radius of the data, i.e. $R = \max_k ||I(k)||$.

THEOREM 3.4   *With separable data, the perceptron learning algorithm converges in at most R^2/γ^2 steps to a weight vector that separates the data (zero training error).*

Proof   The idea of the proof is simply to look at the angle between the current value of the weight vector $w(t)$ and w^* and how it evolves in time. Let us suppose that example $I(k) = I$ with target $T(k) = T$ is selected at step t, considering that only misclassified examples need to be selected. Then: $w(t + 1) = w(t) + TI$ and so:

$$w(t + 1) \cdot w^* - w(t) \cdot w^* = (w(t) + TI) \cdot w^* - w(t) \cdot w^* = TI \cdot w^* \geq \gamma. \tag{3.37}$$

Thus, since $w(0) = 0$, after n learning steps we have:

$$w(n) \cdot w^* \geq n\gamma. \tag{3.38}$$

To estimate the angle, we also need an estimate of the size of w. Since $w(t+1) = w(t)+TI$, we have:

$$||w(t + 1)||^2 \leq ||w(t)||^2 + ||TI||^2 \leq ||w(t)||^2 + R^2. \tag{3.39}$$

Therefore after n steps, we have:

$$||w(n)||^2 \leq nR^2. \tag{3.40}$$

Hence the cosine between $w(n)$ and w^* satisfies:

$$\cos\left(w(n), w^*\right) = \frac{w(n) \cdot w^*}{||w(n)||||w^*||} \geq \frac{n\gamma}{\sqrt{n}R}, \tag{3.41}$$

and thus by the time n reaches the value R^2/γ^2 (or its floor) the cosine of the angle is equal or close to 1, thus the angle is equal or close to 0, and it is easy to check that all the training examples are correctly classified. It is also easy to see that the result remains true even if $w(0) \neq 0$, although in general the convergence may be slower. If the data is not linearly separable, one can show the so-called perceptron cycling theorem which states that with the perceptron learning algorithm the weight vector w remains bounded and does not diverge to infinity [130, 295], and likewise the number of errors is bounded [542].

3.3.5 Data Normalization, Weight Initializations, Learning Rates, and Noise

Even in the simple case of gradual learning in a single unit there are a number of important practical issues.

First, everything else being equal, there is no reason to favor a particular component of the input vector. Doing so may actually slow down learning. Thus it is useful to preprocess the training data by normalizing each component in the same way through some affine transformation. Typically this is done by subtracting the mean and rescaling the range of each component to some fixed interval, or normalizing the standard deviations to one.

Second, everything else being equal, there is no reason to favor any synaptic weight, and doing so may actually slow down learning. A large bias, for instance, is associated with a hyperplane that is likely to be far from the cloud of normalized data points and thus likely to perform poorly, requiring larger modifications during learning. Thus all the weights, including the bias, should be initialized to small values. This can be done efficiently by initializing each weight independently using a uniform or normal distribution with small standard deviation.

Third, there is the issue of the learning rate, or step size, which must be decreased as learning progresses in order to converge to the optimum. In simple convex cases, it is possible to estimate the time of convergence to the global minimum with a given rate schedule and derive effective rate schedules. In more complex and realistic deep learning cases, the schedules must be set in advance or adjusted somewhat empirically at training time as a function of the data.

And fourth, in tandem with the third point, gradient descent changes are often applied using mini-batches. The size of the mini-batches is one way to control the degree of stochasticity of the learning process. In the case of a single unit, or a shallow layer, we have seen that the error functions are typically convex thus the use of stochastic gradient descent is less critical than for deep networks. A classical result due to Robbins and

Monro [614] is that, in the convex case, following noisy gradients with a decreasing step size provably reaches the optimum.

The true gradient is a sum of many terms, the gradients computed on each example. Thus stochastic gradient can be viewed as a drawing from a Gaussian random variable with mean equal to the true gradient, and standard deviation inversely proportional to the square root of the batch size. The larger the mini-batches, the closer the gradient estimate is to the true gradient. In this way, stochastic gradient descent can be modeled as an Ornstein–Uhlenbeck Brownian motion process [739] leading to a stochastic differential equation [551, 482].

3.4   Extensions of Shallow Learning

In this chapter we have studied the design and learning algorithms for shallow $A(n, 1)$ or $A(n, m)$ architectures. However, the same ideas can be applied immediately to a number of other settings. In Chapter 9, we will consider an example of shallow recurrent network called the Hopfield model, consisting of n symmetrically connected linear threshold gates, which are all visible. This enables the implementation of shallow learning using the simple Hebb's rule. Here we consider other examples within the class of layered feedforward networks.

3.4.1   Top Layer of Deep Architectures

In this chapter, we have seen how to design a shallow network for regression or classification and derived a gradient descent learning rule for it. However the design solution is far more general and can be applied to the design of the top layer of *any* deep feedforward architecture for regression or classification purposes. Thus the general design problem for deep forward architectures is basically solved for the output layer. Furthermore, if all the weights in the lower layers are frozen, the same learning algorithm can be applied. Indeed, freezing the weights of the lower layers simply provides a transformation of the original input vectors into a new set of input vectors for the top layer. Thus logically the next level of architectural complexity to be explored is provided by feedforward architectures $A(n, m, p)$ with two layers of weights, but where the lower layer weights are fixed and only the upper layer is adaptive. This actually happens in two well-known cases: extreme machines where the lower weights are random, and support vector machines where the lower weights are equal to the training examples.

3.4.2   Extreme Machines

In the so-called extreme machines [364, 166], the weights in the lower layer are chosen at random and thus provide a random transformation of the input data. In the case where the hidden layer consists of linear units and is smaller in size than the input layer ($n > m$), this can be justified by the the Johnson–Lindenstrauss Lemma and other related theorems [382, 279, 225]. The basic idea implemented by this first layer is the idea of dimensionality reduction with little distortion. The Johnson–Lindenstrauss Lemma states that a properly-scaled random projection from a high-dimensional space to a lower-dimensional space tends to maintain pairwise distances between data points. More precisely:

LEMMA 3.5 (JOHNSON–LINDENSTRAUSS)   *Given $0 < \epsilon < 1$, a set X of K points in $\mathbb{R}^n$, and a number $m > 8\ln(K)/\epsilon^2$, there is a linear map $f : \mathbb{R}^n \longrightarrow \mathbb{R}^m$ such that:*

$$(1 - \epsilon)||u - v||^2 \le ||f(u) - f(v)||^2 \le (1 + \epsilon)||u - v||^2 \tag{3.42}$$

for all $u, v \in X$. Here f can be a suitably scaled orthogonal projection onto a random subspace of dimension m.

Thus the first random layer reduces the dimensionality of the data without introducing too much distortion. The next layer can address classification or regression problems based on the more compact representation generated in the hidden layer. The theory derived in this chapter (e.g. design, learning algorithm, and learning convergence) applies immediately to the top layer of this case without any changes. Note that this remains true even if non-linear transfer functions are used in the hidden layer, as long as the random projection weights remain fixed. In some cases, expansive transformations where $m > n$ can also be considered, for instance in order to encode input vectors into sparse hidden vectors (see [59] for related work).

3.4.3   Support Vector Machines

From an architectural standpoint, in support vector machines (SVMs) [211, 217], the units in the hidden layer are also linear as in extreme machines. The weights of these hidden units are identical to the vectors in the training set. Thus each hidden unit is associated with one training example and its activation is equal to the dot product between the input vector and the corresponding training example. More precisely, consider the binary classification problem with input vectors $I(1), \ldots, I(K)$ with corresponding binary targets $T(1), \ldots, T(K)$. It can be shown that the separating hyperplane with maximal margin can be written in the activation form:

$$S(I) = \sum_{i=1}^{K} w_i T(i)(I \cdot I_i) + w_0 = \sum_{i=1}^{K} w_i T(i)(I^\mathsf{T} I_i) + w_0. \tag{3.43}$$

While gradient descent can be applied to learning the weight vector w, SVMs come with their own optimization learning algorithm. In the optimal solution, the vectors associated with non-zero weights are the support vectors. This approach can be generalized to kernel machines where a similarity kernel $K(I, I_j)$ is used to compute the similarity between I and I_j in lieu of the dot product [657].

3.5   Exercises

EXERCISE 3.1   Derive the prior distribution associated with L1 regularization. Extend the analysis to Lp regularization.

EXERCISE 3.2   What happens in linear regression when the matrix Σ_{II} is not invertible?

EXERCISE 3.3   Estimate the expectation of the error that a trained linear unit makes on a new data point, i.e. a data point not in the training set (generalization error)? How does this expectation depend on the size of the training set? Clarify all your assumptions.

EXERCISE 3.4   (1) Prove that the quadratic error function in linear regression is convex with respect to the weights.
(2) Consider k-classification with softmax output units satisfying $O_i = e^{S_i} / \sum_j e^{S_j}$. Is the relative entropy error term associated with O_i convex with respect to the weights w_{ij} associated with S_i? Is the relative entropy error term associated with O_i convex with respect to the other weights w_{kl}, i.e. the weights associated with the other activations S_k, $k \neq i$)?

EXERCISE 3.5   Study the evolution of the weight vector during learning in a single linear unit trained using the simple Hebbian learning rule $\Delta w_i = \eta O I_i$.

EXERCISE 3.6   Prove that any Boolean functions of n variables can be written as a polynomial threshold function of degree n.

EXERCISE 3.7   Let $C_d(n, 1)$ be the logarithm base 2 of the number of Boolean polynomial threshold functions of n variables of degree d, and let $C_d^*(n, 1)$ be the number of Boolean homogeneous (over $H^n = \{-1, 1\}^n$) polynomial threshold functions of n variables of degree d. Prove the following relationships (the degree d is omitted when $d = 1$):

$$C(n, 1) = C^*(n + 1, 1); \tag{3.44}$$

$$C_{d-1}^*(n, 1) < C_d^*(n, 1) < C^* \left(\binom{n}{d}, 1 \right) \quad \text{for} \quad d \geq 2; \tag{3.45}$$

$$C_{d-1}(n, 1) < C_d(n, 1) < C \left(\binom{n}{0} + \binom{n}{1} + \cdots + \binom{n}{d}, 1 \right) \quad \text{for} \quad d \geq 2. \tag{3.46}$$

EXERCISE 3.8 (HYPERPLANE ARRANGEMENTS)   (1) Prove that the number $K(m, n)$ of connected regions created by m hyperplanes in $\mathbb{R}^n$ (passing through the origin) satisfies:

$$K(m, n) \leq 2 \sum_{k=0}^{n-1} \binom{m-1}{k} = 2 \binom{m-1}{\leq n-1}. \tag{3.47}$$

(2) Prove that this bound becomes an equality if the normal vectors to the hyperplanes are in general position.
(3) Prove that the same bound and equality condition remain true for m central hyperplanes (i.e. affine hyperplanes passing through the same point).

(4) Prove that the number $L(m, n)$ of connected regions created by m affine hyperplanes in $\mathbb{R}^n$ satisfies:

$$L(m, n) \le \sum_{k=0}^{n} \binom{m}{k} = \binom{m}{\le n}. \tag{3.48}$$

(5) Prove that $L(m, n)$ is bounded below by the number of all intersection subspaces defined by the hyperplanes. [An intersection subspace refers to the intersection of any subfamily of the original set of hyperplanes. The dimensions of an intersection subspace may range from zero (a single point) to n (intersecting an empty set of hyperplanes gives the entire space $\mathbb{R}^n$).]

(6) Prove that if the hyperplanes are in general position, then the upper bound and the lower bound are the same and each bound becomes and equality. These results are needed for the next few exercises.

EXERCISE 3.9　To see the relevance of hyperplane arrangements, let us fix a finite subset $S \subset \mathbb{R}^n \setminus \{0\}$ and consider all homogeneous linear threshold functions on S, i.e. functions $f : S \to \mathbb{R}$ of the form

$$f_a(x) = \operatorname{sgn}(a \cdot x),$$

where $a \in \mathbb{R}^n$ is a fixed vector. Consider the collection ("arrangement") of hyperplanes

$$\{x^\perp : x \in S\},$$

where $x^\perp = \{z \in \mathbb{R}^n : z \cdot x = 0\}$ is the hyperplane through the origin with normal vector x. Two vectors a and b define the same homogeneous linear threshold function $f_a = f_b$ if and only if a and b lie on the same side of each of these hyperplanes. In other words, $f_a = f_b$ if and only if a and b lie in the same open component of the partition of $\mathbb{R}^n$ created by the hyperplanes $x^\perp$, with $x \in S$. Such open components are called the *regions* of the hyperplane arrangement. Prove that: the number of homogeneous linear threshold functions on a given finite set $S \subset \mathbb{R}^n \setminus \{0\}$ equals the number of regions of the hyperplane arrangement $\{x^\perp : x \in S\}$.

EXERCISE 3.10　Prove the following theorem originally obtained by Wendel [785].

THEOREM 3.6　*Let K points in $\mathbb{R}^n$ be drawn i.i.d from a centrosymmetric distribution such that the points are in general position. Then the probability that all the points fall in some half space is:*

$$P_{n,K} = 2^{-K+1} \binom{K-1}{\le n-1} = 2^{-K+1} \sum_{i=0}^{n-1} \binom{K-1}{i}. \tag{3.49}$$

EXERCISE 3.11　Prove that for any $n > 1$, the following upper bound holds:

$$C(n, 1) \le n^2. \tag{3.50}$$

EXERCISE 3.12　Prove that for any $n > 1$ and all degrees d such that $1 \le d \le n$, the following upper bound holds:

$$C_d(n, 1) \le n \binom{n}{\le d}. \tag{3.51}$$

EXERCISE 3.13 (CAPACITY OF SETS)　The capacity $C(S)$ of a finite set $S \subset \mathbb{R}^n$ containing $|S|$ points is defined to be the logarithm base 2 of the number of possible ways the set can be split by linear threshold functions. Likewise, the capacity $C_d(S)$ of order d ($d > 1$) of S is defined to be the logarithm base 2 of the number of possible ways the set can be split by polynomial threshold functions of degree d. More generally, we can define the capacity $C(S, n_1, \ldots, n_L)$ to be the logarithm base 2 of the number of linear threshold functions that can be defined on the set S using a feedforward architecture $A(n_1, \ldots, n_L)$ of linear threshold function (with $n = n_1$). Obviously $C(S) = C(S, n, 1)$. Prove that this notion of set capacity satisifes the following properties:

(1) Affine invariance: For any invertible affine transformation $F \colon \mathbb{R}^{n_1} \to \mathbb{R}^{n_1}$, we have:

$$C(F(S), n_1, n_2, \ldots, n_L) = C(S, n_1, n_2, \ldots, n_L).$$

(2) Single layer: For any set $S \subset \mathbb{R}^n$:

$$C(S, n, m) = C(S)m.$$

(3) Replacement by image: For any set $S \subset \mathbb{R}^{n_1}$ and a threshold map from $\mathbb{R}^{n_1}$ to H^{n_2}, we have:

$$C(f(S), n_2, n_3, \ldots, n_L) \leq C(S, n_1, n_2, \ldots, n_L).$$

Derive lower and upper bounds on $C(S)$ and $C_d(S)$ when $S \in \mathbb{R}^n$ and when $S \in \{-1, +1\}^n$. In particular, show that for any such set in $\mathbb{R}^n$:

$$C(S) \leq 2\binom{|S| - 1}{\leq n} \tag{3.52}$$

and

$$1 + \log_2 |S| \leq C(S) \leq 1 + n\log_2\left(\frac{e|S|}{n}\right),$$

where the lower bound is true as soon as $|S| > 2^{17}$. The upperbound can be simplified to $n\log_2 |S|$ as soon as $n > 4$. To prove this result, you will need to prove the following inequality as an intermediate result:

$$\sum_{k=0}^{n} \binom{N}{k} \leq \left(\frac{eN}{n}\right)^n, \tag{3.53}$$

which is valid for all integers $1 \leq n \leq N$. Show that the lower bound is attained by a particular choice of S. If S is a subset of the Boolean hypercube, the lower bound can be improved to:

$$\frac{1}{16}\log_2^2 |S| \leq C(S) \leq 1 + n\log_2\left(\frac{e|S|}{n}\right).$$

EXERCISE 3.14　Prove a lower bound of the form $\alpha n^2 \leq C(n, 1)$ for some positive constant α less than 1. For example, use a recursive construction to show that the number of linear threshold functions of n variables is greater than $2^{n(n-1)/2}$.

EXERCISE 3.15 (CAPACITY WITH BINARY WEIGHTS)   Let $C_B(n, 1)$ be the capacity of a linear threshold gate with n inputs with binary weights restricted to $\{-1, 1\}$. Let $C_B^*(n, 1)$ be the capacity of a linear homogeneous threshold gate (i.e. with no bias) with n inputs, with binary weights restricted to $\{-1, 1\}$. Prove that for any n:

$$C_B^*(n, 1) = n \qquad \text{if } n \text{ is odd}$$
$$C_B(n, 1) = n + 1 \qquad \text{if } n \text{ is even.}$$

Show that if one extends the definition of a threshold function by arbitrarily deciding that $\text{sgn}(0) = +1$, then each formula above is true for every n.

Show that the capacity of polynomial threshold gates of degree $d > 1$ with binary weights satisfies

$$C_{B,d}(n, 1) \leq \sum_{k=1}^{d} \binom{n}{k} = \binom{n}{\leq d} - 1.$$

Derive a similar upper bound in the homogeneous case, where homogeneous is defined over H^n. Derive a similar upper bound in the homogeneous case, where homogeneous is defined over $\mathbb{R}^n$.

EXERCISE 3.16 (CAPACITY WITH POSITIVE WEIGHTS)   Let $C_P(n, 1)$ be the capacity of a linear threshold gate with n inputs with weights restricted to be positive (≥ 0), and similarly $C_P^*(n, 1)$ for linear threshold gate with n inputs but no bias. Prove that:

$$C_P^*(n, 1) = \frac{C^*(n, 1)}{2^n}$$

and

$$C_P^*(n, 1) \leq C_P(n, 1) \leq C_P^*(n + 1, 1).$$

As a result, using Zuev's result, show:

$$C_P(n, 1) = n^2 \left(1 + o(1)\right).$$

In short, for $d = 1$, when the synaptic weights are forced to be positive the capacity is still quadratic. Write down a conjecture for the case $d > 1$ corresponding to polynomial threshold gates of degree d with positive weights.

EXERCISE 3.17   Estimate the capacity of an architecture $A(n, 1, 1)$ where the hidden unit is a ReLU unit, and the output unit is a linear threshold unit.

EXERCISE 3.18   Study the perceptron algorithm when $w(0) \neq 0$. Prove that, in the linearly separable case, the algorithm is still convergent, but the convergence in general may be slower. Study the perceptron algorithm in the case of training data that is not linearly separable. Prove that in this case, the weight vector remains bounded and does not diverge to infinity.

EXERCISE 3.19 (SATISFIABILITY OF THRESHOLD GATES)   Consider m linear threshold gates $f_1, \ldots, f_m$ of n binary variables, i.e. the common input is in $\{-1, +1\}^n$, with binary weights restricted to the set $\{-1, +1\}$. These threshold functions are said to be satisfiable if there exists a vector x in $\{-1, +1\}^n$ such that $f_i(x) = 1$ for $i = 1, \ldots, m$. Is the satisfiability of threshold gates problem NP-complete?

EXERCISE 3.20   Study by simulations and analytically, whenever possible, the behavior of stochastic gradient descent in shallow learning, including: the effect of data normalization, the effect weight initialization, the effect of the learning rate, the effect of noise (e.g. online versus batch learning), and the speed and accuracy of convergence to the global minimum. Begin with the simplest case of a single linear unit with a single weight acting as a multiplier (i.e. $O = wI$) and generalize to a linear unit with n weights. Then proceed with a logistic unit with a single weight (i.e. $O = \sigma(wI)$, σ is the logistic function) and then generalize to n weights.

EXERCISE 3.21   Study by simulations and analytically, whenever possible, the learning behavior of a single linear or logistic unit with probabilistic output, i.e. where the output O' is sampled from the normal distribution with mean $O = \sum_i w_i I_i$ in the linear regression case, or from the Bernoulli distribution with parameter $p = O = \sigma(\sum_i w_i I_i)$ (σ is the logistic function) in the binary classification case. Start with a single weight and generalize to n weights. For learning, consider the quadratic (linear case) or relative entropy (classification case) error functions based on O, or on O', in combination with two learning rules: $\Delta w_i = \eta(T - O)I_i$ and $\Delta w_i = \eta(T - O')I_i$, for a total of four error/rule combinations. For each combination, examine both online and batch learning.

EXERCISE 3.22   Show that there exists a differentiable transfer function such that the Boolean XOR function can be implemented by a single unit with linear activation. More broadly, show that for every Boolean function of n variables that is symmetric, i.e. invariant under any permutation of its input entries, there exists a differentiable transfer function such that the function can be implemented by a single unit with linear activation and identical weights. Even more broadly, show that for every Boolean function of n variables, there exists a differentiable transfer function and a set of weights (with a corresponding linear activation) that can realize the function exactly.

EXERCISE 3.23   Prove the Johnson–Lindenstrauss Lemma.

4 Two-Layer Networks and Universal Approximation

In the preceding chapter, we have acquired a fairly good understanding of shallow architectures of the form $A(n, m)$ with a single adaptive layer. We know how to design these architectures, how to train them, and we broadly understand their capabilities and know how to compute their capacity. Thus in this chapter we begin to turn to deep architectures with hidden layers, starting with the case of a single hidden layer, thus corresponding to $A(n, m, p)$ architectures. We first look at the functional capacity in two simple cases: the linear model and the unrestricted Boolean model. Although simple, these cases reveal the important role played by bottleneck layers, a phenomenon that extends to deeper architectures and will play an important role in Chapter 5 on autoencoders. We then examine the universal approximation properties of $A(n, m, p)$ architectures in the discrete and continuous cases, when there are no restrictions on m. Thus, with a slight abuse of notation, we look at the limiting case of $A(n, \infty, m)$ architectures first. By universal approximation property with respect to a class of functions $\mathcal{F}$ we refer to the property of whether any function in $\mathcal{F}$ can be approximated to any arbitrary degree of precision by a feedforward neural network, in this case with a single hidden layer. We also look at universal approximation properties in terms of training sets, i.e. how well training sets can be learnt by architectures with a single hidden layer. Finally, we estimate the cardinal capacity of the $A(n, m, 1)$ architecture, leaving the general $A(n, m, p)$ case for Chapter 5.

4.1 Functional Capacity

4.1.1 The Linear Model

In the linear setting, with no biases to simplify the discussion, it is easy to see that, if $m \geq n$, then the $A(n, m, p)$ linear architecture implements exactly all linear functions from $\mathbb{R}^n$ to $\mathbb{R}^p$. If instead $m < n$, then the functional capacity depends on the value of p. If $p \leq m$, then the architecture can still implement any linear function from $\mathbb{R}^n$ to $\mathbb{R}^p$. However, if $p > m$ (i.e. $m < \min(n, p)$), then the overall linear function implemented by the network is restricted to have at most rank m. By contrast, the maximum possible rank imposed by the input and output layers is equal to $\min(n, p)$. Any linear function from $\mathbb{R}^n$ to $\mathbb{R}^p$ with rank m can be implemented by such a network, as long as there are no connectivity restrictions. In terms of training capacity, any training set containing at most m independent vectors can be realized with zero training error. Beyond that, from a learning standpoint, in the supervised case one is left with the problem of learning the best rank m approximations to the mapping defined by the input–output pairs in the training set. This will be an essential point in Chapter 5 in the study of linear compressive autoencoders. In particular, although the error function can be quadratic and the overall function W linear, the set of linear functions W with rank restricted to m is *not* a convex set. Thus, the overall optimization problem is not convex, and therefore it is significantly more difficult than in the shallow linear case where it is convex.

In the next chapter, we will be able to solve the learning optimization problem for all $A(n, m, p)$ linear architectures, which in turn leads to the solution of the learning optimization problem and functional capacity characterization for all feedforward, layered, linear architectures of any depth, as long as there is full connectivity between the layers. If additional connectivity restrictions are imposed, then the problem becomes significantly harder, with no known general solutions.

4.1.2   The Unrestricted Boolean Model

As a first step towards the case of non-linear architectures, we begin with the unrestricted Boolean model, i.e. $A(n, m, p)$ architectures where each unit in the hidden layer and in the output layer is capable of implementing any possible Boolean function of its inputs. In this case, one obtains a result that is similar to the linear case (with no connectivity restrictions).

More precisely, if $m \geq n$, then the $A(n, m, p)$ unrestricted Boolean architecture can implement any Boolean function from $\{-1, +1\}^n$ to $\{-1, +1\}^p$. If instead $m < n$, then the functional capacity depends on the value of p. If $p \leq m$, then the architecture can still implement any Boolean function from $\{-1, +1\}^n$ to $\{-1, +1\}^p$. However, if $p > m$ (i.e. $m < \min(n, p)$), then the overall Boolean function implemented by the network is restricted to have at most "rank m" in the sense that the hidden layer can take only 2^m binary values. This is less than the total number of possible states for the input or output layers. In terms of training capacity, if the training set contains at most 2^m points it can be realized with zero training error. However, it the training set contains more than 2^m points, then several states in the input layer are forced to be mapped to the same hidden representation in the hidden layer, and thus to the same output vector in the output layer. Moreover, there are vectors in H^p corresponding to the output layer that do not have an inverse image in the input layer. Thus, again the hidden layer acts as a bottleneck layer.

In Chapter 5, we will be able to solve the functional capacity of all $A(n, m, p)$ architectures which, as in the fully linear case, leads to the solutions of the functional capacity of all feedforward, layered, unrestricted Boolean architectures of any depth, as long as there is full connectivity between the layers. If additional connectivity restrictions are imposed, then the problem becomes significantly harder, with no known general solutions.

4.2   Universal Approximation Properties

4.2.1   Boolean Setting and Threshold Gates

We now look at the capacity of two-layer networks in the sense of their universal approximation properties, i.e. their ability to approximate any reasonable function. This can be done in various non-linear settings. We begin with the Boolean case.

The following universal approximation results are easy to prove and the proofs are left as exercises:

1. Every Boolean function can be expressed in terms of AND, OR, and NOT gates. AND, OR, and NOT can be written as linear threshold functions. Thus, every Boolean function can be computed by a circuit of linear threshold gates.
2. Every Boolean function can be written in disjunctive or conjunctive normal form using essentially a two-layer Boolean network, allowing negation of input variables. By replacing the corresponding gates using threshold gates, every Boolean function can be computed by a two-layer feedforward network of threshold gates.
3. These results can be extended immediately to every Boolean function from $\{-1, +1\}^n$ to $\{-1, +1\}^p$, i.e. to Boolean maps.

4.2.2   The Classification Setting

Consider a classification problem with n inputs and K training examples in H^n or $\mathbb{R}^n$. We leave it as an exercise to show that there is a layered feedforward network $A(n, m, 1)$ consisting entirely of linear threshold gates, with a single hidden layer and a single output unit, that can classify the training set perfectly, i.e. with no errors. This is true both with binary-valued or real-valued input components. In the binary-valued case, this result is just a special case of the result above on implementing Boolean functions using threshold gates. We leave the case of real-valued inputs as an exercise. One approach for proving this result is to use the theorems about the regression case in the next section.

4.2.3   The Regression Setting

We now look at regression settings, in particular the approximation of smooth real-valued functions. Some of the basic ideas here go back to the original work of Kolmogorov and Arnold on Hilbert's 13th problem [418, 45] and subsequent refinements [556, 697] showing that any multivariate continuous function can be implemented by a shallow network using only continuous functions of a single variable and addition. Universal approximation theorems specific to neural networks can be found in [359, 220]. Here we provide very simple constructive proofs of the main results. These are based on the following theorem.

THEOREM 4.1   *Every continuous function $f : [0, 1] \longrightarrow \mathbb{R}$ can be approximated to any degree of precision $\epsilon > 0$ (with respect to the sup norm) by a two-layer neural network where the output unit is linear and the units in the hidden layer are linear threshold units.*

Proof   First, as a reminder, the supremum (sup) norm of a real-valued function h defined over a set S is given by: $||h||_\infty = \sup\{|h(x)| : x \in S\}$. Thus, our goal is to construct a suitable neural network that implements a function g satisfying $|f(x) - g(x)| < \epsilon$ everywhere for $x \in [0, 1]$. Next we construct g, essentially as a lookup table.

Since f is continuous over a compact interval, it is uniformly continuous which means that for every real number $\epsilon > 0$ there exists a real number $\alpha > 0$ such that:

$$|x_1 - x_2| < \alpha \implies |f(x_1) - f(x_2)| < \epsilon. \tag{4.1}$$

We then choose m large enough so that $\alpha > 1/m$ and subdivide the $[0, 1]$ interval into m consecutive intervals, each of length $1/m$, of the form: $[0, 1/m), [1/m, 2/m)$, and so forth. Within any such interval, the function f cannot vary by more than ϵ and therefore it can be approximated by the value of f taken at any point in that interval. We now create a hidden layer with $m + 1$ linear threshold gates with output in $\{0, 1\}$ and, for a given input x in $[0, 1]$, we encode the sub-interval it belongs to by the number of threshold gates that are turned on. So the input unit is connected to each hidden unit, and all these connections have the same weight $+1$. In addition, the linear threshold gates in the hidden layer have increasing thresholds equal to: $-1/m, 0, 1/m, \ldots, (m - 1)/m$. For instance, if $0 \le x < (1/m)$, the first threshold gate is the only gate to output a $+1$ (all the other gates output a zero); and if $x = 1$, all the gates in the hidden layer are turned on.

Finally, the output unit is linear with the following weights. The weight coming from the first threshold gate is equal to $f(0)$; the weight coming from the second threshold gate is equal to $f(1/m) - f(0)$; the weight coming from the third threshold gate is equal to $f(2/m) - f(1/m)$; and so forth. In this way, if $(k/m) \le x < ((k + 1)/m)$, then the output of the network is equal to $f(k/m)$, and for $x = 1$ the output of the network is equal to $f(1)$. Thus, by construction, for every $x \in [0, 1]$): the value $g(x)$ produced by the network satisfies $|f(x) - g(x)| < \epsilon$, completing the proof. $\square$

Remark

It is essential to note that this is a constructive proof that builds an actual neural network with a single hidden layer to approximate the target function f. The neural network operates essentially like a lookup table. In this sense, no learning is required. However, note that the number $m + 1$ of hidden units could be exponentially large (depending on the function f and ϵ), leading to a construction that in general is not practical. This is a major concern, and a major reason for looking into deeper architectures with more than one hidden layer. A second, less important, issue is that we have used real values for the weights from the hidden layer to the output unit (and for the thresholds in the hidden layer), and in principle these may require infinite precision. However, it is easy to see that these could be replaced by rational values (with numerator and denominator bounded by a constant depending on ϵ). Finally, depending on the function f, the value of α may not be easy to estimate, although only a lower bound is needed for the construction. If the function f satisfies the Lipschitz condition, then there is a constant $c \in \mathbb{R}$ such that $\alpha = c\epsilon$. The number of units, and hence of parameters, in this $A(n, m, 1)$ network scales like $m \approx 1/\alpha$. In the Lipschitz case, and up to the small multiplicative constant c, the number of units or parameters scales like $m \approx 1/\epsilon$.

Extensions

This simple proof can easily be extended in several important directions, left as exercises:

(1) Allowing f to have a finite number of points where it is discontinuous.
(2) Allowing f to be defined on more complex sets, such as any finite union of closed intervals, i.e. any compact set.
(3) Replacing the threshold functions in the hidden layer with either:
    (a) sigmoidal functions (logistic or tanh);
    (b) ReLU or leaky ReLU transfer functions; or
    (c) a polynomial function of degree d, for a suitable value of d.
(4) Allowing f to be vector valued, i.e. take its values in $\mathbb{R}^l$ for some l.
(5) Allowing f to be multivariate, i.e a function of n real variables defined on $[0, 1]^n$ (or any compact subset of $\mathbb{R}^n$).

By putting these elements together, one obtains the following more general theorem:

THEOREM 4.2   *Every continuous function $f : C \longrightarrow \mathbb{R}^p$, where C is any compact subset of $\mathbb{R}^n$, can be approximated to any degree of precision $\epsilon > 0$ (with respect to the sup norm) by a two-layer neural network where the output units are linear and the units in the hidden layer are linear threshold units, or alternatively have one of the following transfer functions: sigmoidal (logistic or* tanh*), ReLU (or leaky ReLU), or a suitable polynomial of degree d.*

REMARK   The same scaling analysis done above shows that the number of parameters in this case scales like $(1/\epsilon)^n$ which is exponential in the number n of dimensions (the "curse of dimensionality").

Spectral Approach

There is another way of proving similar universal approximation theorems that involves Fourier series. Consider the problem of approximating a function f defined on a real interval $[-L, L]$ which itself is equal to (or well approximated by) a truncated Fourier series. Thus:

$$f(x) = \frac{a_0}{2} + \sum_{n=1}^{N} a_n \cos\left(\frac{n\pi x}{L}\right) + b_n \sin\left(\frac{n\pi x}{L}\right). \tag{4.2}$$

We can use the theorem above to approximate the cos and sin functions with a single hidden layer of threshold gates and linear output units for each component. The final linear combination with the coefficients a_n and b_n adds a third layer to the architecture, but this layer can be collapsed with the previous layer since both layers are purely linear. By doing so, the entire approximation uses a single non-linear hidden layer of threshold gates and a linear output. In short, this approach requires only proving that the sine and cosine basis functions can be approximated by a neural network with a single hidden layer. The same approach can be applied to other bases of functions besides the sine and cosine functions, e.g. orthogonal polynomials, as well as non-orthogonal polynomial, such as monomials.

The Connection to Gaussian Processes

There is yet another possible way of proving the universal approximation properties of neural networks with a single hidden layer using Gaussian processes [604, 522] in two steps. In rough terms, one needs to first prove that in the limit of very large hidden layers, $A(n, m, 1)$ networks converge to a Gaussian process [532] and, second, that Gaussian processes themselves have universal approximation properties.

4.3   The Capacity of *A(n, m, 1)* Architectures

Here we look at the cardinal capacity $C(n, m, 1)$, i.e. the logarithm base 2 of the number of different Boolean functions that can be implemented by a feedforward architecture of threshold gates with a single hidden layer. We have the theorem:

THEOREM 4.3   *The capacity of an $A(n, m, 1)$ architecture of threshold gates satisfies:*

$$C(n, m, 1) = mn^2 (1 + o(1)) \tag{4.3}$$

for $n \to \infty$ and for any choice of $m \in [1, 2^{o(n)}]$.

Proof   Let us denote by f the map between the input layer and the hidden layer and by ϕ the map from the hidden layer to the output layer. We first prove an upper bound and then a lower bound. As usual, we use the notation:

$$\binom{n}{\leq m} = \binom{n}{0} + \binom{n}{1} + \cdots + \binom{n}{m}. \tag{4.4}$$

For the upper bound, we first note that the total number of possible maps f is bounded by $2^{mn^2(1+o(1))}$, since f consists of m threshold gates, and each threshold gate corresponds to $2^{n^2(1+o(1))}$ possibilities by Zuev's theorem. Any fixed map f produces at most $2n$ distinct vectors in the hidden layer. Thus, using the result of one of the exercises of Chapter 3, the number of threshold functions ϕ of m variables defined on at most 2^n points is bounded by:

$$2\binom{2^n - 1}{\leq m} = 2^{nm(1+o(1))}, \tag{4.5}$$

using the assumption $m \leq 2^{o(n)}$. Thus, under our assumptions, the total number of functions of the form $\phi \circ f$ is bounded by the product of the bounds above which yields immediately:

$$C(n, m, 1) \leq mn^2 (1 + o(1)). \tag{4.6}$$

To prove the lower bound, we use a filtering (or multiplexing) procedure, concisely summarized in Figure 4.1. For this, we decompose:

$$n = n^- + n^+ \quad \text{where} \quad n^- = \lceil \log_2 m \rceil \tag{4.7}$$

and each input vector $I = (I_1, \ldots, I_n) \in \{-1, +1\}^n$ as $I = (I^-, I^+)$, where:

$$I^- = (I_1, \ldots, I_{n^-}) \in \{-1, +1\}^{n^-} \quad \text{and} \quad I^+ = (I_{n^-+1}, \ldots, I_n) \in \{-1, +1\}^{n^+}. \tag{4.8}$$

For any Boolean linear threshold map f^+ from $\{-1, +1\}^{n^+}$ to $\{-1, +1\}^m$, we can uniquely derive a map $f = (f_1, \ldots, f_m)$ from $\{-1, +1\}^n$ to $\{-1, +1\}^m$ defined by:

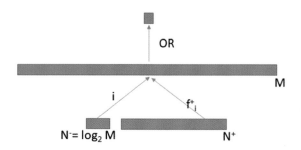

Figure 4.1 The filtering procedure used to prove the lower bound.

$$f_i(I^-, I^+) = [I^- = i] \quad \text{AND} \quad [f_i^+(I^+)]. \tag{4.9}$$

Here $I^- = i$ signifies that the binary vector I^- represents the digit i. In other words, $I^- = i$ acts as a selector for the digit i. Note that this selection procedure can be written as a threshold function with a single positive example. We say that f is obtained from f^+ by filtering. From an exercise in a previous chapter, each component f_i of the filtering process can be expressed as a single linear threshold gate, and thus f is a threshold map. It is easy to see that the filtering of two distinct maps f^+ and g^+ results into two distinct maps f and g. Now let us use $\phi = OR$ in the top layer – note that OR can be expressed as a linear threshold function. Then it is also easy to see that $\phi \circ f \neq \phi \circ g$. Thus, the total number of Boolean functions that can be implemented using linear threshold gates in the $A(n, m, 1)$ architecture is lower bounded by the number of all Boolean maps f^+. This yields:

$$C(n, m, 1) \geq m(n^+)^2 (1 + o(1)) \geq mn^2 (1 + o(1)), \tag{4.10}$$

using the fact that $n^+ = n - \lceil \log_2 m \rceil$, and $\lceil \log_2 m \rceil = o(n)$ by assumption. This lower bound completes the proof. □

We leave it as a non-trivial follow-up exercise to estimate the capacity of the $A(n, m, p)$ architecture of threshold gates.

4.4 Exercises

EXERCISE 4.1 What is the functional capacity of linear $A(n, m, p)$ networks when bias units are allowed in the hidden layer, output layer, or both?

EXERCISE 4.2 Compute the cardinal capacity of the $A(n, m, p)$ unrestricted Boolean architecture. Consider different cases ($m \geq \min(n, p)$ and $m < \min(n, p)$).

EXERCISE 4.3 Build a two-layer network of threshold gates that computes the PARITY function. How many gates and connections are needed? Explore alternative circuits for computing PARITY, in particular circuits with greater depth and fewer units.

EXERCISE 4.4 Identify the smallest set of integers S such that every Boolean function of n variables be implemented by a feedforward network of linear threshold gates with weights and bias in S.

EXERCISE 4.5 Prove that every Boolean map from H^n to H^p can be implemented by a layered feedforward network of linear threshold gates with a single hidden layer.

EXERCISE 4.6 (CLASSIFICATION)   Prove that any classification training set of the form $I(t), T(t)$, with $t = 1, \ldots, K$, where the input I is in $\mathbb{R}^n$ and the target T is in $\{0, 1\}$, can be realized with zero error by an $A(n, m, 1)$ architecture where the hidden units and the output unit are linear threshold gates.

EXERCISE 4.7   Let $\epsilon = 0.1$. Construct a neural network with a single hidden layer that can approximate the function $f(x) = x^2$ within ϵ everywhere over the interval $[0, 2]$.

EXERCISE 4.8   Show that the proof of Theorem 4.1 can be modified so that all the weights (including the thresholds) are rational numbers.

EXERCISE 4.9   Show that the proof of Theorem 4.1 can be extended in the following ways:
(1) Allowing f to have a finite number of points where it is discontinuous.
(2) Allowing f to be defined on more complex sets, such as any finite union of closed intervals (any compact set).
(3) Replacing the threshold functions in the hidden layer with other transfer functions, such as: (a) sigmoidal functions (logistic or tanh); (b) ReLU or leaky ReLU functions; or (c) polynomial functions of degree d, for a suitable value of d.

EXERCISE 4.10   Show that the proof of Theorem 4.1 can be extended in the following ways:
(1) Allowing f to be vector-valued, i.e. take its values in $\mathbb{R}^l$ for some l.
(2) Allowing f to be multivariate, for instance a function of n real variables defined on $[0, 1]^n$.

EXERCISE 4.11   Provide a detailed proof of the spectral approach to proving universal approximation properties of neural networks with a single hidden layer.

EXERCISE 4.12   Consider a real-valued, continuous function, f defined over a closed interval $[a, b] \in \mathbb{R}$. The Bolzano–Weierstrass (BW) theorem is equivalent to the statement that for d large enough, there exists a single neuron with polynomial activation (or transfer function) of degree d that can approximate f to any degree of precision $\epsilon > 0$ (in the sup norm). Use this result to prove that: f can be approximated to any degree of precision $\epsilon > 0$ (in the sup norm) by a suitable $A(1, m, 1)$ neural network, where all the units have linear activations (which implies that at least some of the transfer functions must be non-linear). Likewise, prove the following training capacity result. For any $\epsilon > 0$, use the BW theorem to prove that for any finite training set consisting of input–output pairs $(I(t), T(t)) \in \mathbb{R}^2$ with $t = 1, \ldots, K$, there exists an $A(1, m, 1)$ neural network, where all the units have linear activations, capable of fitting each data point with error at most ϵ.

EXERCISE 4.13   Consider the $A(n, m, p)$ feedforward architecture with linear threshold gates. Prove that if $n \geq 2\lceil \log_2 m \rceil$ and $m \geq 2\lceil \log_2 p \rceil$, then the capacity is given by:

$$C(n, m, p) \asymp n^2 m + \min(n, m)mp.$$

Here the notation $a \asymp b$ means that there exists two positive absolute constants c_1, c_2 such that $c_1 b \leq a \leq c_2 b$. In fact show that here the inequality is satisfied with $c_2 = 1$ and $c_1 \in (0, 1)$.

5   Autoencoders

So far, we have acquired a good understanding of $A(n, m)$ and $A(n, \infty, m)$ architectures. Thus we now begin to turn towards the study of $A(n, m, p)$ architectures. We can remove some degrees of freedom from the problem by having $p = n$ and letting the input data also be the target data. This is the case of autoencoder networks.

   Thus in this chapter we focus on autoencoder networks. The basic original idea behind autoencoders is to use the input data as the target, i.e. to try to reconstruct the input data in the output layer. As described in [9], the idea was originally suggested by Sanjaya Addanki and further developed by the PDP group [627, 490]. The basic idea of training a network to reproduce an input that is already available may seem silly at first sight, until one realizes that what is of interest in such a network is not so much its output, but rather the representations that emerge in the hidden layers. Autoencoders can have recurrent connections and multiple hidden layers, but in this chapter we will focus primarily on feedforward autoencoders with a single hidden layer, and thus on $A(n, m, n)$ architectures. This is for simplicity, but also because we want to further the study of $A(n, m, p)$ networks with a single hidden layer started in Chapter 4. Furthermore, in certain important cases such as the linear case, the solution of the single-hidden layer regime is sufficient to understand what happens in the multiple-hidden layer regime. An example of recurrent autoencoder will be studied in Section 8.7 on recirculation algorithms.

   To be more precise, there are several important reasons for spending an entire chapter on autoencoders. Among the main ones are:

1. Autoencoders provide an essential bridge between supervised and unsupervised learning, basically by turning an unsupervised problem into a supervised problem. As such, they are a canonical example of self-supervised learning.
2. Autoencoders are useful in practice and can be used in different tasks ranging from dimensionality reduction, to denoising, to deep architecture initialization.
3. Autoencoders provide a natural bridge to several other areas, such as data compression, coding and information theory, principal component analysis and generative and latent-variable models in statistics, to name a few.
4. Autoencoders building blocks can be composed in many ways in order to design more complex networks. For instance, they can be stacked vertically to create certain kinds of deep architectures, which can be trained predominantly in self-supervised ways.
5. Finally, they are essential for the theory of deep learning. After understanding shallow networks and the universal properties of deep networks with a single hidden layer, it

is natural to look at specific networks $A(n, m, p)$ with a single hidden layer. Using the input data as the target is a natural way to reduce the degrees of freedom of the problem and results in $A(n, m, n)$. As we shall see, this reduction is not very limiting: in all the cases where one can obtain a full understanding of the corresponding autoencoder, it is relatively easy to move from the auto-association case to the general case of hetero-association. Moreover, in a similar way, we shall see that in all the cases where one can obtain a full understanding of the corresponding autoencoder, it is relatively easy to move from the single hidden layer to the multiple hidden layer case and thereby derive important insights about deeper architectures. We will present a complete treatment of autoencoders in the linear case and the unrestricted Boolean case. This will provide a complete solution to the problem of understanding the functional capacity of these models, and will also lead to key insights on issues of local minima and complexity in more general cases.

We begin by describing a general framework for organizing the study of various autoencoders.

5.1   A General Autoencoder Framework

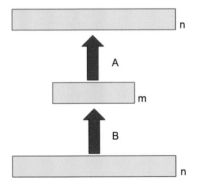

Figure 5.1 An $A(n, m, n)$ Autoencoder Architecture.

To derive a fairly general framework, an autoencoder with architecture $A(n, m, n)$ (Figure 5.1) is defined by a tuple $n, m, K, \mathbb{F}, \mathbb{G}, \mathcal{A}, \mathcal{B}, X, \Delta$ where:

1. n, m and K are positive integers.
2. $\mathbb{F}$ and $\mathbb{G}$ are sets.
3. $\mathcal{A}$ is a class of functions from $\mathbb{G}^m$ to $\mathbb{F}^n$.
4. $\mathcal{B}$ is a class of functions from $\mathbb{F}^n$ to $\mathbb{G}^m$.
5. $X = \{x_1, \ldots, x_K\}$ is a set of K training vectors in $\mathbb{F}^n$. When external targets are present (hetero-association), we let $\mathcal{Y} = \{y_1, \ldots, y_K\}$ denote the corresponding set of target vectors in $\mathbb{F}^n$. In the hetero-associative case, it is also possible for the targets to be in $\mathbb{F}^p$, for some $p \neq n$.

6. Δ is a distance or distortion function (e.g. L_p norm, Hamming distance) defined over $\mathbb{F}^n$.

For any $A \in \mathcal{A}$ and $B \in \mathcal{B}$, the autoencoder transforms an input vector $x \in \mathbb{F}^n$ into an output vector $A \circ B(x) \in \mathbb{F}^n$ (Figure 5.1). The corresponding *autoencoder problem* is to find $A \in \mathcal{A}$ and $B \in \mathcal{B}$ that minimizes the overall error or distortion function:

$$\min_{A,B} \mathcal{E}(A, B) = \min_{A,B} \sum_{k=1}^{K} \mathcal{E}(x_k) = \min_{A,B} \sum_{k=1}^{K} \Delta(A \circ B(x_k), x_k). \qquad (5.1)$$

In the hetero-associative case, when external targets y_k are provided, the minimization problem becomes:

$$\min_{A,B} \mathcal{E}(A, B) = \min_{A,B} \sum_{k=1}^{K} \mathcal{E}(x_k, y_k) = \min_{A,B} \sum_{k=1}^{K} \Delta(A \circ B(x_k), y_k). \qquad (5.2)$$

The framework above is not meant to capture all possible kinds of autoencoders, but only a sufficiently large subset, in order to get us started. Within this framework, many different kinds of autoencoders can be considered. For instance, in the linear case, the functions A and B are represented by matrices with entries over a field. In this case, the most relevant autoencoders for this book are the linear autoencoders over the real numbers [80] with the usual quadratic distance. But one can also consider linear autoencoders over the complex numbers [83], or linear autoencoders over finite fields [70]. The theory of linear autoencoders over the complex numbers is very similar to the theory of linear autoencoders over the real numbers (simply by replacing "transpose" by "conjugate transpose" everywhere). The theory of autoencoders over finite fields is closely related to coding theory and is beyond the scope of this book. Similarly, in the non-linear case, one can consider different kinds of non-linear functions, such as Boolean functions (e.g. unrestricted or linear threshold), or differentiable functions (e.g. sigmoidal). Here we will focus primarily on the Boolean unrestricted case, which is the only non-linear case that has received a complete treatment so far.

When $n > m$ the autoencoder is called compressive, and when $n \leq m$ the autoencoder is called expansive. Expansive autoencoders are of interest, for instance in a biological context [59], but in general require additional assumptions in order to avoid trivial solutions based on the identity function and their theory is under-developed. Thus, in the next sections, we are going to focus on compressive autoencoders, and specifically on the linear autoencoder over the real numbers and the unrestricted Boolean autoencoder with binary $\{0, 1\}$ variables.

5.2 General Autoencoder Properties

One of the main benefits of studying different classes of autoencoders within this general framework is the identification of a list of common properties that may be investigated in each specific case. This general list is thus a *result* of the analysis which emerges, by generalization, only after careful consideration of several individual cases. With the benefit of hindsight, however, it is given here upfront before delving into the details of each specific case.

1: Invariances
What are the relevant group actions for the problem? What are the transformations of $\mathbb{F}^n$ and $\mathbb{G}^p$, or A and B, that leave the problem or the learning algorithm invariant?

2: Fixed Layer Solutions
Is it possible to optimize A (resp. B), fully or partially, while B (resp. A) is held constant?

3: Problem Complexity
How complex is the autoencoder optimization problem? Is there an overall analytical solution? Is the corresponding decision problem NP-complete?

4: Landscape of $\mathcal{E}$
What is the landscape of the overall error $\mathcal{E}$? Are there any symmetries and critical points (maxima, minima, saddle points)? How can they be characterized?

5: Clustering
Especially in the compressive case where $m < n$, what is the relationship to clustering?

6: Transposition
Is there a notion of symmetry or transposition between the decoding and coding transformations A and B, in particular around critical points?

7: Recirculating
What happens if the values from the output layer are recycled into the input layer, in particular around critical points?

8: Learning Algorithms
What are the learning algorithms and their properties? In particular, can A and B be fully, or partially, optimized in alternation? And if so, is the algorithm convergent? And if so, at what speed and what are the properties of the corresponding limit points?

9: Generalization
What are the generalization properties of the autoencoder after learning?

10: External Targets
How does the problem change if external targets are provided?

11: Composition
What are the effects of composing autoencoders horizontally or vertically?

Not all these properties can be addressed analytically for all types of autoencoders. But they can be addressed for several important classes of autoencoders, including the linear autoencoders over the real and complex numbers, the linear autoencoders over finite fields, and the non-linear unrestricted Boolean or unrestricted probabilistic autoencoders.

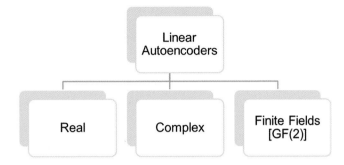

Figure 5.2 Classification of Linear Autoencoders. Linear autoencoders can be defined over different fields, in particular infinite fields such as $\mathbb{R}$ or $\mathbb{C}$, or finite fields such as the Galois Field with two elements GF(2) ($\mathbb{F}_2 = \{0, 1\}$).

5.3 Linear Autoencoders

Here we consider the compressive, real-valued, linear case (Figure 5.2) where $\mathbb{F} = \mathbb{G} = \mathbb{R}$ and the goal is the minimization of the squared Euclidean distance:

$$\min_{A,B} \mathcal{E}(A, B) = \min_{A,B} \sum_{t=k}^{K} ||x_k - ABx_k||^2 = \sum_{k=1}^{K} (x_k - ABx_k)^{\mathrm{T}}(x_k - ABx_k). \quad (5.3)$$

Unless otherwise specified, all vectors are column vectors and we use x^{T} (resp. X^{T}) to denote the transpose (or conjugate transpose in order to deal with the complex case) of a vector x (resp. of a matrix X). As we shall see, one can also address the hetero-associative case where external targets are available, in which case the goal is the minimization of the distance:

$$\min_{A,B} \mathcal{E}(A, B) = \min_{A,B} \sum_{k=1}^{K} ||y_k - ABx_k||^2 = \sum_{k=1}^{K} (y_k - ABx_k)^{\mathrm{T}}(y_k - ABx_k). \quad (5.4)$$

The following covariance matrices will be useful. In general, we define:

$$\Sigma_{XY} = \sum_{k} x_k y_k^{\mathrm{T}}. \quad (5.5)$$

Using this definition, Σ_{XX}, Σ_{YY} are symmetric (Hermitian in the complex case) matrices $(\Sigma_{XX})^{\mathrm{T}} = \Sigma_{XX}$ and $(\Sigma_{YY})^{\mathrm{T}} = \Sigma_{YY}$, and $(\Sigma_{XY})^{\mathrm{T}} = \Sigma_{YX}$. We also define:

$$\Sigma = \Sigma_{YX}\Sigma_{XX}^{-1}\Sigma_{XY}; \quad (5.6)$$

Σ is also symmetric. In the *auto-associative* case, $x_k = y_k$ for all k resulting in $\Sigma = \Sigma_{XX}$.

Note that any symmetric matrix admits a set of orthonormal eigenvectors and all its eigenvalues are real. Finally, we let I_m denote the $m \times m$ identity matrix.

For several results, we will make the assumption that Σ is invertible. This is not a very restrictive assumption for several reasons. First, by adding a small amount of noise to the data, a non-invertible Σ could be converted to an invertible Σ. More importantly, in many settings one can expect the training vectors to span the entire input space and thus Σ to be invertible. If the training vectors span a smaller subspace, then the original problem can be transformed to an equivalent problem defined on the smaller subspace.

5.3.1   Useful Reminders

Here we provide a few reminders that will be useful to solve the linear autoencoder from first principles in a general, coordinate-invariant, way.

Standard Linear Regression
Consider the standard linear regression problem of minimizing $\mathcal{E}(B) = \sum_k ||y_k - Bx_k||^2$, where B is an $m \times n$ matrix, corresponding to a linear neural network without any hidden layers. Then we can write:

$$\mathcal{E}(B) = \sum_k x_k^T B^T B x_k - 2 y_k^T B x_k + ||y_k||^2. \tag{5.7}$$

Thus $\mathcal{E}$ is a convex function in B because the associated quadratic form is equal to:

$$\sum_k x_k^T C^T C x_k = \sum_k ||C x_k||^2 \geq 0. \tag{5.8}$$

Let B be a critical point. Then by definition for any $m \times n$ matrix C we must have $\lim_{\epsilon \to 0}$ $[\mathcal{E}(B + \epsilon C) - \mathcal{E}(B)]/\epsilon = 0$. Expanding and simplifying this expression gives:

$$\sum_k x_k^T B^T C x_k - y_k^T B C x_k = 0 \tag{5.9}$$

for all $m \times n$ matrices C. Using the linearity of the trace operator and its invariance under circular permutation of its arguments[1], this is equivalent to:

$$\text{Tr}((\Sigma_{XX} B^T - \Sigma_{XY})C) = 0 \tag{5.10}$$

for any C. Thus we have $\Sigma_{XX} B^T - \Sigma_{XY} = 0$ and therefore:

$$B\Sigma_{XX} = \Sigma_{YX}. \tag{5.11}$$

If Σ_{XX} is invertible, then $Cx_k = 0$ for any t is equivalent to $C = 0$, and thus the function $\mathcal{E}(B)$ is strictly convex in B. The unique critical point is the global minimum given by $B = \Sigma_{YX} \Sigma_{XX}^{-1}$. This is just another way of deriving the linear regression result obtained by looking at gradient descent in shallow networks in Chapter 3. As we shall see, the solution to the standard linear regression problem, together with the general approach given here to solve it, is also key for solving the more general linear autoencoder problem. The solution will also involve projection matrices.

---

[1] It is easy to show directly that for any matrices A and B of the proper size, $\text{Tr}(AB) = \text{Tr}(BA)$ [431]. Therefore for any matrices A, B, and C of the proper size, we have $\text{Tr}(ABC) = \text{Tr}(CAB) = \text{Tr}(BCA)$.

Projection Matrices

For any $n \times m$ matrix A with $m \leq n$, let P_A denote the orthogonal projection onto the subspace generated by the columns of A. Then P_A is a symmetric matrix and $P_A^2 = P_A$, $P_A A = A$ since the image of P_A is spanned by the columns of A and these are invariant under P_A. The kernel of P_A is the space $A^\perp$ orthogonal to the space spanned by the columns of A. Obviously, we have $P_A A^\perp = 0$ and $A^T P_A = A^T$. The projection onto the space orthogonal to the space spanned by the columns of A is given by $I_n - P_A$. In addition, if the columns of A are independent (i.e. A has full rank m), then the matrix of the orthogonal projection is given by $P_A = A(A^T A)^{-1} A^T$ [499] and $P_A^T = P_A$. Note that all these relationships are true even when the columns of A are not orthonormal.

Some Misconceptions

As we shall see, the global minimum of the linear autoencoder corresponds to Principal Component Analysis (PCA). While the global minimum solution of linear autoencoders over $\mathbb{R}$ and $\mathbb{C}$ can be expressed analytically, it is often not well appreciated that there is more to be understood about linear autoencoders. In particular, if one is interested in learning algorithms that proceed through incremental and somewhat "blind" weight adjustments, then one must study the entire landscape of $\mathcal{E}$, including all the critical points of $\mathcal{E}$, and derive and compare different learning algorithms. A second misconception is to believe that the problem is a convex optimization problem, hence somewhat trivial, since after all the error function is quadratic and the transformation $W = AB$ is linear. As previously mentioned, the difficulty with this argument is that the bottleneck layer forces W to be of rank m or less, and the set of matrices of rank at most m is *not* convex. What is true, and crucial for solving the linear autoencoders over infinite fields, is that the problem becomes convex when A or B is fixed.

5.3.2 Group Invariances

For any autoencoder, it is important to investigate whether there is any group of transformations on the data or on the weights that leave its properties invariant.

Change of Coordinates in the Hidden Layer

Note that for any invertible $m \times m$ matrix C, we have $W = AB = ACC^{-1}B$ and $\mathcal{E}(A, B) = \mathcal{E}(AC, C^{-1}B)$. Thus all the properties of the linear autoencoder are invariant with respect to any change of coordinates in the hidden layer.

Change of Coordinates in the Input/Output Spaces

Consider an orthonormal change of coordinates in the output space defined by an orthogonal (or unitary) $n \times n$ matrix D, and any change of coordinates in the input space defined by an invertible $N \times N$ matrix C. This leads to a new autoencoder problem with input vectors $Cx_1, \ldots, Cx_K$ and target output vectors of the form $Dy_1, \ldots, Dy_K$ with reconstruction error of the form:

$$\mathcal{E}(A', B') = \sum_k ||Dy_k - A'B'Cx_k||^2. \tag{5.12}$$

If we use the one-to-one mapping between pairs of matrices (A, B) and (A', B') defined by $A' = DA$ and $B' = BC^{-1}$, we have:

$$\mathcal{E}(A', B') = \sum_k ||Dy_k - A'B'Cx_k||^2 = \sum_k ||Dy_k - DABx_k||^2 = \mathcal{E}(A, B); \quad (5.13)$$

the last equality follows from using the fact that D is an isometry which preserves distances. Thus, using the transformation $A' = DA$ and $B' = BC^{-1}$ the original problem and the transformed problem are equivalent and the function $\mathcal{E}(A, B)$ and $\mathcal{E}(A', B')$ have the same landscape. In particular, in the auto-associative case, we can take $C = D$ to be a unitary matrix. This leads to an equivalent autoencoder problem with input vectors Cx_k and covariance matrix $C\Sigma C^{-1}$. For the proper choice of C there is an equivalent problem where the basis of the space is provided by the eigenvectors of the covariance matrix and the covariance matrix is a diagonal matrix with diagonal entries equal to the eigenvalues of the original covariance matrix Σ (see exercises).

5.3.3   Fixed-Layer and Convexity Results

A key technique for studying any autoencoder, is to simplify the problem by fixing all its transformations but one. Thus in this section we study what happens to the linear autoencoder problem when either A or B is fixed, essentially reducing the problem to standard linear regression.

THEOREM 5.1 (FIXED A)   *For any fixed $n \times m$ matrix A, the function $\mathcal{E}(A, B)$ is convex in the coefficients of B and attains its minimum for any B satisfying the equation:*

$$A^{\mathrm{T}} A B \Sigma_{XX} = A^{\mathrm{T}} \Sigma_{YX}. \quad (5.14)$$

If Σ_{XX} is invertible and A is of full rank m, then $\mathcal{E}$ is strictly convex and has a unique minimum reached when:

$$B = (A^{\mathrm{T}} A)^{-1} A^{\mathrm{T}} \Sigma_{YX} \Sigma_{XX}^{-1}. \quad (5.15)$$

In the auto-associative case, if Σ_{XX} is invertible and A is of full rank m, then the optimal B has full rank M and does not depend on the data. It is given by:

$$B = (A^{\mathrm{T}} A)^{-1} A^{\mathrm{T}}, \quad (5.16)$$

and in this case, $W = AB = A(A^{\mathrm{T}} A)^{-1} A^{\mathrm{T}} = P_A$ and $BA = I_m$.

Proof   We write:

$$\mathcal{E}(A, B) = \sum_k x_k^{\mathrm{T}} B^{\mathrm{T}} A^{\mathrm{T}} A B x_k - 2(y_k^{\mathrm{T}} A B x_k) + ||y_k||^2. \quad (5.17)$$

Then for fixed A, $\mathcal{E}$ is a convex function because the associated quadratic form is equal to:

$$\sum_k x_k^{\mathrm{T}} C^{\mathrm{T}} A^{\mathrm{T}} A C x_k = \sum_k ||ACx_k||^2 \geq 0 \quad (5.18)$$

for any $m \times n$ matrix C. Let B be a critical point. Then by definition for any $m \times n$ matrix

C, we must have $\lim_{\epsilon \to 0} [\mathcal{E}(A, B + \epsilon C) - \mathcal{E}(A, B)]/\epsilon = 0$. Expanding and simplifying this expression gives:

$$\sum_k x_k^\mathrm{T} B^\mathrm{T} A^\mathrm{T} A C x_k - y_k^\mathrm{T} A C x_k = 0 \tag{5.19}$$

for all $m \times n$ matrices C. Using the linearity of the trace operator and its invariance under circular permutation of its arguments, this is equivalent to:

$$\mathrm{Tr}((\Sigma_{XX} B^\mathrm{T} A^\mathrm{T} A - \Sigma_{XY} A) C) = 0 \tag{5.20}$$

for any C. Thus we have $\Sigma_{XX} B^\mathrm{T} A^\mathrm{T} A - \Sigma_{XY} A = 0$ and therefore:

$$A^\mathrm{T} A B \Sigma_{XX} = A^\mathrm{T} \Sigma_{YX}. \tag{5.21}$$

Finally, if Σ_{XX} is invertible and if A is of full rank, then $A C x_k = 0$ for any k is equivalent to $C = 0$, and thus the function $\mathcal{E}(A, B)$ is strictly convex in B. Since $A^\mathrm{T} A$ is invertible, the unique critical point is obtained by solving Equation 5.14.   □

In similar fashion, we have the following theorem.

THEOREM 5.2 (FIXED B)   *For any fixed $m \times n$ matrix B, the function $\mathcal{E}(A, B)$ is convex in the coefficients of A and attains its minimum for any A satisfying the equation:*

$$A B \Sigma_{XX} B^\mathrm{T} = \Sigma_{YX} B^\mathrm{T}. \tag{5.22}$$

If Σ_{XX} is invertible and B is of full rank, then $\mathcal{E}$ is strictly convex and has a unique minimum reached when:

$$A = \Sigma_{YX} B^\mathrm{T} (B \Sigma_{XX} B^\mathrm{T})^{-1}. \tag{5.23}$$

In the auto-associative case, if Σ_{XX} is invertible and B is of full rank, then the optimal A has full rank m and depends on the data. It is given by:

$$A = \Sigma_{XX} B^\mathrm{T} (B \Sigma_{XX} B^\mathrm{T})^{-1} \tag{5.24}$$

and $BA = I_m$.

Proof   From Equation 5.17, the function $\mathcal{E}(A, B)$ is a convex function in A. The condition for A to be a critical point is:

$$\sum_k x_k^\mathrm{T} B^\mathrm{T} A^\mathrm{T} C B x_k - y_k^\mathrm{T} C B x_k = 0 \tag{5.25}$$

for any $m \times n$ matrix C, which is equivalent to:

$$\mathrm{Tr}((B \Sigma_{XX} B^\mathrm{T} A^\mathrm{T} - B \Sigma_{XY}) C) = 0 \tag{5.26}$$

for any matrix C. Thus $B \Sigma_{XX} B^\mathrm{T} A^\mathrm{T} - B \Sigma_{XY} = 0$ which implies Equation 5.22. The other statements in the theorem follow immediately.   □

REMARK   Note that from Theorems 5.1 and 5.2 and their proofs, we have that (A, B) is a critical point of $\mathcal{E}(A, B)$ *if and only if* Equations (5.14) and (5.22) are simultaneously satisfied, that is if and only if $A^\mathrm{T} A B \Sigma_{XX} = A^\mathrm{T} \Sigma_{YX}$ and $A B \Sigma_{XX} B^\mathrm{T} = \Sigma_{YX} B^\mathrm{T}$.

5.3.4   Critical Points and the Landscape of $\mathcal{E}$

We now study in more depth the landscape of $\mathcal{E}$, its critical points, and the properties of $W = AB$ at those critical points.

THEOREM 5.3 (CRITICAL POINTS) *Assume that Σ_{XX} is invertible. Then two matrices (A, B) define a critical point of $\mathcal{E}$, if and only if the global map $W = AB$ is of the form:*

$$W = P_A \Sigma_{YX} \Sigma_{XX}^{-1}, \tag{5.27}$$

with A satisfying:

$$P_A \Sigma = P_A \Sigma P_A = \Sigma P_A. \tag{5.28}$$

In the auto-associative case, this becomes:

$$W = AB = P_A \tag{5.29}$$

and

$$P_A \Sigma_{XX} = P_A \Sigma_{XX} P_A = \Sigma_{XX} P_A. \tag{5.30}$$

If A is of full rank, then the pair (A, B) defines a critical point of $\mathcal{E}$ if and only if A satisfies Equation 5.28 and B satisfies Equation 5.16. Hence B must also be of full rank.

Proof   If (A, B) is a critical point of $\mathcal{E}$, then from Equation 5.14, we must have:

$$A^T(AB - \Sigma_{YX}\Sigma_{XX}^{-1}) = 0. \tag{5.31}$$

Let:

$$S = AB - P_A\Sigma_{YX}\Sigma_{XX}^{-1}. \tag{5.32}$$

Then since $A^T P_A = A^T$, we have $A^T S = 0$. Thus the space spanned by the columns of S is a subset of the space orthogonal to the space spanned by the columns of A (i.e. $S \in A^\perp$). On the other hand, since:

$$P_A S = S, \tag{5.33}$$

then S is also in the space spanned by the columns of A (i.e. $S \in Span(A)$). Taken together, these two facts imply that $S = 0$, resulting in $W = AB = P_A \Sigma_{YX} \Sigma_{XX}^{-1}$, which proves Equation 5.27. Note that for this result, we need only B to be critical (i.e. optimized with respect to A). Using the definition of Σ, we have:

$$P_A \Sigma P_A = P_A \Sigma_{YX} \Sigma_{XX}^{-1} \Sigma_{XX} \Sigma_{XX}^{-1} \Sigma_{XY} P_A. \tag{5.34}$$

Since $S = 0$, we have $AB = P_A \Sigma_{YX} \Sigma_{XX}^{-1}$ and thus:

$$P_A \Sigma P_A = P_A \Sigma_{YX} \Sigma_{XX}^{-1} \Sigma_{XX} \Sigma_{XX}^{-1} \Sigma_{XY} P_A = AB\Sigma_{XX} B^T A^T. \tag{5.35}$$

Similarly, we have:

$$P_A \Sigma = AB\Sigma_{XY} \tag{5.36}$$

and

$$\Sigma P_A = \Sigma_{YX} B^T A^T. \tag{5.37}$$

Then Equation 5.28 result immediately by combining Equations 5.35, 5.36, and 5.37 using Equation 5.22. The rest of the theorem follows easily.   □

REMARK   The above proof unifies the cases when AB is of rank m and strictly less than m.

THEOREM 5.4 (CRITICAL POINTS OF FULL RANK)   *Assume that Σ is of full rank with n distinct eigenvalues $\lambda_1 > \cdots > \lambda_n$ and let $u_1, \ldots, u_n$ denote a corresponding basis of orthonormal eigenvectors. If $I = \{i_1, \ldots, i_m\}$ $(1 \le i_1 < \cdots < i_m \le n)$ is any ordered set of indices of size m, let $U_I = (u_{i_1}, \ldots, u_{i_m})$ denote the matrix formed using the corresponding column eigenvectors. Then two full rank matrices A, B define a critical point of $\mathcal{E}$ if and only if there exists an ordered m-index set I and an invertible $m \times m$ matrix C such that:*

$$A = U_I C \quad \text{and} \quad B = C^{-1} U_I^T \Sigma_{YX} \Sigma_{XX}^{-1}. \tag{5.38}$$

For such critical point, we have:

$$W = AB = P_{U_I} \Sigma_{YX} \Sigma_{XX}^{-1} \tag{5.39}$$

and

$$\mathcal{E}(A, B) = \operatorname{Tr} \Sigma_{YY} - \sum_{i \in I} \lambda_i. \tag{5.40}$$

In the auto-associative case, these equations reduce to:

$$A = U_I C \quad \text{and} \quad B = C^{-1} U_I^T, \tag{5.41}$$

$$W = AB = P_{U_I}, \tag{5.42}$$

and

$$\mathcal{E}(A, B) = \operatorname{Tr} \Sigma - \sum_{i \in I} \lambda_i = \sum_{i \in \bar{I}} \lambda_i, \tag{5.43}$$

where $\bar{I} = \{1, \ldots, N\} \setminus I$ is the complement of I.

Proof   Since $P_A \Sigma = \Sigma P_A$, we have

$$P_A \Sigma A = \Sigma P_A A = \Sigma A. \tag{5.44}$$

Thus the columns of A form an invariant space of Σ. Thus A is of the form $U_I C$. The conclusion for B follows from Equation 5.27 and the rest is easily derived. Equation 5.43 can be derived easily by using the reminders given at the beginning of this section on linear autoencoders and using the unitary change of coordinates under which Σ_{XX} becomes a diagonal matrix. In this system of coordinates, we have:

$$\mathcal{E}(A, B) = \sum_k \|y_k\|^2 + \sum_k \operatorname{Tr}(x_k^T (AB)^T AB x_k) - 2 \sum_k \operatorname{Tr}(y_k^T AB x_k).$$

Therefore, using the invariance property of the trace under circular permutations, we have:

$$\mathcal{E}(A, B) = \operatorname{Tr}(\Sigma) + \operatorname{Tr}((AB)^2 \Sigma) - 2 \operatorname{Tr}(AB\Sigma).$$

Since AB is a projection operator, this yields Equation 5.43. In the auto-associative case with these coordinates it is easy to see that Wx_k and $\mathcal{E}(A, B) = \sum_k \mathcal{E}(x_k)$ are easily computed from the values of Wu_i. In particular, $\mathcal{E}(A, B) = \sum_{i=1}^n \lambda_i(u_i - Wu_i)^2$. In addition, at the critical points, we have $Wu_i = u_i$ if $i \in I$, and $Wu_i = 0$ otherwise.   □

REMARK   All the previous theorems are true in the hetero-associative case with targets y_k. Thus they can readily be applied to address the linear denoising autoencoder [765, 764] over $\mathbb{R}$ or $\mathbb{C}$. The linear denoising autoencoder is an autoencoder trained to remove noise by having to associate noisy versions of the inputs with the correct inputs. In other words, using the current notation, it is an autoencoder where the inputs x_k are replaced by $x_k + n_k$ where n_k is the noise vector and the target outputs y_k are of the form $y_k = x_k$. Thus the previous theorems can be applied using the following replacements: $\Sigma_{XX} = \Sigma_{XX} + \Sigma_{NN} + \Sigma_{NX} + \Sigma_{XN}, \Sigma_{XY} = \Sigma_{XX} + \Sigma_{NX}, \Sigma_{YX} = \Sigma_{XX} + \Sigma_{XN}$. Further simplifications can be obtained using particular assumptions on the noise, such as $\Sigma_{NX} = \Sigma_{XN} = 0$.

THEOREM 5.5 (ABSENCE OF LOCAL MINIMA)   *The global minimum of the linear autoencoder is achieved by full rank matrices A and B associated with the index set $1, \ldots, m$ of the m largest eigenvalues of Σ with $A = U_I C$ and $B = C^{-1} U_I^T$ (and where C is any invertible $m \times m$ matrix). When $C = I$, $A = B^T$. All other critical points are saddle points associated with corresponding projections onto non-optimal sets of eigenvectors of Σ of size m or less.*

Proof   Note that this theorem provides a fairly complete description of the landscape of the error function $\mathcal{E}$ (Figure 5.3). The proof is by a perturbation argument showing that, for the critical points that are not associated with the global minimum, there is always a direction of escape that can be derived using unused eigenvectors associated with higher eigenvalues in order to lower the error $\mathcal{E}$ (see [80] for more details). The proof can be simplified by using the group invariance properties under transformation of the coordinates by a unitary matrix. With such a transformation, it is sufficient to study the landscape of $\mathcal{E}$ when Σ is a diagonal matrix and $A = B^T = U_I$.   □

REMARK   At the global minimum, if C is the $m \times m$ identity matrix ($C = I$), in the auto-associative case then the activities in the hidden layer are given by $u_1^T x, \ldots, u_p^T x$, corresponding to the coordinates of x along the first m eigenvectors of Σ_{XX}. These are the so-called principal components of x and the autoencoder implements Principal Component Analysis (PCA), also closely related to the Singular Value Decomposition (SVD), establishing another bridge between neural networks and statistics.

The theorem above shows that when Σ is full rank, there is a special class of critical points associated with $C = I$. In the auto-associative case, this class is characterized by the fact that A and B are the transpose of each other ($A = B^T$).

THEOREM 5.6 (CONJUGATE TRANSPOSITION)   *Assume Σ_{XX} is of full rank in the auto-associative case. Consider any point (A, B) where B has been optimized with respect to A, including all critical points. Then:*

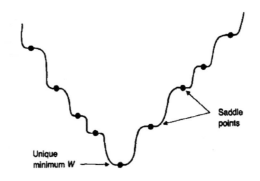

Figure 5.3 Landscape of $\mathcal{E}$.

$$W = AB = B^{\mathrm{T}} A^{\mathrm{T}} AB = B^{\mathrm{T}} A^{\mathrm{T}} = W^{\mathrm{T}} \quad \text{and} \quad \mathcal{E}(A, B) = \mathcal{E}(B^{\mathrm{T}}, A^{\mathrm{T}}). \tag{5.45}$$

Furthermore, when A is full rank:

$$W = P_A = P_A^{\mathrm{T}} = W^{\mathrm{T}}. \tag{5.46}$$

Proof By Theorem 5.1, in the auto-associate case, we have:

$$A^{\mathrm{T}} AB = A^{\mathrm{T}}.$$

Thus, by taking the transpose of each side, we have:

$$B^{\mathrm{T}} A^{\mathrm{T}} A = A.$$

It follows that:

$$B^{\mathrm{T}} A^{\mathrm{T}} = B^{\mathrm{T}} A^{\mathrm{T}} AB = AB,$$

which proves Equation 5.45. If in addition A is full rank, then by Theorem 5.1, $W = AB = P_A$ and the rest follows immediately. $\qquad\square$

REMARK Starting from a pair (A, B) with $W = AB$ and where B has been optimized with respect to A, let $A' = B^{\mathrm{T}}$ and optimize B again so that $B' = (A' A'^{\mathrm{T}})^{-1} A'^{\mathrm{T}}$. Then we also have:

$$W' = A'B' = W^{\mathrm{T}} = W = P_A \quad \text{and} \quad \mathcal{E}(A, B) = \mathcal{E}(A', B'). \tag{5.47}$$

5.3.5 Learning Algorithms

Although mathematical formulas for the global minimum solution of the linear autoencoder have been derived, it is still useful to study alternative incremental learning algorithms for several reasons. First, the global solution may not be available immediately to a physical, self-adjusting, learning circuit capable of making only small adjustments at each learning step. In addition, small adjustments may also be preferable in a non-stationary environment where the set X of training vectors changes with time, or in memory-limited situations where the entire training set cannot be stored. Finally, the study of incremental learning algorithms in linear circuits may shed some light on similar incremental algorithms applied to non-linear circuits where the global optimum cannot be derived analytically.

For the linear autoencoder, several such algorithms can be conceived, including: (stochastic) gradient descent studied in the exercises and in the next chapter; recirculation (studied in Chapter 8); and alternative partial or full optimization of A and B. Here we provide one theorem on the latter, leaving the proof as an exercise (see, also [83] for additional details).

THEOREM 5.7 (ALTERNATE MINIMIZATION) *Consider the algorithm where A and B are optimized in alternation (starting from A or B), holding the other one fixed. This algorithm will converge to a critical point of $\mathcal{E}$. Furthermore, if the starting value of A or B is initialized randomly, then with probability one the algorithm will converge to a critical point where both A and B are full rank.*

5.3.6   Generalization Properties

One of the most fundamental problems in machine learning is to understand the generalization properties of a learning system. Although in general this is not a simple problem, in the case of the autoencoder the generalization properties can easily be understood. After learning, A and B must be at a critical point. Assuming without much loss of generality that A is also full rank and Σ_{XX} is invertible, then from Theorem 5.1 we know in the auto-associative case that $W = P_A$. Thus we have the following result.

THEOREM 5.8 (GENERALIZATION PROPERTIES) *Assume in the auto-associative case that Σ_{XX} is invertible. For any learning algorithm that converges to a point where B is optimized with respect to A and A is full rank (including all full rank critical points), then for any vector x we have $Wx = ABx = P_A x$ and:*

$$\mathcal{E}(x) = ||x - ABx||^2 = ||x - P_A x||^2. \tag{5.48}$$

REMARK   Thus the reconstruction error of any vector is equal to the square of its distance to the subspace spanned by the columns of A, or the square of the norm of its projection onto the orthogonal subspace. The general hetero-associative case can also be treated using Theorems 5.1 and 5.2. In this case, under the same assumptions, we have $W = P_A \Sigma_{YX} \Sigma_{XX}^{-1}$.

5.4   Non-Linear Autoencoders: Unrestricted Boolean Case

5.4.1   Analysis of the Unrestricted Boolean Autoencoder

The unrestricted Boolean autoencoder where the classes $\mathcal{A}$ and $\mathcal{B}$ correspond to unrestricted Boolean transformations is the most extreme form of non-linear autoencoder. In the purely Boolean case, we have $\mathbb{F} = \mathbb{G} = \{0, 1\}$, A and B are unrestricted Boolean functions, and Δ is the Hamming distance. The only case of interest is the compressive case when $m < n$ (to avoid the identity with zero training error) and $2^m < K$. If $2^m \geq K$, it is easy to see that the training data can be implemented with zero error by associating each training vector with a unique hidden representation. Many variants of this problem can be obtained by restricting the classes $\mathcal{A}$ and $\mathcal{B}$ of Boolean functions, for instance by bounding the connectivity of the hidden units, or restricting them to particular classes of Boolean functions such as threshold gates or monotone Boolean functions. The linear case discussed in the previous section, where $\mathbb{F} = \mathbb{G} = \{0, 1\} = \mathbb{F}_2$ is the Galois field with two elements, is also a special case of the general Boolean case.

1: Invariances.

Permutations in the Hidden Layer. Every solution is defined up to arbitrary permutations of the 2^m points of the hypercube $\mathbb{H}^m$. This is because the Boolean functions are unrestricted and therefore their lookup tables can accommodate any such permutation, or relabeling of the hidden states.

Change of Coordinates in the Input/Output Layers. Likewise, any change of coordinates in $\mathbb{H}^n$ that preserves Hamming distances (these are generated by coordinate permutations and bit flips) leads to an equivalent problem.

2: Fixed Layer Solution.
The best way to understand this autoencoder is to look at what happens when one of the two transformations A or B is fixed. In each case, one can assume that the transformations are defined on the training set alone, or on the entire input space. Here we will choose the latter, although the reader should also examine the other cases and the small adjustments they require.

First, note that since $2^m < K$, the mapping B clusters the K training points in at most 2^m clusters. The hidden vectors $h_i = B(x_i)$ are the labels for each cluster and the outputs $A(h_i)$ ought to be cluster centroids to minimize the reconstruction error. It is easy to see that in order to be optimal B ought to be surjective, i.e. use all the 2^m possible hidden values. If a hidden value h is not used, A and B can be improved by taking any training point x_i with non-zero distortion and setting $B(x_i) = h$ and $A(h) = x_i$. By isolating x_i into its own cluster, $\mathcal{E}(x_i)$ decreases to 0, while $\mathcal{E}(x)$ remains unchanged for all the other training points, thus the overall reconstruction error decreases. Similarly, one can see that in order to be optimal A ought to be injective. Under the safe assumption that A is injective and B surjective, we can now show that if A is fixed, then it is easy to find the optimal B. Conversely, if B is fixed, it is easy to find the optimal A.

To see this more precisely, assume first that A is fixed and defined over the entire space $\mathbb{H}^m$. Then for each of the 2^m Boolean vectors $h_1, \ldots, h_{2^M}$ of the hidden layer, $A(h_1), \ldots, A(h_{2^m})$ provide 2^m distinct points (centroids) in the hypercube $\mathbb{H}^n$. One can build the corresponding Voronoi partition by assigning each point of $\mathbb{H}^n$ to its closest centroid, breaking ties arbitrarily, thus forming a partition of $\mathbb{H}^n$ into 2^m corresponding clusters $C_1, \ldots, C_{2^m}$, with $C_i = C^{Vor}(A(h_i))$. The optimal mapping B^* is then easily defined by setting $B^*(x) = h_i$ for any x in $C_i = C^{Vor}(A(h_i))$ (Figure 5.4). Note that this provides not only a definition of $B*$ over X, but also a unique and optimal generalization for $B*$ and hence $W = A \circ B*$ over the entire input space $\mathbb{H}^n$. The hetero-associative case can be handled similarly.

Conversely, assume that B is fixed and defined over the entire space $\mathbb{H}^n$. Then for each of the 2^m possible Boolean vectors $h_1, \ldots, h_{2^m}$ of the hidden layer, let $C^B(h_i) = \{x \in \mathbb{H}^n : B(x) = h_i\} = B^{-1}(h_i)$. To minimize the reconstruction error over the training set, the optimal A^* must map h_i onto a point y of $\mathbb{H}^n$ minimizing the sum of Hamming distances to points in $X \cap C^B(h_i)$. It is easy to see that the minimum over the training set is realized by the component-wise majority vector $A^*(h_i) = Majority[X \cap C^B(h_i)]$, breaking ties arbitrarily (e.g. by a coin flip) (Figure 5.5). Note that it is also possible to take the vector in the training set that is closest to the centroid if it is required that the output vector be in the training set. The optimal generalization over the entire hypercube, however, is achieved by taking the centroid of the entire cluster $C^B(h_i)$, rather than over the training vectors in the cluster. Note again that this provides a definition of $A*$ over the entire space $\mathbb{H}^m$ with an option for optimizing the training error or the generalization error of W over $\mathbb{H}^n$. The centroid of the training vectors in a Voronoi cluster provides the optimum for training whereas the centroid of the entire cluster provides the optimum for generalization. The hetero-associative case can be handled similarly.

3:Problem Complexity.

In general, the overall optimization problem is NP-hard. To be more precise, one must specify the regime of interest characterized by which variables among n, m, and K are going to infinity. Obviously one must have $n \to \infty$. If m does not go to infinity, then the problem can be polynomial, for instance when the centroids must belong to the training set. If $m \to \infty$ and K is a polynomial in n, which is the case of interest in machine learning where typically K is a low degree polynomial in n, then the problem of finding the best Boolean mapping (i.e. the Boolean mapping that minimizes the distortion $\mathcal{E}$ associated with the Hamming distance on the training set) is NP-hard, or the corresponding decision problem is NP-complete. More precisely the optimisation problem is NP-hard in the regime where $m \sim \epsilon \log_2 K$ with $\epsilon > 0$. A proof of this result is given below.

4: The Landscape of $\mathcal{E}$.

In general $\mathcal{E}$ has many local minima (e.g with respect to the Hamming distance applied to the lookup tables of A and B). Critical points are defined to be the points satisfying simultaneously the equations above for A^* and B^*.

5: Clustering.

The overall optimization problem is a problem of optimal clustering. The clustering is defined by the transformation B. Approximate solutions can be sought by many algorithms, such as k-means, belief propagation [283], minimum spanning paths and trees [688], and hierarchical clustering.

6: Transposition.

In the case of the Boolean autoencoder, it is not entirely clear what a notion of transposition ought to be around optimal points. On the other hand, consider an optimal point where B maps several points $x_1, \ldots, x_q$ onto a vector h in the hidden layer. Then $A(h)$ must be the majority vector of $x_1, \ldots, x_q$ and one should have $B(A(h)) = h$. Thus $A(h)$ must be an element of $B^{-1}(h)$ and this could be used to define some notion of "transposition" around optimal points.

7: Recycling.

At any critical point, recycling outputs is stable at the first pass so that for any x $(AB)^n(x) = AB(x)$ (and is equal to the majority vector of the corresponding Voronoi cluster).

8: Learning Algorithms.

A possible learning algorithm is again to alternate the optimization of A and B while holding the other one fixed.

9: Generalization.

At any critical point, for any x, $AB(x)$ is equal to the centroid of the corresponding Voronoi cluster and the corresponding error can be expressed easily.

10: External Targets.

With the proper adjustments, the results above remain essentially the same if a set of target output vectors $y_1, \ldots, y_m$ is provided, instead of $x_1, \ldots, x_m$ serving as the targets. To see this, consider a deep architecture consisting of a stack of autoencoders along the lines of [343]. For any activity vector h in the last hidden layer before the output layer, compute the set of points $C(h)$ in the training set that are mapped to h by the stacked architecture. Assume, without any loss of generality, that $C(h) = \{x_1, \ldots, x_k\}$ with corresponding targets $\{y_1, \ldots, y_k\}$. Then it is easy to see that the final output for h produced by the top layer ought to be the centroid of the targets given by Majority$(y_1, \ldots, y_k)$.

11: Composition.

The global optimum remains the same if additional Boolean layers of size equal to or greater than p are introduced between the input layer and the hidden layer and/or the hidden layer and the output layer. Thus there is no reduction in overall distortion $\mathcal{E}$ by adding such layers (see Section 6.3). For instance, consider a Boolean autoencoder network with layers of size n, p_1, p, p_1, n (Figure 5.7) with $n > p_1 > p$. Then any optimal solution of this network induces an optimal solution for the corresponding n, p, n autoencoder and conversely, any optimal solution of the n, p, n autoencoder induces (usually in many ways) an optimal solution of the n, p_1, p, p_1, n autoencoder. Finding an optimal solution for the n, p_1, n autoencoder network, and combining it with the optimal solution of the p_1, p, p_1 autoencoder network derived using the activity in the hidden layer of the first network as the training set, exactly as in the case of stacked RBMs, is a reasonable strategy but it is not clear that it is guaranteed to provide the global optimum of the n, p, n problem in all cases. In other words, clustering the data first into 2^{p_1} clusters, and then clustering these clusters into 2^p clusters, may not always provide the best clustering of the data into 2^p clusters. However, in practice, each clustering problem is NP-complete and thus combining clustering algorithms in a hierarchical fashion, or equivalently stacking autoencoders, should provide a reasonable approximate algorithm.

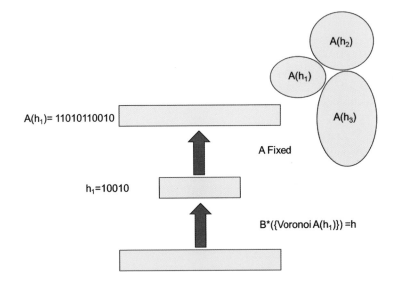

Figure 5.4 $A(n, m, n)$ Unrestricted Boolean Autoencoder with Fixed Transformation A. For each vector h, in the hidden layer, A produces an output vector $A(h)$. The vectors $A(h)$ induce a Voronoi partition of the output space, hence of the input space. Any vector $x \in \mathbb{F}^n$ is in a partition of the form $A(h)$, for some h. In order to minimize the final distortion, one must have $B^*(x) = h$.

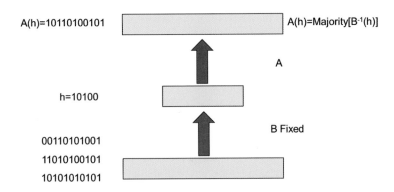

Figure 5.5 $A(n, m, n)$ Unrestricted Boolean Autoencoder with Fixed Transformation B. As shown, consider the set of vectors $B^{-1}(h)$ in the input space that are mapped to the same vector vector h in the hidden layer. Then the vector $A(h)$ must have minimal average Hamming distance to all the vectors in $B^{-1}(h)$. This is achieved if $A^*(h)$ is the Majority vector of $B^{-1}(h)$.

5.4.2   Boolean Autoencoder Problem Complexity

To deal with the hypercube clustering problem one must first understand which quantities are allowed to go to infinity. If n is not allowed to go to infinity, then the number m of training examples is also bounded by 2^n and, since we are assuming $p < n$, there is no quantity that can scale. Thus by necessity we must have $n \to \infty$. We must also have $m \to \infty$. The case of interest for machine learning in general is when m is a low degree polynomial of n. Obviously the hypercube clustering problem is in NP, and it is a special case of clustering in $\mathbb{R}^n$. Thus the only important problem to be addressed is the reduction of a known NP-complete problem to a hypercube clustering problem. For the reduction, it is natural to start from a known NP-complete graphical or geometric clustering problem. In both cases, one must find ways to embed the original problem with its original metric into the hypercube with the Hamming distance.

Problem [Hypercube Clustering]

Instance: K binary vectors $x_1, \ldots, x_K$ of length n and an integer k.

QUESTION   *Can we identify k binary vectors $c_1, \ldots, c_k$ of length n (the centroids) and a function f from $\{x_1, \ldots, x_K\}$ to $\{c_1, \ldots, c_K\}$ that minimizes the distortion $E = \sum_{t=1}^{K} \Delta(x_t, f(x_t))$ where Δ is the Hamming distance?*

THEOREM 5.9   *The hypercube clustering problem is NP-hard when $k \sim K^\epsilon$, where $\epsilon > 0$.*

Proof   To sketch the reduction, we start from the optimization problem of clustering K points in the plane $\mathbb{R}^2$ using cluster centroids and the L_1 distance, which is NP-hard [497] by reduction from 3-SAT [293] when $k \sim K^\epsilon$ for $\epsilon > 0$ (see also related results in [478] and [756]). Without any loss of generality, we can assume that the points in these problems lie on the vertices of a square lattice. Using the theorem in [331], one can show that a $n_1 \times n_2$ square lattice in the plane can be embedded into the hypercube $\mathbb{H}^{n_1 + n_2}$ (i.e. $n = n_1 + n_2$). More precisely, an explicit embedding is given in Figure 5.6 associating one distinct hypercube component to each horizontal step and each vertical step in the lattice. It is easy to check that the L_1 or Manhattan distance between any two points on the square lattice is equal to the corresponding Hamming distance in $\mathbb{H}^{n_1 + n_2}$. Thus a solution of the clustering problem on the hypercube would yield a solution of the clustering problem on the 2D lattice. This polynomial reduction completes the proof that if the number of cluster satisfies $k = 2^m \sim K^\epsilon$, or equivalently $m \sim \epsilon \log_2 K \sim C \log n$, then the hypercube clustering problem associated with the Boolean autoencoder is NP-hard.   □

If the number k of clusters is fixed and the centroids must belong to the training set, there are only $\binom{K}{k} \sim K^k$ possible choices for the centroids inducing the corresponding Voronoi clusters. This yields a trivial, albeit not efficient, polynomial-time algorithm.

There is another significant result about the NP-completeness of learning in neural networks. In [132], it is shown that the problem of training an $A(n, 2, 1)$ architecture of threshold gates, to achieve zero-error on a training set of size $O(n)$ is NP-complete.

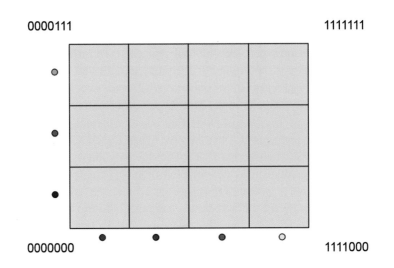

Figure 5.6 Embedding of a 3×4 Square Lattice onto $\mathbb{H}^7$ by Edge Coloring. All edges in the same row or column are given the same color. Each color corresponds to one of the dimensions of the 7-dimensional hypercube. For any pair of points, their Manhattan distance on the lattice is equal to the Hamming distance between their images in the 7-dimensional hypercube.

This remains true in the case of number of variations, for instance even if the weights are restricted to be binary. None of these NP-completeness results should worry practitioners, however, for several well-known reasons. In particular, for many applications, zero-error is not achievable, but also not necessary.

5.5   Other Autoencoders and Autoencoder Properties

5.5.1   Threshold Gate, Sigmoidal, and Mixed Autoencoders

Within the general framework described above, a number of different autoencoders can be considered with different constraints on $\mathbb{F}$ and $\mathbb{G}$, or different constraints on $\mathcal{A}$ and $\mathcal{B}$, for instance by varying the transfer functions in the hidden layer (e.g. Boolean unrestricted, Boolean linear threshold, linear, sigmoidal), the transfer functions in the output layer (e.g. Boolean unrestricted, Boolean linear threshold, linear, sigmoidal), the kinds of training data (binary versus real-valued), and the error function (e.g. Hamming, relative entropy, quadratic). We leave it as an exercise to examine some of the main combinations, however many of these can be understood, at least at an intuitive level, using the results derived above in the linear and unrestricted Boolean case. A simple example is when the input and output layers are real $\mathbb{F} = \mathbb{R}$ and the hidden layer is binary $\mathbb{G} = \{0, 1\}$ (and $\Delta = L_2^2$). It is easy to check that in this case, as long as $2^m < K$, the autoencoder aims at clustering the real data into $k = 2^m$ clusters and all the results obtained in the Boolean case are applicable with the proper adjustments. For instance, the centroid associated with a hidden state h should be the center of mass of the input vectors mapped onto h.

In general, the optimization decision problem for these autoencoders is also NP-complete and, more importantly, from a probabilistic viewpoint, they correspond exactly to a mixture of k-Gaussians model with hard cluster assignments in the deterministic case, and soft cluster assignments in the probabilistic case. More generally, as pointed out in [167], a number of classical problems and algorithms can be recovered by forcing one of the two classes $\mathcal{A}$ or $\mathcal{B}$ to be the class of linear functions, leaving the other one fully unrestricted (or with other non-linear constraints).

Within the general class of Boolean autoencoders, one can study different subclasses by restricting the sets of allowed Boolean functions. We have seen one such example in the case of the linear autoencoders over GF(2). Another interesting example corresponds to the Boolean autoencoder made exclusively of threshold gates [70]. These can be viewed as the limiting case of standard sigmoidal neural network autoencoders when the gain of the sigmoidal functions is taken to infinity. A further interesting restricted class of Boolean functions is that of monotone functions, i.e. Boolean functions that can be built using only the AND and OR operators (these are called monotone because if the number of 1s in the input is increased, the output can only remain identical, or go from 0 to 1.)

More importantly for this book, the solution of the real-valued linear autoencoder and the Boolean unrestricted autoencoder provide at least an intuitive picture of how learning may proceed in a compressive neural network autoencoder with sigmoidal transfer functions in the hidden layer. In the early stages of training, when the weights are small, the hidden neurons operate in their linear regime and learning may proceed toward PCA. As the weights increase and the hidden neurons begin to operate in the saturated portions of the sigmoidal transfer functions, learning may proceed towards optimal clustering in, or near, the PCA space.

5.5.2   Inverting, Redressing, and De-Noising Autoencoders

As a starting point, consider having a data set $D = \{x_1, \ldots, x_K\}$ where the points x_i are in a set A, and $A \subset \mathbb{R}^n$ or $A \subset H^n$ ($H = \{0, 1\}$). Assume that there is a (easily computable) function f from A to B, where $B \subset \mathbb{R}^p$ or $B \subset H^p$. We can use an $A(n, m, p)$ architecture to try to learn f using the pairs $(x, f(x))$ and, more importantly, an $A(p, m, n)$ architecture to learn f^{-1} when f can be inverted. If $p = n$, this leads to several different kinds of $A(n, m, n)$ autoencoders which somehow interpolate between the auto-associative and the hetero-associative cases. In these inverting autoencoders, the input $f(x)$ can often be viewed as a perturbed version of the data and the network is trained to restore or redress the input towards the unperturbed version $x = f^{-1}f(x)$. For instance if f is a rotation by α degrees, the corresponding redressing autoencoder would learn to rotate by $-\alpha$ degrees. Note that f does not need to be a function, it can also be a relation or process, as long as it is injective (i.e. $f(x)$ can take more than one value, but $f(x) = f(y)$ must imply $x = y$). When the function or process f corresponds to the addition of some kind of noise (e.g. Gaussian noise, random erasures) to the data, this approach is often called denoising autoencoder [765, 766].

Thus denoising autoencoders can be trained with the purpose of cleaning up noisy data, or reconstructing data (e.g. images or text) with missing or occluded entries (pattern completion). Denoising autoencoders can also be viewed in the context of regularization or data augmentation in order to prevent overfitting. This is particularly relevant if the autoencoder has a large number of parameters relative to the training data available initially. The denoising procedure can be viewed as a form of data augmentation by adding new training data, or as a form of dropout applied to the input layer [699, 91] (see Chapter 6). In the linear and unrestricted Boolean cases with $m < n$ the denoising autoencoder can be analyzed with the techniques described above, since these techniques work in the hetero-associative case, where the inputs and the targets differ.

Related to denoising autoencoders is also the idea of deblurring or training autoencoder architectures to produce high-resolution version of low resolution inputs. It is also possible to train autoencoder architectures in the reverse direction, to produce low resolution versions of the input in the output layer through a bottle neck. This is the basic idea behind the U-Net architectures for image segmentation [617] where images are presented in the input and segmented images are used as the targets for the output layer.

Along these lines, there are other ways for using an $A(n, m, n)$ architecture with supervised learning, where the input and the output target are slightly different and related through a simple process. For example, when dealing with sequences or time series, one could learn to predict x_{t+1} as a function of x_t. More generally, for a given fixed window of size k, one could learn to predict: $x_{t+1}, x_{t+2}, \ldots, x_{t+k}, x_{t+k+1}$ as a function of the input $x_t, x_{t+1}, \ldots, x_{t+k}$ where the size of the input and output layers is now kn (e.g. [564] and references therein). All the variations in this subsection are examples of self-supervised learning, where supervised learning is used with inputs and targets that are both derived from the original data through some operations.

5.5.3   Probabilistic Autoencoders and Variational Autoencoders

Probabilistic autoencoders with shape $A(n, m, n)$ (auto-associative), or even $A(n, m, p)$ (hetero-associative) can be incorporated into the above framework by considering that the input I, hidden H, or output O vectors are random variables and $\mathcal{A}$ and $\mathcal{B}$ represent classes of possible conditional distributions $P(O|H)$ and $P(H|I)$ over the right spaces. For instance, in the unrestricted probabilistic case, $\mathcal{A}$ and $\mathcal{B}$ are the classes of all possible conditional distributions over the right spaces. If all the units are binary and $m < n$, one obtains the binary compressive unrestricted probabilistic autoencoder where each A consists of a table of conditional probability distributions $P(O = y|H = h)$, where O denotes the binary output random variable and H the binary hidden layer random variable, and each B consists of a table of conditional probability distributions $P(H = h|I = x)$. The most relevant case here is when neural networks are used to parameterize one, or both, of the conditional distributions above. As described in Chapter 3, this can easily be done via sampling. A special case of this approach is the variational autoencoder described below. Different error functions can be used in the output layer. For instance, in the auto-associative case, one can consider the average error:

$$\mathcal{E} = \sum_x \sum_y P(I = x)P(O = y|I = x)\Delta(x, y), \tag{5.49}$$

where $\Delta(x, y)$ measures the degree of distortion between x and y (e.g. Hamming distance, quadratic error) and $P(O = y|I = x) = \sum_h P(H = h|I = x)(P(O = y|H = h)$, or the average relative entropy:

$$\mathcal{E} = -\sum_x P(I = x) \log P(O = x|I = x), \qquad (5.50)$$

or the relative entropy between $P(I = x)$ and $P(O = y)$.

For brevity we will not further discuss these autoencoders here but it should be clear that some of the previous results can be extended to this case. For instance, the binary compressive unrestricted probabilistic autoencoder has the same invariances as the unrestricted Boolean autoencoder and similar considerations can be made for the unrestricted real-valued probabilistic autoencoder. The binary compressive unrestricted probabilistic autoencoder implements probabilistic clustering over the 2^m clusters indexed by the hidden layer activities in the sense that each input x has some probability $P(H = h|I = x)$ of being associated with the cluster labeled by h.

With a compressive layer, in both the auto-and hetero-associative case, it is also useful to consider the error function:

$$\mathcal{E} = I(X, H) - \beta I(H, T)$$

to be minimized over the free, or constrained, or parameterized, set of conditional distributions $P(H|I)$. Here β is positive weighting parameter which controls the relative role of the mutual information I between the input, renamed X to avoid any confusion, and the hidden variable H, and between the H and a target distribution variable T. When $T = X$, one simply seeks to maximize the mutual information between X and H. These probabilistc autoencoders correspond to the bottleneck method [731] and the Blahut–Arimoto alternate optimization algorithm [128, 44] to try to find the optimal solution.

Note that since deterministic autoencoders can be viewed as special cases of probabilistic autoencoders, learning in probabilistic autoencoders is in general also NP-complete.

Variational Autoencoder

The variational autoencoder [407] is a special case of probabilistic autoencoder where the hidden layer is probabilistic. As we have seen in Chapter 3, the hidden layer of a feedforward neural network can be made stochastic by sampling. Thus in the variational autoencoder, the hidden layer vector H is a deterministic function of the input vector I. This function is parameterized by an encoding neural network. This vector H represents the parameters of a latent distribution over a latent space. During the forward propagation H is used to produce a sample $\tilde{H}$. The final output O is a deterministic function of $\tilde{H}$, which is also parameterized by a generative neural network. Once trained, the generative portion of the variational autoencoder can be used to provide a generative model of the data. Variational autoencoders can be trained by gradient descent using the methods described in the next chapter. As we shall see, the propagation of gradients through stochastic layers is facilitated if one can provide a simple parameterization of the relationship between the hidden activities and the corresponding sample. As a simple example, imagine that H is a two-dimensional vector encoding the mean μ and standard deviation σ of a normal distribution $\mathcal{N}(\mu, \sigma)$ over the latent space. Then, the sample $\tilde{H}$ can be parameterized in the form $\tilde{H} = \mu + \epsilon\sigma$, where the sampling variable ϵ follows a standard normal $\mathcal{N}(0, 1)$ distribution.

5.5.4   Expansive Autoencoders

When the hidden layer is larger than the input layer $(m > n)$ and $\mathbb{F} = \mathbb{G}$, there is in general an optimal 0-distortion solution to the autoencoder problem based on using the identity function between the layers. Thus in general this case is interesting only if additional constraints are added to the problem to prevent trivial solutions. These can come in many forms, for instance in terms of restrictions on the classes of functions $\mathcal{A}$ and $\mathcal{B}$, in terms of noise and robustness, or in terms of regularization. Restrictions could exclude the identity function and any other closely related functions. Noise could lead to the need for additional "parity check" bits, as in coding and communication theory. Regularization could be used, for instance to ensure sparsity of the hidden-layer representation, or to constrain the Jacobian or the Hessian of the data representation [483, 203, 612]. When these constraints force the hidden layer to assume only k different values then some of the previous analyses hold and the problem may reduce to clustering into k clusters. Another possibility for creating large hidden layer is the horizontal composition of autoencoders (see below). It is worth mentioning that expansive layers with sparse encoding are frequently found in the early stages of biological sensory systems [59]. While sparsity can be enforced artificially by regularization (e.g. L1 regularization), it is more interesting to explore biophysical or computational reasons for why layer size expansion, coupled with sparse encoding, could be advantageous in a physical neural system.

5.5.5   Composition of Autoencoders

Autoencoders can be composed both vertically (Figure 5.7) and horizontally. When autoencoders are stacked vertically, the hidden layer at one level of the stack can be used as the input layer for the next level of the stack. Thus the stack can be trained in an unsupervised layer from bottom to top. This approach can be used to initialize the layers of a deep architecture in an unsupervised way. When the hidden layers of the autoencoders are compressive, the results in this section suggest that the stack approximates some kind of hierarchical clustering of the data (at least when the hidden layers are binary, or close to binary when sigmoidal functions are in their saturated regimes). This can be viewed as a way of extracting increasingly more abstract representations of the data, as one goes up the hierarchy.

In addition to vertical composition, autoencoders can also be composed horizontally in various ways. For instance, two autoencoders with architectures $A(n_1, m_1, n_1)$ and $A(n_2, m_2, n_2)$ can be trained and combined into an $A(n_1 + n_2, m_1 + m_2, n_1 + n_2)$ architecture. It is also possible to share the same input and output layer and combine an

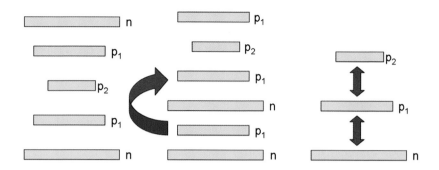

Figure 5.7 Left: Compressive autoencoder with multiple hidden layers. Middle and right: Vertical Composition of Autoencoders.

$A(n, m_1, n)$ autoencoder with an $A(n, m_2, n)$ autoencoder in order to create an $A(n, m_1 + m_2, n)$ autoencoder with an expanded hidden layer representation (Figure 5.8), which in turn can be fed to other subsequent layer of the overall architecture. If $m_1 + m_2 < n$, the expanded hidden layer representation can still be compressive. Differences in the two hidden representations associated with the layers of size m_1 and m_2 can be introduced by many different mechanisms, for instance by using different learning algorithms, different initializations, different training samples, different learning rates, or different distortion measures. It is also possible to envision algorithms that incrementally add (or remove) hidden units to the hidden layer [608, 428]. In the linear case over $\mathbb{R}$, for instance, a first hidden unit can be trained to extract the first principal component, a second hidden unit can then be added to extract the second principal component, and so forth.

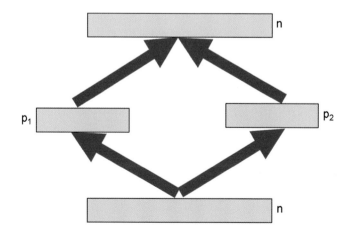

Figure 5.8 Horizontal Composition of Autoencoders to Expand the Hidden Layer Representation.

5.6   Exercises

EXERCISE 5.1   Consider the linear autoencoder over the real numbers. Show that all the information about the data is contained in the mean and covariance matrix of the data. Show that the standard least square error function is a quadratic function (parabola) in each individual weight, if all the other weights are assumed to be constant.

EXERCISE 5.2   Consider the $A(n, m, n)$ linear autoencoder over the real numbers with matrices A and B. Derive the gradient descent equation for the top matrix A using the results of Chapter 3. Derive the gradient descent equations for the matrix B (this becomes easy after seeing Chapter 6 on backpropagation).

EXERCISE 5.3   Consider the $A(n, m, n)$ linear autoencoder over the real numbers with matrices A and B. Show directly that if B is fixed, the problem is convex in A and similarly if A is fixed the problem is convex in B. Derive the gradient descent learning equations for A and B in matrix form. Convert the corresponding difference equations into a system of differential equations. In general, does the system have a closed form solution? If not, can you find a closed form solution in some special cases?

EXERCISE 5.4   In this chapter, we solved the linear autoencoder in a coordinate-independent way. An alternative approach is to solve the problem in a specific coordinate system, and then generalize the approach. Solve the linear autoencoder problem when the data mean is zero and the covariance matrix is diagonal. Solve the linear autoencoder problem when the data mean is not zero and the covariance matrix is diagonal. Generalize these results in order to solve the linear autoencoder problem when the data mean is zero, or non-zero, and the covariance matrix is not diagonal.

EXERCISE 5.5   Consider a linear $A(n, m, n)$ autoencoder over the real numbers with partial connectivity, i.e. some of the entries of the matrices A or B are forced to be 0 at all times. Show that the total number of connectivity patterns is given by $2^{nm} 2^{nm}$. Is there a choice of a partial connectivity pattern for which the corresponding linear autoencoder can exhibit true spurious local minima (i.e. local minima where the quadratic error is strictly larger than the error achieved at the global minima)?

EXERCISE 5.6   Consider a linear $A(n, m, n)$ autoencoder over the real numbers with a training set of the form $I(k)$ for $k = 1, \ldots, K$ and matrices A and B. Thus the output has the form: $O = ABI$, and the quadratic error function is given by $\mathcal{E} = \sum_k ||I(k) - ABI(k)||^2 / 2$. Write down, in matrix form, the learning equations for A and B under simple Hebbian learning. Write down, in matrix form, the learning equations for A and B under gradient descent learning. Convert all the previous learning equations into differential equations and compare the two forms of learning.

EXERCISE 5.7   Study the linear $A(n, m, n)$ autoencoder problem over the complex field $\mathbb{C}$.

EXERCISE 5.8   Study the linear $A(n, m)$ regression problem over any finite field, for instance over the finite field $\mathbb{F}_2$ with two elements. Study the linear $A(n, m, n)$ autoencoder problem over any finite field, for instance over $\mathbb{F}_2$.

EXERCISE 5.9   Consider the $A(n, m, n)$ autoencoder problem with linear threshold gates in the hidden and output layers, the Hamming distance as the error function $\mathcal{E}$, and a training set of polynomial size in n and m. Is the problem of minimizing $\mathcal{E}$ NP-hard?

EXERCISE 5.10   Consider the $A(n, m, n)$ autoencoder problem with monotone Boolean gates in the hidden and output layers, the Hamming distance as the error function $\mathcal{E}$, and a training set of polynomial size in n and m. Is the problem of minimizing $\mathcal{E}$ NP-hard?

EXERCISE 5.11   Consider an unrestricted Boolean autoencoder $A(n, m, n)$ where the K binary training examples are generated as follows. First, k_1 centroids are generated using independent Bernoulli coin flips with probability $p_1 = 0.5$. Then, starting from each centroid, k_2 examples are generated by perturbing the centroid using independent Bernoulli coin flips with small probability $p_2 = \epsilon$ of changing the corresponding bit, so that $K = k_1 k_2$. Examine different regimes for N, M, K, k_1 and ϵ and estimate the expected training and generalization errors.

EXERCISE 5.12   Consider an unrestricted Boolean autoencoder $A(n, m, n)$ where the connectivity is local. In general, compared to the fully connected case, is it easier or harder to solve it? Why? Which algorithm would you use to try to minimize the Hamming error?

EXERCISE 5.13   Consider different compressive autoencoders by varying the type of units (e.g. unrestricted Boolean, threshold, sigmoidal, linear) in the hidden layer or the output layer, the kind of training data (binary or real-valued), and the error function (e.g. Hamming distance, relative entropy, quadratic). Using the results in the chapter, for each autoencoder type develop an intuitive understanding of its behavior and confirm or disprove your intuition by mathematical analyses or simulations.

EXERCISE 5.14   Formalize a notion of binary, compressive, unrestricted, probabilistic $A(n, m, n)$ autoencoder and analyze its properties. Here unrestricted means that any probabilistic table between input and hidden vectors, or hidden and output vectors, can be realized.

EXERCISE 5.15   Assume that the n-dimensional input vectors x of a linear channel have a normal distribution with mean zero and covariance matrix Σ_{xx}. The output of the channel are constrained to be p-dimensional vectors y of the form $y = Bx$ for some $p \times n$ matrix B with $p < n$. The differential entropy of x is defined by:

$$H(x) - \int P(x) \log P(x) dx. \tag{5.51}$$

Prove the following.
(1) y has a normal distribution with mean 0 and covariance matrix $\Sigma_{yy} = B\Sigma_{xx}B^{\mathrm{T}}$.
(2)

$$H(x) = \frac{1}{2} \log \left[(2\pi e)^n \det(\Sigma_{xx}) \right], \tag{5.52}$$

and

$$H(y) \frac{1}{2} \log \left[(2\pi e)^p \det(B\Sigma_{xx}B^{\mathrm{T}}) \right]. \tag{5.53}$$

(3) The conditional distribution of x given y is normal with mean: $\Sigma_{xy}\Sigma yy^{-1}y$, and covariance matrix: $\Sigma = \Sigma_{xx} - \Sigma_{xy}\Sigma yy^{-1}\Sigma_{yx}$.

(4) The conditional entropy of x given y is given by:

$$H(x|y) = \frac{1}{2}\log\left[(2\pi e)^{n-p}\gamma_1\gamma_2\cdots\gamma_{n-p}\right], \qquad (5.54)$$

where $\gamma_1 \geq \gamma_2 \geq \cdots \geq \gamma_{n-p} > 0$ are the non-zero eigenvalues of Σ.

(5) Maximizing $I(x, y)$ is equivalent to minimizing $H(x|y)$ and this is achieved by PCA, i.e. by having $B = CU_p^T$ where C is an invertible $p \times p$ matrix and U is a matrix of column vectors $U_p = [u_1, \ldots, u_p]$. Here $u_1, \ldots, u_p$ denote p principal normalized eigenvectors of Σ_{xx} with eigenvalues $\lambda_1, \ldots, \lambda_p$.

(6) At this maximum:

$$I_{PCA}(x, y) = \frac{1}{2}\log\left[(2\pi e)^p \lambda_1\lambda_2\cdots\lambda_p\right]. \qquad (5.55)$$

EXERCISE 5.16   Derive critical or consistency relations for the bottleneck method in simple cases, for instance, when the variables have Gaussian distributions.

EXERCISE 5.17   In a variational autoencoder, assume that the hidden variable H encodes the parameters of a Beta distribution

$$B(a, b) = \frac{\Gamma(a + b)}{\Gamma(a)\Gamma(b)}x^{a-1}.(1 - x)^{b-1}.$$

How can one parameterize a sample $\tilde{H} \in [0, 1]$?

EXERCISE 5.18   Prove a variational bound for the variational autoencoder.

6 Deep Networks and Backpropagation

Chapters 4 and 5 provided a fairly complete treatment of the design and properties of $A(n, m)$, $A(n, \infty, m)$, and $A(n, m, p)$ architectures. Next, we want to consider the general case of deep feedforward architectures $A(n_1, \ldots, n_L)$ with arbitrary many layers. However, we have seen that $A(n, \infty, m)$ architectures have universal approximation properties. Thus one must first consider what may be good reasons for using deeper architectures in the first place.

6.1 Why Deep?

The first reason for considering deep architectures with more than one hidden layer is that the constructive proof of universal approximation properties for $A(n, \infty, m)$ architectures leads to solutions that are not practical, in that they may require an exponentially large hidden layer. There are functions that require far fewer neurons, or connections, when implemented by a circuit with multiple hidden layers, as opposed to a single one. A good example is the parity function, which can be implemented with a linear number of neurons when depth is allowed.

A second reason is that architectures with more than one hidden layer are very common in biology. While this argument provides no explanation, it does carry some weight from an engineering standpoint: as good reasons may exist for why evolution – with its massive combinatorial tinkering – ended up using deeper networks.

A third reason is that if we consider a feedforward architecture where the first hidden layer consists of linear threshold neurons, each such neuron is associated with a hyperplane that partitions the input space into two regions. A very large first hidden layer will partition the input space in many regions which potentially leads to an overall function that is not smooth. For the same total number of parameters, a deeper architecture with a smaller first-hidden-layer provides the basis for implementing functions that are smoother. In essence, this is the structural regularization advantage of deeper architectures [105].

A fourth reason is our intuition that complex functions – such as recognizing a cat in an image – should not be computed in a single layer, but rather through multiple, hierarchically organized stages of processing. Simple features ought to be extracted in the early layers, followed by more complex representations, involving combinations of features, in the successive layers. Indeed, intelligent systems are generally not expected to solve complex problems in a single step. The human visual system, for instance, contains dozens of different areas intricately interconnected [269]. To make some aspects of this argument more precise, consider the class of functions f that have a hierarchical and modular architecture with L layers. Let us assume that the modules have fan-in $k > 1$ and fan-out 1. And let us assume also that each module is relatively simple, in the sense that it can be implemented with sufficient precision by a single neuron, or a small network of neurons with at most m neurons and w connections. Here we assume that k, m, and w are constants, although one can also consider cases where these quantities grow mildly with the size n of the input. Let us denote by $\mathcal{F}(L, k, m, w)$ the class of such functions. We are going to assume that all the modules in one layer have different inputs, i.e. there are no inputs that are common to two modules. Cases where there is overlap, or where some modules have less than k inputs can be handled similarly. Thus when $L = 3$ and $k = 3$, we are considering functions of the form:

$$f(x_1, x_2, x_3, x_4, \ldots, x_9) = h_4\left(h_1(x_1, x_2, x_3), h_2(x_4, x_5, x_6), h_3(x_7, x_8, x_9)\right); \quad (6.1)$$

and when $L = 4$ and $k = 2$ we are considering functions of the form:

$$f(x_1, x_2, x_3, x_4, \ldots, x_8) = h_7\left(h_5\left(h_1(x_1, x_2), h_2(x_3, x_4)\right), h_6\left(h_3(x_5, x_6), h_4(x_7, x_8), \right)\right) \quad (6.2)$$

where the functions h represent the various modules. It is easy to see that such a hierarchical modular function must have k^{L-1} inputs in the input layer, and a total of $T = 1 + k + k^2 + \cdots + k^{L-2} = (k^{L-1} - 1)/(k - 1) = (n - 1)/(k - 1)$ modules. Thus we have immediately the following theorem:

THEOREM 6.1 *Any function $f \in \mathcal{F}(L, k, m, w)$ can be computed by a deep architecture with $Tm = (n-1)m/(k-1)$ neurons and $T(w+k) = (n-1)(w+k)/(k-1)$ connections.*

This shows that such a function f requires a number of neurons and connections that are linear in the input size n, as opposed to exponential. In contrast, recall from Chapter 4 that approximating a continuous function f with precision ϵ using a single hidden layer typically requires an exponential number of units and weights that scale like $1/\epsilon^n$. This result is not too surprising, since in essence it is saying something tautological: a hierarchical modular function is "deep" by definition, and thus its natural conversion to a neural network yields a deep neural network. One may wonder why many functions of practical interest seem to be hierarchical and modular. At least a partial explanation can be made from physics principles in the sense that most interactions in the world tend to be local and thus ought to be captured by local modules, which can then be hierarchically aggregated to capture longer interactions.

Yet another way to see this is to think in terms of polynomials. Imagine an $A(n_1, \ldots, n_{L-1}, 1)$ architecture where all the transfer functions are fixed polynomials of degree k (most of the standard transfer functions can be approximated well using $k \leq 10$). The entire architecture computes a polynomial of degree $m = k^{L-1}$ in the n_1 input variables: however it is parsimonious. In general, a polynomial of degree m in n_1 variables requires

K coefficients, with:

$$K = \binom{m + n_1 - 1}{m} + \binom{m + n_1 - 2}{m - 1} + \cdots + 1 = \sum_{i=0}^{m} \binom{m + n_1 - 1 - i}{m - i} \qquad (6.3)$$

coefficients. However, the neural architecture with its linear activation operations, computes only a small fraction of all possible such polynomials, using $W \approx \sum_{i=1}^{L-1} n_i n_{i+1}$ parameters. In general, for typical architectures, W is much smaller than K.

We can now address the problem of understanding the functional capacity of deep, feedforward, fully connected architectures in the linear and unrestricted Boolean cases, with the quadratic and Hamming error functions respectively. The results are direct consequences of the results in Chapter 5 on autoencoders.

6.2   Functional Capacity: Deep Linear Case

We begin with a definition. We say that two architectures $A(n_1, \ldots, n_L)$ and $A(m_1, \ldots, m_J)$ with specified transfer functions are *equivalent* if they have exactly the same functional capacity, i.e. if they can implement exactly the same class of functions. In this case, we write: $A(n_1, \ldots, n_L) \equiv A(m_1, \ldots, m_J)$. In both the linear and unrestricted Boolean cases, the functional capacity depends critically on the size of the smallest hidden layer. Let m denote the size of such a layer: $m = \min(n_2, \ldots, n_{L-1})$. In the linear case, we have the following theorem.

THEOREM 6.2   *In the case of a feedforward layered, fully connected, linear architecture, we have:*

$$A(n_1, \ldots, n_L) \equiv \begin{cases} A(n_1, n_L), & m \geq \min(n_1, n_L) \\ A(n_1, m, n_L), & m < \min(n_1, n_L). \end{cases} \qquad (6.4)$$

Furthermore, we can charaterize the landscaper of the quadratic error function in each case. For any training set, in both equivalence cases, the landscapes of the error functions $\mathcal{E}$ are similar in both architectures, up to trivial transformations. In the first equivalence case ($m \geq \min(n_1, n_L)$), the error functions have a unique, up to trivial transformations, global minimum. In the second equivalence case ($m < \min(n_1, n_L)$), the error functions have a unique, up to trivial transformations, global minimum. All other critical points in the two equivalent architectures are saddle points, also defined up to trivial transformations. There is a one-to-one mapping between the corresponding equivalence classes of saddle points. Thus, in all cases, $\mathcal{E}$ can never have any spurious local minima.

Proof   In the linear fully connected case, the only restrictions that any hidden layer can pose are rank restrictions. If $m \geq \min(n_1, n_L)$ there are no rank restrictions and thus $A(n_1, \ldots, n_L) \equiv A(n_1, n_L)$. If $m < \min(n_1, n_L)$ then the smallest hidden layers of size m (there could be more than one) impose a rank m restriction and thus $A(n_1, \ldots, n_L) \equiv A(n_1, m, n_L)$. The rest of the theorem follows easily from the results in Chapter 5 and the properties of linear transformations. For brevity, here we focus on the most interesting property from a deep learning perspective: the absence of spurious local minima. This results immediately from two facts. First, in the linear fully connected case with quadratic loss function, if two architectures A and B are equivalent ($A \equiv B$), then any spurious local minimum in A results in a spurious local minimum in B, and vice versa. Second, as we have seen in Chapter 5, in the linear fully connected case, both $A(n_1, n_L)$ and $A(n_1, m, n_L)$ cannot have any spurious local minima.

The absence of local minima is obvious for the first equivalence case ($m \geq \min(n_1, n_L)$). Therefore we focus on the case where there is at least one bottleneck layer ($m < \min(n_1, n_L)$). There is a trivial mapping f that maps the matrices $A_1, \ldots, A_{L-1}$, of the deep architecture into the matrices D and C of the shallow architecture simply by multiplying the corresponding matrices on each side of the bottleneck layer of size m. This map is obviously surjective and continuously differentiable. In addition, for any point x (or any set of points) in $\mathbb{R}^{n_1}$ the outputs produced by the two architectures are identical, and therefore the errors are identical. Now suppose that the deep architecture had a spurious local minima associated with the matrices $A_1^*, \ldots, A_{L-1}^*$, which are mapped into the matrices D^*, C^* by f. Any small compact set around $A_1^*, \ldots, A_{L-1}^*$ is mapped into a small compact set around D^*, C^* by continuity of f. Furthermore, the values of the error function for the corresponding points of these compact sets are the same. Thus D^*, C^* would itself be a spurious local mimina of the quadratic error function of the equivalent shallow architecture, which is a contradiction.   □

As an aside, the absence of spurious local minima for deep linear architectures is fairly obvious given the results [80], and was already known in the 1980s [95, 81], contrary to highly cited claims made more recently.

6.3   Functional Capacity: Deep Unrestricted Boolean Case

A similar result is true for feedforward, layered, fully-connected, unrestricted Boolean architectures of the form $A(n_1, n_2, \ldots, n_L)$ with $m = \min(n_2, \ldots, n_{L-2})$.

THEOREM 6.3   *In the case of feedforward, layered, fully-connected, unrestricted Boolean architectures, we have:*

$$A(n_1, \ldots, n_L) \equiv \begin{cases} A(n_1, n_L), & m \geq \min(n_1, n_L) \\ A(n_1, m, n_L), & m < \min(n_1, n_L). \end{cases} \tag{6.5}$$

Furthermore, in the first equivalence case ($m \geq \min(n_1, n_L)$), any training set can be realized exactly by both architectures (zero Hamming error). In the second equivalence case ($m < \min(n_1, n_L)$), let K denote the size of the training set. If $2^m \geq K$ then there exist exact solutions with zero Hamming error in both equivalent architectures, and these solutions can be partitioned according to the corresponding mapping from the training set to the binary states of one of the hidden bottleneck layers of size m (there could be more than one), such as the first one. If $2^m < K$, then for both equivalent architectures there is no solution with zero error. All implementations, including optimal solutions, *can be be partitioned in terms of the clustering of the training set into 2^m clusters in the first bottleneck layer of size m.*

Proof   The proof is left as an exercise, which is easy given the results of the previous chapter.

6.4   Cardinal Capacity: Deep Feedforward Architectures

The characterization of the functional capacity of other feedforward deep architectures of the form $A(n_1, \ldots, n_L)$ so far has remained an open problem. If we use polynomial transfer functions of degree d everywhere in the architecture, each component of the overall function implemented by the architecture is a polynomial of degree d^{L-1} in the n_1 input variables. However it is not any arbitrary polynomial of such degree because of the way variables are combined linearly inside each activation, and because the output components are not independent of each other.

However some progress has been made in determining the cardinal capacity of deep feedforward, fully-connected architectures, at least in the case of linear threshold transfer functions [105] where it is proven that under certain mild conditions:

$$C(n_1, \ldots, n_L) \approx \sum_{k=1}^{L-1} \min(n_1, \ldots, n_k) n_k n_{k+1}. \tag{6.6}$$

Thus, in short, the capacity is a cubic polynomial in the layer sizes, where the bottleneck layers play a special role.

We now give a more precise statement of this result, referring the reader to [105] for the proof of the lower bound. The proof of the upper bound is included in the exercises.

THEOREM 6.4 (CAPACITY FORMULA)   *Consider a layered, fully connected, neural architecture $A(n_1, \ldots, n_L)$ of linear threshold gates with $L \geq 2$ layers. Assume that the number of nodes in each layer satisfies $n_j > 18 \log_2(Ln_k)$ for any pair j, k such that $1 \leq j < k \leq L$. Then:*

$$C(n_1, \ldots, n_L) \asymp \sum_{k=1}^{L-1} \min(n_1, \ldots, n_k) n_k n_{k+1}.$$

Here the notation $a \asymp b$ means that there exists two positive absolute constants c_1, c_2 such that $c_1 b \leq a \leq c_2 b$. The upper bound in Theorem 6.4 holds with constant $c_2 = 1$ provided each hidden layer has at least four neurons, and it does not require the assumption $n_j \gtrsim \log_2(Ln_k)$. This mild assumption is important in the lower bound though as it prevents layer sizes from expanding too rapidly. Although this assumption has an almost optimal form, it can be slightly weakened, which is important when accounting for small top layers [105]. The absolute constant $c_1 \in (0, 1)$ hidden in the lower bound may not depend on anything, in particular it is independent of the depth L of the network, or the widths n_k of the layers. We conjecture that, at least asymptotically, $c_1 = c_2 = 1$.

For the special single-neuron case $A(n, 1)$, Theorem 6.4 gives:

$$C(n, 1) \asymp n^2. \tag{6.7}$$

Since $C(n, 1) = C(H^n)$, this recovers Zuev's result up to a constant factor. Zuev's original proof, however, does not offer any insights on how to compute the capacity of deeper networks.

The simplest new case of Theorem 6.4 is for networks $A(n, m, 1)$ with one hidden layer, where it states that $C(n, m, 1) \asymp n^2 m + \min(n, m)m \asymp n^2 m$. The constant factor implicit in this bound can be tightened for large n. Indeed, as we have seen in Chapter 4, $C(n, m, 1) = n^2 m(1 + o(1))$ if $n \to \infty$ and $\log_2 m = o(n)$.

An immediate and somewhat surprising consequence of Theorem 6.4 is that multiple output neurons can always be "channeled" through a single output neuron without a significant change in the capacity, namely:

THEOREM 6.5   *Under the assumptions of Theorem 6.4, we have:*

$$C(n_1, \ldots, n_{L-1}, 1) \asymp C(n_1, \ldots, n_{L-1}).$$

Proof   Comparing the capacity formulas for these two architectures, we see that all the terms in the two sums match except for the last (extra) term in $C(n_1, \ldots, n_{L-1}, 1)$, which is $\min(n_1, \ldots, n_{L-1})n_{L-1}$. However, this term is clearly bounded by:

$$\min(n_1, \ldots, n_{L-2})n_{L-2}n_{L-1}, \tag{6.8}$$

which is the last term in the capacity sum for $C(n_1, \ldots, n_{L-1})$. Therefore, the capacity sums for the two architectures are within a factor of 2 from each other.   □

Finally, let us mention that the capacity formula in Theorem 6.4 obtained for inputs in H^{n_1} can be extended to inputs from other finite sets $C(S, n_1, n_2, \ldots, n_L)$ [105].

6.5   Other Notions of Capacity

There are several notions other than cardinal capacity in the literature that try to capture the capacity of a class of functions. These include the VC dimension and the growth function, the Rademacher and Gaussian complexity, the metric entropy, and the Kolgomorov complexity and related minimum description length (MDL) (e.g. [754, 401, 109, 753, 668]). There are connections between these measures, some of which are explored in the exercises and much of computational learning theory has focused on deriving bounds on generalization errors based on these metrics. While theoretically significant, in general these bounds are not sharp enough to be practically useful.

If neural learning is to be viewed as a communication and storage process, where information is transferred from the data to the synaptic weights, we may need a better theory of "impedance" between data and neural architectures relating the information content of the data, relative to a particular task, and the cardinal capacity or the number of bits that can be stored in a given architecture. Clearly counting the raw number of bits contained in the training data is not satisfactory as it provides at best an upper bound on the number of useful bits contained in the data relative to the task at hand. This is an area of ongoing research.

Finally, to conclude this section let us mention the notion of training capacity, which is connected to the other notions above. For simplicity, let us consider a feedforward architecture A for binary classification. We say that A shatters a set of k input vectors if all possible classifications of those input vectors can be realized by A. There are 2^k such classifications. Using the notion of shattering, we can define two related notions of capacity:

- The *training capacity* TC(A) is the largest m, such that any training set of size m can be shattered by A.
- The *VC dimension* VC(A) is the largest m, such that there is a set of size m than can be shattered by A.

Obviously, from the definition, TC(A) $\leq$ VC(A). Furthermore, an architecture A can implement at least $2^{VC(A)}$ different functions, and thus VC(A) $\leq$ C(A). In short, we have:

$$TC(A) \leq VC(A) \leq C(A). \tag{6.9}$$

Other related results are that for an architecture $(A(n_1, \ldots, n_L)$ with a number of parameters $W \approx n_1 n_2 + \cdots + n_{L-1} n_L$:

$$VC(A) = O(W \log W), \tag{6.10}$$

[112]. With ReLU transfer functions, it has been shown [110] that:

$$VC(A) = O(LW \log W). \tag{6.11}$$

Finally, there are also results trying to further tighten these results and showing that, under various caveats and restrictions, TC(A) $\approx W$ [806, 763].

6.6 Learning by Backpropagation

Backpropagation is the most widely used and most efficient algorithm for computing gradients in neural networks, and thus for learning by gradient descent. The algorithm is a straightforward application of the chain rule for computing derivatives.

6.6.1 Backpropagation

Recall the **Chain Rule**:
If $y = f(u_1, \ldots, u_m)$ then for every i $u_i = g_i(x_1, \ldots, x_n)$, assuming that all the functions are differentiable, we have:

$$\frac{\partial y}{\partial x_i} = \sum_{j=1}^{m} \frac{\partial y}{\partial u_j} \frac{\partial u_i}{\partial x_i}. \tag{6.12}$$

The chain rule is easy to prove since, to first order, a small perturbation Δx_i of x_i will lead to a small perturbation Δu_j of u_j with $\Delta u_j = \partial u_j / \partial x_i \Delta x_i$. In turn, this perturbation, will lead to a small perturbation Δy of y with $\Delta y = \sum_{j=1}^{m} \partial y / \partial u_j \Delta u_j$.

We can now derive the gradient descent learning equations. For a single training example, we have:

$$\frac{\partial \mathcal{E}}{\partial w_{ij}^h} = \eta \frac{\partial \mathcal{E}}{\partial S_i^h} \frac{\partial S_i^h}{\partial w_{ij}^h} = A_i^h O_j^{h-1}. \tag{6.13}$$

Thus the gradient is the product of two terms: the presynaptic activity O_j^{h-1} and the postsynaptic term $A_i^h = \partial \mathcal{E} / \partial S_i^h$. The postsynaptic term can be computed recursively by applying the chain rule in the form:

$$\frac{\partial \mathcal{E}}{\partial S_i^h} = \sum_{k=1}^{n_{h+1}} \frac{\partial \mathcal{E}}{\partial S_k^{h+1}} \frac{\partial S_k^{h+1}}{\partial S_i^h} = \sum_{k=1}^{n_{h+1}} \frac{\partial \mathcal{E}}{\partial S_k^{h+1}} \frac{\partial S_k^{h+1}}{\partial O_i^h} \frac{\partial O_i^h}{\partial S_i^h} = \sum_{k=1}^{n_{h+1}} \frac{\partial \mathcal{E}}{\partial S_k^{h+1}} . w_{ki}^{h+1} f'(S_i^h). \tag{6.14}$$

Therefore the recursive equation for computing the postsynaptic term is:

$$A_i^h = \sum_{k=1}^{n_{h+1}} A_k^{h+1} w_{ki}^{h+1} f'(S_i^h), \tag{6.15}$$

initialized with $A_i^L = \partial \mathcal{E} / \partial S_i^L$. With the error functions and transfer functions seen in Chapter 3 on shallow networks, we typically have:

$$A_i^L = -(T_i - O_i^L). \tag{6.16}$$

Thus, we have the following:

THEOREM 6.6   *For a given training example, the gradient of the error function is given by Equation 6.13, where the backpropagated error is computed recursively using Equation 6.15, with the initial condition given by Equation 6.16.*

It is customary to define $B_i^h = -A_i$ and call it the backpropagated error. The backpropagated error is initialized with $B_i^L = T_i - O_i^L$ and satisfies the same linear propagation equation as A_i^h given by Equation 6.14. With this notation, the stochastic gradient descent equation is given by:

$$\Delta w_{ij}^h = -\eta \frac{\partial \mathcal{E}}{\partial w_{ij}^h} = \eta B_i^h O_j^{h-1}, \tag{6.17}$$

where η is the learning rate. The backpropagation equations above are derived for a single example. In full gradient descent (batch learning), these equations must be averaged over the entire training set, and likewise for any batches of intermediary size.

Thus, starting with the initialization in Equation 6.16, the backpropagated error is computed top down using a linear propagation process (hence computable in an asynchronous manner within each training example) where the vector of errors in one layer is backpropagated to the previous layer by multiplying it by the transpose of the corresponding forward matrix. The resulting vector is then multiplied, component-wise, by the derivatives of the corresponding activation functions at each node.

In matrix notation, the stochastic gradient descent learning equation with learning rate η can be written as:

$$\Delta W_h = \eta \left(D_h W_{h+1}^{\mathrm{T}} \cdots D_{L-1} W_L^{\mathrm{T}} (T - O) \right) (O^{h-1})^{\mathrm{T}} = \eta B^h (O^{h-1})^{\mathrm{T}}, \qquad (6.18)$$

where, for any h, W_h is the matrix of forward connections going into the layer of units numbered h. Likewise, for any h, the matrix D_h denotes the diagonal matrix whose diagonal entries correspond to the derivatives of the outputs of the units in the layer numbered h. The initial error vector associated with the output layer is equal to $T - O$ in the usual cases (i.e. quadratic error function with linear transfer functions, or relative entropy error function with logistic or softmax transfer functions). Otherwise this term needs to be adjusted, knowing that it must correspond to $\partial \mathcal{E}/\partial S^L$ where S^L is the vector of activations in the output layer. The vector B^h is the backpropagated error for the post-synaptic layer h. The vector O^{h-1} is the output for the pre-synaptic layer $h - 1$.

It is important to note that to a first order of approximation the computational complexity of the forward pass is the same as the computational complexity of the backward pass, and both scale like $O(W)$ where W is the total number of weights in the architecture. This is because both the forward and backward pass require multiplying each weight by the presynaptic activity or the posynaptic backpropagated error, thus leading to W multiplications. To compute the forward and backward activations requires on the order of one operation per neuron. In addition, the transfer function must be computed one time per neuron in the forward pass. Likewise, one multiplication by the derivative of the activation is required in the backward pass for each neuron. Assuming costs that are within constant factors for each elementary operation (such as additions, multiplications, computation of transfer functions, computation of derivatives of transfer functions) we see that the complexity scales like $O(W + N) = O(W)$, where N is the total number of neurons.

6.6.2   Deep Targets

It is useful to note that computing the backpropagation error is *equivalent* to assigning a target to the neurons in each deep layer. To see this, consider neuron i in layer h and assume that a target T_i^h is available. Then:

$$\frac{\partial \mathcal{E}}{\partial w_{ij}^h} = \frac{\partial \mathcal{E}}{\partial S_i^h} \frac{\partial S_i^h}{\partial w_{ij}^h} = -B_i^h O_j^{h-1} = -(T_i^h - O_i^h) O_j^{h-1}, \qquad (6.19)$$

where the last equality uses the standard assumptions used in Chapter 3 regarding the local error associated with the target T_i^h and the transfer function of neuron i in layer h. Thus, in short, the equivalence between targets and backpropagated errors is given by:

$$T_i^h = O_i^h + B_i^h, \qquad (6.20)$$

which intuitively makes since B_i^h is the backpropagated error.

6.6.3   Backpropagation through Probabilistic Layers

As we have seen, probabilistic neural network layers can be introduced by assuming that the activities of a given layer represent the parameter of a distribution and then sampling from that distribution. Let $P_\theta^h = P_{O^h}^h$ represent that distribution, and let us assume that a sample Q^h is produced and propagated forward to the upper layers. When the backpropagated signal comes back, we have seen that it can be converted to a target T^h. Thus, one can propagate a gradient by trying to increase the likelihood $P_\theta^h(T^h)$ or its logarithm, assuming P_θ^h is differentiable in θ. As pointed out for the variational autoencoder, there are also other possibilities for backpropagating gradient through probabilistic layers, for instance through reparameterization of the sampling operation (e.g. [626]).

6.6.4   Backpropagation in Linear Networks

By now, it should be clear that linear feedforward networks have interesting properties and cannot be dismissed because they only compute linear functions. We have seen that linear, fully connected, compressive autoencoders perform PCA, and that fully connected feedforward linear networks with the quadratic error function have no spurious local minima. Another interesting property of linear feedforward networks is that propagation can occur in a completely asynchronous fashion. As an exercise, and because it will be useful in later chapters, here we derive the backpropagation learning equations for a linear feedforward network in matrix notation. Assume that $A_1, \ldots, A_{L-1}$ denote the weight matrices of such a network, so that $O = A_{L-1} \cdots A_1(I)$ where I is the input vector and O the output vector. Using Theorem 6.6, the gradient descent learning equation for matrix h is given in matrix form immediately by:

$$\Delta A_h = \eta \left(A_{h+1} \cdots A_{L-1}(T - O) \right) \left(A_{h-1} \cdots A_1(I) \right)^\mathsf{T}, \tag{6.21}$$

when computed on-line on a single input–output example vector pair (I, T). Note how one must use the product of the postsynaptic, back-propagated, error with the *transpose* of the presynaptic, forward-propagated, activity.

The gradient descent equation is obtained by taking expectations on both sides of Equation 6.21:

$$E(\Delta A_h) = \eta A_{h+1} \cdots A_{L-1} E[(T - O)I^\mathsf{T}] A_1^\mathsf{T} \cdots A_{h-1}^\mathsf{T}. \tag{6.22}$$

The middle term can be written as:

$$E[(T - O)I^\mathsf{T}] = \Sigma_{TI} - F\Sigma_{II}, \tag{6.23}$$

with the data covariance matrices $\Sigma_{TI} = E(TI^\mathsf{T})$ and $\Sigma_{II} E(II^\mathsf{T})$, and the overall matrix $F = A_{L-1} \cdots A_1$. For small learning rates ($\eta \approx \Delta t$), the dynamic of gradient descent learning is given by a system of polynomial equations:

$$\frac{dA_h}{dt} = A_{h+1} \cdots A_{L-1}(\Sigma_{TI} - F\Sigma_{II}) A_1^\mathsf{T} \cdots A_{h-1}^\mathsf{T}. \tag{6.24}$$

In the general case, no closed form solutions are known, even in the case of a single hidden layer.

6.7 The Optimality of Backpropagation

In practice, backpropagation learning works exceedingly well. To better understand some of the underlying reasons, it is useful to group them into two separate components: (1) stochastic gradient descent (SGD) for optimization; and (2) the backpropagation algorithm for computing gradients.

6.7.1 Stochastic Gradient Descent

There is growing evidence that in high-dimensional spaces stochastic gradient descent is a powerful algorithm for optimizing differentiable functions. One reason for this is the realization that in general, in high-dimensional spaces, spurious local minima are relatively rare; most critical points where the gradient is zero correspond to saddle points, or to the global optimum. While this is not a theorem, we have proven that this is true for the quadratic error functions of any feedfoward, fully connected, linear neural network. There is also evidence from physics that this may be the case also in other situations [149, 290]. And intuitively, in n dimensions, at a minimum the gradient must be zero and the function must increase locally in *all* directions. For a saddle point, the gradient must be zero but the function may go up in some directions, and down in some others. In a local orthogonal basis centered at the critical point, there are $\binom{n}{k}$ ways of choosing $k > 0$ directions along the axis for the function to go down, for a total of $2^n - 2$ possible ways of realizing a set of downward directions characterizing a saddle point – as opposed to only one way for a minimum where all the directions must go up, or a maximum where all the directions must go down. In short, everything else being equal, it is far more likely for a critical point to be a saddle point rather than an optimum (maximum or minimum), and increasingly so in an exponential way as the dimension of the space is increased. Due to its stochastic nature, SGD may be particularly good at jumping out of saddle points, especially those associated with high error values and having many possible directions of escape. As learning progresses, escaping from saddle points associated with low error and fewer and fewer directions of escape may take longer. However, it seems to be the case that as long as the error is below some level, it does not really matter which saddle point has been reached. In addition to the number of escape directions, there may be a subtle effect related to their steepness. Gradient descent is likely to move first along steep directions where the decrease in error is maximal – think of directions associated with high eigenvalues in the case of PCA implemented by a linear compressive autoencoder. Thus, everything else being equal, as the error decreases during SGD, the saddle points that SGD encounters not only have fewer directions of escape, but these directions may also be less steep, i.e. the saddle points become flatter.

As we have seen, in the convex case, following noisy gradients with a decreasing step size provably reaches the optimum [614]. In the non-convex case, SGD may still converge towards flat regions associated with saddle points (if not global minima) and stay there for periods of time that increase as the number k of escape directions decreases. Furthermore, in both the convex and non-convex cases, SGD can be modeled as an Ornstein–Uhlenbeck Brownian motion process [739] leading to a stochastic differential equation [551, 482]. Together with the remarks above, SGD may have a tendency of settling around equilibrium points that are particularly flat and thus robust, in the sense that most small perturbations of the weights do not significantly affect the error.

6.7.2   Using Backpropagation to Compute Gradients

The second component is the efficiency of the backpropagation algorithm which computes the gradient in $O(W)$ operations for a single example, or $KO(W)$ for K examples. Suppose that we consider the family of iterative learning algorithms which modify the weights at each iteration according to some rule. By definition, such an algorithm requires at least $O(W)$ operations at each iteration to compute the modification of the weights. Locally, this modification is most efficient if it follows the gradient. Thus, within this framework and up to factors hidden in the "O" notation, backpropagation computes the best direction with the least number of operations and, as such, is optimal [102].

It is instructive to compare backpropagation to several other algorithms for changing the weights at each iteration. For instance:

Definition of Derivatives In order to compute $\partial\mathcal{E}/\partial w_{ij}^h$ one can resort to the definition and approximate it by $\left(E(\ldots, w_{ij}^h + \epsilon, \ldots) - E(\ldots, w_{ij}^h, \ldots)\right)/\epsilon$ for ϵ small. This approach, however, essentially requires one forward propagation for each weight perturbation and thus scales like $O(W^2)$ in order to obtain the gradient.

Random Direction Descent In this algorithm one perturbs all the weights by a small random amount ϵ (here ϵ is a vector). If the resulting error decreases the perturbation is accepted. If the resulting error increases, the perturbation is rejected or, alternatively, the opposite perturbation $-\epsilon$ is accepted. This algorithm requires $O(W)$ operations for each iteration. The main issue, however, is that in a high-dimensional space a random perturbation is essentially orthogonal to the gradient and thus in general it leads to improvements that are exceedingly small.

Optimized Random Direction Descent In this algorithm, k small random perturbation of the weights are selected for some fixed integer $k > 1$, and the direction leading to the greatest reduction in error is retained. As an exercise, show that the best-of-k strategy is not sufficient to overcome the problem of random directions being essentially orthogonal to the gradient.

Hessian-based methods In these methods, the full Hessian is computed in order to optimize the direction or the step size. The problem here is that computing the Hessian requires at least $O(W^2)$ operations, which is often impractical on a digital computer.

Simulated Annealing In this algorithm, at each iteration, a random, and not-necessarily, small perturbation of the weights is created according to some distribution. If the resulting error is smaller, the perturbation is accepted. If the resulting error is not smaller, then the pertubation is accepted with some small probability which depends on a temperature parameter which follows some annealing schedule. Although in principle this algorithm could minimize the error function better than backpropagation, in practice in general it is computationally inefficient for large networks.

Thus, in short, all these algorithms are less efficient than backpropagation, either in terms of the number of operations, or in terms of determining a direction of descent that is not locally optimal. This is not to say that small improvements to backpropagation cannot be found, within for instance the approximations of the $O(W)$ notation or the optimization of its hyperparameters (e.g. better learning rates schedules, better weight initializations, and so forth). For instance, in the framework of Hessian methods, attempts have been made to compute and leverage only the diagonal of the Hessian, which can be done in $O(W)$ steps. However, in practice, the increase in computational time, hidden in the $O(W)$ notation, seems too large to justify this approach.

6.8   Architecture Design

6.8.1   Design

There is no comprehensive theory that will prescribe in detail how to design a single layered, feedforward architecture for a given task, training data, and desired level of performance. In particular, there is no theory for the exact number of layers and their sizes. Generally speaking, however, there are a few considerations one can follow.

First, in general, it is unlikely for an architecture to require multiple bottle-neck layers. From the theory, we know that in the fully-connected linear case, and in the unrestricted Boolean case, a single bottleneck layer is always sufficient. In most practical cases, the input layer tends to be large, relative to the output layer where some kind of compact decision, in terms of classification or regression, is achieved. Thus the corresponding architectures will either have a compressive profile, or an expansive–compressive profile. In the first case, starting from the input layers, the size of the layers will progressively taper off. In the second case, the architecture will have an initial shallow expansion, for instance to better separate the input examples and facilitate the tasks of the upper layers, followed by a compressive profile.

Second, generally speaking the depth of the architecture should be dictated by the complexity of the task and the training set. Although there is no satisfying theory yet, and no substitute for experience and experimentation, it is advisable to always keep track of the overall number of parameters in the architecture in relation to the number of training examples. If the number of examples significantly exceeds the number of parameters, overfitting is unlikely. However, even when the number of parameters exceeds the number of training examples, there are many documented examples showing that neural architectures have a tendency to behave well and not to easily overfit. In practice, in all regimes, one ought to monitor whether overfitting is occurring or not; it just that the monitoring should be even more careful in the second regime.

6.8.2   Invariances

In many situations, one is trying to learn or approximate a function $f : X \to Y$ and there is a group G of transformations acting on X, or both X and Y. Furthermore, the function f is known to have some invariance property with respect to the group of transformations and the general question is how to leverage this knowledge when using a neural network approach.

To be more precise, we say that the function f is *invariant* with respect to the transformations in G if and only if: $f(\sigma(x)) = f(x)$ for every $\sigma \in G$. For instance, in image processing one may be interested in recognizing objects in ways that are invariant with respect to translations, or small elastic deformations, or rotations. Recognition by our own visual system is invariant with respect to translations and small deformations, but not to large rotations (e.g. recognizing inverted faces is difficult). Likewise, when processing inputs that represent the elements of a set (as opposed to the elements of a sequence), it may be desirable for the output to be invariant under all possible permutations of the inputs.

When the group G acts on both the input space X and the output space Y we say that f is *equivariant* with respect to the tranformations in G if and only if: $f(\sigma(x)) = \sigma(f(x))$ for every $\sigma \in G$. In other words, when a transformation is applied to the input, the output changes in a predictable manner, by applying the same transformation to the output. A typical example is provided by convolutional layers in a convolutional neural network for computer vision. A translation in the input causes the hidden representation produced by a convolutional layer to be translated by the same amount (assuming that boundary and other effects, such as those dependent on the stride, are small and can be ignored). Likewise, when processing inputs that represent the elements of a set, if the same neural network is applied to each element (weight sharing) then a permutation of the inputs will cause a corresponding permutation of the outputs. Thus invariant recognition often uses intermediate processing steps that are equivariant, as a prerequisite for building invariant recognition.

There are at least three ways to try to create supervised neural network models that are invariant with respect to a group (in some cases it could be just a set) of tranformations: (1) canonicalization; (2) data-augmentation; and (3) architecture design.

Canonicalization
In this approach, the effect of the transformations is in some sense nullified by a pre-processing stage where the input is mapped to some cannonical reference frame. For example, in computer vision, all the images can be centered or rotated in a particular, deterministically-chosen, fashion before being processed by a neural architecture. In cases where the inputs consist, for instance, of sets of distinct numbers, these could be ordered by their size. Likewise, for sets of words these could be ordered lexico-graphically, and so forth. One potential disadvantages of this approach is that there is

nothing canonical about most frames of references: in other words the choice of frame can be arbitrary and mask the information contained in the group of tranformations. Another potential drawback is that the canonicalization can introduce discontinuities in the function to be learned.

Data-Augmentation
In data-augmentation, the training data is expanded by applying the tranformations to the training examples. For example, in object-detection tasks it is common to augment the data during training with random translations, rotations, and mirroring operations. In practice, rather than applying all possible transformation to all elements of the initial training set offline, it is often more efficient to apply a transformation chosen at random (e.g. a rotation by a random angle) to each training example during online training. Either way, the network is forced to learn how to be invariant to the corresponding class of operations. The disadvantage of this approach is that the model must learn that the output should be invariant – this requirement is not enforced by the model itself.

Architecture Design
The third way to achieve equivariance and invariance in deep learning is through architecture design, where the hypothesis space is constrained to functions that satisfy the invariance condition. When feasible, this approach is generally more elegant and efficient. For example, convolution and pooling layers in a convolutional architecture help achieve good translational invariant recognition. The convolutional idea for translations can be extended to other classes of transformations using the theory of Lie groups (e.g. [480, 205, 481, 206]). One can also trivially define neural network architectures that guarantee invariance to any transformation by defining an ensemble model that applies identical subnetworks to every possible transformation of the input, then pooling the results into the final output. Clearly this becomes intractable – or at least inefficient – for applications where the number of elements in the group is large or infinite. For inputs corresponding to sets, a permutation-invariant architecture can be constructed by applying the same shared network to each element and then combining the outputs in a symmetric way, for instance using max or mean pooling. Of course, only a particular subset of symmetric functions can be realized by such an architecture. More complex functions could require subnetworks capable of processing pairs, triplets, etc. of elements rapidly increasing the cost and complexity of the overall architecture.

6.8.3 Ensembles

Ensemble methods [240], where multiple models are trained and combined together, are another way of improving performance when applicable. It can be shown that when the error function is convex up, the performance of an ensemble can be expected to perform better than the average of the performance of the individual predictors, and that ensemble methods require a diversity of models (see [693] and exercises). In deep learning, such diversity can be obtained in many ways, for instance by varying: the architectures of the networks in the ensemble; the training sets of the networks in the ensemble; or the training procedure and its parameters [426, 152].

Common methods for organizing the learning of classifiers and creating diversity include boosting, bagging, and adaptive boosting. Bagging [150], which stands for boot-strap aggregating, is one of the earliest, most intuitive and perhaps simplest ensemble-based algorithms, with a surprisingly good performance. Diversity of classifiers in bagging is obtained by using bootstrapped replicas of the training data [251, 624, 252], i.e. by randomly drawing different training data subsets with replacement and treating them as if they were independently drawn from the underlying distribution. Each training data subset is used to train a different classifier of the same type. Individual classifiers are then combined by taking a simple majority vote of their decisions.

Similar to bagging, boosting [649, 281] also creates an ensemble of classifiers by resampling the data, which are then combined by majority voting. However, in boosting, resampling is strategically geared to provide the most informative training data for each consecutive classifier. Finally, adaptive boosting (AdaBoost) [650] extends boosting to multi-class and regression problems.

Models in an ensemble can be combined in different ways, by taking the average, the product, the max etc. The simplest way for combining models is a static way, by taking a weighted average of the model. Usually the weights are taken uniformly (average or majority rule), but it is also possible to train their values. Static average of models can be shown to improve performance (see exercises). Models can also be combined in a dynamic way, where the weights are adjusted dynamically as a function of the input through some kind of gating mechanism (see below).

6.9   Practical Training Issues

In this section, we go over some of the practical issues encountered when training neural networks. The treatment is somewhat superficial for several reasons. In particular, several of these issues do not have a complete theory, or are still evolving, or are well addressed in current software packages and tutorials. Furthermore, when designing and training neural networks, some degree of experimentation is to be expected.

Weights Initialization
We have already seen in the chapters on shallow networks that the data should be normalized and the weights should be randomly initialized to small values, typically using independent uniform or normal distributions. To see how to select the standard deviation of the initial distributions, one can look at the activation

$$S_j^h = \sum_{j=1}^{n_{h-1}} w_{ij}^h O_j^{h-1} \tag{6.25}$$

of the units in layer h. Assuming that $E(O_j) = 0$ (which is true with normalized data and odd activation functions), that $E(w_{ij}^h) = 0$, and that the weights are independent of the activations, in the fully connected case we have:

$$\text{Var}(S_j^h) = n_{h-1} \, \text{Var}(w_{ij}^h) \, \text{Var}(O_j^{h-1}). \tag{6.26}$$

Thus it makes sense to choose: $\text{Var}(w_{ij}^h) = 1/n_{h-1} = 1/\text{fan\_in}$. However, a similar argument based on the backpropagation would yield: $\text{Var}(w_{ij}^h) = 1/n_{h1} = 1/\text{fan\_out}$. Thus a reasonable compromise is to use [303]:

$$\text{Var}(w_{ij}^h) = \frac{2}{n_{h-1} + n_h} = \frac{2}{\text{fan\_in} + \text{fan\_out}}. \tag{6.27}$$

If all the layers have the same size, this is equivalent to scaling the variance according to the fan-in only. Also note that the variance needs to be comparatively smaller for bottleneck layers, which makes some sense, as these layers should be trained with particular care.

Minibatch and Layer Normalizations
In experiments with very deep networks, minibatch and layer normalizations [367, 56] have sometimes been found to be beneficial. Let S_i^h be the activation of neuron i in layer h. The normalized activation N_i^h is given by:

$$N_i^h = \frac{S_i^h - E(S_i^h)}{\sqrt{\text{Var}(S_i^h)}}. \tag{6.28}$$

In batch normalization, the average and variance are computed over minibatches. It is also possible to introduce two additional parameters to scale and shift the normalized values [367]. If the minibatches have size m and if $S_i^h(k)$ denotes the activation for the kth example in the minibatch, then:

$$E(S_i^h) = \frac{1}{m} \sum_{k=1}^{m} S_i^h(k) \quad \text{and} \quad \text{Var}(S_i^h) = \frac{1}{m-1} \sum_{k=1}^{m} \left(S_i^h(k) - E(S_i^h)\right)^2. \tag{6.29}$$

Ultimately some degree of experimentation on the size of the minibatches is usually necessary as it depends on many tradeoffs, not only with the learning rate and the stage of learning but also, for instance, on whether mini-batches can be processed in parallel or not.

In layer normalization, the mean and variance are computed for a fixed input example across the units in a given layer. Layer normalization does not depend on batch size and can be applied even in the pure on-line case.

Gradient clipping
Another simple approach that has been used for a long time for stabilizing learning and preventing gradients from becoming too large or too small while training deep networks is simply gradient clipping (e.g. [576]), where the magnitude of the components of the gradient, or the gradient itself, are forced to remain within a lower and upper bound, clipping them to the corresponding bound whenever it is attained.

Learning Rates

From the theory of gradient descent, it is easy to infer that the learning rate should decrease according to some exponential schedule. Thus typically the learning rate is reduced by a factor k_1 every k_2 epochs. While software packages may calculate default values for k_1 and k_2, these are often dependent on the problem at hand and require some degree of experimentation. As previously mentioned, the size of the learning rate is also related to other parameters, such as as the size of the minibatches and whether one uses minibatch or layer normalization.

Momentum

Momentum terms combine the current value of the gradient with past values of the gradient. This can speed up convergence, for instance inside long elliptic valleys. It can be implemented in different ways, depending on how many past values are included and the corresponding coefficients. For instance, one can use descent equations of the form:

$$\Delta w_{ij}^h(t) = -\left(\sum_{k=1}^{\infty} \eta^k \frac{\partial \mathcal{E}}{\partial w_{ij}^h}(t+1-k)\right) \quad \text{or} \quad \Delta w_{ij}^h(t) = -\left(\eta \frac{\partial \mathcal{E}}{\partial w_{ij}^h}(t) + \alpha \frac{\partial \mathcal{E}}{\partial w_{ij}^h}(t-1)\right),$$

(6.30)

with $\eta \geq 0$ and $\alpha \geq 0$. Often in practice only the value of the gradient at the previous time step is included (right expression in Equation 6.30). This still introduces one additional hyperparameter α that may be optimized together with all other hyperparameters.

Regularizers

We have seen that the addition of regularizing terms to the error function is essentially equivalent to the inclusion of probabilistic priors on the model parameters. These regularizing terms can be added to the error function to further constrain learning and combat overfitting. Regularizers that are often used, in isolation or in combination, include the L2 and L1 regularizers. Each regularizing term comes with its associated coefficient that controls its strength and must be included in the list of hyperparameters that can be optimized. For instance, for a deep weight w_{ij}^h the L2 regularizer associated with a Gaussian prior leads to a descent equation with weight decay of the form:

$$\Delta w_{ij}^h = -\eta \frac{\partial \mathcal{E}}{\partial w_{ij}^h} - \alpha w_{ij}^h,$$

(6.31)

with $\eta \geq 0$ and $\alpha \geq 0$.

Training, Validation, and Testing:

It is standard practice to divide the available data into at least three different subsets for training, validation and testing. The training set is used for parameter optimization (by backpropagation), the validation set is used for hyperparameter optimization, and the testing set is used to estimate the performance of the network on new data (generalization). Hyperparameters include things like the number and size of the layers, the learning rates, or the coefficients attached to each regularizer. There are several software packages for hyperparameter optimization: our own version (Sherpa, [340]) is freely available at `https://github.com/sherpa-ai/sherpa`. Even for a fixed setting of the hyperparameters, there is some stochastic variability in the overall performance due to random factors such as weight initialization and the ordering of the training examples. This variability can be explored: however hyperparameter exploration and optimization are computationally expensive, and thus one has to deal with the corresponding trade-offs. Likewise, with a single training and testing set, it is difficult to get a sense of the variability in the network performance. Thus, whenever possible, one ought to run full cross-validation experiments in order to get error bars on any performance measure. As an added benefit, sometimes this can also help develop ensembles (see below).

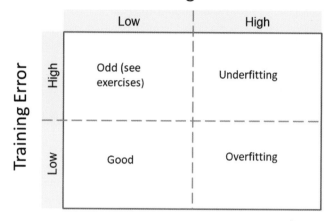

Figure 6.1 Four basic regimes. If the training error is low and the testing error is high, this is generally a sign of overfitting: the model is probably too complex and you need to simplify it, or provide additional data or additional regularization. If the training error is high, and the testing error is high, this is generally a sign of underfitting: the model is probably too simple and you need a bigger model. If the training error is high, and the testing error is low, then something very odd is occurring and you need to investigate it. The fourth regime is the good one. Obviously the notions of "high" and "low" are relative to the task.

Underfitting and Overfitting:

Two of the most basic problems one can encounter in deep learning are underfitting and overfitting (Figure 6.1). In underfitting, the performance on both the training sets and the testing sets are poor. In general, this is a sign that the model being used is not powerful enough and thus one of the first things to try is to use a larger model with more units, more layers, etc. Sometimes it can also be a sign of lack of structure in the data. In overfitting, the performance on the testing set is significantly worse than the performance on the training set. This is usually a sign that the model used may be too powerful for the available data and that it ends up learning spurious correlation in the data that are not beneficial for generalization purposes. There are several general directions that can be used to combat overfitting, including:

1. Reducing the complexity of the model which is typically done by reducing the number of parameters. This can be achieved by reducing the number of layers, or the size of the layers, or through some form of weight sharing.
2. Data augmentation by gathering more data, producing additional data by applying suitable transformations (e.g. translations, rotations, symmetries, addition of Gaussian or other kinds of noise, deletion of input values), where "suitable" is problem-dependent.
3. *Early stopping* techniques where training is stopped as soon as the error begins to increase on a separate validation set, which generally signals the onset of overfitting.
4. Regularization by adding suitable regularizing terms to the error functions.
5. Adding randomness to the data (as in data augmentation), or to the model or training procedure, to increase overall robustness. A standard algorithm for doing that is dropout which is discussed in more detail in Section 6.11.
6. Using some form of transfer learning by either using additional data pertaining to a different, but related, task, or by reusing network components that have already been trained for other tasks, possibly in unsupervised ways. One example is when autoencoders are stacked vertically to initialize a deep architecture. Another example, widely used in computer vision applications, is to reuse a (large) model that has been trained for a different computer vision task using a large data set of images. Typically, the lower layers of the pre-trained model and their weights are retained, while the upper layer(s) are replaced with new neurons and new connections. The new combined model, or just its top layers, are then retrained for the specific task at hand. Examples of widely used, publicly available, model families included in Keras are VGG [683], Inception [717], and ResNet [334].

6.10   The Bias–Variance Decomposition

The bias–variance decomposition is a simple generalization of the basic variance equality $\text{Var}(X) = E((X - E(X))^2) = E(X^2) - (E(X))^2$ which captures some aspects of the tradeoffs between underfitting and overfitting discussed in the previous section. Intuitively it can be visualized using the game of throwing darts at a dartboard, in 2D or any other number of dimensions. If the bull's eye is at 0, we can let X denote the random vector associated with where the dart lands for a given player (or even for a group of players). Then the average square distance to the bull's eye is given by:

$$E(X^2) = E(X - E(X) + E(X))^2 = E(X - E(X))^2 + (E(X))^2 = (E(X))^2 + \text{Var}\,X,$$

(6.32)

the cross-product term being equal to zero. This is just a way of rewriting the variance equation above. In short, the square of the distance to the target can be decomposed into the sum of two terms: the square of the distance between the average and the target, plus the square of the distance to the average. The first term is the square of the bias, and the second term is the variance, hence the name bias–variance decomposition. The term bias comes from the field of statistics where the bias is defined as the difference between the expectation (across samples) of an estimator and the true value being estimated. For instance, the average of a sample is an unbiased (bias = 0) estimator of the true mean.

In terms of machine learning [693], imagine that you are trying to learn a function $y = f(x)$. For *any* given point x, you have multiple predictions $O_1, \ldots, O_n$ with a distribution $P = (p_1, \ldots, p_n)$, uniform or other. Note that there is no conceptual difference between a predictor and an estimator. You can imagine that these predictions are produced by an ensemble of neural networks, for instance neural networks trained on different training examples of the function f. They could also be produced by a single neural network with an added element of stochasticity – it does not really matter. Then, by taking the expectation over the predictions we find:

$$(y - E(O))^2 \leq E(y - O)^2 = (y - E(O))^2 + E(O - E(O))^2 . \qquad (6.33)$$

The inequality results from the convexity of the quadratic error function $\mathcal{E}$, namely: $\mathcal{E}(E(O)) \leq E(\mathcal{E}(O))$. The equality is simply the bias–variance decomposition and it remains true when averaged also across points x, for instance to estimate the generalization error. It is important to note that the variance term can be estimated from unlabeled data, since it does not involve the target y. Furthermore a higher variance, $E(O - E(O))^2$, among the predictors will reduce the error, $(y - E(O))^2$, made by the average of the predictors, provided the errors, $(y - O)^2$, of the individual predictors are roughly constant. High bias is related to underfitting the data, and high variance is related to overfitting the data. There is a tradeoff between the bias and the variance in the sense that a simple approach will tend to have lower variance but higher bias, and vice versa. In the darts analogy, a player may try to use the exact same motion of the arm at each throw to reduce the variance: however in general this will come at the cost of having a non-zero bias. The bias–variance decomposition can be generalized to other situations, including classification settings rather than regression settings (see exercises).

6.11   Dropout

Overfitting results from learning spurious correlations present in the data. Adding randomness to the data or the training procedure is one way to combat overfitting, and dropout is one such method [699]. In its simplest form, at each presentation of each training example, each neuron is deleted randomly with probability $q = 1 - p = 0.5$. The remaining weights are trained by backpropagation. The procedure is repeated for each example and each training epoch, sharing the weights at each iteration. After the training phase is completed, predictions are produced by halving all the weights. The dropout procedure can also be applied to the input layer by randomly deleting some of the input-vector components – typically an input component is deleted with a smaller probability (i.e. $q' = 1 - p' = 0.2$). There are many possible variations on this basic idea. For instance, it is possible to apply dropout to edges rather than neurons, to apply it selectively to subsets of neurons (e.g. layers), to use different dropout probabilities for different neurons, or different forms of noise such as adding Gaussian noise to the activations of the neurons or the connection weights.

The motivation and intuition behind dropout in general is to prevent overfitting associated with the co-adaptation of feature detectors. By randomly dropping out neurons, the procedure prevents any neuron from relying excessively on the output of any other neuron, forcing it instead to rely on the population behavior of its inputs. Another way to look at dropout is to view it as a cheap approximation to training the corresponding ensemble of possible subnetworks and using ensemble averaging at prediction time. Yet another possible interpretation is that it is a form of adaptive regularization. In this section, we review some of the basic analytical results that support these intuitions [91].

To better understand the averaging and adaptive regularization properties of dropout, we can first formalize dropout in a layered feedforward network using equations of the form:

$$O_i^h = f_i^h(S_i^h) = f_i^h\left(\sum_j w_{ij}^h \delta_j^{h-1} O_j^{h-1}\right),$$
(6.34)

where δ_j^{h-1} is a Bernoulli random variable with mean p_j^{h-1}, for modeling dropout for unit j in layer $h-1$. In general, we assume that the Bernoulli random variables are independent of each other, and independent of the neuronal weights and outputs, as well as the network inputs. Similar equations can be written for dropout applied to connections, or for other forms of noise injection.

The ensemble-averaging properties of dropout can be understood precisely in the linear case and, in the non-linear case, for a logistic unit.

6.11.1   Ensemble Averaging: Linear Networks

To study dropout's ensemble-averaging properties in linear networks, for a fixed input we can simply propagate expectations from layer to layer, using the independence assumptions described above. Thus, in the case of a linear feedforward network, allowing even skip connections, we can take the expectation over the dropout Bernoulli variables:

$$E(S_i^h) = \sum_{l<h} \sum_j w_{ij}^{hl} p_j^l E(S_j^l) \qquad \text{for} \quad h > 1.$$
(6.35)

This formula can be applied recursively across the entire network, starting from the input layer. For the input layer, $E(S_j^1) = I_j$ when no dropout is applied to that layer, otherwise I_j should be replaced by $E(I_j)$. Similarly, for dropout applied to the connections, one obtains:

$$E(S_i^h) = \sum_{l<h} \sum_j p_{ij}^{hl} w_{ij}^{hl} E(S_j^l) \qquad \text{for} \quad h > 1.$$
(6.36)

In summary, for linear feedforward networks, the ensemble-averaging properties of dropout applied to the units (or the connections) using Bernoulli gating variables that are independent of the weight values, of the activities, and of each other (but not necessarily identically distributed) can be fully understood. For any input, the expectations of the outputs over all possible networks induced by the Bernoulli gating variables are computed using the recurrence equations 6.35 and 6.36, by simple feedforward propagation in the same network, where each weight is multiplied by the appropriate probability associated with the corresponding Bernoulli gating variable. The variances and covariances can also be computed recursively in a similar way (this is left as an exercise).

6.11.2   Ensemble Averaging: Non-linear Networks

In the non-linear case, let us consider the simple case of a single logistic unit with:

$$O = \sigma(S) = \frac{1}{1 + ce^{-\lambda S}} \quad \text{and} \quad S = \sum_i w_i I_i. \tag{6.37}$$

In this case, applying dropout to the inputs is equivalent to applying dropout to the connections. Each time dropout is applied, a different set of connections, or subnetwork, $\mathcal{N}$ is selected. We can even generalize the Bernoulli dropout model to assume that there is a general selection distribution $P(\mathcal{N})$. This is more general than assuming that P is the product of n independent Bernoulli selector variables. Note that in general $E(f(S)) \neq f(E(S))$; however, for the logistic function, this relationship is almost true. To study the ensemble-averaging properties, we need to introduce the notion of normalized weighted geometric mean.

Given m numbers $x_1, \ldots, x_m$ and associated probability vector $p_1, \ldots, p_m$ we define the corresponding weighted geometric mean G by: $G = \prod_i x_i^{p_i}$. In our case, we want to apply this definition to the outputs of the logistic unit under the distribution $P(\mathcal{N})$. Thus the weighted geometric means of the outputs are defined by:

$$G(O(\mathcal{N})) = \prod_{\mathcal{N}} O_{\mathcal{N}}^{P(\mathcal{N})}. \tag{6.38}$$

The outputs of the logistic unit are between 0 and 1 and thus we can equally define the weighted geometric mean of the complements by:

$$G'(O(\mathcal{N})) = \prod_{\mathcal{N}} (1 - O_{\mathcal{N}})^{P(\mathcal{N})}. \tag{6.39}$$

Finally, we can define the normalized weighted geometric mean (NWGM) by:

$$NWGM = \frac{G}{G + G'}. \tag{6.40}$$

For the logistic unit, we can now compute the normalized weighted geometric mean NWGM in the form:

$$NWGM\,(O(\mathcal{N})) = \frac{\prod_{\mathcal{N}} \sigma(S(\mathcal{N}))^{P(\mathcal{N})}}{\prod_{\mathcal{N}} \sigma(S(\mathcal{N}))^{P(\mathcal{N})} + \prod_{\mathcal{N}} (1 - \sigma(S(\mathcal{N})))^{P(\mathcal{N})}} \tag{6.41}$$

which yields:

$$NWGM\,(O(\mathcal{N})) = \frac{1}{1 + \prod_{\mathcal{N}} (\frac{1 - \sigma(S(\mathcal{N}))}{\sigma(S(\mathcal{N}))})^{P(\mathcal{N})}} = \frac{1}{1 + ce^{-\lambda \sum_{\mathcal{N}} P(\mathcal{N})S(\mathcal{N})}} = \sigma(E(S)), \tag{6.42}$$

where here $E(S) = \sum_{\mathcal{N}} P(\mathcal{N})S(\mathcal{N})$. This formula shows exactly what kind of averaging is associated with the dropout procedure and, in the Bernoulli case, NWGM $(O) = \sigma(\sum_i p_i w_i I_i) = \sigma(E(S))$.

Thus, in summary, with any distribution $P(\mathcal{N})$ over all possible subnetworks $\mathcal{N}$, including the case of independent but not identically distributed input unit Bernoulli selector variables δ_i with probability p_i of being equal to one, the NWGM of the outputs is simply obtained by applying the logistic function to the expectation of the activation S. The expectation of S can be computed simply by keeping the same overall network but replacing each weight w_i by p_i so that $E(S) = \sum_{i=1}^{n} p_i w_i I_i$.

In short, for a logistic unit, the dropout algorithm combines the elements of the corresponding ensemble using the NWGM. In [91], it is shown that: (1) for all convex error functions, the error of the NWGM ensemble is less than the NWGM of the errors of the individual models; and (2) in general NWGM (O) provides also a good approximation of $E(O)$, which is the standard way of combining the ensemble elements. Thus:

$$E(\sigma(S)) \approx \text{NWGM}(\sigma(S)) = \sigma(E(S)). \tag{6.43}$$

Within the limitations of this approximation, in the multi-layer case expectations can be propagated across layers of logistic units, as previously done in the linear case.

6.11.3   Adaptive Regularization: Linear Unit

It is instructive to first consider the simplest case of a single linear unit. In the case of a single linear unit trained with dropout with an input I, an output $O = S$, and a target T, the error is typically quadratic of the form Error $= \frac{1}{2}(T - O)^2$. Let us consider the two error functions E_{ENS} and E_{D} associated with the ensemble of all possible subnetworks and the network with dropout. In the linear case, the ensemble network is identical to the deterministic network obtained by scaling the connections by the dropout probabilities. For a single input I, these error functions are defined by:

$$E_{\text{ENS}} = \frac{1}{2}(T - O_{\text{ENS}})^2 = \frac{1}{2}\left(T - \sum_{i=1}^{n} p_i w_i I_i\right)^2 \tag{6.44}$$

and

$$E_{\text{D}} = \frac{1}{2}(T - O_{\text{D}})^2 = \frac{1}{2}\left(T - \sum_{i=1}^{n} \delta_i w_i I_i\right)^2. \tag{6.45}$$

Here δ_i are the Bernoulli selector random variables with $P(\delta_i = 1) = p_i$, hence E_{D} is a random variable, whereas E_{ENS} is a deterministic function. We use a single training input I for notational simplicity, otherwise the errors of each training example can be combined additively. The learning gradients are of the form $\frac{\partial E}{\partial w} = \frac{\partial E}{\partial O}\frac{\partial O}{\partial w} = -(T-O)\frac{\partial O}{\partial w}$, yielding:

$$\frac{\partial E_{\text{ENS}}}{\partial w_i} = -(T - O_{\text{ENS}})p_i I_i \tag{6.46}$$

and

$$\frac{\partial E_{\text{D}}}{\partial w_i} = -(T - O_{\text{D}})\delta_i I_i = -T\delta_i I_i + w_i \delta_i^2 I_i^2 + \sum_{j \neq i} w_j \delta_i \delta_j I_i I_j. \tag{6.47}$$

The last vector is a random vector variable and we can take its expectation. Assuming as usual that the random variables δ_i are pairwise independent, we have:

$$E\left(\frac{\partial E_D}{\partial w_i}\right) = -(T - E(O_D|\delta_i = 1))\, p_i I_i = -t p_i I_i + w_i p_i I_i^2 + \sum_{j \neq i} w_i p_i p_j I_i I_j \quad (6.48)$$

and thus:

$$E\left(\frac{\partial E_D}{\partial w_i}\right) = -(T - O_{ENS})\, p_i I_i + w_i I_i^2 (p_i)(1 - p_i). \quad (6.49)$$

This yields:

$$E\left(\frac{\partial E_D}{\partial w_i}\right) = \frac{\partial E_{ENS}}{\partial w_i} + w_i I_i^2 \operatorname{Var} \delta_i = \frac{\partial E_{ENS}}{\partial w_i} + w_i \operatorname{Var}(\delta_i I_i). \quad (6.50)$$

Thus, in general the dropout gradient is well aligned with the ensemble gradient. Remarkably, the expectation of the gradient with dropout is the gradient of the regularized ensemble error:

$$E = E_{ENS} + \frac{1}{2} \sum_{i=1}^{n} w_i^2 I_i^2 \operatorname{Var} \delta_i. \quad (6.51)$$

The regularization term is the usual weight decay or Gaussian prior term based on the square of the weights and ensuring that the weights do not become too large and overfit the data. Dropout provides immediately the magnitude of the regularization term which is adaptively scaled by the square of the input terms and by the variance of the dropout variables.

Note that $p_i = 0.5$ is the value that provides the highest level of regularization and the regularization term depends only on the inputs, and not on the target outputs. Furthermore, the expected dropout gradient is on-line also with respect to the regularization term since there is one term for each training example. Obviously, the same result holds for an entire layer of linear units. The regularization effect of dropout in the case of generalized linear models is also discussed in [771] where it is also used to derive other regularizers.

6.11.4 Adaptive Regularization: Linear Networks

Similar calculations can be made for deep feedforward linear networks. For instance, the previous calculation can be adapted immediately to the top layer of a linear network with L layers with:

$$\frac{\partial E_D}{\partial w_{ij}^{L,l}} = -(T_i - O_i^L)\delta_j^l O_j^l \quad (6.52)$$

and:

$$E\left(\frac{\partial E_D}{\partial w_{ij}^{L,l}}\right) = \frac{\partial E_{ENS}}{\partial w_{ij}^{L,l}} + w_{ij}^{L,l} \operatorname{Var}(\delta_j^l O_j^l), \quad (6.53)$$

which corresponds again to an adaptive quadratic regularization term in $w_{ij}^{l,l}$, with a coefficient associated for each input with the corresponding variance of the dropout pre-synaptic neuron $\mathrm{Var}(\delta_j^l O_j^l)$.

To study the gradient of *any* weight w in the network, let us assume without any loss of generality that the deep network has a single output unit. Let us denote its activity by S in the dropout network, and by U in the deterministic ensemble network. Since the network is linear, for a given input the output is a linear function of w:

$$S = \alpha w + \beta \quad \text{and} \quad U = E(S) = E(\alpha)w + E(\beta). \tag{6.54}$$

The output is obtained by summing the contributions provided by all possible paths from the inputs to the output. Here α and β are random variables and α corresponds to the sum of all the contributions associated with paths from the input layer to the output layer that contain the edge associated with w. Likewise, β corresponds to the sum of all the contributions associated with paths from the input layer to the output layer that do not contain the edge associated with w. Thus the gradients are given by:

$$\frac{\partial E_D}{\partial w} = -(t - S)\frac{\partial S}{\partial w} = (\alpha w + \beta - t)\alpha \tag{6.55}$$

and

$$\frac{\partial E_{ENS}}{\partial w} = -(t - U)\frac{\partial U}{\partial w} = (E(\alpha)w + E(\beta) - T)E(\alpha). \tag{6.56}$$

The expectation of the dropout gradient is given by:

$$E\left(\frac{\partial E_D}{\partial w}\right) = (\alpha w + \beta - T)\alpha = E(\alpha^2)w + E(\alpha\beta) - T(\alpha). \tag{6.57}$$

This yields the expression:

$$E\left(\frac{\partial E_D}{\partial w}\right) = \frac{\partial E_{ENS}}{\partial w} + w\,\mathrm{Var}(\alpha) + \mathrm{Cov}(\alpha, \beta). \tag{6.58}$$

Thus again the expectation of the dropout gradient is the gradient of the ensemble plus an adaptive regularization term which has two components. The component $w\,\mathrm{Var}(\alpha)$ corresponds to a weight decay, or quadratic regularization term in the error function. The adaptive coefficient $\mathrm{Var}(\alpha)$ measures the dropout variance of the contribution to the final output associated with all the input-to-output paths which contain w. The component $\mathrm{Cov}(\alpha, \beta)$ measures the dropout covariance between the contribution associated with all the paths that contain w and the contribution associated with all the paths that do not contain w. In general, this covariance is small and equal to zero for a single layer linear network. Both α and β depend on the training inputs, but not on the target outputs.

6.12   Model Compression/Distillation and Dark Knowledge

In some applications, for instance in neuromorphic computing or applications that must be deployed on devices with limited memory or power, it may be necessary to reduce the complexity of the model. This can be in terms of the depth of the network, or the number of connections, or the precision of the connection weights. From the theory of capacity alone one can already expect that for an architecture A, in general weights with precision $C(A)/W$ should suffice. But sometimes it is desirable to achieve an even lower precision and there is quite a bit of empirical work on this topic showing how it is possible to get networks to work with lower precision weights. Here we will mention a different method that can be used sometimes to convert a deep network into a shallower network with somewhat similar performance. This method goes by the names of model compression, distillation, or dark knowledge. It was originally introduced in [159], and subsequently applied in, for instance, [347, 635].

Dark knowledge refers to the knowledge hidden in the analog values of the output units in multi-classification tasks. For example, consider training a deep network to recognize 100 image classes, such as car, truck, pedestrian, etc. In the presence of a car, the corresponding outputs may look something like: 0.8, 0.15, 0.2, etc. In other words, this output implicitly contains additional information that was not contained in the original binary targets of the training set, namely that a car is more similar to a truck than a pedestrian. Thus one can use this additional dark knowledge that has been learnt by the deep network to train a shallow network to recognize the same image categories, but using the richer analog targets provided by the deep network as opposed to the binary targets of the original training set. Thus, in short, one first trains a deep network then uses the analog outputs of this deep network as the targets for training a shallower network. While empirically this can work, it is clear that there are fundamental limitations related to the capacity of the architectures and the amount of information contained in the data in order to achieve the required level of performance.

6.13 Multiplicative Interactions: Gating and Attention

In the basic neural network model we have used so far, the main operations that are used are:

1. the multiplication of neuronal outputs by synaptic weights;
2. the additive aggregation of such products to compute activations; and
3. the linear or non-linear transformation of activations into outputs, using transfer functions.

New operations can be introduced to create more powerful architectures with greater expressiveness, or to model specific mechanisms of interest. The new operation at the root of the concept of gating is the *multiplication* of neuronal outputs or synaptic weights (Figure 6.2). In essence, if neuron i is gated by neuron j, then its output becomes $O_i O_j$ instead of O_i. If the synaptic weight w_{ki} is gated by neuron j, its value becomes $w_{ki} O_j$. These multiplicative mechanisms effectively modulate how neuron i affects its downstream neurons in a dynamic way, as a function of additional information (context) that is not available at, or fully used by, neuron i. Next, we stress some important points.

1. As a multiplication, the gating operation is differentiable and thus can easily be incorporated into the backpropagation algorithm and SGD learning.

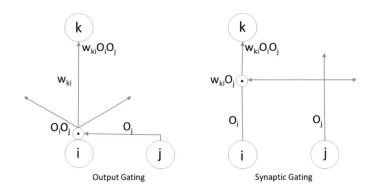

Figure 6.2 Output and Synaptic Gating. In output gating, neuron j gates the output of neuron i producing a new effective output $O_i O_j$. The signal $O_i O_j$ is broadcasted to all the neurons donwstream of neuron i, including neuron k. In synaptic gating, neuron j gates the synapse between neuron i and neuron k, producing a new effective synaptic weight $w_{ki} O_j$. The signal O_j can be transmitted to other neurons and other synapses. In both cases, neuron k received the same signal $w_{ki} O_i O_j$. However the effects of output versus synaptic gating on the rest of the network are different.

2. In output gating, neuron i broadcasts its gated value $O_i O_j$ to all its downstream neurons. In terms of neural propagation, this is equivalent to multiplying all outgoing synaptic weights w_{ki} by O_j, i.e. replacing w_{ki} by $w_{k_i} O_j$ for all neurons k to which neuron i is connected. In contrast, the synaptic gating operation is more selective and affects only the connection that is being gated.

3. In a sense, the gating operation is a special case of quadratic activation for neuron j since, in both the output and synaptic cases, it produces a term of the form $w_{ki} O_i O_j$. However, compared to a full quadratic activation, it can be very sparse and selective. For instance, if the output of n neurons are gated in this way by n other neurons, only n pairwise products are formed.

4. While in our definition we allow O_j to be arbitrary, the term gating is often used in a more restrictive sense where O_j is binary, e.g. either 0 or 1. This can be implemented using a threshold transfer function for neuron j. A softer form of gating can use a sigmoidal transfer function instead.

5. Gating mechanisms are sometimes referred to, or rebranded, as attention mechanisms, especially when a layer of neurons is gated by another layer of neurons called the attention layer. Semantically, the term gating places an emphasis on the downstream information – what information is being passed downstream – whereas the term attention places an emphasis on the upstream information – what information is being attended to. Neurons in the attention layer dynamically influence which neurons in the original layer should be attended to. Thus a neural attention mechanism equips a neural network with the ability to focus on a subset of its inputs (or features).

6. More generally, one can introduce mechanisms by which synaptic weights can be modulated by the activities of other neurons, in the form $w_{k_i} = f(O_{i_1}, O_{i_2}, \ldots, O_{i_k})$ for some function f, and some subset $\{i_1, \ldots, i_k\}$ of modulating neurons, which

typically include neuron i. This is one implementation of the idea of fast weights, or fast synaptic modulation, since the value of w_{ki} changes with the neuronal activity of other neurons.

7. A MaxPool neuron i, which chooses the maximum among its n inputs, can be viewed as one of the simplest cases of this idea. In this case, all the incoming synaptic weight w_{ik} are set to 0, except the one associated with the maximum of all the inputs which is set to 1. In this case, each synapse w_{ik} has its own function f_k which is 1 if the kth input is the maximum, and 0 otherwise. Such function is relatively easy to compute in a digital neural network simulations time proportional to n.

8. A more complex version of this idea is, for instance, to have w_{ik} proportional to the rank of the input O_k among all the other inputs to neuron i. In this case, computing all the ranks is quadratic in n. For reasonably small n, this can still be implemented in a digital neural network simulation. However, in a physical neural network, the issue of the physical implementation of the functions f becomes paramount and, to the best of our knowledge, has not been studied extensively.

9. In some cases, an attention mechanism can make a network more interpretable, or easier to debug, since the mechanism helps identify which information is being used in order to produce a certain output.

Gating and attention mechanisms are not new concepts but they have been used effectively in recent years in many applications ranging, for example, from natural language processing [61, 466] to chemoinformatics [710, 467].

6.14   Unsupervised Learning and Generative Models

Given a data set of point $D = \{d_i : i = 1, \ldots, K\}$ with typically $d_i \in \mathbb{R}^n$ or $d_i \in \{0, 1\}^n$, one may be interested in different unsupervised tasks that do not require having targets. In simple terms, these can include the following non-exclusive tasks:

1. Clustering the data.
2. Finding patterns in the data (of which clustering is a special case).
3. Generating new representations $y_i = f(d_i)$ of the data with useful characteristics. Depending on the situation, the function f may be: injective, surjective, or bijective; deterministic or probabilistic. Examples of useful characteristics with respect to the input data include: (a) compressibility; (b) visualization in a low-dimensional space, typically in dimension 1, 2, or 3; (c) simplicity – for instance, one may require the induced distribution $P(y)$ to be factorial; and (d) usefulness for for other downstream tasks.
4. Modeling the underlying distribution $P(d)$.
5. Generating new samples y of the data.

Clearly these tasks have overlaps and we have already seen methods for addressing some of them. For instance, autoencoders can be used for compressing the data or for visualizing the data by PCA. Here we focus on the application of deep learning to creating generative models of the data, i.e on the last two tasks. In Chapter 5, we saw that autoencoders, and in particular variational autoencoders (VAEs), can be used as generative models. Thus here we briefly describe three other methods for building generative neural networks:

(1) Generative Adversarial Networks (GANs);
(2) Autoregressive Generative Models; and
(3) Flow Generative Models.

It is essential to note that backpropagation, the main topic of this chapter, is not reserved for supervised tasks only. It can be applied to all these unsupervised tasks, usually through some form of self-supervised learning, where the data itself is used to create targets.

Consider, for example, that the points d_i consist of images of buildings, sampled from some distribution. The goal is to generate new points, i.e. new images of buildings, from the same distribution. To create a new sample, a simple idea would be to take the average of two other points in the data set, or more generally a convex combination of several such points. In general, however, the average of two images of buildings is not an image of a building. This indicates that the high-dimensional distribution is far more subtle and, given a point in the high-dimensional space, one needs to be able to recognize whether it is an image of a building or not. In turn, this suggests the idea of training a generator and discriminator pair together.

6.14.1   Generative Adversarial Networks (GANs)

In the basic GAN approach [308], one trains two models together, a generator and a discriminator. Both the generator and the discriminator are implemented using deep feedforward neural networks. The generator receives random inputs and the goal of learning is to generate new samples y of the distribution P, i.e. new images of buildings. The discriminator receives true or generated samples in its input, and must discriminate in its output between true and generated samples, i.e. classify true images versus generated images. Typically the output layer of the discriminator consists of a logistic unit with relative entropy error function. The key idea is to train the two networks together, adversarially, i.e. with opposite goals. The goal of the generator is to fool the discriminator, and thus its goal is to maximize the classification error. The goal of the discriminator is to detect the fake generated data, and thus its goal is to minimize the classification error. As a result the weights of the discriminator are updated by gradient descent on the error function, which typically is the relative entropy. In contrast, the weights of the generator are updated by gradient *ascent* over the same error function. In practice, the two architecture can be concatenated. True or artificially generated points can be fed as inputs to the discriminator. The backpropagation algorithm can then be used to train the weights of the discriminator first; and then, after changing the sign of the backpropaged error, the weights of the generator (Figure 6.3). Note that GANs do not attempt to maximize the data likelihood directly.

6.14.2 Autoregressive Generative Models (ARMs)

For this second approach to building a generative model of the data, consider the data to be of the form $d = (x_1, \ldots, x_n)$, in other words the variables x_i represent the pixels. The starting point for autoregressive models [312, 554, 640, 463] is the observation that any multi-dimensional distribution P can be factored in the form:

$$P(d) = P(x_1, \ldots, x_n) = P(x_1)P(x_2|x_1) \cdots P(x_n|x_1, s_2, \ldots, x_{n-1}). \tag{6.59}$$

The key idea then behind ARM is to first parameterize these conditional distributions by letting:

$$P(x_i|x_1, \ldots, x_{i-1}) = P_{\theta_i}(x_i|x_1, \ldots, x_{i-1}), \tag{6.60}$$

where θ_i is a parameter vector, for $i = 1, \ldots, n-1$); and second to use neural networks to learn these parameterizations, i.e. to estimate θ_i from the data. In practice, in most basic cases, all the conditional distributions are parameterized in the same way (e.g. Bernoulli with parameter $\theta_i = p_i$, or Gaussian with parameter $\theta_i = (\mu_i, \sigma_i)$) and a single shared neural network, as opposed to multiple neural networks, is used to compute θ_i, as a function of an input vector of the form $(x_1, \ldots, x_{i-1}, 0, \ldots, 0)$ with zero padding on the right. The weights are shared across different examples and different values of i using the proper masking. The dependence of pixel i on pixels $j > i$, which seems to be absent from the factorization of Equation 6.60, is taken into account during learning. This is because in general the weights involved in the computation of θ_i are trained using all observations, including observations x_j with $j > i$.

The overall training error is the sum (or average) of the negative log probabilities:

$$\mathcal{E}(w) = - \sum_{d=(x_1, \ldots, x_n)} \sum_i \log P_{\theta_i}(x_i|x_1, \ldots, x_{i-1}), \tag{6.61}$$

where w denotes the weights of the neural network(s) used to compute the parameters θ_i. Thus the network is trained to maximize the likelihood of the data (Figure 6.3). At generation time, starting from the fixed distribution $P(x_1)$, the components x_i are generated one at a time by first computing the corresponding P_{θ_i} and then sampling it. Thus x_1 is sampled first, then θ_2 is computed, then x_2 is sampled, then θ_3 is computed, and so forth. One of the key "hyperparameters" of an ARM is the ordering of the components, as it can make a significant difference. The ARM idea can easily be applied to different contexts such as having different ARM models for different components of the data (e.g. center versus surround), or producing sparse data by modeling the conditional distribution P_{θ_i} of each component as a mixture with a point mass at zero [463].

6.14.3 Flow Models

Flow models are another class of generative models based on likelihood maximization. Consider a random variable $z \in \mathbb{R}^n$ with a density $Q(z)$. As a reminder, if f is an

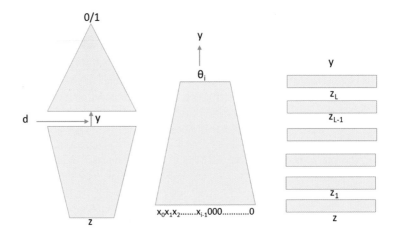

Figure 6.3 Left: Basic Generative Adversarial Network (GAN) Architecture. It comprises a generator network, followed by a discrminator network. The discriminator can be presented with real data d, or with the outputs y of the generator. The discriminator is trained to discriminate between true and fake data by minimizing the classification error. The generator is trained to fool the discriminator, by maximing the classification error. Training is done by backpropagation with respect to the relative entropy classification error, with a sign reversal of the backpropagated error when propagating back from the discriminator to the generator. Middle: Basic AutoRegressive Generative Architecture. The network computes the parameter vector θ_i which parameterizes the probability $P_{\theta_i}(x_i|x_1, \ldots, x_{i-1})$. Weights are trained by backpropagation in order to minimize the negative log-likelihood of the data, and are shared across different values of i. At generation time, y is generated by sequentially sampling the conditional distributions. Right: Basic Flow Architecture. A learnable invertible transformation from z to y is decomposed into a sequence of learnable and invertible transformations that can be implemented using neural networks, possibly with weight sharing. The distribution $Q(z)$ induces a distribution $P(y)$. The stack is trained to minimize the relative entropy between $P(d)$ and $P(y)$ or, equivalently, to minimize the negative log-likelihood of the generated data y.

invertible function transforming z into y ($y \in \mathbb{R}^n$) then the density $P(y)$ of y is given by:

$$P(y) = Q(f^{-1}(y))|\det \frac{\partial z}{\partial y}| = Q(f^{-1}(y))|\det \frac{df^{-1}}{\partial \partial y}| = Q(f^{-1}(y))|\det J^{-1}|, \quad (6.62)$$

where $J = (\partial y_i/\partial z_j)$ is the Jacobian matrix associated with f, and $J^{-1} = (\partial z_i/\partial y_j)$ is the Jacobian associated with f^{-1}. Since JJ^{-1} is the identity matrix, we have: $\det J^{-1} = 1/\det J$. The basic idea of flow models is to create a sequence of invertible functions $f_1, f_2, \ldots, f_L$ that can be composed to progressively transform z into $y = z_L$ so that the induced distribution on y is as close as possible to the target distribution $P(d)$ of the data. If we let $z_1 = f_1(z), z_2 = f_2(z_1), \ldots, z_L = f_L(z_{L-1})$ the sequence of random variables z_i is called the flow and the corresponding chain of distributions $P(z_i)$ is called a normalizing flow. By repeated application of Equation 6.62, the end-to-end transformation of the probability distribution is given by:

$$\log P(y) = \log Q(z) - \sum_{i=1}^{L} \log \left| \det \frac{df_i}{dz_{i-1}} \right|. \tag{6.63}$$

In order to build a useful flow the key points are that: (1) the functions f_i should be invertible; and (2) the determinants of the Jacobians should be easy to compute. The functions f_i can be implemented by, preferably shallow, neural networks, possibly with weight sharing across the layers (Figure 6.3). Because the flow is invertible, for each data point d we can calculate its log-likelihood $\log P(d)$ according to the flow model using Equation 6.63. Thus the flow model can be trained by minimizing the negative log-likelihood of the data:

$$\mathcal{E}(w) = - \sum_{d} \log P(d), \tag{6.64}$$

where w denotes the parameters of the flow. i.e. the weights of the neural networks used to parameterize the functions f_i. There a several approaches in the literature for choosing the form of the functions f_i. In [242], d components are replicated at each stage of the flow, and the remaining $n - d$ components undergo a simple affine transformation. This is extended in [408] using 1×1 invertible convolutions. The flow approach can also be combined with autoregressive models [562].

6.15   Exercises

EXERCISE 6.1   Consider the problem of optimizing a fully connected $A(n_1, \ldots, n_L)$ linear architecture with a fixed training set with respect to the quadratic error function.
(1) Show that without any loss of generality we can assume that $n_1 = n_L$.
(2) Show that this problem reduces to the problem of optimizing an $A(n_1, n_2, n_1)$ linear and fully connected architecture, where $n_2 = \min(n_2, n_3, \ldots, n_{L-1})$. Furthermore, the only interesting case is when $n_2 < n_1$.
(3) Show that without any loss of generality, it is enough to solve the problem in the autoencoder case, where the targets are equal to the inputs.

EXERCISE 6.2   Complete the proof of Theorem 6.2.

EXERCISE 6.3   Prove Theorem 6.3.

EXERCISE 6.4   Prove that for all integers $1 \le n \le N$:

$$\sum_{k=0}^{n} \binom{N}{k} \le \left(\frac{eN}{n} \right)^n. \tag{6.65}$$

Use this inequality and the hyperplane counting results in the exercises of Chapter 3 to prove that the number of distinct linear threshold functions on a given set $S \in \mathbb{R}^n$ is bounded by:

$$2 \sum_{k=0}^{n} \binom{|S| - 1}{k}. \tag{6.66}$$

In particular, if $n \geq 4$, show:

$$C(S) \leq 1 + n \log_2 \left(\frac{e|S|}{n} \right) \leq n \log_2 |S|. \qquad (6.67)$$

Use these results together with the sub-additivity of capacity to prove the upperbound in Theorem 6.4.

EXERCISE 6.5   Derive the gradient descent learning equations:
(1) for weights associated with connections that skip layers;
(2) for weights that are shared, within a layer or across several layers, including the case of a convolutional layer;
(3) for the hinges and slopes of APL (adaptive piecewise linear) transfer functions; and
(4) for the incoming weights of two deep neurons i and j, where neuron j gates the output of neuron i.

EXERCISE 6.6   Derive the gradient descent learning equations in matrix form for a linear $A(n, m, n)$ autoencoder, with matrices A ($n \times m$) and B ($m \times n$). Derive and solve the critical equations.

EXERCISE 6.7   Derive the gradient descent learning equations for a deep feedforward architecture $A(n_1, \ldots, n_L)$ where the output units are linear, and the error function for a single example is quartic, rather than quadratic, i.e. $\mathcal{E} = \sum (T_i - O_i^L)^4 / 4$, the sum being over all the units in the output layer. Repeat the exercise when all the output units are logistic and the error function is quadratic, and again if all the output units are logistic and the error function is quartic.

EXERCISE 6.8   Derive the gradient descent equations with respect to the individual input components. This can be used, for instance, to create adversarial examples, i.e. examples that resemble a training pattern but lead to an output that is significantly different from the target of that pattern.

EXERCISE 6.9   Derive the gradient descent equations in the case of batch normalization. Derive the gradient descent equations in the case of layer normalization.

EXERCISE 6.10   We have seen that the derivative of the sigmoidal logistic function $y = f(x)$ satisfies $f'(x) = f(x)(1 - f(x))$. Use this property to obtain a Taylor expansion of $f(x)$ around 0, as well as a Taylor expansion of the sigmoidal tanh function around 0. Derive also a polynomial approximation for a softmax function (with k classes) . Consider a feedforward neural network consisting of units with such sigmoidal activation functions. By truncating the Taylor series, show that the network can be approximated by a polynomial map of suitable degree. Identify a suitable data set, train a corresponding neural network and its corresponding polynomial approximation, and compare the results in terms of training time and stability, training set performance, and test set performance.

EXERCISE 6.11   Construct a differentiable function f from $\mathbb{R}^n$ to R with multiple spurious local minima. Examine both the strict and non-strict cases (x_0 is a strict spurious local minimum if and only if x_0 is a spurious local minimum and there is an open neighborhood of x_0 such that $f(x_0) < f(x)$ in that neighborhood).

EXERCISE 6.12   Derive two or more algorithms for computing the diagonal of the Hessian, i.e. the tensor of second-order derivatives $\partial^2 \mathcal{E}/\partial(w^h_{ij})^2$ and estimate and compare their computational complexities.

EXERCISE 6.13   Derive two or more algorithms for computing the Hessian, i.e. the tensor of second-order derivatives $\partial^2 \mathcal{E}/\partial w^g_{ij} \partial w^h_{kl}$ and estimate and compare their computational complexities.

EXERCISE 6.14 (SADDLE POINTS)   Consider a saddle point s of the training error function $\mathcal{E}(w)$. Show that without any loss of generality, we can assume that $s = 0$ and that, around $s = 0$, $\mathcal{E}$ can be written as: $\mathcal{E}(w) = \sum_{i \in P} \lambda_i w_i^2 + \sum_{i \in N} \lambda_i w_i^2$, where P (resp. N) represents the indices associated with positive (resp. negative) eigenvalues of the Hessian. Imagine using SGD (stochastic gradient descent), starting from a point ϵ very close to s, using a fixed and small learning rate η. Show that SGD can be decomposed into independent random walks along each axis and compute the expected time required to exit the saddle point as a function of ϵ, η and the eigenvalues λ_i.

EXERCISE 6.15   The question of finding good learning algorithms for feedforward networks of linear threshold gates has not been studied systematically. Through simulations, explore the following three possible algorithms.
(1) Train the same architecture using sigmoidal transfer functions (possibly with a fixed steep slope), and then replace the sigmoidal transfer functions with linear threshold gates, keeping the exact same weights.
(2) Train the same architecture using sigmoidal transfer functions, but progressively increase the slope of the sigmoidal functions according to some schedule to be determined, and then replace the sigmoidal transfer functions with linear threshold gates, as above.
(3) Use the backpropagation algorithm, as above, to produce a deep target for each deep linear threshold gate, and then apply the perceptron learning algorithm to adjust its weights.
    Can you think of better alternatives?

EXERCISE 6.16   Consider a linear, feedforward, fully-connected architecture $A(n_1, \ldots, n_L)$ with, to simplify things, $n_1 = \cdots = n_L = n$. Assume that all the weights are initialized independently using a Gaussian with mean 0 and variance σ^2. Assume that the n inputs are also independent Gaussian variables with mean 0 and variance s^2. Estimate the expectation and variance of the activation S^h_i of any unit i in any layer h. Estimate the covariance between the activations S^h_i and S^l_j of any two units in the network. Extend the analysis as much as possible to the cases where the transfer functions of the neurons are: (1) sigmoidal tanh; and (2) ReLU.

EXERCISE 6.17   Study through mathematical analysis or simulations the following alternative ways of learning the weights of a neural network:
(1) gradient descent using the definition of derivatives to compute the gradient;

(2) random descent using randomly generated directions (if the random direction r locally points uphill, then $-r$ locally points downhill);

(3) optimized random direction descent (choose k random directions and use the best (steepest) one);

(4) Hessian-based methods; and

(5) simulated annealing.

Come up with at least one other algorithm for optimizing the weights. In each case, estimate the computational complexity of the algorithm and compare the weight change to the gradient.

EXERCISE 6.18   After training a network, you observe that its performance on the test set is *better* than on the training set. What are some of the possible explanations?

EXERCISE 6.19 (BIAS–VARIANCE ANALYSIS)   Extend the bias–variance decomposition analysis to the following cases:

(1) The target function is of the form $f(x) = y + \epsilon$ where ϵ is a noise term with mean zero and variance σ^2.

(2) The classification case where the classifiers produce class membership probabilities and the error function is the KL divergence.

(3) The classification case where the classifiers produce 0–1 classifications with the 0–1 loss function which, for each example, takes value 0 if the example is classified correctly, and the value 1 if the classifier is classified incorrectly

EXERCISE 6.20 (ENSEMBLES)   Prove that for any convex error function, the error of the expectation, weighted geometric mean, and normalized weighted geometric mean of an ensemble of predictors is always less than the expected error.

EXERCISE 6.21 (DROPOUT)   Consider the class C of functions f defined on the real line with range in $[0, 1]$ and satisfying

$$\frac{G}{G + G'}(f) = f(E) \tag{6.68}$$

for any distribution $p(x)$ with finite support over $[0, 1]$. Here the left hand side represents the weighted normalized geometric mean of f, and the right hand side represents the image under f of the expectation under p. Prove that for any set of points and any distribution, C consists exactly of the union of all constant functions $f(x) = K$ with $0 \le K \le 1$ and all logistic functions $f(x) = 1/(1 + ce^{-\lambda x})$. As a reminder, G denotes the geometric mean and G' denotes the geometric mean of the complements. Also note that all the constant functions with $f(x) = K$ with $0 \le K \le 1$ can also be viewed as logistic functions by taking $\lambda = 0$ and $c = (1 - K)/K$ ($K = 0$ is a limiting case corresponding to $c \to \infty$).

EXERCISE 6.22 (INFORMATION PLANE)   Consider a multilayer, feedforward architecture $A(n_1, \ldots, n_L)$ and a training set of input–output target pairs of the form (I, T). Let O^i represent the vector of outputs of layer i. The information plane is used to represent the output of each layer by a point in a plane with two coordinates corresponding to its mutual information with the input data $I(I, O^i)$ and the target data $I(T, O^i)$. During training, each hidden layer produces a corresponding trajectory in the information plane. After training such an architecture on some data (e.g. MNIST, CIFAR) explain how to compute the mutual information coordinates and plot the trajectories of each hidden layer in the information plane.

EXERCISE 6.23 (VC DIMENSION)   Let A be a set of functions from a set S to $\{0, 1\}$. The VC dimension of A, written VC(A), is the size of the largest subset $V \in S$ that can be shattered using functions in A, i.e. such that any possible assignments of zeros and ones over V is realized by at least one function in A.
(1) Estimate the VC dimension of linear threshold functions over $S = H^n = \{0, 1\}^n$.
(2) Prove by induction the Sauer–Shelah lemma:

LEMMA 6.7 (SAUER–SHELAH)   *Let A be a set of functions from a set S to $\{0, 1\}$. Then:*

$$2^{VC(A)} \leq |A| \leq \binom{|S|}{\leq VC(A)}. \tag{6.69}$$

EXERCISE 6.24 (VC DIMENSION)   Consider an architecture $A(n_1, \ldots, n_L)$ with a number of parameters $W \approx n_1 n_2 + \cdots n_{L-1} n_L$.
(1) If the transfer functions are linear threshold functions, prove that: $VC(A) = O(W \log W)$.
(2) If the transfer functions are ReLu functions, prove that: $VC(A) = O(LW \log W)$.

EXERCISE 6.25   Let $A(n_1, \ldots, n_L = 1)$ denote a feedforward architecture of linear threshold gates with n_1 binary inputs and a single output node (classification). We have seen in Equation 6.9 that $TC(A) \leq VC(A) \leq C(A)$. When a set of size m can be shattered by A it is tempting to state that the corresponding $m(n_1 + 1)$ bits are stored in A, and therefore to infer that the capacity $C(A)$ is either greater than $m(n_1 + 1)$, or equal to $m(n_1 + 1)$ (depending on whether $m = TC(A)$ or $m = VC(A)$). Examine this argument carefully and explain why it is not correct.

EXERCISE 6.26 (GROWTH FUNCTION)   The *growth function* is a measure of the richness of a family of sets, including a family of functions or hypotheses. It can be viewed as a refinement of the notion of VC dimension. Let $\mathcal{F}$ be a family of sets, and C be a set. The intersection family $\mathcal{F}_C$ is the family of the corresponding intersection sets: $\mathcal{F}_C = \{f \cap C : f \in \mathcal{F}\}$. The index (or intersection size) of $\mathcal{F}$ with respect to C is: $I_C(\mathcal{F}) = |\mathcal{F}_C|$. Show that if $|C| = m$, then $I_C(\mathcal{F}) \leq 2^m$. If $I_C(\mathcal{F}) = 2^m$ then C is shattered by $\mathcal{F}$. The growth function G measures $|\mathcal{F}_C|$ as a function of $|C|$. More precisely:

$$G(\mathcal{F}, m) \doteq \max_{C:|C|=m} |\mathcal{F}_C|. \tag{6.70}$$

We can apply this notion to sets of Boolean or other functions. That is, let $\mathcal{F}$ be a set of functions from a set S to a set R (e.g. $S = \mathbb{R}^n$ or $S = \{0, 1\}^n$ and $R = 0, 1$). Let C be a subset of S with m elements $x_1, \ldots, x_m$. Then we can define the restriction of $\mathcal{F}$ to C to be the set of functions defined on C (i.e. from C to R) that can be derived from $\mathcal{F}$:

$$\mathcal{F}_C = \{f(x) : f \in F, x \in C\} = \{(f(x_1), \ldots, f(x_m)) : f \in F, x_i \in C\}. \tag{6.71}$$

The growth function measures the size of $\mathcal{F}_C$ as a function of $|C| = m$:

$$G(\mathcal{F}, m) = \max_{C:|C|=m} |\mathcal{F}_C|. \tag{6.72}$$

(1) Let $\mathcal{F}$ be the set of all possible closed intervals over $\mathbb{R}$. Let C be any finite subset of $\mathbb{R}$ of size m. Compute $G(\mathcal{F}, m)$.

(2) Assume that $S = \mathbb{R}^n$ and $R = 0, 1$ and $\mathcal{F}$ is the class of all linear threshold functions. Estimate $G(\mathcal{F}, m)$.

(3) What is the relationhip between the growth function and the cardinal capacity of a class of functions?

(4) Show that $VC(\mathcal{F}) \geq d$ if and only if $G(\mathcal{F}, d) = 2^d$.

(5) Show that if $VC(\mathcal{F}) = d$ then $G(\mathcal{F}, m) \leq \binom{m}{\leq d}$. Show that this upperbound is tight (see also the Sauer–Shelah lemma above).

(6) Show that the growth function is either exponential and $G(\mathcal{F}, m) = 2^m$ identically, or it is polynomial with $G(\mathcal{F}, m) \leq m^n + 1$, where n is the smallest integer for which: $G(\mathcal{F}, n) < 2^n$.

EXERCISE 6.27   Using the same setting as for the definition of the growth function G (Exercise 6.22), we can define another measure of complexity of the class $\mathcal{F}$ called the *entropy*. While the notion of growth function is related to the maximum intersection size, this notion of entropy is related to the average intersection size. The entropy H is defined by:

$$H(\mathcal{F}, m) = E_{C:|C|=m}[\log_2 |\mathcal{F}_C|]. \tag{6.73}$$

(1) Show that $H(\mathcal{F}, m_1 + m_2) \leq H(\mathcal{F}, m_1) + H(\mathcal{F}, m_2)$.

(2) Show that the sequence: $H(\mathcal{F}, m)/m$ converges to a constant $c \in [0, 1]$ when $m \to \infty$.

EXERCISE 6.28   Compile and organize a list, as comprehensive as possible, of all possible ways different neural network modules can be combined and trained (e.g. sequential, parallel, ensemble, Siamese, autoencoder, cooperative, adversarial).

EXERCISE 6.29 (GENERATIVE MODELS)

(1) One of the reason the averaging approach to generating new data does not work is that in high dimensions points have a tendency to be equidistant. To see this, consider generating random points $d = (x_1, \ldots, x_n)$ where the components x_i are independent, identically distributed, normal $N(0, \sigma^2)$. Compute the expectation and the standard deviation of the distance between any two points.

(2) Select a data set and build deep VAE, GAN, ARM, and flow generative models of the data. Explore the effect of how the components are ordered in the ARM. Propose an algorithm for selecting the ordering.

7   The Local Learning Principle

Chapters 7 and 8 leverage the principle of local learning [102] and use it to answer several fundamental questions, including:

(1) What is the relationship between Hebbian learning and backpropagaton, in particular is backpropagation "Hebbian"?
(2) What is the space of learning rules?
(3) Why has no one been able to carry out the Fukushima program of training convolutional neural networks using Hebbian learning?
(4) Why is backpropagation challenging to implement in a physical system, and what are some possible alternatives?

7.1   Virtualization and Learning in the Machine

Although straightforward, the principle of local learning has remained somewhat hidden because of the ambiguity of Hebb's original formulation and because of virtualization issues. Virtualization is a fundamental concept in computer science which refers to the use of a computational machine or process to simulate another computational machine or process. Modern computing centers are full of virtual machines and, for instance, UNIX interfaces can be simulated on Windows machines and vice versa. However, the concept of virtualization goes back to the foundations of computer science, since the very concept of a computer relies on mapping computations or algorithms, such as adding two binary integers, from a Platonic world of mathematical abstractions to the state-space dynamics of a physical system. Moreover, in the theory of Turing machines, one first develops special-purpose Turing machines dedicated to solving specific tasks, such as detecting whether a binary input represents an even or odd integer, or adding two binary inputs. This is followed by the realization that all such special-purpose Turing machines, or programs, can be simulated – or virtualized – on a single, general-purpose Turing machine, the so-called universal Turing machine. In addition, virtualization is in essence also what one uses to prove NP-completeness results by polynomially mapping one NP decision problem onto another NP decision problem. For instance, in Chapter 5, we showed that clustering on a 2D lattice with respect to the Manhattan distance can be "virtualized" to clustering on the hypercube with respect to the Hamming distance. Finally, one may suspect that several different forms of virtualization may be present in the brain. For instance, what is empathy if not the ability to virtualize the feelings of others, and feel the pain of others as if it were your own? This ability alone may have played a fundamental role in the evolution of not only morality, but also intelligence by enabling the transition from cold-blooded to warm-blooded animals that require far more food, hence far longer periods of learning, hence far longer periods of parental care [196].

But why is virtualization relevant to neural networks and deep learning? The reason is simple. Every time you run a neural network on a standard digital computer, you are in fact running a virtual neural network, i.e. a fantasy of neurons and synapses stored in digital, Turing-tape-style, format. While virtualizations are useful, they can also lead to misleading illusions if one starts to believe in them, as if they were the real thing. An obvious example is the typical desktop interface which gives us the illusion of the existence of folders, of moving files to folders, and so forth. And these illusions can sometimes become hard to detect (see, for instance, Donald Hoffman's analogy between our perceptual systems and the Windows desktop interface in light of evolution [350]).

In the case of neural networks, the virtualization aspect is routinely forgotten; but recognizing it is going to enable us to answer the key questions mentioned above. To recognize it, you must use your imagination and do like Einstein who imagined how the world would look like if he were a ray of light. In the case of neural networks, this is what can be called "learning in the machine", as opposed to machine learning, i.e. trying to imagine how things work in a native, physical, neural system, as opposed to a simulated one. You must imagine how the world would look like if you were a neuron or, even better, a synapse.

7.2   The Neuronal View

Putting oneself in the shoes of a neuron reveals, for instance, why the CONNECTED problem[1] seen in Chapter 3 is much harder than what it appears to be on the surface. At first sight, the problem seems easy, or at least much easier than the PARITY problem, as we humans can solve it effortlessly using our visual system. But the point is precisely that a neuron does not have a visual system, just a set of incoming connections and signals that can be permuted. Thus, to solve the problem, a neuron would have to learn the particular permutation associated with the ordering of the vector components, a task that is too hard for a single neuron.

In the same vein, imagining that neurons have a high rate of failure could lead immediately to the dropout learning algorithm [698, 91] where, for each training example, neurons are randomly dropped from the training procedure. As a side note, in standard dropout, neurons are unrealistically assumed to function perfectly at production time.

Another example of learning-in-the-machine thinking applied at the neuronal level leads one to think about patterns of connectivity between neuronal layers that are local, as opposed to full, as well as receptive fields that are not perfectly rectangular and perfectly

---

[1] Given a binary input vector, determine whether the 0s are all adjacent to each other (with or without wrap around).

arranged on a square lattice, as is routinely done in convolutional neural networks and computer vision applications.

In fact, the whole notion of exact weight sharing at the center of convolutional architectures may not be realistic for certain machines, including the brain. Thus one may want to consider convolutional architectures with a relaxed form of weight sharing, where neurons may have similar, but not identical, receptive fields, and similar, but not identical, connections at the beginning of learning [557]. An argument can be made that as long as the system is presented with video data, i.e. essentially with images of identical objects translated at different positions, then the approximate weight sharing should be preserved throughout learning by stochastic gradient descent. Indeed the corresponding connections of two neurons located in the same array would be receiving similar initialization at the beginning of learning, up to small random noise, and evolve along parallel paths during learning as the corresponding neurons would see roughly the same stimuli and the same backpropagated errors at almost the same times.

These are examples of insights that can be gained from thinking about the physical neuronal level. However, for the purpose of understanding learning and answering the questions posed at the beginning of this chapter, it is even more productive to imagine the world from the point of view of a physical synapse, which yields the local learning principle.

7.3 The Synaptic View: the Local Learning Principle

As we have seen in the Introduction, if we resize a synapse by a factor of 10^6, it becomes the size of a fist. And if the synapse is in Los Angeles, the tennis racket it must learn to control is in San Francisco. This highlights the fundamental problem of deep learning and leads to the local learning principle.

Local Learning Principle
In a physical neural system, the learning rule of a synapse can only depend on quantities available locally at the synapse, in both space and time.

The local learning principle can easily be stated in layman terms and may seem obvious, but it has significant technical consequences. A simple analogy, with all the necessary caveats to keep things in proportion, is the relativity principle, originally introduced by Galilei, which states that the laws of physics are the same in all frames of reference. Again this statement is simple and understandable by a layman. However, when applied to inertial frames together with the invariance of the speed of light in vacuum, it leads immediately to the Lorentz transformation and special relativity. When applied to non-inertial frames, allowing for rotations and accelerations, it leads to general relativity.

To study the consequences of this principle, in this chapter, we focus primarily on locality in space (see Appendix in [66]). Locality in time is briefly discussed in Chapters 8 and 9. However, it should be obvious that even for the backpropagation algorithm, issues of what is local in time come up immediately: for instance, the backward pass must remember the derivatives associated with the outputs of each layer during the forward pass. More broadly, for a deep weight w_{ij}^h the presynaptic output O_j^{h-1} and the postsynaptic backpropagated error B_i^h must be close in time, where the definition of closeness depends on the kind of physical neural system.

To begin with, it is worth asking which known learning rules are local in space. The space of learning rules found in the literature is rather sparse. In fact most familiar rules, including for instance the perceptron learning rule [618], the delta learning rule [786], and Oja's rule [550], can be viewed as special cases of, or variations on, backpropagation or simple Hebbian learning (Table 7.1).

Learning Rule	Expression
Simple Hebb	$\Delta w_{ij} \propto O_i O_j$
Oja	$\Delta w_{ij} \propto O_i O_j - O_i^2 w_{ij}$
Perceptron	$\Delta w_{ij} \propto (T - O_i) O_j$
Delta	$\Delta w_{ij} \propto (T - O_i) f'(S_i) O_j$
Backprogation	$\Delta w_{ij} \propto B_i O_j$

Table 7.1 Common learning rules and their on-line expressions. O_i represents the activity of the postsynaptic neuron, O_j the activity of the presynaptic neuron, and w_{ij} the synaptic strength of the corresponding connection. B_i represents the back-propagated error in the postsynaptic neuron. The perceptron and delta learning rules were originally defined for a single unit (or single layer), in which case T is the locally available output target.

To understand which rules are local, we must provide a precise definition of locality. In a model, one is of course free to decide which variables are local. Considering first locality in space, using the formalism of this book, it is reasonable to assume that the local variables of a deep synapse with strength w_{ij}^h are the pre-and post-synaptic outputs (or activations), as well as the synaptic strength itself. Thus typically, in the present formalism, a local learning rule for a deep layer of a feedforward architecture should have the functional form:

$$\Delta w_{ij}^h = F(O_i^h, O_j^{h-1}, w_{ij}^h), \tag{7.1}$$

where O_i^h and O_j^{h-1} represent the outputs of the post- and pre-synaptic neurons respectively. Assuming that the targets are local variables at the output layer, local learning rules for the output layer L must have the functional form:

$$\Delta w_{ij}^L = F(T_i, O_i^L, O_j^{L-1}, w_{ij}^L). \tag{7.2}$$

Under these definitions of spatial locality, we see that the simple Hebb rule, Oja's rule, the perceptron rule, and the Delta rule are local learning rules. It should also be obvious that in any $A(n, m)$ architecture with local learning, all the units learn independently of each other. However the backpropagation rule is *not local*.

This alone reveals one of the main reasons for the lack of clarity in Hebb's original formulation, with its implicit focus on the neuronal level ("neurons that fire together, wire together") rather than the synaptic level. Hebb implicitly combined two different concepts that ought to be clearly separated:

(1) the locality of synaptic learning rules; and
(2) the functional form of synaptic learning rules (e.g. quadratic form).

Among other things, separating these two concepts immediately suggests many possible different learning rules, and ways to stratify them by their complexity. It is, for instance, reasonable to consider learning rules that are polynomial in the local variables, and stratify these rules by their degree [66, 102].

7.4 Stratification of Learning Rules

Within the general assumption that $\Delta w_{ij} = F(O_i, O_j, w_{ij})$, or $\Delta w_{ij} = F(T_i, O_i, O_j, w_{ij})$ in the supervised case, one must next consider the functional form of F. Here we consider only the case where F is a polynomial function of degree n (e.g. linear, quadratic, cubic) in the local variables, although other functional forms can easily be considered within this framework. Indeed, most rules that are found in the neural network literature correspond to low-degree polynomial rules. Thus we consider functions F comprising a sum of terms of the form $\alpha O_i^{n_i} O_j^{n_j} w_{ij}^{n_{w_{ij}}}$ (or $\alpha T_i^{n_{T_i}} O_i^{n_i} O_j^{n_j} w_{ij}^{n_{w_{ij}}}$) where α is a real coefficient; n_{T_i}, n_i, n_j, and $n_{w_{ij}}$ are non-negative integers satisfying $n_{T_i} + n_i + n_j + n_{w_{ij}} \leq n$. In this term, the *apparent* degree of w is $n_{w_{ij}}$ but the *effective* degree d of w may be higher because O_i depends also on w_{ij}, typically in a linear way at least around the current value. In this case, the effective degree of w_{ij} in this term is $n_i + n_{w_{ij}}$. For instance, consider a rule of the form $\Delta w_{ij} = \eta w_{ij} O_i^2 I_j$, with a linear unit $O_i = \sum_k w_{ik} I_k$. The apparent degree of the rule in w_{ij} is 1, but the effective degree is 3. Finally, we let d ($d \leq n$) denote the highest effective degree of w, among all the terms in F. As we shall see, n and d are the two main numbers of interest used to stratify the polynomial learning rules.

As we have seen, one of the best ways to understand the behavior of learning rules is to convert them to difference, or differential, equations by taking averages over the training set and assuming the learning rate is small. Because we are restricting ourselves to learning rules with a polynomial form, the initial goal is thus to estimate expectations of the form $E(O_i^{n_i} O_j^{n_j} w_{ij}^{n_{w_{ij}}})$ in the unsupervised case, or $E(T_i^{n_{T_i}} O_i^{n_i} O_j^{n_j} w_{ij}^{n_{w_{ij}}})$ in the supervised case. Because of the time-scale assumption, within an epoch we can assume that w_{ij} is constant and therefore the corresponding term factors out of the expectation. Thus we are left with estimating terms of the form $E(O_i^{n_i} O_j^{n_j})$ in the unsupervised case, or $E(T_i^{n_{T_i}} O_i^{n_i} O_j^{n_j})$ in the supervised case. Estimation of these terms can be carried out, especially in the linear case [102] where, by averaging over the training set, one can derive a differential equation for the learning dynamics (see exercises).

In the linear case, to understand the behavior of any local learning rule, one must compute expectations over the training data of the form

$$E(T^{n_T} O^{n_O} I_i^{n_{I_i}} w_i^{n_i}) = w_i^{n_i} E\left[T^{n_T} (\sum_k w_k I_k)^{n_O} I_i^{n_{I_i}}\right]. \qquad (7.3)$$

This encompasses also the unsupervised case by letting $n_T = 0$. Thus this expectation is a polynomial in the weights, with coefficients that correspond to the statistical moments of the training data of the form $E(T^{n_T} I_i^{n_\alpha} I_k^{n_\beta})$. When this polynomial is linear in the weights ($d \leq 1$), the differential equation associated with the learning dynamics can be solved exactly using standard methods. When the effective degree is greater than 1 (i.e., $d > 1$), then the learning equation can be solved in some special cases, but not in the general case. Systematic examples can be found in the exercises at the end of this chapter and in [102].

So far, the principle of local learning has allowed us to precisely define and stratify the space of learning rules. The study of local learning rules in single units is interesting per se, and some rules may lead to useful statistical functions, such as PCA. However, this can only go so far, because the use of local learning rules in feedforward networks faces fundamental limitations.

7.5   Deep Local Learning and its Fundamental Limitations

Here we consider deep layered feedforward networks, where local learning is applied layer-by-layer, starting from the layer closest to the inputs (asynchronous local learning would not change much of the main conclusions). We call this form of learning, which stacks local learning rules in a deep architecture, deep local learning (Figure 7.1). As we saw in the introduction, deep local learning is what had been proposed for instance by Fukushima [288] to train the neocognitron architecture using Hebbian learning.

In principle such networks can be analyzed since they reduce to the study done above, and in the exercises, of local learning in single units. This is because within any single layer of units, all the units learn independently of each other given the inputs provided by the previous layer. Deep local learning may be able to perform simple statistical operations on the data (e.g. PCA) and learn simple functions. However, in deep local learning, information about the targets is not propagated to the deep layers and therefore in general deep local learning cannot learn complex functions.

To see this more precisely, consider deep local learning in a deep layered feedforward architecture (Figure 7.1) $A(n_0, n_1, \ldots, n_L)$ with $L + 1$ layers of size $n_0, n_1, \ldots n_L$ where here layer 0 is the input layer, and layer L is the output layer. We let O_i^h denote the activity of unit i in layer h with $O_i^h = f(S_i^h) = f(\sum_j w_{ij}^h O_j^{h-1})$. The non-linear transfer functions can be arbitrary, as long as they are continuous and differentiable (except possibly for a finite number of points of non-differentiability, e.g. ReLU transfer functions). It is also possible to extend the analysis to threshold functions by taking the limit of very steep differentiable sigmoidal functions. We consider the supervised learning framework with a training set of input–output vector pairs of the form $(I(k), T(k))$ for $k = 1, \ldots, K$

and the goal is to minimize a differentiable error function $\mathcal{E}(w)$. The main learning constraint is that we can only use local learning rules in each adaptive layer (Figure 7.1).

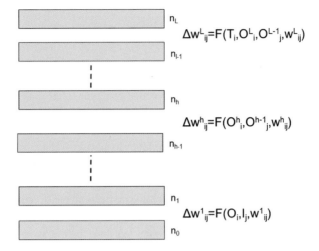

Figure 7.1 Deep Local Learning. In this case, local learning rules, such as the simple Hebb's rule, are applied to each synaptic weight in each adaptive layer of a deep feedforward architecture. For all the hidden units, the local learning rules are unsupervised and thus of the form: $\Delta w_{ij}^h = F(O_i^h, O_j^{h-1}, w_{ij}^h)$. For all the output units, the local learning rules can be supervised since the targets are considered to be local variables for the output layer, and thus can have the form: $\Delta w_{ij}^L = F(T, O_i^L, O_j^{L-1}, w_{ij}^L)$.

RESULT (FUNDAMENTAL LIMITATION OF DEEP LOCAL LEARNING)

Consider the supervised learning problem in a deep feedforward architecture with differentiable error function and transfer functions. Then, in most cases, deep local learning cannot find weights associated with critical points of the error function where the gradient is zero. Thus, in particular, it cannot find locally or globally optimal weights.

Proof If we consider any weight w_{ij}^h in a deep layer h (i.e. $0 < h < L$), by the backpropagation algorithm we know that:

$$\frac{\partial \mathcal{E}}{\partial w_{ij}^h} = E\left[B_i^h(t)O_j^{h-1}(t)\right] = \frac{1}{K}\sum_{k=1}^{K}B_i^h(k)O_j^{h-1}(k), \tag{7.4}$$

where $B_i^h(k)$ is the backpropagated error of unit i in layer h, which depends in particular on the targets $T(k)$ and the weights in the layers above layer h. Likewise, $O_j^{h-1}(k)$ is the presynaptic activity of unit j in layer $h - 1$ which depends on the inputs $I(k)$ and the weights in the layers below layer $h - 1$. In short, the gradient is a large sum over all training examples of product terms, each product term being the product of a target/output-dependent term with an input-dependent term. As a result, in most cases, the deep weights w_{ij}^h, which correspond to a critical point where $\partial E/\partial w_{ij}^h = 0$, must depend *on both the inputs and the targets*. In particular, this must be true at any local or global optimum, as well as any saddle point, including low-error saddle points. However, by using any strictly local learning scheme, all the deep weights w_{ij}^h ($h < L$) depend on the *inputs only*, and thus cannot correspond to such a critical point.

This shows that applying local Hebbian learning to a feedforward architecture, whether a simple autoencoder architecture or Fukushima's complex neocognitron architecture, cannot achieve optimal weights, regardless of which local learning rules, including all possible Hebbian rules, are used. For the same reasons, an architecture consisting of a stack of autoencoders trained using unlabeled data only [343, 257] cannot be optimal in general, even when the top layer is trained by gradient descent. It is of course possible to use local learning, shallow or deep autoencoders, Restricted Boltzmann Machines, and other related techniques to compress data, or to initialize the weights of a deep architecture. However, these steps alone cannot learn complex functions optimally because learning a complex function optimally necessitates the reverse propagation of information from the targets back to the deep layers. Even more importantly, although the limitation above is stated in terms of supervised learning, it applies immediately to any form of deep self-supervised learning for the same reasons. For instance, each autoencoder in a feedforward stack of autoencoders requires the transmission of self-supervised training data information to its hidden layers.

The fact above is correct at a level that would satisfy a physicist and is consistent with empirical evidence. It is not completely tight from a mathematical standpoint due to the phrase "in most cases". This expression is meant to exclude trivial cases where a majority of the weights may not depend on the targets. These cases are not important in practice, but they are not easy to capture exhaustively with mathematical precision. For example, they include the case when the training set is too small with respect to the architecture (e.g. $K = 1$). In this case, the training set can be loaded trivially into the architecture by using random weights in all the lower layers (so they are independent of the targets) and adjusting just the top layer.

Use of the local learning principle has allowed us to stratify the space of local learning rules. Then it has allowed us to provide an explanation for the Fukishima–Hebb problem and why local learning rules alone cannot do much in a feedforward architecture. Together with the relative optimality of backpropagation seen in Chapter 6, this also explains the sparsity of the space of learning rules as there is little incentive to search for new local earning rules, outside of biological or other hardware specific settings. Next, the local learning principle leads to the deep learning channel.

7.6   Local Deep Learning: the Deep Learning Channel

The fundamental limitation above has significant consequences. In particular, if a con-strained feedforward architecture is to be trained on a complex task in some optimal way, the deep weights of the architecture must depend on both the training inputs and the targets. Thus:

Deep Learning Channel(DLC)
In a physical feedforward neural system, in order to be able to reach a locally optimal configuration, where $\partial \mathcal{E} / \partial w_{ij}^h = 0$ for all the weights, there must exist a backward

physical channel that conveys information about the targets back to the deep synapses so that they can be updated using a local learning algorithm depending on this information. We call this channel the **Deep Learning Channel**.

The necessary existence of the DLC immediately leads to fundamental predictions for biology. First, if the learning frameworks discussed in this book have any relevance to biology, then the prediction is that there must exist backward channels, implemented as chains of neurons and axons, going from peripheral neurons where some notion of target may be available all the way back to almost every single deep neuron in the corresponding circuit. Second, one may think of the signal carried by the DLC as some form of "feedback". However, one must be careful to distinguish different kinds of feedback signals, such as dynamic and learning feedback. These different feedback signals may, or may not (or only partially), use the same physical connections. For instance, in the visual of sensory-motor systems one may consider fast dynamic feedback signals for vision or motor control. These feedback signals are different from the learning feedback signals in the DLC which may include fast electrical components, but also much slower bio-chemical components.

The corresponding DLC-based learning is called local deep learning (Figure 7.2), as opposed to deep local learning which simply stacks local learning rules (Figure 7.1). Backpropagation is a local deep learning algorithm but, as we shall see in Chapter 8, it is not the only one. In a physical neural system, deep local learning raises several questions regarding the DLC:

(1) What is the physical nature of the backward channel?
(2) What is the nature of the information being transmitted through the DLC?
(3) What is the rate at which this information can be transmitted and its maximum (the capacity of the DLC)?

The physical nature of the DLC depends on the physical nature of the neural system and, as such, it will not be our focus here. However it should at least be noted that there are a number of different possibilities, such as:

(1) the forward and backward channels use different kinds of physical channels (e.g. electrical in one direction and optical in the other one);
(2) the forward and backward channels use exactly the same physical channel (e.g. wires), but this channel is bidirectional and, at least for backpropagation, it is also symmetric with the same weights in both directions;
(3) the forward and backward channels are similar, but physically separate (e.g. different wires) and symmetric, i.e. with the same weights in both directions, as in backpropagation; and
(4) the forward and backward channels are similar, but physically separate (e.g. different wires) and non-symmetric, i.e. with different weights in both directions.

For biological neural systems, the last case seems the most plausible, as it is hard to imagine having connections with exactly the same synaptic weights in both directions. Finally, although we call it the DLC, in principle there could be on the order of $W \times n_L$ different DLCs, one for each synapse and each output component. In general this is not efficient and some form of multiplexing is preferable and possible, as exemplified by

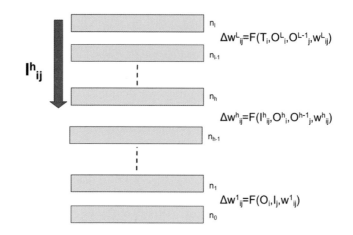

$$\mathsf{I}^h_{ij}$$

$\Delta w^L_{ij}=F(T_i,O^L_i,O^{L-1}_j,w^L_{ij})$

$\Delta w^h_{ij}=F(I^h_{ij},O^h_i,O^{h-1}_j,w^h_{ij})$

$\Delta w^1_{ij}=F(O_i,I_j,w^1_{ij})$

Figure 7.2 Local Deep Learning. In general, deep local learning in a deep feedforward architecture cannot learn complex functions optimally since it leads to architectures where only the weights in the top layer depend on the targets. For optimal learning, some information I^h_{ij} about the targets must be transmitted to each corresponding synapse, so that it becomes a local variable that can be incorporated into the corresponding local learning rule $\Delta w^h_{ij} = F(I^h_{ij}, O^h_i, O^{h-1}_j, w^h_{ij})$.

the backpropagation algorithm. Backpropagation also shows that it can be enough to backpropagate the error signal to the postsynaptic neuron, rather than each one of its impinging synapses. This alone provides a huge saving as it avoids having a separate DLC wire for each synapse, keeping in mind that synapses are more abundant than neurons by several orders of magnitude (about 4 orders of magnitude for the brain).

Next we turn to the question of the nature of the information that must be transmitted through the DLC. This question will also occupy most of Chapter 8. In particular, we are interested in identifying which information is absolutely necessary, and which is not. Let us denote by I^h_{ij} the information that needs to be transmitted by the DLC to the synapse w^h_{ij} in order to enable any effective local deep learning of the form (Figure 7.2):

$$\Delta w^h_{ij} = F(I^h_{ij}, O^h_i, O^{h-1}_j, w^h_{ij}). \tag{7.5}$$

The upper and lower indexes on I distinguish it clearly from the inputs associated with the input layer. From Equation 7.4, we know that in principle at a critical point I^h_{ij} could depend on the inputs, the outputs, the targets, and all the weights of the entire architecture. However, backpropagation shows that this can be simplified in two ways: (1) all the necessary information about the lower layers of the architecture and its weights is contained in O^{h-1}_j; and (2) the information carried by the DLC can be written as:

$$I^h_{ij} = I^h_i(T, O^L, w^l_{rs}(l > h), f'(l \geq h)). \tag{7.6}$$

In other words, rather than having to send a signal through the DLC to each individual synapse impinging onto neuron i in layer h, it is possible to multiplex the signals and, in particular, send a single error signal to neuron i. Neuron i can then broadcast it to all its impinging synapses. This broadcasting operation will not concern us here: it is essentially invisible when we think about the backpropagation algorithm; however, in a biological neuron it requires a major undertaking. In addition, backpropagation, shows that one additional level of simplification is possible: the dependence on both T and O^L can be mediated by the single error term $T - O^L = -\partial \mathcal{E}/\partial S^L$. Therefore:

$$I_{ij}^h = I_i^h (T - O^L, w_{rs}^l (l > h), f'(l \geq h)), \tag{7.7}$$

under the usual assumptions on the error function and the transfer functions for the top layer. Additional simplifications of I_{ij}^h will be examined in Chapter 8.

7.7 Local Deep Learning and Deep Targets Equivalence

Since I_{ij}^h need not depend directly on j, we can define the corresponding class of local deep learning algorithms and show a basic equivalence between having post-synaptic backpropagated errors and deep targets that are local.

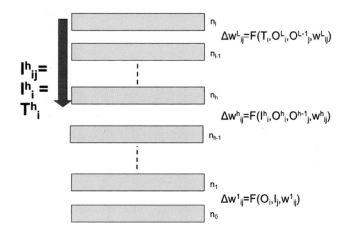

Figure 7.3 Deep Targets Learning. This is a special case of local deep learning, where the transmitted information I_{ij}^h about the targets does not depend on the presynaptic unit $I_{ij}^h = I_i^h$. In this chapter, it is shown that this is equivalent to providing a deep target T_i^h for training the corresponding unit by a local supervised rule of the form $\Delta w_{ij}^h = F(T_i^h, O_i^h, O_j^{h-1}, w_{ij}^h)$. In typical cases (linear, threshold, or sigmoidal units), this rule is $\Delta w_{ij}^h = \eta (T_i^h - O_i^h) O_j^{h-1}$.

DEFINITION 7.1   Within the class of local deep learning algorithms, we define the subclass of deep targets local learning algorithms as those for which the information I_{ij}^h transmitted about the targets depends only on the postsynaptic unit: in other words $I_{ij}^h = I_i^h$. Thus in a deep targets learning algorithm we have

$$\Delta w_{ij}^h = F(I_i^h, O_i^h, O_j^{h-1}, w_{ij}^h), \tag{7.8}$$

for some function F (Figure 7.3).

We have also seen that when proper targets are available, there are efficient local learning rules for adapting the weights of a unit. In particular, the rule $\Delta w = \eta(T - O)I$ works well in practice for both sigmoidal and threshold transfer functions. Thus the deep learning problem can in principle be solved by providing good targets for the deep layers. We can introduce a second definition of deep targets algorithms:

DEFINITION 7.2   A learning algorithm is a deep targets learning algorithm if it provides targets for all the trainable units.

THEOREM 7.3   *Definition 7.1 is equivalent to Definition 7.2. Furthermore, backpropagation can be viewed as a deep targets algorithm.*

Proof Starting from Definition 7.2, if some target T_i^h is available for unit i in layer h, then we can set $I_i^h = T_i^h$ in Definition 7.1. Conversely, starting from Definition 7.1, consider a deep targets algorithm of the form

$$\Delta w_{ij}^h = F(I_i^h, O_i^h, O_j^{h-1}, w_{ij}^h). \tag{7.9}$$

If we had a corresponding target T_i^h for this unit, it would be able to learn by gradient descent in the form

$$\Delta w_{ij}^h = \eta(T_i^h - O_j^h)O_j^{h-1}. \tag{7.10}$$

This is true both for sigmoidal transfer functions and for threshold gates, otherwise the rule should be modified to accommodate other transfer functions accordingly. By combining Equations 7.9 and 7.10, we can solve for the target

$$T_i^h = \frac{F(I_i^h, O_i^h, O_j^{h-1}, w_{ij}^h)}{\eta O_j^{h-1}} + O_i^h, \tag{7.11}$$

assuming the presynaptic activity $O_j^{h-1} \neq 0$ (note that $T^L = T$) (Figure 7.3). As seen in Chapter 6, as a special case, backpropagation can be viewed as a deep targets algorithm providing targets for the hidden layers according to Equation 7.11 in the form:

$$T_i^h = I_i^h + O_i^h, \tag{7.12}$$

where $I_i^h = B_i^h = -\partial \mathcal{E}/\partial S_i^h$ is the backpropagated error.   □

In summary, we started this chapter by introducing the notion of local learning, noticing that Hebbian learning is a special case of local learning. This notion allows us to get a clear view of the space of learning rules, and its stratification by complexity. Backpropagation is not a local learning rule, and therefore it is not Hebbian in this simple sense. By stacking local learning rules in a feedforward architecture, one obtains deep local learning. Deep local learning however is unable to learn complex functions. In order to learn complex functions, local deep learning is necessary. Local deep learning requires sending information about the targets back to the deep synapses through a channel, called the DLC. With the introduction of a DLC, backpropagation is a deep local learning algorithm, and in that sense the resulting learning rule is local. In Chapter 8, we take a closer look at the information that must be sent over the DLC and at alternative local deep learning algorithms that do not require symmetric weights in the forward and backward directions.

7.8 Exercises

EXERCISE 7.1 Compile a list, as exhaustive as possible, of examples of the concept of virtualization.

EXERCISE 7.2 Suppose you have two Windows computers A and B connected to the Internet. You can run the Windows Remote Desktop application on computer B to view the computer screen of A, as if you were sitting in front of computer A. Which command(s) should you type on computer B in order to execute the command 'Ctrl-Alt-Del" on computer A?

EXERCISE 7.3 (1) List all possible terms of degree $d = 1$ of a local polynomial learning rule, in both the supervised and unsupervised cases.
(2) Compute their expectations.
(3) Solve the corresponding differential equations in the linear case.
(4) Study non-linear cases, analytically whenever possible, or through simulations.

EXERCISE 7.4 (1) List all possible terms of degree $d = 2$ of a local polynomial learning rule, in both the supervised and unsupervised cases.
(2) Compute their expectations.
(3) Solve the corresponding differential equations in the linear case.
(4) Study non-linear cases, analytically whenever possible, or through simulations.

EXERCISE 7.5 (1) List all possible terms of degree $d = 3$ of a local polynomial learning rule, in both the supervised and unsupervised cases.
(2) Compute their expectations.
(3) Solve the corresponding differential equations in the linear case.
(4) Study non-linear cases, analytically whenever possible, or through simulations.

EXERCISE 7.6 Learning rules often lead to synaptic weights that diverge over time to infinity. Find at least two different ways for creating polynomial learning rules of arbitrary degree that will keep the synaptic weights bounded.

EXERCISE 7.7 Study the simple Hebbian learning rule $\Delta w_i = \eta O I_i$ with $n = 2$ and $d = 1$ analytically, or by simulations, in both linear and non-linear (threshold gate, sigmoidal, ReLU) neurons. Study the supervised version of the rule when O is replaced by T.

EXERCISE 7.8 Study the simple anti-Hebbian learning rule $\Delta w_i = -\eta O I_i$ with $n = 2$ and $d = 1$ analytically, or by simulations, in both linear and non-linear (threshold gate, sigmoidal, ReLU) neurons. Study the supervised version of the rule when O is replaced by T.

EXERCISE 7.9   Study the learning rule $\Delta w_i = \eta(1 - w_i^2)I_i$ with $n = 3$ and $d = 2$ analytically, or by simulations, in both linear and non-linear (threshold gate, sigmoidal, ReLU) neurons.

EXERCISE 7.10   Study the gradient descent learning rule $\Delta w_i = \eta(T - O)I_i$ with $n = 2$ and $d = 1$ analytically, or by simulations, in both linear and non-linear (threshold gate, sigmoidal, ReLU) neurons.

EXERCISE 7.11   Study Oja's learning rule $\Delta w_i = \eta(OI_i - O^2 w_i)$ with $n = 3$ and $d = 3$ analytically, or by simulations, in both linear and non-linear (threshold gate, sigmoidal, ReLU) neurons.

EXERCISE 7.12   Could batch or layer normalization be easily implemented in a physical neural system?

EXERCISE 7.13   If the DLC theory can be applied to biological neural systems, what is its main prediction? Can you state the prediction in terms of the analogy made in the Introduction where, by rescaling lengths by a factor of one million, a synapse is the size of a fist? Does such a prediction violate any known facts about the anatomy of the brain? Which assumptions in the DLC theory are most questionable in relation to biology?

EXERCISE 7.14   (1) Recall the analogy made in the Introduction where, by rescaling lengths by a factor of one million, a synapse is the size of a fist. In this rescaling, what would correspond to a neuron? Use this to provide a corresponding analogy for deep learning algorithms, where $I_{ij}^h = I_i^h$, for instance by equating the function of the DLC to mail delivery.

(2) Likewise, what would correspond to an entire brain under this rescaling of a factor of 10^6. Assuming there are on the order of 10^{14} synapses in the brain, explain the fundamental role of the locality principle within this rescaled model.

EXERCISE 7.15   Consider a multilayer, feedforward architectures $A(n_1, \ldots, n_L)$ and a training set of input–output target pairs of the form (I, T). Consider two learning rules: backpropagation (local deep learning) and the simple Hebb rule (deep local learning). Using a standard training set (e.g. MNIST or CIFAR) plot in each case the trajectories of the hidden layers in the information plane. What are the main differences?

8   The Deep Learning Channel

In this chapter, we continue to study the local learning principle and the nature of the information I_i^h that must be sent over the DLC. At the same time, we tackle the problem that backpropagation requires perfectly symmetric weights in the forward and backward pass, something that is very easy to implement in digitally simulated neural networks, but very hard to implement in biological and other physical neural networks. This question is part of a broader set of concerns regarding backpropagation in relation to learning in the machine, and in particular to learning in biological networks. These include:

(1) the nature of supervised learning and whether it is a reasonable approximation to some form of biological learning;
(2) the continuous real-valued nature of the gradient information and its ability to change sign, violating Dale's Law;
(3) the need for some kind of teacher's signal to provide targets;
(4) the need for implementing all the linear operations involved in backpropagation;
(5) the need for multiplying the backpropagated signal by the derivatives of the forward activations each time a layer is traversed;
(6) the timing and orchestration of alternating forward and backward passes; and
(7) the complex geometry of biological neurons and the problem of transmitting error signals with precision down to individual synapses.

However, perhaps the most formidable obstacle is that the standard backpropagation algorithm requires propagating error signals backwards using synaptic weights that are *identical* to the corresponding forward weights. Furthermore, a related problem that has not been sufficiently recognized is that this weight symmetry must be maintained at most times during learning, and not just during early neural development. It is hard to imagine mechanisms by which biological neurons could both create and maintain such perfect symmetry.

To address the problem of symmetric weights, as well as the nature of I^h, recall that the backpropagation learning equations in vector form can be written as:

$$\Delta W_h = \eta \left(D_h W_{h+1}^{\mathrm{T}} \cdots D_{L-1} W_L^{\mathrm{T}} (T - O) \right) (O^{h-1})^{\mathrm{T}} = \eta B^h (O^{h-1})^{\mathrm{T}}. \qquad (8.1)$$

The backpropagated error vector is obtained by a series of matrix multiplications. In this series, the matrices W^{T} are the transposes of the forward matrices, and these matrices are fixed, or changing slowly, during one epoch. By contrast, the diagonal matrices D_h, corresponding to the derivatives of the forward activities, are changing somewhat erratically on a rapid time scale, i.e. with each training example. This observation leads one to consider an idea that may seem far-fetched at first sight: what about using random matrices in the backward pass [449]? This would certainly get rid of the problem of requiring the weights in the DLC to be exactly equal to the corresponding weights in the forward direction.

8.1   Random Backpropagation (RBP) and its Variations

A remarkable result is that the symmetry of the weights may not be required after all, and that in fact backpropagation works more or less as well when *random* weights are used to backpropagate the errors. Thus, our next goal is to investigate backpropagation with random weights and to better understand why it works [449, 84, 85].

Standard random backpropagation operates exactly like backpropagation except that the weights used in the backward pass are completely random and fixed. Thus, the learning rule becomes:

$$\Delta w_{ij}^h = \eta R_i^h O_j^{h-1}, \tag{8.2}$$

where the randomly backpropagated error satisfies the recurrence relation:

$$R_i^h = (f_i^h)' \sum_k R_k^{h+1} c_{ki}^{h+1}, \tag{8.3}$$

and the weights c_{ki}^{h+1} are random and fixed. The boundary condition at the top remains the same:

$$R_i^L = \frac{\partial \mathcal{E}_i}{\partial S_i^L} = T_i - O_i^L, \tag{8.4}$$

with the usual correspondence between error functions and transfer functions for the output layer. Thus, in random backpropagation (RBP), the weights in the top layer of the architecture are updated by gradient descent, identically to the backpropagation (BP) case. Random backpropagation shows that the information that needs to be sent to the deep layer does not need to depend explicitly on the weights in the upper layers, namely that one can write:

$$I_{ij}^h = I_i^h(T - O^L, w_{rs}^l(l > h), f'(l \geq h)) = I = I_i^h(T - O^L, f'(l \geq h)). \tag{8.5}$$

8.1.1   Variations

There are many variations on the basic idea of random backpropagation. We are going to focus on algorithms where the information required for the deep weight updates $I_i^h(T - O^L, f'(S_r^l))$ for $l \geq h$) is produced essentially through a *linear* process whereby the vector $T - O$, computed in the output layer, is processed through linear operations, i.e. additions and multiplications by constants, which can include multiplication by the derivatives of the forward activation functions. We are interested in the case where the propagation matrices are random. Even within this restricted setting, there are several possibilities, depending for instance on:

(1) whether the information is progressively propagated through the layers (as in the case of BP), or broadcasted directly to the deep layers by skipping intermediary layers;

(2) whether multiplication by the derivatives of the forward activation functions is included or not; and

(3) the properties of the random matrices in the learning channel (e.g. sparse vs. dense, Gaussian vs. binary vs. other models of randomness).

This leads to several possible algorithms:

- BP= (standard) backpropagation.
- RBP= random backpropagation, where the transpose of the feedforward matrices are replaced by random matrices.
- SRBP = skipped random backpropagation, where the backpropagated signal arriving onto layer h is given by $C^h(T - O)$ with a random matrix C^h directly connecting the output layer L to layer h, and this for each layer h.
- SBP = skipped backpropagation where the skip matrix associated with a deep DLC layer is given by the product of the transposes of the corresponding feedforward matrices, ignoring multiplication by the derivative of the forward transfer functions in all the layers above the layer under consideration. Multiplication by the derivative of the current layer can be included or excluded.
- ARBP = adaptive random backpropagation, where the matrices in the learning channel are initialized randomly, and then progressively adapted during learning using, for instance, the product of the corresponding forward and backward signals, so that $\Delta c_{rs}^l = \eta R_s^{l+1} O_r^l$, where R denotes the randomly backpropagated error. In this case, the forward channel becomes the deep learning channel for the backward weights. More broadly, the general idea here is to use the same kind of "hardware", or algorithms, in both the forward and backward channels, without making one channel special relative to the other.
- ASRBP = adaptive skipped random backpropagation, which combines adaptation with skipped random backpropagation.
- The default for each algorithm involves the multiplication at each layer by the derivative of the forward activation functions. The variants where this multiplication is omitted will be denoted by: "(no-f')".
- The default for each algorithm involves dense random matrices, generated for instance by sampling from a normalized Gaussian for each weight. But one can consider also the case of random ± 1 (or $(0,1)$) binary matrices, or other distributions, including sparse versions of the above.
- As we shall see, using random weights that have the same sign as the forward weights is not essential, but can lead to improvements in speed and stability. Thus we will use the phrase "*congruent weights*" to describe this case. Note that with fixed random matrices in the learning channel initialized congruently, congruence can be lost during learning when the sign of a forward weight changes.

We introduce SRBP both for information-theoretic reasons – what happens if the error information is communicated directly? – and because it may facilitate the mathematical analyses by avoiding the propagation process in the DLC. However, through the simulations to be described, we will also show empirically that SRBP is a viable learning algorithm, which in practice can work even better than RBP. Importantly, these simulation results suggest that when learning the synaptic weight w_{ij}^h the information about all the upper derivatives $(f'(S_r^l)$ for $l \geq h)$ is not needed. However, the immediate $(l = h)$ derivative $f'(S_i^h)$ seems to be needed, although this point is still unclear. Simulations of RBP have been reported in the literature that seem to converge without using any derivatives.

In the special case of linear networks, $f' = 1$ for all the units and therefore including or excluding derivative terms makes no difference. Furthermore, for any linear architecture $A(n, \ldots, n, \ldots, n)$ where all the layers have the same size n, then RBP is equivalent to SRBP. However, if the layers do not have the same size, then the layer sizes introduce rank constraints on the information that is backpropagated through RBP that may differ from the information propagated through SRBP. In both the linear and non-linear cases, for any architecture $A(n_1, n_2, n_3)$ with a single hidden layer, RBP is equivalent to SRBP, since in both cases there is only one random matrix in the DLC.

Another possibility is to have a combination of RBP and SRBP in the learning channel, implemented by a combination of long-ranged connections carrying SRBP signals interleaved with short-range connections carrying a backpropagation procedure, when no long-range signals are available. This may be relevant for biology since combinations of long-ranged and short-ranged feedback connections are common in biological neural systems.

Finally, in many cases different hardware or algorithms are used in the forward channel and in the DLC. For instance, neurons may be non-linear in the forward channel, but linear in the DLC. Weight adaptation may used in the forward channel, but not in the DLC. Dropout may be used in the forward channel, but not in the DLC, and so forth. In a physical neural system, it may be desirable to have greater symmetry, in the sense of having the same kind of hardware and algorithms in both channels. These issues are further explored in [84].

8.2   Simulations of Random Backpropagation

The most important high level result is that the DLC seems to be extremely robust in the sense that most of the variations described above can be made to work in simulations. Not surprisingly, none of the variations seems to work better than backpropagation, and none is of interest in virtualized applications of deep learning implemented in digital machines, where the transposes of the forward matrices are readily available. But from both a theoretical and physical neural network perspective, the robustness of the DLC to multiple forms of randomness is remarkable.

Many simulations have been carried on benchmark datasets, such as the CIFAR and MNIST data sets, and these are described in the references. Here we briefly describe simulation results that were obtained with a convolutional architecture on the CIFAR-10 dataset [421]. The specific architecture used is based on previous work [346], and consists of three sets of convolution and max-pooling layers, followed by a densely-connected layer of 1024 tanh units, then a softmax output layer. The input consists of 32×32 pixel 3-channel images; each convolution layer consists of 64 tanh channels with 5×5 kernel shapes and 1×1 strides; max-pooling layers have 3×3 receptive fields and 2×2 strides. All weights are initialized by sampling from a scaled normal distribution [304], and updated using stochastic gradient descent on mini-batches of size 128 and a momentum of 0.9. The learning rate started at 0.01 and decreased by a factor of 10^{-5} after each update. During training, the training images are randomly translated up to 10% in either direction, horizontally and vertically, and flipped horizontally with probability $p = 0.5$. Examples of results are shown in Figure 8.1. Additional simulation results are found in [85]. Overall, these results show that random backpropagation and its multiple variants are capable of learning the task, although in a slower manner than backpropagation, and that including the derivative of the activation of the postsynaptic neuron in the learning rule may be important for learning. However, others have sometimes reported that learning may be possible even in the absence of any derivatives. This point will have to be clarified through future simulations.

8.3   Understanding Random Backpropagation

In this section, we provide a number of simple observations for why RBP and some of its variations may work. Mathematical analyses are provided in the following section.

FACT 8.1   In all the RBP algorithms, the L-layer at the top with parameters w_{ij}^L follows the gradient, as it is trained just like BP, since there are no random feedback weights used for learning in the top layer. In other words, BP=RBP=SRBP for the top layer.

FACT 8.2   For a given input, if the sign of $T - O$ is changed, all the weights updates are changed in the opposite direction. This is true of all the algorithms considered here – BP, RBP, and their variants – even when the derivatives of the activations are included.

FACT 8.3   In all RBP algorithms, if $T - O = 0$ (online or in batch mode) then for all the weights $\Delta w_{ij}^h = 0$ (on-line or in batch mode).

FACT 8.4   Congruence of the weights is not necessary. However, it can be helpful sometimes and speed up learning. This can easily be seen in simple cases. For instance, consider a linear or non-linear $A(n_1, n_2, 1)$ architecture with coherent weights, and denote by a the weights in the bottom layer, by b the weights in the top layer, and by c the weights in the learning channel. Then, for all variants of RBP, all the weights updates are in the same direction as the gradient. This is obvious for the top layer (Fact 8.1 above). For the first layer of weights, the changes are given by $\Delta w_{ij}^1 = \eta(T - O)c_i I_j$, which is very similar to the change produced by gradient descent $\Delta^1 w_{ij} = \eta(T - O)b_i I_j$ since c_i and b_i are assumed to be coherent. So while the dynamics of the lower layer is not exactly in the gradient direction, it is always in the same orthant as the gradient, and thus downhill with respect to the error function.

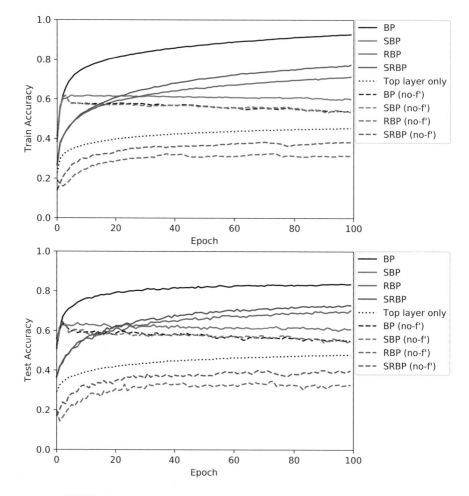

Figure 8.1 CIFAR-10 training (upper) and test (lower) accuracy, as a function of training epoch, for nine different learning algorithms: backpropagation (BP), skip BP (SBP), random BP (RBP), skip random BP (SRBP), the version of each algorithm in which the error signal is not multiplied by the derivative of the post-synaptic transfer function (no-f'), and the case where only the top layer is trained while the lower layer weights are fixed (top layer only). Models are trained five times with different weight initializations; the trajectory of the mean is shown here.

FACT 8.5   SRBP seems to perform well showing that the upper derivatives are not needed. However, the derivatives of the corresponding layer seem to matter. In general, for the activation functions considered here, these derivatives tend to be between 0 and 1. Thus learning is attenuated for neurons that are saturated. So an ingredient that seems to matter is to let the synapses of neurons that are not saturated change more than the synapses of neurons that are saturated (i.e. with f' close to 0).

FACT 8.6   Consider a multi-class classification problem, such as MNIST. All the elements in the same class tend to receive the same backpropagated signal and tend to move in unison. For instance, consider the beginning of learning, with small random weights in the forward network. Then, all the images will tend to produce a more or less uniform output vector similar to $(0.1, 0.1, \ldots, 0.1)$. Hence all the images in the "0" class will tend to produce a more or less uniform error vector similar to $(0.9, -0.1, \ldots, -0.1)$. All the images in the "1" class will tend to produce a more or less uniform error vector similar to $(-0.1, 0.9, \ldots, -0.1)$, which is essentially orthogonal to the previous error vector, and so forth. In other words, the ten classes can be associated with ten roughly orthogonal error vectors. When these vectors are multiplied by a fixed random matrix, as in SRBP, they will tend to produce 10 approximately orthogonal vectors in the corresponding hidden layer. Hence the backpropagated error signals tend to be similar within one digit class, and orthogonal across different digit classes. At the beginning of learning, we can expect roughly half of them (five digits out of ten in the MNIST case) to be in the same direction as BP.

Thus, in conclusion, an intuitive picture of why RBP may work is that:
(1) the random weights introduce a fixed coupling between the learning dynamics of the forward weights (see also mathematical analyses below);
(2) the top layer of weights always follows gradient descent and steers the learning dynamic in the right direction; and
(3) the learning dynamic tends to cluster inputs associated with the same response, and move them away from other similar clusters.

8.4 Mathematical Analysis of Random Backpropagation

For simplicity, we limit ourselves to the simple case of a linear $A(1, 1, 1)$ architecture. More complex cases can be found in the exercises and the literature, although it must be recognized that the number of cases that have been completely solved is limited.

Derivation of the System

The simplest case corresponds to a linear $A(1, 1, 1)$ architecture (Figure 8.2). Let us denote by a_1 and a_2 the weights in the first and second layer, and by c_1 the random weight of the learning channel. In this case, we have $O(t) = a_1 a_2 I(t)$ and the learning equations are given by:

$$
\begin{cases}
\Delta a_1 = \eta c_1 (T - O)I = \eta c_1 (T - a_1 a_2 I)I \\
\Delta a_2 = \eta (T - O)a_1 I = \eta (T - a_1 a_2 I)a_1 I.
\end{cases} \tag{8.6}
$$

When averaged over the training set:

$$
\begin{cases}
E(\Delta a_1) = \eta c_1 E(IT) - \eta c_1 a_1 a_2 E(I^2) = \eta c_1 \alpha - \eta c_1 a_1 a_2 \beta \\
E(\Delta a_2) = \eta a_1 E(IT) - \eta a_1^2 a_2 E(I^2) = \eta a_1 \alpha - \eta a_1^2 a_2 \beta,
\end{cases} \tag{8.7}
$$

where $\alpha = E(IT)$ and $\beta = E(I^2)$. With the proper scaling of the learning rate ($\eta = \Delta t$) this leads to the non-linear system of coupled differential equations for the temporal evolution of a_1 and a_2 during learning:

$$\begin{cases} \frac{da_1}{dt} = \alpha c_1 - \beta c_1 a_1 a_2 = c_1(\alpha - \beta a_1 a_2) \\ \frac{da_2}{dt} = \alpha a_1 - \beta a_1^2 a_2 = a_1(\alpha - \beta a_1 a_2). \end{cases} \tag{8.8}$$

Note that the dynamic of $P = a_1 a_2$ is given by:

$$\frac{dP}{dt} = a_1 \frac{da_2}{dt} + a_2 \frac{da_1}{dt} = (a_1^2 + a_2 c_1)(\alpha - \beta P). \tag{8.9}$$

The error is given by:

$$\mathcal{E} = \frac{1}{2}E(T - PI)^2 = \frac{1}{2}E(T^2) + \frac{1}{2}P^2\beta - P\alpha = \frac{1}{2}E(T^2) + \frac{1}{2\beta}(\alpha - \beta P)^2 - \frac{\alpha^2}{2\beta} \tag{8.10}$$

and

$$\frac{d\mathcal{E}}{dP} = -\alpha + \beta P \quad \text{with} \quad \frac{\partial \mathcal{E}}{\partial a_i} = (-\alpha + \beta P)\frac{P}{a_i}; \tag{8.11}$$

the last equality requires $a_i \neq 0$.

THEOREM 8.1   *The system in Equation 8.8 always converges to a fixed point. Further-more, except for trivial cases associated with $c_1 = 0$, starting from any initial conditions the system converges to a fixed point corresponding to a global minimum of the quadratic error function. All the fixed points are located on the hyperbolas given by $\alpha - \beta P = 0$ and are global minima of the error function. All the fixed points are attractors, except those that are interior to a certain parabola. For any starting point, the final fixed point can be calculated by solving a cubic equation.*

Proof   As this is the first example, we first deal with the trivial cases in detail. For subsequent systems, we will skip the trivial cases entirely.

Trivial Cases: (1) If $\beta = 0$ then we must have $I = 0$ and thus $\alpha = 0$. As a result the activity of the input, hidden, and output neuron will always be 0. Therefore the weights a_1 and a_2 will remain constant ($da_1/dt = da_2/dt = 0$) and equal to their initial values $a_1(0)$ and $a_2(0)$. The error will also remain constant, and equal to 0 if and only if $T = 0$. Thus, from now on, we can assume that $\beta > 0$.

(2) If $c_1 = 0$ then the lower weight a_1 never changes and remains equal to its initial value. If this initial value satisfies $a_1(0) = 0$, then the activity of the hidden and output unit remains equal to 0 at all times, and thus a_2 remains constant and equal to its initial value $a_2 = a_2(0)$. The error remains constant and equal to 0 if and only if T is always 0. If $a_1(0) \neq 0$, then the error is a simple quadratic convex function of a_2 and since the rule for adjusting a_2 is simply gradient descent, the value of a_2 will converge to its optimal value given by: $a_2 = \alpha/\beta a_1(0)$.

General Case: Thus, from now on, we can assume that $\beta > 0$ and $c_1 \neq 0$. Furthermore, it is easy to check that changing the sign of α corresponds to a reflection about the a_2-axis. Likewise, changing the sign of c_1 corresponds to a reflection about the origin (i.e. across both the a_1 and a_2 axis). Thus in short, it is sufficient to focus on the case where: $\alpha > 0$, $\beta > 0$, and $c_1 > 0$.

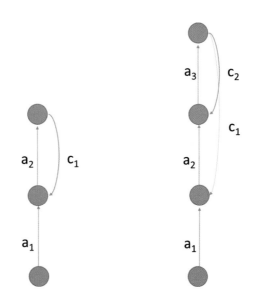

Figure 8.2 Left: $A(1, 1, 1)$ architecture. The weights a_1 and a_2 are adjustable, and the feedback weight c_1 is constant. Right: $A(1, 1, 1, 1)$ architecture. The weights a_1, a_2, and a_3 are adjustable, and the feedback weights c_1 and c_2 are constant.

In this case, the critical points for a_1 and a_2 are given by:

$$P = a_1 a_2 = \frac{\alpha}{\beta} = \frac{E(IT)}{E(I^2)} = 0, \tag{8.12}$$

which corresponds to two hyperbolas in the two-dimensional (a_1, a_2)-plane, in the first and third quadrant for $\alpha = E(IT) > 0$. *Note that these critical points do not depend on the feedback weight c_1.* All these critical points correspond to global minima of the error function $\mathcal{E} = \frac{1}{2} E[(T - O)^2]$. Furthermore, the critical points of P include also the parabola:

$$a_1^2 + a_2 c_1 = 0 \quad \text{or} \quad a_2 = -a_1^2 / c_1 \tag{8.13}$$

(Figure 8.3). These critical points are dependent on the weights in the learning channel. This parabola intersects with the hyperbola $a_1 a_2 = P = \alpha/\beta$ at one point with coordinates: $a_1 = (-c_1 \alpha/\beta)^{1/3}$ and $a_2 = -\alpha^{2/3}/(c_1^{1/3} \beta^{2/3})$.

In the upper half-plane, where a_2 and c_1 are congruent and both positive, the dynamics is simple to understand. For instance in the first quadrant where $a_1, a_2, c_1 > 0$, if $\alpha - \beta P > 0$ then $da_1/dt > 0$, $da_2/dt > 0$, and $dP/dt > 0$ everywhere and therefore the gradient vector flow is directed towards the hyperbola of critical points. If started in this region, a_1, a_2, and P will grow monotonically until a critical point is reached and the error will decrease monotonically towards a global minimum. If $\alpha - \beta P < 0$ then $da_1/dt < 0$, $da_2/dt < 0$, and $dP/dt < 0$ everywhere and again the vector flow is directed towards the hyperbola of critical points. If started in this region, a_1, a_2, and P will decrease monotonically until a critical point is reached and the error will decrease monotonically towards a global minimum. A similar situation is observed in the fourth quadrant where $a_1 < 0$ and $a_2 > 0$.

More generally, if a_2 and c_1 have the same sign, i.e. are congruent as in BP, then $a_1^2 + a_2 c_1 \geq 0$ and P will increase if $\alpha - \beta P > 0$, and decrease if $\alpha - \beta P < 0$. Note however that this is also true in general when c_1 is small regardless of its sign, relative to a_1 and a_2, since in this case it is still true that $a_1^2 + a_2 c_1$ is positive. This remains true even if c_1 varies, as long as it is small. When c_1 is small, the dynamics is dominated by the top layer. The lower layer changes slowly and the top layer adapts rapidly so that the system again converges to a global minimum. When $a_2 = c_1$ one recovers the convergent dynamic of BP, as dP/dt always has the same sign as $\alpha - \beta P$. However, in the lower half-plane, the situation is slightly more complicated (Figure 8.3).

To solve the dynamics in the general case, from Equation 8.8 we get:

$$\frac{da_2}{dt} = a_1 \frac{1}{c_1} \frac{da_1}{dt},$$
(8.14)

which gives $a_2 = \frac{1}{2c_1} a_1^2 + C$ so that finally:

$$a_2 = \frac{1}{2c_1} a_1^2 + b(0) - \frac{1}{2c_1} a_1^2(0).$$
(8.15)

Given a starting point $a_1(0)$ and $a_2(0)$, the system will follow a trajectory given by the parabola in Equation 8.15 until it converges to a critical point (global optimum) where $da_1/dt = da_2/dt = 0$. To find the specific critical point to which it converges to, Equations 8.15 and 8.12 must be satisfied simultaneously which leads to the depressed cubic equation:

$$a_1^3 + (2c_1 a_2(0) - a_1(0)^2) a_1 - 2\frac{c_1 \alpha}{\beta} = 0,$$
(8.16)

which can be solved using the standard formula for the roots of cubic equations. Note that the parabolic trajectories contained in the upper half-plane intersect the critical hyperbola in only one point and therefore the equation has a single real root. In the lower half-plane, the parabolas associated with the trajectories can intersect the hyperbolas in one, twp, or three distinct points corresponding to one real root, two real roots (one being double), and three real roots. The double root corresponds to the point $-(c_1 \alpha/\beta)^{1/3}$ associated with the intersection of the parabola of Equation 8.15 with both the hyperbola of critical points $a_1 a_2 = \alpha/\beta$ and the parabola of additional critical points for P given by Equation 8.13.

When there are multiple roots, the convergence point of each trajectory is easily identified by looking at the derivative vector flow (Figure 8.3). Note on the figure that all the points on the critical hyperbolas are stable attractors, except for those in the lower half-plane that satisfy both $a_1 a_2 = \alpha/\beta$ and $a_2 c_1 + a_1^2 < 0$. This can be shown by linearizing the system around its critical points.

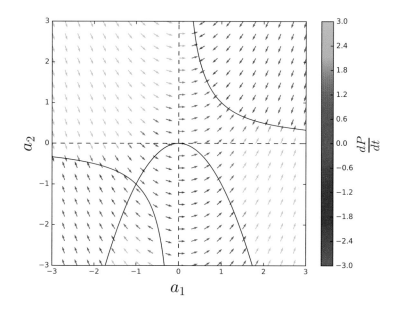

a_1

Figure 8.3 Vector field for the $A(1, 1, 1)$ linear case with $c_1 = 1$, $\alpha = 1$, and $\beta = 1$. a_1 correspond to the horizontal axis and a_2 correspond to the vertical axis. The critical points correspond to the two hyperbolas, and all critical points are fixed points and global minima of the error functions. Arrows are colored according to the value of dP/dt, showing how the critical points inside the parabola $a_2 = -a_1^2/c_1$ are unstable. All other critical points are attractors. Reversing the sign of α, leads to a reflection across the a_2-axis; reversing the sign of c_1, leads to a reflection across both the a_1 and a_2 axes.

Linearization Around Critical Points
If we consider a small deviation $a_1 + u$ and $a_2 + v$ around a critical point a_1, a_2 (satisfying $\alpha - \beta a_1 a_2 = 0$) and linearize the corresponding system, we get:

$$\begin{cases} \frac{du}{dt} = -\beta c_1 (a_2 u + a_1 v) \\ \frac{dv}{dt} = -\beta a_1 (a_2 u + a_1 v), \end{cases} \tag{8.17}$$

with $a_1 a_2 = \alpha/\beta$. If we let $w = a_2 u + a_1 v$ we have:

$$\frac{dw}{dt} = -\beta(c_1 a_2 + a_1^2)w \quad \text{thus} \quad w = w(0)e^{-\beta(c_1 a_2 + a_1^2)t}. \tag{8.18}$$

Hence if $\beta(c_1 a_2 + a_1^2) > 0$, w converges to zero and a_1, a_2 is an attractor. In particular, this is always the case when c_1 is very small, or c_1 has the same sign as a_2. If $\beta(c_1 a_2 + a_1^2) < 0$, w diverges to $+\infty$, and corresponds to unstable critical points as described above. If $\beta(c_1 a_2 + a_1^2) = 0$, w is constant.

Finally, note that in many cases, for instance for trajectories in the upper half-plane, the value of P along the trajectories increases or decreases monotonically towards the global optimum value. However this is not always the case and there are trajectories where dP/dt changes sign, but this can happen only once. □

Other linear architectures that can be solved analytically (see exercises) include:

$A(1, 1, 1, 1)$, and in fact $A(1, 1, 1, \ldots, 1)$ of any depth; $A(1, n, 1)$ for any hidden layer size n; and $A(2, 2, 2)$. The general linear case, even with a single hidden layer $(A(n, m, p))$ remains open. Note that in linear architectures with hidden layers, both BP and RBP with all their variants lead to learning dynamics that are represented by non-linear systems of coupled polynomial differential equations (of degree two or more). Understanding such systems is related to Hilbert's 16th problem of finding a bound for the number of limit cycles such systems can have. The problem is still open, even in the two-dimensional case.

8.5   Further Remarks About Learning Channels

Random backpropagation is one mode for communicating information over the learning channel which completely bypasses the need for symmetric weights. We have derived several variants of RBP and studied them through simulations and mathematical analyses, with additional results in the exercises and the references. In combination, the main emerging picture is that the general concept of RBP is remarkably robust as most of the variants lead to robust learning. Through RBP and its variants, we can refine the analysis, started in Chapter 7, of the information required to effectively change the synaptic weights (Table 8.1).

In supervised learning, the critical equations show that in principle any deep weights must depend on all the training examples and all the other weights of the network. Backpropagation shows that it is possible to derive effective learning rules of the form $\Delta w_{ij}^h = \eta I_{ij}^h O_j^{h-1}$. All the information about the inputs and the lower weights of the architecture is subsumed at the synapse by the presynaptic output O_j^{h-1}. The signal I_{ij}^h is a signal communicated through the deep learning channel that carries information about the outputs and the targets to the deep synapses. Backpropagation shows that information about all the upper weights is subsumed in both the error term $T - O^L$ (e.g. O^L), the backpropagated error B_i^h which is dependent on these upper weights, and the derivatives of the forward activation functions. RBP shows that all the information about the upper weights can be subsumed by just $T - O^L$, with no need for symmetric weights in the DLC, and possibly all the upper derivatives of the transfer functions f^k, for $k \geq h$. SRBP shows that all the information about the upper weights can be subsumed by just $T - O^L$ and possibly the local derivatives of the transfer functions f^h, derivatives for the upper layers $k \geq h$ not being required. Thus, in short, the postsynaptic term must implement gradient descent for the top layer (i.e. random weights in the learning channel for the top layer do not work at all). For any other deep layer h, the postsynaptic term may be of the form $f'F(T - O)$, where:

(1) f' denotes component-wise multiplication by the derivatives of the forward activation functions in the corresponding layer; and

(2) F is a smooth function of the error $T - O$ satisfying $F(0) = 0$. As we have seen, F can be linear, or a composition of linear propagation with non-linear activation functions, it can be fixed or slowly varying, and when matrices are involved these can be random, sparse, etc.

As can be expected, it is better if these matrices are full rank, although gracious degradation – as opposed to catastrophic failure – is observed when these matrices deviate slightly from the full rank case.

Information	Algorithm
$I_{ij}^h = I_{ij}^h(T, O, w_{rs}^l(l > h), f'(l \geq h))$	General Form
$I_{ij}^h = I_i^h(T, O, w_{rs}^l(l > h), f'(l \geq h))$	BP (symmetric weights)
$I_{ij}^h = I_i^h(T - O, w_{rs}^l(l > h), f'(l \geq h))$	BP (symmetric weights)
$I_{ij}^h = I_i^h(T - O, w_{rs}^l(l > h + 1), w_{ki}^{h+1}, f'(l \geq h))$	BP (symmetric weights)
$I_{ij}^h = I_i^h(T - O, r_{rs}^l(l \geq h + 1), r_{ki}^h, f'(l \geq h))$	RBP (random weights)
$I_{ij}^h = I_i^h(T - O, r_{ki}^h, f'(l \geq h))$	SRBP (random skipped weights)
$I_{ij}^h = I_i^h(T - O, r_{ki}^h, f'(l = h))$	SRBP (random skipped weights)
$I_{ij}^h = I_i^h(F(T - O), f'(l = h))$	F sparse/low-prec./adaptive/non-lin.

Table 8.1 Postsynaptic information required by deep synapses for optimal learning. I_{ij}^h represents the signal communicated by the DLC which appears as the postsynaptic term in the learning rules considered here. Different algorithms reveal the essential ingredients of this signal and how it can be simplified (see description in text). In the final row, the function F can be implemented with sparse or adaptive matrices, carry low precision signals, or include non-linear transformations in the learning channel (see also [84]).

We have briefly discussed the physical nature of the DLC and analyzed the nature of the information that should be sent over the DLC. The rate at which this information is sent depends on the details of the physical system and its time scales, and thus is not further discussed. However, the notion of capacity gives us an idea of how much information needs to be sent *in aggregate* over the DLC, in order for the system to select one function among all the functions it can implement.

As a final remark for this section, we have previously discussed the DLC in the context of supervised learning and neural networks. However the situation is more general. Every time a physical learning system can be represented by a deep graph with deep local parameters, in order for it to be able to learn from complex data there must be a physical channel, going from the data to most of the deep parameters. This is true for supervised, self-supervised, and unsupervised learning, as well as for neural networks and for models that are not necessarily neural networks. For instance, in a stack of autoencoders architecture, a DLC is needed for each autoencoder in the stack; interestingly, the DLC connections are local to each autoencoder.

Next, we look at some applications of the previous ideas to unsupervised learning, in particular to autoencoders by studying the connection between learning channels and random backpropagation. We do so in circular autoencoders, where the forward channel and the DLC merge together. Recall that so far we have used the concept of locality, but only in space. Considering circular autoencoders yields also a class of learning algorithms, called recirculation algorithms, which use locality in time in their local learning rules. In essence, this is achieved by encoding local errors using local differences in time (or time derivatives) of neuronal outputs.

8.6   Circular Autoencoders

In addition to the standard feedforward autoencoder architectures seen in Chapter 5, it is also possible to consider circular autoencoder architectures of the form $A^*(n_0, n_1, n_2, \ldots, n_{L-1}, n_L)$ with $n_0 = n_L$, shown in Figure 8.4, with multiple layers numbered $0, 1, \ldots, L$. In a circular architecture, the output units are identical (or spatially very close) to the input units. Thus, we let the index $0 = L$ correspond to the input/output layer. We assume that there is a matrix of weights A^h connecting layer $h - 1$ to layer h for $h = 1, \ldots, L$. [Note: while we use $A^1, \ldots, A^L$ with multiple hidden layers, when only a single hidden layer is present we use A and B instead to improve readability]. In addition, in the non-linear case, there is a vector of non-linear transfer functions F^h associated with each layer h, $h = 1, \ldots, L$. Thus, with a slight abuse of notation, here we can write:

$$O^h(t) = F^h A^h O^{h-1}(t) \qquad \text{for } h = 1, \ldots, L \text{ and } O^0(0) = I. \tag{8.19}$$

The time index t here is used to denote the cycle, with $t = 0$ corresponding to the activations generated by the original input I. In the coming sections, $t = 1$ will be used to index the first cycle of recirculation, and so forth. The abuse of notation is that "$F^h A^h$" does not denote a vector or matrix multiplication, but rather the component-wise application of the transfer functions in F^h to the activations of the layer h. From the DLC theory, something very special happens in the circular autoencoder: since the data are the targets, information about the targets is propagated by the feedforward connections. In other words, it ought to be possible to use the same feedforward connections to implement both the feedforward propagation and the DLC, and derive new corresponding learning algorithms.

To see this more precisely, consider entering an input I in the input layer $O^0(1) = I$) and going around the loop clockwise once to compute the output $O^L(1)$. At this point, we can assume that both the output $O^L(1)$ and the target $O^0(1) = I$ are available and thus in principle the error $I - O^L(1)$ can be computed. Backpropagation would require sending this error in the counter-clockwise direction through a set of connections that are symmetric to the clockwise connections and which, in a physical circular autoencoder, would have to be created. Instead we can use the clockwise connections to send information about the error $I - O^L(1)$ to the deep layers though the matrices $A^1, A^2, \ldots$. As long as there are no biases, this amounts to sending a function of the error to the deep layers, which is zero when the error is zero. Furthermore, the top matrix A^L can be trained by true gradient descent since the target I is local. *As a result, recirculation of the error behaves like random backpropagation or, rather, adaptive random backpropagation since the matrices A are changing slowly (with a small learning rate). In this case, the connections in the deep learning channel are the same as in the forward channel.* Next we look at the case where the output $O^L(1)$ itself is recirculated $(O^0(2) = O^L(1))$, rather than the error. We show that similar considerations can be applied by using the outputs obtained during the first cycle as the targets for the outputs obtained during the second cycle and, more generally, by using differences in time to encode errors. Note that in this way a stack of circular autoencoders, in particular autoencoders with a single hidden layer, can be trained using entirely local learning rules.

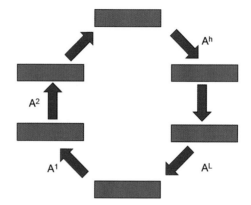

Figure 8.4 Circular autoencoder with multiple hidden layers and connection matrices $A^1, \ldots, A^L$. In the non-linear case, non-linear transformations $F^1, \ldots, F^L$ are associated with each layer.

8.7 Recirculation: Locality in Both Space and Time

The general idea behind the family of recirculation algorithms [344, 92] is to recirculate information, i.e. propagate information, through the circular autoencoder over more than one full cycle, and use information from different cycles to update the weights. Typically earlier cycles are used as targets for later cycles, as information degrades with recirculation.

Several variations can be obtained depending on a number of parameters. In this chapter we focus on the simplest case, leaving some of the variations for the exercises. The parameters to be considered include:

- The nature of the information being recirculated, i.e. outputs versus errors. In the simplest case, and the only one to be considered here, one can simply recirculate outputs, e.g. $O^1(1)$ is computed by propagating $O^L(0)$ forward. However, after completing the first cycle, the error $I - O^L(0) = O^0(0) - O^L(0)$ is available in the input layer and it could be communicated (propagated) to the following layers. In terms of which kind of information is being recirculated, we will consider two different cases, although they turn out to be similar, at least in the case where the biases are set to zero.
  1. **Recirculation of Errors:** where the error $I - O^L$ is computed in the input layer and then recirculated to the other layers.
  2. **Recirculation of Outputs:** where the output O^L is recirculated to the other layers. While we will focus primarily on the first two cycles indexed by $t = 0$

and $t = 1$, it is also possible to recirculate output information over multiple cycles.

3. The manner in which the state of neurons is defined, or updated, across subsequent cycles, for instance by taking convex combinations of activities across two (or more) subsequent cycles [92]. Here, for simplicity, we will consider primarily the case where there are no such combinations.

4. The number of cycles being considered and the interval between cycles used in the learning rules. We will focus on the simplest case where cycle 0 provides the targets for cycle 1.

5. The learning rule being used to adapt the weight using the activities of the neurons taken locally in space (e.g. the pre- and post-synaptic neuron) and locally in time (e.g. across two neighboring cycles).

To derive a learning rule, recall that locality in space has been associated with rules with the functional form:

$$\Delta w_{ij}^h(t) = F\left(O_i(t), O_j(t), w_{ij}(t)\right). \tag{8.20}$$

To extend the concept, we can say that a rule is local in both space and time if it has the functional form:

$$\Delta w_{ij}^h(t) = F\left(O_i(s), O_j(s), w_{ij}(s)\right) \quad \text{for all} \quad t - u \le s \le t, \tag{8.21}$$

where u is the window of time over which spatially local information can be integrated. The key idea behind the recirculation algorithms is to trade off space for time, using differences in the activations of the same units at different times to drive the learning. Thus, in general, one is looking for learning rules that typically are polynomial in the local variables, in fact the product of a presynaptic and a postsynaptic term (simple Hebbian rule), and where the postsynaptic term may be a difference between two activations taken over a relatively short time window. Thus during recirculation we will typically consider rules of the form:

$$\Delta w_{ij}^h(t) = F\left(O_i(s) - O_i(t), O_j(s), w_{ij}(s)\right) \quad \text{for} \quad t - u \le s \le t. \tag{8.22}$$

These learning rules rely on the product of the presynaptic activity times some measure of change in the postsynaptic activity, used to communicate error information. When using spiking neurons, such learning rules are closely related to the concept of spike timedependent synaptic plasticity (STDP). STDP Hebbian or anti-Hebbian learning rules have been proposed using the temporal derivative of the activity of the postsynaptic neuron [797] to encode error derivatives.

$$\Delta w_{ij} = \eta(\Delta O_i^{\text{post}})(O_j^{\text{pre}}), \tag{8.23}$$

with a negative sign in the anti-Hebbian case. In a layered architecture, for a deep weight w_{ij}^h we can write:

$$\Delta w_{ij}^h = \eta(\Delta O_i^h)(O_j^{h-1}). \tag{8.24}$$

As a side note, using time differences in learning rules is just one example of a broader theme of how time may be used in physical neural systems. This theme was already present in the neuromorphic thinking of the 1980s [357, 720, 496, 470, 495]. In digitally simulated neural networks, most issues related to time are taken care of in a manner that is external to the neural networks being simulated. In particular, activities in neurons and layers are updated sequentially in an orderly fashion controlled by a set of computer instructions. Likewise the timing and sequence of example presentations, weight updates, hyperparameter optimizations and so forth are all handled by computer instructions that are external to the neural networks. In contrast, biological neurons must operate in "real time", with limited storage capacity, in an organic, largely asynchronous fashion, and within larger networks. And they must do so not only for learning, but also for all the other activities in which they partake.

8.8   Simulations of Recirculation

In these simulations, output recirculation is compared to backpropagation and random backpropagation using compressive autoencoders on two different data sets:

1. *MNIST*: This well-known benchmark data set contains 70,000 28×28 grayscale images of handwritten digits, with real pixel values in the range $[0, 1]$. In experiments with linear autoencoders, we use a linear output layer with squared error loss, while in the non-linear architectures we use a sigmoid output layer with cross-entropy loss.
2. *Fashion*: This data set contains 70,000 28×28 grayscale images of *Fashion* accessories [795], with real pixel values in the range $[0, 1]$. In experiments with linear autoencoders, we use a linear output layer with squared error loss, while in the non-linear architectures we use a sigmoid output layer with cross-entropy loss.

For each data set, a training epoch consists of 60,000 examples, with another 10,000 examples used for testing. For both data sets, high-dimensional data ($d = 784 = 28 \times 28$) is compressed down to only 20 dimensions. In order to achieve good reconstruction performance on these tasks, deep learning is needed to find good low-dimensional representations of the data. Facilitating the comparison is the fact that all three learning rules perform gradient descent in the last layer, and differ only in how the intermediate-layer weights are updated (see [92] for additional simulations and details).

The experiments demonstrate that recirculation leads to good intermediate representations with small reconstruction error on a variety of data sets and architecture configurations. Figures 8.5 and 8.6 shows that recirculation learns useful intermediate representations on real images, in both linear and non-linear architectures, with one or three hidden layers. Examples of reconstructed *MNIST* digits are shown in Figure 8.7. Thus next we seek an explanation for why recirculation works. The key surprising insight is that recirculation is a form of random backpropagation.

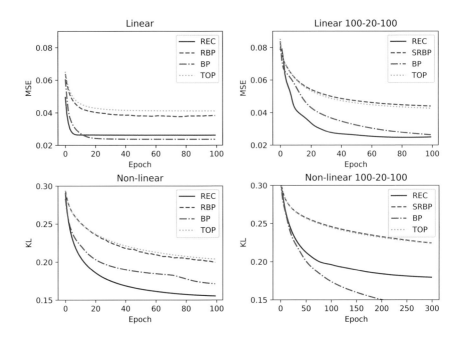

Figure 8.5 *MNIST* test set performance of linear and non-linear compressive autoencoders, with either a single hidden layer of 20 units (left) or three hidden layers of shape 100-20-100 (right), trained with recirculation (REC), random backpropagation (RBP), skip random backpropagation (SRBP), backpropagation (BP), and only training the top layer (TOP).

8.9   Recirculation is Random Backpropagation

Taking the simplest form of recirculation, where outputs are recirculated and only the first and second cycles are considered (Plain Recirculation), we have:

$$\begin{cases} \Delta A^h = \eta(O^h(0) - O^h(1))(O^{h-1}(0))^\mathrm{T} & \text{for} \quad h = 1, \ldots, L-1 \\ \Delta A^L = \eta(O^0(0) - O^0(1))(O^{L-1}(0))^\mathrm{T}. \end{cases} \tag{8.25}$$

Again A^L is being updated by gradient descent. For the other layers, assuming that all the transfer functions are continuous, we can use the mean-value theorem to write:

$$\begin{aligned} O^h(0) - O^h(1) &= F^h A^h O^{h-1}(0) - F^h A^h O^{h-1}(1) \\ &= [F^h]'(R^h)A^h \cdot (O^{h-1}(0) - O^{h-1}(1)), \end{aligned} \tag{8.26}$$

where $[F^h]'(R^h)$ represents the vector of derivatives of the activation functions taken at the appropriate intermediate vector of coordinates R^h. The right-hand side corresponds to the dot product of this vector with the difference of the outputs in layer $h-1$. One key point is that the right-hand side is 0 when $(O^{h-1}(0) - O^{h-1}(1)) = 0$. This relationship and Equation 8.26 hold even when biases are present, which is not the case when errors

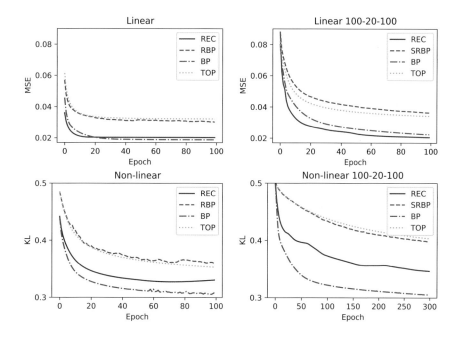

Figure 8.6 *Fashion* test set performance of linear and non-linear compressive autoencoders, with either a single hidden layer of 20 units (left) or three hidden layers of shape 100-20-100 (right), trained with recirculation (REC), random backpropagation (RBP), skip random backpropagation (SRBP), backpropagation (BP), and only training the top layer (TOP).

Figure 8.7 Reconstructed *MNIST* digits from the compressive autoencoder network with 100-20-100 hidden linear units (i.e. $A(784, 100, 20, 100, 784)$), trained with backpropagation (BP), skip random backpropagation (SRBP), and recirculation (REC).

are recirculated. Equation 8.26 can be iterated layer-by-layer to produce:

$$O^h(0) - O^h(1) = [F^h]'(R^h) \cdot A^h[[F^{h-1}]'(R^{h-1}) \cdot A^{h-1}] \cdots [F^1]'(R^1) \cdot A^1(I - O^L(0)).$$

$$(8.27)$$

Thus again the error $[I - O^L(0)]$ is being communicated to each layer through a series of matrix and scalar multiplications, where the matrices are evolving slowly in time (with a small learning rate). This can be viewed as a form of non-linear adaptive random backpropagation and thus in general can be expected to converge [85, 84]. In this case, *the connections in the deep learning channel are identical to the connections in the forward channel.*

8.10 Mathematical Analysis of Recirculation

In the linear case, taking as usual expectations over the training set with a small learning rate, one obtains a polynomial system of ordinary differential equations of the form:

$$\begin{cases} \frac{dA^h}{dt} = P^h(Id - P)\Sigma(P^{h-1})^{\mathrm{T}} & \text{for} \quad h = 1, \ldots, L-1 \\ \frac{dA^L}{dt} = (Id - P)\Sigma(P^{L-1})^{\mathrm{T}}, \end{cases} \tag{8.28}$$

where $P^h = A^h A^{h-1} \cdots A^1$, $P = P^L$, and $\Sigma = E(II^{\mathrm{T}})$. Thus, in the linear case, plain recirculation of error or plain recirculation of output are the same. For consecutive matrices one again has the relationship:

$$\frac{dA^{h+1}}{dt} = A^{h+1}\frac{dA^h}{dt}[A^h]^{\mathrm{T}}. \tag{8.29}$$

As for the similar case in RBP [85, 84], we see that there is a deterministic coupling between consecutive layers, and the top layer follows gradient descent.

It is instructive to look at the case of $L = 2$ and see how it illuminates the connection to both BP and RBP. When $L = 2$, letting $A_1 = B$ and $A_2 = A$, the recirculation learning differential equations are given by:

$$\begin{cases} \frac{dA}{dt} = (Id - AB)\Sigma B^{\mathrm{T}} \\ \frac{dB}{dt} = B(Id - AB)\Sigma. \end{cases} \tag{8.30}$$

By contrast, the usual gradient descent differential equations are given by:

$$\begin{cases} \frac{dA}{dt} = (Id - AB)\Sigma B^{\mathrm{T}} \\ \frac{dB}{dt} = A^{\mathrm{T}}(Id - AB)\Sigma, \end{cases} \tag{8.31}$$

and the RBP differential equations by:

$$\begin{cases} \frac{dA}{dt} = (Id - AB)\Sigma B^{\mathrm{T}} \\ \frac{dB}{dt} = C(Id - AB)\Sigma, \end{cases} \tag{8.32}$$

where C is a random matrix. *Notice that the equation for dA/dt is exactly the same in all three cases. The difference is that BP uses A^{T} to send information about the error, RBP replaces it with a fixed random matrix C, and recirculation uses B itself as the "random matrix".*

The Linear $A^*(1, 1, \ldots, 1)$ Case

In the circular autoencoder $A^*(1, 1, \ldots, 1)$ case, where each layer contains only one linear neuron, the system becomes:

$$\begin{cases} \frac{da_h}{dt} = \beta a_1^2 \cdots a_{h-1}^2 a_h(1 - P) & \text{for} \quad h = 1, \ldots, L-1 \\ \frac{da_L}{dt} = \beta a_1 \cdots a_{L-1}(1 - P), \end{cases} \tag{8.33}$$

where $\beta = E(I^2)$ and $P = a_1 \cdots a_L$. Clearly $P = 1$ corresponds to the optimum. For consecutive weights, we have:

$$\frac{da_{h+1}}{dt} = a_{h+1}a_h \frac{da_h}{dt}, \tag{8.34}$$

for $h = 1, \ldots, L - 2$. Here the coupling can be solved, yielding:

$$\log|a_{h+1}| = \frac{1}{2}a_h^2 + K_h \quad \text{or} \quad |a_{h+1}| = K_h e^{a_h^2/2}, \tag{8.35}$$

for $h = 1, \ldots, L - 2$ and where in either case K_h is a constant that depends only on the initial conditions. The following theorem states that in most cases the system will be able to learn and converge to an optimal set of weights for which $P = 1$.

THEOREM 8.2 *If $\beta > 0$, then for any set of initial conditions satisfying the condition $a_1(0)a_2(0) \cdots a_{L-1}(0) \neq 0$, the system always learns and the weights a_i converge to an optimal equilibrium where $P = 1$. If the initial conditions satisfy $a_1(0)a_2(0) \cdots a_{L-1}(0) = 0$ then $P(t) = 0$ at all times and the system cannot learn. If $\beta = 0$, then for every i $a_i(t) = a_i(0)$ and any choice of initial conditions $a_i(0)$ is optimal.*

Proof First, if $\beta = 0$, then $I = 0$ and $a_i(t) = a_i(0)$ for every i. Thus any set of initial weights provides an optimal solution, including zero weights.

Thus, in the rest of the proof, let us assume that $\beta >= 0$. Let $Q(t) = a_1(t)a_2(t) \cdots a_{L-1}(t)$. Let us assume that $Q(0) = 0$ (rare set of initial conditions). In this case $P(0) = 0$. Let i_0 be the smallest index for which $a_{i_0}(0) = 0$. Then the variables $a_1(t), \ldots, a_{i_0-1}(t)$ evolve in time, but the variables $a_{i_0}(t), \ldots, a_L(t)$ remain constant and equal to 0. Thus $P(t) = 0$ at all times and the system cannot learn.

In the main case of interest, let us assume that $Q(0) \neq 0$, which is easily achieved by any random initialization of the weights.

From the system in Equation 8.33, we immediately have:

$$\begin{cases} \frac{dQ}{dt} = \beta Q(1 - P)(1 + a_1^2 + a_1^2 a_2^2 + \cdots + a_1^2 a_2^2 \cdots a_{L-2}^2) \\ \frac{da_L}{dt} = \beta Q(1 - P). \end{cases} \tag{8.36}$$

As a result:

$$\begin{cases} \frac{dQ}{dt} = \beta Q(1 - P)f \\ \frac{da_L}{dt} = \beta Q(1 - P) \\ P = Qa_L, \end{cases} \tag{8.37}$$

where the function f satisfies $f > 1$ at all times. Hence $dQ/dt = f\, da_L/dt$ and thus the two derivatives always have the same sign. Furthermore note that if $P(0) = 1$, the system is already at an optimal point and all derivatives are 0. Assuming $P(0) \neq 1$, we can examine four possible cases of initial conditions depending on the sign of $Q(0)$ and $a_L(0)$:

$Q(0) > 0$ **and** $a_L(0) \geq 0$: If $P(0) > 1$, then both a_L and Q decrease until they converge to an optimal equilibrium where $P = 1$. If $P(0) < 1$, then both a_L and Q increase until they converge to an optimal equilibrium where $P = 1$.

$Q(0) < 0$ **and** $a_L(0) \leq 0$: If $P(0) > 1$, then both a_L and Q increase and P decreases and converges to an optimal equilibrium where $P = 1$. If $P(0) < 1$, then both a_L and Q decrease, and P increases and converges to an optimal equilibrium where $P = 1$.

$Q(0) > 0$ **and** $a_L(0) \leq 0$: Then initially $P(0) < 1$. Thus both a_L and Q increase, a_L crosses 0 (corresponding to $P = 0$) and then a_L and Q and P keep increasing until P converges to an optimal equilibrium where $P = 1$.

$Q(0) < 0$ **and** $a_L(0) \geq 0$: Then $P(0) < 1$. Thus both a_L and Q decrease, a_L crosses 0 (corresponding to $P = 0$) and then a_L and Q keep decreasing while P increases until P converges to an optimal equilibrium where $P = 1$.

As an example, consider the simple case where $L = 2$. Thus we have:

$$\begin{cases} \frac{da_1}{dt} = \beta a_1(1 - P) \\ \frac{da_2}{dt} = \beta a_1(1 - P), \end{cases} \tag{8.38}$$

and so $a_2 = a_1 + K$ where $K = a_2(0) - a_1(0)$ is a constant that depends only on the initial conditions. As a result, we have the polynomial ordinary differential equation:

$$\frac{da_1}{dt} = \beta a_1(1 - a_1(a_1 + K)). \tag{8.39}$$

The polynomial is of degree three with a negative leading coefficient and thus the ODE is always convergent to a fixed point. The fixed points are given by:

$$a_1 = 0 \quad \text{and} \quad a_1 = \frac{-K \pm \sqrt{K^2 + 4}}{2}. \tag{8.40}$$

By simple inspection of the cubic function, the fixed point $a_1 = 0$ is repulsive and the other two fixed points are attractive. Hence for any initial condition $a_1(0) \neq 0$, a_1 will converge to a non-zero fixed point, and so will a_2. At this fixed point, one must have $P = 1$ corresponding to an optimal solution. $\qquad\square$

Similar results can be obtained with various variants of the algorithms in terms of the number of cycles of recirculation, how activities are combined across cycles, and so forth (see exercises).

In summary, for circular autoencoders, learning algorithms exist that do not require a separate deep learning channel running in the backward direction. In this class of algorithms, named recirculation algorithms, the forward channel is used as the DLC. Analysis of these algorithms reveals a remarkable connection to random backpropagation algorithms, specifically to adaptive random backpropagation. While recirculation algorithms may be of little interest in computer applications of neural networks, they have attractive properties when thinking about learning in physical neural systems, in particular biological neural networks. Not only do they get rid of the need for symmetric weights, as well as the need for a separate DLC altogether, but they also take advantage of time differences, or signal derivatives, in the postsynaptic neurons to encode error information, in a way that is not inconsistent with biological observations and theories of learning, including STDP.

8.11   Exercises

EXERCISE 8.1   Study the computational complexity of random backpropagation and its variants, in particular compare RBP and SRBP.

EXERCISE 8.2   How can the BP or RBP equations be understood as a form of dropout on the backward pass?

EXERCISE 8.3   Consider the $A(1, 1, 1, 1)$ linear architecture with forward weights a_1, a_2, a_3 and random weights c_1 and c_2 in the learning channel. Let $P = a_1 a_2 a_3$ be the overall multiplier, and $\alpha = E(IT)$ and $\beta = E(I^2)$ represent the data statistics. Derive and analyze the differential equations for the dynamics of random backpropagation learning in this linear architecture. In particular, prove the following theorem.

THEOREM 8.3   *Except for trivial cases (associated with $c_1 = 0$ or $c_2 = 0$), starting from any initial conditions the system converges to a fixed point, corresponding to a global minimum of the quadratic error function. All the fixed points are located on the hypersurface given by $\alpha - \beta P = 0$ and are global minima of the error function. Along any trajectory, and for each i, a_{i+1} is a quadratic function of a_i. For any starting point, the final fixed point can be calculated by solving a polynomial equation of degree 7.*

EXERCISE 8.4   Consider the linear $A(1, 1, \ldots, 1)$ architecture, with an arbitrary number L of layers, and forward weights $a_1, a_2, \ldots, a_l$, and random weights $c_1, \ldots, c_{L-1}$ in the learning channel. Let $P = a_1 a_2 a_3 \cdots a_L$ be the overall multiplier, and $\alpha = E(IT)$ and $\beta = E(I^2)$ represent the data statistics. Derive and analyze the differential equations for the dynamics of random backpropagation learning in this linear architecture. In particular, prove the following theorem.

THEOREM 8.4   *Except for trivial cases, starting from any initial conditions the system converges to a fixed point, corresponding to a global minimum of the quadratic error function. All the fixed points are located on the hypersurface given by $\alpha - \beta P = 0$ and are global minima of the error function. Along any trajectory, and for each i, a_{i+1} is a quadratic function of a_i. For any starting point, the final fixed point can be calculated by solving a polynomial equation of degree $2^L - 1$.*

EXERCISE 8.5   Consider the linear $A(1, n, 1)$ architecture. Let $a_1, \ldots, a_n$ be the weights in the lower layer, $b_1, \ldots, b_n$ be the weights in the upper layer, and $c_1, \ldots, c_n$ the random weights of the learning channel. In this case, we have $O = \sum_i a_i b_i I$. We let $P = \sum_i a_i b_i$ be the overall multiplier, and $\alpha = E(IT)$ and $\beta = E(I^2)$ represent the data statistics. Derive and analyze the differential equations for the dynamics of random backpropagation learning in this linear architecture. In particular, prove the following theorem.

THEOREM 8.5   *Except for trivial cases, starting from any initial conditions the system converges to a fixed point, corresponding to a global minimum of the quadratic error function. All the fixed points are located on the hyersurface given by $\alpha - \beta P = 0$ and are global minima of the error function. Along any trajectory, each b_i is a quadratic polynomial function of a_i. Each a_i is an affine function of any other a_j. For any starting* *point, the final fixed point can be calculated by solving a polynomial differential equation of degree 3.*

EXERCISE 8.6   Derive in matrix form the differential equations for the dynamics of random backpropagation learning in:
(1) a general linear $A(n_0, n_1, \ldots, n_L)$ architecture; and
(2) an $A(n_0, n_1, n_0)$ autoencoder architecture.
Derive similar equations for backpropagation learning.

EXERCISE 8.7   Derive and study the differential equation for the dynamics of random backpropagation learning in a non-linear $A(1, 1, 1)$ architecture. Assume that the output unit is linear, but the hidden unit is non-linear with a power transfer function $O(S) = S^\mu$ ($\mu \neq 1$; $\mu = 1$ corresponds to the linear case analyzed in this chapter).

EXERCISE 8.8 (VARIATION OF RECIRCULATION USING CONVEX COMBINATIONS)   In this case, recirculation is still a fast process but the units are assumed to have some memory of the original activity so that the original activity and the recirculated activity are combined through a convex combination (see Table 8.2, containing the equations for the first three layers of a circular autoencoder).

	t=0	t=1
$O^2(t)$	$F^2 A^2 F^1 A^1 I$	$\lambda F^2 A^2 F^1 A^1 I + (1 - \lambda) F^2 A^2 F^1 A^1 O^L(0)$
$O^1(t)$	$F^1 A^1 I$	$\lambda F^1 A^1 I + (1 - \lambda) F^1 A^1 O^L(0)$
$O^0(t)$	I	$O^0(1) = \lambda I + (1 - \lambda) O^L(0)$

Table 8.2 Convex Combination of Recirculation Algorithm (CCR).

Write down the corresponding learning equations and analyze them in the linear $A^*(1, 1, 1)$ case.

EXERCISE 8.9 (RECIRCULATION ACROSS MULTIPLE CYCLES)   Recirculate the output n times through the $A^*(1, 1, \ldots, 1)$ circular linear autoencoder and take, as the error, the difference between the activities in the first circulation and the nth recirculation. Show that the differential equations associated with learning by recirculation are given in this case by:

$$\begin{cases} \frac{da_h}{dt} = \beta a_1^2 \cdots a_{h-1}^2 a_h (1 - P^n) & \text{for} \quad h = 1, \ldots, L - 1 \\ \frac{da_L}{dt} = \beta a_1 \cdots a_{L-1} (1 - P^n), \end{cases} \tag{8.41}$$

where $\beta = E(I^2)$ and $P = a_1 \cdots a_L$. Show that there is a deterministic coupling between consecutive weights which yields:

$$\log |a_{h+1}| = \frac{1}{2} a_h^2 + K_h \quad \text{or} \quad |a_{h+1}| = K_h e^{a_h^2/2}, \tag{8.42}$$

for $h = 1, \ldots, L - 2$ where in either case K_h is a constant that depends only on the initial conditions. Prove the following theorem which states that in most cases the system will be able to learn and converge to an optimal set of weights for which $P = 1$.

THEOREM 8.6 *If $\beta > 0$, then for any set of initial conditions satisfying the condition $a_1(0)a_2(0) \cdots a_{L-1}(0) \neq 0$, the system always learns and the weights a_i converge to an optimal equilibrium where $P = 1$. If the initial conditions satisfy $a_1(0)a_2(0) \cdots a_{L-1}(0) = 0$ then $P(t) = 0$ at all times and the system cannot learn. If $\beta = 0$, then for every i $a_i(t) = a_i(0)$ and any choice of initial conditions $a_i(0)$ is optimal.*

EXERCISE 8.10 (RECIRCULATION ACROSS MULTIPLE CYCLES) One can also recirculate the output m times and compare the activities between cycle m and any earlier cycle n ($n < m$). Specifically, in the learning rate of each weight one can multiply:
(1) the difference in post-synaptic activity between cycle n and cycle m (as the "error" term); with
(2) the presynaptic activity at cycle n.
Show that in the case of the linear $A^*(1, 1, \ldots, 1)$ circular autoencoder, this yields the system of differential equations:

$$\frac{da_h}{dt} = \beta a_1^2 \cdots a_{h-1}^2 a_h P^{2n}(1 - P^{m-n}) \quad \text{for} \quad h = 1, \ldots, L. \tag{8.43}$$

Prove the following theorem which states that in most cases the system will be able to learn and converge to an optimal set of weights for which $P = 1$.

THEOREM 8.7 *If $\beta > 0$, then for any set of initial conditions satisfying the condition $a_1(0)a_2(0) \cdots a_L(0) \neq 0$, the system always learns and the weights a_i converge to an optimal equilibrium where $P = 1$. If the initial conditions satisfy $a_1(0)a_2(0) \cdots a_L(0) = 0$ then $P(t) = 0$ at all times and the system cannot learn. If $\beta = 0$, then for every i $a_i(t) = a_i(0)$ and any choice of initial conditions $a_i(0)$ is optimal.*

EXERCISE 8.11 Study recirculation in the circular $A^*(1, 1, \ldots, 1)$ linear autoencoder with different ways of combining activity across cycles.

EXERCISE 8.12 Study recirculation in the circular $A^*(1, n, 1)$ linear autoencoder, with a vector of weights $a = (a_i)$ between the hidden layer and the output layer, and a vector of weights $b = (b_i)$ between the input and the hidden layer. In particular, show that the system of differential equations associated with simple recirculation learning is given by:

$$\begin{cases} \frac{da_i}{dt} = \beta b_i(1 - \sum a_i b_i) = \beta b_i(1 - P) \\ \frac{db_i}{dt} = \beta b_i(1 - \sum a_i b_i) = \beta b_i(1 - P), \end{cases} \tag{8.44}$$

where $P = \sum_i a_i b_i$ is the global multiplier of the system. Show that any solution satisfies, for every i, $a_i(t) = b_i(t) + c_i$, where the constant vector c satisfies $c_i = a_i(0) - b_i(0)$.

Now let $A = ||a||^2 = \sum_i a_i^2$, $B = ||b||^2 = \sum_i b_i^2$, and $C = ||c||^2 = \sum_i c_i^2$. Show that:

$$\frac{dP}{dt} = \beta(1 - P) \sum_i b_i(a_i + b_i) = \beta(1 - P)(P + B),\qquad(8.45)$$

$$\frac{dA}{dt} = 2\beta(1 - P)P,\qquad(8.46)$$

$$\frac{dB}{dt} = 2\beta(1 - P)B.\qquad(8.47)$$

Prove the following theorem which states that in most cases the system will be able to learn and converge to an optimal set of weights for which $P = 1$.

THEOREM 8.8   *If $\beta > 0$, then for any set of initial conditions satisfying the condition $b(0) \neq 0$, the system always learns and the weights converge to an optimal equilibrium where $P = 1$. If the initial conditions satisfy $b(0) = 0$ then all the weights remain constant, $P(t) = 0$ at all times, and the system cannot learn. If $\beta = 0$, then for every i $a_i(t) = a_i(0)$ and $b_i(t) = b_i(0)$ and any choice of initial conditions is optimal.*

EXERCISE 8.13   Consider a multilayer, feedforward architectures $A(n_1, \ldots, n_L)$ and a training set of input–output target pairs of the form (I, T). Consider two learning rules: backpropagation and random backpropagation (RBP or any of its variants). Using a standard training set (e.g. MNIST or CIFAR) plot in each case the trajectories of the hidden layers in the information plane. Are there any significant differences?

9   Recurrent Networks

Chapters 9 and 10 focus on recurrent and recursive networks. Recurrent networks are networks that contain directed cycles and thus are capable of producing states that evolve over time. The notion of recursive networks is slightly different and more general. Any recurrent network unfolded in time can be viewed as a special case of recursive network. Recursive networks are important in order to deal with variable size structured data.

9.1   Recurrent Networks

A recurrent neural network is a neural network that is represented by a directed graph containing at least one directed cycle.

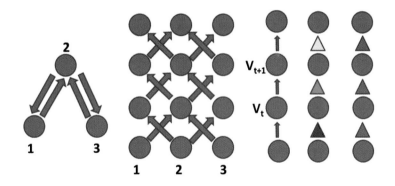

Figure 9.1 From left to right: (a) recurrent networks with three neurons; (b) the same network unfolded in time; (c) a sequence of vectors V_t such that $V_{t+1} = F_{t+1}(V_t)$; (d) the same sequence reparameterized using neural networks, shown as triangles of different colors with $V_{t+1} = NN_{t+1}(V_t)$ [note that each network can be different and include many hidden layers]; (e) corresponding recursive network (see Chapter 10) obtained by using identical networks, or weight sharing, with $V_{t+1} = NN(V_t)$, where $NN()$ represents the shared neural network function.

As soon as a network is recurrent, the question of how its neurons are updated must be addressed. There are at least four main regimes that can be considered:

(1) *synchronous* when all the neurons are updated simultaneously;
(2) *sequential* when all the neurons are updated according to some fixed order;

(3) *stochastic* when neurons are updated randomly.

Variations are obtained depending on whether time is discrete or continuous, whether replacement is allowed in stochastic sampling or not, and so forth. In general, there is no canonical order for updating the neurons sequentially. In a physical neural system without a central clock, the stochastic asynchronous regime may provide a good model. Here, in general, we will use the parallel synchronous mode, which is deterministic, and allows one to unfold recurrent networks in time to derive learning algorithms and other results.

The most widely used approach for learning in recurrent networks is to unfold them in time and then apply backpropagation to the unfolded structure. In the unfolded structure, it is possible to provide targets, fully or partially, at different discrete or continuous times [69]. However there are other learning possibilities, at least in certain special cases, as we have seen in Section 8.7 on recirculation algorithms. After all, a circular autoencoder is a special case of recurrent network. As far as the design of recurrent networks is concerned, the recursive approach described in Chapter 10 provides a systematic way for designing complex recurrent neural networks.

Next we focus on the issue of cardinal capacity of fully connected recurrent networks.

9.2   Cardinal Capacity of Recurrent Networks

Here we consider a fully interconnected recurrent network of n threshold functions of degree d with synchronous updates. We denote by $A_d(n)$ the corresponding architecture. We also consider that all units are visible. Starting from any initial state in $\mathbb{R}^n$ or $\{0, 1\}^n$, the units will be in a binary state at each subsequent update. The sequence of updates will either converge to a fixed point, or to a limit cycle in the n-dimensional hypercube. We let $C_d(n)$ represent the corresponding capacity, i.e. the logarithm base 2 of the number of different functions that can be implemented by the architecture when the initial states (inputs) are restricted to $\{0, 1\}^n$. We say that two such networks are different if there exists at least one binary input that triggers at least one difference in the sequence of updates of the two networks. Note this requires a one-to-one correspondence between the units in the two networks. For instance, if $n = 3$ and the input is the sequence $(0, 0, 0)$, one network may produce the sequence $(0, 0, 0); (0, 0, 0); (0, 0, 0); (0, 0, 0); \ldots$ Any network that produces a different sequence – such as $(0, 0, 0); (1, 1, 1); (0, 0, 0); (1, 1, 1); \ldots$ – when initialized with $(0, 0, 0)$, is considered different. With this definition, two networks are equivalent if and only if each neuron in the first network implements the same threshold gate as the corresponding neuron in the second network. As a result, we have the following capacity theorem:

THEOREM 9.1   *The cardinal capacity of a network of n fully interconnected linear threshold gates of degree d satisfies:*

$$C_d(n) = (C_d(n, 1))^n \tag{9.1}$$

and

$$C_d(n) = \frac{n^{d+2}}{d!} (1 + o(1)).\qquad(9.2)$$

The second equation results immediately from the formula for $C_d(n, 1)$ given in Chapter 3 on shallow networks. In the main case where $d = 1$, this states that the capacity is a cubic function of the number of neurons.

In the rest of this chapter, we focus on a special class of recurrent networks, those with *symmetric* connections ($w_{ij} = w_{ji}$). The key point is that symmetric connections give rise to an energy function that controls the overall behavior of the network. When there are no hidden units, these are called Hopfield networks. The more general case with hidden units corresponds to Boltzmann machines, which can also be viewed as special cases of random Markov fields in the theory of probabilistic graphical models.

9.3 Symmetric Connections: The Hopfield Model

The Hopfield model was originally introduced as a model of associative memory [355]. The key idea behind the model is to combine symmetrically connected linear threshold gates with Hebbian learning. In its basic form, its substrate consists of a network of n linear threshold units with symmetric connections and no self-connections. The units are updated in stochastic asynchronous mode using a uniform distribution over the units, but similar results are obtained with, for instance, sequential update. The activation of unit i is given, as usual, by $S_i = \sum_{j\neq i} w_{ij} O_j + b_i$, where b_i is the bias. Consider the quantity:

$$\mathcal{E} = -\frac{1}{2} \sum_{i,j} w_{ij} O_i O_j - \sum_i b_i O_i.\qquad(9.3)$$

By isolating the contribution of O_i, it can be rewritten as:

$$\mathcal{E} = -\frac{1}{2} \sum_{k,l\neq i} w_{kl} O_k O_l - \sum_{k\neq i} b_k O_k - O_i S_i.\qquad(9.4)$$

One can immediately see that every time unit i is to be updated, either its current output agrees with its current activation and then the value of the unit's output and of the function $\mathcal{E}$ do not change, or the unit output is updated to make it consistent with the activation S_i in which case the function $\mathcal{E}$ must decrease. The magnitude of the decrease is equal to $2|S_i|$ if linear threshold gates with outputs in $\{-1, +1\}$ are used, and to $|S_i|$ if linear threshold gates with outputs in $\{0, 1\}$ are used. Thus in short, the function $\mathcal{E}$ acts like an energy or Lyapounov function for the network and, since the network can only have a finite number 2^n of states, its dynamics always converge to a local minimum, also called stable state, of $\mathcal{E}$.

As an aside, in the previous description the output of a selected unit is updated only when its current activation S_i disagrees with its current output O_i. It is of course possible to use softer update rules where the probability of changing the output is non-zero even when S_i agrees with O_i and is, for instance, proportional to $e^{-\Delta\mathcal{E}/T}$ where T

is a temperature parameter. Alternatively, the unit can be updated probabilistically in all cases, with a probability given by $\sigma(S_i)$, where σ is the logistic function, as in the case of Boltzmann machines (see Section 9.4).

To use this network as a model of associative memory, one would like to sculpt the energy function $\mathcal{E}$ in order to store information, or memories, as energy minima at the bottom of large valleys. Starting from a corrupted version of the memory, the downhill dynamics of the system may restore the full memory. Thus the second key idea in the Hopfield model is to use Hebbian learning to sculpt $\mathcal{E}$ in order to store information, or memories, at the bottom of large valleys of $\mathcal{E}$.

More precisely, suppose we want to store K memories, or training examples, $M^1, \ldots, M^K$, where each M^k is a binary vector of length n. Using linear threshold units with outputs in $\{-1, +1\}$, the synaptic weights are obtained using the outerproduct, or Hebbian, symmetric rule:

$$w_{ij} = \sum_k M_i^k M_j^k. \tag{9.5}$$

In matrix form, this can also be written as $W = \sum_k M^k (M^k)^{\mathrm{T}}$ which explains why the simple Hebbian formula is sometimes also called the outerproduct formula. It is essential to note that all the units in the model are considered to be visible, and therefore this can be viewed as a form of *shallow* learning.

To see why the simple Hebb's rule may be a good idea in this case, we can set the value of the units to a specific memory M^l and check how likely it is to be stable. For this, we need to check how likely the activation S_i of the network is likely to agree with M_i^l, i.e. to have the same sign (we assume zero biases). We have:

$$S_i = \sum_{j \neq i} w_{ij} M_j^l = \sum_{j \neq i} \left(\sum_{k=1}^K M_i^k M_j^k \right) M_j^l. \tag{9.6}$$

We can separate in the sum the contribution resulting from M^l from the rest. Thus we get a signal plus noise equation of the form:

$$S_i = \sum_{j \neq i} M_i^l M_j^l M_j^l + \sum_{j \neq i} \left(\sum_{k=1, k \neq l}^K M_i^k M_j^k \right) M_j^l, \tag{9.7}$$

or:

$$S_i = (n-1) M_i^l + \sum_{j \neq i} \left(\sum_{k=1, k \neq l}^K M_i^k M_j^k \right) M_j^l. \tag{9.8}$$

Thus the magnitude of the signal is $n - 1$. To estimate the noise, imagine that the components of the memories are selected independently using a fair coin flip. The noise term can be approximated with a normal distribution with mean 0 and variance $(n-1)(K-1)$. Thus we see that if K is small relative to n the signal is significantly larger than the noise. It is instructive to study the noise term when the memories are exactly orthogonal [67], as opposed to orthogonal in expectation, as well as the case of sparse memories generated using coin flips with $p < 0.5$.

There are obviously several interesting questions including: How large can K be? How large can the typical radius R of attraction of the memories be? How do these quantities vary with the amount of error tolerated during recall? How do these quantities vary with the way the memories are generated, e.g. by random coin flips with $p = 0.5$ versus $p < 0.5$? How many local minima are there? There is a significant literature addressing these questions (see also some of the exercises). One general answer for the storage is that the maximal number of memories that can be stored scales like $K \approx \alpha n$, where α varies with the details of the storage model. It should be clear that the Hopfield model bears strong connections to spin models in statistical mechanics, in particular spin glasses. This connection was instrumental in bringing physicists to the field in the mid-1980s. The questions above, as well as others, were first addressed using approximate methods, such as mean field theory and replica methods in statistical mechanics (e.g. [25, 26, 103, 28, 27]; see also [492]), followed in time by mathematically rigorous results (e.g. [47, 89, 90, 101, 419, 533, 718, 140]), as well as generalizations to Hopfield networks with polynomial energy functions with degree $d > 2$ (e.g. [68, 156, 761, 760, 104]).

Another way of looking at the Hopfield model is to consider its state space, which is the n-dimensional hypercube, and its orientations. The energy $\mathcal{E}$ assigns a value to each vertex of the hypercube, and edges between two neighboring vertices are oriented from the state with higher energy to the state with lower energy (as usual, in general, ties are rare and not particularly significant). Thus the energy E induces an acyclic orientation of the hypercube and the system dynamics follows directed paths in the hypercube graph. Clearly any real-valued function of the states can be used in a similar way to generate an acyclic orientation. This raises several interesting directions partially covered in the exercises and the literature. These include understanding the symmetry relationships between learning rules and acyclic orientations, estimating the total number of orientations of the hypercube, and the fraction of orientations that can be generated using quadratic functions or, more generally, polynomials of degree d. This is one way of defining a notion of capacity for the Hopfield model and the results are closely related to the notions of capacity seen in Chapter 3 [8, 65, 68, 66].

Finally, in addition to associative memory, a second possible use of the Hopfield model, suggested by its Lyapounov dynamics, is in optimization [357]. While in associative memory the goal is to sculpt $\mathcal{E}$ in order to store memories at the bottom of large valleys and use the dynamics for associative retrieval, in optimization the goal is to map a given optimization problem into the minimization of an energy function $\mathcal{E}$, and let the network dynamics do the minimization. It can be shown that any NP-complete problem can be polynomially reduced to the problem of minimizing a quadratic form on the hypercube [108] (providing a third example in this book connecting NP-completeness to neural networks). Thus, in general, finding the lowest energy state of a Hopfield network is intractable. However, this does not rule out the possibility of being able to carry out the optimization exactly in restricted but important cases, or to carry it out approximately. In the latter case, continuous-time neurons have been considered as potentially a better, smoother option for carrying out the optimization, as opposed to discrete neurons [357].

While the Hopfield model is theoretically elegant and suggestive of how associative storage or optimization could be carried out in a physical neural system, so far it has not proven to be useful when simulated on digital machines. Furthermore, depending on the physical substrate, the requirement of having neurons connected symmetrically may not be easily realizable in a physical neural system.

9.4　Symmetric Connections: Boltzmann Machines

Boltzmann machines [9] can be viewed as generalizations of the Hopfield model to include hidden units in the network. Again the units are symmetrically connected giving rise to the same underlying energy function as in Equations 9.3 and 9.4. Units are selected for updates in a stochastic asynchronous fashion, as in the Hopfield model. The update of a unit is typically probabilistic using a logistic transfer function, i.e. when unit i is selected for update, it is set to 1 with probability given by $1/(1 + e^{-S_i})$, and to 0 (or -1) otherwise. This probability can be generalized to $1/(1 + e^{-S_i/T})$ by introducing a temperature parameter T. If $O = (O_1, \ldots, O_n)$ is the vector describing the state of the system, it can be shown that at equilibrium the system obeys the Boltzmann distribution:

$$P(O) = P(O|W) = \frac{e^{-\mathcal{E}(O)/T}}{\sum_U e^{-\mathcal{E}(U)/T}} = \frac{e^{-\mathcal{E}(O)/T}}{Z}. \qquad (9.9)$$

The normalizing factor $Z = \sum_U e^{-\mathcal{E}(U)/T}$ is also called the *partition function*. Boltzmann machines can also be viewed as examples of Markov random fields [282, 417, 522].

It is important to note that alternatively, starting from the Boltzmann distribution, one can derive the logistic update rule. To see this, consider unit i and using Equation 9.4 to separate its contribution to the energy function:

$$\mathcal{E}(O) = \mathcal{E}(O, W) = -R - O_i S_i, \qquad (9.10)$$

where R is a term that does not depend on unit i. If we represent the rest of the network by the variable $\hat{O}_i = (O_1, \ldots, O_{i-1}, O_{i+1}, \ldots, O_n)$, using the Boltzmann distribution we must have:

$$P(O_i = 1|W, \hat{O}_i) = \frac{e^{(R+S_i)/T}}{Z} \quad \text{and} \quad P(O_i = 0|W, \hat{O}_i) = \frac{e^{R/T}}{Z}, \qquad (9.11)$$

using units valued in $\{0, 1\}$. These two probabilities must add up to one, and thus:

$$P(O_i = 1|W, \hat{O}_i) = \frac{1}{1 + e^{-S_i/T}}. \qquad (9.12)$$

As in the case of the Hopfield model, a Boltzmann machine can be used to address two different computational problems, optimization and learning. In optimization the weights are fixed and the energy function represents a cost function. Simulated annealing [409] can be performed by progressively annealing the temperature towards zero to let the system settle into low-cost states. In learning, the goal is to find the weights that result in a Boltzmann distribution that is as consistent as possible with the training data.

To study learning in more detail, consider that the Boltzmann machine has both visible and hidden units. The visible units are those where the data is entered. The vector of states of the visible units is denoted O^v, and the vector of states for the hidden units is denoted O^h. We assume that the training data consists of a target distribution $T(O^v)$ over the states of the visible units. For a fixed set of weights W, let $P_W(O^v) = P(O^v)$ be the distribution over the visible states of the Boltzmann machine after it reaches equilibrium, after marginalization of the hidden units. The goal of learning is to find the weights that minimize the KL divergence $\mathcal{K}$ between T and P:

$$\min_W \mathcal{K} = \min_W \sum_{O^v} T(O^v) \log \frac{T(O^v)}{P(O^v)}, \tag{9.13}$$

where the sum is over all possible states O^v of the visible units or, in practice, just the training set. As usual, this optimization process is carried by gradient descent. In a typical situation, the data consists of a set of training examples, each weighted equally. Thus minimizing the KL divergence is equivalent to minimizing the negative log-likelihood of the data $-\log P(O^v)$, summed over the training set.

For any state O^v, and assuming for notational simplicity for the rest of this section that $T = 1$, we have:

$$P(O^v) = \sum_{O^h} P(O^v, O^h) = \sum_{O^h} \frac{e^{-\mathcal{E}(O^v, O^h)}}{Z} \tag{9.14}$$

or

$$\log P(O^v) = \log \sum_{O^h} e^{-\mathcal{E}(O^v, O^h)} - \log \sum_{O^{v'}, O^{h'}} e^{-\mathcal{E}(O^{v'}, O^{h'})}, \tag{9.15}$$

where the rightmost term is simply the logarithm of the partition function. A simple calculation, left as an exercise, shows that for any parameter w (weight or bias) and fixed training example O^v, we have:

$$\frac{\partial \log P(O^v)}{\partial w} = \sum_{O^h} P(O^h|O^v) \frac{\partial \mathcal{E}(O^v, O^h)}{\partial w} - \sum_{O^{v'}, O^{h'}} P(O^{v'}, O^{h'}) \frac{\partial \mathcal{E}(O^{v'}, O^{h'})}{\partial w} \tag{9.16}$$

or

$$\frac{\partial \log P(O^v)}{\partial w} = E_{P(O^h|O^v)} \frac{\partial \mathcal{E}(O^v, O^h)}{\partial w} - E_{P(O^{v'}, O^{h'})} \frac{\partial \mathcal{E}(O^{v'}, O^{h'})}{\partial w}. \tag{9.17}$$

The first term in the right-hand side is the expected gradient of the energy function with respect to the conditional distribution $P(O^h|O^v)$. The second term is the expected gradient of the energy function with respect to the joint distribution over all variable states. For a connection parameter w_{ij}, we have: $\partial \mathcal{E}/\partial W_{ij} = O_i O_j$. Thus in this case Equation 9.17 can be written as:

$$\frac{\partial \log P(O^v)}{\partial w} = P_{\text{clamped}}(O_i O_j) - P_{\text{free}}(O_i O_i) \tag{9.18}$$

where $P_{\text{free}}(O_i O_j)$ is the probability that units i and j are both on when the machine is at equilibrium during its free phase, and similarly for the clamped phase.

For any realistic model, in general it is impossible to compute these expectations exactly, since these would require summations over very large numbers of states. Thus in general these expectations are approximated by using Markov Chain Monte Carlo

(MCMC) methods. Thus, for example, for a weight w_{ij}, one uses the approximation:

$$\frac{\partial \log P(v)}{\partial w_{ij}} \approx -\langle O_i O_j \rangle_{\text{clamped}} + \langle O_i O_j \rangle_{\text{free}} \qquad (9.19)$$

ultimately giving rise to the learning rule:

$$\Delta w_{ij} = \eta \left(\langle O_i O_j \rangle_{\text{clamped}} - \langle O_i O_j \rangle_{\text{free}}, \right) \qquad (9.20)$$

where the average correlations $\langle O_i O_j \rangle$ between units i and j are computed using MCMC methods (e.g. Gibbs sampling, Metropolis–Hastings) in the network with the visible units clamped to their training values, and in the free network. A similar equation can be written for the biases and, as usual, these changes are accumulated over the training set. This sampling process is computationally very expensive on a digital machine since it requires first reaching equilibrium and then estimating these correlations.

In short, there are two alternating phases to Boltzmann machine training. One is the clamped phase where the visible units are clamped to a particular binary state vector sampled from the training set. The other is the free phase where the network is allowed to run freely, i.e. no units have their state determined by external data. Learning by approximate gradient descent proceeds using the learning equation 9.20 (and similarly for the biases). These learning equations, with two contrasting phases, are examples of contrastive learning [519, 86, 798, 171].

From a theoretical standpoint, it seems remarkable that the resulting learning rule is entirely local, essentially a form of simple Hebbian learning. Indeed, for any given synapse, all that is required is the correlation between the two neighboring neurons in the clamped and the free phases. However, the existence of such a learning rule can be expected from the theory of local learning given in Chapter 8. Indeed, in a Boltzmann machine, the reciprocal connections implement a deep learning channel which communicates any target information, contained in the clamped visible units, to the deep synapses.

Note that it is also possible to train a conditional Boltzmann machine, where the visible units are further partitioned into input units and output units. During the clamped phase both input and output units are clamped to their training values. During the free phase, only input units are clamped to their training values. It is also possible to consider Boltzmann machines where the stochastic units can assume a larger number of discrete values using softmax probabilistic units, or can assume real values using Gaussian units (i.e. adding Gaussian noise to the activation). More generally, it is possible to consider Boltzmann machines where the distribution of the output of the stochastic units is a member of the exponential family of distributions [153, 784] (see also exercises), so that the log probabilities are linear functions of the parameters.

9.4.1   Restricted Boltzmann Machines (RBMs):

Restricted Boltzmann machines are Boltzmann machines where the only connections allowed are between the visible and hidden units (Figure 9.2). There are no hidden-to-hidden, or visible-to-visible, connections. Thus in restricted Boltzmann machine,

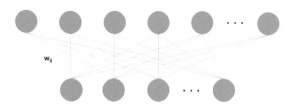

Figure 9.2 The connections in a restricted Boltzmann machine (RBM) form a bipartite graph. Connections run only between the visible units and the hidden units. There are no connections within the visible units, or within the hidden units. All connections are symmetric with $w_{ij} = w_{ji}$.

conditioned on the input vector v, the activities of the hidden units are independent of each other. Conversely, conditioned on the hidden unit activities, the activities of the visible units are independent of each other. This restricted connectivity allows for faster learning, for instance using efficient MCMC methods, such as blocked Gibbs sampling. In practice, for a weight w connecting a visible unit i to a hidden unit j one can use the update rule:

$$\Delta w_{ij} = \eta \left(\langle O_i O_j \rangle_{\text{clamped}} - \langle O_i O_j \rangle_{\text{approx}} \right), \tag{9.21}$$

where the approximation is obtained using only three steps of conditional updates. After initializing the visible units to a training pattern O^v, the three steps compute:
(1) the vector O^h using $P(O^h | O^v)$;
(2) the vector $O^{v'}$ using $P(O^{v'} | O^h)$; and
(3) the vector $O^{h'}$ using $P(O^{h'} | O^{v'})$.

These vectors are then used to compute the averages needed for Equation 9.20. This procedure can also be written as:

$$\Delta w_{ij} = \eta \left(\langle O_i(0) O_j(0) \rangle - \langle O_i(1) O_j(1) \rangle \right) \tag{9.22}$$

and thus can also be viewed as a form of recirculation. This results in an efficient procedure which does approximate gradient descent with respect to a contrastive divergence [171]. Finally, the hidden layers of RBMs can be stacked vertically and trained sequentially, by using the hidden layer of an RBM at level k as the visible layer of the RBM at level $k + 1$, as we did for autoencoders ([345]).

9.5 Exercises

EXERCISE 9.1 Consider a fully recurrent network with n neurons with logistic transfer functions and synchronous updates occurring at times $t = 1, 2, \ldots$. The training data consists of input–output pairs $(I(k), T(k))$ with $k = 1, \ldots, K$. Both inputs and targets are n-dimensional vectors. The learning goal is to set the weights $W = (w_{ij})$ of the network so that, for every k, when the neurons are initialized to $I(k)$ the network is in state $T(k)$ after L synchronous updates. Write down a suitable error function for this task together with the corresponding gradient descent learning equations by unfolding the network in time. Write the learning equations for both the on-line case and the batch case, as well as for w_{ij} and W (in matrix form). Examine how the bias should be handled. How can the learning equations be generalized to the case where, for each example, additional targets are provided also at some intermediary time points (i.e. for some time points t satisfying $1 \le t \le L$), and not necessarily for all the units (i.e. targets may be available only for a subset of the units at such a time point).

EXERCISE 9.2   Consider a Hopfield model with n neurons and K memories. What happens if self-connections are allowed? Assume that all the units are linear threshold gates with outputs in $\{-1, 1\}$. How should the weights be transformed to produce an equivalent networks with outputs in $\{0, 1\}$? How should the simple Hebb learning rule defined for memories with components in $\{-1, 1\}$ be written for memories with components in $\{0, 1\}$?

EXERCISE 9.3   Consider a network with n neurons and K memories. Generalize the concepts of Hopfield networks and Boltzmann machines to the case where the energy function is a polynomial of degree $d > 2$.

EXERCISE 9.4   Consider the problem of minimizing a polynomial of degree d over the n-dimensional cube $\{-1, +1\}^n$. Prove that if $d < 2$ the problem has a trivial solution, and if $d \ge 2$ the problem is NP-complete.

EXERCISE 9.5   Consider a Hopfield network of symmetrically connected, continuous-time, neurons satisfying (see Chapter 2):

$$\frac{dS_i}{dt} = -\frac{S_i}{\tau_i} + \sum_j w_{ij} O_j + I_i \quad \text{and} \quad O_i = f_i(S_i). \tag{9.23}$$

Show that there is a Lyapounov energy function $\mathcal{E}$ that governs the dynamics of the network.

EXERCISE 9.6   Consider the traveling salesman problem (TSP) with m cities and a matrix of pairwise distances d_{ij}. Map the TSP into the problem of minimizing a low degree polynomial over a hypercube of appropriate dimension n.

EXERCISE 9.7   Prove that all the isometries of the n-dimensional hypercube are generated by two elementary operations:
(1) permuting the values associated with any two coordinates i and j; and
(2) flipping the values associated with any coordinate i.
    Let s be an isometry of the hypercube and let $M^1, \ldots, M^K$ be K memories. Show that using Hebb's rule, the acyclic orientation generated by the Hopfield model using $s(M^1), \ldots, s(M^K)$ is the same as the acyclic orientation obtained by applying s to the acyclic orientation generated by $M^1, \ldots, M^K$. In other words, the underlying diagram "commutes". Show that this is true only for Hebb's simple rule.

EXERCISE 9.8   Estimate the total number of acyclic orientations of the hypercube. Estimate the total number of acyclic orientations of the hypercube that can be generated using quadratic energy functions to assign an energy value to each vertex. Similarly, estimate the total number of acyclic orientations of the hypercube that can be generated using polynomial energy functions of degree d.

EXERCISE 9.9   Assign the numbers $1, 2, \ldots, 2^n$ randomly and uniformly to the vertices of the n-dimensional hypercube. Each assignment induces an acyclic orientation of the edges of the hypercube, by orienting each edge from the vertex with the larger number to the vertex with the lower number. For any vertex i, consider the 0–1 random variable X_i, where $X_i = 1$ if i corresponds to a local minimum, and $X_i = 0$ otherwise. Compute the mean and variance of X_i. Compute the covariance between X_i and X_j as a function of the Hamming distance between i and j. What is the expectation and variance of the total number of local minima? Same questions when the values assigned to the vertices are drawn independently from a normal distribution.

EXERCISE 9.10   Consider a network of n threshold gates with symmetric connections $(w_{ij} = w_{ji})$. Assume that the weights w_{ij} are sampled from a standard normal distribution with mean zero and unit variance, and that all biases are set to 0. Estimate the expected number of stable states (i.e. of local minima of the energy function).

EXERCISE 9.11   Consider a Hopfield network with n threshold gate neurons, and K binary memories chosen at random by flipping a fair coin. Estimate, mathematically or through simulations, as a function of K, the expected radius of attraction of the memories and the expected number of stable states. Discuss different regimes.

EXERCISE 9.12   Consider a Hopfield network with n threshold gate neurons, and K binary memories chosen at random by flipping a biased coin with probability p of producing a 1. Estimate, mathematically or through simulations, as a function of K and p, the expected radius of attraction of the memories and the expected number of stable states. Discuss different regimes.

EXERCISE 9.13   Consider a Hopfield network with n neurons, and memories $M^1, \ldots, M^K$ in $\{-1, +1\}^n$ and weights obtained by the simple Hebb rule (outerproduct formula). Assume that the memories are orthogonal to each other. Show that the number of stable states (i.e. minima of the corresponding error function $\mathcal{E}$ is two for $K = 1$, four for $K = 2$, and 14 for $K = 3$ (with $n > 4$). When $K = n$ the memories form a Hadamard matrix. Use a recursive construction to show that Hadamard matrices can be constructed for any $K = 2^m$. It remains an open question whether Hadamard matrices can be constructed for any $K = 4m$. What happens in the Hopfield model when $K = n$ and the memories form a Hadamard matrix?

EXERCISE 9.14   Consider a system that can be in N different states $s_1, \ldots, s_N$ each state s_i occurring with an unknown probability distribution $P(s_i) = p_i$, with $p_i \geq 0$ for very i and $\sum_i p_i = 1$. Assume that there is a known function f that maps each state to a real number and assume the only data available is the average of f: $E(f) = \sum_i f(s_i)p_i$. Show that the probability distribution P with the maximal entropy that is consistent with the data is the Boltzmann distribution. Reformulate this problem in a Bayesian framework with a suitable prior distribution. Show that any probability distribution over a finite set can be written as a Boltzmann distribution for a suitable energy function.

Finally, can any probability distribution over the n-dimensional hypercube $\{0, 1\}^n$ be represented as the equilibrium distribution of a Boltzmann machine with n neurons and quadratic energy function?

EXERCISE 9.15   Consider a set of n symmetrically connected probabilistic binary units with asynchronous stochastic update and logistic transfer function. The state of each unit is either 0 or 1. When unit i is selected, it computes its activation S_i based on the rest of the network and updates its value to 1 with probability $1/(1 + e^{-S_i})$. Show that the states of the network give rise to an irreducible finite Markov chain with aperiodic states and compute the equilibrium distribution.

EXERCISE 9.16   Complete the derivation of Equation 9.17 for computing the gradient of the likelihood in a Boltzmann machine. Derive a similar equation for higher-order Boltzmann machines where the energy function is a polynomial of degree $d > 2$. Show that the learning rule described in Section 9.4 for conditional Boltzmann machines maximizes the log probability of the output vectors conditioned on the input vectors. Show that the recirculation learning rule for RBMs approximates gradient descent on a suitable cost function.

EXERCISE 9.17   A family of distributions is said to belong to a vector exponential family if the probability density function (or probability mass function, for discrete distributions) can be written as:

$$f(x|\theta) = h(x) \exp\left(\sum_{i=1}^{s} g_i(\theta) T_i(x) - A(\theta)\right), \tag{9.24}$$

where $x = (x_1, \ldots, x_k)$ is a k-dimensional real-valued vector, $\theta = (\theta_1, \ldots, \theta_d)$ is a d-dimensional real-valued parameter vector. In most common cases, $s = d$. The functions $T_i(x)$ are the sufficient statistics. For exponential families, the sufficient statistics are functions of the data that contain all the information the data provides with regard to the unknown parameter values.

Write the Gaussian, Poisson, Exponential, Binomial, and Multinomial distributions as exponential distributions. Derive the energy function and the corresponding gradient descent learning equations for Boltzmann machines with unit's output distributions in the exponential family. In particular, show that the gradient can be expressed as the change in the sufficient statistics caused by clamping data on the visible units.

10 Recursive Networks

This chapter focuses on recursive networks, also rebranded as graph neural networks (GNNs). This general concept is essential for desigining recurrent network as well as networks that can handle variable-size structured data and their many applications.

10.1 Variable-Size Structured Data

Many problems in machine learning involve data items represented by vectors or tensors of fixed size. This is the case, for instance, in computer vision with images of fixed size. In these cases, feedforward architectures with fixed-size input can be applied. However, there exist many applications where the data items are not of fixed size. Furthermore, the data items often come with a structure, often represented by a graph, which may also include labels on the nodes or the edges. Examples include:

Sets typically represented by lists, but where the order has no intrinsic meaning. For instance, the representation of a small molecule as a bag of atoms together with the x, y, z coordinates of the corresponding nuclei; the representation of documents as bags of words; the representation of particles showers in high energy physics as lists of objects (e.g. jets, tracks, vertices) and their properties.

Sequences, or ordered lists For instance, time series, sentences in natural language, pieces of software code, mathematical expressions, DNA/RNA sequences, protein sequences, SMILES and SMIRKS strings in chemoinformatics, and various string representations of chemical reactions.

Trees For instance parse trees for text sequences in natural language processing, parse trees for software code, parse trees for mathematical expressions, and evolutionary trees.

Small graphs For instance graphs representing Feynman diagrams in physics, small molecules or chemical reactions in chemistry, and RNA secondary structure in biology.

Large graphs representing networks, such as biological networks associated with biological pathways (e.g. protein-protein interactions, metabolic networks), friendships and other social networks, organization networks.

Grids, or matrices, or tensors For instance 2D contact maps and distance maps for nucleotide or amino acid sequences in computational biology, or 3D atmospheric grids, or grids associated with games and puzzles (e.g. Rubik's cubes of different dimensions and sizes, such as $3 \times 3 \times 3$, $2 \times 2 \times 2 \times 2$, and $4 \times 4 \times 4$).

Note that these variable-size structures can appear at the input level, at the output level, or both. For instance, a translation problem can be viewed as a sequence-to-sequence problem. The input and output sequences need not be of the same length. The prediction of the secondary structure of a protein can be viewed as a translation problem from an alphabet with 20 letters, one for each naturally occurring amino acid, to an alphabet with three letters, corresponding to the three main secondary structure classes (alpha-helix, beta-strand, and coil). In this particular case, the input sequence and the output sequence have the same length. In parsing problems, the input is a sequence and the output is a tree. In protein contact map prediction the input is a sequence, and the output is a matrix, and so forth. In all these problems, labels can exist on the nodes, on the edges, or both. A small molecule in organic chemistry can have labels on the nodes corresponding to the atom type (e.g. C, N, O, H), as well as on the edges, corresponding to the bond type (e.g. single, double, triple, and aromatic).

In some cases, it may be possible to use fixed size vectors, with zeros padding, to represent these objects and process them using feedforward neural networks. However, this is not very elegant and in many cases not efficient, especially if the sizes vary over a wide range. In general, it is better to use recursive neural networks (RNNs), or graph neural networks (GNNs), to process these variable-size structured data. In the next sections, we describe what these are and how to design the corresponding architectures by describing two different approaches, the inner approach and the outer approach [71]. The distinction between inner and outer is not a fundamental one, as discussed further down. Rather it is a convenient way of organizing the heterogenous variety of RNN/GNN approaches described in the literature to help the reader get oriented.

10.2   Recursive Networks and Design

A recursive network is a network that contains connection weights, often entire subnetworks, that are shared, often in a systematic way (Figure 9.1). There is some flexibility in the degree and multiplicity of sharing that is required in order to be called recursive. For instance, at the low end, a convolutional network could be considered a recursive network, although the non-convolutional part of the network could be dominant. Likewise, a Siamese network can also be called recursive, although it may combine only two copies of the same network. At the high end, any recurrent network unfolded in time yields a highly recursive network. Of course, the notion of a recursive network becomes most useful when there is a regular pattern of connections, associated for instance with a lattice (see examples below). The basic idea in recursive approaches is to reuse over and over the same neural network modules to process and pass information between nodes of graphs associated with the data, or derived from the data.

To be more precise, by recursive networks we refer to a general set of approaches for designing and applying neural networks to variable-size data. In these recursive

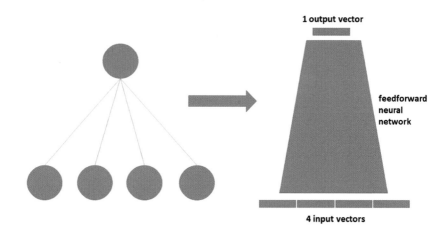

Figure 10.1 The basic building block of recursive approaches. Left: a piece of a graph consisting of four nodes connected to a fifth node which has been selected as the center. Each node comes with an associated vector. Right: a neural network that computes, or updates, the vector at the center node, as a function of the four vectors associated with the four other nodes.

approaches the starting point is a class of graphs associated with the data, or derived from the data, such as a data model (e.g. HMMs). These graphs may have labels associated with the nodes or the edges, and may be directed or undirected. Extensions to hypergraphs are also possible. The recursive approach can be centered on the nodes, or the edges, or both. For simplicity here we will stay centered on the nodes, while still allowing for the possibility of processing labels located on edges.

The basic building block of recursive approaches is illustrated in Figure 10.1. In this approach a vector is attached to each node and the basic idea is that the vector of one node is a function of all the information (e.g. other vectors and node/edge labels) contained in a neighborhood of the node. While larger neighborhoods can be considered, for simplicity we will consider only neighborhoods of radius 1, i.e. immediate neighbors of a node. In the recursive neural network approach, the function associated with each node is parameterized by a neural network. The approach is called recursive because, if the graph has some regular structure, the same neural network can be reused (weight sharing) by all the nodes in the graph that are similar. If the underlying graphs are directed and acyclic, then the node vectors can be updated in an orderly fashion by propagation from the source nodes to the sink nodes. Below, this approach is also called the inner approach. Note that when a recurrent neural network is unfolded in time (Figure 9.1), this can be viewed as the application of an inner approach to a very simple chain graph, where the vector associated with each node is the vector of states of all the units at time t, and the same neural network is applied at all discrete time steps to go from the state at time t to the state at time $t + 1$. In this sense, the recursive approach is more general than the recurrent approach.

If the underlying graphs are not acyclic, then one typically uses synchronous update. This general approach is called the convolutional, or outer, approach, in the literature.

The synchronous update can be repeated but then one must specify how many times as, in general, there is no guarantee of convergence to stable values. It is also possible to use a first set of neural networks during the first pass of synchronous updates, then a second set of neural networks (e.g. with different architectures) during the second pass of asynchronous updates, and so forth. And finally, it is also possible to change the structure of the underlying graphs (e.g. by merging neighboring nodes) from one synchronous pass to the next. The fundamental point of these outer processing approaches is that when properly unfolded they operate on a directed acyclic (operational) graph, although the original data-associated graphs may not be directed, or acyclic. As a result, for each set of input variables they produce a unique set of output variables and, if input-output target pairs are available for training, then backpropagation can be applied through the operational acyclic graph. These approaches for propagating information through graphs using neural networks have broad connections to other areas of machine learning, statistics, and operation research (e.g. belief propagation). In the next sections, we give specific examples of inner and outer approaches.

10.2.1   Inner Approaches

The inner approach requires that the structures of interest be represented by directed acyclic graphs (DAGs) (Figures 10.2). There is no established nomenclature for the the the DAGs but we will use some of corresponding names from the theory of probabilistic graphical models, in particular Bayesian networks which are associated with DAGs, while discarding their probabilistic interpretation. Even then, the nomenclature is not completely established. Important parameters to keep in mind are:

- The presence of inputs, outputs, or both.
- The dimensionality (1D, 2D, 3D, etc) of the inputs, outputs, or both. When the inputs and output have the same dimensionality only one dimension may be mentioned.
- The presence of non visible nodes (hidden factors, hidden chains, or hidden lattices), their number, and connectivity within each group of nodes, and across groups.
- Whether the hidden chains or lattices are oriented in all directions (bidirectional in 1D, omni-directional in higher dimensions) or whether only one subset of the orientations (e.g. left–right in 1D) is represented.

In the case of 1D sequence problems, for instance, these graphs are typically based on left-to-right chains associated with Bayesian network representations such as Markov Chains, Hidden Markov Models (HMMs) (Figure 10.3), Factorial HMMs, and Input–Output HMMs (IOHMMs) (Figure 10.4) [417, 522]. HMMs and factorial HMMs have outputs only, whereas IOHMMs have both inputs and outputs. Factorial HMMs have one, or multiple, chains of hidden factors, all running from left to right. Higher-order Markov versions of all these structures are possible (see exercises). A bidirectional HMM or IOHMM has an additional chain of hidden states running from right to left. A bidirectional multifactorial IOHMMs could have multiple chains, running in both directions (and one would have to specify exactly how many and their exact pattern of connectivity).

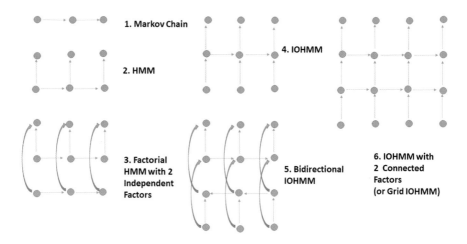

Figure 10.2 Examples of DAGs and their associated probabilistic graphical model names for 1D objects, such as time series or sequences. (1) First-order Markov chain DAG where the state at time t directly depends on the state at time $t - 1$. This is the DAG structure one uses when unfolding a recurrent neural network in time. (2) First-order Hidden Markov Model (HMM) DAG which produces outputs as a function of hidden states. (3) First-order Factorial HMM DAG where the outputs are function of two different kinds of hidden states, corresponding to two separate left-right Markov chains. Connections from one hidden chain to the other can be added without introducing directed cycles. (4) First-order input-output HMM (IOHMM) DAG which produces outputs as a function of both inputs and hidden states. Connections from inputs to outputs can be added without introducing directed cycles. (5) First-order bidirectional IOHMM DAG which produces outputs as a function of both inputs and hidden states. The hidden states are organized in two chains, one running left-to-right and one running right-to-left. Connections from one hidden chain to the other could be added without introducing directed cycles. (6) First-order IOHMM with two Connected Hidden Factors (or Grid IOHMM) DAG which produces outputs as a function of both inputs and hidden states. As the number of hidden factors is increased, this DAG becomes a 2D grid. All edges are oriented towards the North-East corner.

In the inner approach, the variables associated with each node of the DAG are a function of the variables associated with all the parent nodes, and this function is parameterized by a neural network (see, for instance, [99, 306, 280]). Furthermore, the weights of the neural networks sharing a similar functionality can be shared, yielding a recursive neural network approach (Figures 9.1c, 9.1d, 9.1e). For instance, in the case of an HMM DAG, two neural networks can be used, one shared across all outputs, and one shared across all hidden transitions (Figure 10.3). In the case of a factorial HMM DAG with two hiddent factors, three neural networks can be used, and so forth. Thus in this recursive approach the individual networks can be viewed as "crawling" the DAG along its edge the inside – hence the name of the approach – starting from the source nodes and ending in the sink nodes of the DAG. At the end of this crawling process, a well defined vector is assigned to each node in the DAG. The acyclic nature of the overall graph ensures that the forward propagation always converges to a final state and that the backpropagation equations can be applied in order to compute gradients and adjust each parameter during learning. If there is no specific information at the sources nodes, which is typical for hidden source nodes, the corresponding vectors can be initialized to zero. It is also possible to use backpropagation to optimize the initial value of such vectors.

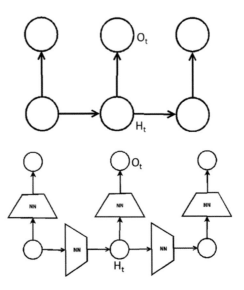

Figure 10.3 The inner approach applied to a hidden Markov model(HMM) DAG for sequences. Top: Bayesian network representation of an HMM, where H_t denotes the hidden state at time t, and O_t the symbol produced at time t. A recursive neural network model derived from the HMM by parameterizing the transitions between hidden states and the production of symbols using neural networks. The transition neural network can be shared for all values of t, and similarly for the production neural network. Note that the output of the production network can either be a deterministic function of H_t or, using a softmax unit, a probabilistic distribution over the symbols of the alphabet dependent on H_t.

The application of the inner approach to a hidden Markov model (HMM) DAG is illustrated in Figure 10.3. In this case, the variable H_t representing the hidden state at time t and the variable O_t representing the output symbol (or the distribution over output symbols) can be parameterized recursively using two neural networks NN_H and NN_O in the form

$$H_t = NN_H(H_{t-1}) \qquad O_t = NN_O(H_t). \tag{10.1}$$

In a second-order HMM DAG, the same relations could be expanded to:

$$H_t = NN_H(H_{t-1}, H_{t-2}) \qquad O_t = NN_O(H_t, H_{t-1}). \tag{10.2}$$

The inner bidirectional IOHMM DAG approach, also known as bidirectional recursive neural networks (BRNNs) was introduced in [75] for the problems of protein secondary structure or relative solvent accessibility prediction. It has been refined over the years and has led to the best predictors in the field (e.g. [185, 515, 475]). In this case, three neural networks are used to refactor the corresponding Bayesian network (Figure 10.4) and compute at each position t the three key variables associated with the output (O_t),

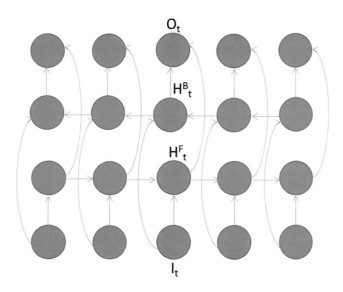

Figure 10.4 Directed acyclic graph depicting a bi-directional Input–Output HMM DAG. The recursive inner approach applied to this DAG relies on three neural networks: one to compute the output O_t, one to compute the forward hidden variable H_t^F, and one to compute the backward hidden variable H_t^B, as a function of the variables associated with the corresponding parent nodes.

the forward hidden state (H_t^F), and the backward hidden state (H_t^B) in the form:

$$O_t = NN_O(I_t, H_t^F, H_t^B) \quad H_t^F = NN_F(I_t, H_{t-1}^F) \quad H_t^B = NN_B(I_t, H_{t+1}^B). \quad (10.3)$$

The same network NN_O is shared by all the outputs O_t, and similarly for the forward network NN_F, and the backward network NN_B.

Without tediously examining other intermediate possibilities, we can directly ask the question of how this approach could be generalized to 2D? In other words, how should a 2D omni-directional IOHMM DAG look like? Note that East–West or North–South chains could be added to the Grid IOHMM of Figure 10.2, but not both. The natural generalization to 2D of a 1D Bidirectional IOHMM was introduced in [87, 576] and subsequently applied to the problem of predicting protein contact or distance maps (see Chapter 13) and learning how to play the game of GO [88, 581, 791, 792]. (A contact map is a 2D matrix representation of a 3D chain, where the (i, j) entry of the matrix is 1 if and only if the corresponding elements i and j in the chain are close to each other in 3D, and 0 otherwise). In this case (Figure 10.5), the corresponding Input–Output HMM Bayesian network DAG comprises four hidden 2D-grids or lattices, each with edges oriented towards one of the four cardinal corners (NE, NW, SE, SW), and one output grid corresponding to the predicted contact map. The complete system can be described in terms of five recursive neural networks computing, at each (i, j) position the output $O_{i,j}$ and the four hidden variables ($H_{i,j}^{NE}, H_{i,j}^{NW}, H_{i,j}^{SE}, H_{i,j}^{SW}$) in the form:

$$O_{i,j} = NN_O(I_{i,j}, H_{i,j}^{NE}, H_{i,j}^{NW}, H_{i,j}^{SE}, H_{i,j}^{SW}), \quad (10.4)$$

with

$$H_{i,j}^{NE} = NN_{NE}(I_{i,j}, H_{i-1,j}^{NE}, H_{i,j-1}^{NE}), \tag{10.5}$$

and similarly for the other three hidden variables. The ideas of bidirectional and grid recursive neural networks can be applied to, and are widely used today in, natural language processing problems in combination with, for instance, LSTMs or attention gating mechanisms (e.g. [705, 236]).

In 3D, in the complete omni-directional case, one would use nine recursive networks associated with nine cubic grids to compute one output variable $O_{i,j,k}$ and eight hidden variables at each position (i, j, k) in each hidden grid. In each hidden cubic lattice, all the edges are oriented towards one of the eight corners. The input at position (i, j, k) is connected to the corresponding positions in the eight hidden cubic grids, as well as in the final output grid. The output at position (i, j, k) receives connections from the corresponding positions in the eight hidden cubic grids, as well as in the input plane.

In d dimensions, the complete system would use 2^d hidden d-dimensional lattices, each with edges oriented towards one of the possible corners, giving rise to $2^d + 1$ recursive neural networks with weight sharing, one for computing outputs, and 2^d networks for propagating context in all possible directions in each of the 2^d hidden lattices. Each input location is connected to the corresponding location in all the 2^d hidden lattices and the output lattice. Each output location received connections from the corresponding locations in all the 2^d hidden lattices and the input hyperplane. To reduce the complexity of these models, it is of course possible to use only a subset of the hidden lattices.

Many of the approaches developed for natural language processing problems are special cases of the inner approach and the models described so far. For instance, in translation problems, an inner approach is used using a DAG corresponding to a multifactorial IOHMM, which ends up looking like a 2D grid. It is also possible to use the inner approach to process trees. For instance, to predict the sentiment of a sentence, one can orient the edges of a parse tree from the leaves to the root, and crawl the directed parse tree with neural networks accordingly [691]. In this case, the basic recursive module is a neural networks that takes two vectors in the input and outputs a single vector.

We can now mention a subtle point hidden in Figure 10.1: in order to apply the recursive approach systematically, one must know in which order to concatenate the vectors associated with the neigbors as input to the corresponding neural network. In all the examples reviewed so far the ordering problem does not come up either because the nodes have a single incoming edge (HMMs) or because they have a small number of edges and each one has a different type associated with it. For instance a node in a 2D grid where all the nodes are oriented towards the NE corner, has two incoming edges, each of a different kind (latitude and longitude). Therefore it is easy to impose an order (e.g. latitude first, longitude second) and share it across all the similar nodes. However this issue can come up in situations characterized by more heterogeneous graphs.

When the graphs associated with, or derived from, the data are undirected, the inner approach can still be used. However its application requires either finding a canonical way of acyclically orienting the edges, as we did above in the case of parse trees, or sampling

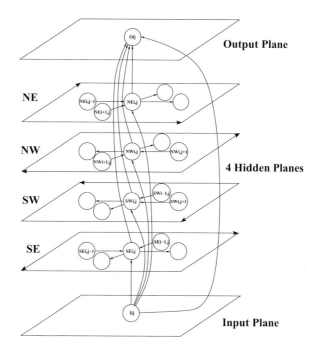

Figure 10.5 Two-dimensional Input-Output DAG for contact or distance map prediction. When the inner approach is applied to this DAG, the output (i, j) is the probability that residues i and j are in contact (or their distance). This probability is computed by a neural network, shared at all (i, j) positions, as a function of the corresponding input vector, and four hidden vectors, one in each of the four hidden planes (North–East, North–West, South–East, South–West). Each hidden vector in each hidden plane is computed by a neural network, shared by all the hidden nodes in the same hidden plane, as a function of the corresponding input vector, and the two neighboring hidden vectors in the same hidden plane.

the possible acyclic orientations in some systematic way, or using all possible acyclic orientations. This problem arises, for instance, in chemoinformatics where molecules are represented by undirected graphs, where the vertices correspond to atoms and the edges correspond to bonds. The typical goal is to predict a particular physical, chemical, or biological property of the molecules. In this case there is no obvious natural way of orienting the corresponding edges in an acyclic fashion. This problem is addressed in [468] for the problem of solubility prediction, using an inner approach that relies on orienting the molecular graphs in all possible ways. Each acyclic orientation is obtained by selecting one vertex of the molecule and orienting all the edges towards that vertex (see Figure 12.2). Considering all possible orientations is computationally feasible for small molecules in organic chemistry because the number of vertices is relatively small, and so is the number of edges due to valence constraints.

10.2.2   Outer Approaches

In the outer approach, the graphs associated with the data can be directed or undirected, and an acyclic orientation is not required. This is because an acyclic orientation is used in a different graph that is built "orthogonally" to the initial graph, hence the outer qualifier. In the simplest form of the approach, illustrated in Figure 10.6 in the case of sequences, consider stacking K copies of the original graph on top of each other into K levels, and connecting the corresponding vertices of consecutive levels with directed edges running from the first to the last level. Additional diagonal edges running from level k to level $k + 1$ can be added to represent neighborhood information. The new constructed graph is obviously acyclic and the inner approach can now be applied to it. So the activity O_i^k of the unit associated with vertex i in layer k is given by:

$$O_i^k = F_i^k \left(O_{\mathcal{N}^{k-1}(i)}^{k-1} \right) = NN_i^k \left(O_{\mathcal{N}^{k-1}(i)}^{k-1} \right) \tag{10.6}$$

where $\mathcal{N}^{k-1}(i)$ denotes the neighborhood of vertex i in layer $k - 1$. The last equality indicates that the function F_i^k is parameterized by a neural network. Furthermore the neural network can be shared, for instance within a layer, so that:

$$O_i^k = NN^k \left(O_{\mathcal{N}(i)}^{k-1} \right). \tag{10.7}$$

It is also possible to have direct connections running from the input layer to each layer k (as in Figure 10.7), or from any layer k to any layer l with $l > k$. In general, as the layer number increases, the corresponding networks are capable of integrating information over large scales in the original graph, as if the graph was being progressively "folded". At the top, the output of the different networks can be summed or averaged. Alternatively, it is also possible to have an outer architecture that tapers off to produce a small output. While this weight sharing is reminiscent of a convolutional neural network, and the outer approach is sometimes called convolutional, this is misleading because the outer approach is different and more general than the standard convolutional approach. In particular the weight sharing is not mandatory, or it can be partial, or it can occur across layers, and so forth. The convolutional approach used in computer vision is a special case of outer approach. The outer approach can also be deployed on the edges of the original graph, rather than its vertices.

For instance, the early work on protein secondary structure prediction [588, 621] can be viewed as a 1D outer approach, albeit a shallow one, where essentially a single network with a relatively small input window (e.g. 11 amino acids) is used to predict the secondary structure classification (alpha-helix, beta-strand, or coil) of the amino acid in the center of the window. The same network is shared across all positions in a protein sequence, and across all proteins sequences.

The first deep outer approach for 2D contact map prediction was described in [237] by stacking neural networks on top of the contact map, as shown in Figure 10.7 (see Chapter 13). In this case, the different layers are literally trying to progressively fold the entire protein. The shapes of the networks are identical across layers. Training can proceed either by providing contact targets at the top and backpropagating through the entire stack, or by providing the same contact targets at each layer. In the latter case, the weights obtained for layer k can be used to initialize the weight of layer $k + 1$ before training.

Another example of outer approach is the application to small molecules [248], obtained by stacking neural networks on top of each atom, using an approach inspired by circular fingerprints [302].

Figure 10.6 Illustration of the outer approach in the case of sequence processing where neural networks are stacked up in a direction perpendicular to the sequence in three layers. In the figure, all the networks in a given layer share the same weights, have the same shape, and neural networks in different layers are distinct. All three conditions can be relaxed. Networks in the higher layers of the hierarchy integrate information over longer scales in the sequences.

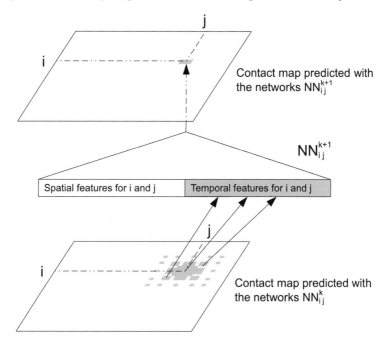

Figure 10.7 Outer approach applied to the problem of protein contact map prediction. Within a layer, the networks have the same weights and receive input both from the networks in the previous layer (temporal features), and fixed input from the input layer (spatial features).

10.3   Relationships between Inner and Outer Approaches

For simplicity, we have organized the main existing approaches for designing recursive architectures into two classes, the inner and the outer class. It is natural to wonder whether the two approaches are fundamentally different and whether one approach is better than the other in general, or on specific classes of problems. As already hinted, the distinction is not fundamental and one approach is not better than the other. To see this in better details, consider the following points.

First, the choice of one approach versus the other in a specific situation may depend on several other considerations, including ease of programming in a particular setting.

Second, given the universal approximation properties of neural networks, it is generally the case that anything that can be achieved using an inner approach can also be achieved using an outer approach, and vice versa. In fact the two approaches are somehow dual to each other. The outer approach can be viewed as an inner approach applied to a directed acyclic graph orthogonal to the original graph. Likewise the inner approach can be viewed as an outer approach applied to the source nodes of the original graph.

Third, the two approaches are not mutually exclusive, in the sense that they can be combined both in parallel or sequentially in a data processing pipeline. For instance, when applied in parallel at the same level, each approach can be applied separately and the predictions produced by the two approaches can be combined by simple averaging. When applied sequentially, one approach can be used at one level and feed its results into the other approach at the next level. For instance in the case of variable-size sets consisting of variable-length vectors, the inner approach can be used at the level of the vectors viewing them as sequences of numbers, and the outer approach can be used at the level of the sets. Likewise, Long Short Term Memory (LSTM) ([349, 299, 410], a kind of recurrent neural network building block capable of learning or storing contextual information over different temporal or spatial length scales, can also be combined with either approach.

Fourth, even when considering the same problem, each approach can be applied in many different ways to different representations of the data. For example, consider the problem of predicting the physical, chemical, or biological properties of small molecules in chemoinformatics (see Chapter 12). In terms of inner approaches, one can:

(1) use the SMILES string representations and apply bidirectional recursive-neural networks (Figure 12.2), or Grid IOHMMs;
(2) use the molecular graph representations and apply the method in [468];
(3) represent the molecular graphs as contact maps (with entries equal to 0,1,2, or 3 depending on the number of bonds) and apply the 2D grid recurrent neural network approach [88] (Figure 10.5);
(4) represent the molecules as unordered lists of atomic nuclei and their 3D coordinates and develop an inner approach for sets; or
(5) represent the molecules by their vector fingerprints (e.g. [302]) and apply an inner approach to these fixed size vectors.

Likewise, a corresponding outer approach can be applied to each one of these representations.

In the case of small molecules, these various representations are "equivalent" in the sense that in general each representation can be recovered from any other one – with some technical details and exceptions that are not relevant for this discussion –

and thus comparable accuracy results should be attainable using different representations with both inner and outer approaches. To empirically exemplify this point, using the inner approach in [468] and the outer approach in [248] on the benchmark solubility data set in [235], we have obtained almost identical RMSE (root mean square error) of 0.61 and 0.60 respectively, in line with the best results reported in the literature.

Finally, the inner/outer distinction is useful for revealing new approaches that have not yet been tried. For instance, to the best of our knowledge, a deep outer approach has not been applied systematically to parse trees and natural language processing, or to protein sequences and 1D feature prediction, such as secondary structure or relative solvent accessibility prediction. Likewise the inner approach Likewise the 2D grid recurrent neural network approach has not been applied systematically to small molecules represented by adjacency matrices. The inner/outer distinction also raises software challenges for providing general tools that can more or less automatically deploy each approach on any suitable problem. As a first step in this direction, general software package implementations of the inner and outer approaches for chemoinformatics problems, based on the molecular graph representation, are available both from github: `www.github.com/Chemoinformatics/InnerOuterRNN`, and from the ChemDB web portal: `cdb.ics.uci.edu`.

10.4   Exercises

EXERCISE 10.1   For the following list of 1D inner approach models:
(a) describe (or draw) the corresponding directed acyclic graphs;
(b) provide a proof that the corresponding graphs are acyclic;
(c) identify edges that, if they were added, would cause the graph to have directed cycles; and
(d) identify the number of recursive neural networks required to implement the corresponding model using the inner approach, identifying each network by its input and output variables.

The list of models is as follows:
(1) Markov chain of order 2 where the state at time t depends on the states at times $t-1$ and $t-2$.
(2) Markov chain of order k where the state at time t depends on the states at times $t-1,\ldots,t-k$.
(3) HMM with hidden states of order 2, where the hidden states form a Markov chain of order 2.
(4) HMM with output states of order 2, where the output at time t depends on the hidden states at time t and $t-1$.
(5) HMM of order 2 where the hidden states from a Markov chain of order 2 and the output at time t depends on the hidden states at time t and $t-1$.
(6) Similarly for an HMM of order k.
(5) Factorial HMM with one hidden factor.

(6) Factorial HMM with k hidden factors.

(7) Factorial HMM of order 2 with k factors.

(8) Input-Output HMM of order 2.

In each case, explain how to initialize the source nodes.

EXERCISE 10.2　For the following list of 1D bidirectional inner approach models:

(a) describe (or draw) the corresponding directed acyclic graphs;

(b) provide a proof that the corresponding graphs are acyclic;

(c) identify edges that, if they were added, would cause the graph to have directed cycles; and

(d) identify the number of recursive neural networks required to implement the corresponding model using the inner approach, identifying each network by its input and output variables.

The list of models is as follows:

(1) Bidirectional Factorial HMM.

(2) Bidirectional Factorial HMM with k bidirectional factors.

(3) Bidirectional Factorial HMM of order 2.

(4) Bidirectional Input-Output HMM of order 2.

(5) Bidirectional Input-Output HMM of order k.

In each case, allow or disallow connections between the hidden factors and explain how to initialize the source nodes.

EXERCISE 10.3　For the following list of 2D inner approach models:

(a) describe (or draw) the corresponding directed acyclic graphs;

(b) provide a proof that the corresponding graphs are acyclic;

(c) identify edges that, if they were added, would cause the graph to have directed cycles; and

(d) identify the number of recursive neural networks required to implement the corresponding model using the inner approach, identifying each network by its input and output variables.

The list of models is as follows:

(1) 2D omni-directional HMM (four hidden factors).

(2) 2D omni-directional HMM of order 2 (four hidden factors).

(3) 2D IOHMM with only two hidden factors (e.g. NE and NW).

(4) 2D IOHMM of order 2 with only two hidden factors (e.g. NE and NW) Input-Output HMM.

(5) 2D omni-directional IOHMM.

(6) 2D omni-directional IOHMM of order 2.

In each case, allow or disallow connections between the hidden factors and explain how to initialize the source nodes.

EXERCISE 10.4　(1) Implement the code to deploy and train a 3D omni-directional IOHMM inner approach (with eight hidden cubes).

(2) Implement the code to deploy and train a 3D omni-directional IOHMM inner approach of order 2 (with eight hidden cubes).

EXERCISE 10.5 (1) Implement the code to deploy and train an omni-directional IOHMM inner approach in d dimensions (with 2^d hidden cubes).
(2) Implement the code to deploy and train an omni-directional IOHMM inner approach in d dimensions of order 2 (with 2^d hidden cubes).
(3) Implement the code to deploy and train an omni-directional IOHMM inner approach in d dimensions of order k (with 2^d hidden cubes).

EXERCISE 10.6 In all the IOHMM DAG models above, the input and output spaces are of the same dimensionality. Explore possible DAGs for IOHMMs between spaces that do not have the same dimensionality, for instance from 1D to 2D, 1D to 3D, 2D to 3D, 2D to 1D, 3D to 1D, 3D to 2D, 1D to trees, and describe possible corresponding recursive neural networks.

EXERCISE 10.7 Can the 2D omni-directional IOHMM inner approach be applied if each input consists of two distinct sequences of different length? Provide examples of problems where this approach could be applied.

EXERCISE 10.8 In all the IOHMM models above, the input and output spaces are of the same dimensionality. Explore possible DAGs for IOHMMs between spaces that do not have the same dimensionality, for instance from 1D to 2D, 1D to 3D, 2D to 3D, 2D to 1 D, 3D to 1D, 3D to 2D and then describe the corresponding recursive neural networks. For each case, provide an example of a problem where this approach could be applied.

EXERCISE 10.9 Consider the general parsing problem (for natural language or for mathematical expressions) as a translation problem going from a sequence to a binary tree. Show that the problem can be converted into a sequence-to-sequence translation problem. Develop at least two different inner approaches and two different outer approaches for dealing with this problem. Identify a publicly available data set of annotated mathematical expressions and test your approaches on this data set.

EXERCISE 10.10 Describe two distinct inner and two distinct outer approaches for the prediction of contact or distance maps in proteins. Estimate the total number of parameters of each corresponding recursive neural network architecture.

EXERCISE 10.11 Design as many recursive neural network architecture as possible for input-to-output problems, where the underlying structure of all the inputs or outputs belongs to one of these four categories: sets, sequences, trees, small graphs (16 possibilities in total). For example, develop a recursive architecture for dealing with a set-to-graph problem. For each case, provide an example of a problem where this approach could be applied. When the input and output structures are in the same category (e.g. sequence to sequence), distinguish the cases where they have the same size (e.g. length) or different sizes.

11 Applications in Physics

As we have seen in Chapter 9, ideas from physics, in particular from statistical mechanics, have played an important role in the development of neural networks, at least since the 1980s. In this chapter, we focus on the applications of neural networks to problems in the physical sciences. An early example of application of neural networks to physics data can be found in [757] where an $A(8, 4, 1)$ neural architecture is trained to distinguish proton and photon showers in a particular experimental set up.

Not unlike AI, physics is today at a crossroads. Current theories, in particular the Standard Model and General Relativity, have been very successful at explaining many phenomena in the universe and ultimately at powering technological developments. However, we know that these theories are incomplete, and essential pieces of the puzzle are missing. In particular, we do not understand how the universe works at extremely small length scales, such as the Planck scale of $\sim 10^{-35} m$, or at extremely high temperatures, such as at the origin of the Big Bang; what is the exact nature of dark matter and dark energy; and the underlying fundamental problem of how to reconcile and unify General Relativity with the Standard Model. This creates remarkable opportunities and challenges for deep learning to help address some of the most fundamental and most beautiful problems about the nature of the universe.

Many of the data sets discussed in this chapter can be downloaded from the UCI Machine Learning Physics Portal `http://mlphysics.ics.uci.edu/`.

11.1 Deep Learning in the Physical Sciences

There are applications of deep learning in all areas of physics, covering all spatial scales, from the subatomic to the cosmological, such as:

(1) particle, nuclear, and plasma physics;
(2) atomic, molecular, and optical physics;
(3) gravitational physics;
(4) astrophysics and cosmology; and
(5) quantum information sciences.

Furthermore, if we take physical sciences in their broadest sense, there are additional applications of deep learning in other areas, such as Earth sciences, including for instance climate and weather prediction [605]. Review papers of some of the literature already exist (e.g. [318]).

Across all these areas of physical sciences, there are recurring classes of problems where deep learning can be applied. These include:

- Processing of raw detector/sensor data, for instance to rapidly eliminate uninteresting data that should not be stored. The Large Hadron Collider (Figure 11.1), for instance, is capable of producing one petabyte of data per second. Most of this data cannot be stored and must be discarded through a combination of fast hardware and software filters (the so-called trigger).

- Classification and regression applied to detector data for instance to identify whether a certain exotic particle may have been produced by a collision or not, or to estimate masses, energy, momenta or other parameters of these particles. In particle physics, the detectors vary greatly in size, geometry, physical composition, layers and so forth across different experiments and collaborations. But, in essence, these detectors consist of arrays of elementary detectors capable of detecting certain particles (e.g. photons, electrons, muons). Each event of potential interest (e.g. collision) paints one or several "images" across the array of elementary detectors. Thus it is natural to apply deep learning methods, including when appropriate convolutional neural networks, to these images for regression and classification problems.

- Current analysis pipelines often process these images and parse them into components (e.g. jets, vertices, tracks). Thus it is also possible to apply deep learning to these other formats, such as sets or lists of features and their characteristics. These sets or lists are variable in size and thus may require recursive approaches. For instance, one may want to infer Feynman diagrams associated with a collision from a list, or set, of four-vectors [273]. Often high-level variables (e.g. momenta of particles) are also computed and deep learning methods can be applied both to produce these high-level representations, or to use them in downstream tasks (e.g. regression, classification). Questions of interpretability, or comparison of information content across different representations, often arise in these settings. In short, in a complex layered detector like the Large Hadron Collider, there are many stages in the processing pipeline where deep learning can be applied using different representations.

- Combining results and evidence from multiple sources, within the same complex detector and experiment, or across different detectors and experiments. For instance, the nature of dark matter can be probed from multiple angles using underground detectors, particle beams, and telescopes.

- Approximating complex phenomena and related functions where the elementary laws are well understood (e.g. Schrödinger equation in quantum mechanics, Navier–Stokes equation in fluid dynamics) but scaling them up to large systems is computationally very challenging. Deep learning methods can be used to help speed up the approximations, for instance in DFT (density functional theory) or climate grid simulations.

- Approximating inverse models, typically in situations where the forward model is computable, and the inverse model is unknown, or computationally intractable. In these situations, the forward model can be used to generate training examples in order to learn the inverse model. One obvious important issue in these cases is whether the models are bijective or not.

- Building fast generative models to generate data or approximate distributions.
- Deriving symbolic regression models. In these problems, one seeks to find a relatively simple mathematical formula in the relevant variables that is consistent with a set of measurements, up to measurement noise [654, 738]. The notion of "simple formula" is of course to be defined, for instance a formula that involve only low degree polynomials, rational fractions, exponential, logarithm, and trigonometric functions.
- Progressing towards more general AI and reasoning. Symbolic regression is just a first step in the direction of trying to build a computer physicist that can reason about the universe and derive physical laws. Physics is particularly interesting from an AI standpoint because it often comes with both a symbolic level and data. For example, in a limited world made of "particles" and "forces" satisfying certain constraints, can one learn to discover the Standard Model using the experimental data available in the late 1960s?

In the rest of this chapter, we focus on several examples from various areas of physics, including: four examples from particle physics in antimatter physics, high-energy physics, neutrino physics, and dark matter physics; one example from astrophysics/cosmology; and one example from climate physics. We emphasize some of the common aspects, from a deep learning perspective, that cut across these different areas.

For now, as an example, let us consider particle physics in more detail. Experiments in this field seek to uncover matter's basic constituents and reveal the forces that determine its structure, stretching from sub-proton distances to the galactic superclusters. The current model of particles and their interactions [719] successfully describes the microscopic nature of matter and its interactions, but important open questions remain. The vast majority of the matter in the Universe, dark matter, is not described by the current theory, and its particle nature is almost completely unknown [270]. Experiments at particle colliders seek to produce particles of dark matter [1], potentially unraveling one of the largest open questions in all of modern science. The asymmetry between matter, which makes up our Universe, and antimatter, which appears to have identical properties but is strangely almost completely absent, remains unexplained [168]. Experiments in many contexts, including particle colliders [3], seek to identify an asymmetry that might account for the preferential conversion of antimatter into matter. The number of particles and their masses are unexplained free parameters of the theory, which strongly suggests that our entire microscopic picture may not be fundamental, but an emergent structure, in the same way that the periodic table emerges from the rules of atomic electron orbitals. A variety of detectors are used to search for evidence of structure [208] in our current set of particles, hoping to reveal a deeper layer of reality.

Measuring the properties of these particles can require highly-sophisticated experiments, some of which recreate extreme conditions and energies that have not existed in nature since the Big Bang. Yet these engineering feats give rise to major data analysis challenges, as the detectors used in these experiments produce a torrent of

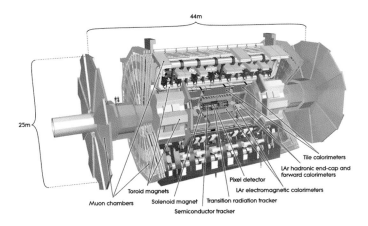

Figure 11.1 The ATLAS detector, surrounding points of collision, at the Large Hadron Collider, which is the largest and most powerful particle accelerator in the world [2]. It includes a tunnel 27 kilometers long, between 50 and 175 meters below the ground. The detector alone is 44m long and 22m in diameter.

high-dimensional data with small signal-to-noise ratios. For example, the ATLAS detector at the Large Hadron Collider (LHC) produces roughly a petabyte of raw data per second, corresponding to 100M channels with collisions occurring every 25ns, which must be carefully analyzed to search for the faint signals of new particles.

The detectors used in these experiments vary in scale and design, but generally consist of layers of sensors that take measurements of traversing particles. The data recorded for a single event – a particle collision for example – is high-dimensional and structured; it roughly corresponds to an image or video, with correlations between adjacent pixels and time steps. From this high-dimensional event data, physicists must reconstruct the underlying physical processes that produced it.

This is typically performed by applying a series of algorithms that reduce and summarize the raw data, each carefully designed by an expert physicist familiar with a particular part of the detector or data-generating process. These include trigger systems that aim to quickly discard uninteresting events in real time, clustering algorithms that group sets of detector hits that were likely caused by the same particle, tracking algorithms that attempt to reconstruct the trajectory of each particle through the detector layers, and classifiers that attempt to discriminate between different types of particles. Each step in this data-processing pipeline transforms the data in some way, distilling the information from the previous step into something more manageable.

Increasingly, machine learning methods are being employed in these data-analysis pipelines. The underlying physical processes that generate the data are often so complex – involving many intermediate unobserved variables – that knowledge of the system alone is insufficient to write a good event-reconstruction algorithm. Instead, machine learning models are trained to perform tasks like particle classification using calibration and/or simulation data for training. Until recently, the machine learning models in common use were not deep learning methods, but rather things like Support Vector Machines or Boosted Decision Trees. In practice, these methods are sensitive to the choice of input features, and usually require the user to engineer a good set of features for optimal performance. This can be a daunting task when the data is high-dimensional and the scientist has little intuition about its shape. Engineering optimal input features to shallow machine learning models has been common practice in the past.

By contrast, the goal of *deep* learning is to *automatically* learn multiple sequential representations and processing steps in an end-to-end manner. Deep learning is a particularly promising approach in experimental physics for multiple reasons. First, training data is abundant in many important applications, either from highly-accurate Monte Carlo simulations or data produced in calibration experiments. Second, the structure of the detector data is often similar to that of images, so that deep learning techniques developed for computer vision can be applied. Third, end-to-end approaches could greatly simplify the development of data-analysis pipelines by aggregating multiple algorithmic steps, each of which usually requires research and testing. And finally, a deep learning approach could alleviate the common problem of early steps losing information that is relevant to the final task. Information is necessarily discarded in each step of the data-processing pipeline, but deep neural networks trained with stochastic gradient descent seem to balance the need to extract useful information about the target while removing irrelevant information [732].

The applications considered next in antimatter, high-energy, neutrino, dark matter, and cosmology physics include examples of supervised regression and classification, unsupervised, and adversarial learning. In general, we compare traditional approaches that rely on "high-level" human-engineered feature representations to an end-to-end deep learning approach that takes in "low-level" features. In each application, the performance of the deep learning approach matches or exceeds that of the traditional approach, with the latter case revealing how much information is lost by the engineered features. These examples demonstrate the potential of deep learning as a powerful tool in scientific data analysis. Ultimately, it could also help us to better understand the limitations of our detectors, and aid in the design of better ones.

11.2   Antimatter Physics

In the Standard Model of physics, every matter particle has a corresponding antimatter particle. Matter and antimatter particles are hypothesized to be symmetric with respect to charge conjugation, parity transformation, and time reversal, a property known as CPT symmetry. One of the big open questions in modern physics is why the universe is unbalanced, consisting of more matter than antimatter, which would appear to violate this symmetry. At the forefront of this investigation is the study of the antihydrogen atom, an atom consisting of a positron-antiproton pair. Measuring the properties of antihydrogen and comparing them to those of its matter counterpart (the hydrogen atom) may reveal asymmetries that would violate the CPT symmetry hypothesis and give rise to new physics beyond the Standard Model. However, experimental studies are difficult because a pair of matter-antimatter particles annihilate whenever they come into contact with each other. Thus, antihydrogen experiments require elaborate electromagnetic traps maintained in almost complete vacuum conditions.

Despite these challenges, multiple experiments in recent years have managed to trap or form a beam of antihydrogen atoms in order to test CPT symmetry [36, 35, 291, 427], or test the effects of gravity on antimatter [11, 569, 29]. Antihydrogen is produced either by injecting antiproton and positron plasmas into cryogenic multi-ring electrode traps where three-body recombination takes place ($\bar{p} + 2e^+ \rightarrow \bar{H} + e^+$), or by the charge exchange processes between positronium, antiproton, and antihydrogen ($Ps^{(*)} + \bar{p} \rightarrow \bar{H} + e^-$ and $\bar{H} + Ps \rightarrow \bar{H}^+ + e^-$). In most cases, the production of an antihydrogen atom is identified by its annihilation signature whereby several charged pions are emitted from the point of annihilation, or vertex [358], and hit a detector system surrounding the trap. These events are distinguished from cosmic or instrumental background events using the hit multiplicity and the inferred positions of the annihilation vertex.

The materials required to maintain the antimatter vacuum trap – layers of vacuum chamber walls, multi-ring electrodes, and thermal isolation – make annihilation detection difficult. The annihilation products are subject to electromagnetic forces and scattering effects before reaching the course-grained detectors, impeding event reconstruction using the traditional tracking and vertex-finding algorithms that have been adopted from other types of physics experiments [31, 30, 812, 702, 209, 210, 595]. Thus, a data analysis pipeline based on traditional tracking and vertex-reconstruction algorithms is likely to be sub-optimal for these experiments. Recently, the authors proposed deep learning as a novel approach to this problem [636], and in the following we discuss its application to the ASACUSA experiment.

11.2.1 ASACUSA

The ASACUSA antihydrogen experiment [427] aims to directly compare the ground-state hyperfine transition frequency of antihydrogen with that of hydrogen. Measurements of the antihydrogen hyperfine transition frequency are performed by measuring the rate of antihydrogen atom production in a Penning–Malmberg trap while controlling the antiproton injection conditions, the overlap time while mixing antimatter plasmas, and other key parameters which constrain the three-body recombination yield and the level population evolution time [596]. Thus, the precision of the measurement depends directly on the ability to detect antihydrogen.

Antihydrogen is detected through the indirect observation of annihilations occurring on the wall of the trap, which must be distinguished from background events where a lone antiproton annihilates with a residual gas particle in the trap. The ASACUSA experiment traps charged antimatter particles (antiprotons and positrons) on the central axis using electro-magnetic fields. When a neutral antihydrogen atom is produced (predominately via three-body recombination of antiprotons and positrons), it may escape these trapping fields and annihilate on the inner wall of the multi-ring electrodes, emitting charged pions that can be detected. However, continuous annihilation of trapped antiprotons on residual gas atoms produces background annihilation events that emit the same pions. The latter tend to be emitted from the central axis, rather than the inner wall, so we can distinguish between antihydrogen and antiproton events if the position of the annihilation can be inferred from the detector data.

The pions are detected by the Asacusa Micromegas Tracker [595], which has a full-cylinder trigger layer of plastic scintillator bars and two detector layers made of gaseous micro-strip Micromegas technology [301, 175]. The two detector layers consist of co-centric half-cylinders, both located on the same side of the detector so that pions can be tracked when they travel through both layers. Each layer is made up of micro-strips, oriented along either the azimuth or axis of the cylinder. When a trigger event occurs, a snapshot of detector activity is recorded. The raw detector data consists of 1,430 binary values per event, one from each micro-strip: 246 inner azimuth strips, 290 outer azimuthal strips, 447 inner axial strips, and 447 outer axial strips.

In the typical vertex-finding approach, each trigger event is processed with a track and vertex reconstruction algorithm, proceeding as follows. First, the single detector channels are searched for entries above threshold, and neighboring channels are iteratively clustered to form hits. The detected hits are used to form and fit tracks, using a Kalman-filtering algorithm [704]. After fitting all hit pair combinations in an event, the track candidates are filtered by their compatibility with the known antiproton cloud position. The filtered track candidates are then paired, and their three-dimensional point of closest approach position is assigned as the vertex position. Finally, event classification is performed based on the radial distance of the reconstructed vertex closest to the central axis (Figure 11.2). However, the reconstruction algorithm only succeeds if two distinct tracks can be identified, and if the reconstructed tracks come within close proximity of each other in three-space (a threshold of 1 cm is used). The failure rate is high because the detector only covers half of the trap, such that roughly half of all pions escape, and the stochastic pion trajectories lead to high uncertainty in the reconstructed tracks.

In the deep learning approach, an artificial neural network was trained to classify annihilations directly from the raw detector data. This automated, end-to-end learning strategy can potentially identify discriminative information in the raw data that is typically discarded by the vertex-reconstruction algorithm. Indeed, this approach will provide predictions for events where vertex-reconstruction completely fails, such as those where only a single track can be reconstructed.

Two neural network architecture design choices were made in order to take advantage of the geometry of the detector and constrain the learning problem. First, data from micro-strips situated along the azimuthal and axial dimensions are processed along separate pathways that are then merged by concatenating the hidden representations higher in the architecture. Second, both pathways employ 1D convolution with locally-connected feature detectors and max-pooling layers. Together, these design choices achieve some amount of translational invariance along each dimension, constraining the learning problem and reducing the total number of network parameters. The highly-correlated inner and outer detector layers are processed together as two associated 'channels' in the first layers of the network, with the outer azimuthal layer downsampled with linear

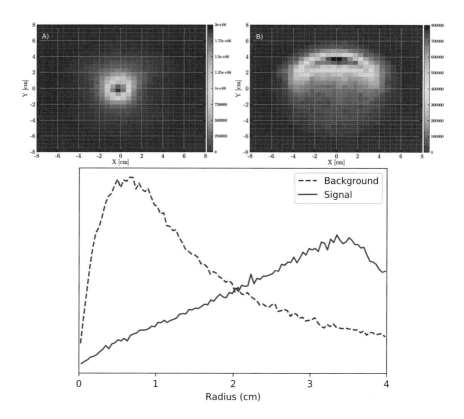

Figure 11.2 Empirical distributions of reconstructed vertices for background events (annihilations on the axis at $R = 0$ cm) and signal events (annihilations on the wall of the trap at $R = 4$ cm). Top left: Heat map of background events in XY-space. Top right: Heat map of signal events in XY-space. Bottom: Empirical histogram of vertex radii. The smearing of these distributions reflects the reconstruction error due to pion scattering effects, low detector precision, and limitations in the track and vertex reconstruction algorithm.

interpolation to match the dimensionality of the inner layer. A diagram of the network architecture is shown in Figure 11.3.

The two approaches were compared on Monte Carlo simulations that reflect realistic conditions in the ASACUSA experiment. One million annihilation events of each type were simulated and randomly divided into training (60%), validation (20%), and test subsets (20%). The vertex finding (VF) algorithm failed on 75% of these events: 20% did not result in any detector hits; 7% had a hit in only one detector; and 48% had hits in both detectors but a vertex could not be reconstructed. Thus, a direct performance comparison was only possible on the 25% of the test events for which the VF algorithm succeeded.

Deep neural networks were trained with a variety of hyperparameter combinations in order to optimize generalization performance on the validation set. The best architecture had five 1D convolutional layers with kernel sizes 7–3–3–3–3 (the size of the receptive fields for neurons in each layer), channel sizes 8–16–32–64–128 (the number of distinct

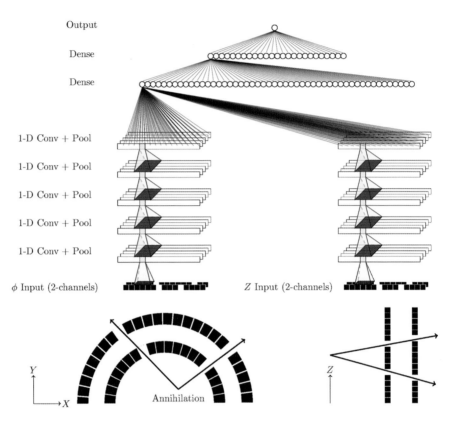

Figure 11.3 Deep neural network architecture consisting of two separate pathways that process data from the micro-strips placed along the azimuthal (ϕ) and axial (Z) dimensions. The inner and outer detector layers are treated as two input channels and processed by a sequence of 1D convolutional layers in each pathway. The two pathways are merged using dense fully-connected layers higher in the network.

feature detectors in each layer), and rectified linear activation [529]. In order to account for translational invariance, each convolution layer is followed by a max-pooling layer with pool size 2 and stride length 2 [307]. The flattened representations from the two pathways are then concatenated and followed by two fully-connected layers of 50 and 25 rectified linear units, then a single logistic output unit with a relative entropy loss. During training, 50% dropout was used in the top two fully-connected layers to reduce overfitting [698, 91]. Data was augmented both at training and test time by translating the hits along the axial direction in order to enforce translational invariance along this dimension (since the true axial distribution in real experiments is unknown). The model weights were initialized from a scaled normal distribution as suggested by He et al. [333], then trained using the Adam optimizer [406] ($\beta_1 = 0.9, \beta_2 = 0.999, \epsilon = 1e - 08$) with mini-batch updates of size 100 and a learning rate that was initialized to 0.0001 and decayed by 1% at the end of each epoch. Training was stopped when the validation objective did not improve within a window of three epochs. The models were implemented in Keras [195] and Theano [726], and trained on a cluster of Nvidia graphics processors.

Performance comparisons were made by plotting the Receiver Operating Characteristic (ROC) curve and summarizing the discrimination by calculating the Area Under the Curve (AUC). On the 25% of test events for which a vertex could be reconstructed, the deep learning approach increases performance from 0.76 to 0.87 AUC (Figure 11.4). On the disjoint set of events for which a vertex could *not* be reconstructed, deep learning achieves 0.78 AUC. This effectively triples the event coverage – to 73% of all events – while *simultaneously* improving overall AUC by more than 0.05 (to 0.82 on the union set).

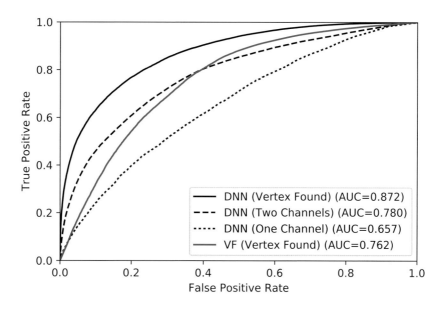

Figure 11.4 ROC curves for the vertex finding algorithm (VF) and a deep convolutional neural network (DNN) on the subset of events for which an annihilation vertex can be reconstructed ('Vertex Found,' 25% of all events). Also shown are the curves for DNN predictions on the subset of events in which both the inner and outer detector channels are hit, but no vertex could be reconstructed (48% of all events), and on events in which only one channel is hit (7% of all events).

These results provide a clear demonstration of the advantages provided by the deep learning approach. The traditional track and vertex reconstruction algorithm is a multi-step process in which relevant information is inevitably discarded at each step, despite the best efforts of the scientists tuning the algorithm. The deep learning approach is capable of learning this classification in an end-to-end manner, and takes advantage of statistical information that is lost in the traditional approach. In particular, for events in which only a single track can be reconstructed (and thus the vertex finder fails), the deep learning approach learns to predict whether the annihilation occurred on the wall based on whether the observed hits suggest a track that travels through the axis. But even for events in which a vertex *can* be reconstructed, the deep learning approach performs better based on the statistical information learned from the raw data.

Preliminary results indicate that deep learning also performs as expected on real ASACUSA calibration data, and we are currently working to improve the experiment sensitivity with this approach. Furthermore, while this study was performed for the ASACUSA experiment, the deep learning approach can easily be deployed to other ongoing antimatter experiments with different instruments. This even offers a potential new direction in the design of future detectors.

11.3   High Energy Collider Physics

11.3.1   The Large Hadron Collider and the ATLAS Detector

The Large Hadron Collider is the most complex experimental instrument ever constructed – designed to produce particle collisions at extremely high energies. Through these collisions, physicists aim to test the fundamental properties of matter and discover new, exotic particles that are not part of the Standard Model. Such discoveries will be necessary to answer the biggest mysteries of modern physics, including how the theory of gravity can be unified with the Standard Model, and what particle(s) consitute the "dark matter" that accounts for 85% of all matter in the universe [573, 271].

The high-energy collisions at the LHC interconvert energy and matter, creating unstable particles that quickly decay into lighter, more stable particles. Thus, exotic particles of interest such as the Higgs boson are not observed directly, but rather indirectly via subtle signatures in the trajectories of their decay products. Furthermore, the vast majority of collision events do not produce particles of interest. The LHC produces approximately 10^{11} collisions per hour [53], but for example, only 300 of these collisions will result in a Higgs boson. Therefore, a massive engineering effort is required to record, process, store, and analyze this data.

A single collision event will produce many decay products that travel outward from the point of collision and through the many-layered detector [52]. In ATLAS, over 100 million detector elements capture a "snapshot" of the event – similar to a 3D image. In order to identify collisions that produce particles of interest, each event snapshot must be carefully analyzed using a multitude of algorithms to identify the different decay products, their trajectories [121], and the particle interactions that produced them.

In the following, we describe three different applications of deep learning to this data-processing pipeline. First, we describe the use of deep learning in exotic particle searches, in which the momentum of the decay products is used to classify collisions of interest from background processes. Second, we describe the analysis of calorimeter data, the outer layer of the detector, which lends itself to deep learning strategies used for computer vision. Third, we describe the use of adversarial neural networks to train classifiers that are robust to systematic uncertainties in the experiment.

11.3.2   Exotic Particle Searches

The goal of exotic particle search studies is to find evidence for new particles or particle interactions buried in mountains of collision data. This evidence typically manifests as a faint "bump" in a high-dimensional distribution due to a rare event, such as the production of a Higgs boson, in an ocean of background events that produce the same stable decay products but with slightly different signatures. While a classifier might not be able to distinguish between signal vs. background events with certainty, the probabilistic output can be used for dimensionality reduction to aid in the statistical analysis when measuring the evidence for a new discovery. Here we demonstrate deep learning as an alternative to the combination of feature-engineering and shallow machine learning that are traditionally employed [93, 94, 635].

We evaluated the deep learning approach on three benchmark tasks:

(1) detecting Higgs boson production;
(2) detecting the production of supersymmetrical particles; and
(3) detecting Higgs-to-$\tau^+\tau^-$ decay (Figures 11.5–11.7).

Each task was formulated as a binary classification problem to distinguish between two physical processes with identical decay products. The input features could be separated into two distinct categories: "low-level" features that comprised the 3D momenta the observed decay products and other measurements that contain additional information, and "high-level," *derivative* features – functions of the low-level features that were engineered to aid in classification.

Deep and shallow neural network architectures – networks with a single hidden layer – were trained and tested on each task with millions of simulated training samples. The hyperparameters were optimized separately for each task and architecture, using the Spearmint Bayesian optimization algorithm [690], on the complete set of 18–28 input features then tested on each feature subset. The results demonstrate that the deep architectures significantly outperform the shallow architectures in terms of AUC (Table 11.1), and similarly in terms of discovery significance (Table 11.2), a measure of statistical power. Furthermore, the deep learning models do almost as well on the low-level feature sets as they do with the complete feature set, indicating that the deep learning approach is *automatically* learning useful intermediate data representations, without the aid of high-level engineered features (Figure 11.8). In fact, deep architectures trained on low-level features for benchmarks (1) and (3) actually outperform the shallow models trained on the complete feature set.

11.3.3   Jet Substructure Classification

The cylindrical ATLAS detector's outer layer consists of a giant calorimeter, which captures showers of energy released by fragmenting quark and gluon particles called "jets." Sometimes, massive particles can be produced at such high velocities that their hadronic decays are collimated and multiple jets overlap. Classifying jets that are due to single low-mass particles or due to the decay of a massive particle is an important problem in the analysis of collider data [10, 7, 19, 20].

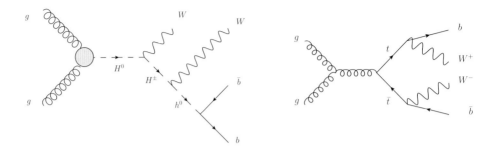

Figure 11.5 Feynman diagrams describing the processes in the HIGGS classification task. The signal involves new exotic Higgs bosons H^0 and $H^\pm$ (left) and the background process involves top-quarks t (right). In both cases, the resulting particles are two W bosons and two b-quarks.

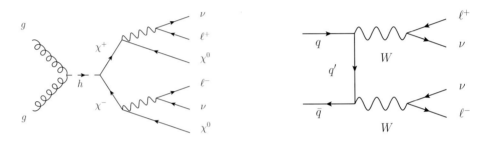

Figure 11.6 Feynman diagrams describing the processes in the SUSY classification task. The signal involves hypothetical supersymmetric particles $\chi^\pm$ and χ^0 along with charged leptons $\ell^\pm$ and neutrinos ν (left) and the background process involves W bosons (right). In both cases, the resulting observed particles are two charged leptons, as neutrinos and χ^0 escape undetected.

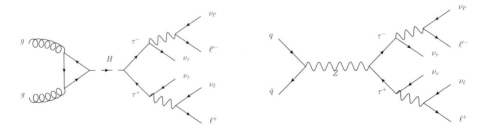

Figure 11.7 Feynman diagrams describing the processes in the Higgs-to-$\tau^+\tau^-$ classification task. The signal process (left) involves a Higgs H decaying to leptons $\tau^+\tau^-$, while the dominant background process (right) produces the same decay products.

There does not exist a complete analytical model for classifying jets directly from theoretical principles, so traditional approaches to this problem have relied on engineered features that were designed to detect patterns of energy deposition in the calorimeter [574, 393, 432, 724, 434, 221, 633, 472, 223, 224]. However, the complexity of the data makes this task an excellent application for machine learning. Indeed, state-of-the-art approaches use shallow machine learning models such as shallow neural networks and boosted decision trees (BDTs) to aggregate information from multiple expert features.

Table 11.1 Performance of shallow and deep neural network architectures on low-level vs. high-level features. The same neural network model was trained on three sets of input features: low-level features, high-level features and the complete set of features. Neural network was trained five times with different random initializations; the table displays the mean AUC, with standard deviations in parentheses.

Data Set	Model	AUC		
		Low-level	High-level	Complete
HIGGS	Shallow NN	0.790 (< 0.001)	0.794 (< 0.001)	0.844 (< 0.001)
	Deep NN	0.891	0.801	0.896
SUSY	Shallow NN	0.875 (< 0.001)	0.868 (< 0.001)	0.879 (< 0.001)
	Deep NN	0.876 (< 0.001)	0.870 (< 0.001)	0.879 (< 0.001)
Higgs-to-$\tau^+\tau^-$	Shallow NN	0.789 (0.001)	0.792 (< 0.001)	0.797 (< 0.001)
	Deep DNN	0.798 (< 0.001)	0.798 (< 0.001)	0.802 (< 0.001)

Table 11.2 Discovery significance. Performance in terms of expected significance of a discovery, estimated using 100 signal events and 5000 background events.

Data Set	Model	Discovery significance		
		Low-level	High-level	Complete
HIGGS	Shallow NN	2.16σ (0.03)	2.64σ (0.01)	3.28σ (0.02)
	Deep NN	4.57σ	2.87σ	4.82σ
SUSY	Shallow NN	7.86σ (0.06)	7.22σ (0.02)	7.81σ (0.05)
	Deep NN	7.73σ (0.07)	7.58σ (0.08)	7.94σ (0.08)
Higgs-to-$\tau^+\tau^-$	Shallow NN	2.57σ (< 0.01)	2.92σ (< 0.01)	3.02σ (< 0.01)
	Deep DNN	3.16σ (< 0.01)	3.24σ (< 0.01)	3.37σ (< 0.01)

Training data can be produced using tools that simulate the microphysics of jet formation and how these jets deposit energy in the calorimeter [687, 62].

Recently, we and others proposed deep learning with the low-level calorimeter data itself, rather than with high-level engineered features [97, 231]. Calorimeter data can be treated as a two-dimensional image, lending itself to the natural application of the deep-learning strategies developed for computer vision. The following experiments demonstrate this approach on the problem of classifying single jets produced in quark or gluon fragmentation from two overlapping jets produced when a high-velocity W boson decays to a collimated pair of quarks.

A simulated data set was produced with standard physics packages [21, 687, 559]. Dijets from boosted $W \rightarrow qq'$ were generated with a center of mass energy $\sqrt{s} = 14$ TeV using the diboson production, decay process $pp \rightarrow W^+W^- \rightarrow qqqq$ leading to two pairs of quarks, and with each pair of quarks collimated and leading to a single jet. Jets originating from single quarks and gluons were generated using the $pp \rightarrow qq, qg, gg$

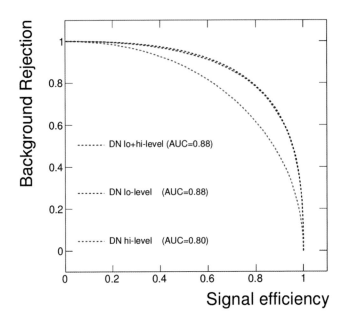

Figure 11.8 ROC plot comparing the same deep neural network trained on the HIGGS task using the low-level feature subset, high-level feature subset, and the complete feature set. The high-level engineered features no longer aid in classification, because the model is able to automatically learn useful intermediate representations. This is not the case with the shallow machine learning models trained on the same problem.

process. In addition, a separate data set was produced that included the effects of pile-up events, a source of noise in which additional pp interactions overlap in time.

To compare our approach to the current state-of-the-art, we calculated six high-level jet-substructure features commonly used in the literature: the invariant mass of the trimmed jet, N-subjettiness [724, 725] $\tau_{21}^{\beta=1}$, and the energy correlation functions [434, 433] $C_2^{\beta=1}, C_2^{\beta=2}, D_2^{\beta=1}$, and $D_2^{\beta=2}$. Each of these individual quantities were outperformed by a BDT trained with all six as input.

In the deep learning approach, each jet was represented as a 32×32 pixel image, approximating the resolution of the calorimeter cells. Jets were translated and rotated into a canonical position based on the center of mass and the principal axis (Figure 11.9). Because this canonicalization removes the translational and rotational invariance of the original data, the deep neural network structure used locally-connected layers (without the parameter-sharing of convolutional layers). The neural network architecture and learning hyperparameters, as well as the BDT hyperparameters, were optimized on the no-pileup data set using the Spearmint Bayesian Optimization algorithm [690].

Our experiments demonstrate that even without the aid of expert features, deep neural networks match or modestly outperform the current state-of-the-art approach (Table 11.3, Figure 11.10). Furthermore, these performance gains persist when our simulations include pileup effects. Similar results have been reported for other jet classification tasks, and with recurrent neural networks trained on tracking data instead of images [319, 459].

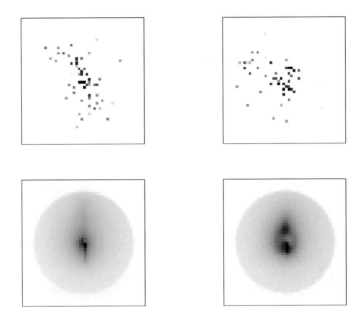

Figure 11.9 Top: Typical jet images from class 1 (single QCD jet from q or g) on the left, and class 2 (two overlapping jets from $W \rightarrow qq'$) on the right. Bottom: Averages of 100,000 jet images from each class.

Table 11.3 Performance results for BDT and deep networks. Shown for each method are both the signal efficiency at background rejection of 10, as well as the Area Under the Curve (AUC), the integral of the background efficiency versus signal efficiency. For the neural networks, we report the mean and standard deviation of three networks trained with different random initializations.

Technique	Performance	
	Signal efficiency	AUC
No pileup		
BDT on derived features	86.5%	95.0%
Deep NN on images	87.8%(0.04%)	95.3%(0.02%)
With pileup		
BDT on derived features	81.5%	93.2%
Deep NN on images	84.3%(0.02%)	94.0%(0.01%)

11.3.4   Decorrelated Tagging with Adversarial Neural Networks

This section considers decorrelated jet-substructure tagging with adversarial neural networks. An additional challenge in jet-substructure classification is the systematic uncertainty in the jet invariant mass distribution of the background process. The simulations used to train classifiers necessarily have a fixed distribution, so in order for a classifier to be robust against this uncertainty, it should not use information about the invariant

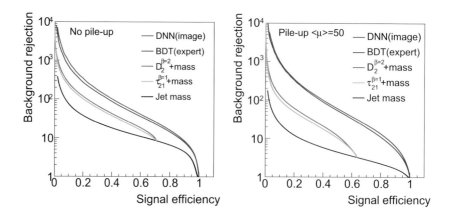

Figure 11.10 ROC plots showing performance of deep neural networks (DNN) trained on the images, BDTs trained on the expert features, both with (bottom) and without pile-up (top). Typical choices of signal efficiency in real applications are in the 0.5–0.7 range. Also shown are the performance of jet mass feature, as well as two other expert variables in conjunction with a mass window.

mass in its prediction. However, most of the features used to classify jets are correlated with this quantity, so models fit to these features will learn to take advantage of these correlations when classifying the jets. One proposed solution is to perform classification based on a single engineered feature that can be "decorrelated," but this sacrifices the boost in classification performance that comes from combining information from multiple features [244, 202].

Another strategy is to incorporate the decorrelation requirement directly into the machine learning model by penalizing the jet classifier for using information about the nuisance variable. This can be achieved with adversarial training [652, 292, 250], and has been proposed to solve the problem of nuisance parameters in physics problems by Ref. [461]. This approach involves training two models together – the original classifier, and a separate, adversarial model – such that the adversary adaptively shapes the loss function of the first model.

For the jet substructure classification problem, we proposed an adversarial neural network classifier that attempts to predict the jet-invariant mass from the output of the jet classifier (Figure 11.11) [674]. The loss of the adversary is included as a linear term with a negative coefficient in the loss of the jet classifier, such that it acts as a regularizer. That is, the jet tagger must find a balance between minimizing the classification loss, and maximizing the loss of the adversary:

$$L_{tagger} = L_{classification} - \lambda L_{adversary}.$$

Results on the classification task from [674] show that this approach yields a jet tagger that is only slightly less powerful in terms of classification performance, but much more robust to changes in the distribution of the background invariant mass (Figure 11.12).

This approach can be generalized to include the case where both the classifier and its adversary are parameterized by some external quantity, such as a theoretical hypothesis

Classifier Adversary

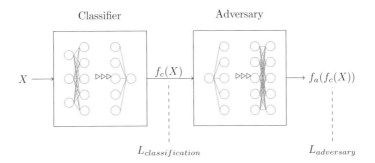

Figure 11.11 Adversarial training approach with a jet-substructure classifier network and an adversary network that attempts to predict the invariant mass from the classifier output. The entire system is trained simultaneously with stochastic gradient descent, with a gradient reversal layer in between the classifier and adversary segments. In this experiment, the classifier is a deep neural network with eleven high-level input features and a sigmoid output; the adversarial network has a single input and a softmax output, with the invariant jet mass quantized into ten bins. See [674] for details.

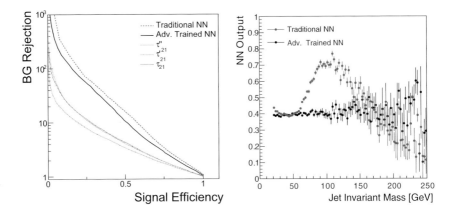

Figure 11.12 **Left:** Signal efficiency and background rejection (1/efficiency) curves for several jet-tagging discriminants: neural networks trained with and without the adversarial strategy to optimize classification while minimizing impact on jet mass, the unmodified τ_{21}, and two "decorrelated" variables τ'_{21} and τ''_{21} [244]. In these experiments, the signal samples have mass $m_{Z'} = 100$ GeV. **Right:** Box plot showing the distribution of tagger predictions for different values of the jet mass. The adversarial training encourages the classifier output to be flat with respect to this quantity.

for the mass of a new particle or a field coupling strength. This is motivated by the fact that resonance searches, such as the one described here, are often performed as a scan over a range of potential particle masses. Generally the optimal classifier for each hypothesized mass will differ; but the simulations used for training can usually only be sampled from a small number of hypothesized values due to computational expense. By including the hypothesized particle mass as an input, we enable the model to interpolate between the discrete values observed in the training data [216, 100]. In this case, we condition both the classifier and the adversary networks on the hypothesized particle mass (Figure 11.13). Again, the adversarially-training keeps the classifier decorrelated with the jet invariant mass over the range of values upon which it is trained, leading to discovery significance that is robust to uncertainty in the background (Figure 11.14).

In these experiments, we have demonstrated an ability to exert *control* over the representations that are learned in deep neural networks. By including an adversarial objective in the loss function, we are able to constrain what information is used to perform the classification task and remove a source of systematic uncertainty from the classifier. This is a powerful technique, both for physics applications and more generally.

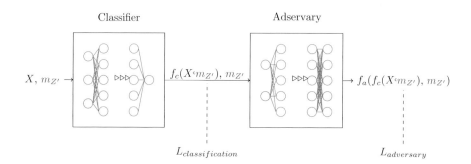

Figure 11.13 Architecture for adversarial training approach, parameterized on the mass of the simulated signal particle $m_{Z'}$. Parameterizing the system in this way allows us to train on a discrete set of simulated particle masses and interpolate to intermediate values.

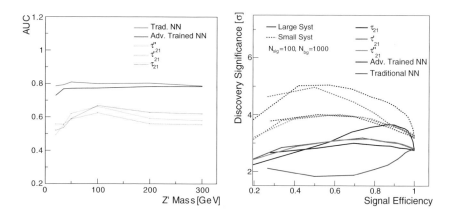

Figure 11.14 Left: AUC vs. particle mass for the jet-tagging discriminants. As in Figure 11.11, the neural network classification performance is only slightly decreased by adversarial training. **Right:** Statistical significance of a hypothetical signal for varying thresholds on the neural network output. Two scenarios are shown, in which the uncertainty on the background level is either negligible or large, both with $N_{sig} = 100$, $N_{bg} = 1000$. In each case, the adversarial training increases discovery significance over the other approaches.

11.3.5 Building Sparse Generative Models

Generation of simulated data is important for data analysis in particle physics. However, current Monte Carlo methods can be computationally expensive, and deep generative models can be helpful to speed up the generation process [232]. One specific challenge is that certain classes of images, such as calorimeter jet images, are very sparse. In addition, the distribution of the pixel values is not homogeneous across the entire image: typically it is significantly higher around the center of the image [231] (Figure 11.15a).

One effective solution [463] to address these problems is to use deep autoregressive generative models that are tuned for sparsity. Furthermore, different models can be used for different parts of the images, for instance one model for the central region, and one model for the peripheral region (Figure 11.15b).

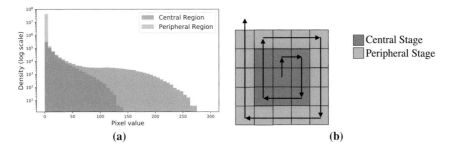

(a)   (b)

Figure 11.15 (a) Distribution of pixel values in a jet substructure study for the nine pixels in the center of the images (central region) and the rest of the pixels (peripheral region). Note that the majority of the pixels in the peripheral region are zero-valued and in general have lower variance than pixels in the central region. (b) Two-stage generation process for a deep sparse autoregressive model for the central and peripheral regions using a spiral path. Using different networks for each region improves performance [463].

A deep autoregressive generative model tuned to sparsity can easily be formed by writing its conditional probability distributions for the pixel values as a mixture, with a non-zero mass component at zero. In other words, letting $P_{\theta_i}(x_i|x_1, \ldots, x_{i-1}) = P(x_i|\theta_i)$, we use the decomposition:

$$P(x_i|\theta_i) = \lambda_i \delta_{x_i=0} + (1 - \lambda_i)\delta_{x_i \neq 0} \cdot P(x_i|\phi_i), \tag{11.1}$$

where the parameters $\theta_i = \{\lambda_i, \phi_i\}$ are produced by a deep neural network taking $x_1, \ldots, x_{i-1}$ as its input (or $(x_1, \ldots, x_{i-1}, 0, \ldots, 0)$) when padding is used). There are different ways of modeling $P(x_i|\phi_i)$ as a discrete or continuous distribution, depending on the situation [463].

SARM (Sparse Autoregressive Models) are shown to outperform GANs and other generative models on these tasks in [463] using different metrics. One metric is to compare the distributions of jet observable produced by different models to the "ground truth" distribution produced by the physics simulator package PYTHIA [687] (Figure 11.16).

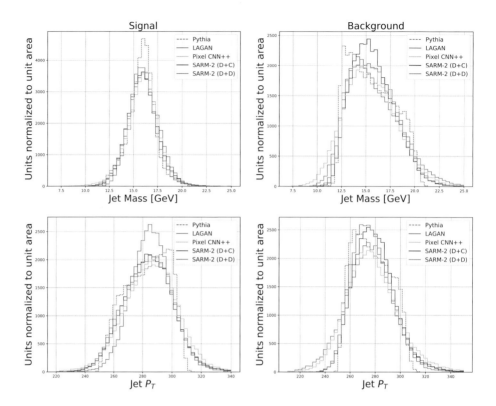

Figure 11.16 Comparison of distributions of jet observables produced using different SARMs (sparse autoregressive models), as well as GANs (LAGAN [232]) and Pixel CNN++ [641], an autoregressive model not tuned for sparsity. In all cases, the distribution produced by the SARMs is closer to the ground truth distribution associated with images produced using the physics simulator package PYTHIA [687].

11.4   Neutrino Physics

Neutrinos are uncharged elementary particles that only interact with other matter through the weak subatomic force and gravity – thus they are very elusive. In nature, they are produced by nuclear power plants, cosmic rays, and stars. They are a topic of intense interest due to the discoveries that they have non-zero mass and that they oscillate between three active *flavor* states, or lepton *flavors* (electron ν_e, muon ν_μ, or tau ν_τ) [260]. Each is a different superposition of three mass states ν_1, ν_2, and ν_3. The relationship between flavor and mass states, and the oscillation between flavors are commonly described by the Pontecorvo–Maki–Nakagawa–Sakata (PMNS) matrix [584, 585, 479]. As it travels through space, a neutrino created with a specific lepton flavor can later be measured to have a different one. Neutrino oscillations are so far the only experimental observation beyond the Standard Model. Neutrino oscillations are of great theoretical and experimental interest: for instance, they imply that the neutrino has non-zero mass, requiring a revision of the Standard Model. At least two fundamental questions remain to be settled by studying neutrino oscillations. First, what is the CP phase δ? The CP phase δ relates to the difference in oscillation behavior between neutrinos and anti-neutrinos. CP violation in the lepton sector holds implications for matter-antimatter asymmetry in the universe through leptogenesis. Second, what is the mass ordering ($m_3 > m_{1,2}$ or $m_{1,2} > m_3$) between neutrinos? The mass hierarchy provides key information for future searches of the neutrino-less double beta decay. Observing the neutrino-less double beta decay would imply that the neutrino is a Majorana particle meaning it is its own anti-particle. The mass hierarchy will also constrain the so far undetermined absolute neutrino masses.

Because neutrinos rarely interact with other particles, detecting them in experiments is a challenge. Detectors commonly consist of large volumes of dense materials, such that neutrinos traveling through the volume occasionally hit the nucleus of an atom and initiate a cascade of events that produce photons or other radiation that can be detected by surrounding instruments. The data produced by these detectors require sophisticated processing and analysis. Deep learning is being explored as a tool for this analysis in at least three areas:

(1) unsupervised learning for anomaly detection and clustering;
(2) event classification; and
(3) measuring the energy of decay products.

Energy reconstruction plays a key role in high energy Physics, as it converts detector unit readout into kinematics of interactions. One of the key challenges is thus a good estimation of electron neutrino energy. The accuracy of neutrino energy reconstruction in turn influences how precisely neutrino oscillation parameters can be estimated [98]. Next, we briefly discuss examples of each application.

Experiments sometimes produce unexpected results, and there is a need for tools that automaticaly flag anomalies. For example, in the Daya Bay Reactor Neutrino Experiment, post-data-collection analysis revealed an unexpected source of light flashes that turned out to be a malfunction in the detector's photo-multiplier tubes. This required alert physicists to pour through the data and notice a pattern – there is a need for *automated* tools for detecting such anomalies. Deep learning can help in this task by representing complex data distributions in a new way that makes such anomalies more apparent. In one study, unsupervised deep neural networks were used to learn new representations of high-dimensional image-like data from the Daya Bay experiment [593]; a convolutional autoencoder was trained and the low-dimensional embedding was used to visualize and cluster events, revealing structure that corresponded to the different types of physical processes in the detector (Figure 11.17).

Deep learning is also being explored as a way to perform the central measurements of neutrino experiments. For example, the NOvA experiment aims to measure the probability of $v_\mu \rightarrow v_e$ oscillations by sending a beam of muon neutrinos from Fermilab in Illinois to a far detector in Ash River, Minnesota. Observing electron neutrinos in the far detector provides a measurement of the oscillation rate, which also depends on the energy of the neutrinos. Thus, the precision of the experiment depends directly on the ability to classify and measure the energy of neutrinos from the high-dimensional data collected by the far detector.

Recent preliminary work with simulated data from the NOvA experiment has

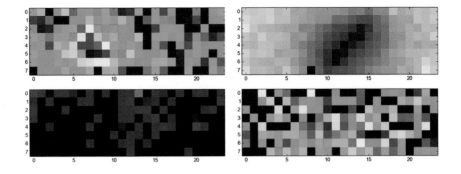

Figure 11.17 Example detector data from the Daya Bay Reactor Neutrino experiment, in which a neutrino hits a liquid scintillator and produces a flash of light that is recorded by the surrounding detector elements, producing an image. Deep learning can be used in both a supervised or unsupervised manner to distinguish events of interest (top left) from different types of background events including muons (top right), mechanical malfunctions (lower left), and random fluctuations (lower right).

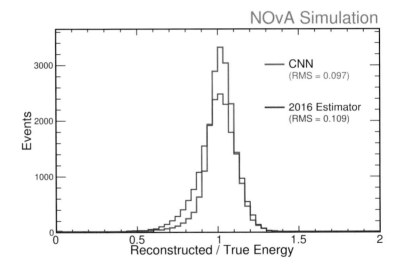

Figure 11.18 Empirical distributions of the predicted energy relative to the true energy (reconstructed / ground truth) on a simulated test set. A deep convolutional neural network (CNN) is compared to the standard approach used in a previous analysis (2016 Estimator). Reprinted from [339].

demonstrated that deep learning improves performance over standard methods in both tasks: classification [54] and energy estimation [339, 98]. In the latter, millions of neutrino shower events in the NOνA far detector were simulated, each producing a pair of 896×384 pixel images, where each pixel measures the energy deposited in the corresponding detector cell. These images capture two views of a single inbound particle showering into secondary particles. A simple cropping procedure was used to reduce the dimensionality of each image to 141×151 pixels, and then a Siamese neural network was trained to combine the information from the two detector views and make a prediction. Deep learning improved performance by 11% compared to the specialized algorithms engineered for a previous NOνA analysis (Figure 11.18).

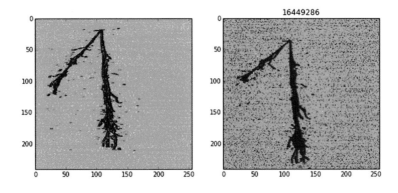

Figure 11.19 A simulated LArIAT event. The two panels show the same particle shower from two separate sections of the detector. Each pixel is a single detector element at a particular location (y-axis) and time (x-axis). The shape of the shower can be used to classify the type of incident particle and predict its energy. In the experiments discussed, the two images were fed into separate arms of a siamese convolutional neural network in order to classify the type of particle and predict its energy.

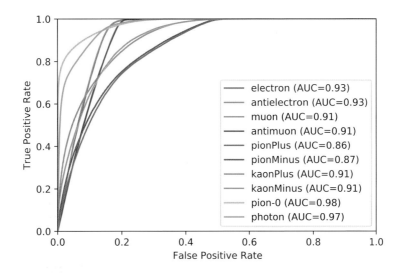

Figure 11.20 Performance of the Siamese convolutional neural network on a 10-way particle classification task, trained on four million simulated LArIAT events of the type in Figure 11.19. One-vs-all ROC curves are shown for a test set of 400,000 events.

Our own preliminary work with the DUNE and LArIAT neutrino experiments show similar results. Like NOνA, the LArIAT detector produces data that can be treated as

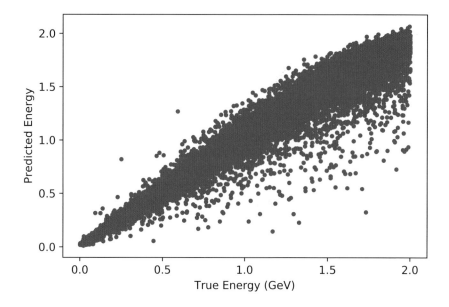

Figure 11.21 Predicted energy vs. true energy for a Siamese convolutional neural network trained to predict the energy of simulated electron showers from raw detector data. The mean squared error of these predictions is 0.02 GeV.

a pair of high-resolution images (Figure 11.19). In classification experiments, we used a Siamese convolutional neural network where each arm is based on the GoogLeNet architecture [716], and demonstrated that the deep learning approach trained on the low-level detector data achieves better performance than a BDT trained on derived features (Figure 11.20). For the energy estimation task, the architecture was adapted for a heteroskedastic regression task by replacing the sigmoid output layer with two outputs, $\hat{y}_1$ and $\hat{y}_2$, and a loss function proportional to the negative log-likelihood of the target value under a Gaussian distribution with mean $\hat{y}_1$ and standard deviation $e^{\hat{y}_2}$. This allows the network to model the uncertainty in its predictions [541]. Preliminary results show that this approach works well (Figure 11.21) and deep learning, as well as other machine learning methods [446], are playing a growing role in the analysis of data from neutrino experiments.

11.5   Dark Matter Physics

Dark matter is invisible matter, i.e. matter that does not emit, absorb, or reflect electromagnetic radiation. There is ample evidence for its existence, for instance through its gravitational effect, and it is estimated that approximately 85% of the matter in the universe consists of dark matter. Several collaborations aim to identify the nature and properties of the particles dark matter may be made of. One of the most widely supported ideas is that dark matter is most likely composed of weakly interacting massive particles, or *WIMPs*, that interact with other matter only through gravity and the weak nuclear force. The XENON1T experiment [41] at the Italian Gran Sasso laboratory is attempting to detect these WIMPs directly. Located in an underground facility shielded from cosmic rays by 1,400 meters of rock, the XENON1T consists of a cylindrical tank containing 3.5 tons of ultra-radio-pure liquid xenon scintillator, achieving record low levels of background radiation [794, 793]. Any radiation above the expected background level would indicate the presence of a hypothesized WIMP particle.

When an inbound particle collides with a Xenon atom in the XENON1T detector, recoiling against either the nucleus or an electron, the interaction releases photons that are observed by the photo multiplier tubes (PMTs) located at the top and bottom of the tank (Figure 11.22). From the pattern of observed photons, the data is analyzed to determine the type and location of the collision. The standard approach relies on algorithms hand-tuned by physicists on a number of high-level descriptive features, but this approach discards potentially-useful information. Thus, a deep learning approach might be able to improve performance by extracting additional information from the raw data.

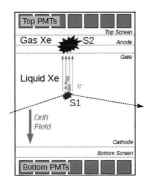

Figure 11.22 Diagram of the XENON1T detector cross-section, showing the PMT arrays located at the top and bottom of the cylindrical tank of Xenon. An incoming particle (dotted black line) recoils against a Xe atom, causing an initial scintillation (S1), as well as releasing electrons that rise to the top of the tank and cause a second scintillation (S2). Reprinted from "The XENON1T Dark Matter Experiment," XENON Collaboration, *The European Physical Journal C*, 77(1434–6052), 2017.

We have explored deep learning for performing both event localization and classification in the XENON1T. The raw data from the detector consists of real-valued measurements from the 248 PMTs sampled at 10 nanosecond intervals (Figure 11.23). The S2 scintillation response can last up to 15 microseconds, so the dimensionality of the low-level data is approximately 248×1500. From this input, we trained one deep neural network to predict the X, Y location of the collision, and another network to classify examples as containing a single collision or multiple overlapping collisions. The networks were each trained on 180,000 simulated events and tested on a held out set of another 20,000 simulated events. On the event location prediction, the deep learning approach achieves a root mean squared error of 0.68 cm (the cylindrical volume has a radius of 48 cm), and on the classification task the deep learning approach achieves 90% accuracy on a balanced test set.

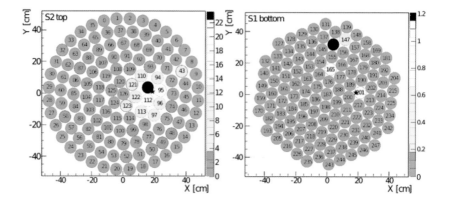

Figure 11.23 Example data from a low-energy single-scatter nuclear recoil event recorded by XENON1T during a calibration run. Shown here is the S2 response at the top of the detector (Left), and the S1 response on the bottom of the detector (Right), summed over time. The inferred X, Y position of the event is indicated by the star marker. In the deep learning approach, the readout from each PMT (circle) at each timestep is treated as an input to a neural network. Adapted from "The XENON1T Dark Matter Experiment," XENON Collaboration, *The European Physical Journal C*, 77(1434–6052), 2017.

Our deep learning approach takes advantage of two important invariances in the data. First, the hexagonal arrangement of the PMTs result in a symmetry isomorphic to the dihedral group of order 6 (under the assumption that the PMTs operate at roughly the same efficiency). To account for this, we augmented our training data set by randomly applying rotation and mirror permutations to the input data in each training batch. Second, we account for a limited amount of translational invariance in the time dimension with 1D convolutions and pooling in the network architecture. Note that while the detector data is essentially a video, the PMTs are not arranged in a grid, so standard 2D or 3D convolutions cannot be applied. However, the arrangement of the PMTs does induce local structure, which could be accounted for with graph convolution architectures in future work.

These results are preliminary but they indicate that deep learning is a promising approach to improving the sensitivity at XENON1T as well as future dark matter experiments.

11.6   Cosmology and Astrophysics

There are many applications of deep learning in cosmology, in particular to process and extract signals from complex images in various ways, to identify and analyze complex phenomena and probe the nature of, for instance, black holes, gravitational waves, and dark matter (e.g. [297, 746]). Here we describe one project ultimately aimed at detecting dark matter in our own galaxy.

Another predicted outcome from a WIMPs model for dark matter is the emission of gamma rays via annihilation or decay of these particles [125]. The inner region of the Milky Way is predicted to be rich in dark matter, and we therefore expect to see an excess gamma signal towards the galactic center. Indeed, observation performed by the Fermi Large Area Telescope find a greater presence of gamma rays matching the expected profile of dark matter annihilation [16]. However, this excess may also be explained by yet unobserved contributions from other, more conventional, astrophysical processes. Studying sources of gamma rays in this region is a difficult task, complicated by the fact that observations towards the galactic center may be tainted by sources outside of our galaxy. Several competing theories for the source of this excess emission have been proposed, with one explanation arguing that point sources such as pulsars my emit this surplus signal. These rapidly spinning and extremely bright neutron stars release gamma rays with a similar profile to dark matter. They are also very common throughout the galaxy, with over 2000 such point sources catalogued, and possibly many more not yet detected.

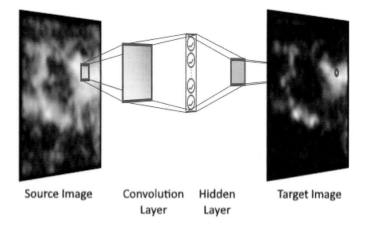

Source Image   Convolution   Hidden   Target Image
                  Layer   Layer

Figure 11.24 Convolutional neural network to predict a gas concentration at a single point given information from an $n \times n$ window surrounding that point.

Another significant contributor to this excess could be interstellar gas that permeates the galaxy. High-energy cosmic particles, released by many commonplace events in the galaxy, may sometimes collide with this diffuse gas to emit light of various wavelengths. Specifically, the interactions between these cosmic particles and the abundant molecular gas clouds (H_2) release gamma radiation with the required profile in a process known as galactic diffuse emission [437]. The brightness of this emission from a region of space would be proportional to the concentration of H_2 in that region. If we could accurately know the concentration of H_2 throughout the galactic center, then we could subtract its contribution. Measuring this concentration directly is difficult, however, and often astronomers measure another indicator gas that can be used to model H_2 instead.

Carbon monoxide is a common gas used for modeling hydrogen because it is simple to measure via radio telescope and produces very accurate models. The most common variant of carbon monoxide ($^{12}C^{16}O$) may be detected with telescopes sensitive to 115 GHz, and we have detailed surveys of its concentration across the entirety of the galactic center [222]. However, the less common isotopologues of carbon monoxide, $^{13}C^{16}O$ and $^{12}C^{18}O$, are also vital for accurately modeling the presence of molecular hydrogen. These variants are more difficult to detect, and we only have high-resolution surveys of these gasses in small sections of the galactic center [161, 148].

We attempt to model the concentration of the rare isotopologues knowing only the concentration of the most common form of carbon monoxide. This relationship is subtly non-linear, likely caused by the isotopologues' larger mass encouraging higher concentration around dense regions of interstellar gas. Learning this relationship accurately would allow us model background gamma emissions attributed to molecular hydrogen knowing only the concentration of $^{12}C^{16}O$. We learn this mapping with a deep convolutional network trained on the complete high-resolution MOPRA [148] survey containing information on all three isotopologues.

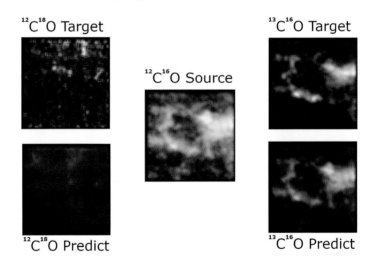

Figure 11.25 Example outputs comparing predicted and ground-truth gas concentrations.

Immediately, we run into a problem when training a deep neural network on this data. The MOPRA dataset is comprised of only 40 images, making it difficult to train an entire image-to-image model on such a small number of examples. Deep learning requires many samples in order to train a competent model, and one key challenge in designing deep learning models is determining how to extract as much information as possible from the available data. In order to generate more training examples from this limited source, we assume that the relationship between the gasses is localized. That is, the concentration of the isotopologues at a particular location in space is only influenced by the concentration of $^{12}C^{16}O$ in a small surrounding region. Therefore, we simplify this modeling task to the goal of predicting the concentration of single point in space given a $n \times n$ window centered at that point. Since the images are high resolution and our values for n are small, we suddenly find that we have over 100,000 low dimensional samples to train on. This relationship can be accurately learned with the convolutional neural network shown in Figure 11.24. The network consists of a single convolution layer with K different kernels and a kernel size equal to the window size n. Throughout the experiment, we compared window sizes between $n = 3$ and $n = 20$, and we find that windows larger than $n = 7$ do not improve performance, supporting the locality assumption. The outputs of these kernels are then fed through a ReLU nonlinearity before being linearly combined to produce a single output prediction.

The network is trained by minimizing the Poisson log-likelihood between the predicted output and the true output. This optimization goal trains a more robust model on this dataset when compared to the regular mean squared error. First, because most of the data is near-zero with clusters of high-density regions, the logarithmic scaling of the Poisson loss better handles these large fluctuations in output value. Furthermore, the Poisson distribution is designed to model the expected number of events that occur in a given timespan. Concentration data is generated by a telescope collecting photons over a fixed exposure period, naturally lending itself to a Poisson likelihood.

The network achieved a mean absolute error of 0.44 on $^{13}C^{16}O$ and 0.27 on $^{12}C^{18}O$. Measuring naive percent error is difficult with this dataset due to the aforementioned prevalence of near-zero values. Instead, we may compare these absolute errors to the maximum value present in each image to create a notion of percent error. Following this metric, the network achieved 1.5% and 4.1% scaled absolute error on $^{13}C^{16}O$ and $^{12}C^{18}O$ respectively. Example outputs and a visual comparison to the true concentrations is given in Figure 11.25.

11.7   Climate Physics

There are many other applications of deep learning in the physical sciences. As another example, here we briefly describe an application to climate modeling and prediction. Current climate models partition the surface of the Earth into a grid with an horizontal resolution of 50–100 km. Many of the most important processes in the atmosphere, such as clouds, occur on smaller scales. Clouds, in particular, can be as small as 100 m, and play an essential role by transporting heat and moisture, absorbing and reflecting radiation, and producing rain [655]. Physical approximations, called parameterizations, have been heuristically developed to represent the effects of such sub-grid processes, however significant inaccuracies persist in the parameterization of clouds and their interactions with other processes [362]. As a result, large uncertainties remain in how much the Earth will warm up due to the greenhouse effects [655, 139, 673].

Cloud-resolving models (CRMs) at finer resolutions of a few kilometers or less have been developed. Such models are beginning to be used over relatively short periods of time (months to a few years) but remain computationally too expensive for exploring climate change over longer periods [508, 151, 803, 413]. Deep learning is the obvious candidate for trying to speed up these calculations.

This approach was first demonstrated in [605], using a deep feedforward neural network to predict subgrid tendencies as a function of the atmospheric state at every time step and grid column. The input variables include: temperature, specific humidity, wind profiles, surface pressure, incoming solar radiation, and latent heat fluxes, corresponding to 94 variables in total. The output variable include: radiative heating rates, moistening rate, net radiative fluxes at the top of the atmosphere and at the surface, and precipitation, corresponding to 65 variables in total. The network used has nine fully-connected layers, with 256 nodes in each layer, corresponding to a total of 0.5M parameters with a data set of 140M examples. The model makes a number of approximations and uses an aquaplanet set up, corresponding to an Earth covered by oceans and with no continents [605].

Name	Options	Parameter Type
Batch Normalization	[yes, no]	Binary Choice
Dropout	[0, 0.25]	Continuous
Leaky ReLU coefficient	[0 - 0.4]	Continuous
Learning Rate	[0.00001 - 0.01]	Continuous (log)
Nodes per Layer	[128,256,512]	Discrete
Number of layers	[4 - 11]	Discrete
Optimizer	[Adam, RMSProp, SGD]	Choice

Table 11.4 Hyperparameter Space

Two important issues are left unresolved in the otherwise pioneering work of Rasp et al., the optimization of the hyperparameters of the network and the deployment of the network in a realistic simulation environment. The latter is not a trivial issue, as much of the software infrastructure for climate simulations is written in Fortran. We address both issues using a model provided by Rasp et al. which has the same architecture as in their published work, but is trained on a different, more complex data set.

For the optimization problem, we use the hyperparameter optimization Python library Sherpa [340]. We detail the hyperparameters of interest in Table 11.4, as well as the range of available options during the search. The hyperparameters of interest consist of whether or not to use batch normalization, the amount of dropout, the leaky ReLU coefficient, the learning rate, the number of nodes per layer, the number of layers, and the optimizer. Over one hundred model configurations are trained for 25 epochs with early stopping monitoring the validation loss. Following the hyperparameter search, the best model, determined by validation loss, is compared against the model of Rasp et al. The compared performance of the two models is shown in Figure 11.26. The model produced by the hyperparameter search outperforms the single model provided to us at all latitudes and pressures, in some cases by substantial margins.

To study the deployment issue, we deployed all the trained models in the Superparameterized Community Atmospheric Model version 3.0 (SPCAM3) simulator, where performance is evaluated by the number of steps until failure. Inside SPCAM3, the neural network models are coupled to the host model dynamics, so that neural network predictions at one time step affect the state of the system at the next time step. However, SPCAM3 is written exclusively in Fortran and thus we leverage the FKB library [558] to convert the Keras models into Fortran neural networks. The Rasp et al. model provided by the authors, ran for 128 steps before crashing due to instability issues. The best model achieved in this study ran for more than 50,000 steps, a 500-fold improvement. In short, hyperparameter searches produce models that not only perform better on test sets but that are also more stable when deployed in the full simulation environment. Efficient training and deployment of deep learning models in scientific environments that are built in Fortran is now possible using the Fortran–Keras Bridge (FKB) library, providing a two-way bridge between Fortran and Keras.

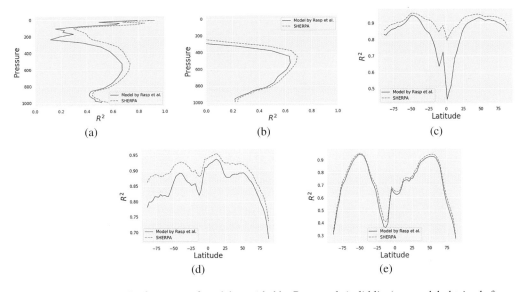

Figure 11.26 Performance of model provided by Rasp et al. (solid line) vs model obtained after hyperparameter optimization using Sherpa (dotted line). (a) Convective heating rate. (b) Convective moistening rate. (c) Long wave flux at the surface. (d) Long wave flux at the top of the atmosphere. (e) Precipitation. In all cases, the dotted line is associated with a better (larger) coefficient of determination R^2.

11.8   Incorporating Physics Knowledge and Constraints

In applying machine learning to physics problems, one is often presented with the challenge of bringing physics knowledge to bear on the machine learning models. This situation can present itself in several different forms such as having to: choose the relevant input and output variables, incorporate prior knowledge, bias solutions towards particular directions, and ensure that particular laws or constraints are satisfied. In many cases, these situations can be addressed through the choice of the architecture or the choice of the error functions.

Physics-aware architectures can be designed that account for additional physics knowledge by taking advantages of architectural motifs, such as such as local connectivity, weight sharing and convolutions, Siamese structures, pooling, skip connections, gating, and attention. In particular, as discussed in Chapter 6, neural networks architectures can be designed to take into account invariances with respect to physically relevant transformations, such as translations or permutations. Likewise, in some cases, prior physics knowledge can be converted into a regularizing term that can be included in the error function. Next we discuss a few examples.

Decaying particles in a detector typically result in decay products that are hierarchically clustered in space and time (jet substructures). Thus, sets of four-vectors often have additional structure that can be exploited. When the clustering hierarchy of each event can be reconstructed, for example using a sequential recombination jet algorithm, this additional information can be incorporated into the network [460]. In particular, recursive neural network architectures can be constructed to match the topology of the jet clustering algorithms, in a way that is analogous to models in natural language processing that take advantage of sentence parse trees. The recursive physics neural network architecture is constructed on a per-event basis to reflect the tree structure of that event. In addition to the properties of permutation invariance (assuming each node is permutation invariant) and scalability to an arbitrary number of set elements, this model has the additional property of local connectivity among related elements in the set, which can lead to better generalization. Finally, in [273], transformer and attention mechanisms are used for permutation-invariant complex-jet event reconstruction from four vectors.

Another example are the Lorentz-boosted neural networks described in [256], in which the first hidden layer of the network is interpreted as "composite particles" and corresponding "rest frames," and represented as linear combinations of the input four-vectors. Each learned composite particle is then boosted into its corresponding rest frame using the non-linear Lorentz transformation. The resulting feature representations are then fed into a neural network, and the entire system is trained using backpropagation. The major advantage of this architecture is that it constrains the representation of the data into a form that can be readily interpreted by physicists (i.e. Lorentz-transformed four vectors) and for which physically meaningful features can be extracted such as invariant masses, pseudorapidities, and so forth.

11.8.1   Incorporating Physics Constraints

Here we consider the situation where there are physical laws, in the form of exact equations, relating the values of some of the relevant variables. In addition to physics, many fields of science and engineering (e.g., fluid dynamics, hydrology, solid mechanics, chemistry kinetics) have exact, often *analytic*, closed-form constraints, i.e. constraints that can be explicitly written using analytic functions of the system's variables. Examples include translational or rotational invariance, conservation laws, or equations of state. While physically-consistent models should enforce constraints to within machine precision, data-driven algorithms often fail to satisfy well-known constraints that are not explicitly enforced. In particular, while neural networks may provide powerful classification and regression tools for non-linear systems, they may optimize overall performance while violating these constraints on individual samples.

Despite the need for physically-informed neural networks for complex physical systems ([609, 120, 394, 787]), enforcing constraints ([485]) has been limited mostly to physical systems governed by specific equations, such as advection equations ([597, 107, 229]), Reynolds-averaged Navier–Stokes equations ([452, 790]), or quasi-geostrophic equations ([138]). Thus it is necessary to have methods that can enforce analytic constraints in more general settings. Here we describe two general ways for enforcing constraints, first in a soft way, and then in a hard way.

In general, let us assume that there is a constraint of the form $C(x, y, z) = 0$ that must be satisfied by the input variables x, the output variables y, and possibly some auxiliary variables z, where x, y and z are vector variables. If $\mathcal{E}$ is the error function of the neural network trained on the pairs (x, y), we can enforce the constraints in a soft way by adding a penalty term to the loss function, e.g. using a new loss function of the form $\mathcal{E}' = \mathcal{E} + \lambda C^2$ where λ is an additional hyperparameter. This regularization approach has been used for instance in climate modeling ([395, 379, 598]). While this approach can be effective, there is no guarantee that the constraints will not be violated.

A general way for enforcing constraints in a hard way is described in [127]. There are several possible implementations of this idea, but the gist of it is to augment the basic neural architecture with an additional neural network to enforce the constraints. For this we can first decompose y non-uniquely as $y = (y_1, y_2)$. Then we introduced a first neural network with adaptive weights that produces an output y_1', trying to predict y_1 from x. This is followed by a second network which computes y_2' from x, y_1' and z, enforcing the constraint C to machine precision. The weights of the second network are fixed and determined by the knowledge of C. For instance, the second network can be linear if the constraint C is linear. We can then combine the two networks into a single overall architecture whose final output is the vector (y_1', y_2'). This output always satisfies the constraint C by construction. Furthermore, it can be compared to the target (y_1, y_2) and the errors can be backpropagated through the combined network, through both the fixed and adjustable weights. As a result of this approach, the constraint C is satisfied at all times, both during and after learning.

11.9 Conclusion: Theoretical Physics

In closing this chapter, we know that the Standard Model and General Relativity, the two most fundamental theories of physics, are at best incomplete. In the quest to go beyond them, this chapter has explored how deep learning is being applied to diverse data analyses and prediction pipelines in antimatter, collider, neutrino, dark matter, and cosmology experiments, as well as in other areas such as climate physics. One common theme is that sophisticated data-processing pipelines and predictive models can be automatically *learned* rather than *engineered*. In many of the studies presented, deep learning is able to extract information from the low-level data that is lost in more traditional approaches, leading to improved performance and speedup of scientific discoveries, while simultaneously reducing the labor required to analyze the data.

Deep learning is also being used to influence the design and optimization of future experiments. Detectors are designed to satisfy the constraints of the algorithms used to process the data, such as tracking algorithms. These designs are likely sub-optimal from an information theory perspective, and deep learning may enable one to optimize detector properties at multiple levels (e.g. their structure, composition, location, geometry) as well as the related detection algorithms.

In addition to its many applications to experimental physics, deep learning is bound to play a role in theoretical physics at multiple interconnected levels. At one level, deep learning is used to try to accelerate complex models, and explore the landscape of complex parameter spaces and theories, in regimes that are currently intractable or poorly understood. In lattice chromodynamics, for instance, physicists have been able to derive the mass of the electron to great precision, but deriving the mass of the proton is a different story. There are ongoing efforts to apply deep learning to a variety of such related areas including various parameterized versions of the Standard Model and families of models derived from it (e.g. [284]), of string theory (e.g. [523]), of supersymmetry theories, and of models of the early universe and Big Bang nucleosynthesis [646]. This is in addition to applications in more "traditional" areas such as quantum mechanics (density functional theory), or fluid dynamics and turbulence.

At another level, deep learning can be used to try to learn and discover symbolic theories, in the same way it can be used to learn specific areas of mathematics, such as symbolic integration. Perhaps the most simple version of this in physics is symbolic regression, where deep learning can be used to seek a particular symbolic formula that fits a specific set of measurements. A more challenging example would be to derive the Standard Model from the experimental data that was available around 1970 or so. Building a computer physicist, as well as the related task of building a computer mathematician, are far from reach but incremental steps in that direction can be taken by progressively increasing the domain over which learning methods can be applied.

12 Applications in Chemistry

In spite of its central role between physics, biology, and other areas of science and technology [154], chemistry has remained in a backward state of informatics development compared to its close relatives. Public downloadable repositories, open software, and large collaborative projects have become the hallmark of research in physics and biology. In contrast, these are relatively absent from chemical research. This is not to say that chemists do not use computers or databases. In fact, some of the first scientific databases arose precisely in the chemical sciences (the Beilstein data base) – but these uses have remained somewhat limited and often commercial in nature. With very few exceptions, these have not led to large public repositories, open software, and large-scale collaborative projects. By and large, chemistry has remained the business of individual investigators and their laboratories. Suffice it to say that until recently, there was no publicly available repository of all known molecules, and that today there is still no publicly available repository of all known chemical reactions.

This unfortunate state of affairs is unlikely to have resulted from some intrinsic properties of chemistry as a science. Rather, it is the product of complex historical and sociological factors, that are beyond the scope of this book, going back at least to the middle ages and the secretive research projects of alchemists seeking to convert base metals into gold. Other contributing factors include the early commercialization of chemical research (e.g. the German chemical industry in the 1800s), the naive perception by the general public that patenting chemicals is more acceptable than patenting molecules associated with life, and the development of powerful companies and societies that often resist the dissemination of information beyond their control. Needless to say, the paucity of large, publicly available, datasets is an obstacle for the large-scale application of AI and machine learning methods in the chemical sciences. However, and although the process is taking decades to unfold, there has been some progress and more can be expected in the future. Many of the required methods for mining chemical data, including deep learning methods, have already been developed and tested, often using relatively small datasets, and are ready to be scaled as more data becomes available.

While there are applications of deep learning in all areas of chemistry, in this chapter we will focus primarily on organic chemistry applications. Even within organic chemistry alone, there are many different problems and we will focus primarily on two main classes: (1) the prediction of the properties of small molecules; and (2) the prediction of chemical reactions. Several of the datasets and programs mentioned in this chapter are available from the UCI chemoinformatics web portal `http://cdb.ics.uci.edu/`.

12.1   Chemical Data and Chemical Space

The term 'small molecules' in organic chemistry refers to molecules with a relatively small number of atoms, consisting primarily of carbon, nitrogen, oxygen, and hydrogen. There is no hard bound on the number of atoms, but typically one considers molecules with up to a few dozens atoms, with an upper bound of say ~ 100 atoms. Many small molecules may also include other elements such sulfur, phosphorus, halogens (e.g. fluorine, chlorine, bromine), and so on. Typical examples of small molecules are water, methane, all the building blocks of life including all amino acids, nucleotides, metabolites and natural products, as well as most drugs. In contrast, large organic molecules are typically polymeric molecules such as proteins with thousands of atoms, or even millions of atoms in the case of DNA molecules. Peptides molecules sit at the boundary between small molecules and proteins.

Small molecules have many applications and can be used as combinatorial building blocks for chemical synthesis [658, 15], as molecular probes for perturbing and analyzing biological systems in chemical genomics and systems biology [659, 700, 243], and for the screening, design, and discovery of useful compounds, including new drugs [453, 385]. Furthermore, huge arrays of new small molecules can be produced in a relatively short period of time [361, 658].

	Astronomical Space	Chemical Space
Visited Universe	0-1 star	10^7 compounds
Existing Universe	10^{22} stars	10^8 molecules
Virtual Universe	10^{22} stars	10^{60} molecules
Travel	very difficult	relatively easy

Table 12.1 Comparison of astronomical and chemical spaces.

Because carbon is capable of easily forming bonds with other atoms, including itself, the space of small molecules is truly astronomical (Table 12.1). Astronomical space contains on the order of 10^{22} stars, i.e. roughly 10^{11} galaxies each containing 10^{11} stars. The number of known small molecules, identified in biological systems or synthesized by man, is on the order of 100 million. However, estimates in the literature of the size of the virtual space of small molecules that could be created vary between 10^{50} and 10^{100}, with 10^{60} being a frequently quoted estimate [137]. Thus by any of these estimates, chemical space remains largely unexplored. A second essential difference between chemical and astronomical space is the ease of travel. Chemical space is comparatively easy to travel! Small molecules can be recursively enumerated in silico and synthesized in vitro from known building blocks and known reactions. By contrast, reaching any star even only a few light years away is out of the question. In short, with $\sim 10^{60}$ enumerable and synthesizable small molecules remaining to be explored, it is likely that computers and machine learning methods will play an increasingly central role.

For a long time, no free public database of small molecules existed. By aggregating molecules found in the catalogs of chemical vendors, the first public databases were created relatively recently [368, 179], these in turn seeded the creation of NIH PubChem [779, 405], not without considerable resistance from the American Chemical Society [486]. In any case, PubChem is now becoming the main public repository of small molecules. Methods for defining similarity between small molecules and using them to efficiently search large repositories have been in place for quite some time (e.g. [712, 531, 530]).

In addition to PubChem, there is also the publicly available and downloadable GDB-n series of datasets, enumerating small organic molecules with up to n atoms (excluding hydrogen atoms). For instance, GDB-13 enumerates small organic molecules up to 13 atoms of C, N, O, S and Cl following simple chemical stability and synthetic feasibility rules [133]. It contains about 1 billion molecules. The latest version in the series is GDB-17 containing about 166 billion organic molecules of up to 17 atoms [625].

As previously discussed, one central problem is to be able to predict the physical, chemical, and biological properties of real or virtual small molecules in order to search them effectively for various applications. The list of such properties is virtually infinite including, as a small set of examples:

(1) 3D structure;
(2) response to electromagnetic waves of various wave lengths;
(3) response to temperature (e.g. melting points);
(4) various aspects of reactivity;
(5) solubility in water, or other solvents, often an important consideration for drugs;
(6) degree of affinity for binding to a particular molecule, including all proteins;
(7) degree of mutagenicity or toxicity, for various definitions of these terms and other bioactivity properties.

Many of these prediction problems can be cast as classification or regression problems. For some of these properties, very little empirical data, public or private, is available. For others, a significant amount of empirical data is available privately or commercially, but only small data sets are available publicly. For a few rare cases, mostly in connection with PubChem, large collaborative annotation efforts and data sets are becoming available.

In parallel to the GDB-n computational efforts mentioned above, aimed at enumerating all small molecules containing up to n heavy atoms, there are similar effort based on quantum mechanical (QM) calculations to computationally estimate a number of properties (e.g. most stable conformations, atomization energies) for systematically generated small organic molecules, giving rise to the QMn series of data sets [600, 601].

For the second broad problem of predicting the outcome of chemical reactions, the data situation is even worse than for small molecules. Today, there is simply no freely downloadable repository of all known chemical reactions. Large repositories of chemical reactions, and some of their annotations, exist (e.g. Elsevier's REAXYS, InfoChem's SPRESI, ACS's CAS system) but these are all commercial. Even when a license is purchased, access to the data, and its use, are often limited and controlled by narrow interfaces allowing searches one-query-at-a-time, which is of course not useful for machine learning purposes where the entire repository needs to be accessible for various training and mining purposes. There are a few isolated and relatively small data sets of reactions. Perhaps the largest one, which is still far from being comprehensive, is the one that can be constructed using reactions extracted by text-mining methods from United States patents [462], currently containing, after some filtering, on the order of half a million reactions.

12.2   Prediction of Small Molecule Properties

Machine learning methods, including deep learning methods, for the prediction of the properties of small molecules have been developed, leveraging in particular the variety of different representations available to represent small molecules (Figure 12.1).

12.2.1   Representations

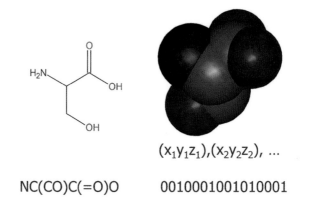

$$(x_1y_1z_1),(x_2y_2z_2), \ldots$$

NC(CO)C(=O)O   0010001001010001

Figure 12.1 Four different representations a small molecule using the amino acid Serine as an example. Top left: graphs (or adjacency matrices) labeled by atom and bond types. Note that alternatively this representation could also come in the form of an image using a standard format (e.g. .png of .pdf). Bottom left: SMILES strings. Note that hydrogen atoms are omitted, carbon atoms are implicit, parentheses denote branching, and "=" denotes double bonds. Top right: 3D structures which can be described by a list, or set, of atoms with the (x, y, z) coordinates of their nuclei. Bottom right: fingerprints consisting of long, sparse, binary vectors of fixed length where a "1" denotes the presence of a particular feature in the molecule. A typical basis of combinatorial features consists of labeled paths or labeled trees up to a certain size.

Indeed molecules can be represented by:

- Labeled graphs. In turn, these graphs can be represented by an adjacency matrix specifying for each atom the atoms it is bonded to, and the type of bond (e.g. single, double, triple, aromatic). This representation is variable in size.

- Images of the labeled graph. This representation can be fixed in size.

- SMILES strings. SMILES [783, 374] is a widely used language that allows one to represent molecules by strings. This representation is variable in size.

- The list, or set, of the atoms in the molecules with the coordinates (x, y, z) of the corresponding nuclei. This representation of course assumes that the coordinates be available, either through experimental methods or computational prediction methods (see below). This representation is variable in size.

- Fingerprints. Fingerprints are usually binary vectors over a basis of features, where for each feature, the corresponding component is 1 if the feature is present in the molecules, and 0 otherwise. The first fingerprints used relatively small hasis of features, corresponding primarily to chemical groups, often handpicked by human experts. Over time, a variety of fingerprints have been developed with larger basis. These larger basis are typically combinatorial in natures, corresponding for instance to all possible labeled paths of a certain length, or to all labeled trees of a certain depth ([276, 277, 374, 800, 801, 436, 302, 73, 616, 531]. Instead of binary entries, it is also possible to use integer entries counting how many time a given feature is found in a molecule. The fingerprint representation is fixed in size.

while these are the most common representations, other representations can be envisioned focusing, for instance, on the electron cloud of each atom, or the "surface" of the molecule. Deep learning methods have been developed and can be applied to each one of these representations.

12.2.2 Similarity Measures and Kernels

In part because the training sets can be small, it is useful to consider first other shallow methods, in particular kernel methods based on similarity. Similarity metrics have been defined for all the representations above and can be used to search existing databases, for instance in ligand-based screening where one seeks to identify molecules that are similar to a set of molecules that are known to be active. Perhaps the most widely used similarity metric for fast database searches is the Jaccard–Tanimoto similarity metric applied to the binary fingerprints, Given two binary fingerprint vectors a and b, this similarity is given by the number of bits in common, divided by the total number of bits in the two fingerprints ("intersection over union"), $S(a, b) = (a \wedge b)/(a \vee b)$ [63]. Other similarity metrics can be defined on the molecular graphs [711]. Using these similarity metrics, kernel-based predictive methods have been developed, both for classification and regression problems, to predict, for instance, the mutagenicity, toxicity, and solubility of small molecules [711, 55].

12.2.3   Prediction of 3D Structures

Before delving into deep learning methods, it is worth briefly discussing the 3D structure prediction problem. The 3D structures of small molecules can in principle be predicted from scratch using Quantum Mechanics and Molecular Dynamics calculations. However, these methods are still too slow for producing predictions on a very large scale. A faster approach, is to leverage the wealth of information contained in structural databases, matching fragments of the query molecule to similar fragments of known structure in the database, and then inputing the overall structure of the query molecule by stitching together the structure of the various fragments. The main repository of 3D structures for molecules is the Cambridge Structural Database (CSD) maintained by the company Cambridge Crystallographic Data Centre, containing the 3D coordinates for the atoms of many millions of molecules. The CSD was used in this way to produce an effective 3D structure predictor [96]. However the CSD comes with a number of restrictions [37], and thus an alternative is to use a smaller, but open, repository called the Crystallography Open Database (formerly CrystalEye) [228] to produce a similar predictor [637].

The 3D structure prediction problem for small molecules, bears many similarities to the 3D structure prediction for proteins addressed in Chapter 13. Thus, although to the best of our knowledge this has not yet been done systematically, one ought to be able also to use deep learning methods to predict the 3D structure of small molecules. However, using a neural network to directly predict the (x, y, z) coordinates is probably not a good idea because the structure of the molecule is invariant under rotations and translations, but the coordinates are not. As a minimum, one would have to define somewhat arbitrarily a fixed frame of coordinates for all the molecules. A more natural approach, is to predict a representation of the molecular structure that is rotation and translation invariant, such as the distance map. The distance map provides all the pairwise distances between the atoms in the molecule. Feedforward or recursive neural networks should be applicable to the various molecular representations discussed above in order to predict the distance map, from which the full 3D structure can be derived.

12.2.4   Deep Learning: Feedforward Networks

Deep learning methods to predict the physical, chemical, and biological properties of small molecules can be applied to any of the representations above. Feedforward neural networks, including convolutional feedforward neural networks, can be applied to the fixed-size representations: images or fingerprints. If the fingerprints vectors are very long, however, it may be necessary to go first through a dimensionality reduction step which can be implemented, for instance, using an autoencoder approach.

There is another option which leverages the similarity measures that exist for small molecules. This option is in fact more general and can be applied anytime there is a good similarity/kernel or distance on the input data. It is presented here in combination with feedforward networks, but it can also be used with recursive networks. The basic idea is that the neural network used to predict the property of interest should look at the entire neighborhood of a molecule and its geometry, rather than just at the representation of the molecule of interest. In this option, rather than applying a feedforward neural network to the native representation of the objects of interest (e.g. the molecular fingerprints), a feedforward neural network is applied to a different representation, describing the neighborhood of each object in the data manifold. In this case, the neighborhood of a molecule can be represented, for instance, by selecting its k-nearest (most similar) molecules in the training data. The neighborhood is then represented numerically by the k similarity values, together with the binary (classification), or real-valued (regression), values of the property of interest for the corresponding molecules (e.g. degree of solubility, activity). This approach,combining similarity measures with neural networks, is developed in [710, 467].

For the variable-size representations of molecules (e.g. graphs, SMILES), it is natural to use recursive neural networks, in particular inner and outer (or convolutional) approaches [741].

12.2.5   Deep Learning: Recursive Inner Approaches

For instance, inner approaches in the form of bi-directional recursive networks and LSTMs can readily be applied to the SMILES sequence format, and similarly for outer approaches. Applications of the inner approach at the level of the molecular graphs require acyclic directed graphs and thus are faced by two major challenges:

(1) the edges of the molecular graphs are not directed; and
(2) the molecular graphs are not acyclic (e.g. benzene rings).

One solution [468] for addressing this problem is essentially to use *all* possible acyclic orientations of a molecule with a single sink-node, using a shared neural network to crawl all these orientations, and pass the aggregated crawling results through a final neural network to produce the final prediction (Figure 12.2). Skipping some technical details, each such orientation can be obtained by selecting a single atom in the molecule as the sink, and orienting all the edges towards that sink. Considering all such orientations is feasible because small organic molecules are associated with sparse graphs, with relatively few atoms and bonds.

12.2.6   Deep Learning: Recursive Outer Approaches

Alternatively, one can apply an outer, or convolutional approach, to the variable-size representations of molecules, e.g. to the SMILES strings or the graphs. An example of outer approach applied to the molecular graph is described in [248]. The inner and outer approaches for molecular graphs are shown side to side in Figure 12.3. Both methods can also be combined.

12.3   Prediction of Chemical Reactions

The prediction of chemical reactions is a fundamental scientific and technological problem to address issues of chemical synthesis and retro-synthesis, identification of likely

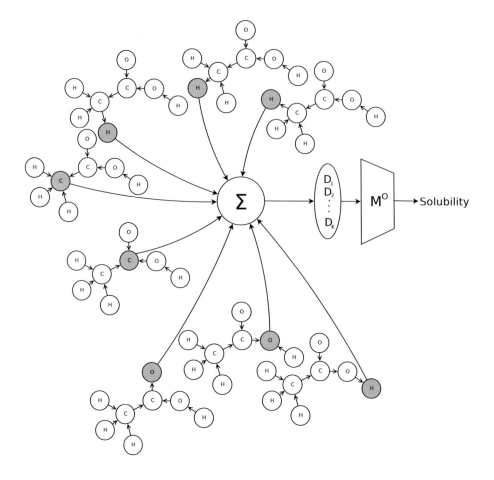

Figure 12.2 Example of directed acyclic graph associated with the inner approach applied to a small molecule (acetic acid in this case) in organic chemistry where the overall goal is to predict solubility. The same neural network is used to crawl the molecular graph in all possible orientations and the corresponding outputs are added and fed to the final prediction neural network.

mechanisms, identification of side-products, and reaction optimization to name a few. These all have applications in areas ranging from materials science, to drug discovery, to ocean and atmospheric chemistry.

12.3.1   Representations

The very concept of a "reaction" can be ambiguous, as it typically corresponds to a macroscopic abstraction and simplification of a complex underlying microscopic reality, ultimately driven by the laws of quantum mechanics. By definition, chemical reactions involve changes in electronic orbitals, as opposed to atomic nuclei, and are driven by a complex physical interplay of electronic and structural attributes of the reactants along

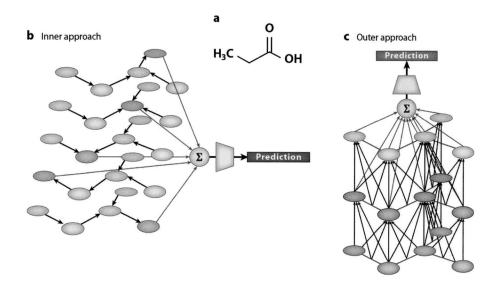

Figure 12.3 Schematic representation of inner (left) and outer approaches (right) for small molecules represented by labeled graphs (a). (b) In the inner approach, several copies of the graph are used. In each copy, a different sink node (red) is used, and all the edges are oriented towards the sink node. A shared neural network is used to crawl each acyclic graph from the inside, starting from the source nodes and producing an output vector at each sink node. The resulting output vectors are aggregated and passed to a final prediction neural network. (c) In the outer approach, neural networks are stacked in a direction perpendicular to the molecular graph. The shared network in the first layer (purple) receives inputs from a node and its immediate neighbors and produces an output vector associated with each node. A similar process is repeated in the following layers of the stack. The outputs from all layers, or just from the top layer (green), are aggregated and passed to a final prediction neural network. Reprinted, with permission, from the Annual Review of Biomedical Data Science, Volume 1, ©2018 by Annual Reviews Inc., www.annualreviews.org.

with the reaction conditions, such as temperature, phase, concentration, presence of catalysts, and so forth.

As in the case of small molecules, there are several ways of representing the simplified concept of a reaction. To fix the ideas, consider a reaction of the form "A + B → C + D" where A and B are the reactants and C and D are the products. In principle one could use any of the representations we have seen above for small molecules, and apply them to this case by concatenation, with the proper delimiters. In practice, however, the main representations are:

- Labeled graphs, something like: G(A) + G(B) → G(C) + G(D), where G(X) is the representation of the labeled graph associated with molecule X. This representation is variable in size.
- Images of the labeled graph, for instance in pdf format. This representation can be fixed in size.
- SMIRKS and SMARTS [374]. These are extensions of SMILES, essentially of the

form $S(A) + S(B) \gg S(C) + S(D)$, where $S(X)$ is the SMILES representation of molecule X. A fully explicit representation, must indicate which atoms among the reactants correspond to which atom among the products. Thus a complete SMIRKS notation must number all the atoms on the reactant side, and use corresponding numbers on the product side. It is also possible to use this string notation to write down reaction patterns, as opposed to specific reactions. This string representation is variable in size. See Figure 12.4 and Tables 12.2 and 12.3.

A reaction equation is balanced if the same atoms appear on the reactant and product sides. It is important to note that the majority of reactions in current repositories are not balanced, which of course creates additional challenges. It would be useful to create a tool that automatically balances reactions; however such a tool would need to understand chemical reactions and thus it would have to be developed in synergy with reaction predictors. Likewise, very often repositories of reactions do not provide atom-mapping between the reactants and the products. Atom-mapping a balanced reaction equation is easier than balancing the equation, and algorithm for addressing this task have been developed [278].

An even more fundamental issues is the distinction between global reactions and elementary reactions. Chemists tend to think and explain global chemical reactions in terms of elementary reactions or elementary steps, also called arrow-pushing mechanisms. An elementary reaction can be thought of as a "movement" of electrons from a source to a sink. A global reaction consists of a chain of elementary reactions. Some of these concepts are illustrated in Figure 12.4 depicting the reaction of an alkene, i.e. a molecule containing a double bond between two carbons and hydrobromic acid – a solution of hydrogen bromide (HBr) with water. Electron movements can easily be added to the SMIRKS/SMARTS representation by using the numbering of the atoms (see Table 12.3 for examples). Somewhat informally, this reaction can be written as:

$$RCH=CH2 \ + \ HBr \ \longrightarrow \ RCH(Br)\text{-}CH3.$$

SMIRKS	**Description**
[C:1]=[C:2].[H:3][Cl,Br,I,$(OS=O):4]≫	Alkene,
[H:3][C:1][C+:2].[-:4]	Protic Acid Addition
[C+:1].[-:2]≫ [C+0:1][+0:2]	Carbocation,
	Anion Addition

Table 12.2 SMIRKS transformation rules corresponding to a simple alkene hydrobromination reaction model. Each item in brackets corresponds to an atom in the reaction equation. The "≫" symbol delimits reactants from products. The numbers following colons are atom-map indexes used to specify which reactant atoms correspond to which product atoms. Further specification of the SMIRKS language can be found in the Daylight tutorial at www.daylight.com.

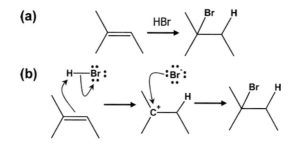

Figure 12.4 Example overall transformation and corresponding elementary, mechanistic reactions. (a) The overall transformation of an alkene with a hydrobromic acid. This is a single graph rearrangement representation of a multi-step reaction. (b) The details of the two mechanistic reactions which compose the overall transformation. The first involves a proton transfer reaction, and the second involves the addition of the bromide anion. Each detailed mechanism is an example of an "arrow-pushing" diagram [316] involving a single transition state, in which each arrow denotes the movement of a pair of electrons, and multiple arrows on a single diagram denote concerted movement.

We can now turn to methods for reaction prediction. Note however that this term hides many different problems such as the prediction of reaction in the forward or reverse direction, at the global or elementary level, together with the prediction of reaction rates, reaction conditions, and so forth.

12.3.2   Quantum-Mechanical Approaches

Ideally, one would like to derive molecular properties, as well as reaction equations and properties, from first principles starting from Schrödinger's equation. While the Schrödinger equation cannot be solved exactly even for somewhat small systems, approximations methods based in particular on DFT (Density Functional Theory) have made significant progress over the last few decades and, together with the advances in computer power have allowed the successful application of QM to modeling some chemical reactions. A clear benefit of these methods, when successful, is their ability to quantitatively predict important reaction parameters such as free energies, energy barriers, transition states, and reaction rates. Still, they require considerable human intervention and are not suitable yet for making high-throughput predictions.

While the QM route may be the most satisfactory, when it is applicable, it is still fraught with problems and limitations. First, QM simulations are computationally demanding – scaling exponentially with the size of the molecule, even when only a small part of the molecule is reactive – and thus this approach cannot be used in high-throughput fashion, or to study really complex reactions. Indeed, many recent studies involving QM-based prediction of reaction pathways are narrowly limited to a single chemical system [448, 583, 4, 34, 676]. Second, this approach is more or less independent of the training data that may be available and thus it does not scale with, and cannot take advantage of, big data although this has begun to change. Third, QM methods can be very sensitive to initial conditions and other parameters and the corresponding information is not always available. Fourth, QM methods are very different from the way a synthetic organic chemist may approach chemical reactions. Finally, there is always a danger that the approximations made in the treatment of Schrödinger's equation may lead to significant deviations from physical reality. With DFT calculations, accuracies for many molecules are limited to 2–3 kcal/mol with presently-available functionals. *Ab initio* methods, such as coupled-cluster, can yield more accurate predictions at a significant cost. However deep learning methods are now being applied to create new density functionals which can attain accuracies below 1 kcal/mol) [136], and to provide efficient approximate solutions to the electronic Schrödinger's equation with up to 30 electrons [337]. Thus, deep learning has important applications in chemistry by helping accelerate QM (or Molecular Dynamics) applications. While useful for certain systems, these hybrid methods are not yet suitable for the high-throughput prediction of chemical reactions.

12.3.3   Rule-Based Approaches

Rule-based approaches to reaction prediction [294, 135, 178] have a fairly long history. The majority of rule-based approaches in the past have focused on global reactions, viewed as graph rearrangements reflecting only the net change of several successive mechanistic reactions. For example, Figure 12.4 shows the overall transformation of an alkene interacting with hydrobromic acid to yield the alkyl bromide along with the two underlying elementary reactions which compose the transformation. Rule-based approaches are meant to approximate decision making rules of human chemists using libraries of graph of graph rearrangement patterns.

Seminal work in the area of rule-based reaction prediction is encapsulated in the CAMEO [387] and EROS [352] systems. CAMEO is based on a complex set of heuristics divided over different classes of chemistry to predict multi-step reactions. EROS uses a more configurable system composed of multi-step reaction graph based rule libraries with extra modules to add more constraints based on heats of formation, physicochemical properties, or kinetic simulations. Other approaches since CAMEO and EROS have contributed their own ideas to the problem. Beppe [666] and Sophia [647] focus on first identifying reactive sites before identifying reactions, though both work with multi-step reactions. ToyChem [119] and Robia [692] build on the EROS idea of physicochemical constraints by explicitly defining reaction energy functions.

One rule-based system focused on elementary reactions is the ReactionExplorer system [180, 178]. The ReactionExplorer system [178] uses detailed graph rewrite rules for individual mechanistic steps rather than the common practice of a single transformation for an overall reaction from starting materials to final products (see Table 12.2). ReactionExplorer comprises 2000 hand-written rules and roughly covers the chemical reactions typically encountered in an undergraduate college curriculum. It has been used to develop an interactive, adaptive, system for teaching chemical reactions which is currently used by Wiley in its chemistry education suite.

Rule-based systems can be fast (compared to QM). However, and while there has been progress with rule-based system, many such systems are no longer maintained, and none so far has been able to equal or surpass human expert performance. Such systems,

SMIRKS	Description	Electron Flow
[H:10][CH1:1][C+;!H0:2]≫ [C+:1][C+0:2][H:10]	Carbocation, Hydride Shift from Tertiary	1,10=10,2
[C:10][CH0:1][C+;!H0:2]≫ [C+:1][C+0:2][C:10]	Carbocation, Methyl Shift from Quaternary	1,10=10,2
[H:10][CH2:1][CH2+:2]≫ [C+:1][C+0:2][H:10]	Carbocation, Hydride Shift from Secondary	1,10=10,2
[C+:1].[-:2]≫ [C+0:1][+0:2]	Carbocation, Anion Addition	2=1
[C:1]=[C;$(*O):2].[H:3][Cl,Br,I,$(OS=O):4]≫ [H:3][C:1][C+:2].[-:4]	Alkene, Protic Acid Addition, Alkoxy	2,1=1,3;3,4=4
[C:1]=[C;$(*a):2].[H:3][Cl,Br,I,$(OS=O):4]≫ [H:3][C:1][C+:2].[-:4]	Alkene, Protic Acid Addition, Benzyl	2,1=1,3;3,4=4
[C:1]=[C;$(**=*):2].[H:3][Cl,Br,I,$(OS=O):4]≫ [H:3][C:1][C+:2].[-:4]	Alkene, Protic Acid Addition, Allyl	2,1=1,3;3,4=4
[C:1]=[CH0:2].[H:3][Cl,Br,I,$(OS=O):4]≫ [H:3][C:1][C+:2].[-:4]	Alkene, Protic Acid Addition, Tertiary	2,1=1,3;3,4=4
[C:1]=[CH1:2].[H:3][Cl,Br,I,$(OS=O):4]≫ [H:3][C:1][C+:2].[-:4]	Alkene, Protic Acid Addition, Secondary	2,1=1,3;3,4=4
[C:1]=[C:2].[H:3][Cl,Br,I,$(OS=O):4]≫ [H:3][C:1][C+:2].[-:4]	Alkene, Protic Acid Addition	2,1=1,3;3,4=4

Table 12.3 Example of 10 prioritized transformation rules, relating to alkene hydrobromination reactions, out of the 92 rules used in the complete robust HBr reagent model. Included for each transformation rule is not only the SMIRKS pattern and description, but a relative priority rank to indicate the order in which the rules should be attempted. The top rule has priority 10, the bottom rule priority 1. The existence of several variants for similar rules, and their customized priority ordering, enable robust reaction predictions. However, this is also what makes it difficult to add new rules in order to scale up the system. An electron flow specification accompanies each rule to support curved arrow mechanism diagrams.

requiring manually-implemented rules and exceptions, require painstaking maintenance and thus suffer from two related limitations: coverage and scalability. It is tedious to manually add new rules to increase the coverage, especially if every time a new rule is added there is a chance it may break previously introduced rules. For instance, in the ReactionExplorer system, adding new transformations is already a challenging undertaking with 80 reagent modules although several hundreds would be required to cover the breadth of modern chemistry [178] (see Table 12.3). One possible solution would be to try to use a symbolic machine-learning approach to learn the rules directly [744] in terms of SMIRKS/SMARTS or some kind of graph grammar rules. To the best of our knowledge, this has not yet been attempted systematically.

12.3.4   Deep Learning Approaches

Machine learning approaches [398, 399, 782] are fast and scalable, but ideally require large data sets from which to learn. Obtaining such data sets of chemical reactions is a significant challenge, as described above. Furthermore, reactions may be unbalanced or not atom-mapped, complicating attempts at statistical learning. Nonetheless, as more data becomes available, deep learning methods will yield increasingly more accurate prediction systems.

Before looking at deep learning for reaction prediction, it is worth observing that the QM, rule-based, and deep learning approaches can be used in complementary ways. Rule-based systems have been used to provide training examples for deep learning approaches [398]. Similarly, deep learning systems can benefit from the implementation of a small number of carefully selected rules [226, 207]. Other work has shown how QM methods can be used to derive new training examples for machine learning algorithms [638], and machine learning methods are being applied intensively to QM and DFT approximations, [630, 328, 629, 375, 663, 193, 631].

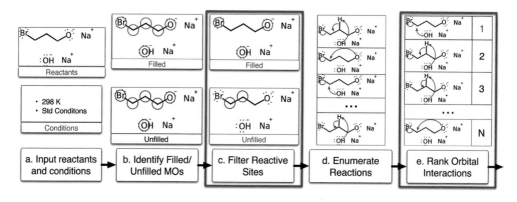

Figure 12.5 Overall reaction prediction framework of the ReactionPredictor system. (a) A user inputs the reactants and conditions. (b) The system identifies potential electron donors and acceptors using coarse approximations of electron filled and electron unfilled molecular orbitals. (c) Deep neural networks are trained and used to filter out the vast majority of unreactive sites, pruning the space of potential reactions. (d) Reactions are enumerated by pairing filled and unfilled molecular orbitals. (e) A deep learning ranking model is trained and used to order the reactions (i.e. source-sink pairs), where the top ranked reactions contain the major products. The top ranked product can be recursively chained to a new instance of the framework for multi-step reaction prediction.

Reaction prediction at the global or elementary level, in the forward or reverse direction, can be viewed as a translation problem (sequence-to-sequence), between the string representing the reactants and the string representing the products. Alternatively it could be viewed as a graph transformation problem (graph-to-graph). We have seen that several recursive neural network methods exist for these kinds of problems, and one important invariance is that predictions should not depend on the ordering of the reactants or the products. For instance, at the sequence level, one could use bidirectional recursive

networks (in combination with for instance LSTMs, transformer networks, or attention mechanisms) to learn tree-to-tree transformations in natural language processing or
symbolic mathematics [43, 42, 430]. It is worth noting that chemical reactions involve
graphs that are very sparse but slightly more complex than trees. For this reason, and
the added complexity coming from the other factors discussed above, such as the lack
of training data and the importance of reaction conditions, learning to predict chemical
reactions is harder than learning more tree-like tasks, such as symbolic integration, and
poses interesting deep learning challenges.

Deep learning has been used to learn to predict reactions at the global level. A combination of rules with a graph convolutional approach for predicting global reactions is
described in [380, 207]. An alternative approach applies a neural network to the concatenated fingerprints to classify the type of reaction (into 17 most common classes)
and then applies a corresponding set of SMART transformation to derive the products
[782].

Here we describe in some more detail ReactionPredictor [396, 397, 226], a deep
learning-based approach to reaction prediction that operates at the level of elementary
reactions, involving the "movement" of electrons from an electron source to an electron
sink. Given a set of input reactants, the ReactionPredictor pipeline operates in the
following multi-step fashion (Figure 12.5):

1. Enumerate all possible electron sources and electron sinks within the input reactant
   molecules.
2. Filter the list of candidate sources and sinks, predicting a smaller list containing only
   the most reactive sources and sinks.
3. Propose reactions by enumerating all combinations of source–sink pairings.
4. Rank the proposed reactions by favorability.
5. Iterate the above process to identify global reactions, or search for unidentified
   products.

Deep learning can be used to identify and filter sources and sinks, as well as to rank
the source–sink pairs. In the earlier versions of the system, candidate sources and sinks
were described by designed features vectors. The most recent version uses convolutional
graph networks to derive and filter such representations. The ranking can be done using
a Siamese deep neural network (Figure 12.6) to compare source–sink pairs and rank
them by favorability.

From the standpoint of elementary reactions, one can in fact distinguish three different
classes of reactions. In a polar reaction, one reactant (the nucleophile) donates two
electrons to another (the electrophile) to form a bond. In a radical reaction, each reactant
donates one electron. In a pericyclic reaction, only the π bond electrons are involved, and
all bonds are changed in a single cyclic step without any intermediates being formed.
Thus, in the complete architecgure of ReactionPredictor the same architecture described
above is essentially replicated three times for each one of these reaction types, and
trained accordingly (Figure 12.7).

How well do current deep learning approaches do at predicting global or elementary
chemical reactions? Rapid progress is being made, but it is still the case that no existing

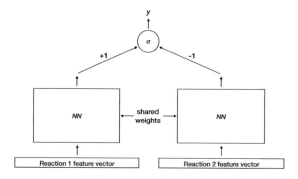

Figure 12.6 Siamese architecture for reaction ranking. Outputs from the left and right instances of the neural network NN have fixed weights of +1 and −1 into a final sigmoid unit. Thus the final output y approaches one if Reaction 1 scores higher than Reaction 2, and zero otherwise. We can think of NN as computing a reaction favorability score that is learned by training on many examples of reaction pairs.

system today achieves or surpasses human-expert performance in all areas of chemical reactions. Examples of success stories (e.g. Figure 12.8), as well as failures, can be found in the references cited. Two main obstacles in assessing and comparing performance are the diversity of problems hidden under the generic theme of reaction prediction, and the current lack of standard benchmark data sets. In terms of diversity of problems, a full-blown expert system ought to be able to address all of them, and for instance couple both elementary and global reaction predictors, and both in the forward and backward directions. As a side note, having elementary reaction predictors provides a direct way to address issues of causality and diagnostic in reaction prediction. In terms of benchmark data sets, the data behind ReactionPredictor and the patent data are publicly available. Opening up existing commercial databases of reactions to deep learning would go a long way in the development of chemical sciences, as well as AI, with significant potential benefits to mankind.

In conclusion, for both the prediction of molecular properties and chemical reactions, effective deep learning methods are in place and awaiting for more data. In addition, there other areas of chemistry where deep learning methods are also being applied, for instance for the classification of crystal structures [816] and the prediction of material properties [796] among many others . Finally, a number of chemical data sets related to this chapter can be downloaded from the ChemDB Portal: `http://cdb.ics.uci.edu`.

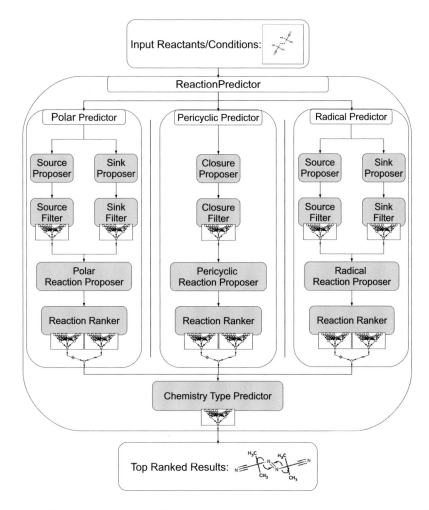

Figure 12.7 High-level ReactionPredictor workflow. Input reactants and conditions are pushed through three separate reaction type ranking models: polar, pericyclic, and radical. In each branch, neural networks are used to identify sources and sinks, and to rank source-sink pairs.

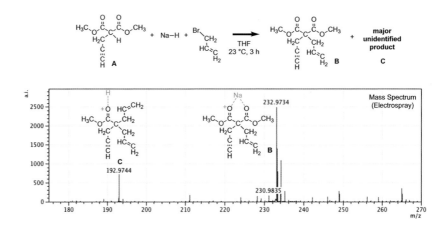

Figure 12.8 The following example demonstrates a typical problem faced by synthetic organic chemists and the importance of a system that can assign plausible product structures to product masses. Chemists at UCI needed an allylated substrate B for use in a new catalytic reaction. They attempted to synthesize B following a procedure of Fensterbank and coworkers [118], which is reported to give the alkylation product in 97% isolated yield with no additional products. When the reaction was applied to reactant A, the reaction generated a low yield of the desired product B along with an unidentified product C, which was difficult to separate and identify using the readily available mass spectrum. When given reactants, reaction predictor was able to assign plausible structures to the masses, including product C. Knowing that the product is undergoing further undesired reactions allows the investigator increase the yield by shortening the reaction time.

13 Applications in Biology and Medicine

Applications of deep learning in the life sciences are even older and more numerous than the applications in the other sciences. There is a strong two-way relationship between deep learning and the life sciences: in one direction, deep learning helps the life sciences, both broadly by providing powerful methods for analyzing biomedical data, and more narrowly by providing simplified but useful computational models for neuroscience. In the other direction, the life sciences help deep learning: it is our knowledge of the human brain that has provided the fundamental source of inspiration for AI and deep learning, and will continue to do so in the future, at least for a subset of AI researchers. What is less appreciated is that some of the earliest applications of deep learning to the natural sciences were precisely in the life sciences, and that the complexity of the problems raised by the life sciences, in particular the problem of protein structure prediction, have inspired over the years the development of novel deep learning methods, in particular the development of recursive (or graph) neural networks.

13.1   Biomedical Data

Biomedical data can be massive, but also extremely heterogeneous ranging from small molecules, to omic data (e.g. genomic, proteomic, transcriptomic, metabolomic), to biomedical imaging data, to clinical and epidemiological data, and to electronic medical records. The data quality can also be very heterogeous and the data types can vary from analog, to digital, to text, and can come with complex associated structures such as sequences, trees, and other graphs which can often vary in size and shape. Central to the application of deep learning methods to biomedical data are methods that can handle different kinds of data, in particular variable-size structured data, and hence recursive neural networks play a central role.

Biomedical data also span many orders of magnitude in both space and time, and cover a myriad of different phenomena. Improvement in sensors and other instruments, as well as computers, databases, and the Internet, coupled with the development of novel methods, such as high-throughput sequencing and high-throughput screening continue to produce a deluge of data. However, even in the era of big data, the landscape remains very variable in terms of the volume of available data. Biologists in general have been good citizens in making data, for instance omic data, as publicly available and downloadable as possible. But data are much less readily available in the chemical, pharmaceutical, or clinical sciences, and much remains to be done in these areas in order to overcome the numerous commercial, legal, and other societal barriers to produce sufficient open data, while also addressing privacy and other legitimate concerns. Overcoming these barriers is essential for enabling real scientific progress powered by deep learning that can benefit everyone. Finally, even in areas where the data appear to be plentiful, it may still not be sufficient to address certain questions. For example, we do have access to thousands of human genome sequences, but not billions, and billions may be required to detect the most subtle effects.

While deep learning applications tend to benefit from the availability of large amounts of data, there are still plenty of areas of research where deep learning ought to be applied in regimes where that is not the case. In these areas, several techniques can be helpful, including:

(1) regularization methods, early stopping, and dropout;
(2) semi-supervised or self-supervised approaches that try to leverage both labeled and unlabeled data;
(3) transfer learning and reuse of pre-trained models; and
(4) data augmentation methods where training and test sets are expanded using natural or artificially generated data, for instance, by adding appropriate noise or applying appropriate group transformations and other manipulations to the original data.

The earliest applications of deep learning in the life sciences are found in molecular biology broadly construed, and these played an important role in the development of bioinformatics. For completeness, we first provide a very brief overview of basic concepts in molecular biology.

13.2   Life in a Nutshell

While biology is very complex, its most basic components are relatively simple. Life as we know it is a form of carbon-based computing that relies on the small organic molecules discussed in Chapter 12, and their reactions. Among these small molecules, two classes stand out: nucleotides and amino acids. Within these two classes of small molecules, life uses primarily five nucleotides denoted by A, C, G, T, U and 20 naturally occurring amino acids. Nucleotides can covalently bond and form polymeric chains of either DNA (using A, C, G, and T) or RNA (using A, C, G, U). Amino acids can covalently bond and form polymeric chains called proteins.

Nucleotides strands can base-pair with complementary strands, where A pairs with T or U, and G pairs with C, by forming hydrogen bonds which are roughly one order of magnitude weaker than covalent bonds. Most of the DNA is double-stranded with a helical structure and digitally encode genetic information. This is the key discovery of Watson and Crick which is at the core of heredity and evolution, and coarsely explains how DNA can be replicated, by opening the double strand and making copies of each separate strand using the base pairing rules. Genetic information in the form of genes is encoded along the DNA molecule. The genome of an organism is the whole of its hereditary information encoded in its DNA (or, RNA for some viruses) (Table 13.1).

Organism	Genome Size	Number of Genes
Virus	10K–100K	10–100
Prokaryote (Bacterium)	5M	3,000
Eukaryote (Yeast)	15M	6,000
Fly	100M	15,000
Mouse	2.5B	25,000
Man	3B	25,000

Table 13.1 Order of magnitude of genome sizes (in base pairs) and number of genes. A small virus like HIV has a genome size of about 10,000. A large virus like smallpox has a genome size of about 300,000. For single-cell organisms, a typical Prokaryote, like *Escherichia Coli* has about 3,000 genes in a 5M-long genome. A typical Eukaryote, such as *Saccharomyces Cerevisiae* has about 6,000 genes in a 15M-long genome. For multi-cellular organisms (Metazoan), *Drosophila Melanogaster* has about 15,000 genes in a 100M-long genome. Mouse *Mus Musculus* and humans *Homo Sapiens* have on the order of 25,000 genes in genomes that are a few billion base-pairs long. There exists organisms, such as plants and amphibians, with even larger genomes, but not many more genes. Numbers are provided for the haploid genome (a single complement of all chromosomes). The double line separates single-cell from multi-cell organisms.

To a first degree of approximation, each gene codes for a protein. The basis for this encoding is the genetic code, which in essence is a lookup table for converting three contiguous nucleotides (a codon) into one of the 20 amino acids, augmented with a stop sign. The code is redundant: since there are 64 possible DNA codons, several different codons can code for the same amino acid. In the typical case, a gene encoded in the DNA is first transcribed to an intermediary RNA form, called messenger RNA (mRNA), and the mRNA is then translated into a protein sequence by a specialized machinery in the cell called a ribosome. The length of protein chains can vary from a few dozens to several thousands amino acids. From Table 13.1, one can see that the size of the genomes grows by five orders of magnitudes when going from viruses to man, but the number of genes grows only by three orders of magnitude. Since the length of proteins is comparable across all organisms, this implies that higher organisms must have a considerable amount of non-protein-coding DNA. DNA that does not code for proteins is found in intergenic regions, but also inside the gene sequences of higher organisms. These gene sequences often consist of an alternation of protein-coding regions called exons, and non-protein-coding regions called introns. Through the mechanism of alternative splicing which is capable, for instance, of excluding a given exon during during gene expression, one single gene has the ability to produce in reality several different proteins.

Protein chains typically fold in complex 3D structures. The 3D structure of a protein largely determines the kinds of interactions it can have with other important molecules – such as other proteins, DNA or RNA molecules, or a variety of small molecules including metabolites – and thus ultimately its function. Several protein chains, as well as nucleotide strands, can assemble together to form a complex which can carry more elaborate functions. In the carbon-based computing analogy, the genome is the Turing tape where information is stored. This information is basically an executable, i.e. a computer program written in machine language (A,C,G,T instead of 0,1) and ready to be executed. The program is executed by proteins which can be viewed as nanoscale machines that carry all the basic functions of life and continuously regulate the concentrations of thousands of molecular species in each cell, in response to internal and external signals. These functions include initiating or inhibiting the transcription and translation of genes, replicating the genome with high fidelity during cell division, orchestrating and maintaining cellular structures over multiple length scales, and processing and controlling all metabolic reactions. These include also fighting pathogens, transmitting electrical signals in the brain by opening and closing ion channels in neuronal membranes, and helping store and modify information at synapses, or in the epigenome (see below).

If unwound, the DNA contained in the chromosomes of one human cell would reach a length of about two meters. This creates significant challenges for folding DNA in the nucleus of a cell into a compact, yet dynamic structure, where genes can be exposed and turned on or off during transcription-translation. The first level of structural compactification is provided by nucleosomes, i.e. sections of DNA wrapped around a core of proteins. The core is formed by histone octamer complexes and the resulting DNA-protein complex is called chromatin. About 146 base pairs of DNA are wrapped around each histone complex. Stretches of linker DNA between adjacent nucleosomes can be up to 80 base pairs long. Each chromosome is thus a long chain of nucleosomes and looks like a string of beads when viewed using an electron microscope. Many chemical groups (e.g. methyl group in the case of methylation, phosphoryl in the case of phosphorylation), can be added to, modified, or removed from both the tails of the histones or the genomic DNA (and also RNA molecules). These modifications are called epigenetic modifications, and the entire set of such modifications is called the epigenome. These modifications, which can be partially inherited, are carried by specialized proteins. Importantly, epigenetic modifications can modify gene expression and how a cell functions. Traditionally, this molecular machinery has been associated with establishing and maintaining cellular diversity and cell fate decisions across the lifespan, X-chromosome inactivation, and genomic imprinting. More recently, various epigenetic processes have been implicated in memory functions (e.g. [568, 713, 274, 311]). Thus the epigenome provides a form of dynamic, partially inheritable, Lamarkian memory, that sits between the environment and the more stable genomic Darwinian memory, which is also changing – but on a slower time scale – as a result of mutations, recombinations, and sexual reproduction.

Modern high-throughput nucleotide sequencing technologies (DNA-seq, RNA-seq, ChIP-seq, Methil-seq, etc.) enable, with different levels of precision, several fundamental tasks including:

(1) sequencing genomic DNA, e.g. a human genome sequence can be obtained in hours at a cost of a few hundred dollars;

(2) sequencing mRNA, in order to measure the level of expression of every gene in the genome, including at the single cell level;

(3) sequencing all the nucleotide sequences that are bound to a given protein to, for instance, identify transcription factor binding sites in promoter and other regulatory regions; and

(4) map epigenetic modifications, such as methylation, along the genome.

Armed with this basic understanding, we can now survey some of the applications of deep learning to biomedical data, organized roughly by spatial scales. from proteins to clinical data. The survey is not meant to be exhaustive as there is already a large and rapidly growing body of literature on this topic, including several other review articles.

13.3 Deep Learning in Proteomics

High-throughput sequencing and other technologies, including synthetic biology technologies, continue to rapidly increase the number of available protein sequences significantly outpacing the rate at which these proteins can be characterized experimentally, for instance using X-ray crystallography. Thus tools for predicting protein structural and functional properties play an important role in high-throughput proteomics to sift through large numbers of protein sequences in order to predict their annotations, for instance in support of integrative systems biology approaches, pathway analyses, drug target discovery, drug side-effect analyses, and to identify relevant candidates that can be targeted for experimental and other followup studies.

13.3.1 Protein Structures

Predicting protein structures from sequences is one of the oldest and most fundamental problems in computational biology. Predicted 3D structures, with different degree of accuracy, can be used for a variety of tasks [64] such as protein classification, inference of functional relationships, identification of functional sites or epitopes, support of site directed mutagenesis experiments, protein engineering, and molecular docking in virtual screening.

The notion of protein structure is complex and multi-faceted and is usually decomposed in multiple levels. The primary structure is simply the sequence of amino acids. The secondary structure corresponds to the segmentation of the sequence into three different kinds of structural motifs, which are recurrently found in crystal and NMR structures: alpha-helices, beta-strands, and coils. For brevity, we are skipping some details associated with finer-grained classification of secondary structure into more classes, as well as the important notion of disordered regions, i.e. regions that do not seem to have a well-defined structure. The backbone tertiary structure corresponds to the x, y, x coordinates of the atoms, in particular the carbons C_α and C_β, along the backbone of the protein associated with the connection of the amino acids via peptide bonds. The full 3D structure must include in addition all the side chains, i.e. all the additional atoms contained in each amino acid that are not part of the backbone. Finally, protein chains can combine to form more complex structures called protein complexes. This level of organization, specifying how each chain combines with each other chain in space, is called the quaternary structure.

Another important distinction to be made is between globular and membrane proteins. Membrane proteins function inside the membrane of cells allowing cells to sense their environmental and react accordingly. The membrane is a lipid bilayer which provides a unique structural environment. Membrane proteins plays important roles and many drugs target membrane proteins. However, here we will focus on globular proteins which represent roughly 75% of a typical proteome, versus 25% for membrane proteins. While membrane proteins are very important, and many of the deep learning methods developed for globular proteins can be applied also to membrane proteins (e.g. [424, 602]), the training sets available for membrane proteins are far smaller due to significantly greater experimental challenges in determining their structures.

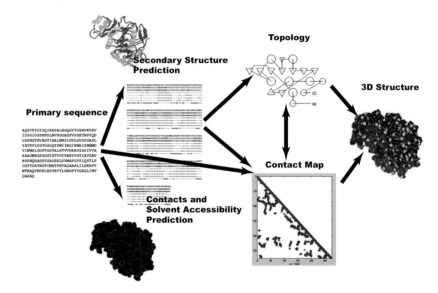

Figure 13.1 Protein 3D structure prediction deep learning pipeline in three main stages, starting from the protein sequence: (1) prediction of structural features such as secondary structure and relative solvent accessibility; (2) prediction of coarse- and fine-grained contact maps invariant to translations and rotations; and (3) prediction of backbone and side-chains 3D coordinates.

Any approach to 3D structure prediction must deal with the fundamental fact that protein structures are invariant under translations and rotations. Thus it would not be a good idea to try to predict 3D coordinates directly from the primary structure alone using a neural network. To address this fundamental issue of invariance, a deep learning strategy must break down the problem modularly into several steps, using intermediate representations that are translation and rotation invariant, such as the protein contact or distance map, or the sequence of its dihedral angles.

A pipeline approach based on contact or distance maps is illustrated in Figure 13.1 [87, 88, 185, 189]. More precisely the first step starts from the protein sequence, possibly in conjunction with evolutionary profiles to leverage evolutionary information, and predicts several structural features such as classification of amino acids into secondary structure membership classes (alpha helices/beta strands/coils), or into relative exposure classes (e.g. surface/buried) [75, 74, 578, 579].

The second step uses the primary structure and the structural features to predict a topological representation in terms of contact or distance maps. The contact map is a 2D representation of neighborhood relationships consisting of an adjacency matrix at some distance cutoff, typically in the range of 6 to 12 at the amino acid level. In other words, the entry i, j of the matrix is equal to 1 if and only if the distance in 3D between the carbons C_α (or C_β) of the amino acids in position i and j along the linear sequence is less than some threshold t in , and 0 otherwise. Clearly contact maps are symmetric and sparse, except of course along the main diagonal. The distance map replaces the binary values with pairwise Euclidean distances. Fine-grained contact or distance maps are derived at the amino acid level, whereas coarse-grained contact or distance maps can be derived at the level of secondary structure elements, for instance from the pairwise distances between the centers of gravity of these elements, providing a coarse view of the overall topology of the protein.

The third step in the pipeline predicts the actual 3D coordinates of the atoms in the protein using the constraints provided by the previous steps, primarily from the 2D contact maps, but also possibly other constraints provided by physical or statistical potentials. Effective methods to address the third step have been developed in the NMR literature [539, 540] and elsewhere [759, 755] and typically use ideas from distance geometry, molecular dynamics, and stochastic optimization, including stochastic gradient descent, to recover 3D coordinates from contacts. Methods exist for recovering a 3D structure, up to mirror symmetries, from a good contact or distance map. Clearly, it is the distant contacts, corresponding to the rare long-range interactions, that are important and difficult to predict and simulation show that recovering about 50% of the distant contacts is sufficient in most cases to derive good 3D structures. Thus deep learning methods must focus primarily on the first and second steps of the pipeline. In terms of contact versus distance map prediction methods, the difference is usually minimal since the same neural network architectures can be used provided the output units are chosen accordingly, logistic for contacts and linear for distances. Historically, contact maps were used more frequently when relatively little data was available. Today the preference is towards distance maps since these are more informative and do not require selecting arbitrary thresholds. Finally, it is worth noting that contact and distance maps can be used for other purposes:

(1) by aligning contact or distance maps one can detect structural homology and identify known templates that can also be used in protein structure prediction (e.g. [440]);

(2) contact maps and distance maps can of course be applied to other molecules, and

even to entire chromosomes to assess chromatin structure during gene expression and other processes (e.g. [734, 457]).

It is worth noting that each major step in the pipeline can be viewed as a variable-size, structure-to-structure, prediction problem and thus should be addressed using recursive neural networks. Secondary structure prediction, for instance, can be viewed as a sequence-to-sequence translation problem, where a variable-length input sequence over a 20-letter alphabet is translated into a sequence of the same length but over a three-letter alphabet. Likewise, contact or distance map prediction, can be viewed as a translation problem from a variable-size 2D input grid to a 2D output grid of the same size.

13.3.2   Protein Secondary Structure and Other Structural Features

In the first step of the pipeline, the prediction of secondary structure, and to a lesser extent relative solvent accessibility, has played a central role in this field. Chou and Fasman developed a simple statistical approach for predicting the location of helices, strands, and coils along the protein sequence – basically by looking at amino acid propensities – using the small data available in the Protein Data Bank (PDB) [122] in the 1970s. The accuracy at the time was around 60%. A first breakthrough, and probably the first application of deep learning in computational biology, came a few years later [588], where a fully connected network with a single hidden layer was able to achieve an accuracy of about 64%, rapidly followed by other similar applications [353]. The next breakthrough [621, 620] brought the accuracy to about 74%. While this work used more sophisticated feedforward deep learning architectures, the major contribution at the time was the realization of the importance of using evolutionary profiles in the input, as opposed to the primary sequence alone. Profiles are derived from multiple sequence alignments of related sequences and represent the probability of observing any one of the 20 amino acids at each position in the sequence. Again other improvements rapidly followed [613]. With the benefit of hindsight, up to this time, all the deep learning applications to secondary structure prediction were essentially based on the outer, or convolutional, approach. In the late 1990s, the first inner approaches, in the form of bidirectional recursive neural networks (BRNNs) were developed and these brought the accuracy to around 80% [75, 579], and similar results were also obtained with large ensembles of feedforward networks [570]. Using ensembles of BRNNs, the best accuracy reported so far, without using alignments to PDB sequences to refine the results at the output level, is 82.3% [515, 506]. Finally using BRNNs, but also alignments to sequences in the Protein Data Bank, the accuracy has been further increased to about 95% [475], suggesting that the problem of secondary structure prediction is now basically solved.

This is because there are fundamental reasons why an accuracy of 100% should not be expected, including:

(1) the presence of disordered regions;
(2) the ambiguities inherent in the definitions of secondary structure or relative solvent accessibility, as reflected by the imperfect correlation between several programs for determining these features from PDB files;

(3) the errors and uncertainties contained in the PDB; and

(4) the role of the solvent and other molecules, from ions to chaperone proteins, in determining structure, and which are not taken into consideration by the current prediction methods.

Thus in about 3.5 decades, through a series of twists and turns, the accuracy for secondary structure prediction has gone from 60% to 95%. Similar trends can be seen for the prediction of secondary structure into eight classes, or for other structural features such as relative solvent accessibility. The challenges have spearheaded the creation of new deep learning methods, in particular bidirectional recursive neural networks for sequences and their generalization to protein maps (see below) which have helped solve the problem. It is also fair to say that the increase in the number of sequences and structures in the protein databases has played a major role in the improvements. Although the main challenges in this highly studied area have been addressed, a few open questions remain. One of them is whether it is possible to achieve similar prediction performances using protein sequences alone, rather than protein profiles. After all, when proteins fold *in vivo*, or even *in vitro*, they do not use sequence or structural similarity at all. This raises subtle questions about the role of profiles in prediction methods and their coverage of protein space. Profiles can be thought of as creating a "ball" around each training protein, but also each test protein. For sequences with little homology to any known protein, profile-based methods do not seem to perform better than sequence-based methods [740].

13.3.3   Protein Contact and Distance Maps

In the second step of the pipeline, there has also been progress on the problem of predicting contact or distance maps using deep learning and, although a harder problem, current trends suggest that at least a partial solution may now be within reach.

Various algorithms for the prediction of amino contacts [675, 552, 263, 264, 578], contact numbers [577] distances [50, 464, 309, 425], and coarse and fine-grained contact maps [265, 576, 580, 183, 777] have been developed. Deep learning methods for special classes of contacts, such as disulphide bridges [186], have also been developed. Many of the early methods to predict the contact or distance between the amino acids at position i and j in the linear sequence, used two similar subnetworks to process the local information contained in two small windows around each position. The local information could include the sequence of amino acids or a corresponding profile, as well as information about the secondary structure or the relative solvent accessibility of the amino acids contained in the corresponding window. A third network is then used to combine the information from the previous two subnetworks into a final prediction of contact or distance for the pair (i, j). The weakness of this approach is that it ignores all the information that lies outside of the two input windows. Attempts to include a third kind of input, containing relevant and more global information – such as the overall composition of the sequence, the length of the protein, or the distance between the two local windows – have led to minor improvements only. The two-window approach can be viewed as the natural generalization in two dimensions of the outer, single-window, deep learning approach first used in 1D for secondary structure prediction [588]. Since this approach had been improved by the introduction of the 1D inner bidirectional recursive neural network approach (BRNNs) [75], this raised the issue of finding the natural generalization of BRNNs to 2D. This problem was solved in [87, 576] for any dimension. In two dimensions, this gives rise to grid recursive neural networks with one input grid, four hidden grids oriented towards each one of the four cardinal corners, and one output grid corresponding to the predicted contacts or distances. Each one of the four hidden grid is a square lattice with all its edges oriented towards one of the four cardinal corners, mimicking the forward and backward hidden chains of the 1D BRNNs. The corresponding deep architecture can be implemented using five recursive neural networks, one for computing the output as a function of the input vector and the four hidden vector, and one for each hidden grid to compute the corresponding hidden vector as a function of its grid neighbors and the input vector (Figure 13.2) [88, 185].

In terms of outer or convolutional approaches, it is possible to consider layered feedforward deep architectures where shared neural networks (within layers or across layers) operate on the 2D inputs to predict contacts or distances across the entire map. The first demonstration of this approach [237] used a stack of neural networks, where the networks are shared within each level thereby performing a convolution. At each level of the stacks, the networks receive both static inputs and dynamic inputs from the previous layer (Figure 13.2). In parallel, as profiles had played a key role for improving the prediction of 1D features (e.g. secondary structure, relative solvent accessibility), these have been generalized to 2D in the form of correlated mutations [384, 484]. Like profiles, correlated mutations are also derived from processing multiple alignments and provide useful information for inferring contact properties. In essence, profiles columns that are highly correlated, or have high mutual information, are indicative of contacts. The combination of: (1) rich input information comprising 1D information (e.g. sequence, profile, predicted secondary structure, predicted relative solvent accessibility) but also correlated mutations information; (2) deep learning for predicting protein maps and resulting potentials; and (3) significant computing power, seems to finally be able to achieve good map and structure predictions (e.g. [814, 667]).

Additional applications of deep learning in this area include:
(1) the prediction of the (x, y, z) coordinates of the side chains using rotamer libraries and global optimization [525, 526];
(2) the prediction of dihedral angles using stacked autoencoders [471]; and
(3) the beginning of the prediction of quaternary structure[266].

Finally, there is also a fairly extensive body of work using similar shallow and deep learning methods to predict other features related to structure including stability [184], solubility [476], disordered regions [187, 769], domains [188], fold recognition [182, 360, 440] (and references therein), short linear binding regions [516], binding regions within disordered regions [404], and bioactive peptides [513] within proteins.

This is also an area where other forms of deep learning, in terms of deep graphical models, have been used. For instance, in [253] an ensemble of stacks of restricted Boltzmann machines is used to predict residue–residue contacts from sequences.

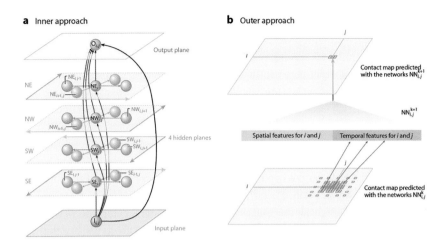

Figure 13.2 Schematic representation of inner (left) and outer approaches (right) for contact or distance map prediction. In the inner approach, the prediction at position (i, j) is computed by a shared neural network as a function of the input vector and four hidden vectors at position (i, j). The input vector may contain information coming from a window around amino acid i and amino acid j, including sequence, profile, and correlated mutation information, as well as predicted features such as secondary structure and relative solvent accessibility. Each of the four hidden vector resides in a different hidden plane. The directed acyclic graph associated with each hidden plane is a grid where all the edges are oriented towards one of the four cardinal corners. For instance, the hidden vector in the North East hidden plane at position (i, j) is computed by a neural network, which is shared within the plane, as a function of the corresponding input vector and the two neighboring hidden vectors in the same grid. Thus this neural networks is used to crawl the North–East hidden grid. In total, five neural networks are first trained and then used recursively to produce the predictions. In the outer approach, neural networks are stacked on top of the contact map plane. Only one level of the stack is shown on the right. At level $k + 1$ of the stack, there is a shared (convolutional) neural network common to all (i, j) positions in that level. The input to the network consists of "spatial or static features" corresponding to the same input vector used in the inner approach, and "temporal or dynamic features" corresponding to a local receptive field of hidden vectors produced at the previous level in the stack. Intuitively, each level tries to refine the predictions produced by the previous level. Reprinted, with permission, from the Annual Review of Biomedical Data Science, Volume 1, ©2018 by Annual Reviews Inc., www.annualreviews.org.

Similarly, deep belief network methods are used in [254] to predict disordered regions, in [695] to predict secondary structures, and in [381] for fold recognition and template ranking (see also [169]).

13.3.4 Protein Functional Features

Here we briefly consider the prediction of other features that are not directly related to the structure of a protein in any obvious way but often inform its function. These include the global classification of a protein into classes (e.g. Kinase, RNA-binding protein) or whether it contains a particular signal or binding site (e.g. signal peptide, glycosylation site). These predictions are often made from the protein sequence, possibly augmented with profiles, protein sequence composition (e.g. frequencies of amino acids and amino acid pairs), protein length, and structural features (e.g. secondary structure, relative solvent accessibility). Seminal early work in this area has been the development of effective deep learning methods for identifying prokaryotic and eukaryotic signal peptides [537] leading to the Signal-P software. Signal peptides control the entry of virtually all proteins to the secretory pathway in both eukaryotes and prokaryotes and the Signal-P software has been one of the most successful software in bioinformatics. Signal-P [537] trains two neural networks from the same data: a signal-peptide/nonsignal-peptide network whose output can be interpreted as the probability of the input position belonging to the signal peptide; and a cleavage-site/non-cleavage site network whose output can be interpreted as the probability of the position being the first in the mature protein (position +1 relative to the cleavage site). Output from the two networks are then combined to produce the final prediction. Similar work has been done for a host of other signals and protein properties, such as post-translational glycosylation and phosphorylation of proteins [131] showing that useful functional properties of proteins can be robustly inferred even when the structure is not known [378]. Outer deep learning approaches have been used also by others to predict, for instance, subcellular localization [517], peptide bioactivity [514, 354], and various forms of protein classification [768, 48].

Finally, inner and outer deep learning methods have also been applied to various problems in computational immunology [465], for instance to predict: T-cell and B-Cell epitopes [538, 714, 715], protein antigenicity [477], and MHC (major histocompatibility complex)-peptide binding [749].

13.4   Deep Learning in Genomics and Transcriptomics

This section looks at deep learning and its applications to DNA, RNA sequences, gene, and genome sequences, as well as gene expression. The earliest precursor in this area is the use of non-linear shallow learning to predict ribosome binding sites using the perceptron algorithm [703]. First systematic applications of deep learning methods in this area were focused on the prediction of splice sites [158, 336] and coding regions [737]. Some of this work has also led to interesting approaches for detecting error in databases [157]. The successful development of HMMs for biological sequence analysis [79, 423] is another form of deep learning that led to a host of applications in bioinformatics, as well as to the combination of neural networks with graphical models [77, 78, 99, 280] and, in turn, the development and application of graph neural networks to protein structure prediction, including secondary structure and contact maps, as described above.

Another early application of deep learning in genomics was the idea of using the discrete or continuous neural network formalism to model gene expression and regulation circuits [509], as opposed to brain circuits, for instance during development. While the regulatory logic of a complex gene [804, 805] may not be linearly separable and hence not amenable to modelization by a single unit, it may still be representable and learnable by a small neural network.

Another relatively early and unrelated application of deep learning to the genomic field was actually for the problem of base calling in early DNA sequencers [305, 261], a problem and approach that continue to evolve today, as new sequencing technologies are being introduced [146].

Not surprisingly, current modern applications of deep learning in genomics are focusing on the analysis of actual DNA or RNA sequences and the inference of functional properties and phenotypic consequences associated with mutations. For instance, convolutional neural networks are used in [17] to predict sequence specificities of DNA- and RNA-binding proteins, and further refinements have used convolutional-recurrent neural networks and LSTMs [776]. In [341], neural network language models are used to predict mutations that allow viruses to escape human immunity and vaccines.

A related cell-specific application using ChIP-seq data is developed in [589], complemented by [592] where convolutional recurrent neural networks, in the form of convolutional bidirectional LSTMs, are used to predict cell type-specific transcription factor binding using reference binding data from ChIP-seq and DNase-seq data. In [815], convolutional neural networks are used to predict chromatin accessibility, histone modification, and transcription factor binding from raw DNA sequences, and the prediction are subsequently used to infer the functional effect of non-coding SNPs (Single Nucleotide Polymorphysms) or indels (insertion/deletion). This work has been complemented [590] using features from annotated data, such as evolutionary scores or distance to the nearest transcription start site, and extended [591] using convolutional-recurrent neural networks, including bidirectional LSTMs (Figure 13.3). Related work [403] has also used convolutional neural networks to predict open chromatin regions from DNase-seq data with the goal of better understanding the regulatory code and assessing the functional effects of SNPs. Deep learning, in the form of convolutional and recurrent neural networks, specifically bidirectional gated recurrent networks, has also been used to predict the methylation state of CpG dinucleotides at the single-cell level [38].

A different application of convolutional neural networks to the problem of predicting and understanding sequence conservation is described in [447]. Finally, a hybrid architecture combining a pre-trained deep neural network and a hidden Markov model has been applied to the identification of replication domains using replication timing profiles [456], and deep restricted Boltzman machines and belief networks have been applied to the prediction of RNA-binding protein binding sites [808] from RNA sequences and their profiles, as well as predicted RNA secondary and tertiary structural features.

Finally, on the gene annotation and trascriptomic sides of things, one of the earliest applications of deep learning is [338], where neural networks are used in an unsupervised manner to cluster gene expression patterns. More recently, deep autoencoders are used in [191] for gene ontology annotation predictions, and deep feedforward networks to predict patterns of alternative splicing using mouse RNA-seq data [442], and to predict splicing in human tissue and its relationship to disease [799]. Feedforward neural networks are also used in [181] for gene expression regression, specifically for inferring the expression level of all the genes using the expression levels of only ~1000 "landmark"

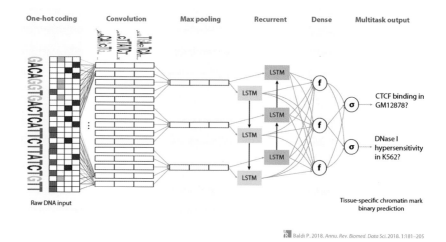

Baldi P. 2018. *Annu. Rev. Biomed. Data Sci.* 2018. 1:181–205

Figure 13.3 Deep hybrid convolutional and bidirectional-LSTM network for DNA sequence analysis [591]. The input DNA sequence is first one-hot encoded into a 4-row bit matrix. A convolution layer acts as a motif scanner across the input matrix to produce an output matrix with a row for each convolution kernel and a column for each position in the input (minus the width of the kernel). Max pooling reduces the size of the output matrix along the spatial axis, preserving the number of channels. The subsequent bidirectional-LSTM layer considers the orientations and spatial distances between the motifs. The bidirectional-LSTMs outputs are flattened into a layer as inputs to a final feedforward neural network which produces a vector of probability predictions of epigenetic marks to be compared via a loss function to the true target vector. For example, the model will predict whether the protein CTCF in the GM12878 cell line binds to the input sequence, or whether the input sequence is DNase-hypersensitive in the K562 cell line. Reprinted, with permission, from the Annual Review of Biomedical Data Science, Volume 1, ©2018 by Annual Reviews Inc., www.annualreviews.org.

genes. Finally, there have been recent applications of deep learning in circadian biology. Deep feedforward neural networks, trained primarily on synthetic data, have been used to identify which species (transcripts, proteins, or metabolites) are periodic in the corresponding omic-time series, in particular to identify circadian patterns of oscillations across millions of omic measurements [176]. In addition, compressive autoencoders with sin and cos bottleneck units have been trained to infer time from single-time-point transcriptome experiments [12] in the GEO database.

13.5   Deep Learning in Biomedical Imaging

It is not surprising that convolutional neural networks are the workhorse of applications of deep learning to biomedical images. The earliest application of deep learning to biomedical image data is found in [76], where deep Siamese convolutional neural networks are developed and used in a biometric application to recognize fingerprints. In recent years, convolutional neural networks and their variants have achieved superhuman performance [198] in image classification and other vision tasks, and thus applications to biomedical images are rapidly expanding. An example of scientific application, is the application of deep neural networks to each pixel of electron microscopy images to segment neuronal membranes [197]. On the medical side, many applications have focused on cancer. For instance, in [200] deep neural networks are used for mitosis detection in breast cancer histology images; in [623] a deep convolutional neural network (CNN) is used in the second tier of a two-tiered, coarse-to-fine cascade framework, to refine the candidate lesions from the first tier for sclerotic spine metastases detection in CT images; in [670] multi-scale convolutional neural networks are developed for lung nodule detection in CT images; in [773] a convolutional neural network method is used for automated detection and diagnosis of metastatic breast cancer in whole slide images of sentinel lymph node biopsies; in [775] a multi-resolution approach using deep Siamese neural networks is developed for spinal metastasis detection; an application to skin cancer identification is described in [259]; an application to classify genetic mutations in gliomas is described in [177]; in addition there are also applications of deep convolutional neural networks to instruments being developed for cancer research and other applications [742]. There are also plenty of applications of deep learning to imaging for other diseases, such as the detection of diabetic retinopathy in retinal fundus photographs [322]; or to regression problems – as opposed to classification problems – for instance in [774] where convolutional neural networks are used to process mammograms and infer the degree of breast calcification and asses the corresponding risk of cardiovascular disease (Figure 13.4).

In addition, efficient deep learning methods have been developed for localization, i.e. to identify regions of interested and create bounding boxes, and for segmentation, i.e. to identify the countours of objects. Generally speaking, there are two approaches for object detection/localization. The first involves training two convolutional neural networks, where one model identifies candidate objects regions in the image and the other model is evaluated on each such region to confirm whether an object of interest is present or not [610, 332]. The second is a transfer learning approach where both tasks (detection and localization) are treated together and carried by a single network [606, 607, 458]. For instance, in the YOLO (you look only once) approach, a single network has both classification output units for the presence/absence of an object of interest, and regression units for the coordinates of the bounding box around the object when it is present.

Likewise, for segmentation problems, one can train a a first network to classify pixels as being inside or outside of the object of interest, and then use this network to scan a region of interest and classify each one of its pixels, which can be slow for real-time applications. Segmentation can also be cast as a a conversion of the image from a high-resolution to a low-resolution version [487, 701]. Often this can be effectively achieved using essentially a convolutional autoencoder where the bottleneck layer learns to compress the high-resolution information. This is the main idea behind the popular U-Net architecture [617] which, in addition, uses skip connections. With the proper training data, such methods can also be used in the reverse direction, to try to increase image resolution.

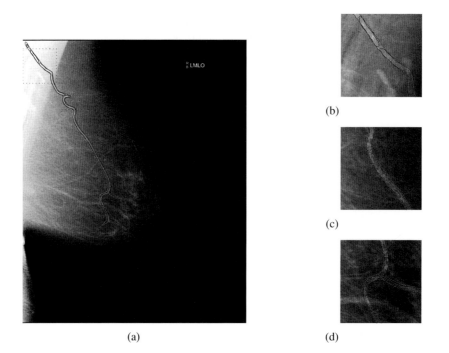

(a)   (b)   (c)   (d)

Figure 13.4 (a) Application of deep learning to the detection of BACs (breast arterial calcifications) in mammogram images, in which the true BACs are marked by red contours, and the automatically detected regions are marked by blue contours. (b)-(d) the magnified views of the three regions of interest in (a) (marked by black dotted squares). Deep learning networks are used to automatically identify BACs and predict the overall level or calcification [774].

Several trends and technical points are worth noticing in this area. First, essentially the same techniques can be applied to several different imaging modalities and scales: such as electron microscopy, ultrasound imaging, photographs, video, Computed Axial Tomograph (CAT) scans, Magnetic Resonance Imaging (MRI) scans, X-ray scans, and so forth.

Second, there are publicly available deep convolutional neural networks that have already been trained on large image datasets for general purpose computer vision, sometimes achieving superhuman performance [198]. These trained networks can easily be reused in many biomedical imaging problems simply by slightly modifying and retraining the top of the architecture, thus reusing the already pre-trained, general-purpose, low level feature detectors. It is also possible to use the pre-trained architecture to initialize the weights but then retrain everything. Using pre-trained architectures often provides excellent performance and also a comparison baseline for training newly designed, problem-specific, architectures. These pretrained architectures usually have a large number of parameters, however the danger of overfitting is limited because they have already been trained with large numbers of images.

Third, in applications where the size or the speed of the architecture becomes an issue (e.g. deep learning on cell phones) then custom architectures need to be trained using, for instance, the techniques for model compression discussed in Chapter 6. For problems of classification into many classes, these include the two-step sequential approach of first training a large deep architecture, and then training a smaller, shallower, architecture using as targets the analog outputs of the trained deep architecture. These analog outputs contain more information (also called "dark knowledge") than the binary targets associated with the original training set in classification tasks [159, 635].

Fourth, biomedical images are often three-dimensional: two spatial dimensions and one temporal dimension (videos), or three spatial dimensions (scans). Training deep architectures can take time, but once trained they can process one image in a few milliseconds. Thus one can process video data in real-time. For instance, in the real-time application of deep learning to colonoscopies [742] (Figure 13.5), after training individual frames are processed in 20ms or so, allowing for identifying the presence/absence and location of polyps in multiple frames within each second, and leveraging the results of neighboring frames to produce more robust inferences. Likewise, in the case of three spatial dimensions, it is possible to process multiple two-dimensional slices, and use one slice and its neighboring slices to derive more robust inferences (e.g. [775]). Finally, it is also possible to use 3D convolutional neural networks. Three-dimensional convolutions are computationally expensive but can be done for relative small volumes (e.g. $3 \times 3 \times 3$) with current technology.

In any case, there is a general sense that this is an area where most of the basic technical problems are already solved. As larger and larger datasets are aggregated and used for training, and as legal, societal, and other barriers are addressed, one can expect an increasing number of deep learning systems to make their way into real biological and medical imaging applications.

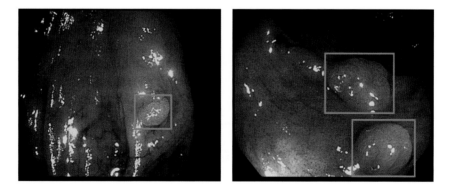

Figure 13.5 Examples of polyps and corresponding bounding boxes produced by deep learning methods [742].

13.6   Deep Learning in Health Care

There is also a rapidly growing set of applications of deep learning to electronic medical records and health care data, recently reviewed in [543, 192], as well as related concerns

[164]. Examples of work in this area include: detection of cardiac arrhythmia [599] from electrocardiograms; prediction of post-operative in-hospital mortality [438, 258] from clinical data; phenotype discovery using clinical data [435]; use of neural network autoencoders and topic modeling techniques to learn compact, useful-for-prediction, representations of electronic health records [505] (see also [113]). One important challenge in the latter area is how to incorporate temporal information, for instance the notion of disease trajectories [377], into end-to-end, specialized or more generic, predictive systems [571, 194].

Many other areas of application of deep learning in the life sciences exist and could not be reviewed. An important example is provided by the growing applications of deep learning to brain-computer interfaces [727, 267, 811]

In short, as should be obvious from this necessarily non-exhaustive review, there have been plenty of deep learning applications to biomedical data over the past four decades and the pace is increasing. As with any exponential growth phase, what remains ahead exceeds what has already been done and one can expect these applications to continue to expand in the coming years and to yield important scientific, biomedical, and clinical breakthroughs. In areas like biomedical imaging, many of the technical problems have already been solved and deep learning may become a commodity. The real challenges lie in the data and the various societal barriers to technological changes. While there is still plenty of room for applying deep learning methods to narrowly focused problems, it is clear that one important direction of research is to broaden their applicability towards general AI for biomedical data and beyond.

14 Conclusion

In AI and machine learning circles, it is not unusual to hear questions about the next wave and how it will look. While deep learning may seem like a wave to some, in reality it is not – it has been progressing steadily for many decades, although not in a linear fashion. Furthermore, it is here to stay, in one form or the other, in the same way that linear regression is not going anywhere any time soon. To conclude, rather than trying to predict the next wave, we briefly discuss two concerns that are often raised in connection to deep learning: (1) the black-box nature of deep learning; and (2) its connection, or lack thereof, to biological neural networks.

14.1 Explainability and the Black-Box Question

The explainability and black-box issue, and the sense of insecurity that arises from not knowing how a trained neural network solves a particular task, is a complex question that requires considering several different points.

- First, one must recognize that this question is also related to the question of adversarial attacks. If we do not know everything about a given algorithm, it may be vulnerable to attacks targeting points of weakness that we are not aware of. Furthermore, in the case of a neural network, it is possible for an attacker to find weak points, without himself knowing what the network does (as long as he has a copy of the network). As seen in one of the exercises, one can for instance apply gradient ascent to the inputs (e.g., image pixels in an image classification problem) to find small perturbations of the input, that create large errors.

- A certain degree of opacity associated with deep learning is inevitable. After all, training is a way of storing the training data into the synapses of a network. But synaptic storage is fundamentally different from the digital, address-based, storage of our computers. It is a holographic form of storage in the sense that each training examples makes a small contribution to each synaptic weight. Unlike digital storage of the training examples, synaptic storage of the training examples is inherently opaque and lossy: the training examples cannot be recovered from the weights. As we have seen, this is already the case for linear regression. The weights in linear regression tell you something about the sufficient statistics of the data (e.g., mean and covariance), but do not allow you to recover the training set.

- If one really wants to, it is possible to open the black box, essentially by conducting neurophysiological experiments and studying the behavior of each neuron under all kinds of different inputs. This is often prohibitively time-consuming and can only be done in favorable circumstances for a subset of neurons (e.g., neurons in the early layers of a convolutional neural network). In addition, the behavior of individual neurons is often meaningless and what matters is the behavior of an entire population of neurons, for instance the behavior of an entire layer. The representations that are being learnt in a deep layer can be very difficult to understand. In practice, one is often forced to operate in a regime where there is not enough time, or computational resources, to study the black box.
- It is reasonable to suspect that there exist fundamental limitations and corresponding theorems stating that as neural networks are being scaled up, it becomes computationally intractable to "understand" them completely, or to have them "explain" themselves automatically. Likewise, it becomes intractable to prevent any vulnerability against any adversarial attack. Consider, for instance, black and white pixel images of size 1000×1000 and the problem of recognizing whether there is a cat in the image or not. How can one reasonably expect a neural network (or any other classifier) to have perfect performance over the space of all possible images, $2^{1,000,000}$ of them? And this is notwithstanding that the boundary between images with and without cats may be fuzzy in some regions of the space, to the point that humans will disagree on the corresponding classifications. And if someone claimed to have a perfect classifier, how would you test his claim given that the number of points to be tested is astronomical? Another reason to suspect fundamental limitations comes from evolution and the primate visual system. Although evolution has had a staggering amount of computing resources and time to produce such a marvel of engineering, it still has failed to make it impervious to errors and adversarial attacks, as easily shown by any visual illusion.
- Nevertheless, there is plenty of work trying to deal, at least in partial fashion with issues of robustness and explainability. For instance, while perfect robustness may be intrinsically unattainable, there may be ways of modifying the adversarial attack tradeoffs of a deep learning system: making it less vulnerable in regions that are more important during deployment, at the cost of making it more vulnerable in regions that are less important. Another example is the use of symmetric transfer functions which may provide some added robustness to certain adversarial attacks [622, 813, 721]. On the explainability side of things, techniques have also been developed to try to explain the behavior of a trained neural network essentially by propagating activations backwards [60] or, locally, by training a simple classifier (e.g., SVM) using examples in the close neighborhood of a test example [611] of interest. While it is commendable to try to develop methods by which deep neural networks could explain how they function to their user, even defining such a goal precisely is not easy, let alone achieving it.
- However, standard engineering design principles of modularity and encapsulation still apply and remain one of the best approaches for improving robustness, explainability, and fault-tolerance of systems that include deep learning components.

Taking a simple example from Chapter 13 on biomedical applications, a deep learning system trained to classify images as containing polyps or no-polyps may be opaque. But if the system also draws bounding boxes around the putative polyps it finds, then in the case of a false positive the bounding box identifies the input regions that leads to misclassification. In this particular example, this led early on to the realization that the corrrelative presence of surgical instruments in the image could be mistaken for the presence of polyps. This provides clues as to why the network fails, and how to fix it, for instance by increasing the number of problematic examples in the training set, or increasing the number of categorical outputs by adding the "surgical instrument" category. Likewise, taking an example from Chapter 12 on chemical applications, a mechanistic system for predicting chemical reactions allows one to isolate which mechanistic step – within a sequence of steps – is wrongly predicted. Furthermore, it can identify within that step which are the sources and sinks of electrons that were mislabeled, or the source-sink pairs that were improperly ranked, again providing important clues for understanding the sources of the errors, and developing means for fixing or isolating them.

- Finally, while the desire to understand and control is fundamental to human nature, one must recognize that most of the objects and processes we use and trust every day are black boxes. Most of us do not know how our cars, computers, or cell phones work in detail. This does not make them unusable. A search engine or an automated translation or recommender system on the Internet may serve hundreds of millions of queries each day, and use deep learning methods that are opaque not only to the users, but also to the engineers who developed it, and perhaps who have to retrain it every day. For many problems, at scale there is just not enough man power to try to understand everything and, up to a certain point, we are going to have to trust deep learning solutions that we do not fully understand. Wonder of wonders, each and everyone of us has no clue of how his own brain works, yet trusts it blindly at every second of his life. As the man who introduced the term synapse, eloquently put it: "*A shower of little electrical leaks conjures up for me, when I look, the landscape; the castle on the height, or when I look at him, my friend's face and how distant he is from me they tell me. Taking their word for it, I go forward and my other senses confirm that he is there.*" (Charles Sherrington in *Man on his Nature*, 1940).

14.2 ANNs versus BNNs

Biological neural networks (BNNs) and the brain have provided the main source of inspiration for artificial neural networks (ANNs) and AI, at least since the 1940s. However, in the reverse direction, the question of how relevant ANNs are for BNNs has been, and remains, controversial.

At one extreme end, there is the view that ANNs have nothing to do with BNNs. Indeed biological neurons, with their complex dendritic arborizations and multiple ion channels, are far more complex than McCulloch and Pitts neurons in both their structures (Figures 14.1 and 14.2) and their functions, by several orders of magnitude [391]. Under

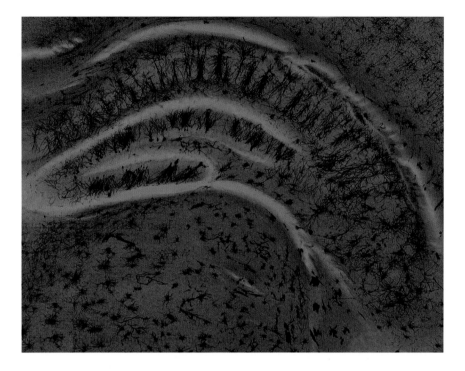

Figure 14.1 Golgi stain of mouse dorsal hippocampus. A small percentage of neurons stain positive (black), which allows for easy visualization of neuronal morphology (courtesy of Dr. A. Vogel Ciernia).

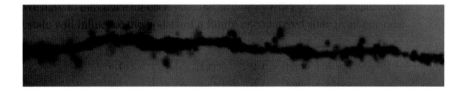

Figure 14.2 Golgi stain of a dendritic branch on a pyramidal neuron within the CA1 region of the mouse hippocampus. Note individual dendritic spines protruding from the dendritic branch (courtesy of Dr. A. Vogel Ciernia).

an electron microscope, a synapse alone may look like a little town (Figure 14.3). In this view, all these intricate details must be there for a reason and ANNs miss them entirely.

At the other extreme end, ANNs provide good approximations of BNNs. Or, even more provocatively, the approximation may be the other way around: it is biological neurons which are (desperately) trying to approximate McCullough and Pitt neurons. However, they struggle in doing so, because of the messiness of carbon-based computing and having to satisfy many other functions and tough constraints that are not directly relevant to their computational essence. After all, some neurons may stay alive for up to a century. Because of this struggle, they end up being fairly lousy and slow approximations.

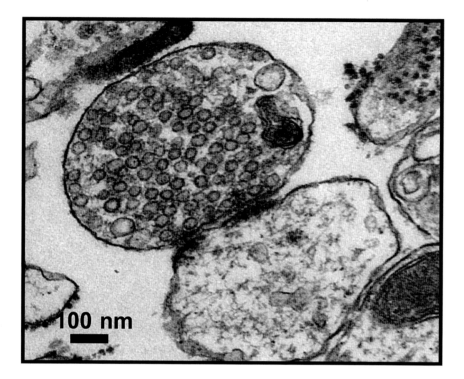

Figure 14.3 Isolated synapse from a brain sample before mass spectrometry analyses. The pre-synapse terminal contains many vesicles carrying neurotransmmitter molecules (courtesy of Okinawa Institute of Sciences and Technology (Z. Taoufiq, OIST 2013)).

Historically, in the wave of excitement of the 1980s produced by the Hopfield model and the work of the PDP group, several papers were published claiming to explain complex cognitive phenomena using connectionist models in overly simplistic terms. This caused a backlash by scientists like Christoph Koch, Tomaso Poggio, and James Bower who argued that ANNs had very little to do with BNNs, and that far more detailed and realistic models had to be created. This led to efforts, that continue to this day, to develop detailed compartmental models of neurons and BNNs, together with the corresponding software simulation tools [415, 498, 141, 342, 142, 170]. This view was influential: in the 1990s, mixing ANNs with biological relevance was often frowned upon and a reason for rejection from various venues, while the distinctive qualifier of "artificial" became almost mandatory for a while.

The truth is somewhere between the two extreme views, although exactly where remains to be better understood. Current evidence does suggest that ANNs are relevant for understanding biology, although perhaps not under a one-to-one match, at least at two different levels. At a more abstract level, to say that ANNs have nothing to do with BNNs is probably as wrong as to say that Turing machines have nothing to do with cell phones. Surely Turing machines do not have antennas, cameras, or GPS. But, on the other hand, Turing machines have played a foundational role in the development of silicon-based computing and its storage model, which is ultimately what cell phones use. Likewise, ANNs provide the simplest model of a neural style of computation and information storage, entirely different from the style of digital computers, where information is both scattered and superimposed across synapses, and storage is intertwined with processing. And this alone enables one to develop and test new ideas, some of which may be relevant for biology. More importantly, at a more concrete level, there is an entire line of work that has used ANNs (and reinforcement learning) to build successful models of BNNs. This line of research goes back at least to the work of Anderson and Zipser in the 1980s [817], followed by several other examples (e.g., [553, 115, 802]). The basic experiment in this line proceeds roughly as follows:

(1) experimentally measure the inputs and outputs of a small brain region;
(2) build an ANN which roughly conforms to the anatomy observed in that region;
(3) train the ANNs by backpropagation (or reinforcement learning) using the inputs and outputs gathered in (1); and
(4) compare relevant properties of the ANN to the properties of the corresponding BNN.

This coarse comparison can be done in different ways depending on the situation, for instance, in terms of receptive fields and synaptic weight patterns (e.g., emergence of edge detectors and Gabor-like filters), firing rates, or response properties to new stimuli. In all these experiments, a remarkable degree of similarity has been reported between the BNNs and the corresponding ANN models, to a degree that cannot be explained by chance alone.

These issues are important not only for those interested in biology, but also to map future directions of AI research. Broadly speaking, there are at least four main, non-independent, directions to try to build better AI systems. First, there is scaling-up, i.e using more or less the current methods but with larger datasets, larger GPU clusters, and so forth. While this approach cannot be ruled out, most experts tend to agree that it is not likely to be sufficient.

Second, there is a variety of symbolic approaches (e.g., [744]) implemented in digital computers, intellectually descending from the AI of the 1970s, which could be further developed and possibly combined with deep learning. A fair discussion of this direction, including the meaning of the term "symbolic", would require a separate book.

Third, there are purely neural approaches, extending beyond the material presented in this book, and based on the premise that the brain is evidence that this is at least one possible way of achieving intelligence. It is within this third class of approaches that looking for additional mechanisms and architectural properties of the brain and finding ways to import them into virtualized, or neuromorphic, neural systems may be useful.

Although we are far from understanding how the brain works, there is indeed no lack of such mechanisms and architectural features. The main challenge here is to filter out what are likely to be details specific to biology from fundamental features that can be exported to digital computers. To name just a few:

(1) Spiking neurons, not only as an energy saving mechanism, but also to encode information in different ways, for instance in the timing of spikes;

(2) Continuous, distributed, asynchronous (i.e., without a central clock) time;

(3) Synapses and synaptic mechanisms with multiple time scales, including fast synapses that can be rapidly written and erased for encoding short-term information and creating some form of a "scratchpad";

(4) Epigenetics forms of memory [274, 469, 568, 713, 311] that can modulate neural memory;

(5) Many other, poorly understood, architectural and procedural aspects of information storage in the brain, including for instance circadian-driven hippocampal replay of information and selective cortical storage involving the adjustment of existing connections and synapses, as well as the creation of new connections and new synapses, potentially to create knowledge graphs of connected entities which evolve constantly as a function of experience and replay [227, 494, 745];

(6) Cognitive architectural ideas such as the Global Workspace theory and its theater metaphor [534, 57, 58] and the related problem of virtualizing Turing-like storage to neural architectures.

One overarching challenge in all these directions is that incorporation of additional biological or cognitive mechanisms into digital virtualized neural networks is likely to slow them down and make them less efficient, at least initially, creating an additional barrier for applications and discovery. Finally, there is a fourth direction, based on other computing frameworks, in particular quantum computing due to its rapid technological progress, its computationally superior power, its holographic superposition of information across multiple qubits vaguely reminiscent of the neural style, its intriguing paradoxes such as entanglement, and its foundational connections to "knowledge" (e.g. the Copenhagen interpretation) and cryptography. Last but not least [327] is its potential, albeit unproven and controversial, connection to the mystery that remains unexplained by any approach – consciousness.

Appendix A Reinforcement Learning and Deep Reinforcement Learning

This appendix, included for completeness, provides a concise overview of reinforcement learning, from its origins to deep reinforcement learning. Thousands of articles have been written on reinforcement learning and we could not cite, let alone survey, most of them. Rather we have tried to focus here on first principles and algorithmic aspects, trying to organize a body of known algorithms in a logical way. A fairly comprehensive introduction to reinforcement learning is provided by [708]. Earlier surveys of the literature can be found in [310, 388, 402].

A.1   Brief History and Background

The concept of reinforcement learning has emerged historically from the combination of two currents of research: (1) the study of the behavior of animals in response to stimuli; and (2) the development of efficient approaches to problems of optimal control.

In behavioral psychology, the term *reinforcement* was introduced by Pavlov in the early 1900s, while investigating the psychology and psychopathology of animals in the context of conditioning stimuli and conditioned responses [391]. One of his experiments consisted in ringing a bell just before giving food to a dog; after a few repetitions, Pavlov noticed that the sound of the bell alone made the dog salivate. In classical conditioning terminology, the bell is the previously neutral stimulus, which becomes a *conditioned stimulus* after becoming associated with the *unconditioned stimulus* (the food). The conditioned stimulus eventually comes to trigger a conditioned response (salivation). Conditioning experiments led to Thorndike's Law of Effect [728] in 1911, which states that:

Of several responses made to the same situation, those which are accompanied or closely followed by satisfaction to the animal will, other things being equal, be more firmly connected with the situation, so that, when it recurs, they will be more likely to recur.

This formed the basis of *operant conditioning* (or instrumental conditioning) in which: (1) the strength of a behavior is modified by the behavior's consequences, such as reward or punishment; and (2) the behavior is controlled by antecedents called "discriminative stimuli" which come to emit those responses. Operant conditioning was studied in the 1930s by Skinner, with his experiments on the behavior of rats exposed to different types of reinforcers (stimuli).

As already discussed in the Introduction, a few years later in 1949, in *The Organization of Behavior* [335], Hebb proposed one of the first theories about the neural basis of learning using the notions of cell assemblies and "Hebbian" learning, encapsulated in the sentence:

When an axon of cell A is near enough to excite cell B and repeatedly or persistently takes part in firing it, some growth process or metabolic change takes place in one or both cells such that A's efficiency, as one of the cells firing B, is increased.

These are some of the biological underpinnings and sources of inspiration for many subsequent developments in reinforcement learning and other forms of learning, such as supervised learning.

In 1954, in the context of optimal control theory, Bellman introduced dynamic programming [117], and the concept of value functions. These functions are computed using a recursive relationship, now called the Bellman equation. Bellman's work was within the framework of Markov Decision Process (MDPs), which were studied in detail by [363]. One of Howard's students, Drake, proposed an extension with partial observability: the POMDP models [247].

In 1961, [504] discussed several issues in the nascent field of reinforcement learning, in particular the problem of *credit assignment*, which is one of the core problems in the field. Around the same period, reinforcement learning ideas began to be applied to games. For instance, Samuel developed his checkers player [642] using the Temporal Differences method. Other experiments were carried by Michie, including the development of the MENACE system to learn how to play Noughts and Crosses [500, 501], and the BOXES controller [502] which has been applied to pole balancing problems.

In the 1970s, Tsetlin made several contributions within the area of automata, in particular in relation to the n-armed bandit problem, i.e. how to select which levers to pull in order to maximize the gain in a game comprising n slot machines without initial knowledge. This problem can be viewed as a special case of a reinforcement learning problem with a single state. In 1975, Holland developed genetic algorithms [351], paving the way for reinforcement learning based on evolutionary algorithms.

In 1988, [788] presented the REINFORCE algorithms, which led to a variety of policy gradient methods. The same year, Sutton introduced TD(λ) [706]. In 1989, Watkins proposed the Q-Learning algorithm [780].

A.1.1 Applications

Reinforcement learning methods have been effective in a variety of areas, in particular in games. Success stories include the application of reinforcement learning to stochastic games (Backgammon [723]), learning by self-play (Chess [429]), learning from games played by experts (Go [678]), and learning without using any hand-crafted features (Atari games [511]).

When the objective is defined by a control task, reinforcement learning has been used to perform low-speed sustained inverted hovering with a helicopter [535], balance a pendulum without a priori knowledge of its dynamics [32], or balance and ride a bicycle [603].

Reinforcement learning has also found plenty of applications in robotics [414], including recent success in manipulation [444] and locomotion [661]. Other notable successes include solutions to the problems of elevator dispatching [218], dynamic communication allocation for cellular radio channels [684], job-shop scheduling [809], and traveling salesman optimization [246]. Other potential industrial applications have included packet routing [144], financial trading [512], job-shop scheduling, and dialog systems [443].

A.1.2   General Idea Behind Reinforcement Learning

Reinforcement learning is used to compute a behavior strategy, a *policy*, that maximizes a satisfaction criteria, a long term sum of *rewards*, by interacting through *trials and errors* with a given environment.

Figure A.1 The agent–environment interaction protocol

A reinforcement learning problem consists of a decision-maker, called the *agent*, operating in an *environment* modeled by *states* $s_t \in S$. The agent is capable of taking certain *actions* $a_t \in \mathcal{A}(s_t)$, as a function of the current state s_t. After choosing an action at time t, the agent receives a scalar *reward* $r_{t+1} \in \mathbb{R}$ and finds itself in a new state s_{t+1} that depends on the current state and the chosen action. At each time step, the agent follows a strategy, called the *policy* π_t, which is a mapping from states to the probability of selecting each possible action: $\pi(s, a)$ denotes the probability that $a = a_t$ if $s = s_t$.

The objective of reinforcement learning is to use the interactions of the agent with its environment to derive (or approximate) an optimal policy to maximize the total amount of reward received by the agent over the long run.

REMARK A.1   This definition is quite general: time can be continuous or discrete, with finite or infinite horizon; the state transitions can be stochastic or deterministic, the rewards can be stationary or not, and deterministic or sampled from a given distribution. In some cases (with an unknown model), the agent may start with partial or no knowledge about its environment.

REMARK A.2   To a first degree of approximation, reinforcement learning in its different forms can be viewed as a generalization of dynamic programming. In the most simple case where time is discrete, the environment can be in a finite and small number of states, the repertoire of actions is also finite and small, and everything is observable and deterministic, then dynamic programming can be applied immediately to find an optimal policy. This is because the most rewarding path from state s_1 at time t_1 to state s_2 at time t_2 that goes through state r at some intermediate time t, consists of the concatenation of the most rewarding paths from (s_1, t_1) to $r, t)$ and from $r, t)$ to (s_2, t_2). Thus, starting from s_1 at time t_1, one can recursively build a table containing for all times t the maximal reward associated with each possible state, as well as backtracking pointer for the corresponding trajectory of optimal actions.

A.1.3 Basic Definitions

Return

To maximize the long-term cumulative reward after the current time t, in the case of a finite time horizon that ends at time T, the *return* R_t is equal to:

$$R_t = r_{t+1} + r_{t+2} + r_{t+3} + \cdots + r_T = \sum_{k=t+1}^{T} r_k.$$

In the case of an infinite time horizon, it is customary instead to use a *discounted* return:

$$R_t = r_{t+1} + \gamma r_{t+2} + \gamma^2 r_{t+3} + \cdots = \sum_{k=0}^{\infty} \gamma^k r_{t+k+1},$$

which will converge if we assume the rewards are bounded and $\gamma < 1$. Here $\gamma \in [0, 1]$ is a constant, called the *discount factor*. In what follows, in general we will use this discounted definition for the return.

Value Functions

In order to find an optimal policy, some algorithms are based on *value functions*, $V(s)$, that represent how beneficial it is for the agent to reach a given state s. Such a function provides, for each state, a numerical estimate of the potential future reward obtainable from this state, and thus depends on the actual policy π followed by the agent:

$$V^\pi(s) = \mathbb{E}_\pi [R_t \mid s_t = s] = \mathbb{E}_\pi \left[\sum_{k=0}^{\infty} \gamma^k r_{t+k+1} \,\middle|\, s_t = s \right],$$

where $\mathbb{E}_\pi [.]$ denotes the expected value given that the agent follows policy π, and t is any time step.

REMARK A.3   The existence and uniqueness of V^π are guaranteed if $\gamma < 1$ or if T is guaranteed to be finite from all states under the policy π [708].

Action–Value Functions

Similarly, we define the value of taking action a in state s under a policy π as the *action–value function Q*:

$$
\begin{aligned}
Q^\pi(s, a) &= \mathbb{E}_\pi [R_t \mid s_t = s, a_t = a] \\
&= \mathbb{E}_\pi \left[\sum_{k=0}^{\infty} \gamma^k r_{t+k+1} \,\middle|\, s_t = s, a_t = a \right].
\end{aligned}
$$

Optimal Policy

An *optimal policy* π^* is a policy that achieves the greatest expected reward over the long run. Formally, a policy π is defined to be better than or equal to a policy π' if its expected return is greater than or equal to that of π' for all states. Thus:

$$\pi^* = \underset{\pi}{\mathrm{argmax}}\, V^\pi(s) \qquad \text{for all} \quad s \in S.$$

REMARK A.4   There is always at least one policy that is better than or equal to all other policies. There may be more than one, but we denote all of them by π^* because they share the same value function and action–value function, denoted:

$$V^*(s) = \max_\pi V^\pi(s) \qquad \text{for all} \quad s \in S,$$

$$Q^*(s,a) = \max_\pi Q^\pi(s,a) \quad \text{for all} \quad s \in S, \qquad \text{for all} \quad a \in \mathcal{A}(s).$$

A.1.4   Markov Decision Processes (MDPs)

A *Markov Decision Process* is a particular instance of reinforcement learning where the set of states is finite, the sets of actions of each state are finite, and the environment satisfies the following Markov property:

$$Pr(s_{t+1} = s' | s_0, a_0, \ldots, s_t, a_t) = Pr(s_{t+1} = s' | s_t, a_t).$$

In other words, the probability of reaching state s' from state s by action a is independent of the other actions or states in the past (before time t). Hence, we can represent a sequence of actions, states, rewards sampled from an MDP by a decision network (see Figure A.2).

Most reinforcement learning research is based on the formalism of MDPs; they provide a simple framework in which to study basic algorithms and their properties. We will continue to use this formalism in Section A.2. Then, we will emphasize its drawbacks in Section A.3 and present potential improvements in Section A.4.

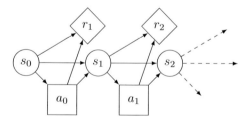

Figure A.2 Decision network representing an episode sampled from an MDP

A.1.5   A Visualization of Reinforcement Learning Algorithms

An overview of the algorithms that will be presented in this chapter can be found in Figure A.3. While this does not cover all reinforcement learning algorithms, we present it as a tool for the reader to get an overview of the reinforcement learning landscape. Each

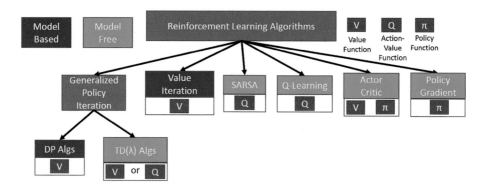

Figure A.3 An overview of the reinforcement learning algorithms that will be presented in this appendix. The functions associated with each reinforcement learning algorithm can take the form of a deep neural network.

algorithm is color-coded according to whether it is *model based* or *model free*. Model-based methods, such as those presented in Sections A.2.2 and A.2.5, require a model of the environment while model-free methods, such as those presented in Sections A.2.3 and A.2.4, do not require a model of the environment. The functions (value function, action–value function, and/or policy function) that each algorithm uses are displayed beneath the algorithm. As shown in Section A.5, these functions can take the form of deep neural networks.

A.2   Main Algorithmic Approaches

Given a reinforcement learning problem, we now are going to present different approaches to computing the optimal policy. There are two main approaches: one based on searching in the space of value functions, and another based on searching in the space of policies.

Value function space search methods attempt to compute the optimal value function V^* and deduce at the end the optimal policy π^* from V^*. These methods include linear programming, dynamic programming, Monte-Carlo methods, and temporal difference methods.

Policy space search methods, on the other hand, maintain explicit representations of policies and update them over the time in order to compute the optimal policy π^*. Such methods typically include evolutionary and policy gradient algorithms. We provide a brief overview of these methods in the following sections.

A.2.1   Linear Programming

In order to cast the goal of finding the optimal value function as a linear programming problem [619], we treat the value function V as a cost function and then try to minimize the cost from each starting state s. In order to minimize a cost, we need to invert the sign of the rewards. We will note the cost function $g_\pi(s_t) = -r_{t+1}$. Thus here we want to minimize:

$$J^\pi(s) = \mathbb{E}_\pi \left[\sum_{k=0}^{\infty} \gamma^k g_\pi(s_k) \,\middle|\, s_0 = s \right].$$

In order to perform this minimization, we define the optimal Bellman operator T:

$$(TJ)(s) = \min_\pi (g_\pi(s) + \gamma P_\pi(s)J),$$

where J is a vector of states, P_π is the transition matrix with the (s, s') entry representing the probability of reaching s' from s under policy π, and the minimization is carried out component-wise.

The solution that minimizes the cost should verify the Bellman equation:

$$J(s) = (TJ)(s).$$

It can be found by solving (using, for example, the simplex algorithm) the linear programming optimization problem :

$$\min_J \quad \mu^T J$$
$$\text{s.t.} \quad TJ \geq J,$$

where μ is a vector of positive weights, known as the *state-relevance weights*.

From a theoretical perspective, linear programming provides the only known algorithm that can solve MDPs in polynomial time, although in general linear programming approaches to reinforcement learning problems do not fare well in practice. In particular, the main problem for linear programming approaches is that the time and space complexity can be extremely high.

A.2.2　Dynamic Programming

Dynamic programming algorithms are the simplest way to tackle a reinforcement learning problem, however, this method requires perfect knowledge of the model and is limited by its computational cost. The idea behind the dynamic programming formulation of reinforcement learning is to choose a policy π, estimate its value function V^π (Algorithm 1), deduce a new policy π' from V^π (Algorithm 2), and iterate this process until a satisfying policy is found (Algorithm 3). This process is known as *policy iteration*. Since each step strictly improves the policy, the algorithm is guaranteed to converge to the optimal policy. For computational convenience, one can decide to stop the policy evaluation step when the change in the value function is small between two iterations, as implemented in Algorithm 1 with the threshold θ.

REMARK A.5　At each step k, the value function V_{k+1} can be computed from the previous one, V_k, in two ways [708]:

- Full Backup: using two distinct arrays to store the two functions V_k and V_{k+1}.

Algorithm 1: Policy Evaluation

Data: π, the policy to be evaluated
Result: $V \approx V^\pi$, an approximation of the value function of π
repeat
    $\Delta \leftarrow 0$
    for $s \in S$ **do**
        $v \leftarrow V(s)$
        $V(s) \leftarrow \sum_a \pi(s, a) \sum_{s'} P^a(s, s')(R^a(s, s') + \gamma V(s'))$
        $\Delta \leftarrow \max(\Delta, |v - V(s)|)$
until $\Delta < \theta$;

- In Place: using only one array, and overwriting V_k when computing V_{k+1} for each state.

The second approach is usually faster.

Algorithm 2: Policy Improvement

Data: π, the policy to be updated
       V, the value function
Result: π, the updated policy
for $s \in S$ **do**
    $\pi(s) \leftarrow \mathrm{argmax}_a \sum_{s'} P^a(s, s')(R^a(s, s') + \gamma V(s'))$

Algorithm 3: Policy Iteration

Result: π^*, the optimal policy
Initialization: π chosen arbitrarily
repeat
    $\pi_0 \leftarrow \pi$
    $V = \text{Policy\_evaluation}(\pi)$
    $\pi = \text{Policy\_improvement}(\pi, V)$
until $\pi_0 = \pi$;

One drawback of policy iteration is the policy evaluation step; which requires multiple iterations over every state. Another way to proceed is to combine policy evaluation and policy improvement in the same loop (Algorithm 4). This process is called value iteration. Value iteration is not always better than policy iteration: the efficiency depends on the nature of the problem and the parameters chosen. These differences are discussed in [566].

Algorithm 4: Value Iteration

Result: π^*, the optimal policy

Initialization: V chosen arbitrarily

repeat

    $\Delta \leftarrow 0$

    for $s \in S$ **do**

        $v \leftarrow V(s)$

        $V(s) \leftarrow \max_a \sum_{s'} P^a(s, s')(R^a(s, s') + \gamma V(s'))$

        $\Delta \leftarrow \max(\Delta, |v - V(s)|)$

until $\Delta < \theta$;

for $s \in S$ **do**

    $\pi(s) \leftarrow \operatorname{argmax}_a \sum_{s'} P^a(s, s')(R^a(s, s') + \gamma V(s'))$

A.2.3   Monte Carlo Methods

The following algorithms correspond to online learning methods that do not require any knowledge of the environment.

To estimate the value function V^π of a policy π, we must generate a sequence of actions and states with π, called an *episode*, compute the total reward at the end of this sequence, then update the estimate of V^π, V, for each state of the episode according to its contribution to the final reward, and repeat this process. One way to achieve this is to compute the average of the expected return from each state (Algorithm 5).

Algorithm 5: MC Policy Evaluation

Data: π, the policy to be evaluated

Result: $V \approx V^\pi$, an approximation of the value function of π

Initialization: V chosen arbitrarily

$$Returns(s) \leftarrow [], \forall s \in S$$

repeat

    $episode = generate\_episode(\pi)$

    for $s \in episode$ **do**

        $R \leftarrow$ Return following first occurrence of s

        $Returns(s).append(R)$

        $V(s) \leftarrow average(Returns(s))$

until;

When one has a model of the environment, state values alone are sufficient to determine a policy. At any state s, the action taken is:

$$\pi(s) \leftarrow \operatorname*{argmax}_a \sum_{s'} P^a(s, s')(R^a(s, s') + \gamma V(s')).$$

However, without a model, we will not have access to the state transition probabilities and/or the expected reward; therefore, we will not be able to find action a that maximizes the aforementioned expression. Therefore, action-value functions are necessary to find the optimal policy. If we are following a deterministic policy, many state-action pairs may never be visited. We present two different methods for addressing this problem: *exploring starts* [708] and *stochastic policies*. Similar to value iteration, the methods we present for *exploring starts* and *stochastic policies* do not wait to complete policy evaluation before doing policy improvement. Instead, policy evaluation and policy improvement are done every episode.

Under the *exploring starts* assumption, each episode starts at a state-action pair and every state-action pair has a nonzero chance of being the starting pair. This algorithm is shown in Algorithm 6.

The exploring starts assumption may often be infeasible in practice. To explore as many state-action pairs as possible, one must consider policies that are stochastic. We distinguish between two different types of policies: The policy that is used to generate episodes (the behavior policy) and the policy that is being evaluated and improved (the estimation policy). The behavior policy must be stochastic in order to ensure new state-action pairs are explored. There are two main types of methods that utilize *stochastic policies*: *on-policy* methods and *off-policy* methods. For *on-policy* methods, the behavior policy and the estimation policy are the same; therefore, the policy that is being evaluated and improved must also be stochastic. Algorithm 7 shows an *on-policy* MC algorithm that utilizes an *ε-greedy* policy: with probability ϵ it chooses an action at random, otherwise, it chooses the greedy action.

On the other hand, *off-policy* methods can have a behavior policy that is separate from the estimation policy. The behavior policy should still be stochastic and must have a nonzero probability of selecting all actions that the estimation policy might select, however, the estimation policy can be greedy and always select the action a at state s that maximizes $Q(s, a)$. The downside of *off-policy* methods is that policy improvement is slower because it can only learn from states where the behavior policy and the estimation policy take the same actions. Differences between *on-policy* and *off-policy* methods are discussed further in [708]. A well-known off-policy algorithm, Q-learning, will be presented in Section A.2.4.

REMARK A.6   The MC methods presented in this appendix are *first-visit* MC methods. The *first-visit* method averages the return following the first visit to a state s in an episode, in the case of MC policy evaluation, or following the first occurrence of the state-action pair s, a, in the case of MC exploring starts and MC on-policy control. There are also *every-visit* methods that use the return from every occurrence of s or s, a. However, these methods are less straightforward because of the introduction of bias [686].

A.2.4   Temporal Difference Methods

TD(0)

Whereas the Monte Carlo algorithms are constrained to wait for the end of an episode to update the value function, the TD(0) algorithm (Algorithm 8) is able to compute an

---

Algorithm 6: MC Exploring Starts

Result: π^*, the optimal policy

Initialization: Q chosen arbitrarily

                 π chosen arbitrarily

                 $Returns(s, a) \leftarrow []$, for all $s \in S$, for all $a \in \mathcal{A}(s)$

repeat

     episode = generate_episode_exploring_starts(π)

     for $s, a \in episode$ **do**

         $R \leftarrow$ Return following first occurrence of s, a

         $Returns(s, a).append(R)$

         $Q(s, a) \leftarrow$ average($Returns(s, a)$)

     for $s \in episode$ **do**

         $\pi(s) \leftarrow \text{argmax}_a Q(s, a)$

until;

Algorithm 7: MC On-Policy Control

Result: π^*, the optimal policy

Initialization: Q chosen arbitrarily

                 π chosen arbitrarily

                 $Returns(s, a) \leftarrow []$, for all $s \in S$, for all $a \in \mathcal{A}(s)$

repeat

     episode = generate_episode(π)

     for $s, a \in episode$ **do**

         $R \leftarrow$ Return following first occurrence of s, a

         $Returns(s, a).append(R)$

         $Q(s, a) \leftarrow$ average($Returns(s, a)$)

     for $s \in episode$ **do**

         $a^* \leftarrow \text{argmax}_a Q(s, a)$

         for $a \in \mathcal{A}(s)$ **do**

$$\pi(s, a) \leftarrow \begin{cases} 1 - \epsilon + \epsilon/|\mathcal{A}(s)| & \text{if } a = a^* \\ \epsilon/|\mathcal{A}(s)| & \text{if } a \neq a^* \end{cases}$$

until;

---

update after every step:

$$V(s_t) \leftarrow V(s_t) + \alpha \left[r_{t+1} + \gamma V(s_{t+1}) - V(s_t) \right].$$

When working with action–value functions, a well-known *off-policy* algorithm known as Q-learning (Algorithm 9) approximates Q^* regardless of the current policy:

$$Q(s_t, a_t) \leftarrow Q(s_t, a_t) + \alpha \left[r_{t+1} + \gamma \max_{a'} Q(s_{t+1}, a') - Q(s_t, a_t) \right]$$

Algorithm 8: TD(0)

Data: π, the policy to be evaluated

Result: $V \approx V^{\pi}$, an approximation of the value function of π

Initialization: V chosen arbitrarily

repeat

    $s \leftarrow get\_initial\_state()$

    while s *not terminal* **do**

        $a \leftarrow get\_action(\pi, s)$

        $s', r \leftarrow get\_next\_state(s, a)$

        $V(s) \leftarrow V(s) + \alpha(r + \gamma V(s') - V(s))$

        $s \leftarrow s'$

until;

Algorithm 9: Q-Learning

Result: π^*, the optimal policy

Initialization: Q chosen arbitrarily

repeat

    $s \leftarrow get\_initial\_state()$

    while s *not terminal* **do**

        $a \leftarrow get\_action(Q, s)$

        $s', r \leftarrow get\_next\_state(s, a)$

        $Q(s, a) \leftarrow Q(s, a) + \alpha(r + \gamma \max_{a'} Q(s', a') - Q(s, a))$

        $s \leftarrow s'$

until;

REMARK A.7   An on-policy variant of the Q-Learning algorithm, called the SARSA algorithm [628], consists of choosing a' with respect to the current policy for selecting the next action, rather than the max of the value function for the next state.

TD(λ) [forward view]

The TD(λ) algorithm, with λ chosen between 0 and 1, is a compromise between the full backup method of the Monte Carlo algorithm and the step-by-step update of the TD(0) algorithm. It relies on backups of episodes that are used to update each state, while assigning a greater importance to the very next step after each state.

We first define an n-step target:

$$R_t^{(n)} = \sum_{k=1}^{n} \gamma^{k-1} r_{t+k} + \gamma^n V(s_{t+n}).$$

Then, we can introduce the particular averaging of the TD(λ) algorithm on a state at time t in an episode ending at time T:

$$R_t^\lambda = (1 - \lambda) \sum_{n=1}^{T-t-1} \lambda^{n-1} R_t^{(n)} + \lambda^{T-t-1} R_t.$$

This can be expanded as:

$$
\begin{aligned}
R_t^\lambda = \ & (1 - \lambda)(r_{t+1} + \gamma V(s_{t+1})) \\
& + (1 - \lambda)\lambda(r_{t+1} + \gamma r_{t+2} + \gamma^2 V(s_{t+2})) \\
& + (1 - \lambda)\lambda^2(r_{t+1} + \gamma r_{t+2} + \gamma^2 r_{t+3} + \gamma^3 V(s_{t+2})) \\
& \ \vdots \\
& + \lambda^{T-t-1}(r_{t+1} + \gamma r_{t+2} + \gamma^2 r_{t+3} + \cdots + \gamma^{T-1} r_T).
\end{aligned}
$$

Finally, the update method used is:

$$V(s_t) \leftarrow V(s_t) + \alpha \left[R_t^\lambda - V(s_t) \right].$$

REMARK A.8   Notice that the sum of the weights $(1 - \lambda)\lambda^{n-1}$ and λ^{T-t-1} is equal to 1. Moreover:

- If $\lambda = 0$, the algorithm corresponds to TD(0).
- If $\lambda = 1$, the algorithm corresponds to the MC algorithm.

TD(λ) [backward view]

The previous description of TD(λ) illustrates the mechanism behind this method. However, it is not computationally tractable. Here, we describe an equivalent approach that leads to an efficient implementation.

We have to introduce for each state the *eligibility trace* $e_t(s)$ that represents how much the state will influence the update of a future encountered state in an episode:

$$
e_t(s) = \begin{cases}
0 & \text{if } t = 0 \\
\gamma \lambda e_{t-1}(s) & \text{if } t > 0 \text{ and } s \neq s_t \\
\gamma \lambda e_{t-1}(s) + 1 & \text{if } t > 0 \text{ and } s = s_t.
\end{cases}
$$

We can now define the update method to be applied at each step t to all states s_i:

$$V(s_i) \leftarrow V(s_i) + \alpha e_t(s_i) \left[r_{t+1} + \gamma V(s_{t+1}) - V(s_t) \right],$$

yielding Algorithm 10.

Actor–Critic Methods

Actor–Critic methods separate the policy and the value function into two distinct structures. The *actor*, or policy structure, is used to select actions; while the *critic*, or the estimated value function V, is used to criticize those actions in the form of a TD error:

$$\delta_t = r_{t+1} + \gamma V(s_{t+1}) - V(s_t).$$

A positive δ_t indicates that the policy's decision to take action a_t in state s_t should be strengthened, on the other hand, a negative δ_t indicates that the policy's decision should be weakened. In a simple case, if the policy for s_t and a_t is just a scalar $p(s_t, a_t)$ that

---

Algorithm 10: TD(λ)

Result: $V \approx V^{\pi}$, an approximation of the value function of π

Initialization: V chosen arbitrarily

$$e(s) = 0, \quad \forall s \in \mathcal{S}$$

repeat

    $s \leftarrow$ get_initial_state()

    while $s \notin$ *Terminal* **do**

        $a \leftarrow$ get_action(π, s)

        $s', r \leftarrow get\_next\_state(s, a)$

        $\delta \leftarrow r + \gamma V(s') - V(s)$

        $e(s) \leftarrow e(s) + 1$

        for $u \in \mathcal{S}$ **do**

            $V(u) \leftarrow V(u) + \alpha \delta e(u)$

            $e(u) \leftarrow \gamma \lambda e(u)$

        $s \leftarrow s'$

until;

---

is then normalized across all actions (i.e. using a softmax function), we can adjust the parameters of the policy using δ_t:

$$p(s_t, a_t) \leftarrow p(s_t, a_t) + \beta \delta_t (1 - \pi_t(s_t, a_t)),$$

where β is a positive scaling factor.

If $\pi_t(s_t, a_t)$ is a more complicated parameterized function, such as a deep neural network, then δ_t is used for computing gradients.

A.2.5 Planning

The key difference between dynamic programming methods and temporal difference methods is the use of a model. Dynamic programming methods use a model of the world to update the value of each state based on state transition probabilities and expectations of rewards. However, temporal difference methods achieve this through directly interacting with the environment.

A model produces a prediction about the future state and reward given a state–action pair. There are two main types of models: *distribution models* and *sample models*. A distribution model, like the one used in dynamic programming methods, produces all the possible next states with their corresponding probabilities and expected rewards, whereas a sample model only produces a sample next state and reward. Distribution models are more powerful than sample models; however, sample models can be more efficient in practice [708].

The benefit of a model is that one can simulate interactions with the environment, which is usually less costly than interacting directly with the environment itself. The downside is that a perfect model does not always exist. A model may have to be approximated by hand or learned through real-world interaction with the environment.

Any sub-optimal behavior in the model can lead to a sub-optimal policy. [707] presented an algorithm that combines reinforcement learning, model learning, and planning (Algorithm 11) [708]. This algorithm requires that the environment be deterministic. The resulting state and reward of each observed state-action pair is stored in the model. The agent can then use the model to improve the action-values associated with each previously seen state-action pair without having to interact with the environment.

Algorithm 11: Dyna-Q

Result: π^*, the optimal policy

Initialization: Q chosen arbitrarily

$\qquad\qquad\qquad$ $Model(s, a)$ chosen arbitrarily for all $s \in \mathcal{S}$, for all $a \in \mathcal{A}$

$\qquad\qquad\qquad$ N some positive integer

repeat

$\quad$ $s \leftarrow$ current (nonterminal) state

$\quad$ $a \leftarrow get\_action(Q, s)$

$\quad$ $s', r \leftarrow get\_next\_state(s, a)$

$\quad$ $Q(s, a) \leftarrow Q(s, a) + \alpha(r + \gamma \max_{a'} Q(s', a') - Q(s, a))$

$\quad$ $Model(s, a) \leftarrow s', r$

$\quad$ $n \leftarrow 0$

$\quad$ **repeat**

$\qquad$ $s \leftarrow$ random previously seen state

$\qquad$ $a \leftarrow$ random action previously taken in s

$\qquad$ $s', r \leftarrow Model(s, a)$

$\qquad$ $Q(s, a) \leftarrow Q(s, a) + \alpha(r + \gamma \max_{a'} Q(s', a') - Q(s, a))$

$\qquad$ $n \leftarrow n + 1$

$\quad$ **until** $n >= N$;

until;

A model can be used to improve a value function and policy or it can be used to pick better actions given the current value function and policy. Heuristic search does this by using the value function and policy as a "heuristic" to search the state-space in order to select better actions. Monte Carlo tree search (MCTS) [212, 416] is a heuristic search algorithm which uses a model to run simulations from the current state. When searching the state-space, the probability of selecting an action a in state s is influenced by the policy as well as the number of times that state-action pair has been selected. In order to encourage exploration, the probability of selecting a state-action pair goes down each time that pair is selected. Backed up values come from either running the simulation until the end of the episode or from the value of the leaf nodes.

A.2.6   Evolutionary Algorithms

We now turn to algorithms that search the policy space, starting with evolutionary algorithms. These algorithms mimic the biological evolution of populations under natural selection (see [518] for more details). In reinforcement learning applications, populations of policies are evolved using a *fitness function*. At each generation, the most fit policies have a better chance of surviving and producing offspring policies in the next generation.

The most straightforward way to represent a policy in an evolutionary algorithm is to use a single chromosome per policy, with a single gene associated with each observed state. Each allele (the value of a gene) represents the action-value associated with the corresponding state. The algorithm (Algorithm 12) first generates a population of policies $P(0)$, then selects the best ones according to a given criterin (*selection*), then randomly perturbs these policies (for instance by randomly selecting a state and then randomly perturbing the distribution of the actions given that state) (*mutation*). The algorithm may also create new policies by merging two different selected policies (*crossover*). This process is repeated until the selected policies satisfy a given criterin.

The fitness of a policy in the population is defined as the expected accumulated rewards for an agent that uses that policy. During the selection step, we keep either the policies with the highest fitness, or use a probabilistic choice in order to avoid local optima, such as:

$$Pr(p_i) = \frac{\text{fitness}(p_i)}{\sum_{j=1}^{n} \text{fitness}(p_j)}.$$

Algorithm 12: Evolutionary Algorithm

Result: $\pi \approx \pi^*$, an approximation of the optimal policy
Initialization: $t = 0$
                population $P(0)$ chosen arbitrarily
repeat
   | $t \leftarrow t + 1$
   | select $P(t)$ from $P(t-1)$
   | apply_mutation($P(t)$)
   | apply_crossover($P(t)$)
until;

A.2.7 Policy Gradient Algorithms

While other approaches tend to struggle with large or continuous state spaces, policy gradient algorithms offer a good alternative for complex environments solvable by relatively simple policies. Starting with an arbitrary policy, the idea behind policy gradient is to modify the policy such that it obtains the largest reward possible. For this purpose, a policy is represented by a parametric probability distribution $\pi_\theta(a|s) = P(a|s, \theta)$ such that in state s action a is selected according to the distribution $P(a|s, \theta)$. Hence, the objective here is to tune the parameter θ to increase the probability of choosing episodes associated with greater rewards. By computing the gradient of the average total return of a batch of episodes sampled from π_θ, we can use this value to update θ step-by-step. This approach is exploited in the REINFORCE algorithm [788].

A.3   Limitations and Open Problems

A.3.1   Complexity Considerations

So far, we have presented several ways of tackling the reinforcement learning problem in the framework of MDPs, but we have not described the theoretical tractability of this problem.

Recall that **P** is the class of all problems that can be solved in polynomial time, and **NC** the class of the problems that can be solved in polylogarithmic time on a parallel computer with a polynomial number of processors. As it seems very unlikely that **NC** = **P**, if a problem is proved to be **P**-complete, one can hardly expect to be able to find a parallel solution to this problem. In particular, it has been proved that the MDP problem is **P**-complete in the case of probabilistic transitions, and is in **NC** in the case of deterministic transitions, by [561]. Furthermore, in the case of high-dimensional MDPs, there exists a randomized algorithm [400] that is able to compute an arbitrary near-optimal policy in a time independent of the number of states.

REMARK A.9   Note that **NC** ⊆ **P**, simply because parallel computers can be simulated on a sequential machine.

Other results for the POMDP framework (see Section A.3.3) are presented in [455]. In particular:

- Computing an infinite (polynomial) horizon undiscounted optimal strategy for a deterministic POMDP is PSPACE-hard (NP-complete).
- Computing an infinite (polynomial) horizon undiscounted optimal strategy for a stochastic POMDP is EXPTIME-hard (PSPACE-complete).

A.3.2   Limitations of Markov Decision Processes (MDPs)

Despite its great convenience as a theoretical model, the MDP model suffers from major drawbacks when it comes to real-world implementations. Here we list the most important ones to highlight common pitfalls encountered in practical applications.

High-dimensional spaces   For high-dimensional spaces, typical of real-world control tasks, using a simple reinforcement learning framework becomes computationally intractable: this phenomenon is known as the *curse of dimensionality*. We can limit this by reducing the dimensionality of the problem [747], or by replacing the lookup table by a *function approximator* [163]. However, some precautions may need to be taken to ensure convergence [143].

Continuous spaces   A variety of real world problems lead to continuous state spaces or action spaces, yet it is not possible to store an arbitrary continuous function. To address this problem, one has to use *function approximators* [643] to obtain tractable models, value functions, or policies. Two common techniques are *tile coding* [672] and fuzzy representation of the space [451].

Convergence While we have good guarantees on the convergence of reinforcement learning methods with lookup tables and linear approximators, our knowledge of the conditions for convergence with non-linear approximators is still very limited [735]. This is unfortunate because non-linear approximators are the most convenient and have been very successful on problems like playing backgammon [723].

Speed One way to speed up the convergence of reinforcement learning algorithms is to modify the reward function during learning to provide guidance toward good policies. This technique, called *shaping*, has been successfully applied to the problem of bike riding, which would not have been tractable without this improvement [603].

Stability Highly dependent on the parameters, the stability of the process of computing an optimal policy has not been studied sufficiently. However, it is a key element in the success of a learning strategy. Stability and stability guarantees have been studied in the context of kernel-based reinforcement learning methods [555].

Exploration vs Exploitation To learn efficiently, an agent in general should navigate the tradeoff between exploration and exploitation. Common heuristics such as ϵ-greedy and Boltzmann (softmax) provide means for addressing this trade-off, yet suffer from major drawbacks in terms of convergence speed and implementation (the choice of the parameters is non-trivial). The R-max algorithm [147], relying on the *optimism under uncertainty* bias, and model-based Bayesian exploration [233] offer convenient alternatives for the *exploration-exploitation dilemma*.

Initialization The choice of the initial policy, or the initial value function, may influence not only whether the algorithm converges, but also the speed of convergence. In some cases, for example, choosing a random initialization leads to drastically long computational times. One way to tackle this issue is to learn first using a simpler but similar task, and then use this knowledge to influence the learning process of the main task. This is the core principle of *transfer learning* which can lead to significant improvements, as shown in [722].

A.3.3   The POMDP Model

The partially observable Markov decision process (POMDP) [810] is a generalization of the MDP model in which the learning agent does not know precisely the current state in which it is operating. Instead, its knowledge relies on *observations* derived from its environment. Formally, a POMDP is an MDP with a finite set of possible observations $\mathcal{Z}$ and an observation model based on the probability $\nu(z|s)$ of observing z when the environment is in state s.

It has been shown in [685], that directly applying the MDP methods to this problem can have arbitrarily poor performance. To address this problem, one has to introduce an internal state distribution for the agent, the *belief state* $b_t(s)$, that represents the probability of being in state s at time t (see Figure A.4). One can then theoretically

Figure A.4 The POMDP model

find an optimal solution to a POMDP problem [174] by defining an equivalent MDP problem, as shown below, and use existing MDP algorithms to solve it.

Assuming that the initial belief state b_0 is known, one can iteratively compute the belief state at any time $t + 1$. We denote this operation by $F(b_t, a_t, z_t) = b_{t+1}$ with:

$$b_{t+1}(s') = \frac{v(z_t|s') \sum_{s \in S} b_t(s) P_{a_t}(s, s')}{\sum_{s' \in S} v(z|s') \sum_{s \in S} b_t(s) P_{a_t}(s, s')}.$$

The rewards are then given by:

$$\bar{r}(b) = \sum_{s \in S} b(s) r(s).$$

In order to compute the transition function, let us first introduce the probability of observing z by applying action a in belief state b:

$$Pr(z|a, b) = \sum_{s' \in S} v(z|s') \sum_{s \in S} b(s) P_a(s, s').$$

Hence, we can define a transition probability function for the POMDP by:

$$\bar{P}_a(b, b') = \sum_{\substack{z \in Z \\ F(b_t, a_t, z_t) = b_{t+1}}} Pr(z_t|a_t, b_t).$$

If $\mathcal{B}$ represents the set of belief states, the value function can then be computed as:

$$\bar{V}_{t+1}(b') = \max_a \left[\bar{r}(b') + \gamma \sum_{b \in \mathcal{B}} \bar{P}_a(b, b') \bar{V}_t(b) \right].$$

REMARK A.10   This approach is obviously quite limited because of the potentially infinite size of $\mathcal{B}$. Several algorithms have been proposed to improve this, such as region-based pruning [272] and point-based algorithms [694], but they are also unable to deal with very large state spaces. VDCBPI [586] is one of the few efficient heuristics that seems to be able to find reasonable approximate solutions.

A.3.4   Multi-Agent Paradigm

There are several reasons for studying the case of multiple agents interacting with each other and seeking to maximize their rewards in a reinforcement learning fashion [162].

Many problems in areas as diverse as robotics, control, game theory, and population modeling lend themselves to such a modeling approach. Furthermore, the ability to parallelize learning across multiple agents is also attractive for several reasons, including speed and robustness. In particular, one may expect that if a particular agent fails, the other agents may be able to adapt without leading to a system-wide failure. Lastly, one may be able to improve or speed up learning of similar tasks by sharing experiences between individual learners (*transfer learning*).

However, as can be expected, the multi-agent model comes with significant challenges. By definition the multi-agent model has more variables and thus the curse of dimensionality is heightened. Furthermore, the environment model is more complex and suffers from non-stationarity during learning because of the constantly evolving behavior of each agent, and the problem of coordination between agents in order to achieve the desired results.

The starting model for the multi-agent paradigm corresponds to a *stochastic game*. For a system with n agents, it is composed of a set of states X, the sets of actions U_i for each agent $i = 1, \ldots, n$ (we let $\mathbf{U} = U_1 \times \cdots \times U_n$), the state transition function $f : X \times \mathbf{U} \times X \to [0, 1]$ and the reward function $\rho_i : X \times \mathbf{U} \times X \to \mathbb{R}$.

There is a large literature with different methods suitable for different multi-agent settings. The two major characteristics of such algorithms are their stability, which is related to their ability to converge to a stationary policy, and their adaptation, which measures how well the agents react to a change in the policy. Usually, it is difficult to guarantee both, and one must favor one over the other. The relationships between the agents can be classified in several classes, including:

- Fully cooperative: all the agents share a common set of objectives that have to be maximized. The *optimal adaptive learning* algorithm [778] has been proven to converge to an optimal Nash equilibrium (a configuration where no agent can improve its expected payoff by deviating to a different strategy) with probability 1. Good experimental results have also been obtained with the *coordinated reinforcement learning* approach [321].

- Fully competitive: the success of each agent directly depends on the failure of the other agents. For such settings, the minimax-Q [454] algorithm has been proposed, combining the minimax strategy (acting optimally while considering that the adversary will also act optimally) with the Q-learning method.

- Mixed: each agent has its own goal. As the objectives of this scenario are not well defined, there exist a significant number of approaches designed to tackle various formulations of this setting. An attempt to organize and clarify this case has been proposed in [587], for instance, along with a comparison of the most popular methods.

A.4   Other Directions of Research

A.4.1   Inverse Reinforcement Learning

Inverse reinforcement learning is the task of determining the reward function given an observed behavior. This observed behavior can be an optimal policy or a teacher's demonstration. Thus, the objective here is to estimate the reward attribution such that when reinforcement learning is applied with that reward function, one obtains the original behavior (in the case of behaviors associated with optimal policies), or even a better one (in the case of demonstrations).

This is particularly relevant in a situation where an expert has the ability to execute a given task but is unable, due to the complexity of the task and the domain, to precisely define the reward attribution that would lead to an optimal policy. One of the most significant success stories of inverse reinforcement learning is the apprenticeship of self driving cars [6].

To solve this problem in the case of MDPs, [536] identifies inequalities such that any reward function satisfying them must lead to an optimal policy. In order to avoid trivial answers, such as the all-zero reward function, these authors propose to use linear programming to identify the reward function that would maximize the difference between the value of an optimal action and the value of the next-best action in the same state. It is also possible to add regularization on the reward function to make it simpler (typically with non-zero reward on few actions). Systematic applications of inverse reinforcement learning in the case of POMDPs have not yet been developed.

A.4.2   Hierarchical Reinforcement Learning

In order to improve the time of convergence of reinforcement learning algorithms, different approaches for reducing the dimensionality of the problem have been proposed. In some cases, these approaches extend the MDP model to semi-Markov Decision Process (SMDP), by relaxing the Markov property, i.e. policies may base their choices on more than just the current state.

The *option* method [709] makes use of local policies that focus on simpler tasks. Hence, along with actions, a policy π can choose an option O. When the option O is chosen, a special policy μ associated with O is followed until a stochastic stop condition over the states and depending on O is reached. After the stop condition is reached, the policy π is resumed. The reward associated with O is the sum of the rewards of the actions performed under μ discounted by γ^τ were τ is the number of steps needed to terminate the option O. These option policies can be defined by an expert, or learned. There has been some work to try to automate this process of creating relevant options, or deleting useless ones [493].

State abstraction [33], used in the MAXQ algorithm [241] and in *hierarchical abstract machines* [563], is a mapping of the problem representation to a new representation that preserves some of its properties, in particular those needed for learning an optimal policy.

A.4.3   Approximate Linear Programming

As noted before, the linear programming approach to reinforcement learning typically suffers from the curse of dimensionality: the large number of states leads to an intractable number of variables for applying exact linear programming. A common way to overcome this issue is to approximate the cost-to-go function [230] by carefully designing some basis functions $\phi_1, \ldots, \phi_K$ that map the state space to rewards, and then constructing a linearly parameterized cost-to-go function:

$$\tilde{J}(\cdot, r) = \sum_{k=1}^{K} r_k \phi_k,$$

where r is a parameter vector to be approximated by linear programming. In this way, the number of variables of the problem is drastically reduced, from the original number of states to K. The work in [366] proposes automated methods for generating a suitable basis functions ϕ for a given problem.

     Using a *dynamic Bayesian network* to represent the transition model leads to the concept of *factored MDP* that can lead to reduced computational times on problems with a large number of states [320].

A.4.4   Relational Reinforcement Learning

Relational reinforcement learning [249] combines reinforcement learning with a relational representation of the state space, for instance by using inductive logic programming [520]. The goal is to propose a formalism that is able to perform well on problems requiring a large number of states, but can be represented compactly using a relational representation. In particular, experiments highlight the ability of this approach to take advantage of learning on simple tasks to accelerate the learning on more complex ones. This representation allows the learning of more "abstract" concepts, which leads to a reduced number of states that can significantly benefit generalization.

A.4.5   Quantum Reinforcement Learning

By taking advantage of the properties of quantum superposition, there is a possibility for considering novel quantum algorithms for reinforcement learning. The study in [245] presents potentially promising results, through simulated experiments, in regards to the speed of convergence and the trade-off between exploration and exploitation. Much work remains to be done in relation to modeling the environment, implementing function approximations, and deriving theoretical guarantees for quantum reinforcement learning.

A.5   Deep Reinforcement Learning

It is natural to try to combine deep learning with reinforcement learning, possibly also in combination with frameworks for massively distributed reinforcement learning, such

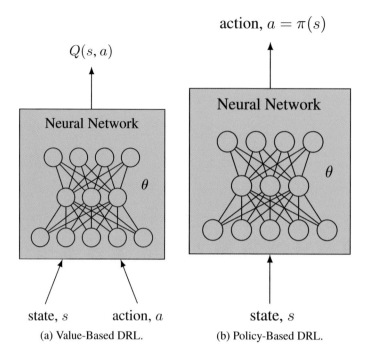

(a) Value-Based DRL.

(b) Policy-Based DRL.

Figure A.5 Deep reinforcement learning uses deep neural networks to approximate functions used in reinforcement learning. Shown here are two examples of such functions.

as Gorila [528]. Deep neural networks can be used to approximate value or policy functions, as shown in Figure A.5; furthermore, deep neural networks can also be used to approximate environment models. While the combination of reinforcement learning with function approximation has been explored in detail over two decades ago [126], the recent success of deep learning has led to a rapid expansion of deep reinforcement learning applications. For instance, deep reinforcement learning has been used to learn how to play the game of Go. The early work in [791, 792] used deep learning methods, in the form of recursive grid neural networks, to evaluate the board or decide the next move. One characteristic of this approach is the ability to transfer learning between different board sizes (e.g. learn from games played on 9×9 or 11×11 boards and transfer the knowledge to larger boards). More recently, reinforcement learning combined with large convolutional neural networks has been used to achieve the AI milestone of building an automated Go player [678, 681] that can outperform human experts.

A.5.1   Model-Free Deep Reinforcement Learning

The early successes of modern deep reinforcement learning came from using deep neural networks to represent action-value functions. In [511], Deep Q-networks that combined Q-learning with deep neural networks are used to teach an agent to play Atari video games without any game-specific feature engineering. In this case, the *state* is represented by the stack of four previous frames, with the deep network consisting of multiple convolutional and fully-connected layers, and the action consisting of the 18 joystick positions. Since directly using neural networks as the function approximator leads to instability or divergence, this work used additional heuristics to address these problems, such as replaying histories to reduce correlations, or using updates that change the parameters only periodically. Agents using this approach learned to play the majority of the games at a level equal or better than the level of professional human players for the same game. There has been subsequent work to improve this approach, such as addressing stability [116], and applying Double Q-Learning [330] to avoid overestimation of the action-value functions in Deep Q-Networks [748]. Other extensions include multi-task learning [651, 632], and rapid learning [134], among others. The work in [510] also investigated asynchronous versions of Q-learning, SARSA, and actor-critic, showing that, in certain cases, it is more efficient to train deep reinforcement learning algorithms using many CPUs instead of just one GPU.

Model-free reinforcement learning has also been applied to many control tasks. Policy-gradient methods, such as trust region policy optimization [660] and proximal policy optimization [662], have been able to learn control policies in simulated environments. The deterministic policy gradient, proposed by [680] and subsequently extended to deep representations by [450], were shown to be more efficient than their stochastic variants, thus directly extending deep reinforcement learning to continuous action spaces. Building off of this work, algorithms such as TD3 [285] and soft actor-critic [326] have also been successful at control tasks.

A.5.2   Model-Based Deep Reinforcement Learning

With the use of a model, planning algorithms can be used to help decide the next move by considering future possibilities. Monte Carlo tree search (MCTS) has been combined with value and policy networks to improve the value and policy networks themselves. When applying deep reinforcement learning to Go, the work in [678] mainly used the MCTS algorithm for action selection, while the value and policy networks relied heavily on examples from games between human experts. However, the work in [681] used MCTS to train a value and policy network from scratch by using the heuristic search algorithm for self-play, which resulted in an agent that outperformed all previous Go agents. This approach was also used to learn how to play chess and shogi [679].

As shown in Figure A.3, access to a model allows us to use algorithms, such as value iteration, that rely on a model of the environment. Value iteration with deep neural networks was used to create DeepCubeA, an algorithm that learned to solve puzzles, such as the Rubik's cube and sliding tile puzzles without human guidance [489, 14] (Figure A.6). These puzzles, or single-player games, are characterized by very large state spaces with single or very few goal states unreachable through random play. The learned value function served as a heuristic with which to guide search algorithms such as MCTS and A* search [329]. Furthermore, despite the large state spaces of these puzzles (i.e. the Rubik's cube has 4.3×10^{19} possible configurations), in the majority of cases, DeepCubeA was able to solve these puzzles in the most efficient way possible.

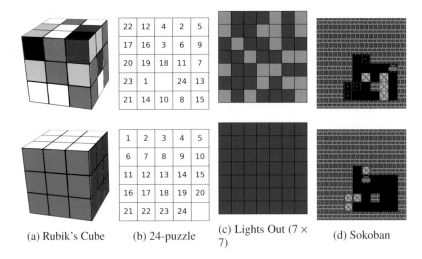

(a) Rubik's Cube   (b) 24-puzzle   (c) Lights Out (7 × 7)   (d) Sokoban

Figure A.6 A visualization of a scrambled state (top) and the goal state (bottom) for four of the puzzles investigated in [14] (see also exercises).

While deep learning can be used to learn a value function or policy function, it can also be used to learn a model of the environment. In 11, a look-up table served as the model of the environment. However, representing high-dimensional environments, such as visual scenes, with a simple look-up table is unfeasible. To address this issue, deep neural networks have been trained to predict the next state and the reward given a state-action pair and, thus, perform the task of the model. When the environment takes the form of an image, deep neural networks have been shown to be able to produce realistic images that the agent can use to plan [781, 548, 439, 190, 565, 594]. However, the predicted images are sometimes noisy and are sometimes missing key elements of the state. An alternative approach is to use a deep neural network to encode the current state into an abstract state and then, given an action, learn to predict the next abstract state along with its value and reward [682, 549]. Furthermore, learning a model can reduce the number of real-world environment interactions needed for proper learning [51], also referred to as the sample complexity. This is very valuable when environment interactions are expensive. Model learning has been successfully applied in domains such as video games [325, 390] and robotics [572], significantly reducing the sample complexity.

A.6   Exercises

EXERCISE A.1   Develop and implement a deep reinforcement learning strategy to solve any of the following combinatorial puzzles (single-player games):
(1) $3 \times 3 \times 3$ Rubik's cube;
(2) $4 \times 4 \times 4$ Rubik's cube;
(3) $2 \times 2 \times 2 \times 2$ Rubik's cube;

(4) n-puzzle for $n = 15, 24, 35, 48$;

(5) $n \times n$ LightsOut for $n = 7$;

(6) Sokoban;

(7) Towers of Hanoi with three pegs and n disks, for increasing values of n.

EXERCISE A.2 Develop and implement a deep reinforcement learning strategy to solve any of the following two-player games:

(1) Backgammon;

(2) Chess;

(3) GO on a $n \times n$ board, with $n = 9, 11, 13, 15, 17$ or 19.

Appendix B Hints and Remarks for Selected Exercises

Chapter 1

EXERCISE 1.1: For example, consider DNA computing.

EXERCISE 1.3: What else there is? Consider, for instance, communicating information using mechanical forces (e.g. sound).

Chapter 2

EXERCISE 2.1: First, to be thorough, you should do this this exercise for both linear threshold functions and linear threshold gates. Second, you should consider the case of feedforward networks and the case of fully recurrent networks (every neuron connected to every other neuron). Finally, in the feedforward case, you should distinguish two subcases, depending on whether the input vectors are identical in both networks, or whether the input vectors are also transformed.

EXERCISE 2.3: This situation occurs in an $A(1, 1, \ldots, 1)$ architecture where the units have logistic or tanh transfer functions.

EXERCISE 2.6: Note that on the $\{0, 1\}^n$ hypercube, for any coordinate x_i, $x_i^2 = x_i$. Likewise, on the $\{-1, +1\}^n$ hypercube, $x_i^2 = 1$. Thus, for example, a degree 3 homogeneous polynomial in H^n may only contain terms of the form $x_i x_j x_k$, whereas a degree 3 homogeneous polynomial in $\mathbb{R}^n$ may also contain other terms of the form $x_i^2 x_j$.

EXERCISE 2.16: For example, meta-learning (learning to learn), active learning, curriculum learning, self-paced learning.

Chapter 3

EXERCISE 3.6: Provide two different proofs: (1) by first proving the results for the basic Boolean operators (e.g. AND and NOT); (2) by using the disjunctive or conjunctive normal form.

EXERCISE 3.8: Use nested induction for the number m of objects (regions, hyperplanes) and the overall dimension n. A set of k points in $\mathbb{R}^n$ is in general position if it contains no two points that are identical, no three points that are on a line (subspace of dimension 1), no four points that are on a plane (subspace of dimension 2), no five points that are contained in a subspace of dimension 3, and so forth.

EXERCISE 3.11: Prove that $P_{n,K}$ satisfies the recurrence relation:

$$P_{n,K} = \frac{1}{2}(P_{n,K-1} + P_{n-1,K-1}), \tag{B.1}$$

then solve the recurrence. Note that a special case of this theorem corresponds to K points scattered at random over the unit sphere in n-dimensional space. Finally, note also that the expression for $P_{n,K}$ corresponds to the probability that in tossing a fair coin, the nth head occurs on or after the Kth toss. Can you find a correspondence between the two problems?

EXERCISE 3.18: This is one way of defining the capacity of a ReLU unit.

EXERCISE 3.23: Fix any two points x and y and consider the random projection $f(x - y)$ and its norm. Then apply the union bound to all the pairs of points among the K points ($\sim K^2$ pairs). This exercise requires some knowledge of high-dimensional probability. Initially, as a simplifying assumption, you can assume that a random subspace of dimension m is selected using $m \times n$ i.i.d. samples of a symmetric Bernoulli distribution.

Chapter 4

EXERCISE 4.3: For example, consider computing parity over the first two bits, then three bits, then four bits, etc. using skip connections.

Chapter 5

EXERCISE 5.2: In matrix form, the derivative is given by the product of a postsynaptic vector by the transpose of a presynaptic vector. On a single input training vector x, the presynaptic vector is x for the matrix B and Bx for the matrix A.

EXERCISE 5.5: To the best of my knowledge, the last question has remained open for the past four decades.

EXERCISE 5.16: Consider also the case of Bernoulli distributions.

Chapter 6

EXERCISE 6.4: To prove the first inequality, multiply both sides by the term $(n/N)^n$, then modify this term in the left-hand side so that you can apply the binomial theorem.

EXERCISE   6.8: Let I_j denote the jth component of the input vector, and S_k^1 denote the activation of the kth unit in the first layer after the input. Use the chain rule to write an expression for $\partial \mathcal{E}/\partial I_j$ and leverage the backpropagation algorithm to compute it effectively.

EXERCISE   6.20: Show that the logistic and constant functions in the Theorem satisfy the property. Then consider a distribution concentrated on two points and analyze the consequences of the equality condition.

Chapter 7

EXERCISE   7.2: Ctrl-Alt-End.

EXERCISE   7.4: For instance, in the unsupervised case, the learning rule must have the form: $\Delta w_i = F(I_i, w_i)$ where F is a polynomial of degree $d = 2$. So, in general: $\Delta w_i = a_{11}I_i^2 + a_{12}I_iw_i + a_{22}w_i^2 + a_{10}I_i + a_{01}w_i + a_{00}$. In the supervised case, the rule must have the form: $\Delta w_i = F(I_i, T, w_i)$ where F is a polynomial of degree $d = 2$.

EXERCISE   7.6: Include a damping term or a term that forces the derivative to be zero when the weights reach a certain size (assuming they are initialized to small values).

Chapter 8

EXERCISE   8.3: First write the learning rule for each weight as a product of a presynaptic activation by a (randomly) backpropagated error. Then convert it to a differential equation assuming the learning rate is small. Then analyze the corresponding system by reducing its dimension (eliminating variables) and looking at the points where all derivatives are equal to zero.

EXERCISE   8.4: As usual, first write the learning rule for each weight as a product of a presynaptic activation by a (randomly) backpropagated error. Then convert it to a differential equation assuming the learning rate is small. Then analyze the corresponding system by reducing its dimension (eliminating variables) and looking at the points where all derivatives are equal to zero. For any differential equation of the form $da/dt = f(a)$ with $a(0) = a_0$, where f is a polynomial, its qualitative behavior can visually be understood by plotting the function f, the points where $f(a) = 0$, and the asymptotic behavior of f (which depends on the degree of f and the sign of its leading coefficient).

EXERCISE   8.5: Same hint as for Exercise 8.4.

EXERCISE   8.11: For instance, use the average or any convex combination of activities across cycles.

Chapter 9

EXERCISE 9.3: The units correspond to polynomial threshold units of degree $d - 1$.

EXERCISE 9.5: The time derivative of S_i or O_i must be proportional to $\partial \mathcal{E} / \partial O_i$.

EXERCISE 9.6: If preferable, you can work with other NP-hard problems.

EXERCISE 9.8: Incidentally, the number of acyclic orientations of a graph is obtained from its chromatic polynomial evaluated at -1. For the hypercube, the total number of orientations can be estimated more directly. With an energy function of degree d over the n-dimensional hypercube, each neuron operates as a polynomial threshold gate of degree $d-1$ in n variables. And we have bounds and asymptotic estimates for the number of polynomial threshold gates of degree $d - 1$ in n variables.

EXERCISE 9.10: Over the hypercube $\{-1, +1\}^n$, there are 2^n states playing a symmetric role. Estimate the probability that one of them is stable, for instance the state where all n of the units are in state $+1$.

EXERCISE 9.11: For a given memory, which you can take to be the vector with n components equal to $+1$ (why?), estimate the corresponding signal and noise for each unit.

EXERCISE 9.12: Again begin by estimating the signal and noise for each unit, and across all K memories.

Chapter 10

EXERCISE 10.6: Note that contact map prediction is a 1D to 2D problem which is converted into a 2D to 2D problem by writing the same 1D sequence along the horizontal and vertical axis.

EXERCISE 10.8: An example where this situation could occur is in the prediction of contacts between two different protein chains.

EXERCISE 10.11: Going from a sequence to a labeled tree occurs, for instance, in parsing. Going from a labeled tree to a labeled tree occurs, for instance, in "translation", when going from the parse tree of a sentence to the parse tree of its translation. Going from a labeled set to a sequence occurs, for instance, when a set of integers is ordered.

Appendix A

EXERCISE A.1: An additional challenge, rather than a hint, is to develop a *symmetric* strategy for solving the Rubik's cube, so that symmetric starting positions are solved in symmetric ways. The first published solution to the Rubik's cube using deep reinforcement learning is only *approximately* symmetric.

References

[1] Morad Aaboud, Georges Aad, Brad Abbott, Dale Charles Abbott, Ovsat Abdinov, Deshan Kavishka Abhayasinghe, Syed Haider Abidi, O.S. AbouZeid, N.L. Abraham, Halina Abramowicz, et al. Constraints on mediator-based dark matter and scalar dark energy model using $\sqrt{s}$ = 13 TeV pp colliion data collected by the ATLAS detector. *Journal of High Energy Physics*, 5:142, 2019.

[2] Georges Aad, J.M. Butterworth, J. Thion, U. Bratzler, P.N. Ratoff, R.B. Nickerson, J.M. Seixas, I. Grabowska-Bold, F. Meisel, S. Lokwitz, et al. The ATLAS experiment at the CERN large hadron collider. *Journal of Instrumentation*, 3:S08003, 2008.

[3] Georges Aad, Alexander Kupco, Samuel Webb, Timo Dreyer, Yufeng Wang, Karl Jakobs, Martin Spousta, Marina Cobal, Peilong Wang, Stefan Schmitt, et al. Measurement of the CP-violating phase phi_s in $b_s^0 \rightarrow j/\psi\phi$ decays in ATLAS at 13 tev. Technical report, ATLAS-BPHY-2018-01-003, 2020.

[4] Enrique Abad, Roland K. Zenn, and Johannes Kästner. Reaction mechanism of monoamine oxidase from qm/mm calculations. *The Journal of Physical Chemistry B*, 117(46):14238–14246, 2013. PMID: 24164690.

[5] Emmanuel Abbe, Amir Shpilka, and Avi Wigderson. Reed–Muller codes for random erasures and errors. *IEEE Transactions on Information Theory*, 61(10):5229–5252, 2015.

[6] Pieter Abbeel and Andrew Y. Ng. Apprenticeship learning via inverse reinforcement learning. In *Proceedings of the Twenty-First International Conference on Machine Learning*, page 1. ACM, 2004.

[7] A. Abdesselam et al. Boosted objects: A Probe of beyond the Standard Model physics. *Eur. Phys. J.*, C71:1661, 2011.

[8] Yaser Abu-Mostafa and J. St. Jacques. Information capacity of the Hopfield model. *IEEE Transactions on Information Theory*, 31(4):461–464, 1985.

[9] D.H. Ackley, G.E. Hinton, and T.J. Sejnowski. A learning algorithm for Boltzmann machines. *Cognitive Science*, 9:147–169, 1985.

[10] D. Adams, A. Arce, L. Asquith, M. Backovic, T. Barillari, et al. Towards an understanding of the correlations in jet substructure. *Eur. Phys. J. C* 75: 409 (2015).

[11] Stefano Aghion, O. Ahlén, C. Amsler, A. Ariga, T. Ariga, A.S. Belov, Karl Berggren, G. Bonomi, P. Bräunig, J. Bremer, et al. A moiré deflectometer for antimatter. *Nature Communications*, 5(1):1–6, 2014.

[12] F. Agostinelli, N. Ceglia, B. Shahbaba, P. Sassone-Corsi, and P. Baldi. What time is it? Deep learning approaches for circadian rhythms. *Bioinformatics*, 32(12):i8–i17, 2016.

[13] Forest Agostinelli, Matthew Hoffman, Peter Sadowski, and Pierre Baldi. Learning activation functions to improve deep neural networks. arXiv:1412.6830, 2014.

[14] Forest Agostinelli, Stephen McAleer, Alexander Shmakov, and Pierre Baldi. Solving the Rubik's cube with deep reinforcement learning and search. *Nature Machine Intelligence*, 1(8):356–363, 2019.

[15] D.K. Agrafiotis, V.S. Lobanov, and F.R. Salemme. Combinatorial informatics in the post-genomics era. *Nature Reviews Drug Discovery*, 1:337–346, 2002.

[16] M. Ajello, A. Albert, W.B. Atwood, G. Barbiellini, D. Bastieri, K. Bechtol, Ronaldo Bellazzini, E. Bissaldi, R.D. Blandford, E.D. Bloom, et al. Fermi-lat observations of high-energy γ-ray emission toward the galactic center. *The Astrophysical Journal*, 819(1):44, 2016.

[17] Babak Alipanahi, Andrew Delong, Matthew T. Weirauch, and Brendan J. Frey. Predicting the sequence specificities of DNA- and RNA-binding proteins by deep learning. *Nat. Biotechnol.*, 33(8):831–8, Aug 2015.

[18] Josh Alman, Timothy M. Chan, and Ryan Williams. Polynomial representations of threshold functions and algorithmic applications. In *2016 IEEE 57th Annual Symposium on Foundations of Computer Science (FOCS)*, pages 467–476. IEEE, 2016.

[19] A. Altheimer et al. Jet substructure at the Tevatron and LHC: new results, new tools, new benchmarks. *J. Phys.*, G39:063001, 2012.

[20] A. Altheimer et al. Boosted objects and jet substructure at the LHC. Report of BOOST2012, held at IFIC Valencia, 23rd-27th of July 2012. *Eur. Phys. J.*, C74(3):2792, 2014.

[21] Johan Alwall et al. MadGraph 5: Going Beyond. *JHEP*, 1106:128, 2011.

[22] Shun-Ichi Amari. Characteristics of random nets of analog neuron-like elements. *IEEE Transactions on Systems, Man, and Cybernetics*, (5):643–657, 1972.

[23] Shun-Ichi Amari. Topographic organization of nerve fields. *Bulletin of Mathematical Biology*, 42(3):339–364, 1980.

[24] Shun-ichi Amari. *Information Geometry and Its applications*, Springer, 2016.

[25] Daniel J. Amit, Hanoch Gutfreund, and Haim Sompolinsky. Spin-glass models of neural networks. *Physical Review A*, 32(2):1007, 1985.

[26] Daniel J. Amit, Hanoch Gutfreund, and Haim Sompolinsky. Storing infinite numbers of patterns in a spin-glass model of neural networks. *Physical Review Letters*, 55(14):1530, 1985.

[27] Daniel J. Amit, Hanoch Gutfreund, and Haim Sompolinsky. Information storage in neural networks with low levels of activity. *Physical Review A*, 35(5):2293, 1987.

[28] Daniel J. Amit, Hanoch Gutfreund, and Haim Sompolinsky. Statistical mechanics of neural networks near saturation. *Annals of physics*, 173(1):30–67, 1987.

[29] C. Amole et al. Description and first application of a new technique to measure the gravitational mass of antihydrogen. *Nature Communications*, 4:1785, 2013.

[30] C. Amole et al. The alpha antihydrogen trapping apparatus. *Nucl. Instr. Meth. A*, 735:319–340, 2014.

[31] M. Amoretti et al. The athena antihydrogen apparatus. *Nucl. Instr. Meth. A*, 518:679–711, 2004.

[32] Charles W. Anderson. Learning to control an inverted pendulum using neural networks. *Control Systems Magazine, IEEE*, 9(3):31–37, 1989.

[33] David Andre and Stuart J. Russell. State abstraction for programmable reinforcement learning agents. In *AAAI/IAAI*, pages 119–125, 2002.

[34] Milica Andrejić and Ricardo A. Mata. Local hybrid qm/qm calculations of reaction pathways in metallobiosites. *Journal of Chemical Theory and Computation*, 10(12):5397–5404, 2014. PMID: 26583223.

[35] G.B. Andresen et al. Confinement of antihydrogen for 1,000 seconds. *Nat. Phys.*, 7:558–564, 2011.

[36] G.B. Andresen, M.D. Ashkezari, M. Baquero-Ruiz, W. Bertsche, Paul David Bowe, E. Butler, C.L. Cesar, S. Chapman, M. Charlton, A. Deller, et al. Trapped antihydrogen. *Nature*, 468(7324):673–676, 2010.

[37] Alessio Andronico, Arlo Randall, Ryan W. Benz, and Pierre Baldi. Data-Driven High-Throughput prediction of the 3-D structure of small molecules: Review and progress. *Journal of Chemical Information and Modeling*, 51(4):760–776, April 2011.

[38] Christof Angermueller, Heather J. Lee, Wolf Reik, and Oliver Stegle. Deepcpg: accurate prediction of single-cell DNA methylation states using deep learning. *Genome Biol.*, 18(1):67, Apr 2017.

[39] Martin Anthony. Classification by polynomial surfaces. *Discrete Applied Mathematics*, 61(2):91–103, 1995.

[40] Martin Anthony. *Discrete Mathematics of Neural Networks: Selected Topics*. SIAM, 2001.

[41] Elena Aprile, J. Aalbers, F. Agostini, M. Alfonsi, F.D. Amaro, M. Anthony, B. Antunes, F. Arneodo, M. Balata, P. Barrow, et al. The XENON1T dark matter experiment. *The European Physical Journal C*, 77(12):881, 2017.

[42] Forough Arabshahi, Sameer Singh, and Animashree Anandkumar. Combining symbolic expressions and black-box function evaluations for training neural programs. In *International Conference on Learning Representations (ICLR)*, 2018.

[43] Forough Arabshahi, Sameer Singh, and Animashree Anandkumar. Towards solving differential equations through neural programming. In *ICML Workshop on Neural Abstract Machines and Program Induction (NAMPI)*, 2018.

[44] S. Arimoto. An algorithm for computing the capacity of arbitrary discrete memoryless channels. *Information Theory, IEEE Transactions on*, 18(1):14–20, 1972.

[45] Vladimir I. Arnold. On functions of three variables. In *Dokl. Akad. Nauk SSSR*, volume 114, pages 679–681, 1957.

[46] Sanjeev Arora and Boaz Barak. *Computational Complexity: A Modern Approach*. Cambridge University Press, 2009.

[47] M. Aschbacher, P. Baldi, E.B. Baum, and R.M. Wilson. Embeddings of ultrametric spaces in finite-dimensional structures. *SIAM Journal of Algebraic and Discrete Methods*, 8(4):564–577, 1987.

[48] E. Asgari and M.R.K. Mofrad. Continuous distributed representation of biological sequences for deep proteomics and genomics. *PLoS ONE*, 10(11):e0141287, 2015.

[49] James Aspnes, Richard Beigel, Merrick Furst, and Steven Rudich. The expressive power of voting polynomials. *Combinatorica*, 14(2):135–148, 1994.

[50] A. Aszodi, M.J. Gradwell, and W.R. Taylor. Global fold determination from a small number of distance restraints. *J. Mol. Biol.*, 251:308–326, 1995.

[51] Christopher G. Atkeson and Juan Carlos Santamaria. A comparison of direct and model-based reinforcement learning. In *Proceedings of International Conference on Robotics and Automation*, volume 4, pages 3557–3564. IEEE, 1997.

[52] ATLAS Collaboration. ATLAS experiment at the CERN Large Hadron Collider. *JINST*, 3:S08003, 2008.

[53] ATLAS Collaboration. Luminosity determination in pp collisions at $\sqrt{s} = 7$ TeV using the ATLAS Detector at the LHC. *Eur. Phys. J*, C73:2518, 2013.

[54] A. Aurisano, A. Radovic, D. Rocco, A. Himmel, M.D. Messier, E. Niner, G. Pawloski, F. Psihas, A. Sousa, and P. Vahle. A convolutional neural network neutrino event classifier. *Journal of Instrumentation*, 11(09):P09001, 2016.

[55] C. Azencott, A. Ksikes, S.J. Swamidass, J. Chen, L. Ralaivola, and P. Baldi. One-to four- dimensional kernels for small molecules and predictive regression of physical, chemical, and biological properties. *Journal of Chemical Information and Modeling*, 47(3):965–974, 2007.

[56] Jimmy Lei Ba, Jamie Ryan Kiros, and Geoffrey E. Hinton. Layer normalization. arXiv:1607.06450, 2016.

[57] Bernard J. Baars et al. *In the Theater of Consciousness: The Workspace of the Mind*. Oxford University Press, USA, 1997.

[58] Bernard J. Baars and Nicole M. Gage. *Cognition, Brain, and Consciousness: Introduction to Cognitive Neuroscience*. Academic Press, 2010.

[59] Baktash Babadi and Haim Sompolinsky. Sparseness and expansion in sensory representations. *Neuron*, 83(5):1213–1226, 2014.

[60] Sebastian Bach, Alexander Binder, Grégoire Montavon, Frederick Klauschen, Klaus-Robert Müller, and Wojciech Samek. On pixel-wise explanations for non-linear classifier decisions by layer-wise relevance propagation. *PloS One*, 10(7):e0130140, 2015.

[61] Dzmitry Bahdanau, Kyunghyun Cho, and Yoshua Bengio. Neural machine translation by jointly learning to align and translate. arXiv:1409.0473, 2014.

[62] M. Bahr et al. Herwig++ Physics and Manual. *Eur. Phys. J.*, C58:639–707, 2008.

[63] Dávid Bajusz, Anita Rácz, and Károly Héberger. Why is tanimoto index an appropriate choice for fingerprint-based similarity calculations? *Journal of chem-informatics*, 7(1):20, 2015.

[64] D. Baker and A. Sali. Protein structure prediction and structural genomics. *Science*, 294:93–96, 2001.

[65] P. Baldi. Symmetries and learning in neural network models. *Physical Review Letters*, 59(17):1976–1978, 1987.

[66] P. Baldi. Group actions and learning for a family of automata. *Journal of Computer and System Sciences*, 36(2):1–15, 1988.

[67] P. Baldi. Neural networks, acyclic orientations of the hypercube and sets of orthogonal vectors. *SIAM Journal Discrete Mathematics*, 1(1):1–13, 1988.

[68] P. Baldi. Neural networks, orientations of the hypercube and algebraic threshold functions. *IEEE Transactions on Information Theory*, 34(3):523–530, 1988.

[69] P. Baldi. Gradient descent learning algorithms overview: A general dynamical systems perspective. *IEEE Transactions on Neural Networks*, 6(1):182–195, 1995.

[70] P. Baldi. Boolean autoencoders and hypercube clustering complexity. *Designs, Codes, and Cryptography*, 65(3):383–403, 2012.

[71] P. Baldi. The inner and outer approaches for the design of recursive neural networks architectures. *Data Mining and Knowledge Discovery*, DOI: 10.1007/s10618-017-0531-0:1–13, 2017. Available at: `http://link.springer.com/article/10.1007/s10618-017-0531-0`.

[72] P. Baldi. Deep learning in biomedical data science. *Annual Review of Biomedical Data Science*, 1:181–205, 2018.

[73] P. Baldi, R. W. Benz, D. Hirschberg, and S.J. Swamidass. Lossless compression of chemical fingerprints using integer entropy codes improves storage and retrieval. *Journal of Chemical Information and Modeling*, 47(6):2098–2109, 2007.

[74] P. Baldi and S. Brunak. *Bioinformatics: The Machine Learning Approach*. MIT Press, Cambridge, MA, 2001. Second edition.

[75] P. Baldi, S. Brunak, P. Frasconi, G. Pollastri, and G. Soda. Exploiting the past and the future in protein secondary structure prediction. *Bioinformatics*, 15:937–946, 1999.

[76] P. Baldi and Y. Chauvin. Neural networks for fingerprint recognition. *Neural Computation*, 5(3):402–418, 1993.

[77] P. Baldi and Y. Chauvin. Smooth on-line learning algorithms for hidden Markov models. *Neural Computation*, 6(2):305–316, 1994.

[78] P. Baldi and Y. Chauvin. Protein modeling with hybrid hidden Markov model/neural networks architectures. In *Proceedings of the 1995 Conference on Intelligent Systems for Molecular Biology (ISMB95), in Cambridge (UK)*. The AAAI Press, Menlo Park, CA, 1995.

[79] P. Baldi, Y. Chauvin, T. Hunkapillar, and M. McClure. Hidden Markov models of biological primary sequence information. *PNAS USA*, 91(3):1059–1063, 1994.

[80] P. Baldi and K. Hornik. Neural networks and principal component analysis: learning from examples without local minima. *Neural Networks*, 2(1):53–58, 1988.

[81] P. Baldi and K. Hornik. Learning in linear networks: a survey. *IEEE Transactions on Neural Networks*, 6(4):837–858, 1994. 1995.

[82] P. Baldi and L. Itti. Of bits and wows: A Bayesian theory of surprise with applications to attention. *Neural Networks*, 23(5):649–666, 2010.

[83] P. Baldi and Z. Lu. Complex-valued autoencoders. *Neural Networks*, 33:136–147, 2012.

[84] P. Baldi, Z. Lu, and P. Sadowski. Learning in the machine: the symmetries of the deep learning channel. *Neural Networks*, 95:110–133, 2017.

[85] P. Baldi, Z. Lu, and P. Sadowski. Learning in the machine: Random backpropagation and the deep learning channel. *Artificial Intelligence*, 260:1–35, 2018. Also: arXiv:1612.02734.

[86] P. Baldi and F. Pineda. Contrastive learning and neural oscillations. *Neural Computation*, 3(4):526–545, 1991.

[87] P. Baldi and G. Pollastri. A machine learning strategy for protein analysis. *IEEE Intelligent Systems. Special Issue on Intelligent Systems in Biology*, 17(2), 2002.

[88] P. Baldi and G. Pollastri. The principled design of large-scale recursive neural network architectures–DAG-RNNs and the protein structure prediction problem. *Journal of Machine Learning Research*, 4:575–602, 2003.

[89] P. Baldi and Y. Rinott. Asymptotic normality of some graph related statistics. *Journal of Applied Probability*, 26:171–175, 1989.

[90] P. Baldi and Y. Rinott. On normal approximations of distributions in terms of dependency graphs. *Annals of Probability*, 17(4):1646–1650, 1989.

[91] P. Baldi and P. Sadowski. The dropout learning algorithm. *Artificial Intelligence*, 210C:78–122, 2014.

[92] P. Baldi and P. Sadowski. Learning in the machine: Recirculation is random backpropagation. *Neural Networks*, 108:479–494, 2018.

[93] P. Baldi, P. Sadowski, and D. Whiteson. Searching for exotic particles in high-energy physics with deep learning. *Nature Communications*, 5, 2014.

[94] P. Baldi, P. Sadowski, and D. Whiteson. Enhanced Higgs boson to $\tau\,\tau$ search with deep learning. *Phys. Rev. Letters*, 114:111801, 2015.

[95] Pierre Baldi. Linear learning: Landscapes and algorithms. In *Advances in Neural Information Processing Systems*, pages 65–72, 1989.

[96] Pierre Baldi. Data-driven high-throughput prediction of the 3-d structure of small molecules: review and progress. a response to the letter by the Cambridge Crystallographic Data Centre. *Journal of Chemical Information and Modeling*, 51(12):3029–3029, 2011.

[97] Pierre Baldi, Kevin Bauer, Clara Eng, Peter Sadowski, and Daniel Whiteson. Jet substructure classification in high-energy physics with deep neural networks. *Phys. Rev. D*, 93:094034, May 2016.

[98] Pierre Baldi, Jianming Bian, Lars Hertel, and Lingge Li. Improved energy reconstruction in nova with regression convolutional neural networks. *Physical Review D*, 99(1):012011, 2019.

[99] Pierre Baldi and Yves Chauvin. Hybrid modeling, HMM/NN architectures, and protein applications. *Neural Computation*, 8(7):1541–1565, 1996.

[100] Pierre Baldi, Kyle Cranmer, Taylor Faucett, Peter Sadowski, and Daniel Whiteson. Parameterized neural networks for high-energy physics. *The European Physical Journal C*, 76(5):235, Apr 2016.

[101] Pierre Baldi, Yosef Rinott, and Charles Stein. A normal approximation for the number of local maxima of a random function on a graph. In *Probability, Statistics, and Mathematics*, pages 59–81. Elsevier, 1989.

[102] Pierre Baldi and Peter Sadowski. A theory of local learning, the learning channel, and the optimality of backpropagation. *Neural Networks*, 83:61–74, 2016.

[103] Pierre Baldi and Santosh S. Venkatesh. Number of stable points for spin-glasses and neural networks of higher orders. *Physical Review Letters*, 58(9):913, 1987.

[104] Pierre Baldi and Santosh S. Venkatesh. Random interactions in higher order neural networks. *IEEE Transactions on Information Theory*, 39(1):274–283, 1993.

[105] Pierre Baldi and Roman Vershynin. The capacity of feedforward neural networks. *Neural Networks*, 1(4):699–729, 2019. Also: arXiv preprint arXiv:1901.00434.

[106] Pierre Baldi and Roman Vershynin. Polynomial threshold functions, hyperplane arrangements, and random tensors. *SIAM Journal on Mathematics of Data Science*, 1(4):699–729, 2019. Also: arXiv preprint arXiv:1803.10868.

[107] Yohai Bar-Sinai, Stephan Hoyer, Jason Hickey, and Michael P. Brenner. Learning data-driven discretizations for partial differential equations. *Proceedings of the National Academy of Sciences*, 116(31):15344–15349, Jul 2019.

[108] Francisco Barahona. On the computational complexity of Ising spin glass models. *Journal of Physics A: Mathematical and General*, 15(10):3241, 1982.

[109] Andrew Barron, Jorma Rissanen, and Bin Yu. The minimum description length principle in coding and modeling. *IEEE Transactions on Information Theory*, 44(6):2743–2760, 1998.

[110] Peter L Bartlett, Nick Harvey, Christopher Liaw, and Abbas Mehrabian. Nearly-tight VC-dimension and pseudodimension bounds for piecewise linear neural networks. *J. Mach. Learn. Res.*, 20:63–1, 2019.

[111] Thomas M. Bartol Jr., Cailey Bromer, Justin Kinney, Michael A. Chirillo, Jennifer N. Bourne, Kristen M. Harris, and Terrence J. Sejnowski. Nanoconnectomic upper bound on the variability of synaptic plasticity. *eLife*, 4, 2015.

[112] Eric B. Baum and David Haussler. What size net gives valid generalization? In *Advances in Neural Information Processing Systems*, pages 81–90, 1989.

[113] Brett K. Beaulieu-Jones, Casey S. Greene, et al. Semi-supervised learning of the electronic health record for phenotype stratification. *Journal of Biomedical Informatics*, 64:168–178, 2016.

[114] Richard Beigel, Nick Reingold, and Daniel Spielman. Pp is closed under intersection. *Journal of Computer and System Sciences*, 50(2):191–202, 1995.

[115] Anthony J. Bell and Terrence J. Sejnowski. The "independent components" of natural scenes are edge filters. *Vision Research*, 37(23):3327–3338, 1997.

[116] Marc G. Bellemare, Georg Ostrovski, Arthur Guez, Philip S. Thomas, and Rémi Munos. Increasing the action gap: New operators for reinforcement learning. In *AAAI*, pages 1476–1483, 2016.

[117] Richard Bellman. *The Theory of Dynamic Programming*. Technical report, DTIC Document, 1954.

[118] Erica Benedetti, Antoine Simonneau, Alexandra Hours, Hani Amouri, Andrea Penoni, Giovanni Palmisano, Max Malacria, Jean-Philippe Goddard, and Louis Fensterbank. (pentamethylcyclopentadienyl) iridium dichloride dimer {[IrCp* Cl2] 2}: A novel efficient catalyst for the cycloisomerizations of homopropargylic diols and n-tethered enynes. *Advanced Synthesis & Catalysis*, 353 (11-12):1908–1912, 2011.

[119] G. Benkö, C. Flamm, and P.F. Stadler. A graph-based toy model of chemistry. *Journal of Chemical Information and Computer Sciences*, 43(4):1085–1093, May 2003.

[120] Karianne J. Bergen, Paul A. Johnson, Maarten V. De Hoop, and Gregory C. Beroza. Machine learning for data-driven discovery in solid-earth geoscience, *Science* 363(6433):eaau0323, 2019. DOI: 10.1126/science.aau0323

[121] J. Beringer et al. Review of particle physics. *Phys. Rev. D*, 86:010001, Jul 2012.

[122] Helen Berman, Kim Henrick, Haruki Nakamura, and John L. Markley. The Worldwide Protein Data Bank (WWPDB): ensuring a single, uniform archive of PDB data. *Nucleic Acids Research*, 35(suppl_1):D301–D303, 2007.

[123] J. Bernardo, J. Berger, A. Dawid, and A. Smith. Some Bayesian numerical analysis. *Bayesian Statistics*, 4:345–363, 1992.

[124] José M. Bernardo and Adrian F.M. Smith. *Bayesian Theory*. IOP Publishing, 2001.

[125] Gianfranco Bertone and David Merritt. Dark matter dynamics and indirect detection. *Modern Physics Letters A*, 20(14):1021–1036, 2005.

[126] Dimitri P. Bertsekas and John N. Tsitsiklis. *Neuro-dynamic Programming*. Athena Scientific Belmont, MA, 1996.

[127] Tom Beucler, Michael Pritchard, Stephan Rasp, Jordan Ott, Pierre Baldi, and Pierre Gentine. Enforcing analytic constraints in neural-networks emulating physical systems. *Phys. Rev. Lett.*, 2021. In press. Also: http://arxiv.org/abs/1909.00912.

[128] R.E. Blahut. Computation of channel capacity and rate-distortion functions. *Information Theory, IEEE Transactions on*, 18(4):460–473, 1972.

[129] R.E. Blahut. *Principles and Practice of Information Theory*. Addison-Wesley, Reading, MA, 1987.

[130] H.D. Block, and S.A. Levin. *On the boundedness of an iterative procedure for solving a system of linear inequalities. Proceedings of the American Mathematical Society*, 26:229–235, 1970.

[131] Nikolaj Blom, Thomas Sicheritz-Pontén, Ramneek Gupta, Steen Gammeltoft, and Søren Brunak. Prediction of post-translational glycosylation and phosphorylation of proteins from the amino acid sequence. *Proteomics*, 4(6):1633–1649, 2004.

[132] A.L. Blum and R.L. Rivest. Training a 3-node neural network is NP-complete. *Neural Networks*, 5(1):117–127, 1992.

[133] Lorenz C. Blum and Jean-Louis Reymond. 970 million druglike small molecules for virtual screening in the chemical universe database GDB-13. *Journal of the American Chemical Society*, 131(25):8732–8733, 2009.

[134] Charles Blundell, Benigno Uria, Alexander Pritzel, Yazhe Li, Avraham Ruderman, Joel Z. Leibo, Jack Rae, Daan Wierstra, and Demis Hassabis. Model-free episodic control. arXiv:1606.04460, 2016.

[135] Edward Blurock. Reaction: system for modeling chemical reactions. *Journal of Chemical Information and Computer Sciences*, 35(3):607–616, 1995.

[136] Mihail Bogojeski, Leslie Vogt-Maranto, Mark E. Tuckerman, Klaus-Robert Mueller, Kieron Burke Density functionals with quantum chemical accuracy: From machine learning to molecular dynamics. DOI: 10.26434/chemrxiv.8079917.

[137] R.S. Bohacek, C. McMartin, and W.C. Guida. The art and practice of structure-based drug design: a molecular modeling perspective. *Medicinal Research Reviews*, 16(1):3–50, 1996.

[138] Thomas Bolton and Laure Zanna. Applications of deep learning to ocean data inference and dubgrid parameterization. *Journal of Advances in Modeling Earth Systems*, 11(1):376–399, 2019.

[139] Sandrine Bony and Jean-Louis Dufresne. Marine boundary layer clouds at the heart of tropical cloud feedback uncertainties in climate models. *Geophysical Research Letters*, 32(20), 2005.

[140] Anton Bovier and Véronique Gayrard. Hopfield models as generalized random mean field models. In A. Bovier and P. Picco, editors, *Mathematical Aspects of Spin Glasses and Neural Networks*. Birkhäuser, pages 3–89, 1998.

[141] James M. Bower and David Beeman. *The Book of GENESIS: Exploring Realistic Neural Models with the GEneral NEural SImulation System*. Electronic Library of Science, 1995.

[142] James M. Bower, David Beeman, and Michael Hucka. The GENESIS simulation system. In: *The Handbook of Brain Theory and Neural Networks*. MIT Press, pages 475–478, 2003.

[143] Justin Boyan and Andrew W. Moore. Generalization in reinforcement learning: safely approximating the value function. *Advances in Neural Information Processing Systems*, pages 369–376, 1995.

[144] Justin A. Boyan, Michael L. Littman, et al. Packet routing in dynamically changing networks: A reinforcement learning approach. *Advances in Neural Information Processing Systems*, pages 671–671, 1994.

[145] Stephen Boyd and Lieven Vandenberghe. *Convex Optimization*. Cambridge University Press, 2004.

[146] Vladimír Boža, Broňa Brejová, and Tomáš Vinař. Deepnano: Deep recurrent neural networks for base calling in minion nanopore reads. *PloS one*, 12(6):e0178751, 2017.

[147] Ronen I. Brafman and Moshe Tennenholtz. R-max – a general polynomial time algorithm for near-optimal reinforcement learning. *The Journal of Machine Learning Research*, 3:213–231, 2003.

[148] Catherine Braiding, Graeme F. Wong, Nigel I. Maxted, Donatella Romano, Michael G. Burton, Rebecca Blackwell, M.D. Filipović, M.S.R. Freeman,

B. Indermuehle, J. Lau, et al. The Mopra Southern Galactic Plane CO Survey–Data Release 3. *Publications of the Astronomical Society of Australia*, 35, 2018.

[149] Alan J. Bray and David S. Dean. Statistics of critical points of Gaussian fields on large-dimensional spaces. *Physical Review Letters*, 98(15):150201, 2007.

[150] Leo Breiman. Bagging predictors. *Machine Learning*, 24(2):123–140, 1996.

[151] Christopher S. Bretherton and Marat F. Khairoutdinov. Convective self-aggregation feedbacks in near-global cloud-resolving simulations of an aquaplanet. *Journal of Advances in Modeling Earth Systems*, 7(4):1765–1787, 2015.

[152] Gavin Brown, Jeremy Wyatt, Rachel Harris, and Xin Yao. Diversity creation methods: a survey and categorisation. *Information Fusion*, 6(1):5–20, 2005.

[153] L.D. Brown. *Fundamentals of Statistical Exponential Families*. Institute of Mathematical Statistics, Hayward, CA, 1986.

[154] T.E. Brown, H.E. LeMay, B.E. Bursten, and C. Murphy. *Chemistry: The Central Science*. Prentice Hall, 2008. 11th Edition.

[155] Jehoshua Bruck. Harmonic analysis of polynomial threshold functions. *SIAM Journal on Discrete Mathematics*, 3(2):168–177, 1990.

[156] Jehoshua Bruck and Mario Blaum. Neural networks, error-correcting codes, and polynomials over the binary n-cube. *IEEE Transactions on Information Theory*, 35(5):976–987, 1989.

[157] Søfren Brunak, Jacob Engelbrecht, and Steen Knudsen. Neural network detects errors in the assignment of mRNA splice sites. *Nucleic Acids Research*, 18(16):4797–4801, 1990.

[158] Søren Brunak, Jacob Engelbrecht, and Steen Knudsen. Prediction of human mRNA donor and acceptor sites from the DNA sequence. *Journal of Molecular Biology*, 220(1):49–65, 1991.

[159] Cristian Bucilua, Rich Caruana, and Alexandru Niculescu-Mizil. Model compression. In *Proceedings of the 12th ACM SIGKDD International Conference on Knowledge Discovery and Data Mining*, pages 535–541. ACM, 2006.

[160] Robert Creighton Buck. Partition of space. *The American Mathematical Monthly*, 50(9):541–544, 1943.

[161] Michael G. Burton, Catherine Braiding, Christian Glueck, Paul Goldsmith, Jarryd Hawkes, David J. Hollenbach, Craig Kulesa, Christopher L. Martin, Jorge L Pineda, Gavin Rowell, et al. The MOPRA southern galactic plane CO survey. *Publications of the Astronomical Society of Australia*, 30, 2013.

[162] Lucian Busoniu, Robert Babuska, and Bart De Schutter. A comprehensive survey of multiagent reinforcement learning. *Systems, Man, and Cybernetics, Part C: Applications and Reviews, IEEE Transactions on*, 38(2):156–172, 2008.

[163] Lucian Busoniu, Robert Babuska, Bart De Schutter, and Damien Ernst. *Reinforcement Learning and Dynamic Programming using Function Approximators*. CRC Press, 2010.

[164] Federico Cabitza, Raffaele Rasoini, and Gian Franco Gensini. Unintended consequences of machine learning in medicine. *JAMA*, 318(6):517–518, 2017.

[165] S Ramón y Cajal. La fine structure des centres nerveux. The Croonian lecture. *Proc. R. Soc. Lond*, 55:444–468, 1894.

[166] Erik Cambria, Qiang Liu, Kuan Li, Victor C.M. Leung, Liang Feng, Yew-Soon Ong, Meng-Hiot Lim, Anton Akusok, Amaury Lendasse, Francesco Corona, et al. Extreme learning machines. *IEEE Intelligent Systems*, (6):30–59, 2013.

[167] G. Canas, T. Poggio, and L. Rosasco. Learning manifolds with K-means and K-flats. In *Proceedings of the 2012 Neural Information Processing Conference (NIPS 2012)*, 2012.

[168] Laurent Canetti, Marco Drewes, and Mikhail Shaposhnikov. Matter and antimatter in the universe. *New Journal of Physics*, 14(9):095012, 2012.

[169] Renzhi Cao, Debswapna Bhattacharya, Jie Hou, and Jianlin Cheng. Deepqa: improving the estimation of single protein model quality with deep belief networks. *BMC bioinformatics*, 17(1):495, 2016.

[170] Nicholas T. Carnevale and Michael L. Hines. *The NEURON book*. Cambridge University Press, 2006.

[171] Miguel A. Carreira-Perpinan and Geoffrey E. Hinton. On contrastive divergence learning. In *AISTATS*, volume 10, pages 33–40. Citeseer, 2005.

[172] Carlos M. Carvalho, Nicholas G. Polson, and James G. Scott. Handling sparsity via the horseshoe. In *Artificial Intelligence and Statistics*, pages 73–80, 2009.

[173] Carlos M. Carvalho, Nicholas G. Polson, and James G. Scott. The horseshoe estimator for sparse signals. *Biometrika*, 97(2):465–480, 2010.

[174] Anthony R. Cassandra, Leslie Pack Kaelbling, and Michael L. Littman. Acting optimally in partially observable stochastic domains. In *AAAI*, volume 94, pages 1023–1028, 1994.

[175] S. Cazaux, T. Lerch, and S. Aune. *Detecteur courbe de particules gazeux*, April 30 2014. Patent App. EP20,130,188,550.

[176] Nicholas Ceglia, Yu Liu, Siwei Chen, Forest Agostinelli, Kristin Eckel-Mahan, Paolo Sassone-Corsi, and Pierre Baldi. Circadiomics: circadian omic web portal. *Nucleic Acids Research*, 46(W1):W157–W162, 2018.

[177] P. Chang, J. Grinband, B.D. Weinberg, M. Bardis, M. Khy, G. Cadena, M.-Y. Su, S. Cha, C.G. Filippi, D. Bota, et al. Deep-learning convolutional neural networks accurately classify genetic mutations in gliomas. *American Journal of Neuroradiology*, 39(7):1201–1207, 2018.

[178] J. Chen and P. Baldi. No electron left behind: a rule-based expert system to predict chemical reactions and reaction mechanisms. *Journal of Chemical Information and Modeling*, 49(9):2034–43, 2009. PMID: 19719121.

[179] J. Chen, S.J. Swamidass, Y. Dou, J. Bruand, and P. Baldi. ChemDB: a public database of small molecules and related chemoinformatics resources. *Bioinformatics*, 21:4133–4139, 2005.

[180] J.H. Chen and P. Baldi. Synthesis explorer: a chemical reaction tutorial system for organic synthesis design and mechanism prediction. *Journal of Chemical Education*, 85(12):1699, December 2008.

[181] Yifei Chen, Yi Li, Rajiv Narayan, Aravind Subramanian, and Xiaohui Xie. Gene expression inference with deep learning. *Bioinformatics*, 32(12):1832–9, Jun 2016.

[182] J. Cheng and P. Baldi. A machine learning information retrieval approach to protein fold recognition. *Bioinformatics*, 22(12):1456–1463, 2006.

[183] J. Cheng and P. Baldi. Improved residue contact prediction using support vector machines and a large feature set. *BMC Bioinformatics*, 8(1):113, 2007.

[184] J. Cheng, A. Randall, and P. Baldi. Prediction of protein stability changes for single-site mutations using support vector machines. *Proteins: Structure, Function, Bioinformatics*, 62(4):1125–1132, 2006.

[185] J. Cheng, A.Z. Randall, M. Sweredoski, and P. Baldi. Scratch: a protein structure and structural feature prediction server. *Nucleic Acids Research*, 33:W72–W76, 2005. Web Servers issue.

[186] J. Cheng, H. Saigo, and P. Baldi. Large-scale prediction of disulphide bridges using kernel methods two-dimensional recursive neural networks, and weighted graph matching. *Proteins*, 62(3):617–629, 2006.

[187] J. Cheng, M. Sweredoski, and P. Baldi. Accurate prediction of protein disordered regions by mining protein structure data. *Data Mining and Knowledge Discovery*, 11(3):213–222, 2005.

[188] J. Cheng, M.J. Sweredoski, and P. Baldi. Dompro: Protein domain prediction using profiles, secondary structure, relative solvent accessibility, and recursive neural networks. *Data Mining and Knowledge Discovery*, 13(1):1–10, 2006.

[189] J. Cheng, A.N. Tegge, and P. Baldi. Machine learning methods for protein structure prediction. *IEEE Reviews in Biomedical Engineering*, 1:41–49, 2008.

[190] Silvia Chiappa, Sébastien Racaniere, Daan Wierstra, and Shakir Mohamed. Recurrent environment simulators. arXiv:1704.02254, 2017.

[191] Davide Chicco, Peter Sadowski, and Pierre Baldi. Deep autoencoder neural networks for gene ontology annotation predictions. In *Proceedings of the 5th ACM Conference on Bioinformatics, Computational Biology, and Health Informatics*, pages 533–540. ACM, 2014.

[192] Travers Ching, Daniel S. Himmelstein, Brett K. Beaulieu-Jones, Alexandr A. Kalinin, Brian T. Do, Gregory P. Way, Enrico Ferrero, Paul-Michael Agapow, Wei Xie, Gail L. Rosen, et al. Opportunities and obstacles for deep learning in biology and medicine. *bioRxiv*, page 142760, 2017.

[193] Stefan Chmiela, Alexandre Tkatchenko, Huziel E. Sauceda, Igor Poltavsky, Kristof T. Schütt, and Klaus-Robert Müller. Machine learning of accurate energy-conserving molecular force fields. *Science Advances*, 3(5):e1603015, 2017.

[194] Edward Choi, Mohammad Taha Bahadori, Andy Schuetz, Walter F. Stewart, and Jimeng Sun. Doctor AI: predicting clinical events via recurrent neural networks. In *Machine Learning for Healthcare Conference*, pages 301–318, 2016.

[195] Francois Chollet. *Keras*. GitHub, 2015.

[196] Patricia S. Churchland. *Braintrust: What Neuroscience Tells us about Morality*. Princeton University Press, 2018.

[197] D.C. Ciresan, A. Giusti, L.M. Gambardella, and J. Schmidhuber. Deep neural networks segment neuronal membranes in electron microscopy images. In *Advances in Neural Information Processing Systems (NIPS)*, pages 2852–2860, 2012.

[198] D.C. Ciresan, U. Meier, and J. Schmidhuber. Multi-column deep neural networks for image classification. In *IEEE Conference on Computer Vision and Pattern Recognition CVPR 2012*, June 2012. Long preprint arXiv:1202.2745v1 [cs.CV], Feb 2012.

[199] Dan CireşAn, Ueli Meier, Jonathan Masci, and Jürgen Schmidhuber. Multi-column deep neural network for traffic sign classification. *Neural networks*, 32:333–338, 2012.

[200] Dan Claudiu Ciresan, Alessandro Giusti, Luca Maria Gambardella, and Jürgen Schmidhuber. Mitosis detection in breast cancer histology images with deep neural networks. In *Proc. MICCAI*, volume 2, pages 411–418, 2013.

[201] P. Clote and E. Kranakis. *Boolean Functions and Computation Models*. Springer Verlag, 2002.

[202] CMS Collaboration. Search for light vector resonances decaying to quarks at 13 TeV. *CMS-PAS-EXO-16-030*, 2016.

[203] Adam Coates, Honglak Lee, and Andrew Y. Ng. An analysis of single-layer networks in unsupervised feature learning. *Ann Arbor*, 1001:48109, 2010.

[204] Michael A. Cohen and Stephen Grossberg. Absolute stability of global pattern formation and parallel memory storage by competitive neural networks. *IEEE Transactions on Systems, Man, and Cybernetics*, (5):815–826, 1983.

[205] Taco Cohen and Max Welling. Group equivariant convolutional networks. In *International Conference on Machine Learning*, pages 2990–2999, 2016.

[206] Taco S. Cohen, Maurice Weiler, Berkay Kicanaoglu, and Max Welling. Gauge equivariant convolutional networks and the icosahedral cnn. arXiv:1902.04615, 2019.

[207] Connor W. Coley, Wengong Jin, Luke Rogers, Timothy F. Jamison, Tommi S. Jaakkola, William H. Green, Regina Barzilay, and Klavs F. Jensen. A graph-convolutional neural network model for the prediction of chemical reactivity. *Chemical Science*, 10(2):370–377, 2019.

[208] ATLAS collaboration et al. Search for new resonances in mass distributions of jet pairs using 139 fb- 1 of pp collisions atv s= 13 tev with the atlas detector. *Journal of High Energy Physics*, 2020(3):145, 2020.

[209] M. Corradini et al. Experimental apparatus for annihilation cross-section measurements of low energy antiprotons. *Nucl. Instr. Meth. A*, 711:12–20, 2013.

[210] M. Corradini et al. Scintillating bar detector for antiproton annihilations measurements. *Hyperfine Interactions*, 233:53–58, 2015.

[211] Corinna Cortes and Vladimir Vapnik. Support-vector networks. *Machine Learning*, 20(3):273–297, 1995.

[212] Rémi Coulom. Efficient selectivity and backup operators in Monte-Carlo tree search. In *International Conference on Computers and Games*, pages 72–83. Springer, 2006.

[213] T.M. Cover and J.A. Thomas. *Elements of Information Theory*. John Wiley, New York, 1991.

[214] Thomas M. Cover. Geometrical and statistical properties of systems of linear inequalities with applications in pattern recognition. *IEEE Transactions on Electronic Computers*, (3):326–334, 1965.

[215] R.T. Cox. Probability, frequency and reasonable expectation. *American Journal of Physics*, 14:1–13, 1964.

[216] Kyle Cranmer, Juan Pavez, and Gilles Louppe. Approximating likelihood ratios with calibrated discriminative classifiers. arXiv:1506.02169, 2015.

[217] N. Cristianini and J. Shawe-Taylor. *An Introduction to Support Vector Machines and other Kernel-Based Learning Methods*. Cambridge University Press, Cambridge, 2000.

[218] Robert Crites and Andrew Barto. Improving elevator performance using reinforcement learning. In *Advances in Neural Information Processing Systems 8*. Citeseer, 1996.

[219] Y. Le Cun, B. Boser, J. Denker, D. Henderson, R. Howard, W. Hubbard, and L. Jackel. Handwritten digit recognition with a back-propagation network. In D. Touretzky, editor, *Advances in Neural Information Processing Systems*, pages 396–404. Morgan Kaufmann, San Mateo, CA, 1990.

[220] George Cybenko. Approximation by superpositions of a sigmoidal function. *Mathematics of Control, Signals, and Systems (MCSS)*, 2(4):303–314, 1989.

[221] J. Thaler D. Krohn and L.-T. Wang. Jet trimming. *JHEP*, 1002:084, 2010.

[222] Thomas M. Dame, Dap Hartmann, and P. Thaddeus. The Milky Way in molecular clouds: a new complete CO survey. *The Astrophysical Journal*, 547(2):792, 2001.

[223] Mrinal Dasgupta, Alessandro Fregoso, Simone Marzani, and Alexander Powling. Jet substructure with analytical methods. *Eur. Phys. J.*, C73(11):2623, 2013.

[224] Mrinal Dasgupta, Alexander Powling, and Andrzej Siodmok. On jet substructure methods for signal jets. *JHEP*, 08:079, 2015.

[225] Sanjoy Dasgupta and Anupam Gupta. An elementary proof of a theorem of Johnson and Lindenstrauss. *Random Structures & Algorithms*, 22(1):60–65, 2003.

[226] Eugene Gutman, Amin Tavakoli, Gregor Urban, Frances Liu, Nancy Huynh, David Van Vranken, David Fooshee, Aaron Mood, and Pierre Baldi. Deep learning for chemical reaction prediction. *Molecular Systems Design & Engineering*, 3:442–452, 2018. DOI: 10.1039/c7me00107j.

[227] Thomas J. Davidson, Fabian Kloosterman, and Matthew A. Wilson. Hippocampal replay of extended experience. *Neuron*, 63(4):497–507, 2009.

[228] Nick Day, Jim Downing, Sam Adams, N.W. England, and Peter Murray-Rust. Crystaleye: automated aggregation, semantification and dissemination of the world's open crystallographic data. *Journal of Applied Crystallography*, 45(2):316–323, 2012.

[229] Emmanuel de Bezenac, Arthur Pajot, and Patrick Gallinari. Deep Learning for Physical Processes: Incorporating Prior Scientific Knowledge. *Journal of Statistical Mechanics*, 124009, 2019.

[230] Daniela Pucci de Farias and Benjamin Van Roy. The linear programming approach to approximate dynamic programming. *Operations Research*, 51(6):850–865, 2003.

[231] Luke de Oliveira, Michael Kagan, Lester Mackey, Benjamin Nachman, and Ariel Schwartzman. Jet-images – deep learning edition. *Journal of High Energy Physics*, 2016(7):69, 2016.

[232] Luke de Oliveira, Michela Paganini, and Benjamin Nachman. Learning particle physics by example: location-aware generative adversarial networks for physics synthesis. *Comput. Softw. Big Sci.*, 2017.

[233] Richard Dearden, Nir Friedman, and David Andre. Model based Bayesian exploration. In *Proceedings of the Fifteenth Conference on Uncertainty in Artificial Intelligence*, pages 150–159. Morgan Kaufmann Publishers Inc., 1999.

[234] Rina Dechter. Reasoning with probabilistic and deterministic graphical models: exact algorithms. *Synthesis Lectures on Artificial Intelligence and Machine Learning*, 13(1):1–199, 2019.

[235] John S. Delaney. Esol: estimating aqueous solubility directly from molecular structure. *Journal of Chemical Information and Computer Sciences*, 44(3):1000–1005, 2004.

[236] Jacob Devlin, Ming-Wei Kenton Lee, and Kristina Toutanova. Bert: Pre-training of deep bidirectional transformers for language understanding, 2018. Preprint arXiv:1810.04805.

[237] P. Di Lena, K. Nagata, and P. Baldi. Deep architectures for protein contact map prediction. *Bioinformatics*, 28:2449–2457, 2012. DOI: 10.1093/bioinformatics/bts475. First published online: July 30, 2012.

[238] Persi Diaconis. Bayesian numerical analysis. *Statistical Decision Theory and Related Topics IV*, 1:163–175, 1988.

[239] Ilias Diakonikolas, Ryan O'Donnell, Rocco A. Servedio, and Yi Wu. Hardness results for agnostically learning low-degree polynomial threshold functions. In *Proceedings of the Twenty-Second Annual ACM–SIAM Symposium on Discrete Algorithms*, pages 1590–1606. SIAM, 2011.

[240] Thomas G Dietterich. Ensemble methods in machine learning. In *International Workshop on Multiple Classifier Systems*, pages 1–15. Springer, 2000.

[241] Thomas G. Dietterich. An overview of MAXQ hierarchical reinforcement learning. In *Abstraction, Reformulation, and Approximation*, pages 26–44. Springer, 2000.

[242] Laurent Dinh, Jascha Sohl-Dickstein, and Samy Bengio. Density estimation using real nvp. arXiv:1605.08803, 2016.

[243] C. M. Dobson. Chemical space and biology. *Nature*, 432:824–828, 2004.

[244] James Dolen, Philip Harris, Simone Marzani, Salvatore Rappoccio, and Nhan Tran. Thinking outside the ROCs: Designing Decorrelated Taggers (DDT) for jet substructure. *JHEP*, 05:156, 2016.

[245] Daoyi Dong, Chunlin Chen, Hanxiong Li, and Tzyh-Jong Tarn. Quantum reinforcement learning. *Systems, Man, and Cybernetics, Part B: Cybernetics, IEEE Transactions on*, 38(5):1207–1220, 2008.

[246] Marco Dorigo and LM Gambardella. Ant-Q: A reinforcement learning approach to the traveling salesman problem. In *Proceedings of ML-95, Twelfth Intern. Conf. on Machine Learning*, pages 252–260, 2014.

[247] Alvin W Drake. *Observation of a Markov process through a noisy channel*. PhD thesis, Massachusetts Institute of Technology, 1962.

[248] David Duvenaud, Dougal Maclaurin, Jorge Aguilera-Iparraguirre, Rafael Gomez-Bombarelli, Timothy Hirzel, Alán Aspuru-Guzik, and Ryan P. Adams. Convolutional networks on graphs for learning molecular fingerprints. In *Neural Information Processing Systems*, 2015.

[249] Sašo Džeroski, Luc De Raedt, and Kurt Driessens. Relational reinforcement learning. *Machine Learning*, 43(1-2):7–52, 2001.

[250] Harrison Edwards and Amos J. Storkey. Censoring Representations with an Adversary. 2016.

[251] B. Efron. Bootstrap methods: Another look at the jacknife. *The Annals of Statistics*, 7(1):1–26, 1979.

[252] Bradley Efron and Robert Tibshirani. Bootstrap methods for standard errors, confidence intervals, and other measures of statistical accuracy. *Statistical science*, pages 54–75, 1986.

[253] Jesse Eickholt and Jianlin Cheng. Predicting protein residue–residue contacts using deep networks and boosting. *Bioinformatics*, 28(23):3066–3072, 2012.

[254] Jesse Eickholt and Jianlin Cheng. DNdisorder: predicting protein disorder using boosting and deep networks. *BMC Bioinformatics*, 14(1):88, 2013.

[255] Samuel A Ellias and Stephen Grossberg. Pattern formation, contrast control, and oscillations in the short term memory of shunting on-center off-surround networks. *Biological Cybernetics*, 20(2):69–98, 1975.

[256] Martin Erdmann, Erik Geiser, Yannik Rath, and Marcel Rieger. Lorentz boost networks: autonomous physics-inspired feature engineering. *Journal of Instrumentation*, 14(06):P06006, 2019.

[257] Dumitru Erhan, Yoshua Bengio, Aaron Courville, Pierre-Antoine Manzagol, Pascal Vincent, and Samy Bengio. Why does unsupervised pre-training help deep learning? *Journal of Machine Learning Research*, 11:625–660, February 2010.

[258] B. Ershoff, C. Lee, C. Wray, V. Agopian, G. Urban, P. Baldi, and M. Cannesson. The Training and Validation of Deep Neural Networks for the Prediction of 90-Day Post-Liver Transplant Mortality Using UNOS Registry Data. *Transplantation Proceedings*, 52(1):246–258, 2020.

[259] Andre Esteva, Brett Kuprel, Roberto A Novoa, Justin Ko, Susan M Swetter, Helen M Blau, and Sebastian Thrun. Dermatologist-level classification of skin cancer with deep neural networks. *Nature*, 542(7639):115–118, 2017.

[260] M. A. Acero *et al.* [NOvA Collaboration]. First Measurement of Neutrino Oscillation Parameters using Neutrinos and Antineutrinos by NOvA. *Physical Review Letters*, 123(15):151803, 2019. Also: arXiv:1906.04907.

[261] Brent Ewing, LaDeana Hillier, Michael C Wendl, and Phil Green. Base-calling of automated sequencer traces usingphred. i. accuracy assessment. *Genome Research*, 8(3):175–185, 1998.

[262] S. Singh F. Agostinelli, G. Hocquet and P. Baldi. From reinforcement learning to deep reinforcement learning: An overview. In Ilya Muchnik, editor, *Key Ideas*

in *Learning Theory from Inception to Current State: Emmanuel Braverman's Legacy*, pages 298–328. Springer, 2018.

[263] P. Fariselli and R. Casadio. Neural network based predictor of residue contacts in proteins. *Protein Engineering*, 12:15–21, 1999.

[264] P. Fariselli and R. Casadio. Prediction of the number of residue contacts in proteins. In *Proceedings of the 2000 Conference on Intelligent Systems for Molecular Biology (ISMB00), La Jolla, CA*, pages 146–151. AAAI Press, Menlo Park, CA, 2000.

[265] P. Fariselli, O. Olmea, A. Valencia, and R. Casadio. Prediction of contact maps with neural networks and correlated mutations. *Protein Engineering*, 14:835–843, 2001.

[266] Piero Fariselli, Florencio Pazos, Alfonso Valencia, and Rita Casadio. Prediction of protein–protein interaction sites in heterocomplexes with neural networks. *The FEBS Journal*, 269(5):1356–1361, 2002.

[267] Oliver Faust, Yuki Hagiwara, Tan Jen Hong, Oh Shu Lih, and U Rajendra Acharya. Deep learning for healthcare applications based on physiological signals: A review. *Computer Methods and Programs in Biomedicine*, 161:1–13, 2018.

[268] Thorsten Fehr, Jochen Weber, Klaus Willmes, and Manfred Herrmann. Neural correlates in exceptional mental arithmetic–about the neural architecture of prodigious skills. *Neuropsychologia*, 48(5):1407–1416, 2010.

[269] Daniel J Felleman and David C Van Essen. Distributed hierarchical processing in the primate cerebral cortex. *Cerebral cortex (New York, NY: 1991)*, 1(1):1–47, 1991.

[270] Jonathan L Feng. Dark matter candidates from particle physics and methods of detection. *Ann. Rev. of Astron. and Astrophys.*, 48:495–545, 2010.

[271] Jonathan L. Feng. Dark Matter Candidates from Particle Physics and Methods of Detection. *Ann. Rev. Astron. Astrophys.*, 48:495–545, 2010.

[272] Zhengzhu Feng and Shlomo Zilberstein. Region-based incremental pruning for POMDPs. In *Proceedings of the 20th conference on Uncertainty in artificial intelligence*, pages 146–153. AUAI Press, 2004.

[273] M. Fenton, A. Shmakov, T. Ho, S. Hsu, D. Whiteson, and P. Baldi. Permutation-less many-jet event reconstruction with symmetry preserving attention networks. *Physical Review Letters*, 2020. Submitted. Also arXiv:2010.0920.

[274] Andre Fischer, Farahnaz Sananbenesi, Xinyu Wang, Matthew Dobbin, and Li-Huei Tsai. Recovery of learning and memory is associated with chromatin remodelling. *Nature*, 447(7141):178–182, 2007.

[275] Richard FitzHugh. Impulses and physiological states in theoretical models of nerve membrane. *Biophysical Journal*, 1(6):445, 1961.

[276] M. A. Fligner, J. S. Verducci, and P. E. Blower. A Modification of the Jaccard/Tanimoto Similarity Index for Diverse Selection of Chemical Compounds Using Binary Strings. *Technometrics*, 44(2):110–119, 2002.

[277] D. R. Flower. On the properties of bit string-based measures of chemical similarity. *J. of Chemical Information and Computer Science*, 38:378–386, 1998.

[278] David Fooshee, Alessio Andronico, and Pierre Baldi. Reactionmap: An efficient atom-mapping algorithm for chemical reactions. *Journal of Chemical information and Modeling*, 53(11):2812–2819, 2013.

[279] Peter Frankl and Hiroshi Maehara. The Johnson–Lindenstrauss lemma and the sphericity of some graphs. *Journal of Combinatorial Theory, Series B*, 44(3):355–362, 1988.

[280] Paolo Frasconi, Marco Gori, and Alessandro Sperduti. A general framework for adaptive processing of data structures. *Neural Networks, IEEE Transactions on*, 9(5):768–786, 1998.

[281] Yoav Freund. An adaptive version of the boost by majority algorithm. *Machine Learning*, 43(3):293–318, 2001.

[282] B. Frey. *Graphical Models for Machine Learning and Digital Communication.* MIT Press, Cambridge, MA, 1998.

[283] B.J. Frey and D. Dueck. Clustering by passing messages between data points. *Science*, 315(5814):972, 2007.

[284] Colin D. Froggatt and Holger Bech Nielsen. Hierarchy of quark masses, Cabibbo angles and CP violation. *Nuclear Physics B*, 147(3-4):277–298, 1979.

[285] Scott Fujimoto, Herke van Hoof, and David Meger. Addressing function approximation error in actor–critic methods. arXiv:1802.09477, 2018.

[286] Kunihiko Fukushima. Visual feature extraction by a multilayered network of analog threshold elements. *IEEE Transactions on Systems Science and Cybernetics*, 5(4):322–333, 1969.

[287] Kunihiko Fukushima. A feature extractor for curvilinear patterns: A design suggested by the mammalian visual system. *Kybernetik*, 7(4):153–160, 1970.

[288] Kunihiko Fukushima. Neocognitron: A self-organizing neural network model for a mechanism of pattern recognition unaffected by shift in position. *Biological Cybernetics*, 36(4):193–202, 1980.

[289] Kunihiko Fukushima, Yoko Yamaguchi, Mitsuru Yasuda, and Shigemi Nagata. An electronic model of the retina. *Proceedings of the IEEE*, 58(12):1950–1951, 1970.

[290] Yan V Fyodorov and Ian Williams. Replica symmetry breaking condition exposed by random matrix calculation of landscape complexity. *Journal of Statistical Physics*, 129(5-6):1081–1116, 2007.

[291] G. Gabrielse, R. Kalra, W. S. Kolthammer, R. McConnell, P. Richerme, D. Grzonka, W. Oelert, T. Sefzick, M. Zielinski, D. W. Fitzakerley, M. C. George, E. A. Hessels, C. H. Storry, M. Weel, A. Mullers, and J. Walz. Trapped antihydrogen in its ground state. *Phys. Rev. Lett.*, 108:113002, Mar 2012.

[292] Yaroslav Ganin, Evgeniya Ustinova, Hana Ajakan, Pascal Germain, Hugo Larochelle, François Laviolette, Mario Marchand, and Victor Lempitsky. Domain-adversarial training of neural networks. *J. Mach. Learn. Res.*, 17(1):2096–2030, January 2016.

[293] M.R. Garey and D.S. Johnson. *Computers and Intractability*. Freeman San Francisco, 1979.

[294] Johann Gasteiger and Clemens Jochum. EROS A computer program for generating sequences of reactions. *Organic Compunds*, pages 93–126, 1978.

[295] A. Gelfand, L. van der Maaten, Y. Chen, and M. Welling. On herding and the perceptron cycling theorem. *Advances of Neural Information Processing Systems (NIPS)*, 23:694–702, 2010.

[296] A. Gelman, J. B. Carlin, H. S. Stern, and D. B. Rubin. *Bayesian Data Analysis*. Chapman and Hall, London, 1995.

[297] Daniel George and EA Huerta. Deep learning for real-time gravitational wave detection and parameter estimation: Results with advanced ligo data. *Physics Letters B*, 778:64–70, 2018.

[298] Edward I George and Robert E McCulloch. Variable selection via Gibbs sampling. *Journal of the American Statistical Association*, 88(423):881–889, 1993.

[299] Felix A Gers, Jürgen Schmidhuber, and Fred Cummins. Learning to forget: Continual prediction with LSTM. *Neural Computation*, 12(10):2451–2471, 2000.

[300] Walter R Gilks, Sylvia Richardson, and David Spiegelhalter. *Markov chain Monte Carlo in Practice*. CRC press, 1995.

[301] Y. Giomataris, Ph. Rebourgeard, J. P. Robert, and G. Charpak. Micromegas: A high-granularity position-sensitive gaseous detector for high particle-flux environments. *Nucl. Instr. Meth. A*, 376, 1996.

[302] Robert C Glen, Andreas Bender, Catrin H Arnby, Lars Carlsson, Scott Boyer, and James Smith. Circular fingerprints: flexible molecular descriptors with applications from physical chemistry to ADME. *IDrugs*, 9(3):199, 2006.

[303] Xavier Glorot and Yoshua Bengio. Understanding the difficulty of training deep feedforward neural networks. In *Proceedings of the Thirteenth International Conference on Artificial Intelligence and Statistics*, pages 249–256, 2010.

[304] Xavier Glorot and Yoshua Bengio. Understanding the difficulty of training deep feedforward neural networks. *In Proceedings of the International Conference on Artificial Intelligence and Statistics (AISTATS10). Society for Artificial Intelligence and Statistics*, 2010.

[305] J. Golden, E. Garcia, and C. Tibbetts. Evolutionary optimization of a neural network-based signal processor for photometric data from an automated DNA sequencer. In *Evolutionary Programming IV. Proceedings of the Fourth Annual Conference on Evolutionary Programming.*, pages 579–601. MIT Press, 1995.

[306] Christoph Goller and Andreas Kuchler. Learning task-dependent distributed representations by backpropagation through structure. In *Neural Networks, 1996., IEEE International Conference on*, volume 1, pages 347–352. IEEE, 1996.

[307] Ian Goodfellow, Yoshua Bengio, and Aaron Courville. *Deep Learning*. MIT Press, 2016. http://www.deeplearningbook.org.

[308] Ian Goodfellow, Jean Pouget-Abadie, Mehdi Mirza, Bing Xu, David Warde-Farley, Sherjil Ozair, Aaron Courville, and Yoshua Bengio. Generative adversarial nets. In *Advances in Neural Information Processing Systems*, pages 2672–2680, 2014.

[309] J. Gorodkin, O. Lund, C. A. Andersen, and S. Brunak. Using sequence motifs for enhanced neural network prediction of protein distance constraints. In *Proceedings of the Seventh International Conference on Intelligent Systems for Molecular*

Biology (ISMB99), La Jolla, CA, pages 95–105. AAAI Press, Menlo Park, CA, 1999.

[310] Abhijit Gosavi. Reinforcement learning: A tutorial survey and recent advances. *INFORMS Journal on Computing*, 21(2):178–192, 2009.

[311] Johannes Gräff, Nadine F Joseph, Meryl E Horn, Alireza Samiei, Jia Meng, Jinsoo Seo, Damien Rei, Adam W Bero, Trongha X Phan, Florence Wagner, et al. Epigenetic priming of memory updating during reconsolidation to attenuate remote fear memories. *Cell*, 156(1-2):261–276, 2014.

[312] Karol Gregor, Ivo Danihelka, Andriy Mnih, Charles Blundell, and Daan Wierstra. Deep autoregressive networks. arXiv:1310.8499, 2013.

[313] Stephen Grossberg. Some networks that can learn, remember, and reproduce any number of complicated space-time patterns, i. *Journal of Mathematics and Mechanics*, 19(1):53–91, 1969.

[314] Stephen Grossberg. Neural pattern discrimination. *Journal of Theoretical Biology*, 27(2):291–337, 1970.

[315] Stephen Grossberg. On the development of feature detectors in the visual cortex with applications to learning and reaction-diffusion systems. *Biological Cybernetics*, 21(3):145–159, 1976.

[316] Robert B Grossman and Robert Grossman. *The Art of Writing Reasonable Organic Reaction Mechanisms*. Springer, 2003.

[317] Zhonghui Guan, Maurizio Giustetto, Stavros Lomvardas, Joung-Hun Kim, Maria Concetta Miniaci, James H Schwartz, Dimitris Thanos, and Eric R Kandel. Integration of long-term-memory-related synaptic plasticity involves bidirectional regulation of gene expression and chromatin structure. *Cell*, 111(4):483–493, 2002.

[318] Dan Guest, Kyle Cranmer, and Daniel Whiteson. Deep learning and its application to LHC physics. *Annual Review of Nuclear and Particle Science*, 68:161–181, 2018.

[319] Daniel Guest, Julian Collado, Pierre Baldi, Shih-Chieh Hsu, Gregor Urban, and Daniel Whiteson. Jet flavor classification in high-energy physics with deep neural networks. *Phys. Rev. D*, 94:112002, Dec 2016.

[320] Carlos Guestrin, Daphne Koller, Ronald Parr, and Shobha Venkataraman. Efficient solution algorithms for factored MDPs. *Journal of Artificial Intelligence Research*, pages 399–468, 2003.

[321] Carlos Guestrin, Michail Lagoudakis, and Ronald Parr. Coordinated reinforcement learning. In *ICML*, volume 2, pages 227–234, 2002.

[322] Varun Gulshan, Lily Peng, Marc Coram, Martin C Stumpe, Derek Wu, Arunachalam Narayanaswamy, Subhashini Venugopalan, Kasumi Widner, Tom Madams, Jorge Cuadros, et al. Development and validation of a deep learning algorithm for detection of diabetic retinopathy in retinal fundus photographs. *Jama*, 316(22):2402–2410, 2016.

[323] J.F. Guzowski, G.L. Lyford, G.D. Stevenson, F.P. Houston, J.L. McGaugh, P.F. Worley, and C.A. Barnes. Inhibition of activity-dependent arc protein expression in the rat hippocampus impairs the maintenance of long-term potentiation and

the consolidation of long-term memory. *Journal of Neuroscience*, 20(11):3993, 2000.

[324] J.F. Guzowski and J.L. McGaugh. Antisense oligodeoxynucleotide-mediated disruption of hippocampal cAMP response element binding protein levels impairs consolidation of memory for water maze training. *Proceedings of the National Academy of Sciences of the United States of America*, 94(6):2693, 1997.

[325] David Ha and Jürgen Schmidhuber. Recurrent world models facilitate policy evolution. In *Advances in Neural Information Processing Systems*, pages 2450–2462, 2018.

[326] Tuomas Haarnoja, Aurick Zhou, Pieter Abbeel, and Sergey Levine. Soft actor–critic: Off-policy maximum entropy deep reinforcement learning with a stochastic actor. arXiv:1801.01290, 2018.

[327] Stuart Hameroff and Roger Penrose. Consciousness in the universe: A review of the 'Orch OR' theory. *Physics of Life Reviews*, 11(1):39–78, 2014.

[328] Katja Hansen, Grégoire Montavon, Franziska Biegler, Siamac Fazli, Matthias Rupp, Matthias Scheffler, O. Anatole von Lilienfeld, Alexandre Tkatchenko, and Klaus-Robert Müller. Assessment and validation of machine learning methods for predicting molecular atomization energies. *Journal of Chemical Theory and Computation*, 9(8):3404–3419, 2013. PMID: 26584096.

[329] Peter E. Hart, Nils J. Nilsson, and Bertram Raphael. A formal basis for the heuristic determination of minimum cost paths. *IEEE Transactions on Systems Science and Cybernetics*, 4(2):100–107, 1968.

[330] Hado V. Hasselt. Double Q-learning. In *Advances in Neural Information Processing Systems*, pages 2613–2621, 2010.

[331] I. Havel and J. Morávek. *B*-valuations of graphs. *Czechoslovak Mathematical Journal*, 22(2):338–351, 1972.

[332] Kaiming He, Georgia Gkioxari, Piotr Dollár, and Ross Girshick. Mask r-cnn. In *Proceedings of the IEEE International Conference on Computer Vision*, pages 2961–2969, 2017.

[333] Kaiming He, Xiangyu Zhang, Shaoqing Ren, and Jian Sun. Delving deep into rectifiers: Surpassing human-level performance on imagenet classification. In *The IEEE International Conference on Computer Vision (ICCV)*, December 2015.

[334] Kaiming He, Xiangyu Zhang, Shaoqing Ren, and Jian Sun. Deep residual learning for image recognition. In *Proceedings of the IEEE Conference on Computer Vision and Pattern Recognition*, pages 770–778, 2016.

[335] Donald Olding Hebb. *The Organization of Behavior: A Neuropsychological Theory*. Wiley, 1949.

[336] Stefan M Hebsgaard, Peter G. Korning, Niels Tolstrup, Jacob Engelbrecht, Pierre Rouzé, and Søren Brunak. Splice site prediction in *arabidopsis thaliana* pre-mRNA by combining local and global sequence information. *Nucleic Acids Research*, 24(17):3439–3452, 1996.

[337] Jan Hermann, Zeno Schätzle, and Frank Noé. Deep-neural-network solution of the electronic Schrödinger equation. *Nature Chemistry*, 12(10):891–897, 2020.

[338] Javier Herrero, Alfonso Valencia, and Joaquın Dopazo. A hierarchical unsupervised growing neural network for clustering gene expression patterns. *Bioinformatics*, 17(2):126–136, 2001.

[339] Lars Hertel, Lingge Li, Pierre Baldi, and Jianming Bian. Convolutional neural networks for electron neutrino and electron shower energy reconstruction in the NOVA detectors. In *Deep Learning for Physical Sciences Workshop at Neural Information Processing Systems*, 2017.

[340] Lars Hertela, Julian Collado, Peter Sadowski, Jordan Ott, and Pierre Baldi. Sherpa: Robust hyperparameter optimization for machine learning. *SoftwareX*, 2020. Also arXiv:2005.04048. Software available at: https://github.com/sherpa-ai/sherpa.

[341] Brian Hie, Ellen Zhong, Bonnie Berger, and Bryan Bryson. Learning the language of viral evolution and escape. *Science*, 371(6526):284–288, 2021.

[342] Michael L Hines and Nicholas T Carnevale. The neuron simulation environment. *Neural Computation*, 9(6):1179–1209, 1997.

[343] G.E. Hinton, S. Osindero, and Y.W. Teh. A fast learning algorithm for deep belief nets. *Neural Computation*, 18(7):1527–1554, 2006.

[344] Geoffrey E Hinton and James L McClelland. Learning representations by recirculation. In *Neural information processing systems*, pages 358–366. New York: American Institute of Physics, 1988.

[345] Geoffrey E. Hinton, Simon Osindero, and Yee-Whye Teh. A fast learning algorithm for deep belief nets. *Neural Computation*, 18(7):1527–1554, 2006.

[346] Geoffrey E. Hinton, Nitish Srivastava, Alex Krizhevsky, Ilya Sutskever, and Ruslan R. Salakhutdinov. Improving neural networks by preventing co-adaptation of feature detectors. *arXiv:1207.0580*, July 2012.

[347] Geoffrey E Hinton, Oriol Vinyals, and Jeff Dean. Distilling the knowledge in a neural network. In *NIPS 2014 Deep Learning Workshop*, 2014.

[348] S. Hochreiter and J. Schmidhuber. Long Short-Term Memory. *Neural Computation*, 9(8):1735–1780, 1997. Based on TR FKI-207-95, TUM (1995).

[349] S. Hochreiter and J. Schmidhuber. Long Short-Term Memory. *Neural Computation*, 9(8):1735–1780, 1997.

[350] Donald Hoffman. *The Case Against Reality: Why Evolution Hid the Truth from Our Eyes*. W.W. Norton & Company, 2019.

[351] John H. Holland. Genetic algorithms and the optimal allocation of trials. *SIAM Journal on Computing*, 2(2):88–105, 1973.

[352] R. Hollering, J. Gasteiger, L. Steinhauer, K.-P. Schulz, and A. Herwig. Simulation of organic reactions: from the degradation of chemicals to combinatorial synthesis. *Journal of Chemical Information and Computer Sciences*, 40(2):482–494, January 2000.

[353] L. Howard Holley and Martin Karplus. Protein secondary structure prediction with a neural network. *Proceedings of the National Academy of Sciences*, 86(1):152–156, 1989.

[354] Thérèse A. Holton, Gianluca Pollastri, Denis C. Shields, and Catherine Mooney. CPPpred: prediction of cell penetrating peptides. *Bioinformatics*, 29(23):3094–3096, 2013.

[355] J.J. Hopfield. Neural networks and physical systems with emergent collective computational abilities. *Proc. of the National Academy of Sciences*, 79:2554–2558, 1982.

[356] J.J. Hopfield and David W. Tank. Neural computation of decisions in optimization problems. *Biological Cybernetics*, 52:141–152, 1985.

[357] John Hopfield and David Tank. Computing with neural circuits: a model. *Science*, 233(4764):625–633, 1986.

[358] M. Hori, K. Yamashita, R.S. Hayano, and T. Yamazaki. Analog cherenkov detectors used in laser spectroscopy experiments on antiprotonic helium. *Nucl. Instr. Meth. A*, 496:102–122, 2003.

[359] K. Hornik, M. Stinchcombe, and H. White. Multilayer feedforward networks are universal approximators. *Neural Netw.*, 2(5):359–366, July 1989.

[360] Jie Hou, Badri Adhikari, and Jianlin Cheng. Deepsf: deep convolutional neural network for mapping protein sequences to folds. arXiv:1706.01010, 2017.

[361] R.A. Houghten. Parallel array and mixture-based synthetic combinatorial chemistry: tools for the next millennium. *Annual Review of Pharmacology and Toxicology*, 40:273–282, 2000.

[362] Frederic Hourdin, Thorsten Mauritsen, Andrew Gettelman, Jean-Christophe Golaz, Venkatramani Balaji, Qingyun Duan, Doris Folini, Duoying Ji, Daniel Klocke, Yun Qian, et al. The art and science of climate model tuning. *Bulletin of the American Meteorological Society*, 98(3):589–602, 2017.

[363] Ronald A. Howard. *Dynamic Programming and Markov Processes*. MIT Press, 1960.

[364] Guang-Bin Huang, Dian Hui Wang, and Yuan Lan. Extreme learning machines: a survey. *International Journal of Machine Learning and Cybernetics*, 2(2):107–122, 2011.

[365] David H. Hubel and Torsten N. Wiesel. Receptive fields, binocular interaction and functional architecture in the cat's visual cortex. *The Journal of Physiology*, 160(1):106, 1962.

[366] Marcus Hutter. Feature reinforcement learning: Part I. unstructured MDPs. *Journal of Artificial General Intelligence*, 1(1):3–24, 2009.

[367] Sergey Ioffe and Christian Szegedy. Batch normalization: Accelerating deep network training by reducing internal covariate shift. arXiv:1502.03167, 2015.

[368] J.J. Irwin and B.K. Shoichet. ZINC – a free database of commercially available compounds for virtual screening. *Journal of Chemical Information and Computer Sciences*, 45:177–182, 2005.

[369] L. Itti and P. Baldi. A principled approach to detecting surprising events in video. In *Computer Vision and Pattern Recognition, 2005. CVPR 2005. IEEE Computer Society Conference on*, volume 1, pages 631–637. IEEE, 2005.

[370] Teresa Iuculano, Miriam Rosenberg-Lee, Kaustubh Supekar, Charles J. Lynch, Amirah Khouzam, Jennifer Phillips, Lucina Q. Uddin, and Vinod Menon. Brain

organization underlying superior mathematical abilities in children with autism. *Biological Psychiatry*, 75(3):223–230, 2014.

[371] A.G. Ivakhnenko. The group method of data handling – a rival of the method of stochastic approximation. *Soviet Automatic Control*, 13(3):43–55, 1968.

[372] A.G. Ivakhnenko. Polynomial theory of complex systems. *Systems, Man and Cybernetics, IEEE Transactions on*, (4):364–378, 1971.

[373] Eugene M. Izhikevich. Simple model of spiking neurons. *IEEE Transactions on Neural Networks*, 14(6):1569–1572, 2003.

[374] C.A. James, D. Weininger, and J. Delany. *Daylight Theory Manual*, 2004. Available at `http://www.daylight.com/dayhtml/doc/theory/theory.toc.html`.

[375] Jon Paul Janet and Heather J. Kulik. Predicting electronic structure properties of transition metal complexes with neural networks. *Chem. Sci.*, 8:5137–5152, 2017.

[376] E.T. Jaynes. *Probability Theory. The Logic of Science*. Cambridge University Press, 2003.

[377] Anders Boeck Jensen, Pope L. Moseley, Tudor I. Oprea, Sabrina Gade Ellesøe, Robert Eriksson, Henriette Schmock, Peter Bjødstrup Jensen, Lars Juhl Jensen, and Søren Brunak. Temporal disease trajectories condensed from population-wide registry data covering 6.2 million patients. *Nature Communications*, 5, 2014.

[378] L. Juhl Jensen, Ramneek Gupta, Nikolaj Blom, D. Devos, J. Tamames, Can Kesmir, Henrik Nielsen, Hans Henrik Stærfeldt, Krzysztof Rapacki, Christopher Workman, et al. Prediction of human protein function from post-translational modifications and localization features. *Journal of molecular biology*, 319(5):1257–1265, 2002.

[379] Xiaowei Jia, Jared Willard, Anuj Karpatne, Jordan Read, Jacob Zwart, Michael Steinbach, and Vipin Kumar. Physics guided RNNs for modeling dynamical systems: A case study in simulating lake temperature profiles. In *SIAM International Conference on Data Mining, SDM 2019*, pages 558–566, 2019.

[380] Wengong Jin, Connor Coley, Regina Barzilay, and Tommi Jaakkola. Predicting organic reaction outcomes with Weisfeiler–Lehman network. In *Advances in Neural Information Processing Systems*, pages 2607–2616, 2017.

[381] Taeho Jo, Jie Hou, Jesse Eickholt, and Jianlin Cheng. Improving protein fold recognition by deep learning networks. *Scientific reports*, 5:srep17573, 2015.

[382] William B. Johnson and Joram Lindenstrauss. Extensions of Lipschitz mappings into a Hilbert space. *Contemporary Mathematics*, 26(189-206):1, 1984.

[383] Catherine R.G. Jones, Francesca Happé, Hannah Golden, Anita J.S. Marsden, Jenifer Tregay, Emily Simonoff, Andrew Pickles, Gillian Baird, and Tony Charman. Reading and arithmetic in adolescents with autism spectrum disorders: Peaks and dips in attainment. *Neuropsychology*, 23(6):718, 2009.

[384] David T. Jones, Daniel W.A. Buchan, Domenico Cozzetto, and Massimiliano Pontil. Psicov: precise structural contact prediction using sparse inverse covariance

estimation on large multiple sequence alignments. *Bioinformatics*, 28(2):184–190, 2011.

[385] S.O. Jonsdottir, F.S. Jorgensen, and S. Brunak. Prediction methods and databases within chemoinformatics: Emphasis on drugs and drug candidates. *Bioinformatics*, 21:2145–2160, 2005.

[386] M.I. Jordan, editor. *Learning in Graphical Models*. MIT Press, Cambridge, MA, 1999.

[387] W.L. Jorgensen, E.R. Laird, A.J. Gushurst, J.M. Fleischer, S.A. Gothe, H.E. Helson, G.D. Paderes, and S. Sinclair. CAMEO: a program from the logical prediction of the products of organic reactions. *Pure and Applied Chemistry*, 62:1921–1932, July 1990.

[388] Leslie Pack Kaelbling, Michael L. Littman, and Andrew W. Moore. Reinforcement learning: A survey. *Journal of Artificial Intelligence Research*, 4:237–285, 1996.

[389] Jeff Kahn, János Komlós, and Endre Szemerédi. On the probability that a random ±1-matrix is singular. *Journal of the American Mathematical Society*, 8(1):223–240, 1995.

[390] Lukasz Kaiser, Mohammad Babaeizadeh, Piotr Milos, Blazej Osinski, Roy H. Campbell, Konrad Czechowski, Dumitru Erhan, Chelsea Finn, Piotr Kozakowski, Sergey Levine, et al. Model-based reinforcement learning for atari. arXiv:1903.00374, 2019.

[391] Eric R Kandel, James H Schwartz, Thomas M Jessell, et al. *Principles of Neural Science*. McGraw-hill New York, 2000.

[392] Daniel Kane et al. A structure theorem for poorly anticoncentrated polynomials of Gaussians and applications to the study of polynomial threshold functions. *The Annals of Probability*, 45(3):1612–1679, 2017.

[393] David E. Kaplan, Keith Rehermann, Matthew D. Schwartz, and Brock Tweedie. Top Tagging: A Method for Identifying Boosted Hadronically Decaying Top Quarks. *Phys. Rev. Lett.*, 101:142001, 2008.

[394] Anuj Karpatne, Gowtham Atluri, James H. Faghmous, Michael Steinbach, Arindam Banerjee, Auroop Ganguly, Shashi Shekhar, Nagiza Samatova, and Vipin Kumar. Theory-guided data science: A new paradigm for scientific discovery from data. *IEEE Transactions on Knowledge and Data Engineering*, 29(10):2318–2331, oct 2017.

[395] Anuj Karpatne, William Watkins, Jordan Read, and Vipin Kumar. Physics-guided Neural Networks (PGNN): An Application in Lake Temperature Modeling. 2017.

[396] M.A. Kayala, C.A. Azencott, J.H. Chen, and P. Baldi. Learning to predict chemical reactions. *Journal of chemical information and modeling*, 51(9):2209–2222, 2011.

[397] M.A. Kayala and P. Baldi. Reactionpredictor: Prediction of complex chemical reactions at the mechanistic level using machine learning. *Journal of Chemical Information and Modeling*, 52(10):2526–2540, 2012.

[398] Matthew A. Kayala, Chloé-Agathe Azencott, Jonathan H. Chen, and Pierre Baldi. Learning to predict chemical reactions. *Journal of Chemical Information and Modeling*, 51(9):2209–2222, 2011. PMID: 21819139.

[399] Matthew A. Kayala and Pierre Baldi. Reactionpredictor: Prediction of complex chemical reactions at the mechanistic level using machine learning. *Journal of Chemical Information and Modeling*, 52(10):2526–2540, 2012. PMID: 22978639.

[400] Michael Kearns, Yishay Mansour, and Andrew Y Ng. A sparse sampling algorithm for near-optimal planning in large Markov decision processes. *Machine Learning*, 49(2-3):193–208, 2002.

[401] Michael J. Kearns and Umesh Vazirani. *An Introduction to Computational Learning Theory*. MIT Press, 1994.

[402] S. Sathiya Keerthi and B. Ravindran. A tutorial survey of reinforcement learning. *Sadhana*, 19(6):851–889, 1994.

[403] David R. Kelley, Jasper Snoek, and John L. Rinn. Basset: learning the regulatory code of the accessible genome with deep convolutional neural networks. *Genome Res.*, 26(7):990–9, 07 2016.

[404] Waqasuddin Khan, Fergal Duffy, Gianluca Pollastri, Denis C. Shields, and Catherine Mooney. Predicting binding within disordered protein regions to structurally characterised peptide-binding domains. *PLoS One*, 8(9):e72838, 2013.

[405] Sunghwan Kim, Paul A. Thiessen, Evan E. Bolton, Jie Chen, Gang Fu, Asta Gindulyte, Lianyi Han, Jane He, Siqian He, Benjamin A. Shoemaker, et al. Pubchem substance and compound databases. *Nucleic Acids Research*, 44(D1):D1202–D1213, 2015.

[406] Diederik P. Kingma and Jimmy Ba. Adam: A method for stochastic optimization. In *Proceedings of the 3rd International Conference on Learning Representations (ICLR)*, 2014.

[407] Diederik P. Kingma and Max Welling. Auto-encoding variational bayes. arXiv:1312.6114, 2013.

[408] Durk P Kingma and Prafulla Dhariwal. Glow: Generative flow with invertible 1x1 convolutions. In *Advances in Neural Information Processing Systems*, pages 10215–10224, 2018.

[409] Scott Kirkpatrick, C Daniel Gelatt, and Mario P Vecchi. Optimization by simulated annealing. *Science*, 220(4598):671–680, 1983.

[410] Jan Koutnik Bas R. Steunebrink Jurgen Schmidhuber Klaus Greff, Rupesh Kumar Srivastava. LSTM: A search space odyssey. *Arxiv*, arXiv:1503.04069, 2015.

[411] Adam R Klivans, Ryan O'Donnell, and Rocco A Servedio. Learning intersections and thresholds of halfspaces. *Journal of Computer and System Sciences*, 68(4):808–840, 2004.

[412] Adam R Klivans and Rocco A Servedio. Learning DNF in time $2^{O(n^{1/3})}$. *Journal of Computer and System Sciences*, 68(2):303–318, 2004.

[413] Daniel Klocke, Matthias Brueck, Cathy Hohenegger, and Bjorn Stevens. Rediscovery of the doldrums in storm-resolving simulations over the tropical Atlantic. *Nature Geoscience*, 10(12):891–896, 2017.

[414] Jens Kober, J Andrew Bagnell, and Jan Peters. Reinforcement learning in robotics: A survey. *The International Journal of Robotics Research*, page 0278364913495721, 2013.

[415] Christof Koch, Tomaso Poggio, and Vincent Torre. Nonlinear interactions in a dendritic tree: localization, timing, and role in information processing. *Proceedings of the National Academy of Sciences*, 80(9):2799–2802, 1983.

[416] Levente Kocsis and Csaba Szepesvári. Bandit based monte-carlo planning. In *European conference on machine learning*, pages 282–293. Springer, 2006.

[417] D. Koller and N. Friedman. *Probabilistic Graphical Models: Principles and Techniques*. The MIT Press, 2009.

[418] Andreĭ Nikolaevich Kolmogorov. The representation of continuous functions of several variables by superpositions of continuous functions of a smaller number of variables. *Doklady Akademii Nauk SSSR*, 108(2):179–182, 1956.

[419] János Komlós and Ramamohan Paturi. Convergence results in an associative memory model. *Neural Networks*, 1(3):239–250, 1988.

[420] Matthias Krause and Pavel Pudlák. Computing Boolean functions by polynomials and threshold circuits. *Computational Complexity*, 7(4):346–370, 1998.

[421] Alex Krizhevsky and Geoffrey Hinton. Learning multiple layers of features from tiny images. 2009.

[422] Alex Krizhevsky, Ilya Sutskever, and Geoffrey E. Hinton. Imagenet classification with deep convolutional neural networks. In F. Pereira, C.J.C. Burges, L. Bottou, and K.Q. Weinberger, editors, *Advances in Neural Information Processing Systems 25*, pages 1097–1105. Curran Associates, Inc., 2012.

[423] A. Krogh, M. Brown, I.S. Mian, K. Sjölander, and D. Haussler. Hidden Markov models in computational biology: Applications to protein modeling. *J. Mol. Biol.*, 235:1501–1531, 1994.

[424] Anders Krogh, BjoÈrn Larsson, Gunnar Von Heijne, and Erik L.L. Sonnhammer. Predicting transmembrane protein topology with a hidden Markov model: application to complete genomes. *Journal of molecular biology*, 305(3):567–580, 2001.

[425] Predrag Kukic, Claudio Mirabello, Giuseppe Tradigo, Ian Walsh, Pierangelo Veltri, and Gianluca Pollastri. Toward an accurate prediction of inter-residue distances in proteins using 2D recursive neural networks. *BMC bioinformatics*, 15(1):6, 2014.

[426] Ludmila I. Kuncheva and Christopher J. Whitaker. Measures of diversity in classifier ensembles and their relationship with the ensemble accuracy. *Machine Learning*, 51(2):181–207, 2003.

[427] N. Kuroda et al. A source of antihydrogen for in-flight hyperfine spectroscopy. *Nature Communications*, 5:3089, 2014.

[428] T. Kwok and D. Yeung. Constructive Algorithms for Structure Learning in Feedforward Neural Networks for Regression Problems. *IEEE Transactions on Neural Networks*, 8:630–645, 1997.

[429] Matthew Lai. Giraffe: Using deep reinforcement learning to play chess. arXiv:1509.01549, 2015.

[430] Guillaume Lample and François Charton. Deep learning for symbolic mathematics. arXiv:1912.01412, 2019.

[431] S. Lang. *Algebra*. Addison-Wesley, Reading, MA, 1984.

[432] Andrew J. Larkoski, Simone Marzani, Gregory Soyez, and Jesse Thaler. Soft Drop. *JHEP*, 1405:146, 2014.

[433] Andrew J. Larkoski, Ian Moult, and Duff Neill. Power Counting to Better Jet Observables. *JHEP*, 12:009, 2014.

[434] Andrew J. Larkoski, Gavin P. Salam, and Jesse Thaler. Energy Correlation Functions for Jet Substructure. *JHEP*, 1306:108, 2013.

[435] Thomas A. Lasko, Joshua C. Denny, and Mia A. Levy. Computational phenotype discovery using unsupervised feature learning over noisy, sparse, and irregular clinical data. *PloS one*, 8(6):e66341, 2013.

[436] A.R. Leach and V.J. Gillet. *An Introduction to Chemoinformatics*. Springer, Dordrecht, The Netherlands, 2005.

[437] Rebecca K. Leane and Tracy R. Slatyer. Dark matter strikes back at the Galactic Center. arXiv:1904.08430, 2019.

[438] Christine K. Lee, Ira Hofer, Eilon Gabel, Pierre Baldi, and Maxime Cannesson. Development and validation of a deep neural network model for prediction of postoperative in-hospital mortality. *Anesthesiology: The Journal of the American Society of Anesthesiologists*, 129(4):649–662, 2018.

[439] Felix Leibfried, Nate Kushman, and Katja Hofmann. A deep learning approach for joint video frame and reward prediction in atari games. arXiv:1611.07078, 2016.

[440] P. Di Lena and P. Baldi. Fold recognition by scoring protein map similarities using the congruence coefficient. *Bioinformatics*, 2021. In press. Also: bioRxiv: doi: https://protect-eu.mimecast.com/s/5xMNC83N3IQNy6Jt24dLc?domain=doi.org

[441] Aurora KR LePort, Aaron T Mattfeld, Heather Dickinson-Anson, James H Fallon, Craig EL Stark, Frithjof Kruggel, Larry Cahill, and James L McGaugh. Behavioral and neuroanatomical investigation of highly superior autobiographical memory (HSAM). *Neurobiology of learning and memory*, 98(1):78–92, 2012.

[442] Michael K K Leung, Hui Yuan Xiong, Leo J Lee, and Brendan J Frey. Deep learning of the tissue-regulated splicing code. *Bioinformatics*, 30(12):i121–9, Jun 2014.

[443] Esther Levin, Roberto Pieraccini, and Wieland Eckert. A stochastic model of human-machine interaction for learning dialog strategies. *IEEE Transactions on speech and audio processing*, 8(1):11–23, 2000.

[444] Sergey Levine, Chelsea Finn, Trevor Darrell, and Pieter Abbeel. End-to-end training of deep visuomotor policies. *Journal of Machine Learning Research*, 17(39):1–40, 2016.

[445] Lingge Li, Andrew Holbrook, Babak Shahbaba, and Pierre Baldi. Neural network gradient hamiltonian monte carlo. *Computational statistics*, 34(1):281–299, 2019.

[446] Lingge Li, Nitish Nayak, Jianming Bian, and Pierre Baldi. Efficient neutrino oscillation parameter inference using Gaussian processes. *Physical Review D*, 101(1):012001, 2020.

[447] Yi Li, Daniel Quang, and Xiaohui Xie. Understanding sequence conservation with deep learning. *bioRxiv*, page 103929, 2017.

[448] Rong-Zhen Liao and Walter Thiel. Comparison of QM-only and QM/MM models for the mechanism of tungsten-dependent acetylene hydratase. *Journal of Chemical Theory and Computation*, 8(10):3793–3803, 2012. PMID: 26593020.

[449] Timothy P Lillicrap, Daniel Cownden, Douglas B Tweed, and Colin J Akerman. Random synaptic feedback weights support error backpropagation for deep learning. *Nature Communications*, 7, 2016.

[450] Timothy P Lillicrap, Jonathan J Hunt, Alexander Pritzel, Nicolas Heess, Tom Erez, Yuval Tassa, David Silver, and Daan Wierstra. Continuous control with deep reinforcement learning. 2016.

[451] Chin-Teng Lin and CS George Lee. Reinforcement structure/parameter learning for neural-network-based fuzzy logic control systems. *Fuzzy Systems, IEEE Transactions on*, 2(1):46–63, 1994.

[452] Julia Ling, Andrew Kurzawski, and Jeremy Templeton. Reynolds averaged turbulence modelling using deep neural networks with embedded invariance. *Journal of Fluid Mechanics*, 807:155–166, nov 2016.

[453] C. Lipinski and A. Hopkins. Navigating chemical space for biology and medicine. *Nature*, 432:855–861, 2004.

[454] Michael L Littman. Markov games as a framework for multi-agent reinforcement learning. In *Proceedings of the Eleventh International Conference on Machine Learning*, volume 157, pages 157–163, 1994.

[455] Michael Lederman Littman. *Algorithms for sequential decision making*. PhD thesis, Brown University, 1996.

[456] Feng Liu, Chao Ren, Hao Li, Pingkun Zhou, Xiaochen Bo, and Wenjie Shu. De novo identification of replication-timing domains in the human genome by deep learning. *Bioinformatics*, 32(5):641–649, 2015.

[457] Sijia Liu, Haiming Chen, Scott Ronquist, Laura Seaman, Nicholas Ceglia, Walter Meixner, Pin-Yu Chen, Gerald Higgins, Pierre Baldi, Steve Smale, et al. Genome architecture mediates transcriptional control of human myogenic reprogramming. *iScience*, 6:232–246, 2018.

[458] Wei Liu, Dragomir Anguelov, Dumitru Erhan, Christian Szegedy, Scott Reed, Cheng-Yang Fu, and Alexander C Berg. Ssd: Single shot multibox detector. In *European conference on computer vision*, pages 21–37. Springer, 2016.

[459] Gilles Louppe, Kyunghyun Cho, Cyril Becot, and Kyle Cranmer. QCD-Aware Recursive Neural Networks for Jet Physics. 2017. arXiv:1702.00748.

[460] Gilles Louppe, Kyunghyun Cho, Cyril Becot, and Kyle Cranmer. QCD-Aware Recursive Neural Networks for Jet Physics. *Journal of High Energy Physics*, 01:057, 2019.

[461] Gilles Louppe, Michael Kagan, and Kyle Cranmer. Learning to Pivot with Adversarial Networks. 2016.

[462] Daniel Lowe. Chemical reactions from US patents (1976-Sep2016). `https://figshare.com/articles/Chemical_reactions_from_US_patents_1976-Sep2016_/5104873`, 2017.

[463] Yadong Lu, Julian Collado, Daniel Whiteson, and Pierre Baldi. SARM: SARM: Sparse Auto-Regressive Models for Scalable Generation of Sparse Images in Particle Physics. *Physical Review D*, 2021. In press. Also arXiv:2009.14017.

[464] O. Lund, K. Frimand, J. Gorodkin, H. Bohr, J. Bohr, J. Hansen, and S. Brunak. Protein distance constraints predicted by neural networks and probability density functions. *Prot. Eng.*, 10:11:1241–1248, 1997.

[465] O. Lund, Nielsen M., C. Lundegaard, C. Kesmir, and S. Brunak. *Immunological Bioinformatics*. MIT press, 2005.

[466] Minh-Thang Luong, Hieu Pham, and Christopher D Manning. Effective approaches to attention-based neural machine translation. arXiv:1508.04025, 2015.

[467] Alessandro Lusci, David Fooshee, Michael Browning, Joshua Swamidass, and Pierre Baldi. Accurate and efficient target prediction using a potency-sensitive influence-relevance voter. *Journal of cheminformatics*, 7(1):63, 2015.

[468] Alessandro Lusci, Gianluca Pollastri, and Pierre Baldi. Deep architectures and deep learning in chemoinformatics: the prediction of aqueous solubility for drug-like molecules. *Journal of Chemical Information and Modeling*, 53(7):1563–1575, 2013.

[469] Frank Lyko, Sylvain Foret, Robert Kucharski, Stephan Wolf, Cassandra Falckenhayn, and Ryszard Maleszka. The honey bee epigenomes: differential methylation of brain DNA in queens and workers. *PLoS Biol*, 8(11):e1000506, 2010.

[470] Richard Lyon and Carver Mead. An analog electronic cochlea. *IEEE Transactions on Acoustics, Speech, and Signal Processing*, 36(7):1119–1134, 1988.

[471] James Lyons, Abdollah Dehzangi, Rhys Heffernan, Alok Sharma, Kuldip Paliwal, Abdul Sattar, Yaoqi Zhou, and Yuedong Yang. Predicting backbone $c\alpha$ angles and dihedrals from protein sequences by stacked sparse auto-encoder deep neural network. *Journal of Computational Chemistry*, 35(28):2040–2046, 2014.

[472] S. Marzani M. Dasgupta, A. Fregoso and G. P. Salam. Towards an understanding of jet substructure. *JHEP*, 1309:029,, 2013.

[473] David J.C. MacKay. The evidence framework applied to classification networks. *Neural Computation*, 4(5):720–736, 1992.

[474] David J.C. MacKay. A practical Bayesian framework for back-propagation networks. *Neural Computation*, 4(3):448–472, 1992.

[475] Christophe N. Magnan and Pierre Baldi. SSpro/ACCpro 5: Almost perfect prediction of protein secondary structure and relative solvent accessibility using profiles, machine learning, and structural similarity. *Bioinformatics*, 30(18):2592–2597, 2014.

[476] C.N. Magnan, A. Randall, and P. Baldi. SOLpro: accurate sequence-based prediction of protein solubility. *Bioinformatics*, 25(17):2200–2207, 2009.

[477] C.N. Magnan, M. Zeller, M.A. Kayala, A. Vigil, A. Randall, P.L. Felgner, and P. Baldi. High-throughput prediction of protein antigenicity using protein microarray data. *Bioinformatics*, 26(23):2936–2943, 2010.

[478] M. Mahajan, P. Nimbhorkar, and K. Varadarajan. The planar k-means problem is NP-hard. *WALCOM: Algorithms and Computation*, pages 274–285, 2009.

[479] Ziro Maki, Masami Nakagawa, and Shoichi Sakata. Remarks on the unified model of elementary particles. *Progress of Theoretical Physics*, 28(5):870–880, 1962.

[480] Stéphane Mallat. Group invariant scattering. *Communications on Pure and Applied Mathematics*, 65(10):1331–1398, 2012.

[481] Stéphane Mallat. Understanding deep convolutional networks. *Philosophical Transactions of the Royal Society A: Mathematical, Physical and Engineering Sciences*, 374(2065):20150203, 2016.

[482] Stephan Mandt, Matthew Hoffman, and David Blei. A variational analysis of stochastic gradient algorithms. In *International Conference on Machine Learning*, pages 354–363, 2016.

[483] Y Marc'Aurelio Ranzato, Lan Boureau, and Yann LeCun. Sparse feature learning for deep belief networks. *Advances in Neural Information Processing Systems*, 20:1185–1192, 2007.

[484] Debora S. Marks, Thomas A. Hopf, and Chris Sander. Protein structure prediction from sequence variation. *Nature Biotechnology*, 30(11):1072–1080, 2012.

[485] Pablo Márquez-Neila, Mathieu Salzmann, and Pascal Fua. Imposing Hard Constraints on Deep Networks: Promises and Limitations. arXiv:1706.02025, 2017.

[486] E. Marris. Chemistry society goes head to head with NIH in fight over public database. *Nature*, 435(7043):718–719, 2005.

[487] Jonathan Masci, Alessandro Giusti, Dan C. Ciresan, Gabriel Fricout, and Jürgen Schmidhuber. A fast learning algorithm for image segmentation with max-pooling convolutional networks. In *International Conference on Image Processing (ICIP13)*, pages 2713–2717, 2013.

[488] Mark Mayford, Steven A. Siegelbaum, and Eric R. Kandel. Synapses and memory storage. *Cold Spring Harbor Perspectives in Biology*, 4(6):a005751, 2012.

[489] Stephen McAleer, Forest Agostinelli, Alexander Shmakov, and Pierre Baldi. Solving the Rubik's cube with approximate policy iteration. *International Conference on Learning Representations (ICLR)*, 2019.

[490] James L. McClelland, David E. Rumelhart, and the PDP Research Group. *Parallel Distributed Processing*, volumes 1 and 2. MIT Press, Cambridge, MA, 1987.

[491] Robert J. McEliece. *The Theory of Information and Coding*. Cambridge University Press, 2002.

[492] Robert J. McEliece, Edward Posner, Eugene Rodemich, and Santosh S. Venkatesh. The capacity of the Hopfield associative memory. *IEEE Transactions on Information Theory*, 33(4):461–482, 1987.

[493] Amy McGovern and Andrew G. Barto. Automatic discovery of subgoals in reinforcement learning using diverse density. In *ICML '01: Proceedings of the Eighteenth International Conference on Machine Learning*, page 8, 2001.

[494] Bruce L McNaughton. Cortical hierarchies, sleep, and the extraction of knowledge from memory. *Artificial Intelligence*, 174(2):205–214, 2010.

[495] Carver Mead and Mohammed Ismail (editors). *Analog VLSI Implementation of Neural Systems*. Springer Science & Business Media, 2012.

[496] Carver Mead and Misha Mahowald. A silicon model of early visual processing. *Neural Networks*, 1(1):91–97, 1988.

[497] N. Megiddo and K.J. Supowit. On the complexity of some common geometric location problems. *SIAM J. Comput.*, 13(1):182–196, 1984.

[498] Bartlett W. Mel. Information processing in dendritic trees. *Neural Computation*, 6(6):1031–1085, 1994.

[499] C.D. Meyer. *Matrix Analysis and Applied Linear Algebra*. SIAM, 2000.

[500] Donald Michie. Trial and error. *Science Survey, Part*, 2:129–145, 1961.

[501] Donald Michie. Experiments on the mechanization of game-learning. Part I. Characterization of the model and its parameters. *The Computer Journal*, 6(3):232–236, 1963.

[502] Donald Michie and Roger A. Chambers. Boxes: An experiment in adaptive control. *Machine intelligence*, 2(2):137–152, 1968.

[503] M. Minsky and S. Papert. *Perceptrons*. MIT Press, Cambridge, MA, 1969.

[504] Marvin Minsky. Steps toward artificial intelligence. *Proceedings of the IRE*, 49(1):8–30, 1961.

[505] Riccardo Miotto, Li Li, Brian A Kidd, and Joel T Dudley. Deep patient: An unsupervised representation to predict the future of patients from the electronic health records. *Scientific reports*, 6:26094, 2016.

[506] Claudio Mirabello and Gianluca Pollastri. Porter, paleale 4.0: high-accuracy prediction of protein secondary structure and relative solvent accessibility. *Bioinformatics*, 29(16):2056–2058, 2013.

[507] Toby J Mitchell and John J Beauchamp. Bayesian variable selection in linear regression. *Journal of the American Statistical Association*, 83(404):1023–1032, 1988.

[508] Yoshiaki Miyamoto, Yoshiyuki Kajikawa, Ryuji Yoshida, Tsuyoshi Yamaura, Hisashi Yashiro, and Hirofumi Tomita. Deep moist atmospheric convection in a subkilometer global simulation. *Geophysical Research Letters*, 40(18):4922–4926, 2013.

[509] Eric Mjolsness, David H Sharp, and John Reinitz. A connectionist model of development. *Journal of theoretical Biology*, 152(4):429–453, 1991.

[510] Volodymyr Mnih, Adria Puigdomenech Badia, Mehdi Mirza, Alex Graves, Timothy P Lillicrap, Tim Harley, David Silver, and Koray Kavukcuoglu. Asynchronous methods for deep reinforcement learning. In *International Conference on Machine Learning (ICML)*, 2016.

[511] Volodymyr Mnih, Koray Kavukcuoglu, David Silver, Andrei A Rusu, Joel Veness, Marc G Bellemare, Alex Graves, Martin Riedmiller, Andreas K Fidjeland, Georg Ostrovski, et al. Human-level control through deep reinforcement learning. *Nature*, 518(7540):529–533, 2015.

[512] John Moody and Matthew Saffell. Reinforcement learning for trading. *Advances in Neural Information Processing Systems*, pages 917–923, 1999.

[513] Catherine Mooney, Niall J Haslam, Thérèse A Holton, Gianluca Pollastri, and Denis C Shields. Peptidelocator: prediction of bioactive peptides in protein sequences. *Bioinformatics*, 29(9):1120–1126, 2013.

[514] Catherine Mooney, Niall J Haslam, Gianluca Pollastri, and Denis C Shields. Towards the improved discovery and design of functional peptides: common features of diverse classes permit generalized prediction of bioactivity. *PloS one*, 7(10):e45012, 2012.

[515] Catherine Mooney and Gianluca Pollastri. Beyond the twilight zone: Automated prediction of structural properties of proteins by recursive neural networks and remote homology information. *Proteins: Structure, Function, and Bioinformatics*, 77(1):181–190, 2009.

[516] Catherine Mooney, Gianluca Pollastri, Denis C Shields, and Niall J Haslam. Prediction of short linear protein binding regions. *Journal of molecular biology*, 415(1):193–204, 2012.

[517] Catherine Mooney, Yong-Hong Wang, and Gianluca Pollastri. SCLpred: protein subcellular localization prediction by N-to-1 neural networks. *Bioinformatics*, 27(20):2812–2819, 2011.

[518] David E. Moriarty, Alan C. Schultz, and John J. Grefenstette. Evolutionary algorithms for reinforcement learning. *J. Artif. Intell. Res.(JAIR)*, 11:241–276, 1999.

[519] Javier R. Movellan. Contrastive Hebbian learning in the continuous Hopfield model. In *Connectionist Models*, pages 10–17. Elsevier, 1991.

[520] Stephen Muggleton and Luc De Raedt. Inductive logic programming: Theory and methods. *The Journal of Logic Programming*, 19:629–679, 1994.

[521] Saburo Muroga. Lower bounds of the number of threshold functions and a maximum weight. *IEEE Transactions on Electronic Computers*, (2):136–148, 1965.

[522] Kevin P. Murphy. *Machine Learning: a Probabilistic Perspective*. MIT press, 2012.

[523] Andreas Mütter, Erik Parr, and Patrick K. S. Vaudrevange. Deep learning in the heterotic orbifold landscape. *Nuclear Physics B*, 940:113–129, 2019.

[524] N.N. Tishby, F. Pereira, and W. Bialek. The information bottleneck method. In *Proceedings of the 37th Annual Allerton Conference on Communcation, Control, and Computing*, pages 368–377. University of Illinois, 1999. Also: arXiv preprint physics/0004057.

[525] K. Nagata, A. Randall, and P. Baldi. SIDEpro: A Novel Machine Learning Approach for the Accurate Prediction of Protein Side Chains. 2011. Server available. Manuscript under preparation.

[526] Ken Nagata, Arlo Randall, and Pierre Baldi. Incorporating post-translational modifications and unnatural amino acids into high-throughput modeling of protein structures. *Bioinformatics*, 30(12):1681–1689, 2014.

[527] Jinichi Nagumo, Suguru Arimoto, and Shuji Yoshizawa. An active pulse transmission line simulating nerve axon. *Proceedings of the IRE*, 50(10):2061–2070, 1962.

[528] Arun Nair, Praveen Srinivasan, Sam Blackwell, Cagdas Alcicek, Rory Fearon, Alessandro De Maria, Vedavyas Panneershelvam, Mustafa Suleyman, Charles Beattie, Stig Petersen, et al. Massively parallel methods for deep reinforcement learning. arXiv:1507.04296, 2015.

[529] Vinod Nair and Geoffrey E. Hinton. Rectified Linear Units Improve Restricted Boltzmann Machines. In Johannes Furnkranz and Thorsten Joachims, editors, *Proceedings of the 27th International Conference on Machine Learning (ICML-10)*, pages 807–814. Omnipress, 2010.

[530] R. Nasr, D.S. Hirschberg, and P. Baldi. Hashing Algorithms and Data Structures for Rapid Searches of Fingerprint Vectors. *Journal of Chemical Information and Modeling*, 50(8):1358–1368, 2011.

[531] Ramzi Nasr, Rares Vernica, Chen Li, and Pierre Baldi. Speeding up chemical searches using the inverted index: The convergence of chemoinformatics and text search methods. *Journal of chemical information and modeling*, 52(4):891–900, 2012.

[532] Radford M Neal. *Bayesian Learning for Neural Networks*. Springer Verlag 1996. Reissued in 2012.

[533] Charles M Newman. Memory capacity in neural network models: Rigorous lower bounds. *Neural Networks*, 1(3):223–238, 1988.

[534] James Newman and Bernard J Baars. A neural attentional model for access to consciousness: A global workspace perspective. *Concepts in Neuroscience*, 4(2):255–290, 1993.

[535] Andrew Y Ng, Adam Coates, Mark Diel, Varun Ganapathi, Jamie Schulte, Ben Tse, Eric Berger, and Eric Liang. Autonomous inverted helicopter flight via reinforcement learning. In *Experimental Robotics IX*, pages 363–372. Springer, 2006.

[536] Andrew Y Ng, Stuart J Russell, et al. Algorithms for inverse reinforcement learning. In *Icml*, pages 663–670, 2000.

[537] Henrik Nielsen, Jacob Engelbrecht, Søren Brunak, and Gunnar von Heijne. Identification of prokaryotic and eukaryotic signal peptides and prediction of their cleavage sites. *Protein engineering*, 10(1):1–6, 1997.

[538] Morten Nielsen, Claus Lundegaard, Peder Worning, Sanne Lise Lauemøller, Kasper Lamberth, Søren Buus, Søren Brunak, and Ole Lund. Reliable prediction of t-cell epitopes using neural networks with novel sequence representations. *Protein Science*, 12(5):1007–1017, 2003.

[539] M. Nilges, G. M. Clore, and A. M. Gronenborn. Determination of three-dimensional structures of proteins from interproton distance data by dynamical simulated annealing from a random array of atoms. *FEBS Lett.*, 239:129–136, 1988.

[540] M. Nilges, G. M. Clore, and A. M. Gronenborn. Determination of three-dimensional structures of proteins from interproton distance data by hybrid distance geometry-dynamical simulated annealing calculations. *FEBS Lett.*, 229:317–324, 1988.

[541] D. A. Nix and A. S. Weigend. Estimating the mean and variance of the target probability distribution. In *Neural Networks, 1994. IEEE World Congress on Computational Intelligence., 1994 IEEE International Conference on*, volume 1, pages 55–60 vol.1, June 1994.

[542] A. B. Novikoff. On convergence proofs for perceptrons. In *Proceedings of the Symposium on the Mathematical Theory of Automata*, volume 12, pages 615–622. Polytechnic Institute of Brooklyn, 1962.

[543] Ziad Obermeyer and Ezekiel J Emanuel. Predicting the future–big data, machine learning, and clinical medicine. *The New England journal of medicine*, 375(13):1216, 2016.

[544] Andrew M Odlyzko. On subspaces spanned by random selections of±1 vectors. *journal of combinatorial theory, Series A*, 47(1):124–133, 1988.

[545] Ryan O'Donnell. *Analysis of Boolean Functions*. Cambridge University Press, 2014.

[546] Ryan O'Donnell and Rocco A Servedio. Extremal properties of polynomial threshold functions. *Journal of Computer and System Sciences*, 74(3):298–312, 2008.

[547] Ryan O'Donnell and Rocco A Servedio. New degree bounds for polynomial threshold functions. *Combinatorica*, 30(3):327–358, 2010.

[548] Junhyuk Oh, Xiaoxiao Guo, Honglak Lee, Richard L Lewis, and Satinder Singh. Action-conditional video prediction using deep networks in atari games. In *Advances in Neural Information Processing Systems*, pages 2863–2871, 2015.

[549] Junhyuk Oh, Satinder Singh, and Honglak Lee. Value prediction network. In *Advances in Neural Information Processing Systems*, pages 6120–6130, 2017.

[550] E. Oja. Simplified neuron model as a principal component analyzer. *Journal of mathematical biology*, 15(3):267–273, 1982.

[551] Bernt Oksendal. *Stochastic differential equations: an introduction with applications*. Springer Science & Business Media, 2013.

[552] O. Olmea and A. Valencia. Improving contact predictions by the combination of correlated mutations and other sources of sequence information. *Fold. Des.*, 2:S25–32, 1997.

[553] Bruno A Olshausen and David J Field. Emergence of simple-cell receptive field properties by learning a sparse code for natural images. *Nature*, 381(6583):607, 1996.

[554] Aaron Van Oord, Nal Kalchbrenner, and Koray Kavukcuoglu. Pixel recurrent neural networks. In Maria Florina Balcan and Kilian Q. Weinberger, editors, *Proceedings of The 33rd International Conference on Machine Learning*, volume 48 of *Proceedings of Machine Learning Research*, pages 1747–1756, New York, New York, USA, 20–22 Jun 2016. PMLR.

[555] Dirk Ormoneit and Śaunak Sen. Kernel-based reinforcement learning. *Machine Learning*, 49(2-3):161–178, 2002.

[556] Phillip A Ostrand. Dimension of metric spaces and Hilbert's problem 13. *Bulletin of the American Mathematical Society*, 71(4):619–622, 1965.

[557] J. Ott, E. Linstead, N. LaHaye, and P. Baldi. Learning in the machine: To share or not to share? *Neural Networks*, 126:235–249, 2020.

[558] Jordan Ott, Mike Pritchard, Natalie Best, Erik Linstead, Milan Curcic, and Pierre Baldi. A Fortran-Keras Deep Learning Bridge for Scientific Computing. *Scientific Programming*, 2020. In press. Also: arXiv:2005.04048.

[559] S. Ovyn, X. Rouby, and V. Lemaitre. DELPHES, a framework for fast simulation of a generic collider experiment. arXiv:0903.2225, 2009.

[560] Christos H. Papadimitriou. *Computational Complexity*. Wiley, 2003.

[561] Christos H. Papadimitriou and John N. Tsitsiklis. The complexity of Markov decision processes. *Mathematics of Operations Research*, 12(3):441–450, 1987.

[562] George Papamakarios, Theo Pavlakou, and Iain Murray. Masked autoregressive flow for density estimation. In *Advances in Neural Information Processing Systems*, pages 2338–2347, 2017.

[563] Ronald Parr and Stuart Russell. Reinforcement learning with hierarchies of machines. *Advances in Neural Information Processing Systems*, pages 1043–1049, 1998.

[564] Luca Pasa and Alessandro Sperduti. Pre-training of recurrent neural networks via linear autoencoders. In *Advances in Neural Information Processing Systems*, pages 3572–3580, 2014.

[565] Razvan Pascanu, Yujia Li, Oriol Vinyals, Nicolas Heess, Lars Buesing, Sebastien Racanière, David Reichert, Théophane Weber, Daan Wierstra, and Peter Battaglia. Learning model-based planning from scratch. arXiv:1707.06170, 2017.

[566] Elena Pashenkova, Irina Rish, and Rina Dechter. Value iteration and policy iteration algorithms for Markov decision problem. In *AAAI 96: Workshop on Structural Issues in Planning and Temporal Reasoning*. Citeseer, 1996.

[567] J. Pearl. *Probabilistic Reasoning in Intelligent Systems: Networks of Plausible Inference*. Morgan Kaufmann, San Mateo, CA., 1988.

[568] Lucia Peixoto and Ted Abel. The role of histone acetylation in memory formation and cognitive impairments. *Neuropsychopharmacology*, 38(1):62–76, 2013.

[569] Patrice Perez, D Banerjee, François Biraben, D. Brook-Roberge, M. Charlton, Pierre Cladé, Pauline Comini, Paolo Crivelli, Oleg Dalkarov, Pascal Debu, et al. The GBAR antimatter gravity experiment. *Hyperfine Interactions*, 233(1):21–27, 2015.

[570] Thomas Nordahl Petersen, Claus Lundegaard, Morten Nielsen, Henrik Bohr, Jakob Bohr, Søren Brunak, Garry P. Gippert, and Ole Lund. Prediction of protein secondary structure at 80% accuracy. *Proteins: Structure, Function, and Bioinformatics*, 41(1):17–20, 2000.

[571] Trang Pham, Truyen Tran, Dinh Phung, and Svetha Venkatesh. Deepcare: A deep dynamic memory model for predictive medicine. In *Pacific-Asia Conference on Knowledge Discovery and Data Mining*, pages 30–41. Springer, 2016.

[572] A.J. Piergiovanni, Alan Wu, and Michael S. Ryoo. Learning real-world robot policies by dreaming. arXiv:1805.07813, 2018.

[573] Planck Collaboration. Planck 2013 results. XVI. Cosmological parameters. 2013.

[574] Tilman Plehn, Michael Spannowsky, Michihisa Takeuchi, and Dirk Zerwas. Stop Reconstruction with Tagged Tops. *JHEP*, 1010:078, 2010.

[575] Tomaso Poggio and Fabio Anselmi. *Visual cortex and deep networks: learning invariant representations*. MIT Press, 2016.

[576] G. Pollastri and P. Baldi. Predition of contact maps by GIOHMMs and recurrent neural networks using lateral propagation from all four cardinal corners. *Bioinformatics*, 18 Supplement 1:S62–S70, 2002. Proceedings of the ISMB 2002 Conference.

[577] G. Pollastri, P. Baldi, P. Fariselli, and R. Casadio. Improved prediction of the number of residue contacts in proteins by recurrent neural networks. *Bioinformatics*, 17:S234–S242, 2001. Proceedings of the ISMB 2001 Conference.

[578] G. Pollastri, P. Baldi, P. Fariselli, and R. Casadio. Prediction of coordination number and relative solvent accessibility in proteins. *Proteins*, 47:142–153, 2001.

[579] G. Pollastri, D. Przybylski, B. Rost, and P. Baldi. Improving the prediction of protein secondary strucure in three and eight classes using recurrent neural networks and profiles. *Proteins*, 47:228–235, 2001.

[580] G. Pollastri, A. Vullo, P. Frasconi, and P. Baldi. Modular DAG-RNN architectures for assembling coarse protein structures. *Journal of Computational Biology*, 13(3):631–650, 2006.

[581] Gianluca Pollastri, Pierre Baldi, Alessandro Vullo, and Paolo Frasconi. Prediction of protein topologies using generalized IOHMMs and RNNs. In S. Thrun S. Becker and K. Obermayer, editors, *Advances in Neural Information Processing Systems 15*, pages 1449–1456. MIT Press, Cambridge, MA, 2003.

[582] Alon Polsky, Bartlett W Mel, and Jackie Schiller. Computational subunits in thin dendrites of pyramidal cells. *Nature neuroscience*, 7(6):621–627, 2004.

[583] Iakov Polyak, Manfred T. Reetz, and Walter Thiel. Quantum mechanical/molecular mechanical study on the mechanism of the enzymatic Baeyer–Villiger reaction. *Journal of the American Chemical Society*, 134(5):2732–2741, 2012. PMID: 22239272.

[584] Bruno Pontecorvo. Mesonium and antimesonium. *JETP*, 6:429, 1958.

[585] Bruno Pontecorvo. Neutrino experiments and the problem of conservation of leptonic charge. *Sov. Phys. JETP*, 26(984-988):165, 1968.

[586] Pascal Poupart and Craig Boutilier. VDCBPI: an approximate scalable algorithm for large POMDPs. In *Advances in Neural Information Processing Systems*, pages 1081–1088, 2004.

[587] Rob Powers and Yoav Shoham. New criteria and a new algorithm for learning in multi-agent systems. In *Advances in Neural Information Processing Systems*, pages 1089–1096, 2004.

[588] N. Qian and T. J. Sejnowski. Predicting the secondary structure of globular proteins using neural network models. *J. Mol. Biol.*, 202:865–884, 1988.

[589] Qian Qin and Jianxing Feng. Imputation for transcription factor binding predictions based on deep learning. *PLoS Comput Biol*, 13(2):e1005403, Feb 2017.

[590] Daniel Quang, Yifei Chen, and Xiaohui Xie. Dann: a deep learning approach for annotating the pathogenicity of genetic variants. *Bioinformatics*, 31(5):761–3, Mar 2015.

[591] Daniel Quang and Xiaohui Xie. Danq: a hybrid convolutional and recurrent deep neural network for quantifying the function of DNA sequences. *Nucleic Acids Research*, 44(11):e107–e107, 2016.

[592] Daniel Quang and Xiaohui Xie. Factornet: a deep learning framework for predicting cell type specific transcription factor binding from nucleotide-resolution sequential data. *bioRxiv*, page 151274, 2017.

[593] E. Racah, S. Ko, P. Sadowski, W. Bhimji, C. Tull, S.Y. Oh, P. Baldi, and Prabhat. Revealing fundamental physics from the Daya Bay Neutrino Experiment using deep neural networks. In *2016 15th IEEE International Conference on Machine Learning and Applications (ICMLA)*, pages 892–897, Dec 2016.

[594] Sébastien Racanière, Théophane Weber, David Reichert, Lars Buesing, Arthur Guez, Danilo Jimenez Rezende, Adria Puigdomènech Badia, Oriol Vinyals, Nicolas Heess, Yujia Li, et al. Imagination-augmented agents for deep reinforcement learning. In *Advances in Neural Information Processing Systems*, pages 5690–5701, 2017.

[595] B. Radics et al. The ASACUSA micromegas tracker: A cylindrical, bulk micromegas detector for antimatter research. *Review of Scientific Instruments*, 86, 2015.

[596] B. Radics, D.J. Murtagh, Y. Yamazaki, and F. Robicheaux. Scaling behavior of the ground-state antihydrogen yield as a function of positron density and temperature from classical-trajectory Monte Carlo simulations. *Physical Review A*, 90(3):032704, September 2014.

[597] Maziar Raissi, Paris Perdikaris, and George Em Karniadakis. Physics informed deep learning (Part I): data-driven solutions of nonlinear partial differential equations. arXiv:1711.10561, 2017.

[598] Maziar Raissi, Alireza Yazdani, and George Em Karniadakis. Hidden fluid mechanics: Learning velocity and pressure fields from flow visualizations. *Science*, 367(6481):1026–1030, feb 2020.

[599] Pranav Rajpurkar, Awni Y. Hannun, Masoumeh Haghpanahi, Codie Bourn, and Andrew Y. Ng. Cardiologist-level arrhythmia detection with convolutional neural networks. arXiv:1707.01836, 2017.

[600] Raghunathan Ramakrishnan, Pavlo O Dral, Matthias Rupp, and O Anatole Von Lilienfeld. Quantum chemistry structures and properties of 134 kilo molecules. *Scientific data*, 1:140022, 2014.

[601] Raghunathan Ramakrishnan, Mia Hartmann, Enrico Tapavicza, and O Anatole Von Lilienfeld. Electronic spectra from TDDFT and machine learning in chemical space. *The Journal of Chemical Physics*, 143(8):084111, 2015.

[602] Arlo Randall, Jianlin Cheng, Michael Sweredoski, and Pierre Baldi. TMBpro: secondary structure, β-contact and tertiary structure prediction of transmembrane β-barrel proteins. *Bioinformatics*, 24(4):513–520, 2008.

[603] Jette Randløv and Preben Alstrøm. Learning to drive a bicycle using reinforcement learning and shaping. In *ICML*, volume 98, pages 463–471. Citeseer, 1998.

[604] Carl Edward Rasmussen. *Gaussian processes for machine learning*. MIT Press, 2006.

[605] Stephan Rasp, Michael S. Pritchard, and Pierre Gentine. Deep learning to represent subgrid processes in climate models. *Proceedings of the National Academy of Sciences*, 115(39):9684–9689, 2018.

[606] Joseph Redmon, Santosh Divvala, Ross Girshick, and Ali Farhadi. You only look once: Unified, real-time object detection. In *Proceedings of the IEEE conference on computer vision and pattern recognition*, pages 779–788, 2016.

[607] Joseph Redmon and Ali Farhadi. Yolov3: An incremental improvement. arXiv:1804.02767, 2018.

[608] R. Reed. Pruning algorithms – a survey. *Neural Networks, IEEE Transactions on*, 4(5):740–747, 1993.

[609] Markus Reichstein, Gustau Camps-Valls, Bjorn Stevens, Martin Jung, Joachim Denzler, Nuno Carvalhais, and Prabhat. Deep learning and process understanding for data-driven Earth system science. *Nature*, 566(7743):195–204, feb 2019.

[610] Shaoqing Ren, Kaiming He, Ross Girshick, and Jian Sun. Faster R-CNN: Towards Real-Time Object Detection With Region Proposal Networks. In *Advances in Neural Information Processing Systems*, pages 91–99, 2015.

[611] Marco Tulio Ribeiro, Sameer Singh, and Carlos Guestrin. "Why should I trust you?": Explaining the predictions of any classifier. In *Knowledge Discovery and Data Mining (KDD)*, 2016.

[612] S. Rifai, G. Mesnil, P. Vincent, X. Muller, Y. Bengio, Y. Dauphin, and X. Glorot. Higher order contractive auto-encoder. *Machine Learning and Knowledge Discovery in Databases*, pages 645–660, 2011.

[613] S.K. Riis and A. Krogh. Improving prediction of protein secondary structure using structured neural networks and multiple sequence alignments. *J. Comput. Biol.*, 3:163–183, 1996.

[614] Herbert Robbins and Sutton Monro. A stochastic approximation method. *The Annals of Mathematical Statistics*, pages 400–407, 1951.

[615] R. Tyrell Rockafellar. *Convex Analysis*. Princeton University Press, 1997.

[616] David Rogers and Mathew Hahn. Extended-connectivity fingerprints. *Journal of Chemical Information and Modeling*, 50(5):742–754, 2010.

[617] Olaf Ronneberger, Philipp Fischer, and Thomas Brox. U-Net: Convolutional Networks for Biomedical Image Segmentation. In *International Conference on Medical Image Computing and Computer-assisted Intervention*, pages 234–241. Springer, 2015.

[618] F. Rosenblatt. The perceptron: A probabilistic model for information storage and organization in the brain. *Psychological Review*, 65(6):386, 1958.

[619] Sheldon M. Ross. *Introduction to Stochastic Dynamic Programming*. Academic press, 2014.

[620] B. Rost and C. Sander. Combining evolutionary information and neural networks to predict protein secondary structure. *Proteins*, 19:55–72, 1994.

[621] B. Rost and C. Sander. Prediction of protein secondary structure at better than 70% accuracy. *J. Mol. Biol.*, 232:584–599, 1997.

[622] Andras Rozsa and Terrance E. Boult. Improved adversarial robustness by reducing open space risk via tent activations, 2019. Preprint arXiv:1908.02435

[623] Holger R Roth, Jianhua Yao, Le Lu, James Stieger, Joseph E Burns, and Ronald M Summers. Detection of sclerotic spine metastases via random aggregation of deep convolutional neural network classifications. In *Recent Advances in Computational Methods and Clinical Applications for Spine Imaging*, pages 3–12. Springer, 2015.

[624] Donald B Rubin. The Bayesian Bootstrap. *The annals of statistics*, pages 130–134, 1981.

[625] Lars Ruddigkeit, Ruud Van Deursen, Lorenz C Blum, and Jean-Louis Reymond. Enumeration of 166 Billion Organic Small Molecules in the Chemical Universe database gdb-17. *Journal of chemical information and modeling*, 52(11):2864–2875, 2012.

[626] Francisco R Ruiz, Michalis Titsias RC AUEB, and David Blei. The generalized reparameterization gradient. In *Advances in Neural Information Processing Systems*, pages 460–468, 2016.

[627] D.E. Rumelhart, G.E. Hintont, and R.J. Williams. Learning representations by back-propagating errors. *Nature*, 323(6088):533–536, 1986.

[628] Gavin A Rummery and Mahesan Niranjan. *On-line Q-learning using connectionist systems*. University of Cambridge, Department of Engineering, 1994.

[629] Matthias Rupp. Machine learning for quantum mechanics in a nutshell. *International Journal of Quantum Chemistry*, 115(16):1058–1073, 2015.

[630] Matthias Rupp, Alexandre Tkatchenko, Klaus-Robert Müller, and O. Anatole von Lilienfeld. Fast and accurate modeling of molecular atomization energies with machine learning. *Phys. Rev. Lett.*, 108:058301, Jan 2012.

[631] Matthias Rupp, O Anatole Von Lilienfeld, and Kieron Burke. Guest editorial: Special topic on data-enabled theoretical chemistry. *The Journal of Chemical Physics*, 148(24), 2018.

[632] Andrei A Rusu, Sergio Gomez Colmenarejo, Caglar Gulcehre, Guillaume Desjardins, James Kirkpatrick, Razvan Pascanu, Volodymyr Mnih, Koray Kavukcuoglu, and Raia Hadsell. Policy distillation. In *International Conference on Learning Representations (ICLR)*, 2016.

[633] C.K. Vermilion S.D. Ellis and J.R. Walsh. Recombination algorithms and jet substructure: pruning as a tool for heavy particle searches. *Phys.Rev.*, D81:094023, 2010.

[634] P. Sadowski and P. Baldi. Deep learning in the natural sciences: Applications to physics. In Ilya Muchnik, editor, *Key Ideas in Learning Theory from Inception to Current State: Emmanuel Braverman's Legacy*, pages 269–297. Springer, 2018.

[635] P. Sadowski, J. Collado, D. Whiteson, and P. Baldi. Deep learning, dark knowledge, and dark matter. *Journal of Machine Learning Research, Workshop and Conference Proceedings*, 42:81–97, 2015.

[636] P. Sadowski, B. Radics, Ananya, Y. Yamazaki, and P. Baldi. Efficient antihydrogen detection in antimatter physics by deep learning. *Journal of Physics Communications*, 1(2):025001, 2017.

[637] Peter Sadowski and Pierre Baldi. Small-Molecule 3D Structure Prediction Using Open Crystallography Data. *Journal of Chemical Information and Modeling*, 53(12):3127–3130, 2013.

[638] Peter Sadowski, David Fooshee, Niranjan Subrahmanya, and Pierre Baldi. Synergies between quantum mechanics and machine learning in reaction prediction. *Journal of Chemical Information and Modeling*, 56(11):2125–2128, 2016. PMID: 27749058.

[639] Michael Saks. Slicing the hypercube. *Surveys in combinatorics*, 1993:211–255, 1993.

[640] Tim Salimans, Andrej Karpathy, Xi Chen, and Diederik P. Kingma. PixelCNN++: Improving the pixelCNN with Discretized Logistic Mixture Likelihood and Other Modifications. arXiv:1701.05517, 2017.

[641] Tim Salimans, Andrej Karpathy, Xi Chen, and Diederik P. Kingma. PixelCNN++: Improving the PixelCNN with Discretized Logistic Mixture Likelihood and Other Modifications. *CoRR*, 2017.

[642] Arthur L Samuel. Some studies in machine learning using the game of checkers. ii. recent progress. *IBM Journal of research and development*, 11(6):601–617, 1967.

[643] Juan C Santamaría, Richard S Sutton, and Ashwin Ram. Experiments with reinforcement learning in problems with continuous state and action spaces. *Adaptive behavior*, 6(2):163–217, 1997.

[644] Valerio Santangelo, Clarissa Cavallina, Paola Colucci, Alessia Santori, Simone Macrì, James L McGaugh, and Patrizia Campolongo. Enhanced brain activity associated with memory access in highly superior autobiographical memory. *Proceedings of the National Academy of Sciences*, 115(30):7795–7800, 2018.

[645] Fadil Santosa and William W Symes. Linear inversion of band-limited reflection seismograms. *SIAM Journal on Scientific and Statistical Computing*, 7(4):1307–1330, 1986.

[646] Subir Sarkar. Big bang nucleosynthesis and physics beyond the standard model. *Reports on Progress in Physics*, 59(12):1493, 1996.

[647] H. Satoh and K. Funatsu. SOPHIA, a knowledge base-guided reaction prediction system - utilization of a knowledge base derived from a reaction database. *Journal of Chemical Information and Modeling*, 35(1):34–44, January 1995.

[648] L. J. Savage. *The foundations of statistics*. Dover, New York, 1972. (First Edition in 1954).

[649] Robert E Schapire. The strength of weak learnability. *Machine Learning*, 5(2):197–227, 1990.

[650] Robert E Schapire. Explaining adaboost. In *Empirical Inference*, pages 37–52. Springer, 2013.

[651] Tom Schaul, Daniel Horgan, Karol Gregor, and David Silver. Universal value function approximators. In *International Conference on Machine Learning (ICML)*, pages 1312–1320, 2015.

[652] Jürgen Schmidhuber. Learning factorial codes by predictability minimization. *Neural Computation*, 4:863–879, 1991.

[653] Jürgen Schmidhuber. Deep learning in neural networks: An overview. *Neural Networks*, 61:85–117, 2015.

[654] Michael Schmidt and Hod Lipson. Distilling free-form natural laws from experimental data. *Science*, 324(5923):81–85, 2009.

[655] Tapio Schneider, João Teixeira, Christopher S. Bretherton, Florent Brient, Kyle G. Pressel, Christoph Schär, and A. Pier Siebesma. Climate goals and computing the future of clouds. *Nature Climate Change*, 7(1):3–5, 2017.

[656] B. Schölkopf, C.J.C. Burges, and A.J. Smola, editors. *Advances in Kernel Methods - Support Vector Learning*. MIT Press, Cambridge, MA, 1998.

[657] B. Scholkopf and A.J. Smola. *Learning with Kernels*. MIT Press, Cambridge, MA, 2002.

[658] S.L. Schreiber. Target-oriented and diversity-oriented organic synthesis in drug discovery. *Science*, 287:1964–1969, 2000.

[659] S.L. Schreiber. The small-molecule approach to biology: chemical genetics and diversity-oriented organic synthesis make possible the systematic exploration of biology. *Chemical and Engineering News*, 81:51–61, 2003.

[660] John Schulman, Sergey Levine, Pieter Abbeel, Michael Jordan, and Philipp Moritz. Trust region policy optimization. In *International Conference on Machine Learning*, pages 1889–1897, 2015.

[661] John Schulman, Philipp Moritz, Sergey Levine, Michael Jordan, and Pieter Abbeel. High-dimensional continuous control using generalized advantage estimation. In *Proceedings of the International Conference on Learning Representations (ICLR)*, 2016.

[662] John Schulman, Filip Wolski, Prafulla Dhariwal, Alec Radford, and Oleg Klimov. Proximal policy optimization algorithms. arXiv:1707.06347, 2017.

[663] Kristof T Schütt, Farhad Arbabzadah, Stefan Chmiela, Klaus R Müller, and Alexandre Tkatchenko. Quantum-chemical insights from deep tensor neural networks. *Nature communications*, 8:13890, 2017.

[664] T.J Sejnowski. On the stochastic dynamics of neuronal interaction. *Biological cybernetics*, 22(4):203–211, 1976.

[665] T.J. Sejnowski and C.R. Rosenberg. Parallel networks that learn to pronounce english text. *Complex systems*, 1(1):145–168, 1987.

[666] G. Sello. Reaction prediction: the suggestions of the Beppe program. *Journal of Chemical Information and Computer Sciences*, 32(6):713–717, 1992.

[667] Andrew W Senior, Richard Evans, John Jumper, James Kirkpatrick, Laurent Sifre, Tim Green, Chongli Qin, Augustin Žídek, Alexander WR Nelson, Alex Bridgland, et al. Improved protein structure prediction using potentials from deep learning. *Nature*, 577(7792):706–710, 2020.

[668] Shai Shalev-Shwartz and Shai Ben-David. *Understanding machine learning: From theory to algorithms*. Cambridge university press, 2014.

[669] C. E. Shannon. A mathematical theory of communication. *Bell System Technical Journal*, 27:379–423, 623–656, 1948.

[670] Wei Shen, Mu Zhou, Feng Yang, Caiyun Yang, and Jie Tian. Multi-scale convolutional neural networks for lung nodule classification. In *International Conference on Information Processing in Medical Imaging*, pages 588–599. Springer, 2015.

[671] Alexander A. Sherstov. Separating ac^0 from depth-2 majority circuits. *SIAM Journal on Computing*, 38(6):2113–2129, 2009.

[672] Alexander A. Sherstov and Peter Stone. On continuous-action Q-learning via tile coding function approximation. *Under Review*, 2004.

[673] Steven C. Sherwood, Sandrine Bony, and Jean-Louis Dufresne. Spread in model climate sensitivity traced to atmospheric convective mixing. *Nature*, 505(7481):37–42, 2014.

[674] Chase Shimmin, Peter Sadowski, Pierre Baldi, Edison Weik, Daniel Whiteson, Edward Goul, and Andreas Søgaard. Decorrelated jet substructure tagging using adversarial neural networks. *Physical Review D*, 96(7):074034, 2017.

[675] I.N. Shindyalov, N.A. Kolchanov, and C. Sander. Can three-dimensional contacts of proteins be predicted by analysis of correlated mutations? *Protein Engineering*, 7:349–358, 1994.

[676] Mitsuo Shoji, Hiroshi Isobe, and Kizashi Yamaguchi. QM/MM study of the S_2 to S_3 transition reaction in the oxygen-evolving complex of photosystem ii. *Chemical Physics Letters*, 636:172 – 179, 2015.

[677] Ravid Shwartz-Ziv and Naftali Tishby. Opening the black box of deep neural networks via information. arXiv:1703.00810, 2017.

[678] David Silver, Aja Huang, Chris J Maddison, Arthur Guez, Laurent Sifre, George Van Den Driessche, Julian Schrittwieser, Ioannis Antonoglou, Veda Panneershelvam, Marc Lanctot, et al. Mastering the game of Go with deep neural networks and tree search. *Nature*, 529(7587):484–489, 2016.

[679] David Silver, Thomas Hubert, Julian Schrittwieser, Ioannis Antonoglou, Matthew Lai, Arthur Guez, Marc Lanctot, Laurent Sifre, Dharshan Kumaran, Thore Graepel, et al. Mastering chess and shogi by self-play with a general reinforcement learning algorithm. arXiv:1712.01815, 2017.

[680] David Silver, Guy Lever, Nicolas Heess, Thomas Degris, Daan Wierstra, and Martin Riedmiller. Deterministic policy gradient algorithms. In *International Conference on Machine Learning (ICML)*, 2014.

[681] David Silver, Julian Schrittwieser, Karen Simonyan, Ioannis Antonoglou, Aja Huang, Arthur Guez, Thomas Hubert, Lucas Baker, Matthew Lai, Adrian Bolton, et al. Mastering the game of Go without human knowledge. *Nature*, 550(7676):354, 2017.

[682] David Silver, Hado van Hasselt, Matteo Hessel, Tom Schaul, Arthur Guez, Tim Harley, Gabriel Dulac-Arnold, David Reichert, Neil Rabinowitz, Andre Barreto, et al. The Predictron: End-To-End Learning and Planning. arXiv:1612.08810, 2016.

[683] Karen Simonyan and Andrew Zisserman. Very deep convolutional networks for large-scale image recognition. arXiv:1409.1556, 2014.

[684] Satinder Singh and Dimitri Bertsekas. Reinforcement learning for dynamic channel allocation in cellular telephone systems. *Advances in Neural Information Processing Systems*, pages 974–980, 1997.

[685] Satinder P. Singh, Tommi S. Jaakkola, and Michael I. Jordan. Learning Without State-Estimation in Partially Observable Markovian Decision Processes. In *ICML*, pages 284–292, 1994.

[686] Satinder P. Singh and Richard S. Sutton. Reinforcement learning with replacing eligibility traces. *Machine Learning*, 22(1-3):123–158, 1996.

[687] T. Sjostrand et al. PYTHIA 6.4 physics and manual. *JHEP*, 05:026, 2006.

[688] J.L. Slagle, C.L. Chang, and S.R. Heller. A clustering and data reorganization algorithm. *IEEE Transactions on Systems, Man and Cybernetics*, 5:121–128, 1975.

[689] Padhraic Smyth, David Heckerman, and Michael I. Jordan. Probabilistic Independence Networks for Hidden Markov Probability Models. *Neural Computation*, 9(2):227–269, 1997.

[690] Jasper Snoek, Hugo Larochelle, and Ryan P. Adams. Practical Bayesian optimization of machine learning algorithms. In *Advances in Neural Information Processing Systems 25*, 2951–2959. Curran Associates, Inc., 2012.

[691] Richard Socher, Alex Perelygin, Jean Y. Wu, Jason Chuang, Christopher D. Manning, Andrew Y. Ng, Christopher Potts, et al. Recursive deep models for semantic compositionality over a sentiment treebank. In *Proceedings of the Conference on Empirical Methods in Natural Language Processing (EMNLP)*, 1631–1642. Association for Computational Linguistics, 2013.

[692] I.M. Socorro, K. Taylor, and J.M. Goodman. ROBIA: a reaction prediction program. *Organic Letters*, 7(16):3541–3544, 2005.

[693] Peter Sollich and Anders Krogh. Learning with ensembles: How overfitting can be useful. In *Advances in Neural Information Processing Systems*, 190–196, 1996.

[694] Matthijs T.J. Spaan and Nikos Vlassis. A point-based POMDP algorithm for robot planning. In *Proceedings of IEEE International Conference on Robotics and Automation (ICRA), 2004*, volume 3, pages 2399–2404. IEEE, 2004.

[695] Matt Spencer, Jesse Eickholt, and Jianlin Cheng. A deep learning network approach to ab initio protein secondary structure prediction. *IEEE/ACM Transactions on Computational Biology and Bioinformatics*, 12(1):103–112, 2015.

[696] David J. Spiegelhalter and Steffen L. Lauritzen. Sequential updating of conditional probabilities on directed graphical structures. *Networks*, 20(5):579–605, 1990.

[697] David A. Sprecher. On the structure of continuous functions of several variables. *Transactions of the American Mathematical Society*, 115:340–355, 1965.

[698] Nitish Srivastava, Geoffrey Hinton, Alex Krizhevsky, Ilya Sutskever, and Ruslan Salakhutdinov. Dropout: A simple way to prevent neural networks from overfitting. *Journal of Machine Learning Research*, 15:1929–1958, 2014.

[699] Nitish Srivastava, Geoffrey E Hinton, Alex Krizhevsky, Ilya Sutskever, and Ruslan Salakhutdinov. Dropout: a simple way to prevent neural networks from overfitting. *Journal of Machine Learning Research*, 15(1):1929–1958, 2014.

[700] B. R. Stockwell. Exploring biology with small organic molecules. *Nature*, 432:846–854, 2004.

[701] Marijn Stollenga, Wonmin Beyon, Markus Liwicki, and Juergen Schmidhuber. Parallel multi-dimensional LSTM, with application to fast biomedical volumetric image segmentation. In *Advances in Neural Information Processing Systems (NIPS)*, 2015. Preprint arXiv:1506.07452 [cs.CV].

[702] J. Storey et al. Particle tracking at 4 k: The fast annihilation cryogenic tracking (fact) detector for the AEgIS Antimatter gravity experiment. *Nucl. Instr. Meth. A*, 732:437–441, 2013.

[703] Gary D. Stormo, Thomas D. Schneider, Larry Gold, and Andrzej Ehrenfeucht. Use of the "Perceptron" algorithm to distinguish translational initiation sites in E. coli. *Nucleic Acids Research*, 10(9):2997–3011, 1982.

[704] A. Strandlie and R. Frühwirth. Track and vertex reconstruction: From classical to adaptive methods. *Rev. Mod. Phys.*, 82, 2010.

[705] Ilya Sutskever, Oriol Vinyals, and Quoc V. Le. Sequence to sequence learning with neural networks. *Advances in Neural Information Processing Systems*, 27:3104–3112, 2014.

[706] Richard S. Sutton. Learning to predict by the methods of temporal differences. *Machine Learning*, 3(1):9–44, 1988.

[707] Richard S. Sutton. Integrated architectures for learning, planning, and reacting based on approximating dynamic programming. In *Machine Learning Proceedings 1990*, pages 216–224. Elsevier, 1990.

[708] Richard S. Sutton and Andrew G. Barto. *Reinforcement Learning: An Introduction*. MIT Press, 1998.

[709] Richard S Sutton, Doina Precup, and Satinder Singh. Between MDPs and semi-MDPs: A framework for temporal abstraction in reinforcement learning. *Artificial Intelligence*, 112(1):181–211, 1999.

[710] S. J. Swamidass, C. Azencott, H. Gramajo, S. Tsai, and P. Baldi. The influence relevance voter: An accurate and interpretable virtual high-throughput screening method. *Journal of Chemical Information and Modeling*, 49(4):756–766, 2009.

[711] S. J. Swamidass, J. Chen, J. Bruand, P. Phung, L. Ralaivola, and P. Baldi. Kernels for small molecules and the prediction of mutagenicity, toxicity, and anti-cancer activity. *Bioinformatics*, 21(Supplement 1):i359–368, 2005. Proceedings of the 2005 ISMB Conference.

[712] S.J. Swamidass and P. Baldi. Bounds and algorithms for exact searches of chemical fingerprints in linear and sub-linear time. *Journal of Chemical Information and Modeling*, 47(2):302–317, 2007.

[713] J. David Sweatt. The emerging field of neuroepigenetics. *Neuron*, 80(3):624–632, 2013.

[714] M.J. Sweredoski and P. Baldi. Pepito: Improved discontinuous B-cell epitope prediction using multiple distance thresholds and half-sphere exposure. *Bioinformatics*, 24(12):1459–1460, 2008.

[715] M.J. Sweredoski and P. Baldi. COBEpro: a novel system for predicting continuous B-cell epitopes. *Protein Engineering Design and Selection*, 22(3):113, 2009.

[716] C. Szegedy, Wei Liu, Yangqing Jia, P. Sermanet, S. Reed, D. Anguelov, D. Erhan, V. Vanhoucke, and A. Rabinovich. Going deeper with convolutions. In *2015 IEEE Conference on Computer Vision and Pattern Recognition (CVPR)*, pages 1–9, June 2015.

[717] Christian Szegedy, Wei Liu, Yangqing Jia, Pierre Sermanet, Scott Reed, Dragomir Anguelov, Dumitru Erhan, Vincent Vanhoucke, and Andrew Rabinovich. Going

deeper with convolutions. In *Proceedings of the IEEE conference on computer vision and pattern recognition*, pages 1–9, 2015.

[718] Michel Talagrand. Self averaging and the space of interactions in neural networks. *Random Structures & Algorithms*, 14(3):199–213, 1999.

[719] Masaharu Tanabashi, K. Hagiwara, K. Hikasa, K. Nakamura, Y. Sumino, F. Takahashi, J. Tanaka, K. Agashe, G. Aielli, C. Amsler, et al. Review of particle physics. *Physical Review D*, 98(3):030001, 2018.

[720] David Tank and John Hopfield. Neural computation by concentrating information in time. *Proceedings of the National Academy of Sciences*, 84(7):1896–1900, 1987.

[721] A. Tavakoli, F. Agostinelli, and P. Baldi. Splash: Learnable activation functions for improving accuracy and adversarial robustness. 2020. arXiv:2006.08947.

[722] Matthew E. Taylor and Peter Stone. Cross-domain transfer for reinforcement learning. In *Proceedings of the 24th International Conference on Machine Learning*, pages 879–886. ACM, 2007.

[723] Gerald Tesauro. Temporal difference learning and TD-Gammon. *Communications of the ACM*, 38(3):58–68, 1995.

[724] Jesse Thaler and Ken Van Tilburg. Identifying boosted objects with N-subjettiness. *JHEP*, 1103:015, 2011.

[725] Jesse Thaler and Ken Van Tilburg. Maximizing boosted top identification by minimizing N-subjettiness. *JHEP*, 02:093, 2012.

[726] Theano Development Team. Theano: A Python framework for fast computation of mathematical expressions. abs/1605.02688, May 2016.

[727] John Thomas, Tomasz Maszczyk, Nishant Sinha, Tilmann Kluge, and Justin Dauwels. Deep learning-based classification for brain-computer interfaces. In *2017 IEEE International Conference on Systems, Man, and Cybernetics (SMC)*, pages 234–239. IEEE, 2017.

[728] Edward Lee Thorndike. *Animal Intelligence: Experimental Studies*. Transaction Publishers, 1965.

[729] Robert Tibshirani. Regression shrinkage and selection via the lasso. *Journal of the Royal Statistical Society: Series B (Methodological)*, 58(1):267–288, 1996.

[730] Michael E. Tipping. Sparse Bayesian learning and the relevance vector machine. *Journal of Machine Learning Research*, 1(Jun):211–244, 2001.

[731] N. Tishby, F.C. Pereira, and W. Bialek. The information bottleneck method. arXiv preprint physics/0004057, 2000.

[732] N. Tishby and N. Zaslavsky. Deep learning and the information bottleneck principle. In *2015 IEEE Information Theory Workshop (ITW)*, pages 1–5, April 2015.

[733] Naftali Tishby and Noga Zaslavsky. Deep learning and the information bottleneck principle. In *2015 IEEE Information Theory Workshop (ITW)*, pages 1–5. IEEE, 2015.

[734] Tuan Trieu and Jianlin Cheng. Large-scale reconstruction of 3D Structures of human chromosomes from chromosomal contact data. *Nucleic Acids Research*, 42(7):e52–e52, 2014.

[735] John N Tsitsiklis and Benjamin Van Roy. An analysis of temporal-difference learning with function approximation. *Automatic Control, IEEE Transactions on*, 42(5):674–690, 1997.

[736] A.M. Turing. On computable numbers, with an application to the Entscheidungsproblem. *Proceedings of the London Mathematical Society, Series 2*, 41:230–267, 1936.

[737] Edward C. Uberbacher and Richard J. Mural. Locating protein-coding regions in human DNA sequences by a multiple sensor-neural network approach. *Proceedings of the National Academy of Sciences*, 88(24):11261–11265, 1991.

[738] Silviu-Marian Udrescu and Max Tegmark. AI Feynman a Physics-Inspired Method for Symbolic Regression. arXiv:1905.11481, 2019.

[739] George E Uhlenbeck and Leonard S Ornstein. On the Theory of the Brownian Motion. *Physical Review*, 36(5):823, 1930.

[740] G. Urban, M. Torrisi, C. Magnan, G. Pollastri, and P. Baldi. Protein profiles: Biases and protocols. *Computational and Structural Biotechnology Journal*, 18:2281–2289, 2020. Also BIORXIV/2020/148718.

[741] Gregor Urban, Niranjan Subrahmanya, and Pierre Baldi. Inner and outer recursive neural networks for chemoinformatics applications. *Journal of chemical information and modeling*, 58(2):207–211, 2018.

[742] Gregor Urban, Priyam Tripathi, Talal Alkayali, Mohit Mittal, Farid Jalali, William Karnes, and Pierre Baldi. Deep learning localizes and identifies polyps in real time with 96% accuracy in screening colonoscopy. *Gastroenterology*, 155(4):1069–1078, 2018.

[743] Leslie G Valiant. A theory of the learnable. *Communications of the ACM*, 27(11):1134–1142, 1984.

[744] Leslie G Valiant. Robust logics. *Artificial Intelligence*, 117(2):231–253, 2000.

[745] Leslie G Valiant. The hippocampus as a stable memory allocator for cortex. *Neural Computation*, 24(11):2873–2899, 2012.

[746] Jeffrey van der Gucht, Jordy Davelaar, Luc Hendriks, Oliver Porth, Hector Olivares, Yosuke Mizuno, Christian M Fromm, and Heino Falcke. Deep horizon: A machine learning network that recovers accreting black hole parameters. *Astronomy & Astrophysics*, 636:A94, 2020.

[747] Laurens Van Der Maaten, Eric Postma, and Jaap Van den Herik. Dimensionality reduction: a comparative. *J Mach Learn Res*, 10:66–71, 2009.

[748] Hado Van Hasselt, Arthur Guez, and David Silver. Deep reinforcement learning with double q-learning. In *AAAI*, pages 2094–2100, 2016.

[749] Yeeleng S Vang and Xiaohui Xie. Hla class i binding prediction via convolutional neural networks. *Bioinformatics*, Apr 2017.

[750] V. Vapnik. *Estimation of Dependences Based on Empirical Data*. Springer-Verlag, 1982.

[751] V. Vapnik. *The Nature of Statistical Learning Theory*. Springer Verlag, New York, 1995.

[752] V. N. Vapnik and A. Y. Chervonenkis. On the uniform convergence of relative frequencies of events to their probabilities. *Theory of Probability and its Applications*, XVI(2):264–280, 1971.

[753] Vladimir N Vapnik and A Ya Chervonenkis. On the uniform convergence of relative frequencies of events to their probabilities. In *Measures of complexity*, pages 11–30. Springer, 2015.

[754] Vladimir Naumovich Vapnik and Aleksei Yakovlevich Chervonenkis. The uniform convergence of frequencies of the appearance of events to their probabilities. In *Doklady Akademii Nauk*, volume 181, pages 781–783. Russian Academy of Sciences, 1968.

[755] M. Vassura, L. Margara, P. Di Lena, F. Medri, P. Fariselli, and R. Casadio. FT-COMAR: fault tolerant three-dimensional structure reconstruction from protein contact maps. *Bioinformatics*, 24(10):1313, 2008.

[756] A. Vattani. A simpler proof of the hardness of k-means clustering in the plane. *UCSD Technical Report*, 2010.

[757] RA Vazquez, Francis Halzen, and E Zas. Improving the Čerenkov imaging technique with neural networks. *Physical Review D*, 45(1):356, 1992.

[758] C.G. Vecsey, J.D. Hawk, K.M. Lattal, J.M. Stein, S.A. Fabian, M.A. Attner, S.M. Cabrera, C.B. McDonough, P.K. Brindle, T. Abel, et al. Histone deacetylase inhibitors enhance memory and synaptic plasticity via CREB: CBP-dependent transcriptional activation. *Journal of Neuroscience*, 27(23):6128, 2007.

[759] M. Vendruscolo, E. Kussell, and E. Domany. Recovery of protein structure from contact maps. *Folding and Design*, 2:295–306, 1997.

[760] Santosh S Venkatesh and Pierre Baldi. Programmed interactions in higher-order neural networks: Maximal capacity. *Journal of Complexity*, 7(3):316–337, 1991.

[761] Santosh S Venkatesht and Pierre Baldi. Programmed interactions in higher-order neural networks: The outer-product algorithm. *Journal of Complexity*, 7(4):443–479, 1991.

[762] Roman Vershynin. *High-Dimensional Probability: An Introduction with Applications in Data Science*. Cambridge University Press, 2018.

[763] Roman Vershynin. Memory capacity of neural networks with threshold and relu activations. arXiv:2001.06938, 2020.

[764] P. Vincent. A connection between score matching and denoising autoencoders. *Neural Computation*, 23(7):1661–1674, 2011.

[765] P. Vincent, H. Larochelle, Y. Bengio, and P.A. Manzagol. Extracting and composing robust features with denoising autoencoders. In *Proceedings of the 25th International Conference on Machine learning*, 1096–1103. ACM, 2008.

[766] Pascal Vincent, Hugo Larochelle, Isabelle Lajoie, Yoshua Bengio, and Pierre-Antoine Manzagol. Stacked denoising autoencoders: Learning useful representations in a deep network with a local denoising criterion. *The Journal of Machine Learning Research*, 11:3371–3408, 2010.

[767] A. Vogel-Ciernia, R. M. Barrett, D. P. Matheos, E. Kramar, S. Azzawi, Y. Chen, C. N. Magnan, M. Zeller, A. Sylvain, J. Haettig, Y. Jia, A. Tran, R. Dang, R. J. Post, M. Chabrier, A. Babayan, J. I. Wu, G. R. Crabtree, P. Baldi, T. Z. Baram,

G. Lynch, and M. A. Wood. The neuron-specific chromatin regulatory subunit BAF53b is necessary for synaptic plasticity and memory. *Nature Neuroscience*, 16:552–561, 2013.

[768] Viola Volpato, Alessandro Adelfio, and Gianluca Pollastri. Accurate prediction of protein enzymatic class by n-to-1 neural networks. *BMC bioinformatics*, 14(1):S11, 2013.

[769] Viola Volpato, Badr Alshomrani, and Gianluca Pollastri. Accurate ab initio and template-based prediction of short intrinsically-disordered regions by bidirectional recurrent neural networks trained on large-scale datasets. *International Journal of Molecular Sciences*, 16(8):19868–19885, 2015.

[770] J. von Neumann. *The Computer and the Brain*. Yale University Press, New Haven, CT, 1958.

[771] Stefan Wager, Sida Wang, and Percy Liang. Dropout training as adaptive regularization. In C.J.C. Burges, L. Bottou, M. Welling, Z. Ghahramani, and K.Q. Weinberger, editors, *Advances in Neural Information Processing Systems 26*, pages 351–359. 2013.

[772] Chi Wang and A.C. Williams. The threshold order of a Boolean function. *Discrete Applied Mathematics*, 31(1):51–69, 1991.

[773] Dayong Wang, Aditya Khosla, Rishab Gargeya, Humayun Irshad, and Andrew H. Beck. Deep learning for identifying metastatic breast cancer. arXiv:1606.05718, 2016.

[774] Juan Wang, Huanjun Ding, FateMeh Azamian, Brian Zhou, Carlos Iribarren, Sabee Molloi, and Pierre Baldi. Detecting cardiovascular disease from mammograms with deep learning. *IEEE Transactions on Medical Imaging*, 36(5): 1172–1181, 2017.

[775] Juan Wang, Zhiyuan Fang, Ning Lang, Huishu Yuan, Min-Ying Su, and Pierre Baldi. A multi-resolution approach for spinal metastasis detection using deep Siamese neural networks. *Computers in Biology and Medicine*, 84:137–146, 2017.

[776] May D. Wang and Hamid Reza Hassanzadeh. Deeperbind: Enhancing prediction of sequence specificities of DNA binding proteins. *bioRxiv*, page 099754, 2017.

[777] Sheng Wang, Siqi Sun, Zhen Li, Renyu Zhang, and Jinbo Xu. Accurate de novo prediction of protein contact map by ultra-deep learning model. *PLoS Computational Biology*, 13(1):e1005324, 2017.

[778] Xiaofeng Wang and Tuomas Sandholm. Reinforcement learning to play an optimal Nash equilibrium in team Markov games. In *Advances in Neural Information Processing Systems*, 1571–1578, 2002.

[779] Y. Wang, J. Xiao, T.O. Suzek, J. Zhang, J. Wang, and S.H. Bryant. PubChem: a public information system for analyzing bioactivities of small molecules. *Nucleic Acids Research*, 37(Web Server issue):W623, 2009.

[780] Christopher J.C.H. Watkins and Peter Dayan. Q-learning. *Machine Learning*, 8(3–4):279–292, 1992.

[781] Manuel Watter, Jost Springenberg, Joschka Boedecker, and Martin Riedmiller. Embed to control: alocally linear latent dynamics model for control from raw images. In *Advances in Neural Information Processing Systems*, pages 2746–2754, 2015.

[782] Jennifer N. Wei, David Duvenaud, and Alán Aspuru-Guzik. Neural networks for the prediction of organic chemistry reactions. *ACS Central Science*, 2(10):725–732, 2016. PMID: 27800555.

[783] David Weininger, Arthur Weininger, and Joseph L. Weininger. Smiles. 2. Algorithm for generation of unique smiles notation. *Journal of Chemical Information and Computer Sciences*, 29(2):97–101, 1989.

[784] Max Welling, Michal Rosen-Zvi, and Geoffrey E. Hinton. Exponential family harmoniums with an application to information retrieval. In *Advances in Neural Information Processing Systems*, 1481–1488, 2005.

[785] James G. Wendell. A problem in geometric probability. *Math. Scand.*, 11:109–112, 1962.

[786] B. Widrow and M.E. Hoff. Adaptive switching circuits. In *Institute of Radio Engineers, Western Electronic Show and Convention, Convention Record, Part 4*, pages 96–104, 1960.

[787] Jared Willard, Xiaowei Jia, Shaoming Xu, Michael Steinbach, and Vipin Kumar. Integrating physics-based modeling with machine learning: a survey. arXiv:2003.04919, 2020.

[788] Ronald J. Williams. Simple statistical gradient-following algorithms for connectionist reinforcement learning. *Machine Learning*, 8(3–4):229–256, 1992.

[789] M.A. Wood, M.P. Kaplan, A. Park, E.J. Blanchard, A.M.M. Oliveira, T.L. Lombardi, and T. Abel. Transgenic mice expressing a truncated form of CREB-binding protein (CBP) exhibit deficits in hippocampal synaptic plasticity and memory storage. *Learning & Memory*, 12(2):111, 2005.

[790] Jin Long Wu, Heng Xiao, and Eric Paterson. Physics-informed machine learning approach for augmenting turbulence models: A comprehensive framework. *Physical Review Fluids*, 7(3):074602, jul 2018.

[791] L. Wu and P. Baldi. A scalable machine learning approach to GO. *Advances in Neural Information Processing Systems*, 19:1521, 2007.

[792] Lin Wu and Pierre Baldi. Learning to play GO using recursive neural networks. *Neural Networks*, 21(9):1392–1400, 2008.

[793] XENON Collaboration. First dark matter search results from the XENON1T experiment. *Physical review letters*, 119(18):181301, 2017.

[794] XENON Collaboration. The XENON1T dark matter experiment. *The European Physical Journal C*, 77(12):881, Dec 2017.

[795] Han Xiao, Kashif Rasul, and Roland Vollgraf. Fashion-MNIST: a novel image dataset for benchmarking machine learning algorithms, arXiv:1708.07747, 2017.

[796] Tian Xie and Jeffrey C Grossman. Crystal graph convolutional neural networks for an accurate and interpretable prediction of material properties. *Physical Review Letters*, 120(14):145301, 2018.

[797] Xiaohui Xie and H. Sebastian Seung. Spike-based learning rules and stabilization of persistent neural activity. In S.A. Solla, T.K. Leen, and K. Müller, editors, *Advances in Neural Information Processing Systems 12*, pages 199–208. MIT Press, 2000.

[798] Xiaohui Xie and H. Sebastian Seung. Equivalence of backpropagation and contrastive Hebbian learning in a layered network. *Neural Computation*, 15(2): 441–454, 2003.

[799] Hui Y. Xiong, Babak Alipanahi, Leo J. Lee, Hannes Bretschneider, Daniele Merico, Ryan K.C. Yuen, Yimin Hua, Serge Gueroussov, Hamed S. Najafabadi, Timothy R. Hughes, et al. The human splicing code reveals new insights into the genetic determinants of disease. *Science*, 347(6218):1254806, 2015.

[800] L. Xue, J.F. Godden, F.L. Stahura, and J. Bajorath. Profile scaling increases the similarity search performance of molecular fingerprints containing numerical descriptors and structural keys. *Journal of Chemical Information and Computer Sciences*, 43:1218–1225, 2003.

[801] L. Xue, F.L. Stahura, and J. Bajorath. Similarity search profiling reveals effects of fingerprint scaling in virtual screening. *Journal of Chemical Information and Computer Sciences*, 44:2032–2039, 2004.

[802] Daniel L.K. Yamins and James J. DiCarlo. Using goal-driven deep learning models to understand sensory cortex. *Nature Neuroscience*, 19(3):356–365, 2016.

[803] Hisashi Yashiro, Yoshiyuki Kajikawa, Yoshiaki Miyamoto, Tsuyoshi Yamaura, Ryuji Yoshida, and Hirofumi Tomita. Resolution dependence of the diurnal cycle of precipitation simulated by a global cloud-system resolving model. *Sola*, 12:272–276, 2016.

[804] C.H. Yuh, H. Bolouri, and E.H. Davidson. Genomic cis-regulatory logic: experimental and computational analysis of a sea urchin gene. *Science*, 279:1896–1902, 1998.

[805] C.H. Yuh, H. Bolouri, and E.H. Davidson. Cis-regulatory logic in the endo16 gene: switching from a specification to a differentiation mode of control. *Development*, 128:617–629, 2001.

[806] Chulhee Yun, Suvrit Sra, and Ali Jadbabaie. Small ReLu networks are powerful memorizers: a tight analysis of memorization capacity. In *Advances in Neural Information Processing Systems*, 15558–15569, 2019.

[807] Thomas Zaslavsky. *Facing up to Arrangements: Face-Count Formulas for Partitions of Space by Hyperplanes*. Memoirs of the American Mathematical Society, volume 154, 1975.

[808] Sai Zhang, Jingtian Zhou, Hailin Hu, Haipeng Gong, Ligong Chen, Chao Cheng, and Jianyang Zeng. A deep learning framework for modeling structural features of RNA-binding protein targets. *Nucleic Acids Research*, 44(4):e32–e32, 2015.

[809] Wei Zhang and Tom G. Dietterich. High-performance job-shop scheduling with a time-delay TD network. *Advances in Neural Information Processing Systems*, 8:1024–1030, 1996.

[810] Weihong Zhang. *Algorithms for partially observable Markov decision processes*. PhD thesis, Citeseer, 2001.

[811] Xiang Zhang, Lina Yao, Xianzhi Wang, Jessica Monaghan, and David McAlpine. A survey on deep learning based brain computer interface: recent advances and new frontiers. arXiv:1905.04149, 2019.

[812] Z. Zhang, W. Oelert, D. Grzonka, and T. Sefzick. The antiproton annihilation detector system of the ATRAP experiment. *Chinese Science Bulletin*, 54:189–195, 2009.

[813] Qiyang Zhao and Lewis D. Griffin. Suppressing the unusual: towards robust CNNS using symmetric activation functions, 2016. Preprint arxiv:1603.05145.

[814] Wei Zheng, Yang Li, Chengxin Zhang, Robin Pearce, S.M. Mortuza, and Yang Zhang. Deep-learning contact-map guided protein structure prediction in CASP13. *Proteins: Structure, Function, and Bioinformatics*, 87(12):1149–1164, 2019.

[815] Jian Zhou and Olga G. Troyanskaya. Predicting effects of noncoding variants with deep learning-based sequence model. *Nature Methods*, 12(10):931–4, Oct 2015.

[816] Angelo Ziletti, Devinder Kumar, Matthias Scheffler, and Luca M. Ghiringhelli. Insightful classification of crystal structures using deep learning. *Nature communications*, 9(1):2775, 2018.

[817] David Zipser and Richard A. Andersen. A back-propagation programmed network that simulates response properties of a subset of posterior parietal neurons. *Nature*, 331(6158):679–684, 1988.

[818] Yu. A. Zuev. Asymptotics of the logarithm of the number of threshold functions of the algebra of logic. *Soviet Mathematics Doklady*, 39(3):512–513, 1989.

[819] Yu. A. Zuev. Combinatorial-probability and geometric methods in threshold logic. *Diskretnaya Matematika*, 3(2):47–57, 1991.

Index